Defect
Detect

Windows
Memory Dump Analysis
Accelerated

Version 6

Part 1: Process User Space

Dmitry Vostokov
Software Diagnostics Services

Published by OpenTask, Republic of Ireland

OpenTask books and magazines are available through booksellers and distributors worldwide. For further information or comments, send requests to press@opentask.com.

A CIP catalog record for this book is available from the British Library.

ISBN-l3: 978-1-912636-92-1 (Paperback)

Revision 6.00 (July 2023)

Contents

About the Author

Dmitry Vostokov is an internationally recognized expert, speaker, educator, scientist, inventor, and author. He is the founder of the pattern-oriented software diagnostics, forensics, and prognostics discipline (Systematic Software Diagnostics), and Software Diagnostics Institute (DA+TA: DumpAnalysis.org + TraceAnalysis.org). Vostokov has also authored more than 50 books on software diagnostics, anomaly detection and analysis, software and memory forensics, root cause analysis and problem solving, memory dump analysis, debugging, software trace and log analysis, reverse engineering, and malware analysis. He has over 25 years of experience in software architecture, design, development, and maintenance in various industries, including leadership, technical, and people management roles. Dmitry also founded Syndromatix, Anolog.io, BriteTrace, DiaThings, Logtellect, OpenTask Iterative and Incremental Publishing (OpenTask.com), Software Diagnostics Technology and Services (former Memory Dump Analysis Services) PatternDiagnostics.com, and Software Prognostics. In his spare time, he presents various topics on Debugging.TV and explores Software Narratology, its further development as Narratology of Things and Diagnostics of Things (DoT), Software Pathology, and Quantum Software Diagnostics. His current interest areas are theoretical software diagnostics and its mathematical and computer science foundations, application of formal logic, artificial intelligence, machine learning and data mining to diagnostics and anomaly detection, software diagnostics engineering and diagnostics-driven development, diagnostics workflow and interaction. Recent interest areas also include cloud native computing, security, automation, functional programming, applications of category theory to software diagnostics, development and big data, and diagnostics of artificial intelligence.

Presentation Slides and Transcript

Windows Memory Dump Analysis

Accelerated

Version 6

Part 1: Process User Space

Dmitry Vostokov
Software Diagnostics Services

Hello, everyone, my name is Dmitry Vostokov, and I teach this training course.

Prerequisites

Basic Windows troubleshooting

These prerequisites are hard to define. Some of you have software development experience, and some do not. However, one thing is certain, to get most of this training, you are expected to have basic troubleshooting experience. Another thing I expect you to be familiar with is hexadecimal notation and that you have seen or can read programming source code in some language. The ability to read assembly language has some advantages but is not necessary for most of this training.

Training Goals

- Part 1A: Review fundamentals
- Part 1B: Review x64 disassembly
- Part 1C: Learn how to analyze process dumps
- Part 2A: Review fundamentals
- Part 2B: Review x64 disassembly
- Part 2C: Learn how to analyze kernel dumps
- Part 2D: Learn how to analyze complete (physical memory) dumps
- Part 2E: Learn how to analyze minidumps

Our primary goal is to learn memory dump analysis in an accelerated fashion. So first, we review absolutely essential fundamentals necessary for memory dump analysis, including x64 disassembly. Then we learn how to analyze different types of memory dumps. Part 1 is concerned with process memory dumps. Part 2 is about kernel, complete (physical memory), and minidumps. Also, this training is about memory dump analysis and not memory dump collection methods, tricks, and tips. Some collection methods and principles are listed in the following presentation's Special Topic section: https://www.patterndiagnostics.com/files/LegacyWindowsDebugging.pdf

Training Principles

◉ Talk only about what I can show
◉ Lots of pictures
◉ Lots of examples
◉ Original content and examples

For me, there were many training formats to consider, and I decided that the best way is to concentrate on exercises. Specifically, for this part of the training, I developed 22 of them. I also left out many concepts traditionally included in such training courses because I felt they were not necessary for accelerated training. More specialized topics for process memory dump analysis are covered in the follow-up training courses "Accelerated .NET Core Memory Dump Analysis" and "Accelerated Windows Malware Analysis with Memory Dumps." See the "Further Training Courses" slide at the end of this training.

Coverage (Part 1)

- Windows 10 and 11
- Both x64* and x86 code, WOW64
- x64 disassembly review
- Preliminary .NET analysis
- Process memory dumps
- Crashes, hangs, memory and handle leaks, CPU spikes

* Most of the exercises are focused on x64 code. For their x86 equivalents from older Windows versions, please refer to the previous fourth edition of this course.

All exercises from this edition focus on memory dumps from Windows 10 x64 platform except seven exercises where process dumps were taken from Windows 11 x64: Exercises 0 – 3, .NET Core dump analysis exercise, the blocked service analysis exercise, and the Rust memory dump analysis exercise. Exercises using memory dumps from .NET Framework, Windows Vista, and Windows 7 are available in the previous editions (4.0 and below).

Part 1A: Fundamentals

So now I show you some pictures. In the previous editions, such as 4.0 and below, we used mostly 32-bit diagram examples since, most of the time, fundamentals do not change when we move to the x64 Windows platform, and the analysis process most of the time is the same. However, in editions starting from 5.0, we added 64-bit diagram examples to reflect changes in virtual memory layout after the initial Windows 10 release and shifted all major slide explanations to them instead of x86.

Process Space (x64)

User Space

`00000000` 00000000`

`00007FFF` FFFFFFFF`
`FFFF8000` 00000000`

Kernel Space

`FFFFFFFF` FFFFFFFF`

For every process, Windows process memory range is divided into kernel space and user space parts. I follow the tradition of using red for the kernel and blue for the user part. Please note that there is a difference between space and mode. The mode is execution privilege attribute; for example, code running in kernel space has higher execution privilege than code running in user space. However, kernel code can access user space and access data there. We say that such code is running in kernel mode. On the contrary, the application code from user space is running in user mode, and because of its lower privilege, it cannot access kernel space. This division prevents accidental kernel modifications. Otherwise, you could easily crash your system. I put addresses on the right, and on 64-bit systems, all kernel addresses start with a hexadecimal digit "F". This uniform memory space is called virtual process space because it is an abstraction that allows us to analyze memory dumps without thinking about how it is all organized in physical memory. When we look at process dumps, we are concerned with virtual space only.

Process Space (x86)

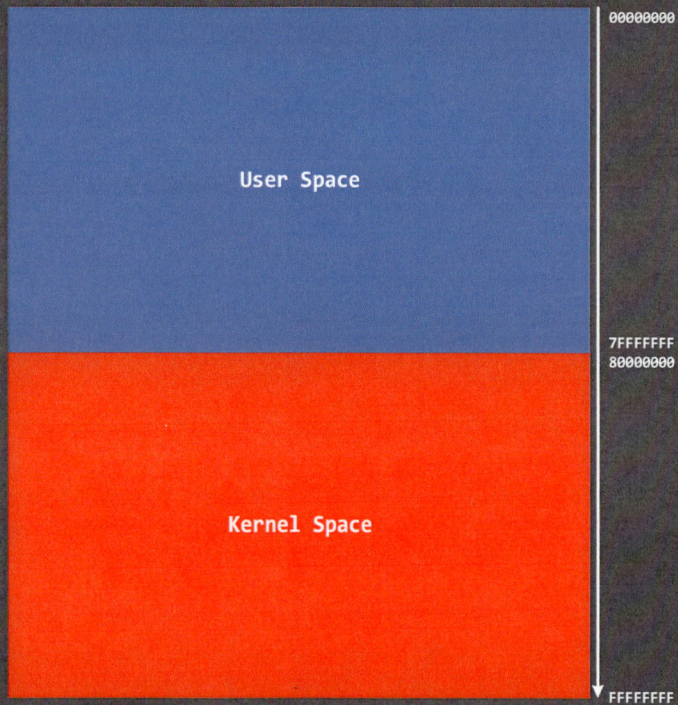

Here's a typical virtual process address space on 32-bit Windows. We see that kernel space addresses start with the digit "8".

Application/Process/Module (x64)

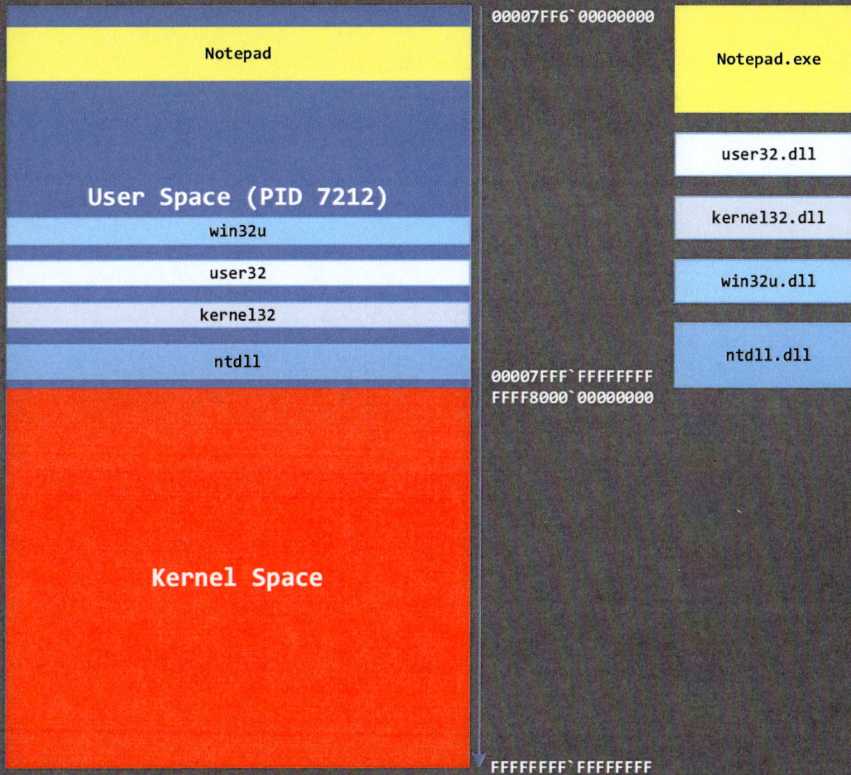

When an application is loaded, all modules (an executable image on a disk and associated DLLs) are organized sequentially in virtual memory space. Some modules can also be loaded twice at different virtual memory locations. A process is then set up for running, and a process ID is assigned to it. If you run another such process, it has a different virtual memory space (it could be exactly the same in layout, but most recent Windows versions put modules in a different order). We see that the main application executable module is usually loaded above the 00007FF0`00000000 address (subject to change with every major update).

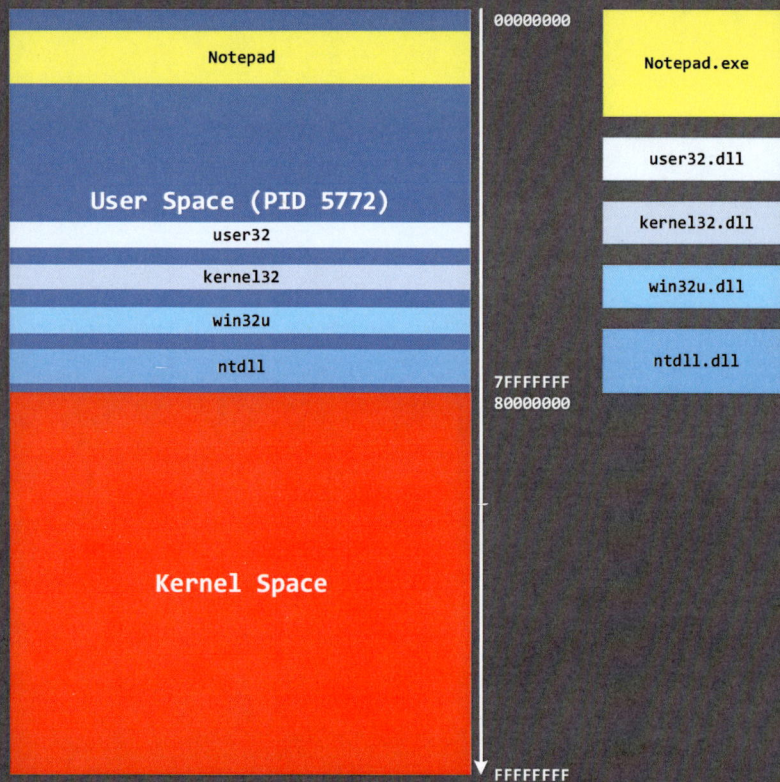

Application/Process/Module (x86)

A 32-bit virtual process space has a slightly different DLL arrangement with the main application executable module, which is usually loaded closer to the lower addresses.

OS Kernel/Driver/Module (x64)

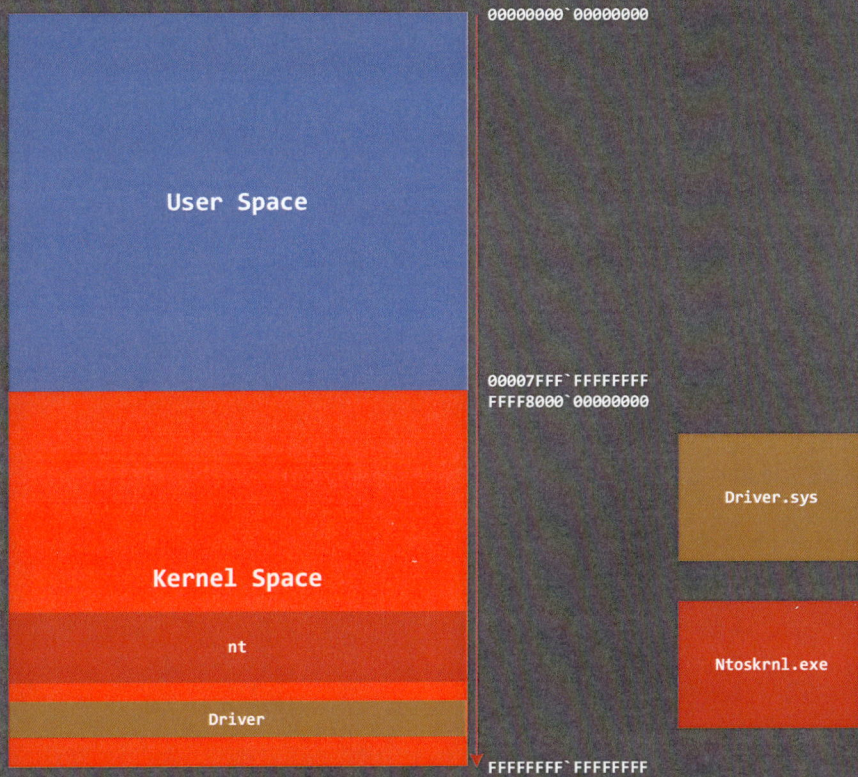

With kernel virtual address space, it is all the same. Actually, the image of the Windows kernel is also .exe, and system drivers have similar if not the same format as DLLs, and just have a different .sys extension.

OS Kernel/Driver/Module (x86)

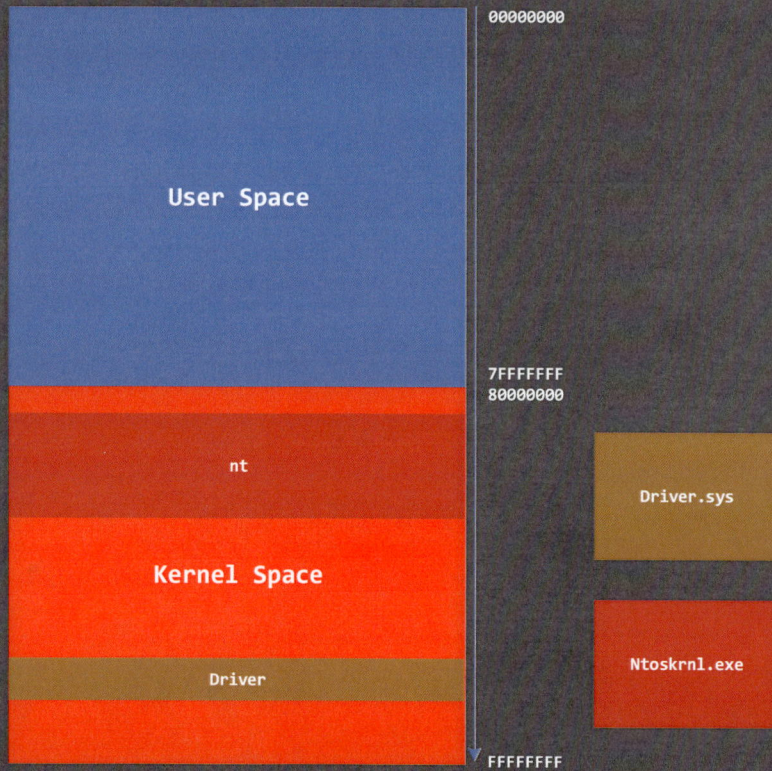

A 32-bit kernel virtual address space layout is similar too.

Process Virtual Space (x64)

```
00000000`00000000



00007FF6`00000000
```

Notepad

User Space (PID 7212)

win32u

user32

kernel32

ntdll

```
00007FFF`FFFFFFFF
FFFF8000`00000000
```

Kernel Space

nt

Driver

```
FFFFFFFF`FFFFFFFF
```

```
00000000`00000000 ...
FFFFFFFF`FFFFFFFF
```

Let's now see the big picture: the whole virtual process memory space and how it all maps to memory dumps.

Process Virtual Space (x86)

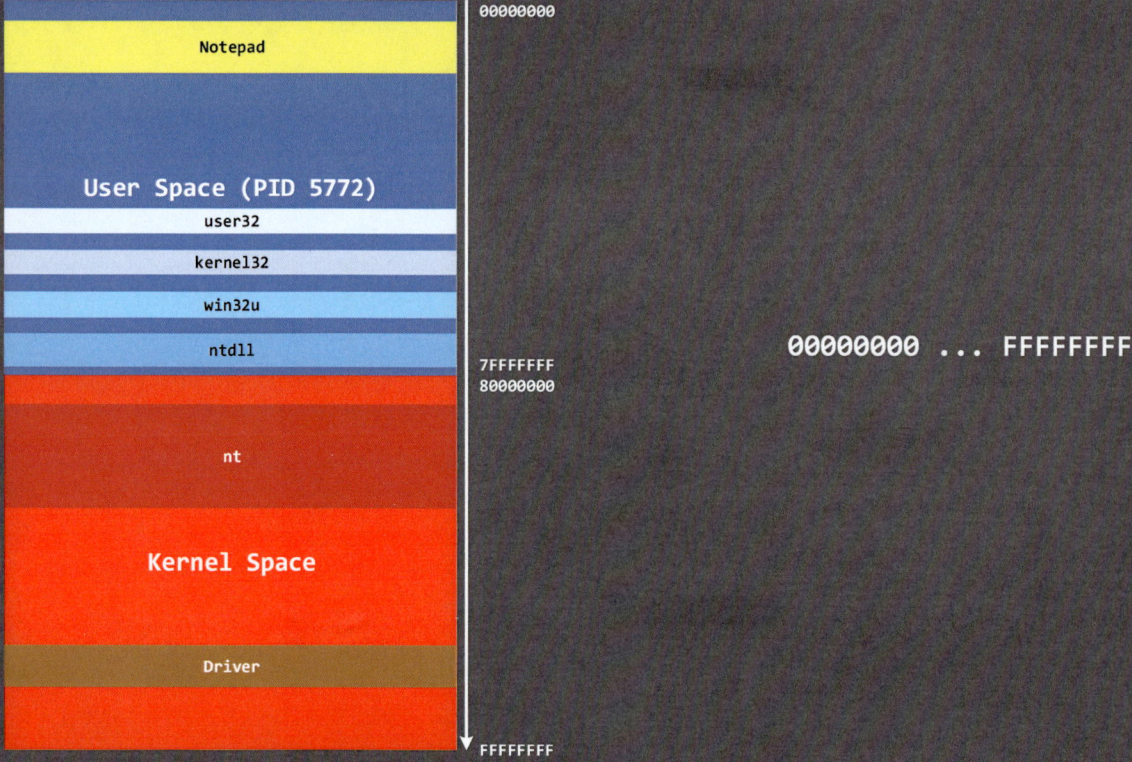

A 32-bit whole process virtual address space has a similar layout.

Process Virtual Space (WOW64)

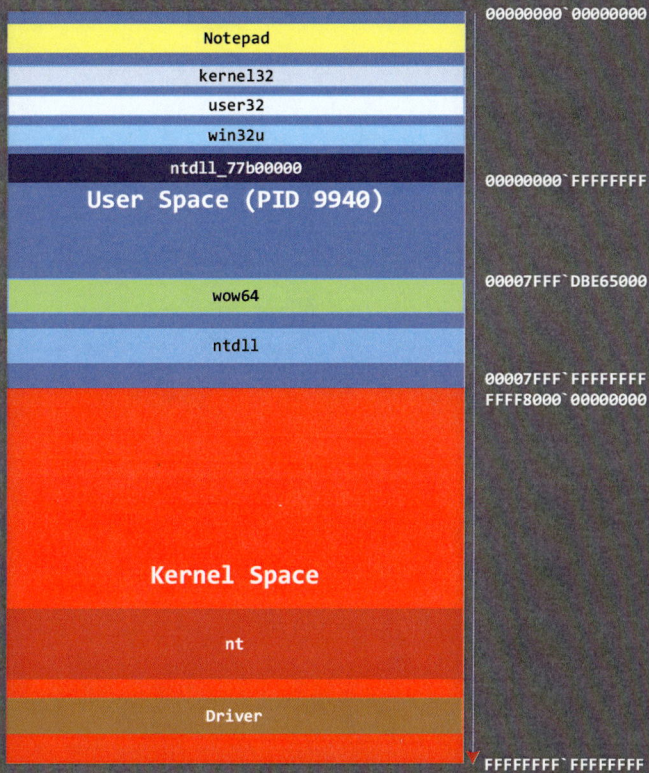

Notepad	00000000`00000000
kernel32	
user32	
win32u	
ntdll_77b00000	00000000`FFFFFFFF
User Space (PID 9940)	
wow64	00007FFF`DBE65000
ntdll	
	00007FFF`FFFFFFFF
	FFFF8000`00000000
Kernel Space	
nt	
Driver	
	FFFFFFFF`FFFFFFFF

On x64 Windows, 32-bit applications are executed as 64-bit processes (the so-called WOW64). The virtual memory layout of the user space part is mostly the same as for x86 space, except that it also includes some 64-bit modules.

Process Memory Dump (x64)

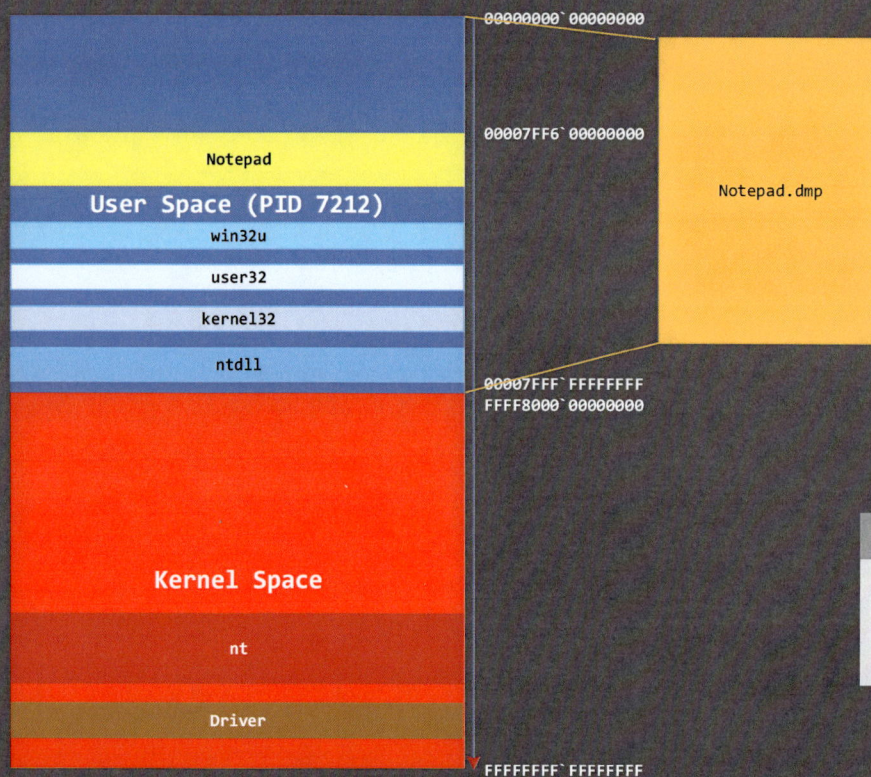

```
00000000`00000000



00007FF6`00000000



                          Notepad.dmp




00007FFF`FFFFFFFF
FFFF8000`00000000




FFFFFFFF`FFFFFFFF
```

Notepad

User Space (PID 7212)

win32u

user32

kernel32

ntdll

Kernel Space

nt

Driver

WinDbg Commands

lmv command lists modules and their description

When we save a process memory dump, a user space portion of the application virtual process space is saved without any kernel virtual space stuff. However, we usually don't see process memory dumps of several gigabytes in size unless we have memory leaks. It is because process space has gaps unfilled with modules and data. These unallocated parts are not saved in a memory dump. However, if some parts were paged out and now reside in a page file, they are usually brought back before saving a memory dump. You may have noticed that sometimes when you save a dump file, for example, by using Task Manager, process memory consumption increases.

Process Memory Dump (x86)

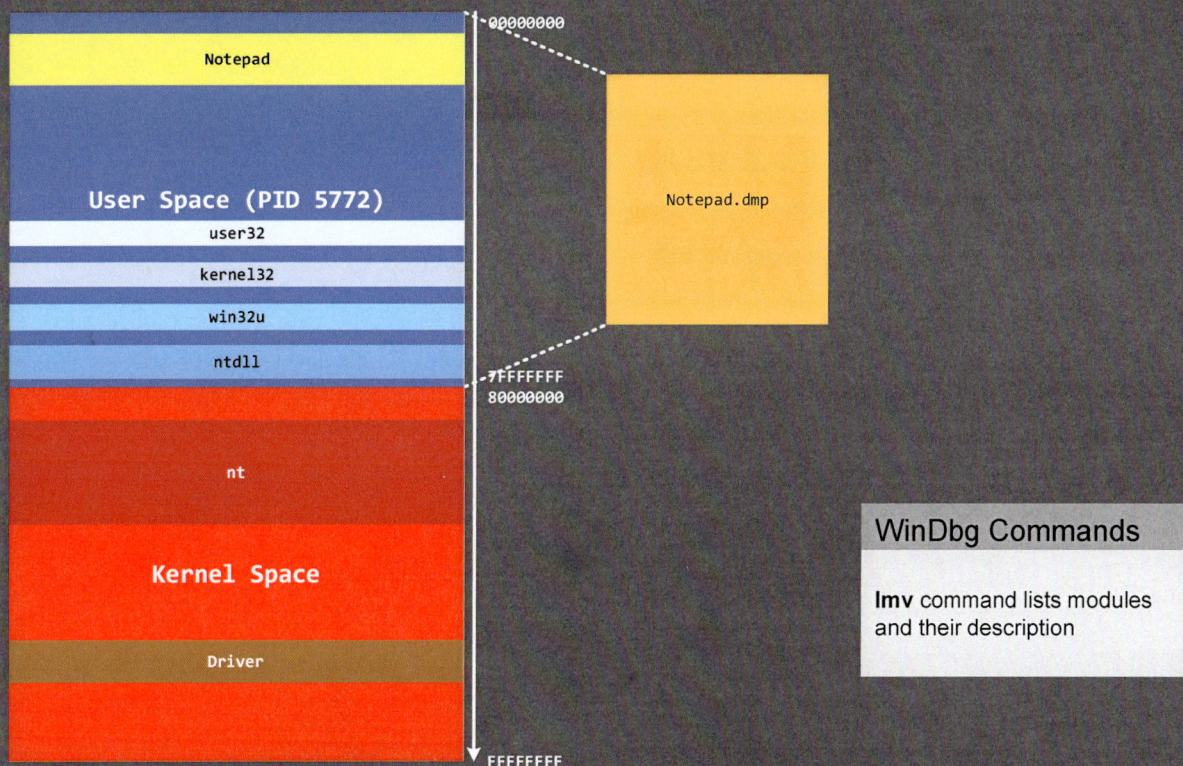

Process memory dumps from 32-bit Windows are usually smaller than their x64 counterparts, and also, we usually don't see 2 GB sizes unless we have memory leaks.

Process Memory Dump (WOW64)

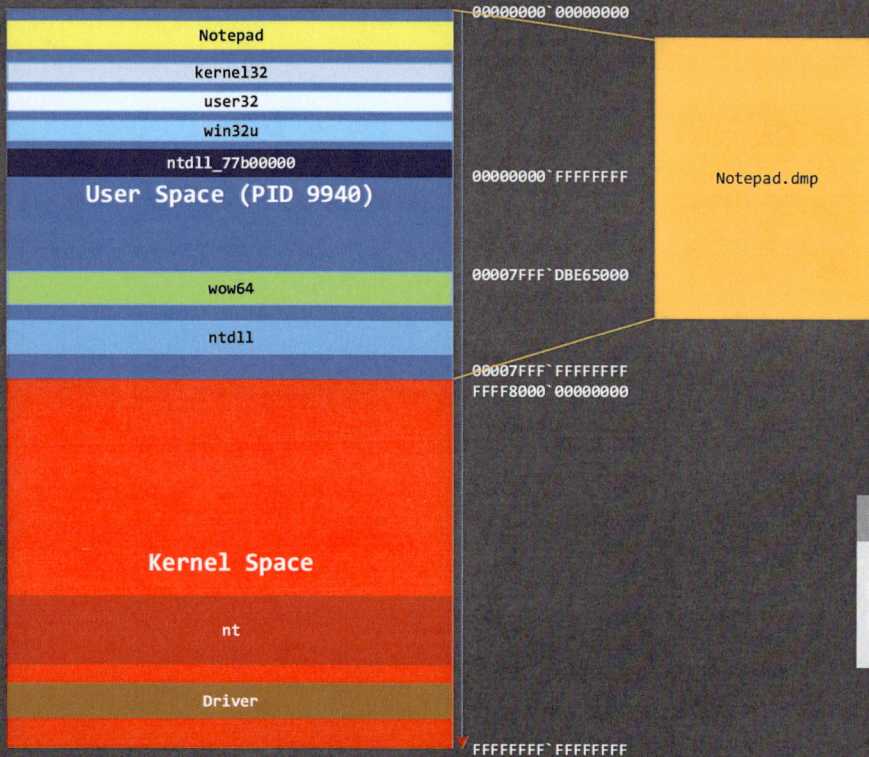

Memory Layout	Address
Notepad	00000000`00000000
kernel32	
user32	
win32u	
ntdll_77b00000	
User Space (PID 9940)	00000000`FFFFFFFF
wow64	00007FFF`DBE65000
ntdll	00007FFF`FFFFFFFF
	FFFF8000`00000000
Kernel Space	
nt	
Driver	
	FFFFFFFF`FFFFFFFF

Notepad.dmp

WinDbg Commands

lmv command lists modules and their description

On x64 Windows, the default 64-bit Task Manager saves 32-bit processes as 64-bit process memory dumps. To save them as x86 32-bit process memory dumps, we need to use the 32-bit Task Manager from the \Windows\SysWOW64 folder.

Process Threads

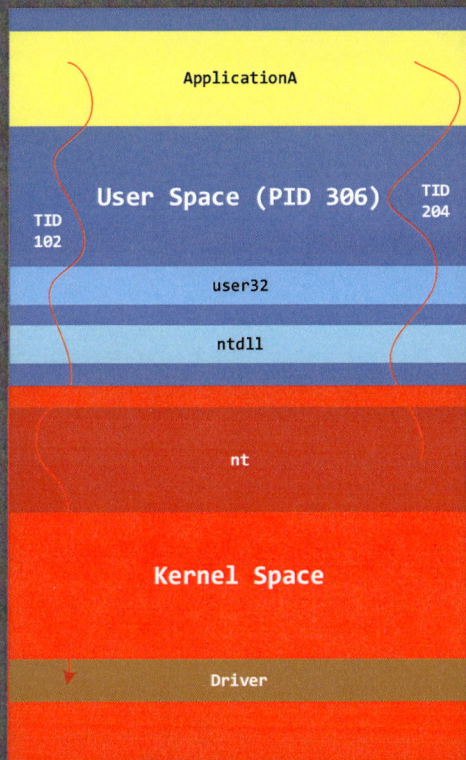

ApplicationA

User Space (PID 306)

TID 102

TID 204

user32

ntdll

nt

Kernel Space

Driver

WinDbg Commands

Process dumps:
~<n>s switches between threads

Now we come to another important fundamental concept in Windows memory dump analysis: thread. It is basically a unit of execution, and there can be many threads in a given process. Every thread just executes some code and performs various tasks; for example, in Microsoft Edge, one thread can download a page, another thread responds to parse JavaScript on a different page, and yet other threads can support Java or .NET virtual machine and execute graphics code. Every thread has its ID. In this training, we also learn how to navigate between process threads. They are called process threads because they originate in user space.

Thread Stack Raw Data

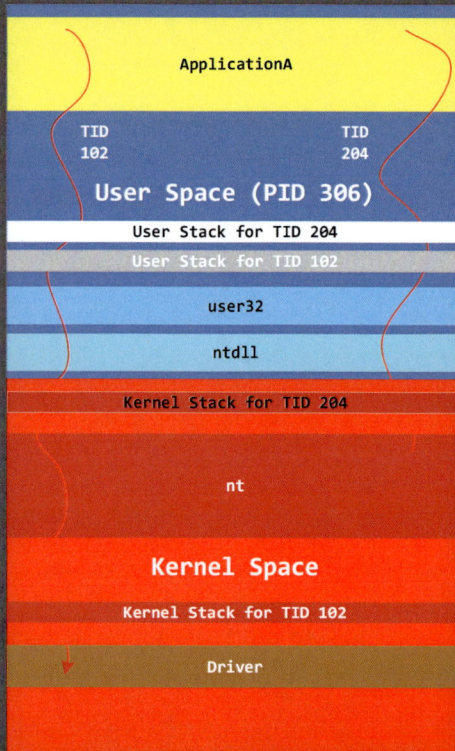

WinDbg Commands

Process dumps:
!teb

Data:
dc / dps / dpp / dpa / dpu

Every thread needs a temporary memory region to store its execution history and temporary data. This region is called a thread stack. To avoid conflict, OS designers split thread stack into 2 parts: user and kernel. In the picture, you see them for both threads with TID 102 and 204. Please note that the stack region is just any other memory region, and you can use any WinDbg data dumping commands there. We also learn how to get the thread stack region address range. Examining raw stack data can hint at the past system behavior: the so-called **Execution Residue** pattern.

Thread Stack Trace

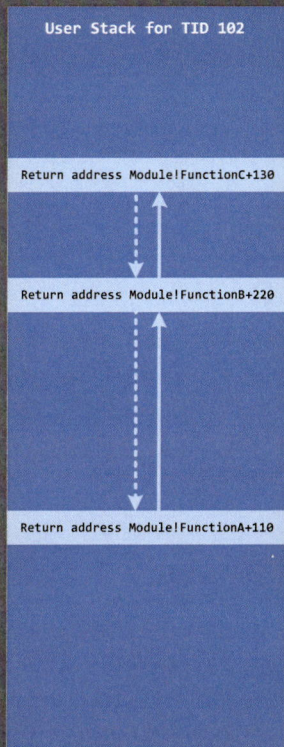

```
FunctionA()
{
  ...
  FunctionB();
  ...
}
FunctionB()
{
  ...
  FunctionC();
  ...
}
FunctionC()
{
  ...
  FunctionD();
  ...
}
```

User Stack for TID 102

Return address Module!FunctionC+130

Return address Module!FunctionB+220

Return address Module!FunctionA+110

Module!FunctionA

Resumes from address Module!FunctionA+110   Saves return address Module!FunctionA+110

Module!FunctionB

Resumes from address Module!FunctionB+220   Saves return address Module!FunctionB+220

Module!FunctionC

Resumes from address Module!FunctionC+130   Saves return address Module!FunctionC+130

Module!FunctionD

WinDbg Commands

```
0:000> k
Module!FunctionD
Module!FunctionC+130
Module!FunctionB+220
Module!FunctionA+110
```

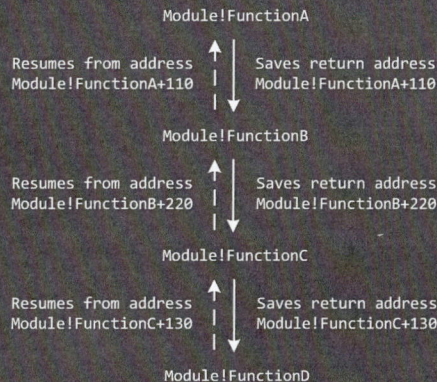

© 2023 Software Diagnostics Services

Now we explain thread stack traces. Suppose we have source code where *FunctionA* calls *FunctionB* at some point, *FunctionB* calls *FunctionC,* and so on: a thread of execution. If *FunctionA* calls *FunctionB*, you expect the execution thread to return to the same place where it left and then resume from there. It is achieved by saving a return address in the thread stack region. So every return address is saved and then restored during the course of thread execution. Although the memory addresses grow from top to bottom in this picture, return addresses are saved from bottom to top: the stack grows from higher to lower addresses. It might seem counter-intuitive to all previous pictures, but this is how you would see the output from WinDbg commands. What WinDbg does when you instruct it to dump a stack trace from a given thread is to analyze thread raw stack data and figure out return addresses, map them to symbolic form according to symbol files and show them from top to bottom. Note that *FunctionD* is not present in the raw stack data on the left because the thread is currently executing the function *FunctionD* called from *FunctionC*. However, *FunctionC* called *FunctionD,* and the return address of *FunctionC* was saved. In the gray box on the right, we see the results of the WinDbg command.

Thread Stack Trace (no PDB)

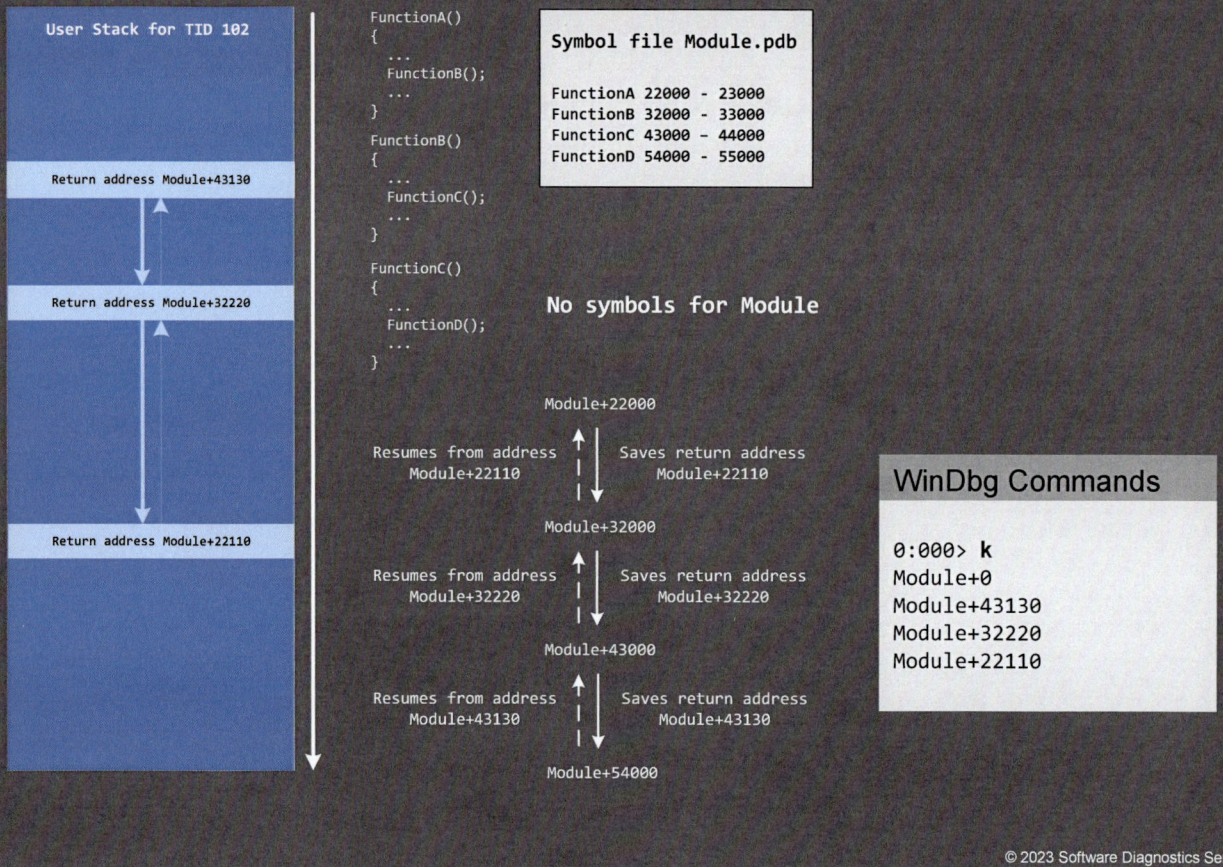

```
User Stack for TID 102


Return address Module+43130



Return address Module+32220



Return address Module+22110
```

```
FunctionA()
{
  ...
  FunctionB();
  ...
}
FunctionB()
{
  ...
  FunctionC();
  ...
}
FunctionC()
{
  ...
  FunctionD();
  ...
}
```

```
Symbol file Module.pdb

FunctionA 22000 - 23000
FunctionB 32000 - 33000
FunctionC 43000 - 44000
FunctionD 54000 - 55000
```

No symbols for Module

```
                         Module+22000
Resumes from address       ↑   Saves return address
   Module+22110            │        Module+22110
                           ↓
                         Module+32000
Resumes from address       ↑   Saves return address
   Module+32220            │        Module+32220
                           ↓
                         Module+43000
Resumes from address       ↑   Saves return address
   Module+43130            │        Module+43130
                           ↓
                         Module+54000
```

WinDbg Commands

```
0:000> k
Module+0
Module+43130
Module+32220
Module+22110
```

Here I'd like to show you why symbol files are important and what stack traces you get without them. Symbol files just provide mappings between memory address ranges and associated symbols, like a table of contents in a book. So in the absence of symbols, we are left with bare module names that are saved in a dump. Dumps with .NET code are much better because .NET assembly modules usually include full code description inside.

Exceptions (Access Violation)

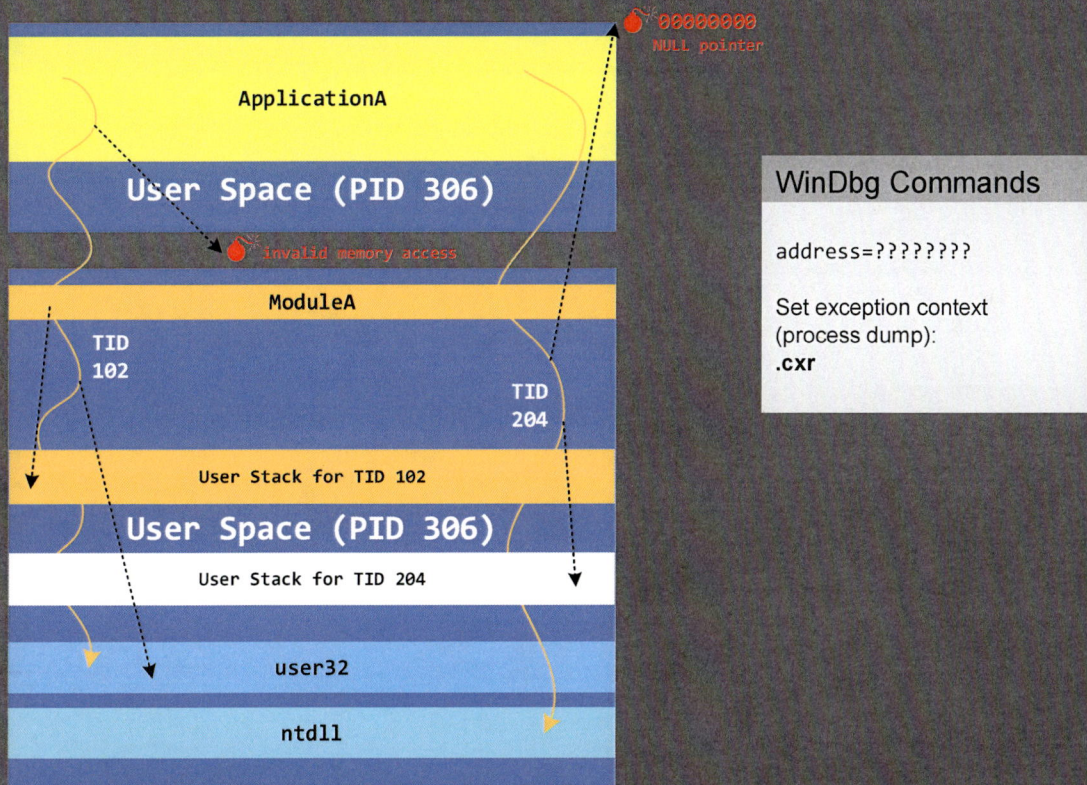

Now we talk about access violation exceptions. During thread execution, it accesses various memory addresses doing reads and writes. Sometimes the memory is not present due to gaps in virtual address space or different protection levels like read-only or no execute memory regions. If a thread tries to violate that, we get an exception, or it is often called fault or trap in kernel space. OS stores an exception context and transfers execution to exception processing code. In practical exercises, we would see how to recover that information because WinDbg is just a tool with its own assumptions and often is wrong in its conclusions when you just execute the default analysis command !analyze –v. A typical example is a page fault when a driver tries to access memory that resides in a page file. Then OS brings that page to memory and restarts that processor instruction. However, in some situations, it is considered invalid to access such paged-out memory, and we have a bugcheck, and a kernel memory dump is saved that allows us to find the driver name and its functions. Certain regions are forbidden to read and write, such as near-zero addresses. If we have an access violation there, it is called NULL pointer access. Note that every thread can have an exception, and it often happens that there are multiple exceptions stored in a dump file. It is also sometimes the case that the code can catch these exceptions preventing a user from seeing error messages. Such exceptions can contribute to corruption, and we call them **Hidden Exceptions**, and we also learn how to recognize them in a dump file.

31

Exceptions (Runtime)

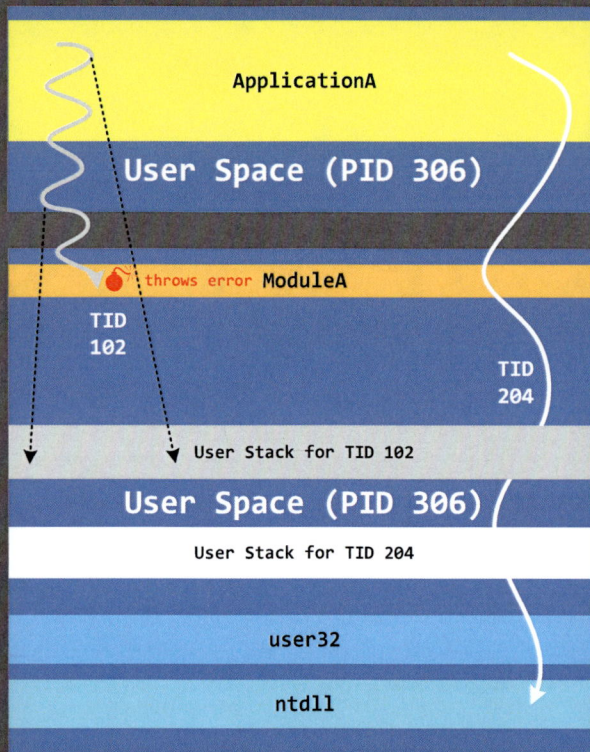

However, not all exceptions happen from invalid access. Many exceptions are generated by the code itself when it checks for some condition and it is not satisfied, for example, when a code checks a buffer or an array to verify whether it is full before trying to add data. If it finds that it is already full, the code throws an exception. In one of our practice examples, we would see that when C++ code throws a C++ exception. Such exceptions are usually called runtime exceptions.

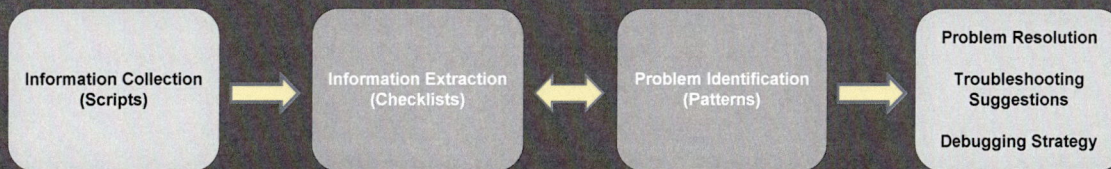

Pattern-Oriented Diagnostic Analysis

Diagnostic Pattern: a common recurrent identifiable problem together with a set of recommendations and possible solutions to apply in a specific context.

Diagnostic Problem: a set of indicators (symptoms, signs) describing a problem.

Diagnostic Analysis Pattern: a common recurrent analysis technique and method of diagnostic pattern identification in a specific context.

Diagnostics Pattern Language: common names of diagnostic and diagnostic analysis patterns. The same language for any operating system: Windows, Mac OS X, Linux, ...

| Information Collection (Scripts) | → | Information Extraction (Checklists) | ↔ | Problem Identification (Patterns) | → | Problem Resolution / Troubleshooting Suggestions / Debugging Strategy |

Checklist: http://www.dumpanalysis.org/windows-memory-analysis-checklist

Patterns: http://www.dumpanalysis.org/blog/index.php/crash-dump-analysis-patterns/

© 2023 Software Diagnostics Services

A few words about logs, checklists, and patterns. Memory dump analysis is usually an analysis of a text for the presence of diagnostic patterns. We run commands; they output text, and then we look at that textual output, and when we find suspicious diagnostic indicators, we execute more commands. Here checklists can be very useful. One such checklist is provided as a link. In some cases (such as complete memory dumps), it is beneficial to collect information into one huge log file by running several commands one by one (like a script) and then doing the first-order analysis.

Checklist: https://www.dumpanalysis.org/windows-memory-analysis-checklist

Patterns: https://www.dumpanalysis.org/blog/index.php/crash-dump-analysis-patterns/

Review of x64 Disassembly

Part 1B: x64 Disassembly

This section provides an overview of disassembly for the x64 platform. Linux developers who know the x64 assembly language may benefit because we use a different flavor than the default in Linux GDB.

x64 CPU Registers

- **RAX** ⊃ **EAX** ⊃ **AX** ⊇ {**AH**, **AL**}

RAX 64-bit	EAX 32-bit

- ALU: **RAX**, **RDX**

- Counter: **RCX**

- Memory copy: **RSI** (src), **RDI** (dst)

- Stack: **RSP**

- Next instruction: **RIP**

- New: **R8** – **R15**, **Rx(D|W|B)**

There are familiar 32-bit CPU register names, such as **EAX,** that are extended to 64-bit names, such as **RAX**. Most of them are traditionally specialized, such as ALU, counter, and memory copy registers. Although, now they all can be used as general-purpose registers. There is, of course, a stack pointer, **RSP**, and it also takes the role of a frame pointer, which is also used to address local variables and saved parameters. It can be used for stack reconstruction. In Microsoft compiler code generation implementations, **RBP** is also used as a general-purpose register. An instruction pointer **RIP** is saved in the stack memory region with every function call, then restored on return from the called function. In addition, the x64 platform features another eight general-purpose registers, from **R8** to **R15**.

Instructions and Registers

- Opcode DST, SRC

- Examples:

```
mov     rax, 10h              ; RAX ← 0x10
mov     r13, rdx              ; R13 ← RDX
add     r10, 10h              ; R10 ← R10 + 0x10
imul    edx, ecx              ; EDX ← EDX * ECX
call    rdx                   ; RDX already contains
                              ;     the address of func (&func)
                              ; PUSH RIP; &func → RIP
sub     rsp, 30h              ; RSP ← RSP-0x30
                              ; make room for local variables
```

This slide shows a few examples of CPU instructions involving operations with registers, such as moving a value and doing arithmetic. The direction of operands is opposite to the AT&T x64 disassembly flavor if you are accustomed to default GDB disassembly on Linux.

Memory and Stack Addressing

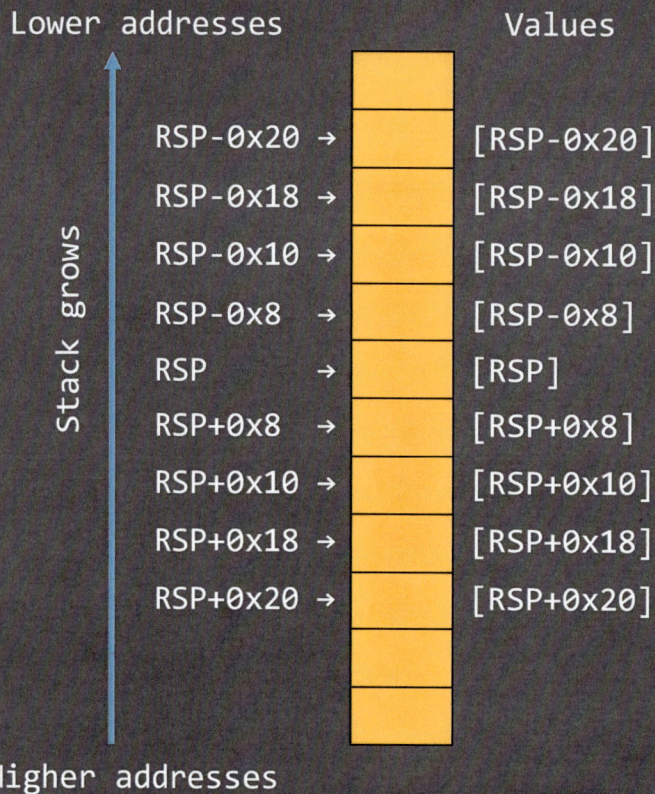

Lower addresses	Values
RSP-0x20 →	[RSP-0x20]
RSP-0x18 →	[RSP-0x18]
RSP-0x10 →	[RSP-0x10]
RSP-0x8 →	[RSP-0x8]
RSP →	[RSP]
RSP+0x8 →	[RSP+0x8]
RSP+0x10 →	[RSP+0x10]
RSP+0x18 →	[RSP+0x18]
RSP+0x20 →	[RSP+0x20]
Higher addresses	

Stack grows

Before we look at operations with memory, let's look at a graphical representation of memory addressing where for simplicity, I use 64-bit (or 8-byte) memory cells. A thread stack is just any other memory region, so instead of **RSP,** any other register can be used. Please note that stack grows towards lower addresses, so to access the previously pushed values, you need to use positive offsets from **RSP**.

Memory Cell Sizes

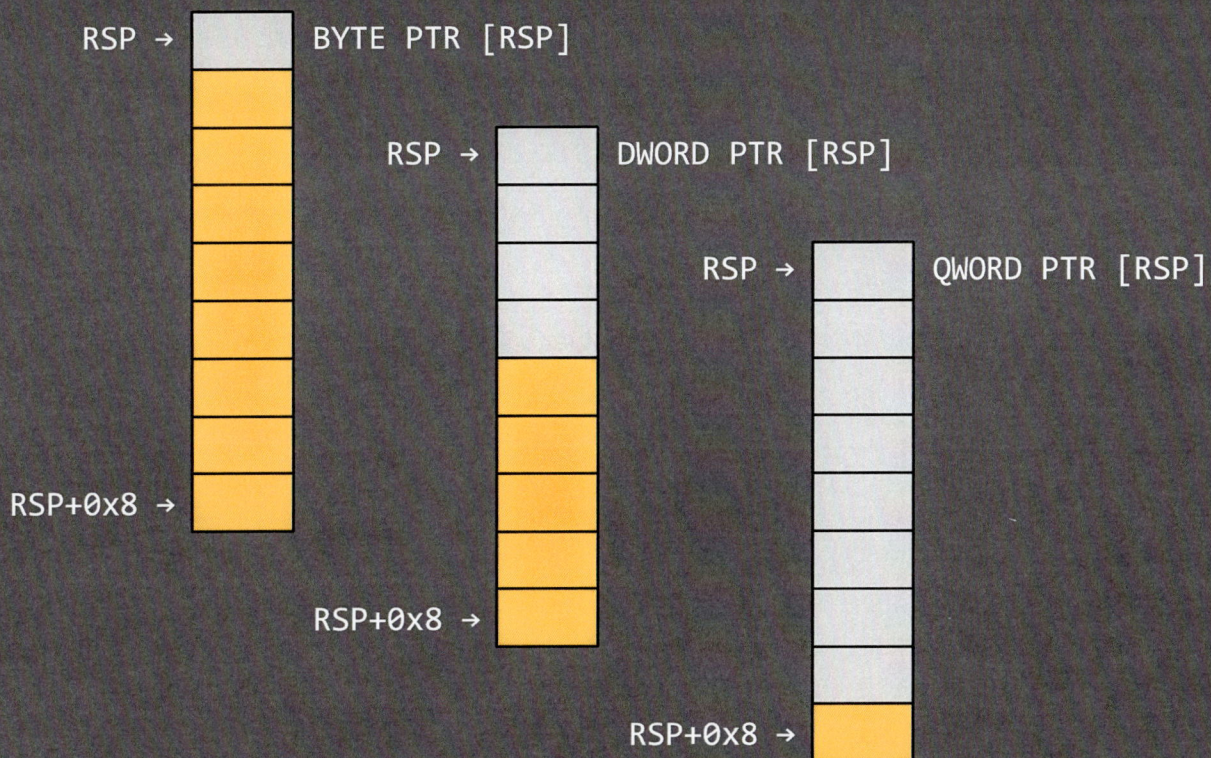

RSP → BYTE PTR [RSP]

RSP+0x8 →

RSP → DWORD PTR [RSP]

RSP+0x8 →

RSP → QWORD PTR [RSP]

RSP+0x8 →

© 2023 Software Diagnostics Services

Here, each memory cell is 8-bit (or one byte). When we have a register pointing to memory, and we want to work with the value at that address, we need to specify the size of memory cells to work with, for example, **BYTE PTR** if we want to work with a byte, **DWORD PTR** if we want to work with 32-bit double words, and **QWORD PTR** if we want to work with 64-bit quad words. There's also **WORD PTR** for 16-bit values. This notation is different from Linux GDB, where we have bytes, half-words, words, and double words.

Memory Load Instructions

- Opcode DST, PTR [SRC+Offset]

- Opcode DST

- Examples:

```
mov    rax, qword ptr [rsp+10h] ; RAX ←
                                ; 64-bit value at address RSP+0x10
mov    ecx, dword ptr [20]      ; ECX ←
                                ; 32-bit value at address 0x20
pop    rdi                      ; RDI ← value at address RSP
                                ; RSP ← RSP + 8
lea    r8, [rsp+20h]            ; R8 ← address RSP+0x20
```

Constants are encoded in instructions, but if we need arbitrary values, we must get them from memory. Square brackets show memory access relative to an address stored in a register.

Memory Store Instructions

- Opcode PTR [DST+Offset], SRC

- Opcode DST|SRC

- Examples:

```
mov    qword ptr [rbp-20h], rcx ; 64-bit value at address RBP-0x20
                                 ;    ← RCX
mov    byte ptr [0], 1           ; 8-bit value at address 0 ← 1
push   rsi                       ; RSP ← RSP - 8
                                 ; value at address RSP ← RSI
inc    dword ptr [rcx]           ; 32-bit value at address RCX ←
                                 ;    1 + 32-bit value at address RCX
```

Storing is similar to loading.

Flow Instructions

- Opcode DST

- Opcode PTR [DST]

- Examples:

```
jmp    00007ff6`9ef2f008    ; RIP ← 0x7ff69ef2f008
                            ; (goto 0x7ff69ef2f008)
jmp    qword ptr [rax+10h]  ; RIP ← value at address RAX+0x10
call   00007ff6`9ef21400    ; RSP ← RSP – 8
00007ff6`9ef21057:          ; value at address RSP ← 0x7ff69ef21057
                            ; RIP ← 0x7ff69ef21400
                            ; (goto 0x7ff69ef21400)
```

Goto (an unconditional jump) is implemented via the **JMP** instruction. Function calls are implemented via **CALL** instruction. For conditional branches, please look at the official Intel documentation. We don't use these instructions in our exercises.

Windows API Parameters

- x86: Right to left PUSH

  `Args to Child` are parameters

- x64: Left to right RCX, RDX, R8, R9, stack

  `Args to Child` are not parameters

```
WinDbg Commands

0:000> kv
 # Child-SP    RetAddr   : Args to Child   : Call Site
 ...
```

Additional calling convention explanation slides are available from the "Accelerated Windows API for Software Diagnostics" presentation:

https://www.patterndiagnostics.com/Training/Accelerated-Windows-API-Slides.pdf

Practice Exercises

Part 1C: Practice Exercises

Now we come to practice. The goal is to show you important commands and how their output helps recognize patterns of abnormal software structure and behavior.

Links

- Memory Dumps:

Included in Exercise 0

- Exercise Transcripts:

Included in this book

Exercise 0

- **Goal:** Install WinDbg or Debugging Tools for Windows, or pull Docker image, and check that symbols are set up correctly

- **Patterns:** Stack Trace; Incorrect Stack Trace

- \AWMDA-Dumps\Exercise-0-Download-Setup-WinDbg.pdf

Exercise 0: Download, setup, and verify your WinDbg or Debugging Tools for Windows installation, or Docker Debugging Tools for Windows image

Goal: Install WinDbg or Debugging Tools for Windows, or pull Docker image, and check that symbols are set up correctly.

Patterns: Stack Trace; Incorrect Stack Trace.

1.   Download memory dump files if you haven't done that already and unpack the archives:

https://www.patterndiagnostics.com/Training/AWMDA/AWMDA-V6-Dumps.zip
https://www.patterndiagnostics.com/Training/AWMDA/AWMDA-V5-Dumps-Part1.zip
https://www.patterndiagnostics.com/Training/AWMDA/AWMDA-V5-Dumps-W11.zip
https://www.patterndiagnostics.com/Training/AWMDA/AWMDA-V5-Dumps-W11-Additional.zip

2.   Install WinDbg (or upgrade existing WinDbg Preview) from https://learn.microsoft.com/en-gb/windows-hardware/drivers/debugger. Run WinDbg.

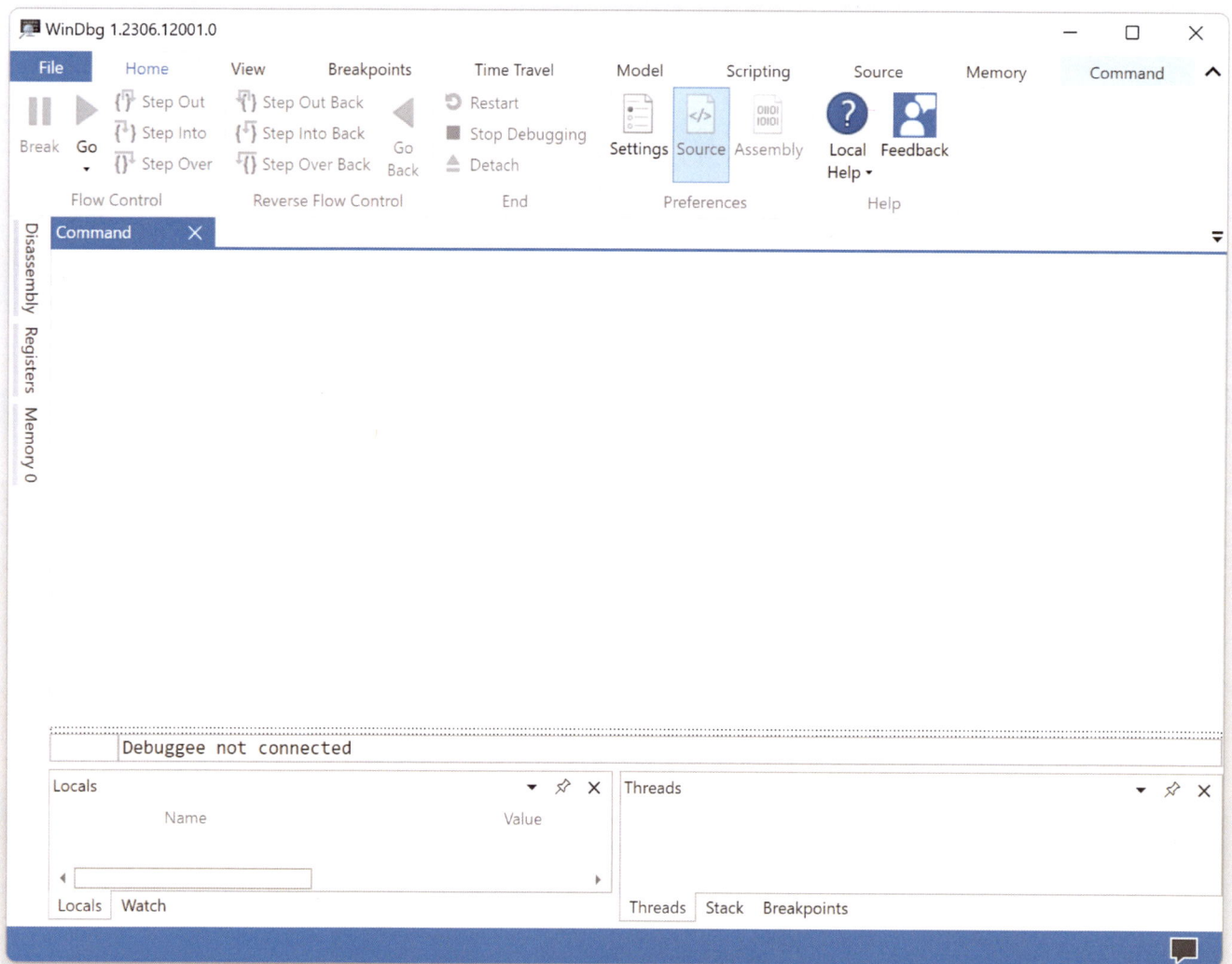

3.   Open \AWMDA-Dumps\Process\x64\wordpad.DMP:

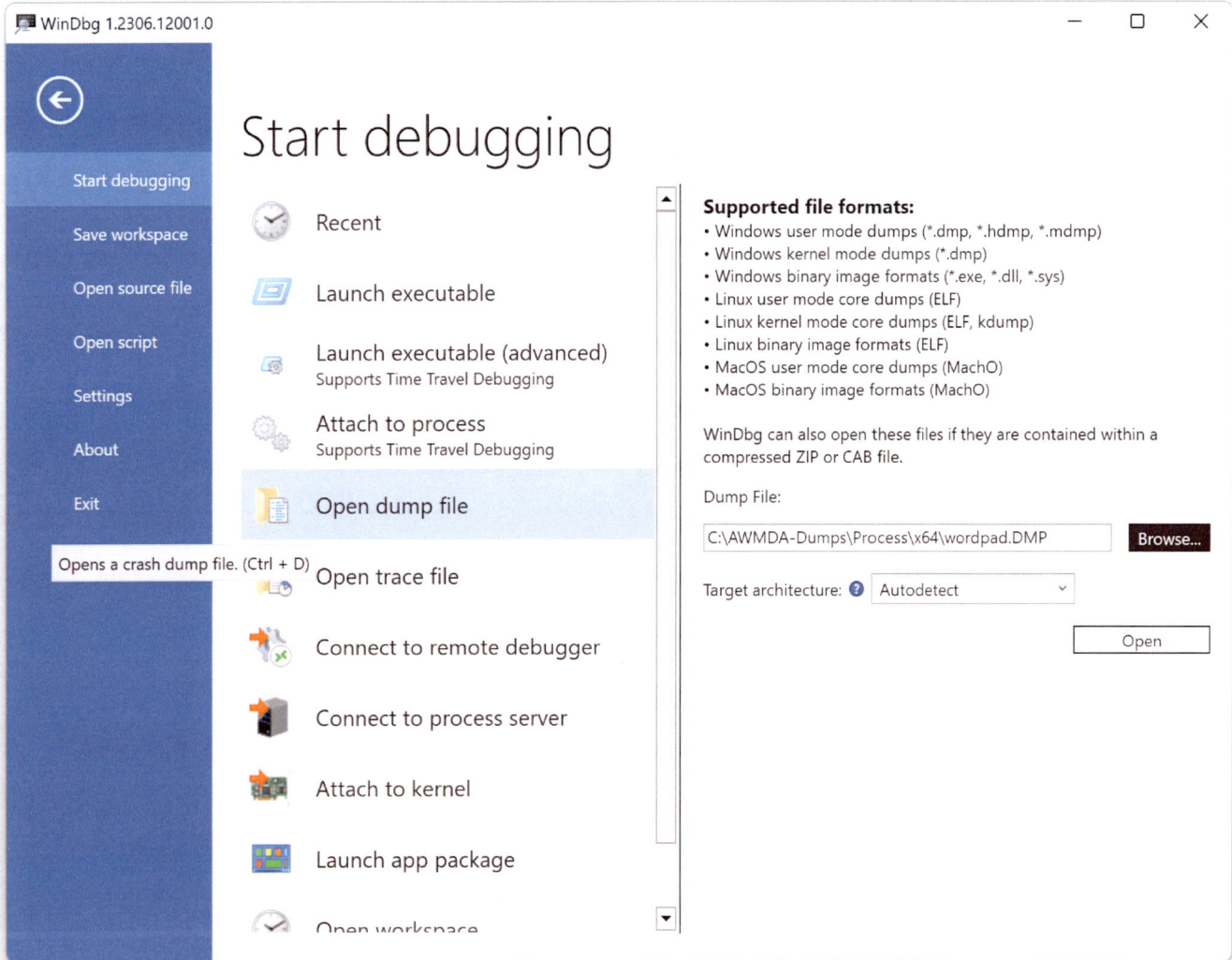

4.   We get the dump file loaded:

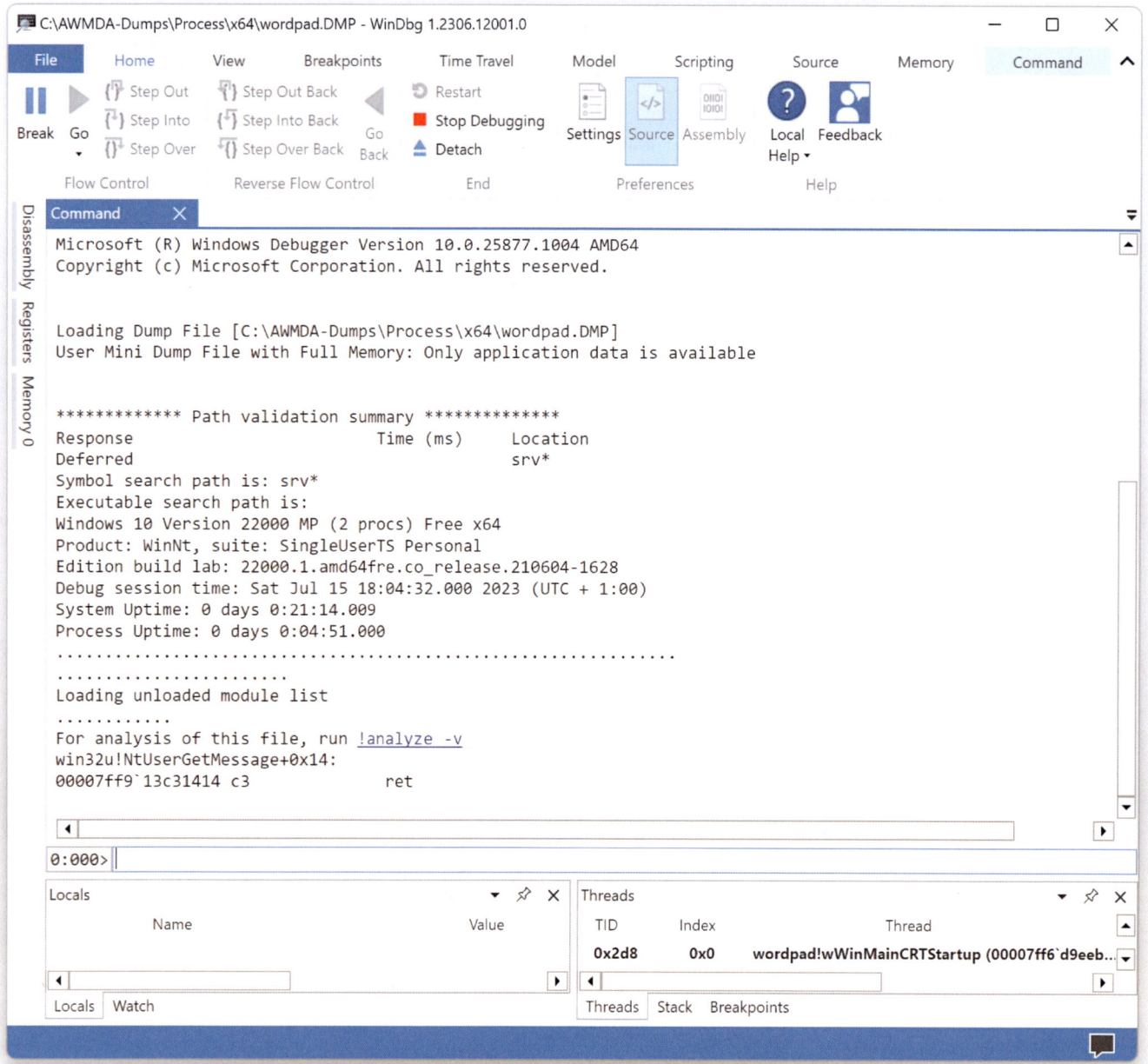

5.   Type the **k** command to verify the correctness of the stack trace:

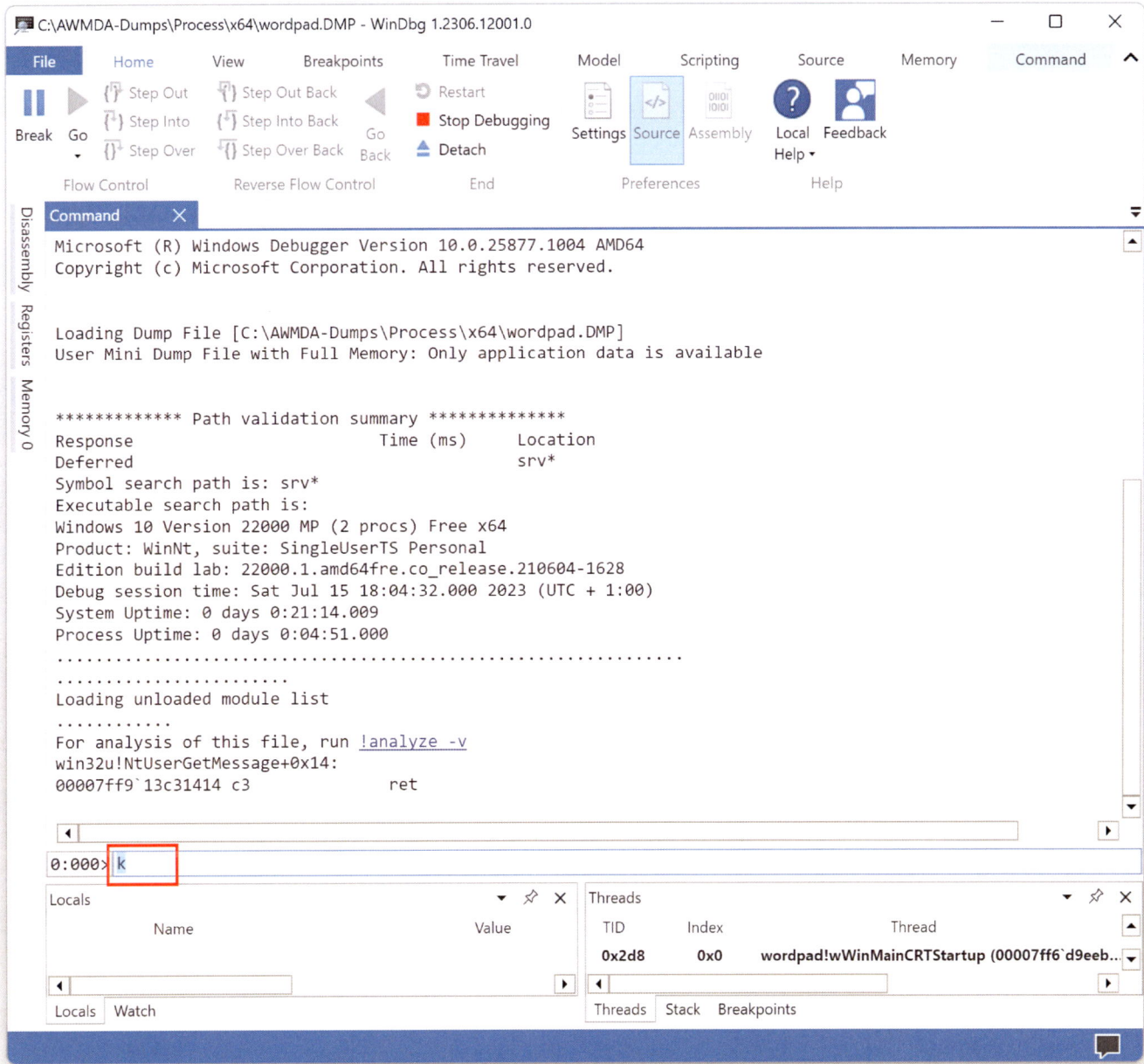

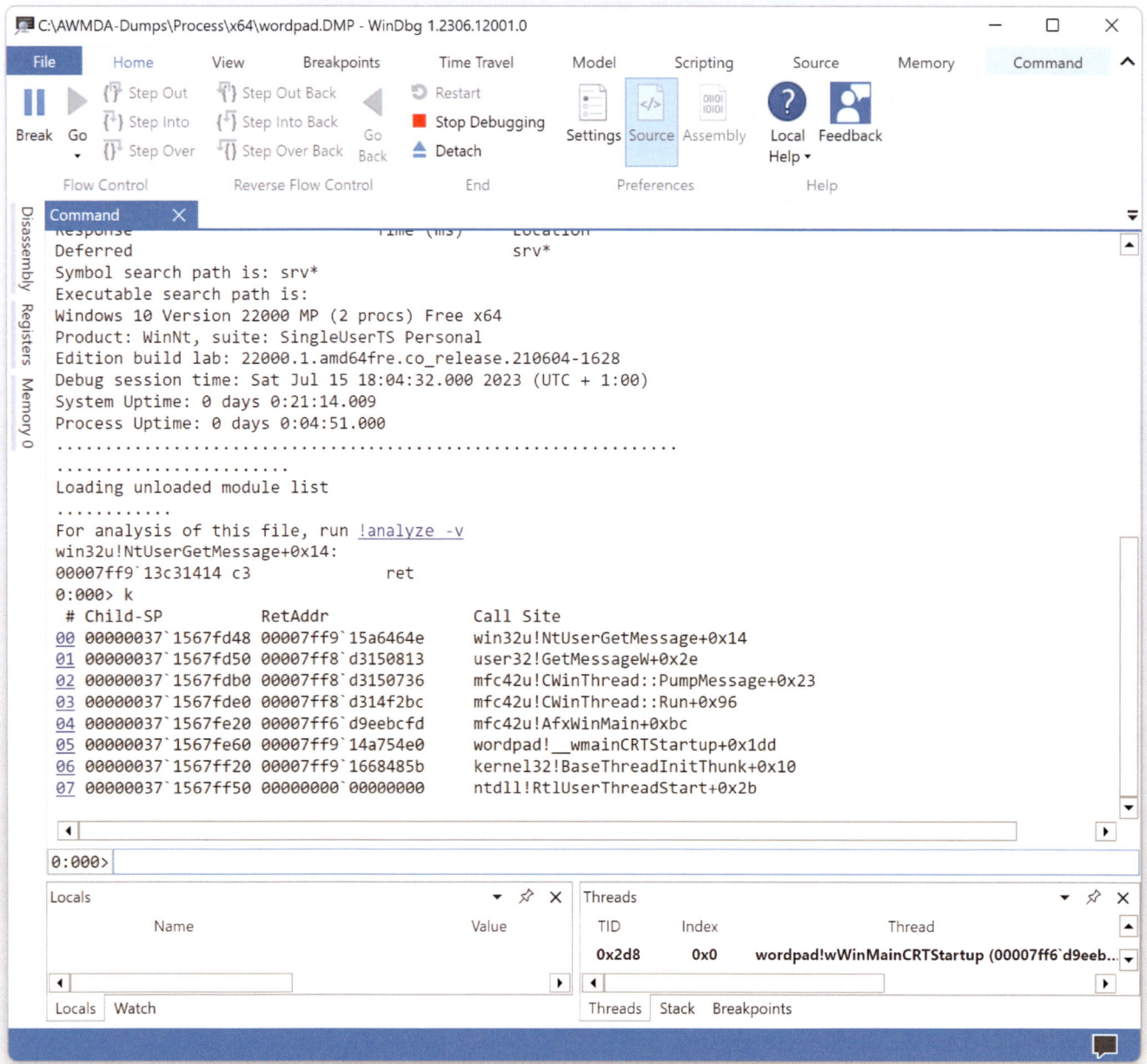

6. The output of the command should be this:

```
0:000> k
# Child-SP          RetAddr            Call Site
00 00000037`1567fd48 00007ff9`15a6464e   win32u!NtUserGetMessage+0x14
01 00000037`1567fd50 00007ff8`d3150813   user32!GetMessageW+0x2e
02 00000037`1567fdb0 00007ff8`d3150736   mfc42u!CWinThread::PumpMessage+0x23
03 00000037`1567fde0 00007ff8`d314f2bc   mfc42u!CWinThread::Run+0x96
04 00000037`1567fe20 00007ff6`d9eebcfd   mfc42u!AfxWinMain+0xbc
05 00000037`1567fe60 00007ff9`14a754e0   wordpad!__wmainCRTStartup+0x1dd
06 00000037`1567ff20 00007ff9`1668485b   kernel32!BaseThreadInitThunk+0x10
07 00000037`1567ff50 00000000`00000000   ntdll!RtlUserThreadStart+0x2b
```

If it has this form below with large offsets, then your symbol files were not set up correctly - **Incorrect Stack Trace** pattern:

```
0:000> k
# Child-SP          RetAddr           Call Site
00 00000037`1567fd48 00007ff9`15a6464e  win32u!NtUserGetMessage+0x14
01 00000037`1567fd50 00007ff8`d3150813  user32!GetMessageW+0x2e
02 00000037`1567fdb0 00007ff8`d3150736  mfc42u+0x10813
03 00000037`1567fde0 00007ff8`d314f2bc  mfc42u+0x10736
04 00000037`1567fe20 00007ff6`d9eebcfd  mfc42u+0xf2bc
05 00000037`1567fe60 00007ff9`14a754e0  wordpad+0xbcfd
06 00000037`1567ff20 00007ff9`1668485b  kernel32!BaseThreadInitThunk+0x10
07 00000037`1567ff50 00000000`00000000  ntdll!RtlUserThreadStart+0x2b
```

7.   [Optional] Download and install Debugging Tools for Windows (See windbg.org for quick links, WinDbg Quick Links \ Download Debugging Tools for Windows). For this part, we use WinDbg 10.0.22621.382 from Windows 11 WDK, version 22H2.

8.   Launch WinDbg from Windows Kits \ WinDbg (X64) or Windows Kits \ WinDbg (X86). For uniformity, we use the X64 version of WinDbg throughout the exercises.

WinDbg:10.0.22621.382 AMD64

File Edit View Debug Window Help

Ln 0, Col 0   Sys 0:<None>   Proc 000:0   Thrd 000:0   ASM   OVR   CAPS   NUM

9.   Open \AWMDA-Dumps\Process\x64\wordpad.DMP:

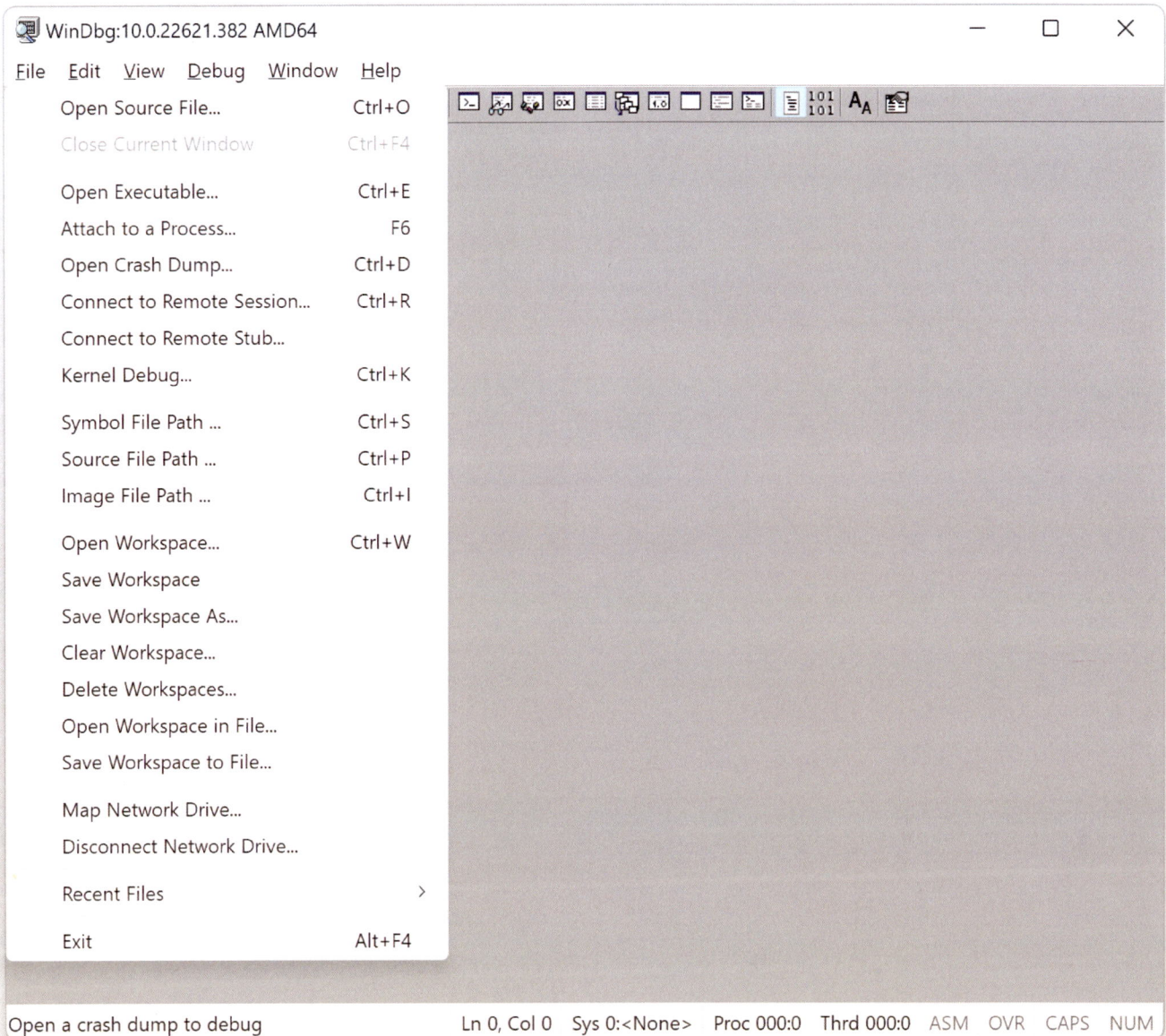

10. We get the dump file loaded:

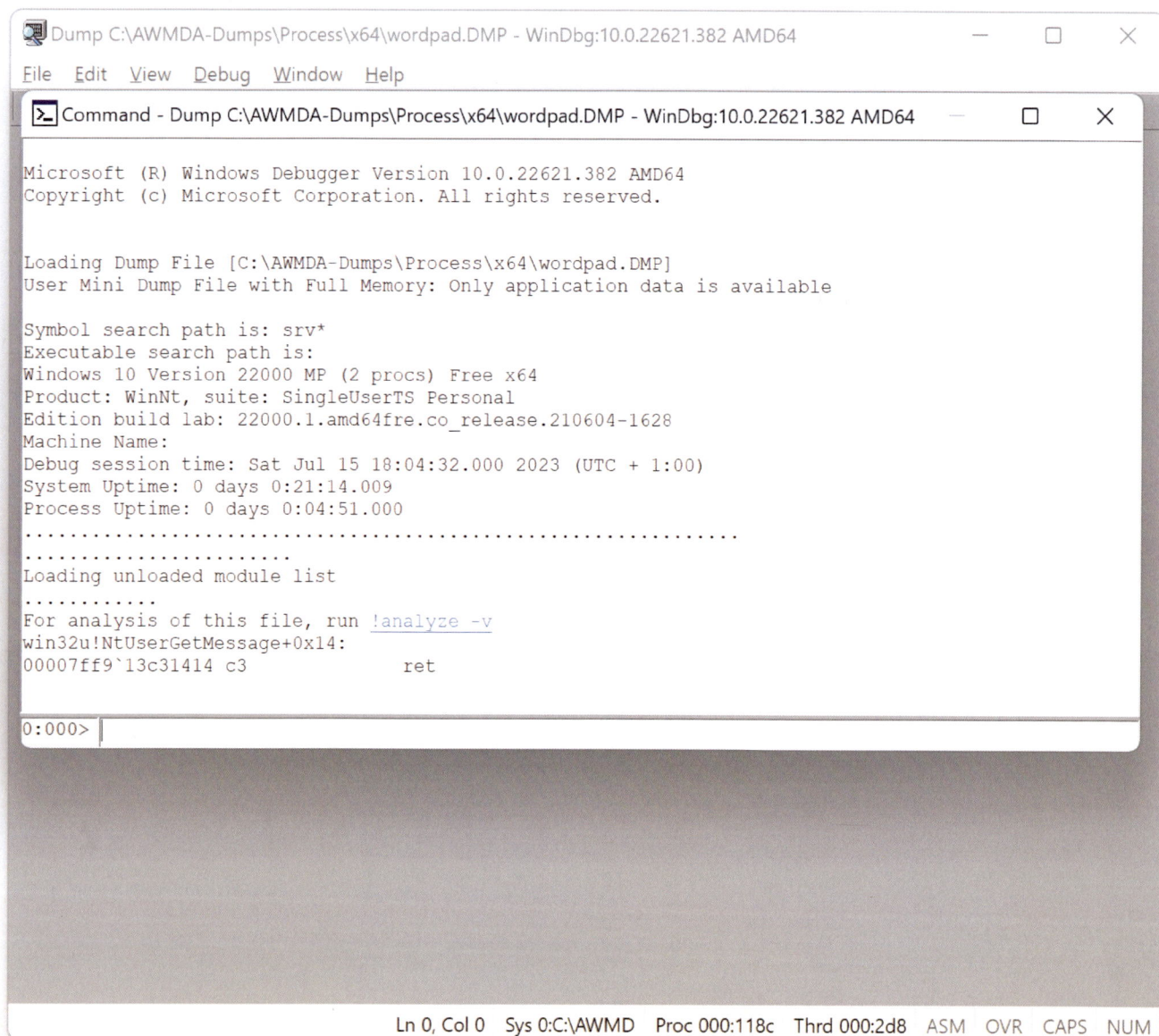

```
Dump C:\AWMDA-Dumps\Process\x64\wordpad.DMP - WinDbg:10.0.22621.382 AMD64          —   □   ✕
File  Edit  View  Debug  Window  Help

Command - Dump C:\AWMDA-Dumps\Process\x64\wordpad.DMP - WinDbg:10.0.22621.382 AMD64    —   □   ✕

Microsoft (R) Windows Debugger Version 10.0.22621.382 AMD64
Copyright (c) Microsoft Corporation. All rights reserved.


Loading Dump File [C:\AWMDA-Dumps\Process\x64\wordpad.DMP]
User Mini Dump File with Full Memory: Only application data is available

Symbol search path is: srv*
Executable search path is:
Windows 10 Version 22000 MP (2 procs) Free x64
Product: WinNt, suite: SingleUserTS Personal
Edition build lab: 22000.1.amd64fre.co_release.210604-1628
Machine Name:
Debug session time: Sat Jul 15 18:04:32.000 2023 (UTC + 1:00)
System Uptime: 0 days 0:21:14.009
Process Uptime: 0 days 0:04:51.000
...........................................................
....................
Loading unloaded module list
............
For analysis of this file, run !analyze -v
win32u!NtUserGetMessage+0x14:
00007ff9`13c31414 c3              ret

0:000> |

                    Ln 0, Col 0   Sys 0:C:\AWMD   Proc 000:118c   Thrd 000:2d8   ASM  OVR  CAPS  NUM
```

60

11.   Type **k** command to verify the correctness of stack trace:

```
Command - Dump C:\AWMDA-Dumps\Process\x64\wordpad.DMP - WinDbg:10.0.22621.382 AMD64     □   ✕

Microsoft (R) Windows Debugger Version 10.0.22621.382 AMD64
Copyright (c) Microsoft Corporation. All rights reserved.


Loading Dump File [C:\AWMDA-Dumps\Process\x64\wordpad.DMP]
User Mini Dump File with Full Memory: Only application data is available

Symbol search path is: srv*
Executable search path is:
Windows 10 Version 22000 MP (2 procs) Free x64
Product: WinNt, suite: SingleUserTS Personal
Edition build lab: 22000.1.amd64fre.co_release.210604-1628
Machine Name:
Debug session time: Sat Jul 15 18:04:32.000 2023 (UTC + 1:00)
System Uptime: 0 days 0:21:14.009
Process Uptime: 0 days 0:04:51.000
............................................................
.......................
Loading unloaded module list
............
For analysis of this file, run !analyze -v
win32u!NtUserGetMessage+0x14:
00007ff9`13c31414 c3              ret

0:000> k
```

```
Command - Dump C:\AWMDA-Dumps\Process\x64\wordpad.DMP - WinDbg:10.0.22621.382 AMD64     □   ✕
Executable search path is.
Windows 10 Version 22000 MP (2 procs) Free x64
Product: WinNt, suite: SingleUserTS Personal
Edition build lab: 22000.1.amd64fre.co_release.210604-1628
Machine Name:
Debug session time: Sat Jul 15 18:04:32.000 2023 (UTC + 1:00)
System Uptime: 0 days 0:21:14.009
Process Uptime: 0 days 0:04:51.000
............................................................
.......................
Loading unloaded module list
............
For analysis of this file, run !analyze -v
win32u!NtUserGetMessage+0x14:
00007ff9`13c31414 c3              ret
0:000> k
 # Child-SP          RetAddr               Call Site
00 00000037`1567fd48 00007ff9`15a6464e     win32u!NtUserGetMessage+0x14
01 00000037`1567fd50 00007ff8`d3150813     user32!GetMessageW+0x2e
02 00000037`1567fdb0 00007ff8`d3150736     mfc42u!CWinThread::PumpMessage+0x23
03 00000037`1567fde0 00007ff8`d314f2bc     mfc42u!CWinThread::Run+0x96
04 00000037`1567fe20 00007ff6`d9eebcfd     mfc42u!AfxWinMain+0xbc
05 00000037`1567fe60 00007ff9`14a754e0     wordpad!__wmainCRTStartup+0x1dd
06 00000037`1567ff20 00007ff9`1668485b     kernel32!BaseThreadInitThunk+0x10
07 00000037`1567ff50 00000000`00000000     ntdll!RtlUserThreadStart+0x2b
0:000>
```

12.   [Optional] Another approach is to use Docker container image that contains preinstalled WinDbg x64 with required symbol files for this course's memory dump files:

```
c:\AWMDA-Dumps> docker pull patterndiagnostics/windbg:10.0.22621.382-awmda6
10.0.22621.382-awmda6: Pulling from patterndiagnostics/windbg
Digest: sha256:ab5632327cd474e886e8bd95bdad71b420e18f1ef1a00c9d32f70d7029c6733b
Status: Image is up to date for patterndiagnostics/windbg:10.0.22621.382-awmda6
docker.io/patterndiagnostics/windbg:10.0.22621.382-awmda6

c:\AWMDA-Dumps>docker run -it -v C:\AWMDA-Dumps:C:\AWMDA-Dumps
patterndiagnostics/windbg:10.0.22621.382-awmda6
Microsoft Windows [Version 10.0.20348.1726]
(c) Microsoft Corporation. All rights reserved.

C:\WinDbg>windbg.bat C:\AWMDA-Dumps\Process\x64\wordpad.DMP

Microsoft (R) Windows Debugger Version 10.0.22621.382 AMD64
Copyright (c) Microsoft Corporation. All rights reserved.


Loading Dump File [C:\AWMDA-Dumps\Process\x64\wordpad.DMP]
User Mini Dump File with Full Memory: Only application data is available


************* Path validation summary **************
Response                        Time (ms)       Location
OK                                              C:\WinDbg\mss
Symbol search path is: C:\WinDbg\mss
Executable search path is:
Windows 10 Version 22000 MP (2 procs) Free x64
Product: WinNt, suite: SingleUserTS Personal
Edition build lab: 22000.1.amd64fre.co_release.210604-1628
Machine Name:
Debug session time: Sat Jul 15 18:04:32.000 2023 (UTC + 1:00)
System Uptime: 0 days 0:21:14.009
Process Uptime: 0 days 0:04:51.000
.............................................................
........................
Loading unloaded module list
...........
For analysis of this file, run !analyze -v
win32u!NtUserGetMessage+0x14:
00007ff9`13c31414 c3              ret

0:000> k
Child-SP          RetAddr               Call Site
00000037`1567fd48 00007ff9`15a6464e     win32u!NtUserGetMessage+0x14
00000037`1567fd50 00007ff8`d3150813     user32!GetMessageW+0x2e
00000037`1567fdb0 00007ff8`d3150736     mfc42u!CWinThread::PumpMessage+0x23
00000037`1567fde0 00007ff8`d314f2bc     mfc42u!CWinThread::Run+0x96
00000037`1567fe20 00007ff6`d9eebcfd     mfc42u!AfxWinMain+0xbc
00000037`1567fe60 00007ff9`14a754e0     wordpad!__wmainCRTStartup+0x1dd
00000037`1567ff20 00007ff9`1668485b     kernel32!BaseThreadInitThunk+0x10
00000037`1567ff50 00000000`00000000     ntdll!RtlUserThreadStart+0x2b

0:000> q
quit:
NatVis script unloaded from 'C:\Program Files\Windows Kits\10\Debuggers\x64\Visualizers\atlmfc.natvis'
NatVis script unloaded from 'C:\Program Files\Windows Kits\10\Debuggers\x64\Visualizers\ObjectiveC.natvis'
NatVis script unloaded from 'C:\Program Files\Windows Kits\10\Debuggers\x64\Visualizers\concurrency.natvis'
```

```
NatVis script unloaded from 'C:\Program Files\Windows Kits\10\Debuggers\x64\Visualizers\cpp_rest.natvis'
NatVis script unloaded from 'C:\Program Files\Windows Kits\10\Debuggers\x64\Visualizers\stl.natvis'
NatVis script unloaded from 'C:\Program Files\Windows Kits\10\Debuggers\x64\Visualizers\Windows.Data.Json.natvis'
NatVis script unloaded from 'C:\Program Files\Windows
Kits\10\Debuggers\x64\Visualizers\Windows.Devices.Geolocation.natvis'
NatVis script unloaded from 'C:\Program Files\Windows
Kits\10\Debuggers\x64\Visualizers\Windows.Devices.Sensors.natvis'
NatVis script unloaded from 'C:\Program Files\Windows Kits\10\Debuggers\x64\Visualizers\Windows.Media.natvis'
NatVis script unloaded from 'C:\Program Files\Windows Kits\10\Debuggers\x64\Visualizers\windows.natvis'
NatVis script unloaded from 'C:\Program Files\Windows Kits\10\Debuggers\x64\Visualizers\winrt.natvis'
```

`C:\WinDbg>`**`exit`**

`c:\AWMDA-Dumps>`

If you find any symbol problems, please use the Contact form on www.patterndiagnostics.com to report them.

13.   We recommend exiting WinDbg after each exercise.

Process Memory Dumps

Exercises P1 – P21

All exercises were modeled on real-life examples using specially constructed applications. All process dumps were saved from Windows 10 and Windows 11 systems[1]. We learn more than 50 memory analysis patterns.

---

[1] Exercises based on WinDbg from Windows 8.1 with process dumps saved from Windows Vista system running under VMware Fusion on Mac OS X or non-virtualized Windows 7 and Windows Server 2008 R2 are available in the previous editions of this course (version 4.0 and below).

Exercise P1

- **Goal:** Learn how to see dump file type and version, get a stack trace, check its correctness, perform default analysis, list threads and modules, check module version information, dump module data, and check the process environment

- **Patterns:** Manual Dump (Process); Stack Trace; Not My Version (Software); Environment Hint; Unknown Component

- \AWMDA-Dumps\Exercise-P1-Analysis-normal-process-dump-wordpad-64.pdf

Exercise P1: Analysis of a normal application process dump (64-bit wordpad)

Goal: Learn how to see dump file type and version, get a stack trace, check its correctness, perform default analysis, list threads and modules, check module version information, dump module data, and check the process environment.

Patterns: Manual Dump (Process); Stack Trace; Not My Version (Software); Environment Hint; Unknown Component.

1.   Launch WinDbg.

2.   Open \AWMDA-Dumps\Process\x64\wordpad.DMP.

3.   We get the dump file loaded:

```
Microsoft (R) Windows Debugger Version 10.0.25877.1004 AMD64
Copyright (c) Microsoft Corporation. All rights reserved.


Loading Dump File [C:\AWMDA-Dumps\Process\x64\wordpad.DMP]
User Mini Dump File with Full Memory: Only application data is available


************* Path validation summary **************
Response                      Time (ms)     Location
Deferred                                    srv*
Symbol search path is: srv*
Executable search path is:
Windows 10 Version 22000 MP (2 procs) Free x64
Product: WinNt, suite: SingleUserTS Personal
Edition build lab: 22000.1.amd64fre.co_release.210604-1628
Debug session time: Sat Jul 15 18:04:32.000 2023 (UTC + 1:00)
System Uptime: 0 days 0:21:14.009
Process Uptime: 0 days 0:04:51.000
..............................................................
.......................
Loading unloaded module list
...........
For analysis of this file, run !analyze -v
win32u!NtUserGetMessage+0x14:
00007ff9`13c31414 c3              ret
```

4.   Open a log file to save all future output using the **.logopen** command:

```
0:000> .logopen C:\AWMDA-Dumps\Process\x64\wordpad.log
Opened log file 'C:\AWMDA-Dumps\Process\x64\wordpad.log'
```

5.   Type **k** command to verify the correctness of the stack trace:

```
0:000> k
 # Child-SP          RetAddr           Call Site
00 00000037`1567fd48 00007ff9`15a6464e win32u!NtUserGetMessage+0x14
01 00000037`1567fd50 00007ff8`d3150813 user32!GetMessageW+0x2e
02 00000037`1567fdb0 00007ff8`d3150736 mfc42u!CWinThread::PumpMessage+0x23
03 00000037`1567fde0 00007ff8`d314f2bc mfc42u!CWinThread::Run+0x96
04 00000037`1567fe20 00007ff6`d9eebcfd mfc42u!AfxWinMain+0xbc
05 00000037`1567fe60 00007ff9`14a754e0 wordpad!__wmainCRTStartup+0x1dd
06 00000037`1567ff20 00007ff9`1668485b kernel32!BaseThreadInitThunk+0x10
07 00000037`1567ff50 00000000`00000000 ntdll!RtlUserThreadStart+0x2b
```

6.   Type the **version** command to get the OS version, system and process uptimes, the dump file timestamp, and its type:

```
0:000> version
Windows 10 Version 22000 MP (2 procs) Free x64
Product: WinNt, suite: SingleUserTS Personal
Edition build lab: 22000.1.amd64fre.co_release.210604-1628
Debug session time: Sat Jul 15 18:04:32.000 2023 (UTC + 1:00)
System Uptime: 0 days 0:21:14.009
Process Uptime: 0 days 0:04:51.000
  Kernel time: 0 days 0:00:01.000
  User time: 0 days 0:00:00.000
Full memory user mini dump: C:\AWMDA-Dumps\Process\x64\wordpad.DMP

Microsoft (R) Windows Debugger Version 10.0.25877.1004 AMD64
Copyright (c) Microsoft Corporation. All rights reserved.

command line: '"C:\Program Files\WindowsApps\Microsoft.WinDbg_1.2306.12001.0_x64__8wekyb3d8bbwe\amd64\EngHost.exe"
npipe:pipe=DbgX_485dd9d6637e46dfbfb0270a9e44d88e,password=0ed044e5d5a4 "C:\Program
Files\WindowsApps\Microsoft.WinDbg_1.2306.12001.0_x64__8wekyb3d8bbwe\amd64" "C:\ProgramData\Dbg"'  Debugger Process 0x21DC
dbgeng:  image 10.0.25877.1004,
        [path: C:\Program Files\WindowsApps\Microsoft.WinDbg_1.2306.12001.0_x64__8wekyb3d8bbwe\amd64\dbgeng.dll]
dbghelp: image 10.0.25877.1004,
        [path: C:\Program Files\WindowsApps\Microsoft.WinDbg_1.2306.12001.0_x64__8wekyb3d8bbwe\amd64\dbghelp.dll]
        DIA version: 32595
Extension DLL search Path:
[...]
Extension DLL chain:
    DbgEngCoreDMExt: image 10.0.25877.1004, API 0.0.0,
        [path: C:\Program Files\WindowsApps\Microsoft.WinDbg_1.2306.12001.0_x64__8wekyb3d8bbwe\amd64\winext\DbgEngCoreDMExt.dll]
    MachOBinComposition: image 10.0.25877.1004, API 0.0.0,
        [path: C:\Program Files\WindowsApps\Microsoft.WinDbg_1.2306.12001.0_x64__8wekyb3d8bbwe\amd64\winext\MachOBinComposition.dll]
    ELFBinComposition: image 10.0.25877.1004, API 0.0.0,
        [path: C:\Program Files\WindowsApps\Microsoft.WinDbg_1.2306.12001.0_x64__8wekyb3d8bbwe\amd64\winext\ELFBinComposition.dll]
    dbghelp: image 10.0.25877.1004, API 10.0.6,
        [path: C:\Program Files\WindowsApps\Microsoft.WinDbg_1.2306.12001.0_x64__8wekyb3d8bbwe\amd64\dbghelp.dll]
    exts: image 10.0.25877.1004, API 1.0.0,
        [path: C:\Program Files\WindowsApps\Microsoft.WinDbg_1.2306.12001.0_x64__8wekyb3d8bbwe\amd64\WINXP\exts.dll]
    uext: image 10.0.25877.1004, API 1.0.0,
        [path: C:\Program Files\WindowsApps\Microsoft.WinDbg_1.2306.12001.0_x64__8wekyb3d8bbwe\amd64\winext\uext.dll]
    ntsdexts: image 10.0.25877.1004, API 1.0.0,
        [path: C:\Program Files\WindowsApps\Microsoft.WinDbg_1.2306.12001.0_x64__8wekyb3d8bbwe\amd64\WINXP\ntsdexts.dll]
```

Note: Debug session time is when the dump was generated. Although the dump is called a "mini dump," it is a full memory user dump with all process memory included.

7.   Type the default analysis command **!analyze -v**:

Note: This command may take some time initially as symbols may be downloaded from the symbol server:

```
0:000> !analyze -v
*******************************************************************************
*                                                                             *
*                        Exception Analysis                                   *
*                                                                             *
*******************************************************************************


KEY_VALUES_STRING: 1

    Key  : Analysis.CPU.mSec
    Value: 702

    Key  : Analysis.Elapsed.mSec
    Value: 8353

    Key  : Analysis.IO.Other.Mb
    Value: 13

    Key  : Analysis.IO.Read.Mb
    Value: 0

    Key  : Analysis.IO.Write.Mb
    Value: 27

    Key  : Analysis.Init.CPU.mSec
    Value: 171

    Key  : Analysis.Init.Elapsed.mSec
    Value: 330539

    Key  : Analysis.Memory.CommitPeak.Mb
    Value: 145

    Key  : Failure.Bucket
    Value: BREAKPOINT_80000003_win32u.dll!NtUserGetMessage

    Key  : Failure.Hash
    Value: {3112b5eb-303b-e877-0655-90bdfa336126}

    Key  : Timeline.OS.Boot.DeltaSec
    Value: 1274

    Key  : Timeline.Process.Start.DeltaSec
    Value: 291

    Key  : WER.OS.Branch
    Value: co_release

    Key  : WER.OS.Version
    Value: 10.0.22000.1

    Key  : WER.Process.Version
    Value: 10.0.22000.1


FILE_IN_CAB:  wordpad.DMP

NTGLOBALFLAG:  400

APPLICATION_VERIFIER_FLAGS:  0

EXCEPTION_RECORD:  (.exr -1)
ExceptionAddress: 0000000000000000
   ExceptionCode: 80000003 (Break instruction exception)
  ExceptionFlags: 00000000
NumberParameters: 0

FAULTING_THREAD:  000002d8

PROCESS_NAME:  wordpad.exe

ERROR_CODE: (NTSTATUS) 0x80000003 - {EXCEPTION}  Breakpoint  A breakpoint has been reached.

EXCEPTION_CODE_STR:  80000003

STACK_TEXT:
00000037`1567fd48 00007ff9`15a6464e     : 00007ff8`d328a460 00007ff8`d314b71b 00007ff8`d328a460 00007ff8`d314ba4b : win32u!NtUserGetMessage+0x14
00000037`1567fd50 00007ff8`d3150813     : 00007ff6`d9fddfd0 00000000`00000000 00000000`ffffffff 00000000`00000000 : user32!GetMessageW+0x2e
00000037`1567fdb0 00007ff8`d3150736     : 00000000`00000002 00000000`00000001 00000000`00000000 00000000`00000000 : mfc42u!CWinThread::PumpMessage+0x23
00000037`1567fde0 00007ff8`d314f2bc     : 00000000`00000001 00007ff6`d9ee0000 00000000`00000000 00000164`9e3d6bec : mfc42u!CWinThread::Run+0x96
00000037`1567fe20 00007ff6`d9eebcfd     : 00000000`00000001 00000000`00000000 00000000`00000000 00000000`0000001f : mfc42u!AfxWinMain+0xbc
00000037`1567fe60 00007ff9`14a754e0     : 00000000`00000000 00000000`00000000 00000000`00000000 00000000`00000000 : wordpad!__wmainCRTStartup+0x1dd
00000037`1567ff20 00007ff9`1668485b     : 00000000`00000000 00000000`00000000 00000000`00000000 00000000`00000000 : kernel32!BaseThreadInitThunk+0x10
00000037`1567ff50 00000000`00000000     : 00000000`00000000 00000000`00000000 00000000`00000000 00000000`00000000 : ntdll!RtlUserThreadStart+0x2b


STACK_COMMAND:  ~0s; .ecxr ; kb

SYMBOL_NAME:  win32u!NtUserGetMessage+14

MODULE_NAME: win32u
```

68

```
IMAGE_NAME:  win32u.dll

FAILURE_BUCKET_ID:  BREAKPOINT_80000003_win32u.dll!NtUserGetMessage

OS_VERSION:  10.0.22000.1

BUILDLAB_STR:  co_release

OSPLATFORM_TYPE:  x64

OSNAME:  Windows 10

IMAGE_VERSION:  10.0.22000.434

FAILURE_ID_HASH:  {3112b5eb-303b-e877-0655-90bdfa336126}

Followup:    MachineOwner
---------
```

Note: "Break instruction exception" can be the sign of a **Manual Dump** pattern, but often WinDbg is not able to figure out an exception that may be on another thread or hidden. STACK_COMMAND shows the sequence commands that WinDbg executed to get STACK_TEXT.

8.   Now we check how many threads there are by using the ~ command:

```
0:000> ~
.  0  Id: 118c.2d8 Suspend: 0 Teb: 00000037`15400000 Unfrozen
   1  Id: 118c.1064 Suspend: 0 Teb: 00000037`15408000 Unfrozen
   2  Id: 118c.2108 Suspend: 0 Teb: 00000037`1540a000 Unfrozen
   3  Id: 118c.50c Suspend: 0 Teb: 00000037`1540c000 Unfrozen
```

Note: **118c** is Process ID (PID), and **2d8** is Thread ID (TID). **118c.2d8** is called CID (Client ID).

9.   Now we dump a stack trace using the **kc** command (only modules and symbols):

```
0:000> kc
 # Call Site
00 win32u!NtUserGetMessage
01 user32!GetMessageW
02 mfc42u!CWinThread::PumpMessage
03 mfc42u!CWinThread::Run
04 mfc42u!AfxWinMain
05 wordpad!__wmainCRTStartup
06 kernel32!BaseThreadInitThunk
07 ntdll!RtlUserThreadStart
```

10.   Now we dump the stack trace of the current thread using the **k** command (with symbols, return addresses, and function offsets):

```
0:000> k
 # Child-SP          RetAddr               Call Site
00 00000037`1567fd48 00007ff9`15a6464e     win32u!NtUserGetMessage+0x14
01 00000037`1567fd50 00007ff8`d3150813     user32!GetMessageW+0x2e
02 00000037`1567fdb0 00007ff8`d3150736     mfc42u!CWinThread::PumpMessage+0x23
03 00000037`1567fde0 00007ff8`d314f2bc     mfc42u!CWinThread::Run+0x96
04 00000037`1567fe20 00007ff6`d9eebcfd     mfc42u!AfxWinMain+0xbc
05 00000037`1567fe60 00007ff9`14a754e0     wordpad!__wmainCRTStartup+0x1dd
06 00000037`1567ff20 00007ff9`1668485b     kernel32!BaseThreadInitThunk+0x10
07 00000037`1567ff50 00000000`00000000     ntdll!RtlUserThreadStart+0x2b
```

Hint: How to check that the stack trace is correct. Use the **ub** command (**u**nassemble **b**ackward) to check if there is a *call* instruction. We check that the *GetMessageW* function was called from the *CWinThread::PumpMessage* function:

```
0:000> k
 # Child-SP          RetAddr               Call Site
00 00000037`1567fd48 00007ff9`15a6464e     win32u!NtUserGetMessage+0x14
01 00000037`1567fd50 00007ff8`d3150813     user32!GetMessageW+0x2e
02 00000037`1567fdb0 00007ff8`d3150736     mfc42u!CWinThread::PumpMessage+0x23
03 00000037`1567fde0 00007ff8`d314f2bc     mfc42u!CWinThread::Run+0x96
04 00000037`1567fe20 00007ff6`d9eebcfd     mfc42u!AfxWinMain+0xbc
05 00000037`1567fe60 00007ff9`14a754e0     wordpad!__wmainCRTStartup+0x1dd
06 00000037`1567ff20 00007ff9`1668485b     kernel32!BaseThreadInitThunk+0x10
07 00000037`1567ff50 00000000`00000000     ntdll!RtlUserThreadStart+0x2b
```

```
0:000> ub 00007ff8`d3150813
mfc42u!CWinThread::PumpMessage+0x9:
00007ff8`d31507f9 20488d          and      byte ptr [rax-73h],cl
00007ff8`d31507fc 59              pop      rcx
00007ff8`d31507fd 68488bf948      push     48F98B48h
00007ff8`d3150802 8bcb            mov      ecx,ebx
00007ff8`d3150804 4533c9          xor      r9d,r9d
00007ff8`d3150807 4533c0          xor      r8d,r8d
00007ff8`d315080a 33d2            xor      edx,edx
00007ff8`d315080c 48ff152dc00f00  call     qword ptr [mfc42u!_imp_GetMessageW
(00007ff8`d324c840)]
```

Then we check that the *NtUserGetMessage* function was called from the *GetMessageW* function:

```
0:000> k
 # Child-SP          RetAddr               Call Site
00 00000037`1567fd48 00007ff9`15a6464e     win32u!NtUserGetMessage+0x14
01 00000037`1567fd50 00007ff8`d3150813     user32!GetMessageW+0x2e
02 00000037`1567fdb0 00007ff8`d3150736     mfc42u!CWinThread::PumpMessage+0x23
03 00000037`1567fde0 00007ff8`d314f2bc     mfc42u!CWinThread::Run+0x96
04 00000037`1567fe20 00007ff6`d9eebcfd     mfc42u!AfxWinMain+0xbc
05 00000037`1567fe60 00007ff9`14a754e0     wordpad!__wmainCRTStartup+0x1dd
06 00000037`1567ff20 00007ff9`1668485b     kernel32!BaseThreadInitThunk+0x10
07 00000037`1567ff50 00000000`00000000     ntdll!RtlUserThreadStart+0x2b
```

```
0:000> ub 00007ff9`15a6464e
user32!GetMessageW+0x9:
00007ff9`15a64629 488bd9          mov      rbx,rcx
00007ff9`15a6462c 458bc8          mov      r9d,r8d
00007ff9`15a6462f 440bc8          or       r9d,eax
00007ff9`15a64632 41f7c10000feff  test     r9d,0FFFE0000h
00007ff9`15a64639 0f85c70b0200    jne      user32!GetMessageW+0x20be6 (00007ff9`15a85206)
00007ff9`15a6463f 448bc8          mov      r9d,eax
00007ff9`15a64642 48897c2460      mov      qword ptr [rsp+60h],rdi
00007ff9`15a64647 48ff158a260700  call     qword ptr [user32!_imp_NtUserGetMessage (00007ff9`15ad6cd8)]
```

Note: Remember the functions call each other from bottom to top. The topmost function from the stack trace is the last one that was called. **ExceptionAddress** may point to the last one. We will come to this in the real exception process dumps later.

11.   Now we check the list of loaded modules using the **lm** command:

```
0:000> lm
start             end               module name
00007ff6`d9ee0000 00007ff6`da1cd000   wordpad    (pdb symbols)          C:\WinDbg.Docker.AWMDA6\mss\wordpad.pdb\B193BA11D609CB39E8D086A748A191651\wordpad.pdb
00007ff8`baf60000 00007ff8`bb39c000   UIRibbon   (deferred)
00007ff8`d3140000 00007ff8`d32b4000   mfc42u     (pdb symbols)          C:\WinDbg.Docker.AWMDA6\mss\mfc42u.pdb\C250069F808FD6D342ADAE9524B0F1EE1\mfc42u.pdb
00007ff8`e0c80000 00007ff8`e0eb5000   opcservices   (deferred)
00007ff8`e0ec0000 00007ff8`e112e000   msxml3     (deferred)
00007ff8`f4cb0000 00007ff8`f4d11000   AcGenral   (deferred)
00007ff8`f5320000 00007ff8`f5596000   xpsservices   (deferred)
00007ff8`f55a0000 00007ff8`f567b000   MXDWDRV    (deferred)
00007ff8`f5680000 00007ff8`f5a3e000   PrintConfig   (deferred)
00007ff8`f6620000 00007ff8`f662d000   atlthunk   (deferred)
00007ff8`f6630000 00007ff8`f67e3000   GdiPlus    (deferred)
00007ff8`f7470000 00007ff8`f77d6000   msftedit   (deferred)
00007ff8`f7d70000 00007ff8`f7d96000   globinputhost   (deferred)
00007ff8`fa3c0000 00007ff8`fa41d000   dataexchange   (deferred)
00007ff8`fa420000 00007ff8`fa489000   oleacc     (deferred)
00007ff8`fb530000 00007ff8`fb59a000   ninput     (deferred)
00007ff8`fb8d0000 00007ff8`fb8f3000   fontsub    (deferred)
00007ff8`fcdf0000 00007ff8`fd072000   msxml6     (deferred)
00007ff8`ff650000 00007ff8`ff6eb000   winspool   (deferred)
00007ff9`00880000 00007ff9`00b25000   comctl32   (deferred)
00007ff9`01170000 00007ff9`01246000   jscript    (deferred)
00007ff9`01840000 00007ff9`0189b000   XpsPushLayer   (deferred)
00007ff9`01df0000 00007ff9`01e6b000   MpOAV      (deferred)
00007ff9`04070000 00007ff9`0408d000   mpr        (deferred)
00007ff9`07360000 00007ff9`0740e000   TextShaping   (deferred)
00007ff9`074e0000 00007ff9`0760d000   textinputframework   (deferred)
00007ff9`08120000 00007ff9`0812a000   version    (deferred)
00007ff9`08130000 00007ff9`08163000   winmm      (deferred)
00007ff9`08360000 00007ff9`08522000   Windows_Globalization   (deferred)
00007ff9`08530000 00007ff9`0878f000   DWrite     (deferred)
00007ff9`08790000 00007ff9`08fa6000   OneCoreUAPCommonProxyStub   (deferred)
00007ff9`0a580000 00007ff9`0a72e000   windowscodecs   (deferred)
00007ff9`0a770000 00007ff9`0a8f8000   Windows_UI   (deferred)
00007ff9`0b5e0000 00007ff9`0b645000   Bcp47Langs   (deferred)
00007ff9`0c0d0000 00007ff9`0c0e2000   npmproxy   (deferred)
00007ff9`0c5b0000 00007ff9`0c816000   twinapi_appcore   (pdb symbols)
C:\WinDbg.Docker.AWMDA6\mss\twinapi.appcore.pdb\4FD957C7E31BBC581E01125EC191B7F81\twinapi.appcore.pdb
00007ff9`0cda0000 00007ff9`0cdc8000   srvcli     (deferred)
00007ff9`0cdd0000 00007ff9`0d082000   iertutil   (deferred)
00007ff9`0d100000 00007ff9`0d2ee000   urlmon     (deferred)
00007ff9`0d850000 00007ff9`0d869000   dhcpcsvc6   (deferred)
00007ff9`0db20000 00007ff9`0db3e000   dhcpcsvc   (deferred)
00007ff9`0e250000 00007ff9`0e2c1000   netprofm   (deferred)
00007ff9`0e670000 00007ff9`0e9dd000   CoreUIComponents   (deferred)
00007ff9`0f140000 00007ff9`0f1d2000   msvcp110_win   (deferred)
00007ff9`0f6a0000 00007ff9`0f6d1000   prntvpt    (deferred)
00007ff9`0f820000 00007ff9`0f857000   xmllite    (deferred)
00007ff9`10930000 00007ff9`10a62000   CoreMessaging   (deferred)
00007ff9`10d70000 00007ff9`10e01000   apphelp    (deferred)
00007ff9`10e30000 00007ff9`10edc000   uxtheme    (deferred)
00007ff9`113c0000 00007ff9`113ef000   dwmapi     (deferred)
00007ff9`118d0000 00007ff9`119c7000   propsys    (deferred)
00007ff9`11b70000 00007ff9`11cd6000   WinTypes   (deferred)
00007ff9`11ce0000 00007ff9`12547000   windows_storage   (deferred)
00007ff9`126b0000 00007ff9`126bc000   netutils   (deferred)
00007ff9`127e0000 00007ff9`1280d000   IPHLPAPI   (deferred)
00007ff9`12860000 00007ff9`12947000   dnsapi     (deferred)
00007ff9`12c70000 00007ff9`12c88000   kernel_appcore   (deferred)
00007ff9`12e90000 00007ff9`12ed2000   sspicli    (deferred)
00007ff9`13200000 00007ff9`13229000   userenv    (deferred)
00007ff9`13350000 00007ff9`1335c000   CRYPTBASE   (deferred)
00007ff9`13550000 00007ff9`13577000   bcrypt     (deferred)
00007ff9`139e0000 00007ff9`13a82000   sxs        (deferred)
00007ff9`13a90000 00007ff9`13ac1000   profapi    (deferred)
00007ff9`13c30000 00007ff9`13c56000   win32u     (pdb symbols)          C:\WinDbg.Docker.AWMDA6\mss\win32u.pdb\045A07FC5CC3A90DFCCC8B4C1918F7421\win32u.pdb
00007ff9`13c60000 00007ff9`13cfd000   msvcp_win   (deferred)
00007ff9`13d00000 00007ff9`13e12000   gdi32full   (deferred)
00007ff9`13f90000 00007ff9`14304000   KERNELBASE   (pdb symbols)
C:\WinDbg.Docker.AWMDA6\mss\kernelbase.pdb\AF202873637A4CAABB4ACB056CE0BCCA1\kernelbase.pdb
00007ff9`14380000 00007ff9`143ff000   bcryptPrimitives   (deferred)
00007ff9`14400000 00007ff9`14511000   ucrtbase   (deferred)
00007ff9`14590000 00007ff9`14908000   combase    (private pdb symbols)  C:\WinDbg.Docker.AWMDA6\mss\combase.pdb\FB29C6C2977E6207AAC857DCE3D9183C1\combase.pdb
00007ff9`14920000 00007ff9`149c3000   msvcrt     (deferred)
00007ff9`14a60000 00007ff9`14b1d000   kernel32   (pdb symbols)
C:\WinDbg.Docker.AWMDA6\mss\kernel32.pdb\DC094362EEB8DA89986E90A2096ACE281\kernel32.pdb
00007ff9`14b20000 00007ff9`14b49000   gdi32      (deferred)
00007ff9`14b70000 00007ff9`1531e000   shell32    (deferred)
00007ff9`15320000 00007ff9`1540c000   comdlg32   (deferred)
00007ff9`15410000 00007ff9`1552e000   msctf      (deferred)
00007ff9`15760000 00007ff9`157bd000   shlwapi    (deferred)
00007ff9`157c0000 00007ff9`158aa000   SHCore     (deferred)
00007ff9`15910000 00007ff9`15a30000   rpcrt4     (deferred)
00007ff9`15a30000 00007ff9`15a39000   nsi        (deferred)
00007ff9`15a40000 00007ff9`15bec000   user32     (pdb symbols)          C:\WinDbg.Docker.AWMDA6\mss\user32.pdb\9479B9C8D8218B8972152084F4D6840C1\user32.pdb
00007ff9`15bf0000 00007ff9`15c9f000   clbcatq    (deferred)
00007ff9`15ca0000 00007ff9`15d3e000   sechost    (deferred)
00007ff9`15d40000 00007ff9`15dee000   advapi32   (deferred)
00007ff9`15e60000 00007ff9`15f36000   oleaut32   (deferred)
00007ff9`15f70000 00007ff9`1610a000   ole32      (private pdb symbols)  C:\WinDbg.Docker.AWMDA6\mss\ole32.pdb\FC5E57B29784316F10EE67D8895FF8341\ole32.pdb
00007ff9`16190000 00007ff9`161c1000   imm32      (deferred)
00007ff9`16680000 00007ff9`16889000   ntdll      (pdb symbols)          C:\WinDbg.Docker.AWMDA6\mss\ntdll.pdb\D522F52AE48D7166E35F4FB492B6398B1\ntdll.pdb

Unloaded modules:
```

```
00007ff9`01e70000 00007ff9`01e8d000   amsi.dll
00007ff9`01e70000 00007ff9`01e8d000   amsi.dll
00007ff9`01e70000 00007ff9`01e8d000   amsi.dll
00007ff9`01e70000 00007ff9`01e8d000   amsi.dll
00007ff9`06000000 00007ff9`06023000   compstui.dll
00007ff9`0f720000 00007ff9`0f727000   MSIMG32.dll
00007ff9`01e70000 00007ff9`01e8d000   amsi.dll
00007ff9`01e70000 00007ff9`01e8d000   amsi.dll
00007ff9`06000000 00007ff9`06023000   compstui.dll
00007ff9`0f720000 00007ff9`0f727000   MSIMG32.dll
00007ff9`01e70000 00007ff9`01e8d000   amsi.dll
00007ff9`02970000 00007ff9`029a8000   fms.dll
```

Note: start and **end** addresses show where modules are loaded in process virtual memory. You can see the module contents by using the **dc** command (**Unknown Component** pattern):

```
0:000> dc 00007ff6`d9ee0000 00007ff6`da1cd000
00007ff6`d9ee0000   00905a4d 00000003 00000004 0000ffff   MZ..............
00007ff6`d9ee0010   000000b8 00000000 00000040 00000000   ........@.......
00007ff6`d9ee0020   00000000 00000000 00000000 00000000   ................
00007ff6`d9ee0030   00000000 00000000 00000000 000000f0   ................
00007ff6`d9ee0040   0eba1f0e cd09b400 4c01b821 685421cd   ........!..L.!Th
00007ff6`d9ee0050   70207369 72676f72 63206d61 6f6e6e61   is program canno
00007ff6`d9ee0060   65622074 6e757220 206e6920 20534f44   t be run in DOS
00007ff6`d9ee0070   65646f6d 0a0d0d2e 00000024 00000000   mode....$.......
00007ff6`d9ee0080   cc9a0e95 9ff46fd1 9ff46fd1 9ff46fd1   .....o...o...o..
00007ff6`d9ee0090   9ef71d02 9ff46fd5 9ef01d02 9ff46fce   .....o.......o..
00007ff6`d9ee00a0   9ef11d02 9ff46fda 9ef51d02 9ff46ff6   .....o.......o..
00007ff6`d9ee00b0   9ff56fd1 9ff46b3f 9efc1d02 9ff46fa2   .o..?k.......o..
00007ff6`d9ee00c0   9f0b1d02 9ff46fd0 9ef61d02 9ff46fd0   .....o.......o..
00007ff6`d9ee00d0   68636952 9ff46fd1 00000000 00000000   Rich.o..........
00007ff6`d9ee00e0   00000000 00000000 00000000 00000000   ................
00007ff6`d9ee00f0   00004550 00078664 b930df5e 00000000   PE..d...^.0.....
00007ff6`d9ee0100   00000000 002200f0 1c0e020b 0009f000   ......".........
00007ff6`d9ee0110   0024d000 00000000 0000bda0 00001000   ..$.............
[...]
00007ff6`da1ccf90   00000000 00000000 00000000 00000000   ................
00007ff6`da1ccfa0   00000000 00000000 00000000 00000000   ................
00007ff6`da1ccfb0   00000000 00000000 00000000 00000000   ................
00007ff6`da1ccfc0   00000000 00000000 00000000 00000000   ................
00007ff6`da1ccfd0   00000000 00000000 00000000 00000000   ................
00007ff6`da1ccfe0   00000000 00000000 00000000 00000000   ................
00007ff6`da1ccff0   00000000 00000000 00000000 00000000   ................
00007ff6`da1cd000   ????????                              ????
```

12.   We can check verbose module information using the **lmv** command or use **lmv m** *<module name>* to check an individual module (**Not My Version** pattern):

```
0:000> lmv m wordpad
Browse full module list
start             end                 module name
00007ff6`d9ee0000 00007ff6`da1cd000   wordpad    (pdb symbols)
C:\WinDbg.Docker.AWMDA6\mss\wordpad.pdb\B193BA11D609CB39E8D086A748A191651\wordpad.pdb
    Loaded symbol image file: wordpad.exe
    Image path: C:\Program Files\Windows NT\Accessories\wordpad.exe
    Image name: wordpad.exe
    Browse all global symbols  functions  data
    Image was built with /Brepro flag.
    Timestamp:        B930DF5E (This is a reproducible build file hash, not a timestamp)
    CheckSum:         002F073E
    ImageSize:        002ED000
    File version:     10.0.22000.1
    Product version:  10.0.22000.1
    File flags:       0 (Mask 3F)
    File OS:          40004 NT Win32
    File type:        1.0 App
    File date:        00000000.00000000
```

```
Translations:     0409.04b0
Information from resource tables:
    CompanyName:      Microsoft Corporation
    ProductName:      Microsoft® Windows® Operating System
    InternalName:     wordpad
    OriginalFilename: WORDPAD.EXE
    ProductVersion:   10.0.22000.1
    FileVersion:      10.0.22000.1 (WinBuild.160101.0800)
    FileDescription:  Windows Wordpad Application
    LegalCopyright:   © Microsoft Corporation. All rights reserved
```

13.   Sometimes **lmv** command doesn't show much and **!lmi** command might give extra information:

```
0:000> !lmi wordpad
Loaded Module Info: [wordpad]
         Module: wordpad
   Base Address: 00007ff6d9ee0000
     Image Name: wordpad.exe
   Machine Type: 34404 (X64)
     Time Stamp: b930df5e (This is a reproducible build file hash, not a true timestamp)
           Size: 2ed000
       CheckSum: 2f073e
Characteristics: 22
Debug Data Dirs: Type  Size      VA  Pointer
           CODEVIEW    24, e7b2c,    e7b2c RSDS - GUID: {B193BA11-D609-CB39-E8D0-86A748A19165}
             Age: 1, Pdb: wordpad.pdb
             POGO   48c, e7b50,    e7b50 [Data not mapped]
             REPRO   24, e7fdc,    e7fdc Reproducible build
     Image Type: MEMORY   - Image read successfully from loaded memory.
    Symbol Type: PDB      - Symbols loaded successfully from symbol server.
             C:\WinDbg.Docker.AWMDA6\mss\wordpad.pdb\B193BA11D609CB39E8D086A748A191651\wordpad.pdb
    Load Report: public symbols , not source indexed
             C:\WinDbg.Docker.AWMDA6\mss\wordpad.pdb\B193BA11D609CB39E8D086A748A191651\wordpad.pdb
```

Note: We can also use the **lmt** command variant if we are interested in timestamps only.

14.   Sometimes **Environment Hint** pattern can give troubleshooting suggestions related to environment variables and DLL paths. **!peb** command (**P**rocess **E**nvironment **B**lock):

```
0:000> !peb
PEB at 00000037155ff000
    InheritedAddressSpace:    No
    ReadImageFileExecOptions: No
    BeingDebugged:            No
    ImageBaseAddress:         00007ff6d9ee0000
    NtGlobalFlag:             400
    NtGlobalFlag2:            0
    Ldr                       00007ff9167fa120
    Ldr.Initialized:          Yes
    Ldr.InInitializationOrderModuleList: 000001649e3d1fd0 . 00000164a097d4d0
    Ldr.InLoadOrderModuleList:           000001649e3d2150 . 00000164a097d4b0
    Ldr.InMemoryOrderModuleList:         000001649e3d2160 . 00000164a097d4c0
              Base TimeStamp                     Module
        7ff6d9ee0000 b930df5e Jun 15 13:11:10 2068 C:\Program Files\Windows NT\Accessories\wordpad.exe
        7ff916680000 931cda92 Mar 18 10:55:14 2048 C:\WINDOWS\SYSTEM32\ntdll.dll
        7ff914a60000 7b65e245 Aug 09 13:17:09 2035 C:\WINDOWS\System32\KERNEL32.DLL
        7ff913f90000 72a6f702 Dec 15 06:00:34 2030 C:\WINDOWS\System32\KERNELBASE.dll
        7ff910d70000 3c3af44a Jan 08 13:29:46 2002 C:\WINDOWS\SYSTEM32\apphelp.dll
        7ff8f4cb0000 0e564edf Aug 16 00:55:11 1977 C:\WINDOWS\SYSTEM32\AcGenral.dll
        7ff914920000 90483ed2 Sep 15 20:49:38 2046 C:\WINDOWS\System32\msvcrt.dll
        7ff915ca0000 31ec7be5 Jul 17 06:36:37 1996 C:\WINDOWS\System32\sechost.dll
        7ff915760000 5d809272 Sep 17 08:59:46 2019 C:\WINDOWS\System32\SHLWAPI.dll
        7ff915a40000 95c2e8f0 Aug 14 19:33:20 2049 C:\WINDOWS\System32\USER32.dll
        7ff913c30000 2eab7211 Oct 24 09:36:33 1994 C:\WINDOWS\System32\win32u.dll
        7ff914b20000 0b2998f3 Dec 08 12:58:27 1975 C:\WINDOWS\System32\GDI32.dll
```

```
7ff913d00000 f03395da Sep 13 13:08:58 2097 C:\WINDOWS\System32\gdi32full.dll
7ff913c60000 1fb7fd57 Nov 12 03:53:59 1986 C:\WINDOWS\System32\msvcp_win.dll
7ff914400000 00e78ce9 Jun 25 16:14:49 1970 C:\WINDOWS\System32\ucrtbase.dll
7ff915f70000 8dfb3d4d Jun 26 02:18:05 2045 C:\WINDOWS\System32\ole32.dll
7ff914590000 426c1ced Apr 24 23:25:49 2005 C:\WINDOWS\System32\combase.dll
7ff915910000 7ff0ec4a Jan 07 16:46:02 2038 C:\WINDOWS\System32\RPCRT4.dll
7ff914b70000 8cba58e5 Oct 25 16:38:13 2044 C:\WINDOWS\System32\SHELL32.dll
7ff915d40000 ce622c7b Sep 21 17:46:51 2079 C:\WINDOWS\System32\ADVAPI32.dll
7ff913200000 a3572516 Nov 02 13:28:54 2056 C:\WINDOWS\SYSTEM32\USERENV.dll
7ff904070000 4ab16881 Sep 16 23:36:49 2009 C:\WINDOWS\SYSTEM32\MPR.dll
7ff912e90000 e2336ada Apr 04 21:21:46 2090 C:\WINDOWS\System32\SspiCli.dll
7ff916190000 356942c7 May 25 11:07:03 1998 C:\WINDOWS\System32\IMM32.DLL
7ff915320000 b5c44fd4 Aug 20 15:53:08 2066 C:\WINDOWS\System32\COMDLG32.dll
7ff9157c0000 d40bc30a Sep 25 06:43:38 2082 C:\WINDOWS\System32\shcore.dll
7ff915e60000 f6e2d5cf Apr 04 13:30:07 2101 C:\WINDOWS\System32\OLEAUT32.dll
7ff90f140000 7a1c0743 Dec 02 07:26:59 2034 C:\WINDOWS\SYSTEM32\msvcp110_win.dll
7ff8d3140000 f91a937d Jun 09 04:54:37 2102 C:\WINDOWS\SYSTEM32\MFC42u.dll
7ff900880000 150b8699 Mar 10 12:54:49 1981 C:\WINDOWS\WinSxS\amd64_microsoft.windows.common-
controls_6595b64144ccf1df_6.0.22000.120_none_9d947278b86cc467\COMCTL32.dll
7ff908130000 4b928681 Mar 06 16:44:49 2010 C:\WINDOWS\SYSTEM32\WINMM.dll
7ff90d100000 cc1588be Jul 02 05:55:26 2078 C:\WINDOWS\SYSTEM32\urlmon.dll
7ff90f820000 ced9ec48 Dec 21 12:44:56 2079 C:\WINDOWS\SYSTEM32\XmlLite.dll
7ff90cdd0000 5a2fa526 Dec 12 09:45:10 2017 C:\WINDOWS\SYSTEM32\iertutil.dll
7ff90cda0000 35be966e Jul 29 04:26:38 1998 C:\WINDOWS\SYSTEM32\srvcli.dll
7ff9118d0000 c2756dbe May 20 04:15:10 2073 C:\WINDOWS\SYSTEM32\PROPSYS.dll
7ff9126b0000 813aa4df Sep 14 20:09:19 2038 C:\WINDOWS\SYSTEM32\netutils.dll
7ff8fb530000 cc168813 Jul 03 00:04:51 2078 C:\WINDOWS\SYSTEM32\ninput.dll
7ff912c70000 fb20135b Jul 06 17:42:03 2103 C:\WINDOWS\SYSTEM32\kernel.appcore.dll
7ff914380000 a34302f0 Oct 18 07:57:52 2056 C:\WINDOWS\System32\bcryptPrimitives.dll
7ff910e30000 e2c027fe Jul 20 15:26:06 2090 C:\WINDOWS\system32\uxtheme.dll
7ff915bf0000 1d473905 Jul 26 07:21:57 1985 C:\WINDOWS\System32\clbcatq.dll
7ff8e0ec0000 9e59ff97 Mar 09 19:44:23 2054 C:\WINDOWS\System32\msxml3.dll
7ff913550000 54fe428f Mar 10 01:02:07 2015 C:\WINDOWS\System32\bcrypt.dll
7ff8f7470000 fc008760 Dec 23 22:44:48 2103 C:\WINDOWS\SYSTEM32\MSFTEDIT.DLL
7ff8baf60000 9a0b9171 Nov 24 14:36:33 2051 C:\WINDOWS\system32\UIRibbon.dll
7ff8f6630000 dc58dab9 Feb 23 03:51:21 2087
C:\WINDOWS\WinSxS\amd64_microsoft.windows.gdiplus_6595b64144ccf1df_1.1.22000.434_none_ce836c1412fb9b57\gdiplus.dll
7ff915410000 81def127 Jan 17 10:06:31 2039 C:\WINDOWS\SYSTEM32\MSCTF.dll
7ff907360000 6627ed04 Apr 23 18:16:52 2024 C:\WINDOWS\SYSTEM32\TextShaping.dll
7ff908360000 10fbb3fc Jan 11 19:31:08 1979 C:\Windows\System32\Windows.Globalization.dll
7ff8f7d70000 c9e14921 Apr 30 06:05:37 2077 C:\WINDOWS\SYSTEM32\globinputhost.dll
7ff90b5e0000 10434404 Aug 24 22:56:20 1978 C:\WINDOWS\SYSTEM32\Bcp47Langs.dll
7ff8fa3c0000 511f48d8 Feb 16 08:52:40 2013 C:\WINDOWS\system32\dataexchange.dll
7ff90c5b0000 d6129e9c Oct 23 20:14:36 2083 C:\WINDOWS\system32\twinapi.appcore.dll
7ff9074e0000 63938554 Dec 09 18:58:28 2022 C:\WINDOWS\SYSTEM32\textinputframework.dll
7ff8fa420000 d4726d59 Dec 12 02:41:29 2082 C:\Windows\System32\oleacc.dll
7ff8f6620000 f95e4869 Jul 30 13:28:25 2102 C:\WINDOWS\SYSTEM32\atlthunk.dll
7ff9113c0000 09360bc9 Nov 24 14:55:05 1974 C:\WINDOWS\system32\dwmapi.dll
7ff8fcdf0000 bd9922fe Oct 19 08:36:30 2070 C:\Windows\System32\msxml6.dll
7ff90a580000 1decf0c2 Nov 28 23:09:54 1985 C:\WINDOWS\system32\windowscodecs.dll
7ff90a770000 2a4aa2e7 Jun 26 05:53:59 1992 C:\Windows\System32\Windows.UI.dll
7ff910930000 9e78ed02 Apr 02 07:45:22 2054 C:\WINDOWS\SYSTEM32\CoreMessaging.dll
7ff90e670000 6685eb5c Jul 04 01:22:52 2024 C:\WINDOWS\SYSTEM32\CoreUIComponents.dll
7ff911b70000 b3354271 Apr 10 19:01:21 2065 C:\WINDOWS\SYSTEM32\wintypes.dll
7ff913350000 14759998 Nov 16 19:35:52 1980 C:\WINDOWS\SYSTEM32\CRYPTBASE.DLL
7ff911ce0000 42c927b5 Jul 04 13:12:37 2005 C:\WINDOWS\SYSTEM32\windows.storage.dll
7ff8ff650000 fdebc754 Dec 30 13:40:36 2104 C:\WINDOWS\SYSTEM32\WINSPOOL.DRV
7ff90e250000 2e513767 Aug 16 23:02:15 1994 C:\WINDOWS\System32\netprofm.dll
7ff90c0d0000 f288926c Dec 10 07:57:32 2098 C:\WINDOWS\System32\npmproxy.dll
7ff9127e0000 8c5d7fee Aug 16 06:23:58 2044 C:\WINDOWS\SYSTEM32\IPHLPAPI.DLL
7ff915a30000 1de8145c Nov 25 06:40:28 1985 C:\WINDOWS\System32\NSI.dll
7ff90d850000 bda0ed88 Oct 25 06:26:32 2070 C:\WINDOWS\SYSTEM32\dhcpcsvc6.DLL
7ff90db20000 7d8aeb85 Sep 29 00:11:01 2036 C:\WINDOWS\SYSTEM32\dhcpcsvc.DLL
7ff912860000 64c37de6 Jul 28 09:35:50 2013 C:\WINDOWS\SYSTEM32\DNSAPI.dll
7ff8f5680000 922ff4f6 Sep 20 19:20:38 2047
C:\WINDOWS\System32\DriverStore\FileRepository\prnms003.inf_amd64_03994fdd96c52654\Amd64\PrintConfig.dll
7ff908120000 12bfcbe0 Dec 20 17:37:36 1979 C:\WINDOWS\SYSTEM32\VERSION.dll
7ff90f6a0000 c491446b Jul 03 15:42:51 2074 C:\WINDOWS\SYSTEM32\prntvpt.dll
7ff901170000 0549fc92 Oct 24 01:34:26 1972 C:\Windows\System32\jscript.dll
7ff913aa0000 47c07815 Feb 23 19:46:29 2008 C:\WINDOWS\System32\profapi.dll
7ff901df0000 8e940251 Oct 19 23:23:13 2045 C:\ProgramData\Microsoft\Windows
Defender\Platform\4.18.23050.5-0\MpOav.dll
7ff9139e0000 a2eb73f0 Aug 12 22:00:32 2056 C:\WINDOWS\SYSTEM32\sxs.dll
7ff8f55a0000 89c5dd1c Mar 31 21:16:28 2043
C:\WINDOWS\System32\DriverStore\FileRepository\ntprint.inf_amd64_69e8e0efb212ba16\Amd64\mxdwdrv.dll
```

```
         7ff908530000 13ccbe72 Jul 11 18:40:02 1980 C:\WINDOWS\SYSTEM32\DWrite.dll
         7ff908790000 9028fb7a Aug 23 03:42:02 2046 C:\Windows\System32\OneCoreUAPCommonProxyStub.dll
         7ff8e0c80000 399cd7ea Aug 18 07:30:02 2000 C:\WINDOWS\SYSTEM32\opcservices.dll
         7ff901840000 50fd98e3 Jan 21 19:37:07 2013 C:\WINDOWS\SYSTEM32\XpsPushLayer.dll
         7ff8f5320000 f6f60cb7 Apr 19 03:17:27 2101 C:\WINDOWS\SYSTEM32\xpsservices.dll
         7ff8fb8d0000 7c246416 Jan 01 00:21:42 2036 C:\WINDOWS\system32\FontSub.dll
SubSystemData:     0000000000000000
ProcessHeap:       000001649e3d0000
ProcessParameters: 000001649e3d64d0
CurrentDirectory:  'C:\Users\dumpa\Documents\'
WindowTitle:  'C:\ProgramData\Microsoft\Windows\Start Menu\Programs\Accessories\Wordpad.lnk'
ImageFile:    'C:\Program Files\Windows NT\Accessories\wordpad.exe'
CommandLine:  '"C:\Program Files\Windows NT\Accessories\wordpad.exe" '
DllPath:      '< Name not readable >'
Environment:  000001649e3d11f0
    =::=::\
    ALLUSERSPROFILE=C:\ProgramData
    APPDATA=C:\Users\dumpa\AppData\Roaming
    CommonProgramFiles=C:\Program Files\Common Files
    CommonProgramFiles(x86)=C:\Program Files (x86)\Common Files
    CommonProgramW6432=C:\Program Files\Common Files
    COMPUTERNAME=DESKTOP-OGPC0LO
    ComSpec=C:\WINDOWS\system32\cmd.exe
    DriverData=C:\Windows\System32\Drivers\DriverData
    FPS_BROWSER_APP_PROFILE_STRING=Internet Explorer
    FPS_BROWSER_USER_PROFILE_STRING=Default
    HOMEDRIVE=C:
    HOMEPATH=\Users\dumpa
    LOCALAPPDATA=C:\Users\dumpa\AppData\Local
    LOGONSERVER=\\DESKTOP-OGPC0LO
    NUMBER_OF_PROCESSORS=2
    OneDrive=C:\Users\dumpa\OneDrive
    OS=Windows_NT

Path=C:\WINDOWS\system32;C:\WINDOWS;C:\WINDOWS\System32\Wbem;C:\WINDOWS\System32\WindowsPowerShell\v1.0\;C:\WINDOWS\Sy
stem32\OpenSSH\;C:\Program Files\dotnet\;C:\Program Files
(x86)\dotnet\;C:\Users\dumpa\AppData\Local\Microsoft\WindowsApps;C:\Users\dumpa\.dotnet\tools;
    PATHEXT=.COM;.EXE;.BAT;.CMD;.VBS;.VBE;.JS;.JSE;.WSF;.WSH;.MSC
    PROCESSOR_ARCHITECTURE=AMD64
    PROCESSOR_IDENTIFIER=Intel64 Family 6 Model 142 Stepping 10, GenuineIntel
    PROCESSOR_LEVEL=6
    PROCESSOR_REVISION=8e0a
    ProgramData=C:\ProgramData
    ProgramFiles=C:\Program Files
    ProgramFiles(x86)=C:\Program Files (x86)
    ProgramW6432=C:\Program Files
    PSModulePath=C:\Program Files\WindowsPowerShell\Modules;C:\WINDOWS\system32\WindowsPowerShell\v1.0\Modules
    PUBLIC=C:\Users\Public
    SESSIONNAME=Console
    SystemDrive=C:
    SystemRoot=C:\WINDOWS
    TEMP=C:\Users\dumpa\AppData\Local\Temp
    TMP=C:\Users\dumpa\AppData\Local\Temp
    USERDOMAIN=DESKTOP-OGPC0LO
    USERDOMAIN_ROAMINGPROFILE=DESKTOP-OGPC0LO
    USERNAME=Training
    USERPROFILE=C:\Users\dumpa
    windir=C:\WINDOWS
```

15.   To launch classic help from the WinDbg app, type the **.hh** command.

16.   We close logging before exiting WinDbg:


```
0:000> .logclose
Closing open log file C:\AWMDA-Dumps\Process\x64\wordpad.log
```

Note: If you close a log and later reopen it using the **.logopen** command, its contents will be lost. To append new
output to an already existing log please use **.logappend** WinDbg command.

Exercise P2

- **Goal:** Repeat exercise P1 using 32-bit notepad process memory dump

- \AWMDA-Dumps\Exercise-P2-Analysis-normal-process-dump-wordpad-32.pdf

Exercise P2: Analysis of a normal application process dump (32-bit wordpad)

Goal: Repeat exercise P1 using a 32-bit wordpad process memory dump.

1.   Launch WinDbg.

2.   Open \AWMDA-Dumps\Process\x86\wordpad.DMP.

3.   We get the dump file loaded:

```
Microsoft (R) Windows Debugger Version 10.0.25877.1004 X86
Copyright (c) Microsoft Corporation. All rights reserved.


Loading Dump File [C:\AWMDA-Dumps\Process\x86\wordpad.DMP]
User Mini Dump File with Full Memory: Only application data is available


************* Path validation summary **************
Response                      Time (ms)     Location
Deferred                                    srv*
Symbol search path is: srv*
Executable search path is:
Windows 10 Version 22000 MP (2 procs) Free x86 compatible
Product: WinNt, suite: SingleUserTS Personal
Edition build lab: 22000.1.amd64fre.co_release.210604-1628
Debug session time: Sat Jul 15 18:08:49.000 2023 (UTC + 1:00)
System Uptime: 0 days 0:25:31.226
Process Uptime: 0 days 0:03:21.000
.............................................................
.....
Loading unloaded module list
.
For analysis of this file, run !analyze -v
eax=00000000 ebx=010393c8 ecx=00000000 edx=00000000 esi=010393fc edi=010393fc
eip=75fd10cc esp=00c3f948 ebp=00c3f980 iopl=0         nv up ei pl nz na pe nc
cs=0023  ss=002b  ds=002b  es=002b  fs=0053  gs=002b             efl=00000206
win32u!NtUserGetMessage+0xc:
75fd10cc c21000          ret     10h
```

Note: The analysis process and the command output are very similar to the previous exercise, except that the virtual memory address range is different. We recommend doing this exercise on your own to reinforce what you learned previously. One difference is that in 32-bit memory dumps, we can use yet another **kv** (or **kb**) stack trace command that shows the first 3 function parameters passed during the function call (which is usually not the case for 64-bit dumps where the values happen to be what was in the stack memory at that time).

```
0:000> kb
 # ChildEBP RetAddr       Args to Child
00 00c3f944 762b0200      010393fc 00000000 00000000 win32u!NtUserGetMessage+0xc
01 00c3f980 747c8f35      010393fc 00000000 00000000 user32!GetMessageW+0x30
02 00c3f99c 747c8fe3      010393c8 010268c0 ffffffff mfc42u!CWinThread::PumpMessage+0x15
03 00c3f9b8 7479a242      00000000 00000020 00000000 mfc42u!CWinThread::Run+0x63
04 00c3f9d0 01026d0c      00f80000 00000000 033657b4 mfc42u!AfxWinMain+0xa2
05 00c3fa60 76926739      00b32000 76926720 00c3fac8 wordpad!__wmainCRTStartup+0x153
```

```
06 00c3fa70 778a8e7f   00b32000 ccaa57de 00000000 kernel32!BaseThreadInitThunk+0x19
07 00c3fac8 778a8e4d   ffffffff 778d8c89 00000000 ntdll!__RtlUserThreadStart+0x2b
08 00c3fad8 00000000   01026e40 00b32000 00000000 ntdll!_RtlUserThreadStart+0x1b
```

Exercise P3

- **Goal:** Learn how to list stack traces, check their correctness, perform default analysis, list modules, check their version information, and check thread age and CPU consumption

- **Patterns:** Stack Trace Collection (Unmanaged Space)

- \AWMDA-Dumps\Exercise-P3-Analysis-normal-process-dump-msedge-64.pdf

Exercise P3: Analysis of a normal application process dump (64-bit Microsoft Edge)

Goal: Learn how to list stack traces, check their correctness, perform default analysis, list modules, check their version information, and check thread age and CPU consumption.

Patterns: Stack Trace Collection (Unmanaged Space).

1.   Launch WinDbg.

2.   Open \AWMDA-Dumps\Process\x64\msedge.DMP.

3.   We get the dump file loaded:

```
Microsoft (R) Windows Debugger Version 10.0.25877.1004 AMD64
Copyright (c) Microsoft Corporation. All rights reserved.


Loading Dump File [C:\AWMDA-Dumps\Process\x64\msedge.DMP]
User Mini Dump File with Full Memory: Only application data is available


************* Path validation summary **************
Response                     Time (ms)      Location
Deferred                                    srv*
Symbol search path is: srv*
Executable search path is:
Windows 10 Version 22000 MP (2 procs) Free x64
Product: WinNt, suite: SingleUserTS Personal
Edition build lab: 22000.1.amd64fre.co_release.210604-1628
Debug session time: Mon Jul 17 23:00:35.000 2023 (UTC + 1:00)
System Uptime: 0 days 0:09:16.500
Process Uptime: 0 days 0:04:03.000
....................
Loading unloaded module list
.
For analysis of this file, run !analyze -v
ntdll!NtRemoveIoCompletion+0x14:
00007ffd`4b023874 c3              ret
```

4.   Open a log file using the **.logopen** command:

```
0:000> .logopen C:\AWMDA-Dumps\Process\x64\msedge.log
Opened log file 'C:\AWMDA-Dumps\Process\x64\msedge.log'
```

5.   Type the **k** command to verify the correctness of stack trace:

```
0:000> k
 # Child-SP          RetAddr               Call Site
00 0000009b`155feef8 00007ffd`484c0a33     ntdll!NtRemoveIoCompletion+0x14
01 0000009b`155fef00 00007ff7`0ce94bdd     KERNELBASE!GetQueuedCompletionStatus+0x53
02 0000009b`155fef60 00007ff7`0ce906df     msedge!crashpad::ExceptionHandlerServer::Run+0x25b
03 0000009b`155ff090 00007ff7`0ce8f2ec     msedge!crashpad::HandlerMain+0xd18
04 0000009b`155ff570 00007ff7`0ce88d0f     msedge!crash_reporter::RunAsCrashpadHandler+0x59e
05 0000009b`155ff720 00007ff7`0cf7e492     msedge!wWinMain+0x677
06 0000009b`155ffc40 00007ffd`4a2654e0     msedge!__scrt_common_main_seh+0x106
07 0000009b`155ffc80 00007ffd`4af8485b     kernel32!BaseThreadInitThunk+0x10
```

```
08 0000009b`155ffcb0 00000000`00000000      ntdll!RtlUserThreadStart+0x2b
```

Note: Some stack traces may have a lot of source code references from runtime components, and to reduce the clutter, we recommend the **kL** command.

6. Type the **version** command to get the OS version, system and process uptimes, the dump timestamp and type:

```
0:000> version
Windows 10 Version 22000 MP (2 procs) Free x64
Product: WinNt, suite: SingleUserTS Personal
Edition build lab: 22000.1.amd64fre.co_release.210604-1628
Debug session time: Mon Jul 17 23:00:35.000 2023 (UTC + 1:00)
System Uptime: 0 days 0:09:16.500
Process Uptime: 0 days 0:04:03.000
  Kernel time: 0 days 0:00:00.000
  User time: 0 days 0:00:00.000
Full memory user mini dump: C:\AWMDA-Dumps\Process\x64\msedge.DMP

Microsoft (R) Windows Debugger Version 10.0.25877.1004 AMD64
Copyright (c) Microsoft Corporation. All rights reserved.

command line: '"C:\Program Files\WindowsApps\Microsoft.WinDbg_1.2306.12001.0_x64__8wekyb3d8bbwe\amd64\EngHost.exe"
npipe:pipe=DbgX_308e8db5ae3b467ca8bc59d926e7916e,password=0ee9e515e5c0 "C:\Program
Files\WindowsApps\Microsoft.WinDbg_1.2306.12001.0_x64__8wekyb3d8bbwe\amd64" "C:\ProgramData\Dbg"'  Debugger Process 0x26E4
dbgeng:   image 10.0.25877.1004,
        [path: C:\Program Files\WindowsApps\Microsoft.WinDbg_1.2306.12001.0_x64__8wekyb3d8bbwe\amd64\dbgeng.dll]
dbghelp: image 10.0.25877.1004,
        [path: C:\Program Files\WindowsApps\Microsoft.WinDbg_1.2306.12001.0_x64__8wekyb3d8bbwe\amd64\dbghelp.dll]
        DIA version: 32595
Extension DLL search Path:
[...]
Extension DLL chain:
    DbgEngCoreDMExt: image 10.0.25877.1004, API 0.0.0,
        [path: C:\Program Files\WindowsApps\Microsoft.WinDbg_1.2306.12001.0_x64__8wekyb3d8bbwe\amd64\winext\DbgEngCoreDMExt.dll]
    MachOBinComposition: image 10.0.25877.1004, API 0.0.0,
        [path: C:\Program Files\WindowsApps\Microsoft.WinDbg_1.2306.12001.0_x64__8wekyb3d8bbwe\amd64\winext\MachOBinComposition.dll]
    ELFBinComposition: image 10.0.25877.1004, API 0.0.0,
        [path: C:\Program Files\WindowsApps\Microsoft.WinDbg_1.2306.12001.0_x64__8wekyb3d8bbwe\amd64\winext\ELFBinComposition.dll]
    dbghelp: image 10.0.25877.1004, API 10.0.6,
        [path: C:\Program Files\WindowsApps\Microsoft.WinDbg_1.2306.12001.0_x64__8wekyb3d8bbwe\amd64\dbghelp.dll]
    exts: image 10.0.25877.1004, API 1.0.0,
        [path: C:\Program Files\WindowsApps\Microsoft.WinDbg_1.2306.12001.0_x64__8wekyb3d8bbwe\amd64\WINXP\exts.dll]
    uext: image 10.0.25877.1004, API 1.0.0,
        [path: C:\Program Files\WindowsApps\Microsoft.WinDbg_1.2306.12001.0_x64__8wekyb3d8bbwe\amd64\winext\uext.dll]
    ntsdexts: image 10.0.25877.1004, API 1.0.0,
        [path: C:\Program Files\WindowsApps\Microsoft.WinDbg_1.2306.12001.0_x64__8wekyb3d8bbwe\amd64\WINXP\ntsdexts.dll]
```

7.   Type the default analysis command **!analyze -v**:

```
0:000> !analyze -v
*******************************************************************
*                                                                 *
*                        Exception Analysis                       *
*                                                                 *
*******************************************************************

KEY_VALUES_STRING: 1

    Key  : Analysis.CPU.mSec
    Value: 655

    Key  : Analysis.Elapsed.mSec
    Value: 1897

    Key  : Analysis.IO.Other.Mb
    Value: 2

    Key  : Analysis.IO.Read.Mb
    Value: 0

    Key  : Analysis.IO.Write.Mb
    Value: 6

    Key  : Analysis.Init.CPU.mSec
    Value: 264

    Key  : Analysis.Init.Elapsed.mSec
    Value: 238489

    Key  : Analysis.Memory.CommitPeak.Mb
    Value: 165
```

```
Key : Failure.Bucket
Value: BREAKPOINT_80000003_msedge.exe!crashpad::ExceptionHandlerServer::Run

Key : Failure.Hash
Value: {94d5016a-0f5e-cec2-8317-92e676323e4d}

Key : Timeline.OS.Boot.DeltaSec
Value: 556

Key : Timeline.Process.Start.DeltaSec
Value: 243

Key : WER.OS.Branch
Value: co_release

Key : WER.OS.Version
Value: 10.0.22000.1

Key : WER.Process.Version
Value: 114.0.1823.82


FILE_IN_CAB: msedge.DMP

NTGLOBALFLAG: 400

APPLICATION_VERIFIER_FLAGS: 0

EXCEPTION_RECORD: (.exr -1)
ExceptionAddress: 0000000000000000
   ExceptionCode: 80000003 (Break instruction exception)
  ExceptionFlags: 00000000
NumberParameters: 0

FAULTING_THREAD: 00001634

PROCESS_NAME: msedge.exe

ERROR_CODE: (NTSTATUS) 0x80000003 - {EXCEPTION}  Breakpoint  A breakpoint has been reached.

EXCEPTION_CODE_STR: 80000003

STACK_TEXT:
0000009b`155feef8 00007ffd`484c0a33     : 00000000`00000000 00007ff7`0cf5317d 000057d0`002ccb40 00007ff7`0ce94fb8 : ntdll!NtRemoveIoCompletion+0x14
0000009b`155fef00 00007ff7`0ce94bdd     : 00000000`00000000 000057d0`00254640 786793eb`fef89fdb 00000000`00000108 : KERNELBASE!GetQueuedCompletionStatus+0x53
0000009b`155fef60 00007ff7`0ce906df     : 0000009b`155ff290 00007ffd`4a2700e0 000057d0`0029c1e0 0000009b`155ff2f8 :
msedge!crashpad::ExceptionHandlerServer::Run+0x25b
0000009b`155ff090 00007ff7`0ce8f2ec     : aaaaaaaa`aaaaaaaa aaaaaaaa`aaaaaaaa 00000000`00000000 00000000`00000070 : msedge!crashpad::HandlerMain+0xd18
0000009b`155ff570 00007ff7`0ce88d0f     : 00000000`0000000a 00079a6`6a3285e8 00000000`00000000 00000000`00000000 :
msedge!crash_reporter::RunAsCrashpadHandler+0x59e
0000009b`155ff720 00007ff7`0cf7e492     : 00000000`00000000 00007ff7`0cf7e509 00000000`00000000 00000000`00000000 : msedge!wWinMain+0x677
0000009b`155ffc40 00007ffd`4a2654e0     : 00000000`00000000 00000000`00000000 00000000`00000000 00000000`00000000 : msedge!__scrt_common_main_seh+0x106
0000009b`155ffc80 00007ffd`4af8485b     : 00000000`00000000 00000000`00000000 00000000`00000000 00000000`00000000 : kernel32!BaseThreadInitThunk+0x10
0000009b`155ffcb0 00000000`00000000     : 00000000`00000000 00000000`00000000 00000000`00000000 00000000`00000000 : ntdll!RtlUserThreadStart+0x2b


STACK_COMMAND: ~0s; .ecxr ; kb

SYMBOL_NAME: msedge!crashpad::ExceptionHandlerServer::Run+25b

MODULE_NAME: msedge

IMAGE_NAME: msedge.exe

FAILURE_BUCKET_ID: BREAKPOINT_80000003_msedge.exe!crashpad::ExceptionHandlerServer::Run

OS_VERSION: 10.0.22000.1

BUILDLAB_STR: co_release

OSPLATFORM_TYPE: x64

OSNAME: Windows 10

IMAGE_VERSION: 114.0.1823.82

FAILURE_ID_HASH: {94d5016a-0f5e-cec2-8317-92e676323e4d}

Followup:    MachineOwner
---------
```

Note: The stack trace in the output above from the **kb** command contains a lot of "noise" in the form of additional columns that usually have no use for analysis of x64 memory dumps.

8.   Now we check how many threads we have by using the **~** command (**.** shows that the current thread is #0):

```
0:000> ~
.  0  Id: c88.1634 Suspend: 0 Teb: 0000009b`14c68000 Unfrozen "CrashpadMainThread"
   1  Id: c88.1e60 Suspend: 0 Teb: 0000009b`14c6e000 Unfrozen "ExitCodeWatcherThread"
   2  Id: c88.1920 Suspend: 0 Teb: 0000009b`14c70000 Unfrozen
```

```
 3  Id: c88.1f9c Suspend: 0 Teb: 0000009b`14c72000 Unfrozen
 4  Id: c88.2fc Suspend: 0 Teb: 0000009b`14c74000 Unfrozen
 5  Id: c88.2270 Suspend: 0 Teb: 0000009b`14c76000 Unfrozen
 6  Id: c88.16f4 Suspend: 0 Teb: 0000009b`14c78000 Unfrozen
 7  Id: c88.d98 Suspend: 0 Teb: 0000009b`14c7a000 Unfrozen
 8  Id: c88.b78 Suspend: 0 Teb: 0000009b`14c7c000 Unfrozen
```

Note: Process ID (PID) and Thread IDs (TIDs) are given for each thread. Threads are also numbered starting from 0. Commands such as **k** work on the current thread. We can switch to other threads using the **~<number>s** command.

9.   Switching to thread #1:

```
0:000> ~1s
ntdll!NtWaitForMultipleObjects+0x14:
00007ffd`4b0242a4 c3              ret


0:001> k
 # Child-SP          RetAddr               Call Site
00 0000009b`16dfea78 00007ffd`484bfb10     ntdll!NtWaitForMultipleObjects+0x14
01 0000009b`16dfea80 00007ffd`484bfa0e     KERNELBASE!WaitForMultipleObjectsEx+0xf0
02 0000009b`16dfed70 00007ff7`0cea939b     KERNELBASE!WaitForMultipleObjects+0xe
03 0000009b`16dfedb0 00007ff7`0cea925c     msedge!base::Process::WaitForExitOrEvent+0x4b
04 0000009b`16dfee20 00007ff7`0ce75e6b     msedge!ExitCodeWatcher::WaitForExit+0x2c
05 0000009b`16dfee90 00007ff7`0ce75524     msedge!base::TaskAnnotator::RunTaskImpl+0x13b
06 0000009b`16dfefd0 00007ff7`0ce730c2
msedge!base::sequence_manager::internal::ThreadControllerWithMessagePumpImpl::DoWorkImpl+0x304
07 0000009b`16dff1d0 00007ff7`0cf7aef9     msedge!base::MessagePumpForIO::DoRunLoop+0x112
08 0000009b`16dff4f0 00007ff7`0ce9e662     msedge!base::MessagePumpWin::Run+0x79
09 0000009b`16dff550 00007ff7`0cf2b22b
msedge!base::sequence_manager::internal::ThreadControllerWithMessagePumpImpl::Run+0xe2
0a 0000009b`16dff5e0 00007ff7`0cf7ab54     msedge!base::RunLoop::Run+0xfb
0b 0000009b`16dff6f0 00007ff7`0ce97299     msedge!base::Thread::Run+0x44
0c 0000009b`16dff750 00007ff7`0cef65c4     msedge!base::Thread::ThreadMain+0xc9
0d 0000009b`16dff7d0 00007ffd`4a2654e0     msedge!base::`anonymous namespace'::ThreadFunc+0x114
0e 0000009b`16dff860 00007ffd`4af8485b     kernel32!BaseThreadInitThunk+0x10
0f 0000009b`16dff890 00000000`00000000     ntdll!RtlUserThreadStart+0x2b
```

Note: We see that 0:000 has changed to 0:001.

10.   Now we can check any module we are interested in using the **lmv m** *<module name>* command:

```
0:001> lmv m msedge
Browse full module list
start               end                 module name
00007ff7`0ce30000 00007ff7`0d232000   msedge     (pdb symbols)
C:\WinDbg.Docker.AWMDA6\mss\msedge.exe.pdb\95B9A5FB5E9A2B194C4C44205044422E1\msedge.exe.pdb
    Loaded symbol image file: msedge.exe
    Image path: C:\Program Files (x86)\Microsoft\Edge\Application\msedge.exe
    Image name: msedge.exe
    Browse all global symbols  functions  data
    Timestamp:         Wed Jul 12 15:16:17 2023 (64AEB5B1)
    CheckSum:          003F5A2B
    ImageSize:         00402000
    File version:      114.0.1823.82
    Product version:   114.0.1823.82
    File flags:        0 (Mask 17)
    File OS:           4 Unknown Win32
    File type:         1.0 App
    File date:         00000000.00000000
    Translations:      0409.04b0
```

Information from resource tables:
        CompanyName: Microsoft Corporation
        ProductName: Microsoft Edge
        InternalName: msedge_exe
        OriginalFilename: msedge.exe
        ProductVersion: 114.0.1823.82
        FileVersion: 114.0.1823.82
        FileDescription: Microsoft Edge
        LegalCopyright: Copyright Microsoft Corporation. All rights reserved.

11.   We can use WinDbg commands on all threads at once using the ~* prefix:

```
0:001> ~*k

# 0  Id: c88.1634 Suspend: 0 Teb: 0000009b`14c68000 Unfrozen "CrashpadMainThread"
 # Child-SP          RetAddr               Call Site
00 0000009b`155feef8 00007ffd`484c0a33     ntdll!NtRemoveIoCompletion+0x14
01 0000009b`155fef00 00007ff7`0ce94bdd     KERNELBASE!GetQueuedCompletionStatus+0x53
02 0000009b`155fef60 00007ff7`0ce906df     msedge!crashpad::ExceptionHandlerServer::Run+0x25b
03 0000009b`155ff090 00007ff7`0ce8f2ec     msedge!crashpad::HandlerMain+0xd18
04 0000009b`155ff570 00007ff7`0ce88d0f     msedge!crash_reporter::RunAsCrashpadHandler+0x59e
05 0000009b`155ff720 00007ff7`0cf7e492     msedge!wWinMain+0x677
06 0000009b`155ffc40 00007ffd`4a2654e0     msedge!__scrt_common_main_seh+0x106
07 0000009b`155ffc80 00007ffd`4af8485b     kernel32!BaseThreadInitThunk+0x10
08 0000009b`155ffcb0 00000000`00000000     ntdll!RtlUserThreadStart+0x2b

  1  Id: c88.1e60 Suspend: 0 Teb: 0000009b`14c6e000 Unfrozen "ExitCodeWatcherThread"
 # Child-SP          RetAddr               Call Site
00 0000009b`16dfea78 00007ffd`484bfb10     ntdll!NtWaitForMultipleObjects+0x14
01 0000009b`16dfea80 00007ffd`484bfa0e     KERNELBASE!WaitForMultipleObjectsEx+0xf0
02 0000009b`16dfed70 00007ff7`0cea939b     KERNELBASE!WaitForMultipleObjects+0xe
03 0000009b`16dfedb0 00007ff7`0cea925c     msedge!base::Process::WaitForExitOrEvent+0x4b
04 0000009b`16dfee20 00007ff7`0ce75e6b     msedge!ExitCodeWatcher::WaitForExit+0x2c
05 0000009b`16dfee90 00007ff7`0ce75524     msedge!base::TaskAnnotator::RunTaskImpl+0x13b
06 0000009b`16dfefd0 00007ff7`0ce730c2
msedge!base::sequence_manager::internal::ThreadControllerWithMessagePumpImpl::DoWorkImpl+0x304
07 0000009b`16dff1d0 00007ff7`0cf7aef9     msedge!base::MessagePumpForIO::DoRunLoop+0x112
08 0000009b`16dff4f0 00007ff7`0ce9e662     msedge!base::MessagePumpWin::Run+0x79
09 0000009b`16dff550 00007ff7`0cf2b22b     msedge!base::sequence_manager::internal::ThreadControllerWithMessagePumpImpl::Run+0xe2
0a 0000009b`16dff5e0 00007ff7`0cf7ab54     msedge!base::RunLoop::Run+0xfb
0b 0000009b`16dff6f0 00007ff7`0ce97299     msedge!base::Thread::Run+0x44
0c 0000009b`16dff750 00007ff7`0cef65c4     msedge!base::Thread::ThreadMain+0xc9
0d 0000009b`16dff7d0 00007ffd`4a2654e0     msedge!base::`anonymous namespace'::ThreadFunc+0x114
0e 0000009b`16dff860 00007ffd`4af8485b     kernel32!BaseThreadInitThunk+0x10
0f 0000009b`16dff890 00000000`00000000     ntdll!RtlUserThreadStart+0x2b

  2  Id: c88.1920 Suspend: 0 Teb: 0000009b`14c70000 Unfrozen
 # Child-SP          RetAddr               Call Site
00 0000009b`175ff9a8 00007ffd`4a7d464e     win32u!NtUserGetMessage+0x14
01 0000009b`175ff9b0 00007ff7`0cea8b73     user32!GetMessageW+0x2e
02 0000009b`175ffa10 00007ff7`0ceaff41     msedge!crashpad::SessionEndWatcher::ThreadMain+0x1d3
03 0000009b`175ffc90 00007ffd`4a2654e0     msedge!crashpad::Thread::ThreadEntryThunk+0x11
04 0000009b`175ffcc0 00007ffd`4af8485b     kernel32!BaseThreadInitThunk+0x10
05 0000009b`175ffcf0 00000000`00000000     ntdll!RtlUserThreadStart+0x2b

  3  Id: c88.1f9c Suspend: 0 Teb: 0000009b`14c72000 Unfrozen
 # Child-SP          RetAddr               Call Site
00 0000009b`17dff838 00007ffd`484b2a4e     ntdll!NtWaitForSingleObject+0x14
01 0000009b`17dff840 00007ff7`0cea856b     KERNELBASE!WaitForSingleObjectEx+0x8e
02 0000009b`17dff8e0 00007ff7`0cea8511     msedge!crashpad::Semaphore::TimedWait+0x4b
03 0000009b`17dff940 00007ff7`0ceaff41     msedge!crashpad::internal::WorkerThreadImpl::ThreadMain+0x61
04 0000009b`17dff980 00007ffd`4a2654e0     msedge!crashpad::Thread::ThreadEntryThunk+0x11
05 0000009b`17dff9b0 00007ffd`4af8485b     kernel32!BaseThreadInitThunk+0x10
06 0000009b`17dff9e0 00000000`00000000     ntdll!RtlUserThreadStart+0x2b

  4  Id: c88.2fc Suspend: 0 Teb: 0000009b`14c74000 Unfrozen
 # Child-SP          RetAddr               Call Site
00 0000009b`185ff5d8 00007ffd`484b2a4e     ntdll!NtWaitForSingleObject+0x14
01 0000009b`185ff5e0 00007ff7`0cea856b     KERNELBASE!WaitForSingleObjectEx+0x8e
02 0000009b`185ff680 00007ff7`0cea84d1     msedge!crashpad::Semaphore::TimedWait+0x4b
03 0000009b`185ff6e0 00007ff7`0ceaff41     msedge!crashpad::internal::WorkerThreadImpl::ThreadMain+0x21
04 0000009b`185ff720 00007ffd`4a2654e0     msedge!crashpad::Thread::ThreadEntryThunk+0x11
05 0000009b`185ff750 00007ffd`4af8485b     kernel32!BaseThreadInitThunk+0x10
06 0000009b`185ff780 00000000`00000000     ntdll!RtlUserThreadStart+0x2b

  5  Id: c88.2270 Suspend: 0 Teb: 0000009b`14c76000 Unfrozen
 # Child-SP          RetAddr               Call Site
00 0000009b`18dffc08 00007ffd`484d6e06     ntdll!NtFsControlFile+0x14
01 0000009b`18dffc10 00007ff7`0cea18b3     KERNELBASE!ConnectNamedPipe+0x66
```

84

```
02 0000009b`18dffc80 00007ffd`4a2654e0     msedge!crashpad::ExceptionHandlerServer::PipeServiceProc+0x43
03 0000009b`18dffe30 00007ffd`4af8485b     kernel32!BaseThreadInitThunk+0x10
04 0000009b`18dffe60 00000000`00000000     ntdll!RtlUserThreadStart+0x2b

   6  Id: c88.16f4 Suspend: 0 Teb: 0000009b`14c78000 Unfrozen
 # Child-SP          RetAddr               Call Site
00 0000009b`195ffaf8 00007ffd`484d6e06     ntdll!NtFsControlFile+0x14
01 0000009b`195ffb00 00007ff7`0cea18b3     KERNELBASE!ConnectNamedPipe+0x66
02 0000009b`195ffb70 00007ffd`4a2654e0     msedge!crashpad::ExceptionHandlerServer::PipeServiceProc+0x43
03 0000009b`195ffd20 00007ffd`4af8485b     kernel32!BaseThreadInitThunk+0x10
04 0000009b`195ffd50 00000000`00000000     ntdll!RtlUserThreadStart+0x2b

   7  Id: c88.d98 Suspend: 0 Teb: 0000009b`14c7a000 Unfrozen
 # Child-SP          RetAddr               Call Site
00 0000009b`19dff758 00007ffd`4af96c2f     ntdll!NtWaitForWorkViaWorkerFactory+0x14
01 0000009b`19dff760 00007ffd`4a2654e0     ntdll!TppWorkerThread+0x2df
02 0000009b`19dffa50 00007ffd`4af8485b     kernel32!BaseThreadInitThunk+0x10
03 0000009b`19dffa80 00000000`00000000     ntdll!RtlUserThreadStart+0x2b

   8  Id: c88.b78 Suspend: 0 Teb: 0000009b`14c7c000 Unfrozen
 # Child-SP          RetAddr               Call Site
00 0000009b`15dffa98 00007ffd`4af96c2f     ntdll!NtWaitForWorkViaWorkerFactory+0x14
01 0000009b`15dffaa0 00007ffd`4a2654e0     ntdll!TppWorkerThread+0x2df
02 0000009b`15dffd90 00007ffd`4af8485b     kernel32!BaseThreadInitThunk+0x10
03 0000009b`15dffdc0 00000000`00000000     ntdll!RtlUserThreadStart+0x2b
```

Note: module names (and functions) can give us an idea of what every thread was doing. For example, thread #1 was possibly related to exit monitoring and was blocked waiting for synchronization object handles. If we have a lot of similar thread stack traces (for example, from some thread pool), we can significantly reduce the output by executing the **!uniqstack** command:

```
0:001> !uniqstack
Processing 9 threads, please wait

.  0  Id: c88.1634 Suspend: 0 Teb: 0000009b`14c68000 Unfrozen "CrashpadMainThread"
      Start: msedge!wWinMainCRTStartup (00007ff7`0cf7e500)
      Priority: 0  Priority class: 32  Affinity: 3
 # Child-SP          RetAddr               Call Site
00 0000009b`155feef8 00007ffd`484c0a33     ntdll!NtRemoveIoCompletion+0x14
01 0000009b`155fef00 00007ff7`0ce94bdd     KERNELBASE!GetQueuedCompletionStatus+0x53
02 0000009b`155fef60 00007ff7`0ce906df     msedge!crashpad::ExceptionHandlerServer::Run+0x25b
03 0000009b`155ff090 00007ff7`0ce8f2ec     msedge!crashpad::HandlerMain+0xd18
04 0000009b`155ff570 00007ff7`0ce88d0f     msedge!crash_reporter::RunAsCrashpadHandler+0x59e
05 0000009b`155ff720 00007ff7`0cf7e492     msedge!wWinMain+0x677
06 0000009b`155ffc40 00007ffd`4a2654e0     msedge!__scrt_common_main_seh+0x106
07 0000009b`155ffc80 00007ffd`4af8485b     kernel32!BaseThreadInitThunk+0x10
08 0000009b`155ffcb0 00000000`00000000     ntdll!RtlUserThreadStart+0x2b

.  1  Id: c88.1e60 Suspend: 0 Teb: 0000009b`14c6e000 Unfrozen "ExitCodeWatcherThread"
      Start: msedge!base::`anonymous namespace'::ThreadFunc (00007ff7`0cef64b0)
      Priority: 0  Priority class: 32  Affinity: 3
 # Child-SP          RetAddr               Call Site
00 0000009b`16dfea78 00007ffd`484bfb10     ntdll!NtWaitForMultipleObjects+0x14
01 0000009b`16dfea80 00007ffd`484bfa0e     KERNELBASE!WaitForMultipleObjectsEx+0xf0
02 0000009b`16dfed70 00007ff7`0cea939b     KERNELBASE!WaitForMultipleObjects+0xe
03 0000009b`16dfedb0 00007ff7`0cea925c     msedge!base::Process::WaitForExitOrEvent+0x4b
04 0000009b`16dfee20 00007ff7`0ce75e6b     msedge!ExitCodeWatcher::WaitForExit+0x2c
05 0000009b`16dfee90 00007ff7`0ce75524     msedge!base::TaskAnnotator::RunTaskImpl+0x13b
06 0000009b`16dfefd0 00007ff7`0ce730c2
msedge!base::sequence_manager::internal::ThreadControllerWithMessagePumpImpl::DoWorkImpl+0x304
07 0000009b`16dff1d0 00007ff7`0cf7aef9     msedge!base::MessagePumpForIO::DoRunLoop+0x112
08 0000009b`16dff4f0 00007ff7`0ce9e662     msedge!base::MessagePumpWin::Run+0x79
09 0000009b`16dff550 00007ff7`0cf2b22b     msedge!base::sequence_manager::internal::ThreadControllerWithMessagePumpImpl::Run+0xe2
0a 0000009b`16dff5e0 00007ff7`0cf7ab54     msedge!base::RunLoop::Run+0xfb
0b 0000009b`16dff6f0 00007ff7`0ce97299     msedge!base::Thread::Run+0x44
0c 0000009b`16dff750 00007ff7`0cef65c4     msedge!base::Thread::ThreadMain+0xc9
0d 0000009b`16dff7d0 00007ffd`4a2654e0     msedge!base::`anonymous namespace'::ThreadFunc+0x114
0e 0000009b`16dff860 00007ffd`4af8485b     kernel32!BaseThreadInitThunk+0x10
0f 0000009b`16dff890 00000000`00000000     ntdll!RtlUserThreadStart+0x2b

.  2  Id: c88.1920 Suspend: 0 Teb: 0000009b`14c70000 Unfrozen
      Start: msedge!crashpad::Thread::ThreadEntryThunk (00007ff7`0ceaff30)
      Priority: 0  Priority class: 32  Affinity: 3
 # Child-SP          RetAddr               Call Site
00 0000009b`175ff9a8 00007ffd`4a7d464e     win32u!NtUserGetMessage+0x14
01 0000009b`175ff9b0 00007ff7`0cea8b73     user32!GetMessageW+0x2e
02 0000009b`175ffa10 00007ff7`0ceaff41     msedge!crashpad::SessionEndWatcher::ThreadMain+0x1d3
03 0000009b`175ffc90 00007ffd`4a2654e0     msedge!crashpad::Thread::ThreadEntryThunk+0x11
04 0000009b`175ffcc0 00007ffd`4af8485b     kernel32!BaseThreadInitThunk+0x10
05 0000009b`175ffcf0 00000000`00000000     ntdll!RtlUserThreadStart+0x2b
```

```
  .  3  Id: c88.1f9c Suspend: 0 Teb: 0000009b`14c72000 Unfrozen
        Start: msedge!crashpad::Thread::ThreadEntryThunk (00007ff7`0ceaff30)
        Priority: 0  Priority class: 32  Affinity: 3
 # Child-SP          RetAddr               Call Site
00 0000009b`17dff838 00007ffd`484b2a4e     ntdll!NtWaitForSingleObject+0x14
01 0000009b`17dff840 00007ff7`0cea856b     KERNELBASE!WaitForSingleObjectEx+0x8e
02 0000009b`17dff8e0 00007ff7`0cea8511     msedge!crashpad::Semaphore::TimedWait+0x4b
03 0000009b`17dff940 00007ff7`0ceaff41     msedge!crashpad::internal::WorkerThreadImpl::ThreadMain+0x61
04 0000009b`17dff980 00007ffd`4a2654e0     msedge!crashpad::Thread::ThreadEntryThunk+0x11
05 0000009b`17dff9b0 00007ffd`4af8485b     kernel32!BaseThreadInitThunk+0x10
06 0000009b`17dff9e0 00000000`00000000     ntdll!RtlUserThreadStart+0x2b

  .  4  Id: c88.2fc Suspend: 0 Teb: 0000009b`14c74000 Unfrozen
        Start: msedge!crashpad::Thread::ThreadEntryThunk (00007ff7`0ceaff30)
        Priority: 0  Priority class: 32  Affinity: 3
 # Child-SP          RetAddr               Call Site
00 0000009b`185ff5d8 00007ffd`484b2a4e     ntdll!NtWaitForSingleObject+0x14
01 0000009b`185ff5e0 00007ff7`0cea856b     KERNELBASE!WaitForSingleObjectEx+0x8e
02 0000009b`185ff680 00007ff7`0cea84d1     msedge!crashpad::Semaphore::TimedWait+0x4b
03 0000009b`185ff6e0 00007ff7`0ceaff41     msedge!crashpad::internal::WorkerThreadImpl::ThreadMain+0x21
04 0000009b`185ff720 00007ffd`4a2654e0     msedge!crashpad::Thread::ThreadEntryThunk+0x11
05 0000009b`185ff750 00007ffd`4af8485b     kernel32!BaseThreadInitThunk+0x10
06 0000009b`185ff780 00000000`00000000     ntdll!RtlUserThreadStart+0x2b

  .  5  Id: c88.2270 Suspend: 0 Teb: 0000009b`14c76000 Unfrozen
        Start: msedge!crashpad::ExceptionHandlerServer::PipeServiceProc (00007ff7`0cea1870)
        Priority: 0  Priority class: 32  Affinity: 3
 # Child-SP          RetAddr               Call Site
00 0000009b`18dffc08 00007ffd`484d6e06     ntdll!NtFsControlFile+0x14
01 0000009b`18dffc10 00007ff7`0cea18b3     KERNELBASE!ConnectNamedPipe+0x66
02 0000009b`18dffc80 00007ffd`4a2654e0     msedge!crashpad::ExceptionHandlerServer::PipeServiceProc+0x43
03 0000009b`18dffe30 00007ffd`4af8485b     kernel32!BaseThreadInitThunk+0x10
04 0000009b`18dffe60 00000000`00000000     ntdll!RtlUserThreadStart+0x2b

  .  7  Id: c88.d98 Suspend: 0 Teb: 0000009b`14c7a000 Unfrozen
        Start: ntdll!TppWorkerThread (00007ffd`4af96950)
        Priority: 0  Priority class: 32  Affinity: 3
 # Child-SP          RetAddr               Call Site
00 0000009b`19dff758 00007ffd`4af96c2f     ntdll!NtWaitForWorkViaWorkerFactory+0x14
01 0000009b`19dff760 00007ffd`4a2654e0     ntdll!TppWorkerThread+0x2df
02 0000009b`19dffa50 00007ffd`4af8485b     kernel32!BaseThreadInitThunk+0x10
03 0000009b`19dffa80 00000000`00000000     ntdll!RtlUserThreadStart+0x2b

Total threads: 9
Duplicate callstacks: 2 (windbg thread #s follow):
6, 8
```

12.   As we can see, all threads are normally waiting (no CPU activity) or blocked:

0:001> ~*kc

```
 #  0  Id: c88.1634 Suspend: 0 Teb: 0000009b`14c68000 Unfrozen "CrashpadMainThread"
 # Call Site
00 ntdll!NtRemoveIoCompletion
01 KERNELBASE!GetQueuedCompletionStatus
02 msedge!crashpad::ExceptionHandlerServer::Run
03 msedge!crashpad::HandlerMain
04 msedge!crash_reporter::RunAsCrashpadHandler
05 msedge!wWinMain
06 msedge!__scrt_common_main_seh
07 kernel32!BaseThreadInitThunk
08 ntdll!RtlUserThreadStart

    1  Id: c88.1e60 Suspend: 0 Teb: 0000009b`14c6e000 Unfrozen "ExitCodeWatcherThread"
 # Call Site
00 ntdll!NtWaitForMultipleObjects
01 KERNELBASE!WaitForMultipleObjectsEx
02 KERNELBASE!WaitForMultipleObjects
03 msedge!base::Process::WaitForExitOrEvent
04 msedge!ExitCodeWatcher::WaitForExit
05 msedge!base::TaskAnnotator::RunTaskImpl
06 msedge!base::sequence_manager::internal::ThreadControllerWithMessagePumpImpl::DoWorkImpl
07 msedge!base::MessagePumpForIO::DoRunLoop
08 msedge!base::MessagePumpWin::Run
09 msedge!base::sequence_manager::internal::ThreadControllerWithMessagePumpImpl::Run
0a msedge!base::RunLoop::Run
0b msedge!base::Thread::Run
0c msedge!base::Thread::ThreadMain
0d msedge!base::`anonymous namespace'::ThreadFunc
0e kernel32!BaseThreadInitThunk
0f ntdll!RtlUserThreadStart
```

```
   2  Id: c88.1920 Suspend: 0 Teb: 0000009b`14c70000 Unfrozen
 # Call Site
00 win32u!NtUserGetMessage
01 user32!GetMessageW
02 msedge!crashpad::SessionEndWatcher::ThreadMain
03 msedge!crashpad::Thread::ThreadEntryThunk
04 kernel32!BaseThreadInitThunk
05 ntdll!RtlUserThreadStart

   3  Id: c88.1f9c Suspend: 0 Teb: 0000009b`14c72000 Unfrozen
 # Call Site
00 ntdll!NtWaitForSingleObject
01 KERNELBASE!WaitForSingleObjectEx
02 msedge!crashpad::Semaphore::TimedWait
03 msedge!crashpad::internal::WorkerThreadImpl::ThreadMain
04 msedge!crashpad::Thread::ThreadEntryThunk
05 kernel32!BaseThreadInitThunk
06 ntdll!RtlUserThreadStart

   4  Id: c88.2fc Suspend: 0 Teb: 0000009b`14c74000 Unfrozen
 # Call Site
00 ntdll!NtWaitForSingleObject
01 KERNELBASE!WaitForSingleObjectEx
02 msedge!crashpad::Semaphore::TimedWait
03 msedge!crashpad::internal::WorkerThreadImpl::ThreadMain
04 msedge!crashpad::Thread::ThreadEntryThunk
05 kernel32!BaseThreadInitThunk
06 ntdll!RtlUserThreadStart

   5  Id: c88.2270 Suspend: 0 Teb: 0000009b`14c76000 Unfrozen
 # Call Site
00 ntdll!NtFsControlFile
01 KERNELBASE!ConnectNamedPipe
02 msedge!crashpad::ExceptionHandlerServer::PipeServiceProc
03 kernel32!BaseThreadInitThunk
04 ntdll!RtlUserThreadStart

   6  Id: c88.16f4 Suspend: 0 Teb: 0000009b`14c78000 Unfrozen
 # Call Site
00 ntdll!NtFsControlFile
01 KERNELBASE!ConnectNamedPipe
02 msedge!crashpad::ExceptionHandlerServer::PipeServiceProc
03 kernel32!BaseThreadInitThunk
04 ntdll!RtlUserThreadStart

   7  Id: c88.d98 Suspend: 0 Teb: 0000009b`14c7a000 Unfrozen
 # Call Site
00 ntdll!NtWaitForWorkViaWorkerFactory
01 ntdll!TppWorkerThread
02 kernel32!BaseThreadInitThunk
03 ntdll!RtlUserThreadStart

   8  Id: c88.b78 Suspend: 0 Teb: 0000009b`14c7c000 Unfrozen
 # Call Site
00 ntdll!NtWaitForWorkViaWorkerFactory
01 ntdll!TppWorkerThread
02 kernel32!BaseThreadInitThunk
03 ntdll!RtlUserThreadStart
```

13.   The application where all threads are waiting can be hung. We can check this with the **!analyze -v -hang**
command:

```
0:001> !analyze -v -hang
*******************************************************************************
*                                                                             *
*                        Exception Analysis                                   *
*                                                                             *
*******************************************************************************

KEY_VALUES_STRING: 1

    Key  : Analysis.CPU.mSec
    Value: 515

    Key  : Analysis.Elapsed.mSec
    Value: 1009

    Key  : Analysis.IO.Other.Mb
    Value: 2

    Key  : Analysis.IO.Read.Mb
    Value: 1

    Key  : Analysis.IO.Write.Mb
    Value: 7
```

```
    Key  : Analysis.Init.CPU.mSec
    Value: 1077

    Key  : Analysis.Init.Elapsed.mSec
    Value: 1425258

    Key  : Analysis.Memory.CommitPeak.Mb
    Value: 175

    Key  : Failure.Bucket
    Value: APPLICATION_HANG_cfffffff_msedge.exe!crashpad::ExceptionHandlerServer::Run

    Key  : Failure.Hash
    Value: {c207630a-19c2-1495-0f75-f28f9e485f79}

    Key  : Timeline.OS.Boot.DeltaSec
    Value: 556

    Key  : Timeline.Process.Start.DeltaSec
    Value: 243

    Key  : WER.OS.Branch
    Value: co_release

    Key  : WER.OS.Version
    Value: 10.0.22000.1

    Key  : WER.Process.Version
    Value: 114.0.1823.82


FILE_IN_CAB:  msedge.DMP

NTGLOBALFLAG:  400

APPLICATION_VERIFIER_FLAGS:  0

CONTEXT:  (.cxr;r)
rax=0000000000000009 rbx=0000009b155fefb8 rcx=0000000000000154
rdx=0000009b155fefa8 rsi=0000009b155ff110 rdi=0000009b155fefec
rip=00007ffd4b023874 rsp=0000009b155feef8 rbp=000057d0002ccb40
 r8=000057d000220c80  r9=0000000000000210 r10=00000ffee19ec10e
r11=0000000000004400 r12=0000009b155fefa8 r13=0000009b155fefb8
r14=0000009b155fefe0 r15=00007ffd4a266320
iopl=0         nv up ei pl zr na po nc
cs=0033  ss=002b  ds=002b  es=002b  fs=0053  gs=002b             efl=00000246
ntdll!NtRemoveIoCompletion+0x14:
00007ffd`4b023874 c3              ret

EXCEPTION_RECORD:  (.exr -1)
ExceptionAddress: 0000000000000000
   ExceptionCode: 80000003 (Break instruction exception)
  ExceptionFlags: 00000000
NumberParameters: 0

FAULTING_THREAD:  00001634

PROCESS_NAME:  msedge.exe

WATSON_BKT_EVENT:  AppHang

BLOCKING_THREAD:  0000000000001634

ERROR_CODE: (NTSTATUS) 0xcfffffff - <Unable to get error code text>

EXCEPTION_CODE_STR:  cfffffff

DERIVED_WAIT_CHAIN:

Dl Eid Cid     WaitType
-- --- ------- -------------------------
   0   c88.1634 (null)

WAIT_CHAIN_COMMAND:  ~0s;k;;

STACK_TEXT:
0000009b`155feef8 00007ffd`484c0a33     : 00000000`00000000 00007ff7`0cf5317d 000057d0`002ccb40 00007ff7`0ce94fb8 : ntdll!NtRemoveIoCompletion+0x14
0000009b`155fef00 00007ff7`0ce94bdd     : 00000000`00000000 000057d0`00254640 786793eb`fef89fdb 00000000`00000108 : KERNELBASE!GetQueuedCompletionStatus+0x53
0000009b`155fef60 00007ff7`0ce906df     : 0000009b`155ff290 00007ffd`4a2700e0 000057d0`0029c1e0 0000009b`155ff2f8 :
msedge!crashpad::ExceptionHandlerServer::Run+0x25b
0000009b`155ff090 00007ff7`0ce8f2ec     : aaaaaaaa`aaaaaaaa aaaaaaaa`aaaaaaaa 00000000`00000000 00000000`00000070 : msedge!crashpad::HandlerMain+0xd18
0000009b`155ff570 00007ff7`0ce88d0f     : 00000000`0000000a 000079a6`6a3285e8 00000000`00000000 00000000`00000000 :
msedge!crash_reporter::RunAsCrashpadHandler+0x59e
0000009b`155ff720 00007ff7`0cf7e492     : 00000000`00000000 00007ff7`0cf7e509 00000000`00000000 00000000`00000000 : msedge!wWinMain+0x677
0000009b`155ffc40 00007ffd`4a2654e0     : 00000000`00000000 00000000`00000000 00000000`00000000 00000000`00000000 : msedge!__scrt_common_main_seh+0x106
0000009b`155ffc80 00007ffd`4af8485b     : 00000000`00000000 00000000`00000000 00000000`00000000 00000000`00000000 : kernel32!BaseThreadInitThunk+0x10
0000009b`155ffcb0 00000000`00000000     : 00000000`00000000 00000000`00000000 00000000`00000000 00000000`00000000 : ntdll!RtlUserThreadStart+0x2b


STACK_COMMAND:  ~0s ; .cxr ; kb

SYMBOL_NAME:  msedge!crashpad::ExceptionHandlerServer::Run+25b

MODULE_NAME: msedge

IMAGE_NAME:  msedge.exe

FAILURE_BUCKET_ID:  APPLICATION_HANG_cfffffff_msedge.exe!crashpad::ExceptionHandlerServer::Run
```

```
OS_VERSION:  10.0.22000.1

BUILDLAB_STR:  co_release

OSPLATFORM_TYPE:  x64

OSNAME:  Windows 10

IMAGE_VERSION:  114.0.1823.82

FAILURE_ID_HASH:  {c207630a-19c2-1495-0f75-f28f9e485f79}

Followup:     MachineOwner
---------
```

Note: WinDbg gives us an indication of a possible application hang. However, we know that Microsoft Edge was not hanging at the time when we saved its memory dump. In real problem scenarios, we need to compare stack traces of a normal process with the problem process memory dump.

14.   We can check how much time each thread had spent in kernel and user modes and also how much time had elapsed since the thread was created by using the **!runaway f** command:

```
0:001> !runaway f
User Mode Time
  Thread       Time
   8:b78      0 days 0:00:00.000
   7:d98      0 days 0:00:00.000
   6:16f4     0 days 0:00:00.000
   5:2270     0 days 0:00:00.000
   4:2fc      0 days 0:00:00.000
   3:1f9c     0 days 0:00:00.000
   2:1920     0 days 0:00:00.000
   1:1e60     0 days 0:00:00.000
   0:1634     0 days 0:00:00.000
Kernel Mode Time
  Thread       Time
   0:1634     0 days 0:00:00.140
   2:1920     0 days 0:00:00.031
   7:d98      0 days 0:00:00.015
   8:b78      0 days 0:00:00.000
   6:16f4     0 days 0:00:00.000
   5:2270     0 days 0:00:00.000
   4:2fc      0 days 0:00:00.000
   3:1f9c     0 days 0:00:00.000
   1:1e60     0 days 0:00:00.000
Elapsed Time
  Thread       Time
   0:1634     0 days 0:04:02.124
   1:1e60     0 days 0:04:01.165
   2:1920     0 days 0:04:01.162
   3:1f9c     0 days 0:04:01.040
   4:2fc      0 days 0:04:01.039
   5:2270     0 days 0:04:01.039
   6:16f4     0 days 0:04:01.039
   7:d98      0 days 0:03:05.105
   8:b78      0 days 0:02:33.117
```

15.   We close logging before exiting WinDbg:

```
0:001> .logclose
Closing open log file C:\AWMDA-Dumps\Process\x64\msedge.log
```

Exercise P4

- **Goal:** Learn to recognize exceptions in process memory dumps and get their context

- **Patterns:** Exception Stack Trace; Exception Module; Multiple Exceptions (User Mode); NULL Pointer (Data)

- \AWMDA-Dumps\Exercise-P4-Analysis-process-dump-AppK-64-no-symbols.pdf

Exercise P4: Analysis of an application process dump (64-bit AppK, no symbols)

Goal: Learn to recognize exceptions in process memory dumps and get their context.

Patterns: Exception Stack Trace; Multiple Exceptions (User Mode); NULL Pointer (Data).

1.   Launch WinDbg.

2.   Open \AWMDA-Dumps\Process\x64\AppK.exe.8484.dmp.

3.   We get the dump file loaded:

```
Microsoft (R) Windows Debugger Version 10.0.25877.1004 AMD64
Copyright (c) Microsoft Corporation. All rights reserved.


Loading Dump File [C:\AWMDA-Dumps\Process\x64\AppK.exe.8484.dmp]
User Mini Dump File with Full Memory: Only application data is available


************* Path validation summary **************
Response                         Time (ms)        Location
Deferred                                          srv*
Symbol search path is: srv*
Executable search path is:
Windows 10 Version 18362 MP (2 procs) Free x64
Product: WinNt, suite: SingleUserTS Personal
Edition build lab: 18362.1.amd64fre.19h1_release.190318-1202
Debug session time: Tue Oct  1 23:54:08.000 2019 (UTC + 1:00)
System Uptime: 0 days 0:04:48.832
Process Uptime: 0 days 0:00:01.000
.......
This dump file has a breakpoint exception stored in it.
The stored exception information can be accessed via .ecxr.
For analysis of this file, run !analyze -v
ntdll!NtWaitForMultipleObjects+0x14:
00007ffe`fd2dcc24 c3              ret
```

4.   Open a log file using the **.logopen** command:

```
0:000> .logopen C:\AWMDA-Dumps\Process\x64\AppK.log
Opened log file 'C:\AWMDA-Dumps\Process\x64\AppK.log'
```

5.   Type the **k** command to verify the correctness of the stack trace:

```
0:000> k
 # Child-SP          RetAddr           Call Site
00 00000032`b51fe788 00007ffe`fb097ff7 ntdll!NtWaitForMultipleObjects+0x14
01 00000032`b51fe790 00007ffe`fb097ede KERNELBASE!WaitForMultipleObjectsEx+0x107
02 00000032`b51fea90 00007ffe`fbd371fb KERNELBASE!WaitForMultipleObjects+0xe
03 00000032`b51fead0 00007ffe`fbd36ca8 kernel32!WerpReportFaultInternal+0x51b
04 00000032`b51febf0 00007ffe`fb13f988 kernel32!WerpReportFault+0xac
05 00000032`b51fec30 00007ffe`fd2e4af2 KERNELBASE!UnhandledExceptionFilter+0x3b8
06 00000032`b51fed50 00007ffe`fd2cc6e6 ntdll!RtlUserThreadStart$filt$0+0xa2
07 00000032`b51fed90 00007ffe`fd2e120f ntdll!_C_specific_handler+0x96
```

91

```
08 00000032`b51fee00 00007ffe`fd2aa299 ntdll!RtlpExecuteHandlerForException+0xf
09 00000032`b51fee30 00007ffe`fd2dfe7e ntdll!RtlDispatchException+0x219
0a 00000032`b51ff540 00007ffe`fb1002b2 ntdll!KiUserExceptionDispatch+0x2e
0b 00000032`b51ffcd8 00007ff7`94981075 KERNELBASE!wil::details::DebugBreak+0x2
0c 00000032`b51ffce0 00007ff7`9498126c AppK+0x1075
0d 00000032`b51ffd10 00007ffe`fbce7bd4 AppK+0x126c
0e 00000032`b51ffd50 00007ffe`fd2acee1 kernel32!BaseThreadInitThunk+0x14
0f 00000032`b51ffd80 00000000`00000000 ntdll!RtlUserThreadStart+0x21
```

Note: The symbols were loaded correctly for MS modules but not for the 3rd-party *AppK*. This is a normal real-life scenario where symbols are not available.

6. Let's review the stack trace again:

```
0:000> k
 # Child-SP          RetAddr           Call Site
00 00000032`b51fe788 00007ffe`fb097ff7 ntdll!NtWaitForMultipleObjects+0x14
01 00000032`b51fe790 00007ffe`fb097ede KERNELBASE!WaitForMultipleObjectsEx+0x107
02 00000032`b51fea90 00007ffe`fbd371fb KERNELBASE!WaitForMultipleObjects+0xe
03 00000032`b51fead0 00007ffe`fbd36ca8 kernel32!WerpReportFaultInternal+0x51b
04 00000032`b51febf0 00007ffe`fb13f988 kernel32!WerpReportFault+0xac
05 00000032`b51fec30 00007ffe`fd2e4af2 KERNELBASE!UnhandledExceptionFilter+0x3b8
06 00000032`b51fed50 00007ffe`fd2cc6e6 ntdll!RtlUserThreadStart$filt$0+0xa2
07 00000032`b51fed90 00007ffe`fd2e120f ntdll!_C_specific_handler+0x96
08 00000032`b51fee00 00007ffe`fd2aa299 ntdll!RtlpExecuteHandlerForException+0xf
09 00000032`b51fee30 00007ffe`fd2dfe7e ntdll!RtlDispatchException+0x219
0a 00000032`b51ff540 00007ffe`fb1002b2 ntdll!KiUserExceptionDispatch+0x2e
0b 00000032`b51ffcd8 00007ff7`94981075 KERNELBASE!wil::details::DebugBreak+0x2
0c 00000032`b51ffce0 00007ff7`9498126c AppK+0x1075
0d 00000032`b51ffd10 00007ffe`fbce7bd4 AppK+0x126c
0e 00000032`b51ffd50 00007ffe`fd2acee1 kernel32!BaseThreadInitThunk+0x14
0f 00000032`b51ffd80 00000000`00000000 ntdll!RtlUserThreadStart+0x21
```

Note: We see various exceptions and fault report calls, including the *DebugBreak* call used to insert a manual break (normally used to invoke a debugger).

7.   Type default analysis command **!analyze -v**:

```
0:000> !analyze -v
*******************************************************************************
*                                                                             *
*                        Exception Analysis                                   *
*                                                                             *
*******************************************************************************

KEY_VALUES_STRING: 1

    Key  : Analysis.CPU.mSec
    Value: 702

    Key  : Analysis.DebugAnalysisManager
    Value: Create

    Key  : Analysis.Elapsed.mSec
    Value: 793

    Key  : Analysis.Init.CPU.mSec
    Value: 468

    Key  : Analysis.Init.Elapsed.mSec
    Value: 377860

    Key  : Analysis.Memory.CommitPeak.Mb
    Value: 224

    Key  : Timeline.OS.Boot.DeltaSec
    Value: 288

    Key  : Timeline.Process.Start.DeltaSec
    Value: 1
```

```
      Key  : WER.OS.Branch
      Value: 19h1_release

      Key  : WER.OS.Timestamp
      Value: 2019-03-18T12:02:00Z

      Key  : WER.OS.Version
      Value: 10.0.18362.1

      Key  : WER.Process.Version
      Value: 2.0.0.1


FILE_IN_CAB:  AppK.exe.8484.dmp

NTGLOBALFLAG:  0

PROCESS_BAM_CURRENT_THROTTLED: 0

PROCESS_BAM_PREVIOUS_THROTTLED: 0

APPLICATION_VERIFIER_FLAGS:  0

CONTEXT:  (.ecxr)
rax=000000000000008c rbx=00000200bcbc2960 rcx=00007ffefd2dcb14
rdx=0000000000000000 rsi=0000000000000000 rdi=00000200bcbc5b70
rip=00007ffefb1002b2 rsp=00000032b51ffcd8 rbp=0000000000000000
 r8=00000032b51ffc68  r9=0000000000000000 r10=0000000000000000
r11=0000000000000246 r12=0000000000000000 r13=0000000000000000
r14=0000000000000000 r15=0000000000000000
iopl=0         nv up ei pl nz na pe nc
cs=0033  ss=002b  ds=002b  es=002b  fs=0053  gs=002b            efl=00000202
KERNELBASE!wil::details::DebugBreak+0x2:
00007ffe`fb1002b2 cc              int     3
Resetting default scope

EXCEPTION_RECORD:  (.exr -1)
ExceptionAddress: 00007ffefb1002b2 (KERNELBASE!wil::details::DebugBreak+0x0000000000000002)
   ExceptionCode: 80000003 (Break instruction exception)
  ExceptionFlags: 00000000
NumberParameters: 1
   Parameter[0]: 0000000000000000

PROCESS_NAME:  AppK.exe

ERROR_CODE: (NTSTATUS) 0x80000003 - {EXCEPTION}  Breakpoint  A breakpoint has been reached.

EXCEPTION_CODE_STR:  80000003

EXCEPTION_PARAMETER1:  0000000000000000

STACK_TEXT:
00000032`b51ffcd8 00007ff7`94981075     : 00000000`00001ce0 00000200`bcbc2960 00000000`00000000 00007ff7`9498c2a0 : KERNELBASE!wil::details::DebugBreak+0x2
00000032`b51ffce0 00007ff7`9498126c     : 00000000`00000001 00000200`bcbc2960 00000000`00000000 00000000`00000000 : AppK+0x1075
00000032`b51ffd10 00007ffe`fbce7bd4     : 00000000`00000000 00000000`00000000 00000000`00000000 00000000`00000000 : AppK+0x126c
00000032`b51ffd50 00007ffe`fd2acee1     : 00000000`00000000 00000000`00000000 00000000`00000000 00000000`00000000 : kernel32!BaseThreadInitThunk+0x14
00000032`b51ffd80 00000000`00000000     : 00000000`00000000 00000000`00000000 00000000`00000000 00000000`00000000 : ntdll!RtlUserThreadStart+0x21


STACK_COMMAND:  ~0s; .ecxr ; kb

SYMBOL_NAME:  appk!wmain+35

MODULE_NAME: AppK

IMAGE_NAME:  AppK.exe

FAILURE_BUCKET_ID:  BREAKPOINT_80000003_AppK.exe!wmain

OS_VERSION:  10.0.18362.1

BUILDLAB_STR:  19h1_release

OSPLATFORM_TYPE:  x64

OSNAME:  Windows 10

IMAGE_VERSION:  2.0.0.1

FAILURE_ID_HASH:  {b3f13783-908c-3b79-52dc-ac6373b9b27a}

Followup:    MachineOwner
---------
```

Note: We see that WinDbg identified a manual break and provided the stack trace (that we show in smaller font below):

ExceptionAddress: 00007ffefb1002b2 (KERNELBASE!wil::details::DebugBreak+0x0000000000000002)

```
STACK_TEXT:
00000032`b51ffcd8 00007ff7`94981075 : 00000000`00001ce0 00000200`bcbc2960 00000000`00000000 00007ff7`9498c2a0 : KERNELBASE!wil::details::DebugBreak+0x2
00000032`b51ffce0 00007ff7`9498126c : 00000000`00000001 00000200`bcbc2960 00000000`00000000 00000000`00000000 : AppK+0x1075
00000032`b51ffd10 00007ffe`fbce7bd4 : 00000000`00000000 00000000`00000000 00000000`00000000 00000000`00000000 : AppK+0x126c
00000032`b51ffd50 00007ffe`fd2acee1 : 00000000`00000000 00000000`00000000 00000000`00000000 00000000`00000000 : kernel32!BaseThreadInitThunk+0x14
00000032`b51ffd80 00000000`00000000 : 00000000`00000000 00000000`00000000 00000000`00000000 00000000`00000000 : ntdll!RtlUserThreadStart+0x21
```

8.   Let's check that WinDbg conclusion was correct:

```
0:000> k
 # Child-SP          RetAddr           Call Site
00 00000032`b51fe788 00007ffe`fb097ff7 ntdll!NtWaitForMultipleObjects+0x14
01 00000032`b51fe790 00007ffe`fb097ede KERNELBASE!WaitForMultipleObjectsEx+0x107
02 00000032`b51fea90 00007ffe`fbd371fb KERNELBASE!WaitForMultipleObjects+0xe
03 00000032`b51fead0 00007ffe`fbd36ca8 kernel32!WerpReportFaultInternal+0x51b
04 00000032`b51febf0 00007ffe`fb13f988 kernel32!WerpReportFault+0xac
05 00000032`b51fec30 00007ffe`fd2e4af2 KERNELBASE!UnhandledExceptionFilter+0x3b8
06 00000032`b51fed50 00007ffe`fd2cc6e6 ntdll!RtlUserThreadStart$filt$0+0xa2
07 00000032`b51fed90 00007ffe`fd2e120f ntdll!_C_specific_handler+0x96
08 00000032`b51fee00 00007ffe`fd2aa299 ntdll!RtlpExecuteHandlerForException+0xf
09 00000032`b51fee30 00007ffe`fd2dfe7e ntdll!RtlDispatchException+0x219
0a 00000032`b51ff540 00007ffe`fb1002b2 ntdll!KiUserExceptionDispatch+0x2e
0b 00000032`b51ffcd8 00007ff7`94981075 KERNELBASE!wil::details::DebugBreak+0x2
0c 00000032`b51ffce0 00007ff7`9498126c AppK+0x1075
0d 00000032`b51ffd10 00007ffe`fbce7bd4 AppK+0x126c
0e 00000032`b51ffd50 00007ffe`fd2acee1 kernel32!BaseThreadInitThunk+0x14
0f 00000032`b51ffd80 00000000`00000000 ntdll!RtlUserThreadStart+0x21
```

```
0:000> ub 00007ff7`94981075
AppK+0x1050:
00007ff7`94981050 33d2             xor     edx,edx
00007ff7`94981052 488d0dc7ffffff   lea     rcx,[AppK+0x1020 (00007ff7`94981020)]
00007ff7`94981059 e806190000       call    AppK+0x2964 (00007ff7`94982964)
00007ff7`9498105e 4533c0           xor     r8d,r8d
00007ff7`94981061 33d2             xor     edx,edx
00007ff7`94981063 488d0d96ffffff   lea     rcx,[AppK+0x1000 (00007ff7`94981000)]
00007ff7`9498106a e8f1800000       call    AppK+0x2964 (00007ff7`94982964)
00007ff7`9498106f ff158baf0000     call    qword ptr [AppK+0xc000 (00007ff7`9498c000)]
```

```
0:000> dps 00007ff7`9498c000
00007ff7`9498c000  00007ffe`fbd059e0 kernel32!DebugBreakStub
00007ff7`9498c008  00007ffe`fbcf28f0 kernel32!WriteConsoleW
00007ff7`9498c010  00007ffe`fbce6a10 kernel32!QueryPerformanceCounterStub
00007ff7`9498c018  00007ffe`fbcf1dc0 kernel32!GetCurrentProcessId
00007ff7`9498c020  00007ffe`fbce5e50 kernel32!GetCurrentThreadId
00007ff7`9498c028  00007ffe`fbce6a20 kernel32!GetSystemTimeAsFileTimeStub
00007ff7`9498c030  00007ffe`fd2b3880 ntdll!RtlInitializeSListHead
00007ff7`9498c038  00007ffe`fbcf1bf0 kernel32!RtlCaptureContext
00007ff7`9498c040  00007ffe`fbcec470 kernel32!RtlLookupFunctionEntryStub
00007ff7`9498c048  00007ffe`fbcd1010 kernel32!RtlVirtualUnwindStub
00007ff7`9498c050  00007ffe`fbcee920 kernel32!IsDebuggerPresentStub
00007ff7`9498c058  00007ffe`fbd06b20 kernel32!UnhandledExceptionFilterStub
00007ff7`9498c060  00007ffe`fbcee5c0 kernel32!SetUnhandledExceptionFilterStub
00007ff7`9498c068  00007ffe`fbcec7f0 kernel32!GetStartupInfoWStub
00007ff7`9498c070  00007ffe`fbcec7d0 kernel32!IsProcessorFeaturePresentStub
00007ff7`9498c078  00007ffe`fbcec460 kernel32!GetModuleHandleWStub
```

9.   Now we check how many threads we have by using the ~ command:

```
0:000> ~
.  0  Id: 2124.2150 Suspend: 0 Teb: 00000032`b52cf000 Unfrozen
   1  Id: 2124.1e4c Suspend: 1 Teb: 00000032`b52d1000 Unfrozen
   2  Id: 2124.1ce0 Suspend: 1 Teb: 00000032`b52d3000 Unfrozen
   3  Id: 2124.11ac Suspend: 1 Teb: 00000032`b52d5000 Unfrozen
   4  Id: 2124.1fc0 Suspend: 1 Teb: 00000032`b52d7000 Unfrozen
```

Note: Exceptions and faults are per thread. There can be other exceptions from other threads. It is usually the case that WinDbg recognizes the first exception (like a breakpoint here) but misses the subsequent ones being processed at the time of the first exception.

10.   We get stack traces from all threads at once using **~*k** command:

```
0:000> ~*k

.  0  Id: 2124.2150 Suspend: 0 Teb: 00000032`b52cf000 Unfrozen
 # Child-SP          RetAddr           Call Site
00 00000032`b51fe788 00007ffe`fb097ff7 ntdll!NtWaitForMultipleObjects+0x14
01 00000032`b51fe790 00007ffe`fb097ede KERNELBASE!WaitForMultipleObjectsEx+0x107
02 00000032`b51fea90 00007ffe`fbd371fb KERNELBASE!WaitForMultipleObjects+0xe
03 00000032`b51fead0 00007ffe`fbd36ca8 kernel32!WerpReportFaultInternal+0x51b
04 00000032`b51febf0 00007ffe`fb13f988 kernel32!WerpReportFault+0xac
05 00000032`b51fec30 00007ffe`fd2e4af2 KERNELBASE!UnhandledExceptionFilter+0x3b8
06 00000032`b51fed50 00007ffe`fd2cc6e6 ntdll!RtlUserThreadStart$filt$0+0xa2
07 00000032`b51fed90 00007ffe`fd2e120f ntdll!_C_specific_handler+0x96
08 00000032`b51fee00 00007ffe`fd2aa299 ntdll!RtlpExecuteHandlerForException+0xf
09 00000032`b51fee30 00007ffe`fd2dfe7e ntdll!RtlDispatchException+0x219
0a 00000032`b51ff540 00007ffe`fb1002b2 ntdll!KiUserExceptionDispatch+0x2e
0b 00000032`b51ffcd8 00007ff7`94981075 KERNELBASE!wil::details::DebugBreak+0x2
0c 00000032`b51ffce0 00007ff7`9498126c AppK+0x1075
0d 00000032`b51ffd10 00007ffe`fbce7bd4 AppK+0x126c
0e 00000032`b51ffd50 00007ffe`fd2acee1 kernel32!BaseThreadInitThunk+0x14
0f 00000032`b51ffd80 00000000`00000000 ntdll!RtlUserThreadStart+0x21

   1  Id: 2124.1e4c Suspend: 1 Teb: 00000032`b52d1000 Unfrozen
 # Child-SP          RetAddr           Call Site
00 00000032`b54feb88 00007ffe`fb086931 ntdll!NtDelayExecution+0x14
01 00000032`b54feb90 00007ffe`fbd36c93 KERNELBASE!SleepEx+0xa1
02 00000032`b54fec30 00007ffe`fb13f988 kernel32!WerpReportFault+0x97
03 00000032`b54fec70 00007ffe`fd2e4af2 KERNELBASE!UnhandledExceptionFilter+0x3b8
04 00000032`b54fed90 00007ffe`fd2cc6e6 ntdll!RtlUserThreadStart$filt$0+0xa2
05 00000032`b54fedd0 00007ffe`fd2e120f ntdll!_C_specific_handler+0x96
06 00000032`b54fee40 00007ffe`fd2aa299 ntdll!RtlpExecuteHandlerForException+0xf
07 00000032`b54fee70 00007ffe`fd2dfe7e ntdll!RtlDispatchException+0x219
08 00000032`b54ff580 00007ff7`94981030 ntdll!KiUserExceptionDispatch+0x2e
09 00000032`b54ffd20 00007ff7`94982888 AppK+0x1030
0a 00000032`b54ffd40 00007ffe`fbce7bd4 AppK+0x2888
0b 00000032`b54ffd70 00007ffe`fd2acee1 kernel32!BaseThreadInitThunk+0x14
0c 00000032`b54ffda0 00000000`00000000 ntdll!RtlUserThreadStart+0x21

   2  Id: 2124.1ce0 Suspend: 1 Teb: 00000032`b52d3000 Unfrozen
 # Child-SP          RetAddr           Call Site
00 00000032`b55fe8c8 00007ffe`fb086931 ntdll!NtDelayExecution+0x14
01 00000032`b55fe8d0 00007ffe`fbd36c93 KERNELBASE!SleepEx+0xa1
02 00000032`b55fe970 00007ffe`fb13f988 kernel32!WerpReportFault+0x97
03 00000032`b55fe9b0 00007ffe`fd2e4af2 KERNELBASE!UnhandledExceptionFilter+0x3b8
04 00000032`b55fead0 00007ffe`fd2cc6e6 ntdll!RtlUserThreadStart$filt$0+0xa2
05 00000032`b55feb10 00007ffe`fd2e120f ntdll!_C_specific_handler+0x96
06 00000032`b55feb80 00007ffe`fd2aa299 ntdll!RtlpExecuteHandlerForException+0xf
07 00000032`b55febb0 00007ffe`fd2dfe7e ntdll!RtlDispatchException+0x219
08 00000032`b55ff2c0 00007ff7`94981010 ntdll!KiUserExceptionDispatch+0x2e
09 00000032`b55ffa40 00007ff7`94982888 AppK+0x1010
0a 00000032`b55ffa60 00007ffe`fbce7bd4 AppK+0x2888
0b 00000032`b55ffa90 00007ffe`fd2acee1 kernel32!BaseThreadInitThunk+0x14
0c 00000032`b55ffac0 00000000`00000000 ntdll!RtlUserThreadStart+0x21
```

```
     3  Id: 2124.11ac Suspend: 1 Teb: 00000032`b52d5000 Unfrozen
 # Child-SP          RetAddr          Call Site
00 00000032`b56ff728 00007ffe`fd274060 ntdll!NtWaitForWorkViaWorkerFactory+0x14
01 00000032`b56ff730 00007ffe`fbce7bd4 ntdll!TppWorkerThread+0x300
02 00000032`b56ffaf0 00007ffe`fd2acee1 kernel32!BaseThreadInitThunk+0x14
03 00000032`b56ffb20 00000000`00000000 ntdll!RtlUserThreadStart+0x21

     4  Id: 2124.1fc0 Suspend: 1 Teb: 00000032`b52d7000 Unfrozen
 # Child-SP          RetAddr          Call Site
00 00000032`b57ff868 00007ffe`fd274060 ntdll!NtWaitForWorkViaWorkerFactory+0x14
01 00000032`b57ff870 00007ffe`fbce7bd4 ntdll!TppWorkerThread+0x300
02 00000032`b57ffc30 00007ffe`fd2acee1 kernel32!BaseThreadInitThunk+0x14
03 00000032`b57ffc60 00000000`00000000 ntdll!RtlUserThreadStart+0x21
```

Note: We see exceptions on two other threads.

11.	We switch to the second (#1, threads are numbered from #0) thread and get its verbose stack trace (**~1s** and **k** commands, the stack trace is shown in smaller font for readability):

```
0:000> ~1s
ntdll!NtDelayExecution+0x14:
00007ffe`fd2dc754 c3              ret
```

```
0:001> kv
 # Child-SP          RetAddr          : Args to Child                                                                          : Call Site
00 00000032`b54feb88 00007ffe`fb086931 : 00000032`b54fec48 004f004e`004d004c 00000000`00000030 00000032`b54febb0 : ntdll!NtDelayExecution+0x14
01 00000032`b54feb90 00007ffe`fbd36c93 : 00000000`00000000 00007ffe`00000000 00007dfc`c00000bb 00000000`00000000 : KERNELBASE!SleepEx+0xa1
02 00000032`b54fec30 00007ffe`fb13f988 : 00000000`00000000 00000032`b54fda0 00007ffe`fbcd0000 00000000`0000036a : kernel32!WerpReportFault+0x97
03 00000032`b54fec70 00007ffe`fd2e4af2 : 00000000`00000000 00007ffe`fd384420 00000000`00000000 00000032`b54ffd40 : KERNELBASE!UnhandledExceptionFilter+0x3b8
04 00000032`b54fed90 00007ffe`fd2cc6e6 : 00000001`00000000 00000000`00000000 00000032`b54ff3c8 00000032`b54ff450 : ntdll!RtlUserThreadStart$filt$0+0xa2
05 00000032`b54fedd0 00007ffe`fd2e120f : 00000000`00000000 00000032`b54ff3b0 00000032`b54ffa70 00000000`00000000 : ntdll!_C_specific_handler+0x96
06 00000032`b54fee40 00007ffe`fd2aa299 : 00000032`00000001 00007ffe`fd240000 00000000`00000000 00007ffe`fd3ae9f0 : ntdll!RtlpExecuteHandlerForException+0xf
07 00000032`b54fee70 00007ffe`fd2dfe7e : 00000200`bce21250 00007ffe`0a00000a 00000200`bcbc6b50 00000000`00000000 : ntdll!RtlDispatchException+0x219
08 00000032`b54ff580 00007ff7`94981030 : 00000000`00000002 00000000`00000005 00000200`bcbc6b50 00007ff7`94982888 : ntdll!KiUserExceptionDispatch+0x2e
(TrapFrame @ 00000032`b54ff9a8)
09 00000032`b54ffd20 00007ff7`94982888 : 00000000`00000000 00000000`00000000 00000000`00000000 00000000`00000000 : AppK+0x1030
0a 00000032`b54ffd40 00007ffe`fbce7bd4 : 00000000`00000000 00000000`00000000 00000000`00000000 00000000`00000000 : AppK+0x2888
0b 00000032`b54ffd70 00007ffe`fd2acee1 : 00000000`00000000 00000000`00000000 00000000`00000000 00000000`00000000 : kernel32!BaseThreadInitThunk+0x14
0c 00000032`b54ffda0 00000000`00000000 : 00000000`00000000 00000000`00000000 00000000`00000000 00000000`00000000 : ntdll!RtlUserThreadStart+0x21
```

Note: We see trap frame reference (processor information saved when an exception had occurred).

12.	Setting the current stack frame to #9 (the next after the frame #8 where we see the *KiUserExceptionDispatch* function) should show CPU information at the time of the exception:

```
0:001> .frame /c 9
09 00000032`b54ffd20 00007ff7`94982888 AppK+0x1030
rax=00000200bcbc8a80 rbx=00000200bcbc6b50 rcx=00007ff79498d770
rdx=00000200bcbc8a80 rsi=0000000000000000 rdi=0000000000000000
rip=00007ff794981030 rsp=00000032b54ffd20 rbp=0000000000000000
 r8=0053005c00530057  r9=0045005400530059 r10=005c00320033004d
r11=006e00720065006b r12=0000000000000000 r13=0000000000000000
r14=0000000000000000 r15=0000000000000000
iopl=0         nv up ei pl zr na po nc
cs=0033  ss=002b  ds=002b  es=002b  fs=0053  gs=002b             efl=00000246
AppK+0x1030:
00007ff7`94981030 c7042500000000000000 mov dword ptr [0],0 ds:00000000`00000000=????????
```

Note: We see that the *AppK* module was at fault, and we see invalid NULL pointer access. Since this is a **mov** instruction and (**ds**, data segment), we see this as data NULL pointer access. We see code NULL pointer access in later exercises.

We can also double-check this information with the trap frame structure instruction pointer RIP and disassemble the instruction it points to (the **dt** command dumps C/C++ structure fields):

```
08 00000032`b54ff580 00007ff7`94981030 : 00000000`00000002 00000000`00000005 00000200`bcbc6b50 00007ff7`94982888 : ntdll!KiUserExceptionDispatch+0x2e
(TrapFrame @ 00000032`b54ff9a8)

0:001> dt ntdll!_KTRAP_FRAME RIP 00000032`b54ff9a8
   +0x168 Rip : 0x00007ff7`94981030

0:001> u 0x00007ff7`94981030
AppK+0x1030:
00007ff7`94981030 c7042500000000000000000 mov     dword ptr [0],0
00007ff7`9498103b 4883c418            add     rsp,18h
00007ff7`9498103f c3                  ret
00007ff7`94981040 4889542410          mov     qword ptr [rsp+10h],rdx
00007ff7`94981045 894c2408            mov     dword ptr [rsp+8],ecx
00007ff7`94981049 4883ec28            sub     rsp,28h
00007ff7`9498104d 4533c0              xor     r8d,r8d
00007ff7`94981050 33d2                xor     edx,edx
```

13.   Now we check the problem module information and get a stack trace prior to the exception (**lmv m** and **k** commands):

```
0:001> lmv m AppK
Browse full module list
start             end               module name
00007ff7`94980000 00007ff7`9499b000   AppK      C (no symbols)
    Loaded symbol image file: AppK.exe
    Image path: Z:\AWMDA-Dumps\Apps\AppK.exe
    Image name: AppK.exe
    Browse all global symbols  functions  data
    Timestamp:        Tue Oct  1 23:52:58 2019 (5D93D8CA)
    CheckSum:         00000000
    ImageSize:        0001B000
    File version:     2.0.0.1
    Product version:  2.0.0.1
    File flags:       0 (Mask 3F)
    File OS:          40004 NT Win32
    File type:        1.0 App
    File date:        00000000.00000000
    Translations:     0809.04b0
    Information from resource tables:
        CompanyName:     Software Diagnostics Technology and Services
        ProductName:     Accelerated Windows Memory Dump Analysis Training
        InternalName:    AppK.exe
        OriginalFilename: AppK.exe
        ProductVersion:  2.0.0.1
        FileVersion:     2.0.0.1
        FileDescription: Models multiple exceptions in user mode
        LegalCopyright:  Copyright (C) 2011-2019

0:001> k
  *** Stack trace for last set context - .thread/.cxr resets it
 # Child-SP          RetAddr           Call Site
09 00000032`b54ffd20 00007ff7`94982888 AppK+0x1030
0a 00000032`b54ffd40 00007ffe`fbce7bd4 AppK+0x2888
0b 00000032`b54ffd70 00007ffe`fd2acee1 kernel32!BaseThreadInitThunk+0x14
0c 00000032`b54ffda0 00000000`00000000 ntdll!RtlUserThreadStart+0x21
```

14.   We repeat the same commands for the 3rd thread (#2):

```
0:001> ~2s
ntdll!NtDelayExecution+0x14:
00007ffe`fd2dc754 c3               ret
```

```
0:002> kv
# Child-SP          RetAddr           : Args to Child                                                        : Call Site
00 00000032`b55fe8c8 00007ffe`fb086931 : 00000032`b55fe988 00000000`00000000 00000000`00000030 00000032`b55fe8f0 : ntdll!NtDelayExecution+0x14
01 00000032`b55fe8d0 00007ffe`fbd36c93 : 00000000`00000000 00007ffe`00000000 00007dfc`c00000bb 00000000`00000000 : KERNELBASE!SleepEx+0xa1
02 00000032`b55fe970 00007ffe`fb13f988 : 00000000`00000000 00000032`b55ffac0 00007ffe`fbcd0000 00000000`00000000 : kernel32!WerpReportFault+0x97
03 00000032`b55fe9b0 00007ffe`fd2e4af2 : 00000000`00000000 00007ffe`fd384420 00000000`00000000 00000032`b55ffa60 : KERNELBASE!UnhandledExceptionFilter+0x3b8
04 00000032`b55fead0 00007ffe`fd2cc6e6 : 00000000`00000000 00000000`00000000 00000032`b55ff108 00000032`b55ff190 : ntdll!RtlUserThreadStart$filt$0+0xa2
05 00000032`b55feb10 00007ffe`fd2e120f : 00000000`00000000 00000032`b55ff0f0 00000032`b55ff7b0 00000032`b55ff7b0 : ntdll!_C_specific_handler+0x96
06 00000032`b55feb80 00007ffe`fd2aa299 : 00000032`00000001 00007ffe`fd240000 00000000`00000000 00007ffe`fd3ae9f0 : ntdll!RtlpExecuteHandlerForException+0xf
07 00000032`b55febb0 00007ffe`fd2dfe7e : 00000000`00000000 00000000`00000000 00000200`bcbc6b80 00000000`00000000 : ntdll!RtlDispatchException+0x219
08 00000032`b55ff2c0 00007ff7`94981010 : 00000000`00000001 00000000`00000005 00000200`bcbc6b80 00007ff7`94982888 : ntdll!KiUserExceptionDispatch+0x2e
(TrapFrame @ 00000032`b55ff6e8)
09 00000032`b55ffa40 00007ff7`94982888 : 00000000`00000000 00000000`00000000 00000000`00000000 00000000`00000000 : AppK+0x1010
0a 00000032`b55ffa60 00007ffe`fbce7bd4 : 00000000`00000000 00000000`00000000 00000000`00000000 00000000`00000000 : AppK+0x2888
0b 00000032`b55ffa90 00007ffe`fd2acee1 : 00000000`00000000 00000000`00000000 00000000`00000000 00000000`00000000 : kernel32!BaseThreadInitThunk+0x14
0c 00000032`b55ffac0 00000000`00000000 : 00000000`00000000 00000000`00000000 00000000`00000000 00000000`00000000 : ntdll!RtlUserThreadStart+0x21
```

```
0:002> .frame /c 9
09 00000032`b55ffa40 00007ff7`94982888 AppK+0x1010
rax=0045005400530059 rbx=00000200bcbc6b80 rcx=005c00320033004d
rdx=006e00720065006b rsi=0000000000000000 rdi=0000000000000000
rip=00007ff794981010 rsp=00000032b55ffa40 rbp=0000000000000000
 r8=0000000000000000  r9=0000000000000000 r10=0000000000000000
r11=0000000000000000 r12=0000000000000000 r13=0000000000000000
r14=0000000000000000 r15=0000000000000000
iopl=0         nv up ei pl zr na po nc
cs=0033  ss=002b  ds=002b  es=002b  fs=0053  gs=002b             efl=00000246
AppK+0x1010:
00007ff7`94981010 c70425000000000000000000 mov dword ptr [0],0 ds:00000000`00000000=????????
```

```
0:002> k
 *** Stack trace for last set context - .thread/.cxr resets it
 # Child-SP          RetAddr           Call Site
09 00000032`b55ffa40 00007ff7`94982888 AppK+0x1010
0a 00000032`b55ffa60 00007ffe`fbce7bd4 AppK+0x2888
0b 00000032`b55ffa90 00007ffe`fd2acee1 kernel32!BaseThreadInitThunk+0x14
0c 00000032`b55ffac0 00000000`00000000 ntdll!RtlUserThreadStart+0x21
```

Note: We see another NULL pointer access exception. If we come back to the previous **!analyze -v** output above, we would see that WinDbg identified only the debug break from the first thread.

We can use the **.cxr** command to reset the exception context:

```
0:002> .cxr
Resetting default scope
```

```
0:002> k
 # Child-SP          RetAddr           Call Site
00 00000032`b55fe8c8 00007ffe`fb086931 ntdll!NtDelayExecution+0x14
01 00000032`b55fe8d0 00007ffe`fbd36c93 KERNELBASE!SleepEx+0xa1
02 00000032`b55fe970 00007ffe`fb13f988 kernel32!WerpReportFault+0x97
03 00000032`b55fe9b0 00007ffe`fd2e4af2 KERNELBASE!UnhandledExceptionFilter+0x3b8
04 00000032`b55fead0 00007ffe`fd2cc6e6 ntdll!RtlUserThreadStart$filt$0+0xa2
05 00000032`b55feb10 00007ffe`fd2e120f ntdll!_C_specific_handler+0x96
06 00000032`b55feb80 00007ffe`fd2aa299 ntdll!RtlpExecuteHandlerForException+0xf
07 00000032`b55febb0 00007ffe`fd2dfe7e ntdll!RtlDispatchException+0x219
08 00000032`b55ff2c0 00007ff7`94981010 ntdll!KiUserExceptionDispatch+0x2e
09 00000032`b55ffa40 00007ff7`94982888 AppK+0x1010
```

```
0a 00000032`b55ffa60 00007ffe`fbce7bd4 AppK+0x2888
0b 00000032`b55ffa90 00007ffe`fd2acee1 kernel32!BaseThreadInitThunk+0x14
0c 00000032`b55ffac0 00000000`00000000 ntdll!RtlUserThreadStart+0x21
```

15.   We close logging before exiting WinDbg:

```
0:002> .logclose
Closing open log file C:\AWMDA-Dumps\Process\x64\AppK.log
```

Exercise P5

- **Goal:** Learn how to load application symbols

- \AWMDA-Dumps\Exercise-P5-Analysis-process-dump-AppK-64-with-symbols.pdf

Exercise P5: Analysis of an application process dump (64-bit AppK, with application symbols)

Goal: Learn how to load application symbols.

1.   Launch WinDbg.

2.   Open \AWMDA-Dumps\Process\x64\AppK.exe.8484.dmp.

3.   We get the dump file loaded:

```
Microsoft (R) Windows Debugger Version 10.0.25877.1004 AMD64
Copyright (c) Microsoft Corporation. All rights reserved.


Loading Dump File [C:\AWMDA-Dumps\Process\x64\AppK.exe.8484.dmp]
User Mini Dump File with Full Memory: Only application data is available


************* Path validation summary **************
Response                         Time (ms)      Location
Deferred                                        srv*
Symbol search path is: srv*
Executable search path is:
Windows 10 Version 18362 MP (2 procs) Free x64
Product: WinNt, suite: SingleUserTS Personal
Edition build lab: 18362.1.amd64fre.19h1_release.190318-1202
Debug session time: Tue Oct  1 23:54:08.000 2019 (UTC + 1:00)
System Uptime: 0 days 0:04:48.832
Process Uptime: 0 days 0:00:01.000
.......
This dump file has a breakpoint exception stored in it.
The stored exception information can be accessed via .ecxr.
For analysis of this file, run !analyze -v
ntdll!NtWaitForMultipleObjects+0x14:
00007ffe`fd2dcc24 c3              ret
```

4.   Open a log file using the **.logopen** command:

```
0:000> .logopen C:\AWMDA-Dumps\Process\x64\AppK-symbols.log
Opened log file 'C:\AWMDA-Dumps\Process\x64\AppK-symbols.log'
```

5.   Type the **k** command to verify the correctness of the stack trace:

```
0:000> k
 # Child-SP          RetAddr           Call Site
00 00000032`b51fe788 00007ffe`fb097ff7 ntdll!NtWaitForMultipleObjects+0x14
01 00000032`b51fe790 00007ffe`fb097ede KERNELBASE!WaitForMultipleObjectsEx+0x107
02 00000032`b51fea90 00007ffe`fbd371fb KERNELBASE!WaitForMultipleObjects+0xe
03 00000032`b51fead0 00007ffe`fbd36ca8 kernel32!WerpReportFaultInternal+0x51b
04 00000032`b51febf0 00007ffe`fb13f988 kernel32!WerpReportFault+0xac
05 00000032`b51fec30 00007ffe`fd2e4af2 KERNELBASE!UnhandledExceptionFilter+0x3b8
06 00000032`b51fed50 00007ffe`fd2cc6e6 ntdll!RtlUserThreadStart$filt$0+0xa2
07 00000032`b51fed90 00007ffe`fd2e120f ntdll!_C_specific_handler+0x96
08 00000032`b51fee00 00007ffe`fd2aa299 ntdll!RtlpExecuteHandlerForException+0xf
```

```
09 00000032`b51fee30 00007ffe`fd2dfe7e ntdll!RtlDispatchException+0x219
0a 00000032`b51ff540 00007ffe`fb1002b2 ntdll!KiUserExceptionDispatch+0x2e
0b 00000032`b51ffcd8 00007ff7`94981075 KERNELBASE!wil::details::DebugBreak+0x2
0c 00000032`b51ffce0 00007ff7`9498126c AppK+0x1075
0d 00000032`b51ffd10 00007ffe`fbce7bd4 AppK+0x126c
0e 00000032`b51ffd50 00007ffe`fd2acee1 kernel32!BaseThreadInitThunk+0x14
0f 00000032`b51ffd80 00000000`00000000 ntdll!RtlUserThreadStart+0x21
```

Note: The symbols were loaded correctly for Microsoft modules but not for the 3rd-party *AppK* module. Now, suppose we got symbols from an application developer in the *C:\AWMDA-Dumps\x64\Symbols* folder.

6.   We specify an additional symbol folder using the **.sympath+ <folder>** command and then reload all necessary symbols (**.reload**):

```
0:000> .sympath+ C:\AWMDA-Dumps\Symbols
Symbol search path is: srv*;C:\AWMDA-Dumps\Symbols
Expanded Symbol search path is:
cache*;SRV*https://msdl.microsoft.com/download/symbols;c:\awmda-dumps\symbols

************* Path validation summary **************
Response                        Time (ms)       Location
Deferred                                        srv*
OK                                              C:\AWMDA-Dumps\Symbols

0:000> .reload
.......
```

Note: In case you specified the wrong additional symbols paths, it is always possible to reset the symbol paths via the **.symfix** command.

7.   Let's get the stack trace again:

```
0:000> k
 # Child-SP          RetAddr           Call Site
00 00000032`b51fe788 00007ffe`fb097ff7 ntdll!NtWaitForMultipleObjects+0x14
01 00000032`b51fe790 00007ffe`fb097ede KERNELBASE!WaitForMultipleObjectsEx+0x107
02 00000032`b51fea90 00007ffe`fbd371fb KERNELBASE!WaitForMultipleObjects+0xe
03 00000032`b51fead0 00007ffe`fbd36ca8 kernel32!WerpReportFaultInternal+0x51b
04 00000032`b51febf0 00007ffe`fb13f988 kernel32!WerpReportFault+0xac
05 00000032`b51fec30 00007ffe`fd2e4af2 KERNELBASE!UnhandledExceptionFilter+0x3b8
06 00000032`b51fed50 00007ffe`fd2cc6e6 ntdll!RtlUserThreadStart$filt$0+0xa2
07 00000032`b51fed90 00007ffe`fd2e120f ntdll!_C_specific_handler+0x96
08 00000032`b51fee00 00007ffe`fd2aa299 ntdll!RtlpExecuteHandlerForException+0xf
09 00000032`b51fee30 00007ffe`fd2dfe7e ntdll!RtlDispatchException+0x219
0a 00000032`b51ff540 00007ffe`fb1002b2 ntdll!KiUserExceptionDispatch+0x2e
*** WARNING: Unable to verify checksum for AppK.exe
0b 00000032`b51ffcd8 00007ff7`94981075 KERNELBASE!wil::details::DebugBreak+0x2
0c 00000032`b51ffce0 00007ff7`9498126c AppK!wmain+0x35 [C:\AWMDA-Examples\AppK\AppK.cpp @ 30]
0d (Inline Function) --------`-------- AppK!invoke_main+0x22
[d:\agent\_work\3\s\src\vctools\crt\vcstartup\src\startup\exe_common.inl @ 90]
0e 00000032`b51ffd10 00007ffe`fbce7bd4 AppK!__scrt_common_main_seh+0x10c
[d:\agent\_work\3\s\src\vctools\crt\vcstartup\src\startup\exe_common.inl @ 288]
0f 00000032`b51ffd50 00007ffe`fd2acee1 kernel32!BaseThreadInitThunk+0x14
10 00000032`b51ffd80 00000000`00000000 ntdll!RtlUserThreadStart+0x21
```

Note: We now see *AppK* functions on the stack trace. Also, the **kL** command can be used to hide source code paths:

```
0:000> kL
 # Child-SP          RetAddr           Call Site
00 00000032`b51fe788 00007ffe`fb097ff7 ntdll!NtWaitForMultipleObjects+0x14
01 00000032`b51fe790 00007ffe`fb097ede KERNELBASE!WaitForMultipleObjectsEx+0x107
02 00000032`b51fea90 00007ffe`fbd371fb KERNELBASE!WaitForMultipleObjects+0xe
03 00000032`b51fead0 00007ffe`fbd36ca8 kernel32!WerpReportFaultInternal+0x51b
04 00000032`b51febf0 00007ffe`fb13f988 kernel32!WerpReportFault+0xac
05 00000032`b51fec30 00007ffe`fd2e4af2 KERNELBASE!UnhandledExceptionFilter+0x3b8
06 00000032`b51fed50 00007ffe`fd2cc6e6 ntdll!RtlUserThreadStart$filt$0+0xa2
07 00000032`b51fed90 00007ffe`fd2e120f ntdll!_C_specific_handler+0x96
08 00000032`b51fee00 00007ffe`fd2aa299 ntdll!RtlpExecuteHandlerForException+0xf
09 00000032`b51fee30 00007ffe`fd2dfe7e ntdll!RtlDispatchException+0x219
0a 00000032`b51ff540 00007ffe`fb1002b2 ntdll!KiUserExceptionDispatch+0x2e
0b 00000032`b51ffcd8 00007ff7`94981075 KERNELBASE!wil::details::DebugBreak+0x2
0c 00000032`b51ffce0 00007ff7`9498126c AppK!wmain+0x35
0d (Inline Function) --------`-------- AppK!invoke_main+0x22
0e 00000032`b51ffd10 00007ffe`fbce7bd4 AppK!__scrt_common_main_seh+0x10c
0f 00000032`b51ffd50 00007ffe`fd2acee1 kernel32!BaseThreadInitThunk+0x14
10 00000032`b51ffd80 00000000`00000000 ntdll!RtlUserThreadStart+0x21
```

8.   Now we repeat commands from the previous exercise for thread #1:

```
0:000> ~1s
ntdll!NtDelayExecution+0x14:
00007ffe`fd2dc754 c3              ret

0:001> kL
 # Child-SP          RetAddr           Call Site
00 00000032`b54feb88 00007ffe`fb086931 ntdll!NtDelayExecution+0x14
01 00000032`b54feb90 00007ffe`fbd36c93 KERNELBASE!SleepEx+0xa1
02 00000032`b54fec30 00007ffe`fb13f988 kernel32!WerpReportFault+0x97
03 00000032`b54fec70 00007ffe`fd2e4af2 KERNELBASE!UnhandledExceptionFilter+0x3b8
04 00000032`b54fed90 00007ffe`fd2cc6e6 ntdll!RtlUserThreadStart$filt$0+0xa2
05 00000032`b54fedd0 00007ffe`fd2e120f ntdll!_C_specific_handler+0x96
06 00000032`b54fee40 00007ffe`fd2aa299 ntdll!RtlpExecuteHandlerForException+0xf
07 00000032`b54fee70 00007ffe`fd2dfe7e ntdll!RtlDispatchException+0x219
08 00000032`b54ff580 00007ff7`94981030 ntdll!KiUserExceptionDispatch+0x2e
09 00000032`b54ffd20 00007ff7`94982888 AppK!thread_two+0x10
0a 00000032`b54ffd40 00007ffe`fbce7bd4 AppK!thread_start<void (__cdecl*)(void *),0>+0x50
0b 00000032`b54ffd70 00007ffe`fd2acee1 kernel32!BaseThreadInitThunk+0x14
0c 00000032`b54ffda0 00000000`00000000 ntdll!RtlUserThreadStart+0x21

0:001> .frame /c 9
09 00000032`b54ffd20 00007ff7`94982888 AppK!thread_two+0x10 [C:\AWMDA-Examples\AppK\AppK.cpp @
20]
rax=00000200bcbc8a80 rbx=00000200bcbc6b50 rcx=00007ff79498d770
rdx=00000200bcbc8a80 rsi=0000000000000000 rdi=0000000000000000
rip=00007ff794981030 rsp=00000032b54ffd20 rbp=0000000000000000
 r8=0053005c00530057  r9=0045005400530059 r10=005c00320033004d
r11=006e00720065006b r12=0000000000000000 r13=0000000000000000
r14=0000000000000000 r15=0000000000000000
iopl=0         nv up ei pl zr na po nc
cs=0033  ss=002b  ds=002b  es=002b  fs=0053  gs=002b             efl=00000246
AppK!thread_two+0x10:
00007ff7`94981030 c704250000000000000000 mov dword ptr [0],0 ds:00000000`00000000=????????
```

103

Note: If you have *AppK* source code in the location *C:\AWMDA-Examples\AppK*, the following window appears in WinDbg highlighting the problem C++ code if you run the **.cxr** command:

```cpp
AppK.cpp                                                           ▾  □  ✕
     1 // AppK - Models multiple exceptions in user mode
     2 // Copyright (c) 2011-2019 Software Diagnostics Technology and Services
     3 // GNU GENERAL PUBLIC LICENSE
     4 // http://www.gnu.org/licenses/gpl-3.0.txt
     5
     6 #include <windows.h>
     7 #include <process.h>
     8
     9 void thread_one(void*)
    10 {
    11     int one{ 1 };
    12
    13     *(int*)nullptr = 0;
    14 }
    15
    16 void thread_two(void*)
    17 {
    18     int two{ 2 };
    19
 ⇨  20     *(int*)nullptr = 0;
    21 }
    22
    23 int wmain(int argc, wchar_t* argv[])
    24 {
    25     _beginthread(thread_two, 0, nullptr);
    26     _beginthread(thread_one, 0, nullptr);
    27
    28     DebugBreak();
    29
    30     return 0;
    31 }
    32
```

For a different source code location, you can set it via the **.srcpath+** *<folder>* command. Now, repeating the stack trace command, we should get the stack trace up to the problem function call:

```
0:001> kL
  *** Stack trace for last set context - .thread/.cxr resets it
 # Child-SP          RetAddr           Call Site
09 00000032`b54ffd20 00007ff7`94982888 AppK!thread_two+0x10
0a 00000032`b54ffd40 00007ffe`fbce7bd4 AppK!thread_start<void (__cdecl*)(void *),0>+0x50
0b 00000032`b54ffd70 00007ffe`fd2acee1 kernel32!BaseThreadInitThunk+0x14
0c 00000032`b54ffda0 00000000`00000000 ntdll!RtlUserThreadStart+0x21
```

9.   We close logging before exiting WinDbg:

```
0:001> .logclose
Closing open log file C:\AWMDA-Dumps\Process\x64\AppK-symbols.log
```

Exercise P6

- **Goal:** Learn how to recognize heap corruption, dump memory contents, follow critical section wait chains, and check error and status codes

- **Patterns:** Dynamic Memory Corruption (Process Heap); Wait Chain (Critical Sections); Execution Residue (Unmanaged Space, User); Last Error Collection

- \AWMDA-Dumps\Exercise-P6-Analysis-process-dump-AppL-64.pdf

Exercise P6: Analysis of an application process dump (AppL, 64-bit)

Goal: Learn how to recognize heap corruption, dump memory contents, follow critical section wait chains, and check error and status codes.

Patterns: Dynamic Memory Corruption (Process Heap); Wait Chain (Critical Sections); Execution Residue (Unmanaged Space, User); Last Error Collection.

1.   Launch WinDbg.

2.   Open \AWMDA-Dumps\Process\x64\AppL.exe.9408.dmp.

3.   We get the dump file loaded:

```
Microsoft (R) Windows Debugger Version 10.0.25877.1004 AMD64
Copyright (c) Microsoft Corporation. All rights reserved.


Loading Dump File [C:\AWMDA-Dumps\Process\x64\AppL.exe.9408.dmp]
User Mini Dump File with Full Memory: Only application data is available


************* Path validation summary **************
Response                        Time (ms)     Location
Deferred                                      srv*
Symbol search path is: srv*
Executable search path is:
Windows 10 Version 18362 MP (2 procs) Free x64
Product: WinNt, suite: SingleUserTS Personal
Edition build lab: 18362.1.amd64fre.19h1_release.190318-1202
Machine Name:
Debug session time: Thu Oct 10 19:37:41.000 2019 (UTC + 1:00)
System Uptime: 0 days 0:11:56.115
Process Uptime: 0 days 0:00:02.000
.......
```
This dump file has an exception of interest stored in it.
The stored exception information can be accessed via .ecxr.
(24c0.243c): Unknown exception - code c0000374 (first/second chance not available)
```
For analysis of this file, run !analyze -v
ntdll!NtWaitForMultipleObjects+0x14:
00007ffe`fd2dcc24 c3              ret
```

4.   Open a log file using the **.logopen** command and load *AppL* symbols (**.sympath+** and **.reload**):

```
0:001> .logopen C:\AWMDA-Dumps\Process\x64\AppL.log
Opened log file 'C:\AWMDA-Dumps\Process\x64\AppL.log'

0:001> .sympath+ C:\AWMDA-Dumps\Symbols
Symbol search path is: srv*;C:\AWMDA-Dumps\Symbols
Expanded Symbol search path is:
cache*;SRV*https://msdl.microsoft.com/download/symbols;c:\awmda-dumps\symbols

************* Path validation summary **************
Response                        Time (ms)     Location
Deferred                                      srv*
```

```
0:001> .reload
.......
```

5.   Type the **kL** command to verify the correctness of the stack trace (we use **L** to suppress the source code information that may clutter the output):

```
0:001> kL
 # Child-SP          RetAddr           Call Site
00 00000046`be8fe068 00007ffe`fd31ce0c ntdll!NtWaitForMultipleObjects+0x14
01 00000046`be8fe070 00007ffe`fd31c40e ntdll!WerpWaitForCrashReporting+0xa8
02 00000046`be8fe0f0 00007ffe`fd31bbcb ntdll!RtlReportExceptionHelper+0x33e
03 00000046`be8fe1c0 00007ffe`fd3392a3 ntdll!RtlReportException+0x9b
04 00000046`be8fe240 00007ffe`fd2cc6e6 ntdll!RtlReportFatalFailure$filt$0+0x33
05 00000046`be8fe270 00007ffe`fd2e120f ntdll!_C_specific_handler+0x96
06 00000046`be8fe2e0 00007ffe`fd2aa299 ntdll!RtlpExecuteHandlerForException+0xf
07 00000046`be8fe310 00007ffe`fd2aa053 ntdll!RtlDispatchException+0x219
08 00000046`be8fea20 00007ffe`fd339269 ntdll!RtlRaiseException+0x153
09 00000046`be8ff290 00007ffe`fd339233 ntdll!RtlReportFatalFailure+0x9
0a 00000046`be8ff2e0 00007ffe`fd341622 ntdll!RtlReportCriticalFailure+0x97
0b 00000046`be8ff3d0 00007ffe`fd34192a ntdll!RtlpHeapHandleError+0x12
0c 00000046`be8ff400 00007ffe`fd34a8e9 ntdll!RtlpHpHeapHandleError+0x7a
0d 00000046`be8ff430 00007ffe`fd341531 ntdll!RtlpLogHeapFailure+0x45
0e 00000046`be8ff460 00007ffe`fd282544 ntdll!RtlpAnalyzeHeapFailure+0x2fd
0f 00000046`be8ff4c0 00007ffe`fd280810 ntdll!RtlpFreeHeap+0xbe4
10 00000046`be8ff620 00007ffe`fd27fc11 ntdll!RtlpFreeHeapInternal+0x790
*** WARNING: Unable to verify checksum for AppL.exe
11 00000046`be8ff6d0 00007ff6`53374ac4 ntdll!RtlFreeHeap+0x51
12 00000046`be8ff710 00007ff6`533710b4 AppL!_free_base+0x1c
13 00000046`be8ff740 00007ff6`53372e88 AppL!thread_two+0x44
14 00000046`be8ff790 00007ffe`fbce7bd4 AppL!thread_start<void (__cdecl*)(void *),0>+0x50
15 00000046`be8ff7c0 00007ffe`fd2acee1 kernel32!BaseThreadInitThunk+0x14
16 00000046`be8ff7f0 00000000`00000000 ntdll!RtlUserThreadStart+0x21
```

Note: In addition to exception processing, we see heap failure analysis and heap manipulation functions.

6.   Let's now double-check our findings with the **!analyze -v** command:

```
0:001> !analyze -v
*******************************************************************
*                                                                 *
*                        Exception Analysis                       *
*                                                                 *
*******************************************************************

KEY_VALUES_STRING: 1

    Key  : Analysis.CPU.mSec
    Value: 717

    Key  : Analysis.DebugAnalysisManager
    Value: Create

    Key  : Analysis.Elapsed.mSec
    Value: 725

    Key  : Analysis.Init.CPU.mSec
    Value: 1280

    Key  : Analysis.Init.Elapsed.mSec
    Value: 321767

    Key  : Analysis.Memory.CommitPeak.Mb
    Value: 238

    Key  : Timeline.OS.Boot.DeltaSec
    Value: 716

    Key  : Timeline.Process.Start.DeltaSec
    Value: 2
```

```
Key  : WER.OS.Branch
Value: 19h1_release

Key  : WER.OS.Timestamp
Value: 2019-03-18T12:02:00Z

Key  : WER.OS.Version
Value: 10.0.18362.1

Key  : WER.Process.Version
Value: 2.0.0.1


FILE_IN_CAB:  AppL.exe.9408.dmp

NTGLOBALFLAG:  0

PROCESS_BAM_CURRENT_THROTTLED:  0

PROCESS_BAM_PREVIOUS_THROTTLED:  0

APPLICATION_VERIFIER_FLAGS:  0

CONTEXT:  (.ecxr)
rax=0000000000000000 rbx=00000000c0000374 rcx=0000000000000000
rdx=0000000000000000 rsi=0000000000000001 rdi=00007ffefd3a27f0
rip=00007ffefd339269 rsp=00000046be8ff290 rbp=000002226cef0000
 r8=0000000000000000  r9=0000000000000000 r10=0000000000000000
r11=0000000000000000 r12=0000000000000001 r13=0000000000000000
r14=000000007ffe0380 r15=0000000000000000
iopl=0         nv up ei pl nz na po nc
cs=0033  ss=002b  ds=002b  es=002b  fs=0053  gs=002b             efl=00000206
ntdll!RtlReportFatalFailure+0x9:
00007ffe`fd339269 eb00            jmp     ntdll!RtlReportFatalFailure+0xb (00007ffe`fd33926b)
Resetting default scope

EXCEPTION_RECORD:  (.exr -1)
ExceptionAddress: 00007ffefd339269 (ntdll!RtlReportFatalFailure+0x0000000000000009)
   ExceptionCode: c0000374
  ExceptionFlags: 00000001
NumberParameters: 1
   Parameter[0]: 00007ffefd3a27f0

PROCESS_NAME:  AppL.exe

ERROR_CODE: (NTSTATUS) 0xc0000374 - A heap has been corrupted.

EXCEPTION_CODE_STR:  c0000374

EXCEPTION_PARAMETER1:  00007ffefd3a27f0

STACK_TEXT:
00000046`be8ff290 00007ffe`fd339233     : 00000046`be8ff748 00000046`be8ff420 00000000`00000200 00000046`be8ff500 : ntdll!RtlReportFatalFailure+0x9
00000046`be8ff2e0 00007ffe`fd341622     : 00007ff6`5337e870 00007ffe`fd3a27f0 00000000`00000003 000002222`6cef0000 : ntdll!RtlReportCriticalFailure+0x97
00000046`be8ff3d0 00007ffe`fd34192a     : 00000000`00000003 00000222`6cef0000 00000222`6cef0000 00000000`0000000e : ntdll!RtlpHeapHandleError+0x12
00000046`be8ff400 00007ffe`fd34a8e9     : 00000222`6cef0000 00000000`00100000 00000000`00000018 00000000`00000008 : ntdll!RtlpHpHeapHandleError+0x7a
00000046`be8ff430 00007ffe`fd341531     : 00000000`00000000 00000222`6cef0150 00000222`6cefc140 00000000`00000000 : ntdll!RtlpLogHeapFailure+0x45
00000046`be8ff460 00007ffe`fd282544     : 00000222`6cef0000 00000222`6cefc140 00000222`6cef0000 00000222`6cefc140 : ntdll!RtlpAnalyzeHeapFailure+0x2fd
00000046`be8ff4c0 00007ffe`fd280810     : 00000222`6cef0000 00000222`6cef0000 00000222`6cefc140 00000222`6cefc150 : ntdll!RtlpFreeHeap+0xbe4
00000046`be8ff620 00007ffe`fd27fc11     : 00000000`00000000 00000222`6cef0000 00000000`00000000 00000000`00000000 : ntdll!RtlpFreeHeapInternal+0x790
00000046`be8ff6d0 00007ff6`53374ac4     : 00000222`6cef7040 00000000`00000000 00000000`00000000 00007ffe`fb0b62d5 : ntdll!RtlFreeHeap+0x51
00000046`be8ff710 00007ff6`533710b4     : 00000000`00000000 00000000`00000000 00000000`00000001 00007ff6`5337583a : AppL!_free_base+0x1c
00000046`be8ff740 00007ff6`53372e88     : 00000000`00000000 00000000`00000000 00000000`00000000 00000000`00000000 : AppL!thread_two+0x44
00000046`be8ff790 00007ffe`fbce7bd4     : 00000000`00000000 00000000`00000000 00000000`00000000 00000000`00000000 : AppL!thread_start<void (__cdecl*)(void
*),0>+0x50
00000046`be8ff7c0 00007ffe`fd2acee1     : 00000000`00000000 00000000`00000000 00000000`00000000 00000000`00000000 : kernel32!BaseThreadInitThunk+0x14
00000046`be8ff7f0 00000000`00000000     : 00000000`00000000 00000000`00000000 00000000`00000000 00000000`00000000 : ntdll!RtlUserThreadStart+0x21


STACK_COMMAND:  ~1s; .ecxr ; kb

FAULTING_SOURCE_LINE:  minkernel\crts\ucrt\src\appcrt\heap\free_base.cpp

FAULTING_SOURCE_FILE:  minkernel\crts\ucrt\src\appcrt\heap\free_base.cpp

FAULTING_SOURCE_LINE_NUMBER:  105

FAULTING_SOURCE_CODE:
No source found for 'minkernel\crts\ucrt\src\appcrt\heap\free_base.cpp'


SYMBOL_NAME:  appl!_free_base+1c

MODULE_NAME: AppL

IMAGE_NAME:  AppL.exe

FAILURE_BUCKET_ID:  HEAP_CORRUPTION_c0000374_AppL.exe!_free_base

OS_VERSION:  10.0.18362.1

BUILDLAB_STR:  19h1_release

OSPLATFORM_TYPE:  x64

OSNAME:  Windows 10

IMAGE_VERSION:  2.0.0.1
```

FAILURE_ID_HASH: {2e238f93-cfaa-a6fc-071a-c1c8394ff03b}

Followup: MachineOwner

Note: We see that WinDbg correctly diagnosed heap corruption and error code 0xc0000374 - A heap has been corrupted. We can also check the process heap for any errors using the **!heap -s -v** command:

```
0:001> !heap -s -v


*******************************************************************************
                              NT HEAP STATS BELOW
*******************************************************************************
***************************************************************
*                                                             *
*                  HEAP ERROR DETECTED                        *
*                                                             *
***************************************************************

Details:

Heap address:  000002226cef0000
Error address: 000002226cefc140
Last known valid blocks: before - 000002226cefc110, after - 000002226cefc220
Error type:    HEAP_FAILURE_BUFFER_OVERRUN
Details:       The heap manager detected an error whose features are
               consistent with a buffer overrun.
Follow-up:     Enable pageheap.

Stack trace:
Stack trace at 0x00007ffefd3a2848
    00007ffefd34a8e9: ntdll!RtlpLogHeapFailure+0x45
    00007ffefd341531: ntdll!RtlpAnalyzeHeapFailure+0x2fd
    00007ffefd282544: ntdll!RtlpFreeHeap+0xbe4
    00007ffefd280810: ntdll!RtlpFreeHeapInternal+0x790
    00007ffefd27fc11: ntdll!RtlFreeHeap+0x51
    00007ff653374ac4: AppL!_free_base+0x1c
    00007ff6533710b4: AppL!thread_two+0x44
    00007ff653372e88: AppL!thread_start<void (__cdecl*)(void *),0>+0x50
    00007ffefbce7bd4: kernel32!BaseThreadInitThunk+0x14
    00007ffefd2acee1: ntdll!RtlUserThreadStart+0x21

LFH Key                   : 0x9684b109a9336c37
Termination on corruption : ENABLED
          Heap     Flags   Reserv  Commit  Virt   Free  List   UCR  Virt  Lock  Fast
                            (k)     (k)     (k)    (k) length       blocks cont. heap
-------------------------------------------------------------------------------------
.HEAP 000002226cef0000 (Seg 000002226cef0000) At 000002226cf75440 Error: invalid block size

000002226cef0000 00000002    1072      60    1020      7     5      1     0     2   LFH
.000002226cdf0000 00008000      64       4      64      2     1      1     0     0
.000002226d210000 00001002     112      32      60      7     2      1     0     0   LFH
-------------------------------------------------------------------------------------
```

Note: The command output shows the last valid heap block before the failure is detected: 000002226cefc110. Let's check its data:

```
0:001> !heap -x 000002226cefc110
HEAP 000002226cef0000 (Seg 000002226cef0000) At 000002226cf75440 Error: invalid block size

Entry            User             Heap             Segment               Size  PrevSize  Unused   Flags
-------------------------------------------------------------------------------------------------------
000002226cefc110  000002226cefc120  000002226cef0000  000002226cef0000        30       20      10  busy
```

Since we know this block size (**30**), we can check the next block:

```
0:001> !heap -x 000002226cefc110+30
HEAP 000002226cef0000 (Seg 000002226cef0000) At 000002226cf75440 Error: invalid block size

Entry            User             Heap             Segment               Size  PrevSize  Unused   Flags
-------------------------------------------------------------------------------------------------------
000002226cefc140  000002226cefc150  000002226cef0000  000002226cef0000     79300       30      18  busy
```

Note: Values for **Size** and **PrevSize** are hexadecimal.

We see that its size is very big, but the **PrevSize** looks valid for the previous block we inspected. Let's dump its memory contents:

```
0:001> dc 000002226cefc140
00000222`6cefc140  00000000 00000000 9b7a3232 1800849a  ........22z.....
00000222`6cefc150  6cefbd90 00000222 6cefbff0 00000222  ...l"......l"...
00000222`6cefc160  be9ff560 00000046 00000000 00000000  `...F...........
00000222`6cefc170  00108020 00000000 be9ff3b8 00000046  .......... ....F...
00000222`6cefc180  6cef7310 00000222 6cefc230 00000222  .s.l"...0..l"...
00000222`6cefc190  fd3a52f0 00007ffe fd3a52f0 00007ffe  .R:......R:.....
00000222`6cefc1a0  00000000 00000000 6cefc3b0 00000222  ...........l"...
00000222`6cefc1b0  0000001b 00000000 fba89000 00007ffe  ................
```

We see '22' in the block header (which is 16 bytes, 0x10), which corresponds to the *thread_two* function in the *AppL* source code:

```
void thread_two(void*)
{
    auto p = new short [100];
    *(p - 4) = '22';
    delete[] p;
}
```

The correspondence to the source code is more visible if we dump short values (words) using the **dw** command:

```
0:001> dw 000002226cefc140
00000222`6cefc140  0000 0000 0000 0000 3232 9b7a 849a 1800
00000222`6cefc150  bd90 6cef 0222 0000 bff0 6cef 0222 0000
00000222`6cefc160  f560 be9f 0046 0000 0000 0000 0000 0000
00000222`6cefc170  8020 0010 0000 0000 f3b8 be9f 0046 0000
00000222`6cefc180  7310 6cef 0222 0000 c230 6cef 0222 0000
00000222`6cefc190  52f0 fd3a 7ffe 0000 52f0 fd3a 7ffe 0000
00000222`6cefc1a0  0000 0000 0000 0000 c3b0 6cef 0222 0000
00000222`6cefc1b0  001b 0000 0000 0000 9000 fba8 7ffe 0000
```

00000222`6cefc150 address here (**User** from the table header) corresponds to the address returned by C++ *new*. If we try to get the next block information using the corrupt *Size* value, we fail:

```
0:001> !heap -x 000002226cefc140+79300
HEAP 000002226cef0000 (Seg 000002226cef0000) At 000002226cf75440 Error: invalid block size
```

The memory for it is also invalid:

```
0:001> dc 000002226cefc140+79300
00000222`6cf75440  ???????? ???????? ???????? ????????  ????????????????????
00000222`6cf75450  ???????? ???????? ???????? ????????  ????????????????????
00000222`6cf75460  ???????? ???????? ???????? ????????  ????????????????????
00000222`6cf75470  ???????? ???????? ???????? ????????  ????????????????????
00000222`6cf75480  ???????? ???????? ???????? ????????  ????????????????????
00000222`6cf75490  ???????? ???????? ???????? ????????  ????????????????????
00000222`6cf754a0  ???????? ???????? ???????? ????????  ????????????????????
00000222`6cf754b0  ???????? ???????? ???????? ????????  ????????????????????
```

This memory region belongs to the process heap but has not yet been committed:

```
0:001> !address 000002226cefc140+79300

Mapping file section regions...
Mapping module regions...
Mapping PEB regions...
Mapping TEB and stack regions...
Mapping heap regions...
Mapping page heap regions...
Mapping other regions...
Mapping stack trace database regions...
Mapping activation context regions...

Usage:                Heap
Base Address:         00000222`6cefe000
End Address:          00000222`6cfef000
Region Size:          00000000`000f1000 ( 964.000 kB)
State:                00002000           MEM_RESERVE
Protect:              <info not present at the target>
Type:                 00020000           MEM_PRIVATE
Allocation Base:      00000222`6cef0000
Allocation Protect:   00000004           PAGE_READWRITE
More info:            heap owning the address: !heap 0x2226cef0000
More info:            heap segment
More info:            heap entry containing the address: !heap -x 0x2226cf75440

Content source: 0 (invalid), length: 7abc0
```

7.   Let's now check all threads to see if there are any anomalies:

```
0:001> ~*kL

   0  Id: 24c0.9f4 Suspend: 1 Teb: 00000046`be7f9000 Unfrozen
 # Child-SP          RetAddr               Call Site
00 00000046`be5cf628 00007ffe`fb086931 ntdll!NtDelayExecution+0x14
01 00000046`be5cf630 00007ff6`5337111a KERNELBASE!SleepEx+0xa1
02 00000046`be5cf6d0 00007ff6`53371364 AppL!wmain+0x3a
03 (Inline Function) --------`-------- AppL!invoke_main+0x22
04 00000046`be5cf700 00007ffe`fbce7bd4 AppL!__scrt_common_main_seh+0x10c
05 00000046`be5cf740 00007ffe`fd2acee1 kernel32!BaseThreadInitThunk+0x14
06 00000046`be5cf770 00000000`00000000 ntdll!RtlUserThreadStart+0x21

 #  1  Id: 24c0.243c Suspend: 0 Teb: 00000046`be7fb000 Unfrozen
 # Child-SP          RetAddr               Call Site
00 00000046`be8fe068 00007ffe`fd31ce0c ntdll!NtWaitForMultipleObjects+0x14
01 00000046`be8fe070 00007ffe`fd31c40e ntdll!WerpWaitForCrashReporting+0xa8
```

```
02 00000046`be8fe0f0 00007ffe`fd31bbcb ntdll!RtlReportExceptionHelper+0x33e
03 00000046`be8fe1c0 00007ffe`fd3392a3 ntdll!RtlReportException+0x9b
04 00000046`be8fe240 00007ffe`fd2cc6e6 ntdll!RtlReportFatalFailure$filt$0+0x33
05 00000046`be8fe270 00007ffe`fd2e120f ntdll!_C_specific_handler+0x96
06 00000046`be8fe2e0 00007ffe`fd2aa299 ntdll!RtlpExecuteHandlerForException+0xf
07 00000046`be8fe310 00007ffe`fd2aa053 ntdll!RtlDispatchException+0x219
08 00000046`be8fea20 00007ffe`fd339269 ntdll!RtlRaiseException+0x153
09 00000046`be8ff290 00007ffe`fd339233 ntdll!RtlReportFatalFailure+0x9
0a 00000046`be8ff2e0 00007ffe`fd341622 ntdll!RtlReportCriticalFailure+0x97
0b 00000046`be8ff3d0 00007ffe`fd34192a ntdll!RtlpHeapHandleError+0x12
0c 00000046`be8ff400 00007ffe`fd34a8e9 ntdll!RtlpHpHeapHandleError+0x7a
0d 00000046`be8ff430 00007ffe`fd341531 ntdll!RtlpLogHeapFailure+0x45
0e 00000046`be8ff460 00007ffe`fd282544 ntdll!RtlpAnalyzeHeapFailure+0x2fd
0f 00000046`be8ff4c0 00007ffe`fd280810 ntdll!RtlpFreeHeap+0xbe4
10 00000046`be8ff620 00007ffe`fd27fc11 ntdll!RtlpFreeHeapInternal+0x790
11 00000046`be8ff6d0 00007ff6`53374ac4 ntdll!RtlFreeHeap+0x51
12 00000046`be8ff710 00007ff6`533710b4 AppL!_free_base+0x1c
13 00000046`be8ff740 00007ff6`53372e88 AppL!thread_two+0x44
14 00000046`be8ff790 00007ffe`fbce7bd4 AppL!thread_start<void (__cdecl*)(void *),0>+0x50
15 00000046`be8ff7c0 00007ffe`fd2acee1 kernel32!BaseThreadInitThunk+0x14
16 00000046`be8ff7f0 00000000`00000000 ntdll!RtlUserThreadStart+0x21

   2  Id: 24c0.1f1c Suspend: 1 Teb: 00000046`be7fd000 Unfrozen
 # Child-SP          RetAddr               Call Site
00 00000046`be9ff178 00007ffe`fd247619 ntdll!NtWaitForAlertByThreadId+0x14
01 00000046`be9ff180 00007ffe`fd2474d2 ntdll!RtlpWaitOnAddressWithTimeout+0x81
02 00000046`be9ff1b0 00007ffe`fd2472fd ntdll!RtlpWaitOnAddress+0xae
03 00000046`be9ff220 00007ffe`fd25b5f6 ntdll!RtlpWaitOnCriticalSection+0xfd
04 00000046`be9ff300 00007ffe`fd25b440 ntdll!RtlpEnterCriticalSectionContended+0x1a6
05 00000046`be9ff360 00007ffe`fd27daf3 ntdll!RtlEnterCriticalSection+0x40
06 00000046`be9ff390 00007ffe`fd27babb ntdll!RtlpAllocateHeap+0xc03
07 00000046`be9ff570 00007ff6`53377908 ntdll!RtlpAllocateHeapInternal+0x1cb
08 00000046`be9ff680 00007ff6`5337158b AppL!_malloc_base+0x44
09 00000046`be9ff6b0 00007ff6`53371013 AppL!operator new+0x1f
0a 00000046`be9ff6e0 00007ff6`53372e88 AppL!thread_one+0x13
0b 00000046`be9ff730 00007ffe`fbce7bd4 AppL!thread_start<void (__cdecl*)(void *),0>+0x50
0c 00000046`be9ff760 00007ffe`fd2acee1 kernel32!BaseThreadInitThunk+0x14
0d 00000046`be9ff790 00000000`00000000 ntdll!RtlUserThreadStart+0x21

   3  Id: 24c0.1f04 Suspend: 1 Teb: 00000046`be600000 Unfrozen
 # Child-SP          RetAddr               Call Site
00 00000046`beaff608 00007ffe`fd247619 ntdll!NtWaitForAlertByThreadId+0x14
01 00000046`beaff610 00007ffe`fd2474d2 ntdll!RtlpWaitOnAddressWithTimeout+0x81
02 00000046`beaff640 00007ffe`fd2472fd ntdll!RtlpWaitOnAddress+0xae
03 00000046`beaff6b0 00007ffe`fd25b5f6 ntdll!RtlpWaitOnCriticalSection+0xfd
04 00000046`beaff790 00007ffe`fd25b440 ntdll!RtlpEnterCriticalSectionContended+0x1a6
05 00000046`beaff7f0 00007ffe`fd27daf3 ntdll!RtlEnterCriticalSection+0x40
06 00000046`beaff820 00007ffe`fd27babb ntdll!RtlpAllocateHeap+0xc03
07 00000046`beaffa00 00007ffe`fd270239 ntdll!RtlpAllocateHeapInternal+0x1cb
08 00000046`beaffb10 00007ffe`fd273e06 ntdll!TppAllocThreadData+0x41
09 00000046`beaffb40 00007ffe`fbce7bd4 ntdll!TppWorkerThread+0xa6
0a 00000046`beafff00 00007ffe`fd2acee1 kernel32!BaseThreadInitThunk+0x14
0b 00000046`beafff30 00000000`00000000 ntdll!RtlUserThreadStart+0x21
```

Note: We see that in addition to **Exception Thread** #1, there are threads #2 and #3 that try to allocate dynamic memory and are waiting for a critical section.

8.	We now check if there is any wait chain, and if there is, what is its owner thread (a thread that entered a critical section and blocked other threads trying to access it)? We can do it using the **!cs -l -o -s** command:

```
0:001> !cs -l -o -s
-----------------------------------------
DebugInfo          = 0x00007ffefd3a3d70
Critical section   = 0x000002226cef02c0 (+0x2226CEF02C0)
LOCKED
LockCount          = 0x2
WaiterWoken        = No
OwningThread       = 0x000000000000243c
RecursionCount     = 0x1
LockSemaphore      = 0xFFFFFFFF
SpinCount          = 0x00000000020007d0
OwningThread DbgId = ~1s
OwningThread Stack =
        Child-SP          RetAddr           : Args to Child                                                           : Call Site
        00000046`be8fe068 00007ffe`fd31ce0c : 00000000`00000000 00000000`00000000 00000000`00000000 00000000`00000000 : ntdll!NtWaitForMultipleObjects+0x14
        00000046`be8fe070 00007ffe`fd31c40e : 00000000`00000000 00000000`000024c0 00000046`be8ff310 00000000`00001000 :
ntdll!WerpWaitForCrashReporting+0xa8
        00000046`be8fe0f0 00007ffe`fd31bbcb : 00000000`00000000 00000046`be8fea60 00000000`00000000 00000000`00000000 :
ntdll!RtlReportExceptionHelper+0x33e
        00000046`be8fe1c0 00007ffe`fd3392a3 : 00007ffe`fd38b13c 00000046`be8ff290 00000000`00000000 00000000`00000000 : ntdll!RtlReportException+0x9b
        00000046`be8fe240 00007ffe`fd2cc6e6 : 00000000`00000000 00000000`00000000 00000000`00000000 00000000`00000000 :
ntdll!RtlReportFatalFailure$filt$0+0x33
        00000046`be8fe270 00007ffe`fd2e120f : 00000000`00000000 00000046`be8fe850 00000046`be8ff310 00000046`be8ff310 : ntdll!_C_specific_handler+0x96
        00000046`be8fe2e0 00007ffe`fd2aa299 : 00000046`00000001 00007ffe`fd240000 00000000`00000000 00007ffe`fd3b7cfc :
ntdll!RtlpExecuteHandlerForException+0xf
        00000046`be8fe310 00007ffe`fd2aa053 : 80000000`00000000 00007ffe`fd240000 00000000`00000000 00007ffe`fd3ae81c : ntdll!RtlDispatchException+0x219
        00000046`be8fea20 00007ffe`fd339269 : 00000000`00000330 00000000`c0000374 00000000`00000001 00000000`00000000 : ntdll!RtlRaiseException+0x153
        00000046`be8ff290 00007ffe`fd339233 : 00000046`be8ff748 00000046`be8ff420 00000000`00000200 00000046`be8ff500 : ntdll!RtlReportFatalFailure+0x9
        00000046`be8ff220 00007ff6`5337e870 : 00007ff6`5337e870 00007ffe`fd3a27f0 00000000`00000003 00002222`6cef0000 : ntdll!RtlReportCriticalFailure+0x97
        00000046`be8ff3d0 00007ffe`fd34192a : 00000000`00000003 00002222`6cef0000 00002222`6cef0000 00000000`0000000e : ntdll!RtlpHeapHandleError+0x12
        00000046`be8ff400 00007ffe`fd34a8e9 : 00002222`6cef0000 00000000`00100000 00000000`00000018 00000000`00000008 : ntdll!RtlpHpHeapHandleError+0x7a
        00000046`be8ff430 00007ffe`fd341531 : 00000000`00000000 00002222`6cef0150 00002222`6cefc140 00000000`00000000 : ntdll!RtlpLogHeapFailure+0x45
        00000046`be8ff460 00007ffe`fd282544 : 00002222`6cef0000 00002222`6cefc140 00002222`6cef0000 00002222`6cefc140 : ntdll!RtlpAnalyzeHeapFailure+0x2fd
        00000046`be8ff4c0 00007ffe`fd280810 : 00002222`6cef0000 00002222`6cef0000 00002222`6cefc140 00002222`6cefc150 : ntdll!RtlpFreeHeap+0xbe4
        00000046`be8ff620 00007ffe`fd27fc11 : 00000000`00000000 00002222`6cef0000 00000000`00000000 00000000`00000000 : ntdll!RtlpFreeHeapInternal+0x790
        00000046`be8ff6d0 00007ff6`53374ac4 : 00002222`6cef7040 00000000`00000000 00000000`00000000 00007ffe`fb0b62d5 : ntdll!RtlFreeHeap+0x51
        00000046`be8ff710 00007ff6`533710b4 : 00000000`00000000 00000000`00000000 00000000`00000001 00007ff6`5337583a : AppL!_free_base+0x1c
        00000046`be8ff740 00007ff6`53372e88 : 00000000`00000000 00000000`00000000 00000000`00000000 00000000`00000000 : AppL!thread_two+0x44
ntdll!RtlpStackTraceDataBase is NULL. Probably the stack traces are not enabled.
```

Note: We see **LockCount** is 2 (means 2 threads are waiting), and **OwningThread** is thread #1 that detected hear corruption. We also see a critical section address and can double-check that threads #2 and #3 are indeed the ones that were waiting (we see it from the execution residue left in the stack region):

```
0:001> ~2kvL
 # Child-SP          RetAddr           : Args to Child                                                           : Call Site
00 00000046`be9ff178 00007ffe`fd247619 : 00000000`00000000 00002222`6cefc150 00000000`00000000 00007ffe`fd28083d : ntdll!NtWaitForAlertByThreadId+0x14
01 00000046`be9ff180 00007ffe`fd2474d2 : 00000000`00000000 00000000`00000000 00000046`be9ff268 00002222`6cef02c8 : ntdll!RtlpWaitOnAddressWithTimeout+0x81
02 00000046`be9ff1b0 00007ffe`fd2472fd : 00000222`6cef02c0 00000000`00001722 00000000`00000000 00000046`be9ff268 : ntdll!RtlpWaitOnAddress+0xae
03 00000046`be9ff220 00007ffe`fd25b5f6 : 00002222`6cefb501 00007ffe`fd25c398 00000000`ffffffa 00000046`be9ff338 : ntdll!RtlpWaitOnCriticalSection+0xfd
04 00000046`be9ff300 00007ffe`fd25b440 : 00000046`be9ff508 00000000`00000000 00002222`6cef0000 00002222`6cef7310 :
ntdll!RtlpEnterCriticalSectionContended+0x1a6
05 00000046`be9ff360 00007ffe`fd27daf3 : 00007ffe`fa1200f8 00000000`00000000 00002222`6cefb580 00000046`be9ff471 : ntdll!RtlEnterCriticalSection+0x40
06 00000046`be9ff390 00007ffe`fd27babb : 00002222`6cef0000 00000000`00000002 00000000`000000c8 00000000`000000d0 : ntdll!RtlpAllocateHeap+0xc03
07 00000046`be9ff570 00007ff6`53377908 : 00000000`00000003 00000000`000000c8 00000000`00000000 00000000`00000000 : ntdll!RtlpAllocateHeapInternal+0x1cb
08 00000046`be9ff680 00007ff6`5337158b : 00000000`00000000 00000000`00000000 00000000`00000000 00007ffe`fb0b62d5 : AppL!_malloc_base+0x44
09 00000046`be9ff6b0 00007ff6`53371013 : 00000000`00000000 00000000`00000000 00000000`00000001 00007ff6`5337583a : AppL!operator new+0x1f
0a 00000046`be9ff6e0 00007ff6`53372e88 : 00000000`00000000 00000000`00000000 00000000`00000000 00000000`00000000 : AppL!thread_one+0x13
0b 00000046`be9ff730 00007ffe`fbce7bd4 : 00000000`00000000 00000000`00000000 00000000`00000000 00000000`00000000 : AppL!thread_start<void (__cdecl*)(void
*),0>+0x50
0c 00000046`be9ff760 00007ffe`fd2acee1 : 00000000`00000000 00000000`00000000 00000000`00000000 00000000`00000000 : kernel32!BaseThreadInitThunk+0x14
0d 00000046`be9ff790 00000000`00000000 : 00000000`00000000 00000000`00000000 00000000`00000000 00000000`00000000 : ntdll!RtlUserThreadStart+0x21

0:001> ~3kvL
 # Child-SP          RetAddr           : Args to Child                                                           : Call Site
00 00000046`beaff608 00007ffe`fd247619 : 00000000`00000000 00000000`00000000 00000000`00000000 00000000`00000000 : ntdll!NtWaitForAlertByThreadId+0x14
01 00000046`beaff610 00007ffe`fd2474d2 : 00000000`00000000 00000000`00000000 00000046`beaff6f8 00002222`6cef02c8 : ntdll!RtlpWaitOnAddressWithTimeout+0x81
02 00000046`beaff640 00007ffe`fd2472fd : 00000222`6cef02c0 00000000`00001722 00000000`00000000 00000000`00000000 : ntdll!RtlpWaitOnAddress+0xae
03 00000046`beaff6b0 00007ffe`fd25b5f6 : 00000000`00000000 00000000`00000000 00000000`ffffff6 00000000`00000000 : ntdll!RtlpWaitOnCriticalSection+0xfd
04 00000046`beaff790 00007ffe`fd25b440 : 00000000`00000000 00000000`00000000 00002222`6cef0000 00000000`00000000 :
ntdll!RtlpEnterCriticalSectionContended+0x1a6
05 00000046`beaff7f0 00007ffe`fd27daf3 : 00000000`00000000 00000000`00000000 00000000`00000000 00000000`00000000 : ntdll!RtlEnterCriticalSection+0x40
06 00000046`beaff820 00007ffe`fd27babb : 00002222`6cef0000 00000000`002c000a 00000000`00000088 00000046`00000090 : ntdll!RtlpAllocateHeap+0xc03
07 00000046`beaffa00 00007ffe`fd270239 : 00000046`00000003 00000046`be600000 00002222`6cef2c50 00000046`beaffbc8 : ntdll!RtlpAllocateHeapInternal+0x1cb
08 00000046`beaffb10 00007ffe`fd273e06 : 00000000`00000000 00000000`00000000 00002222`6cef2c50 00000000`00000000 : ntdll!TppAllocThreadData+0x41
09 00000046`beaffb40 00007ffe`fbce7bd4 : 00000000`00000000 00000000`00000000 00000000`00000000 00000000`00000000 : ntdll!TppWorkerThread+0xa6
0a 00000046`beafff00 00007ffe`fd2acee1 : 00000000`00000000 00000000`00000000 00000000`00000000 00000000`00000000 : kernel32!BaseThreadInitThunk+0x14
0b 00000046`beafff30 00000000`00000000 : 00000000`00000000 00000000`00000000 00000000`00000000 00000000`00000000 : ntdll!RtlUserThreadStart+0x21
```

9.	At the end of this exercise, we check error codes manually (**!error** command):

```
0:001> !error c0000374
Error code: (NTSTATUS) 0xc0000374 (3221226356) - A heap has been corrupted.
```

113

```
0:001> !error c0000005
```
Error code: (NTSTATUS) 0xc0000005 (3221225477) - The instruction at 0x%p referenced memory at 0x%p. The memory could not be %s.

Note: 0x%p is not "corruption" garbage. It's a formatting instruction (code), and real address values are usually substituted by applications into this generic error code message.

10.   We can also check the last errors for every thread (most last errors can be ignored – always compare with a normal memory dump):

```
0:001> !gle -all
```
Last error for thread 0:
LastErrorValue: (Win32) 0 (0) - The operation completed successfully.
LastStatusValue: (NTSTATUS) 0xc00700bb - <Unable to get error code text>

Last error for thread 1:
LastErrorValue: (Win32) 0xbb (187) - The specified system semaphore name was not found.
LastStatusValue: (NTSTATUS) 0xc000000d - An invalid parameter was passed to a service or function.

Last error for thread 2:
LastErrorValue: (Win32) 0xbb (187) - The specified system semaphore name was not found.
LastStatusValue: (NTSTATUS) 0xc000000d - An invalid parameter was passed to a service or function.

Last error for thread 3:
LastErrorValue: (Win32) 0 (0) - The operation completed successfully.
LastStatusValue: (NTSTATUS) 0 - STATUS_SUCCESS

11.   We close logging before exiting WinDbg:

```
0:001> .logclose
```
Closing open log file C:\AWMDA-Dumps\Process\x64\AppL.log

Exercise P7

⊙ **Goal:** Learn how to debug heap corruption using page heap

⊙ **Patterns:** Invalid Pointer (General); Instrumentation Information

⊙ \AWMDA-Dumps\Exercise-P7-Analysis-process-dump-AppL2-64.pdf

Exercise P7: Analysis of an application process dump (AppL2, 64-bit)

Goal: Learn how to debug heap corruption using page heap.

Patterns: Invalid Pointer (General); Instrumentation Information.

1. Launch WinDbg.

2. Open \AWMDA-Dumps\Process\x64\AppL2.exe.10156.dmp.

3. We get the dump file loaded:

```
Microsoft (R) Windows Debugger Version 10.0.25877.1004 AMD64
Copyright (c) Microsoft Corporation. All rights reserved.


Loading Dump File [C:\AWMDA-Dumps\Process\x64\AppL2.exe.10156.dmp]
User Mini Dump File with Full Memory: Only application data is available


************* Path validation summary **************
Response                      Time (ms)     Location
Deferred                                    srv*
OK                                          C:\AWMDA-Dumps\Symbols
Symbol search path is: srv*;C:\AWMDA-Dumps\Symbols
Executable search path is:
Windows 10 Version 18362 MP (2 procs) Free x64
Product: WinNt, suite: SingleUserTS Personal
Edition build lab: 18362.1.amd64fre.19h1_release.190318-1202
Machine Name:
Debug session time: Tue Oct 29 20:51:40.000 2019 (UTC + 1:00)
System Uptime: 0 days 0:13:48.825
Process Uptime: 0 days 0:00:16.000
........
This dump file has an exception of interest stored in it.
The stored exception information can be accessed via .ecxr.
(27ac.27b0): Unknown exception - code c0000374 (first/second chance not available)
For analysis of this file, run !analyze -v
ntdll!NtWaitForMultipleObjects+0x14:
00007ffe`fd2dcc24 c3              ret
```

4. Open a log file using the **.logopen** command and load symbols (**.symfix** and **.reload**):

```
0:001> .logopen C:\AWMDA-Dumps\Process\x64\AppL2.log
Opened log file 'C:\AWMDA-Dumps\Process\x64\AppL2.log'

0:001> .sympath+ C:\AWMDA-Dumps\Symbols
Symbol search path is: srv*;C:\AWMDA-Dumps\Symbols
Expanded Symbol search path is:
cache*;SRV*https://msdl.microsoft.com/download/symbols;c:\awmda-dumps\symbols

************* Path validation summary **************
Response                      Time (ms)     Location
Deferred                                    srv*
OK                                          C:\AWMDA-Dumps\Symbols
```

```
0:001> .reload
........
```

Note: WinDbg may remember symbol and source paths from the previous sessions.

5.   Type the **k** command to verify the correctness of the stack trace:

```
0:001> kL
 # Child-SP          RetAddr           Call Site
00 00000041`9fafe808 00007ffe`fd31ce0c ntdll!NtWaitForMultipleObjects+0x14
01 00000041`9fafe810 00007ffe`fd31c40e ntdll!WerpWaitForCrashReporting+0xa8
02 00000041`9fafe890 00007ffe`fd31bbcb ntdll!RtlReportExceptionHelper+0x33e
03 00000041`9fafe960 00007ffe`fd3392a3 ntdll!RtlReportException+0x9b
04 00000041`9fafe9e0 00007ffe`fd2cc6e6 ntdll!RtlReportFatalFailure$filt$0+0x33
05 00000041`9fafea10 00007ffe`fd2e120f ntdll!_C_specific_handler+0x96
06 00000041`9fafea80 00007ffe`fd2aa299 ntdll!RtlpExecuteHandlerForException+0xf
07 00000041`9fafeab0 00007ffe`fd2aa053 ntdll!RtlDispatchException+0x219
08 00000041`9faff1c0 00007ffe`fd339269 ntdll!RtlRaiseException+0x153
09 00000041`9faffa30 00007ffe`fd339233 ntdll!RtlReportFatalFailure+0x9
0a 00000041`9faffa80 00007ffe`fd341622 ntdll!RtlReportCriticalFailure+0x97
0b 00000041`9faffb70 00007ffe`fd34192a ntdll!RtlpHeapHandleError+0x12
0c 00000041`9faffba0 00007ffe`fd34a8e9 ntdll!RtlpHpHeapHandleError+0x7a
0d 00000041`9faffbd0 00007ffe`fd2e646d ntdll!RtlpLogHeapFailure+0x45
0e 00000041`9faffc00 00007ffe`fd27fc11 ntdll!RtlpFreeHeapInternal+0x663ed
0f 00000041`9faffcb0 00007ff7`98afc2b8 ntdll!RtlFreeHeap+0x51
10 00000041`9faffcf0 00007ff7`98af1464 AppL2!_free_base+0x1c
11 00000041`9faffd20 00007ff7`98af1ef5 AppL2!thread_one+0x74
12 00000041`9faffd90 00007ff7`98af1e0b AppL2!std::_Invoker_functor::_Call<void
(__cdecl*)(void)>+0x15
13 00000041`9faffdc0 00007ff7`98af1a84 AppL2!std::invoke<void (__cdecl*)(void)>+0x1b
14 00000041`9faffdf0 00007ff7`98af9c58 AppL2!std::thread::_Invoke<std::tuple<void
(__cdecl*)(void)>,0>+0x64
15 00000041`9faffe40 00007ffe`fbce7bd4 AppL2!thread_start<unsigned int (__cdecl*)(void
*),1>+0x50
16 00000041`9faffe70 00007ffe`fd2acee1 kernel32!BaseThreadInitThunk+0x14
17 00000041`9faffea0 00000000`00000000 ntdll!RtlUserThreadStart+0x21
```

Note: In addition to exception processing functions, we see heap manipulation functions. So we check the heap for any errors:

```
0:001> !heap -s -v

************************************************************************************************
                                  NT HEAP STATS BELOW
************************************************************************************************
*******************************************************************
*                                                                 *
*                      HEAP ERROR DETECTED                        *
*                                                                 *
*******************************************************************

Details:

Heap address:  000001f59a830000
Error address: 000001f59a831680
Last known valid blocks: before - 000001f59a831550, after - 000001f59a831960
Error type:    HEAP_FAILURE_MULTIPLE_ENTRIES_CORRUPTION
Details:          The heap manager detected multiple corrupt heap entries.
```

Follow-up: Enable pageheap.

```
Stack trace:
Stack trace at 0x00007ffefd3a2848
    00007ffefd34a8e9: ntdll!RtlpLogHeapFailure+0x45
    00007ffefd2e646d: ntdll!RtlpFreeHeapInternal+0x663ed
    00007ffefd27fc11: ntdll!RtlFreeHeap+0x51
    00007ff798afc2b8: AppL2!_free_base+0x1c
    00007ff798af1464: AppL2!thread_one+0x74
    00007ff798af1ef5: AppL2!std::_Invoker_functor::_Call<void (__cdecl*)(void)>+0x15
    00007ff798af1e0b: AppL2!std::invoke<void (__cdecl*)(void)>+0x1b
    00007ff798af1a84: AppL2!std::thread::_Invoke<std::tuple<void (__cdecl*)(void)>,0>+0x64
    00007ff798af9c58: AppL2!thread_start<unsigned int (__cdecl*)(void *),1>+0x50
    00007ffefbce7bd4: kernel32!BaseThreadInitThunk+0x14
    00007ffefd2acee1: ntdll!RtlUserThreadStart+0x21
```

```
LFH Key                 : 0xd1c4c76356732878
Termination on corruption : ENABLED
```

Heap	Flags	Reserv (k)	Commit (k)	Virt (k)	Free (k)	List length	UCR	Virt blocks	Lock cont.	Fast heap
.000001f59a830000	00000002	1072	100	1020	1	6	1	0	0	LFH
.000001f59a680000	00008000	64	4	64	2	1	1	0	0	
.000001f59aa80000	00001002	112	32	60	7	2	1	0	0	LFH

Note: This is detected heap corruption, but sometimes, heap corruption results in memory access violation during internal heap manipulation, like when free heap blocks are joined together (heap coalescence). For example, this is a stack trace and **!analyze -v** output from Legacy.P6 exercise from the previous edition of this book:

```
0:001> kL
ChildEBP RetAddr
0070f2e0 770d0bdd ntdll!NtWaitForMultipleObjects+0x15
0070f37c 7529162d KERNELBASE!WaitForMultipleObjectsEx+0x100
0070f3c4 75291921 kernel32!WaitForMultipleObjectsExImplementation+0xe0
0070f3e0 752b9b2d kernel32!WaitForMultipleObjects+0x18
0070f44c 752b9bca kernel32!WerpReportFaultInternal+0x186
0070f460 752b98f8 kernel32!WerpReportFault+0x70
0070f470 752b9875 kernel32!BasepReportFault+0x20
0070f4fc 77b10df7 kernel32!UnhandledExceptionFilter+0x1af
0070f504 77b10cd4 ntdll!__RtlUserThreadStart+0x62
0070f518 77b10b71 ntdll!_EH4_CallFilterFunc+0x12
0070f540 77ae6ac9 ntdll!_except_handler4+0x8e
0070f564 77ae6a9b ntdll!ExecuteHandler2+0x26
0070f614 77ab010f ntdll!ExecuteHandler+0x24
0070f614 77ad3b30 ntdll!KiUserExceptionDispatcher+0xf
0070f98c 77ad2d07 ntdll!RtlpCoalesceFreeBlocks+0x268
0070fa84 77ad2bf2 ntdll!RtlpFreeHeap+0x1f4
0070faa4 752914d1 ntdll!RtlFreeHeap+0x142
0070fab8 010b11f0 kernel32!HeapFree+0x14
0070faf8 010b1274 ApplicationL!free+0x6e
0070fb30 010b1310 ApplicationL!_callthreadstart+0x1b
0070fb38 75293677 ApplicationL!_threadstart+0x76
0070fb44 77ad9f02 kernel32!BaseThreadInitThunk+0xe
0070fb84 77ad9ed5 ntdll!__RtlUserThreadStart+0x70
0070fb9c 00000000 ntdll!_RtlUserThreadStart+0x1b
```

```
0:001> !analyze -v

[...]

EXCEPTION_RECORD:  ffffffff -- (.exr 0xffffffffffffffff)
ExceptionAddress: 77ad3b30 (ntdll!RtlpCoalesceFreeBlocks+0x00000268)
   ExceptionCode: c0000005 (Access violation)
  ExceptionFlags: 00000000
NumberParameters: 2
   Parameter[0]: 00000000
   Parameter[1]: 00000003
Attempt to read from address 00000003

[...]
```

6.   Let's check other threads:

```
0:001> ~*kL

   0  Id: 27ac.20b8 Suspend: 1 Teb: 00000041`9f9f0000 Unfrozen
 # Child-SP          RetAddr               Call Site
00 00000041`9f7ff648 00007ffe`fb078ba3 ntdll!NtWaitForSingleObject+0x14
01 00000041`9f7ff650 00007ff7`98af3623 KERNELBASE!WaitForSingleObjectEx+0x93
02 00000041`9f7ff6f0 00007ff7`98af13af AppL2!_Thrd_join+0x1f
03 00000041`9f7ff720 00007ff7`98af159a AppL2!std::thread::join+0x5f
04 00000041`9f7ff780 00007ff7`98af4060 AppL2!wmain+0x4a
05 (Inline Function) --------`-------- AppL2!invoke_main+0x22
06 00000041`9f7ff7f0 00007ffe`fbce7bd4 AppL2!__scrt_common_main_seh+0x10c
07 00000041`9f7ff830 00007ffe`fd2acee1 kernel32!BaseThreadInitThunk+0x14
08 00000041`9f7ff860 00000000`00000000 ntdll!RtlUserThreadStart+0x21

 #  1  Id: 27ac.27b0 Suspend: 0 Teb: 00000041`9f9f2000 Unfrozen
 # Child-SP          RetAddr               Call Site
00 00000041`9fafe808 00007ffe`fd31ce0c ntdll!NtWaitForMultipleObjects+0x14
01 00000041`9fafe810 00007ffe`fd31c40e ntdll!WerpWaitForCrashReporting+0xa8
02 00000041`9fafe890 00007ffe`fd31bbcb ntdll!RtlReportExceptionHelper+0x33e
03 00000041`9fafe960 00007ffe`fd3392a3 ntdll!RtlReportException+0x9b
04 00000041`9fafe9e0 00007ffe`fd2cc6e6 ntdll!RtlReportFatalFailure$filt$0+0x33
05 00000041`9fafea10 00007ffe`fd2e120f ntdll!_C_specific_handler+0x96
06 00000041`9fafea80 00007ffe`fd2aa299 ntdll!RtlpExecuteHandlerForException+0xf
07 00000041`9fafeab0 00007ffe`fd2aa053 ntdll!RtlDispatchException+0x219
08 00000041`9faff1c0 00007ffe`fd339269 ntdll!RtlRaiseException+0x153
09 00000041`9faffa30 00007ffe`fd339233 ntdll!RtlReportFatalFailure+0x9
0a 00000041`9faffa80 00007ffe`fd341622 ntdll!RtlReportCriticalFailure+0x97
0b 00000041`9faffb70 00007ffe`fd34192a ntdll!RtlpHeapHandleError+0x12
0c 00000041`9faffba0 00007ffe`fd34a8e9 ntdll!RtlpHpHeapHandleError+0x7a
0d 00000041`9faffbd0 00007ffe`fd2e646d ntdll!RtlpLogHeapFailure+0x45
0e 00000041`9faffc00 00007ffe`fd27fc11 ntdll!RtlpFreeHeapInternal+0x663ed
0f 00000041`9faffcb0 00007ff7`98afc2b8 ntdll!RtlFreeHeap+0x51
10 00000041`9faffcf0 00007ff7`98af1464 AppL2!_free_base+0x1c
11 00000041`9faffd20 00007ff7`98af1ef5 AppL2!thread_one+0x74
12 00000041`9faffd90 00007ff7`98af1e0b AppL2!std::_Invoker_functor::_Call<void
(__cdecl*)(void)>+0x15
13 00000041`9faffdc0 00007ff7`98af1a84 AppL2!std::invoke<void (__cdecl*)(void)>+0x1b
14 00000041`9faffdf0 00007ff7`98af9c58 AppL2!std::thread::_Invoke<std::tuple<void
(__cdecl*)(void)>,0>+0x64
15 00000041`9faffe40 00007ffe`fbce7bd4 AppL2!thread_start<unsigned int (__cdecl*)(void
*),1>+0x50
16 00000041`9faffe70 00007ffe`fd2acee1 kernel32!BaseThreadInitThunk+0x14
```

```
17 00000041`9faffea0 00000000`00000000 ntdll!RtlUserThreadStart+0x21

    2  Id: 27ac.2480 Suspend: 1 Teb: 00000041`9f9f4000 Unfrozen
 # Child-SP          RetAddr           Call Site
00 00000041`9fbffbd8 00007ffe`fb086931 ntdll!NtDelayExecution+0x14
01 00000041`9fbffbe0 00007ff7`98af36a8 KERNELBASE!SleepEx+0xa1
02 00000041`9fbffc80 00007ff7`98af1985 AppL2!_Thrd_sleep+0x3c
03 00000041`9fbffcd0 00007ff7`98af168d
AppL2!std::this_thread::sleep_until<std::chrono::steady_clock,std::chrono::duration<__int64,std
::ratio<1,1000000000> > >+0x65
04 00000041`9fbffd30 00007ff7`98af1500
AppL2!std::this_thread::sleep_for<__int64,std::ratio<1,1000> >+0x2d
05 00000041`9fbffd70 00007ff7`98af1ef5 AppL2!thread_two+0x60
06 00000041`9fbffde0 00007ff7`98af1e0b AppL2!std::_Invoker_functor::_Call<void
(__cdecl*)(void)>+0x15
07 00000041`9fbffe10 00007ff7`98af1a84 AppL2!std::invoke<void (__cdecl*)(void)>+0x1b
08 00000041`9fbffe40 00007ff7`98af9c58 AppL2!std::thread::_Invoke<std::tuple<void
(__cdecl*)(void)>,0>+0x64
09 00000041`9fbffe90 00007ffe`fbce7bd4 AppL2!thread_start<unsigned int (__cdecl*)(void
*),1>+0x50
0a 00000041`9fbffec0 00007ffe`fd2acee1 kernel32!BaseThreadInitThunk+0x14
0b 00000041`9fbffef0 00000000`00000000 ntdll!RtlUserThreadStart+0x21

    3  Id: 27ac.ed8 Suspend: 1 Teb: 00000041`9f9f6000 Unfrozen
 # Child-SP          RetAddr           Call Site
00 00000041`9fcff808 00007ffe`fd274060 ntdll!NtWaitForWorkViaWorkerFactory+0x14
01 00000041`9fcff810 00007ffe`fbce7bd4 ntdll!TppWorkerThread+0x300
02 00000041`9fcffbd0 00007ffe`fd2acee1 kernel32!BaseThreadInitThunk+0x14
03 00000041`9fcffc00 00000000`00000000 ntdll!RtlUserThreadStart+0x21

    4  Id: 27ac.bac Suspend: 1 Teb: 00000041`9f9f8000 Unfrozen
 # Child-SP          RetAddr           Call Site
00 00000041`9fdff408 00007ffe`fd274060 ntdll!NtWaitForWorkViaWorkerFactory+0x14
01 00000041`9fdff410 00007ffe`fbce7bd4 ntdll!TppWorkerThread+0x300
02 00000041`9fdff7d0 00007ffe`fd2acee1 kernel32!BaseThreadInitThunk+0x14
03 00000041`9fdff800 00000000`00000000 ntdll!RtlUserThreadStart+0x21
```

Note: We don't see any other threads having exception or heap processing functions on their call stacks.

7.   In the **!heap** checking command output, we see a follow-up recommendation to **enable pageheap**. This means running the application under conditions when a special version of process heap management runtime is used instead of the default version. It's done using the *gflags* GUI tool from Debugging Tools for Windows (although a command-line version can also be used or even direct registry manipulation). We need to launch the appropriate version of *gflags.exe* based on your process bitness; for example, we use the following Start menu option: Windows Kits \ Global Flags (X64) to launch *gflags.exe* and choose Enable page heap option there in the Image File tab for *AppL2.exe*:

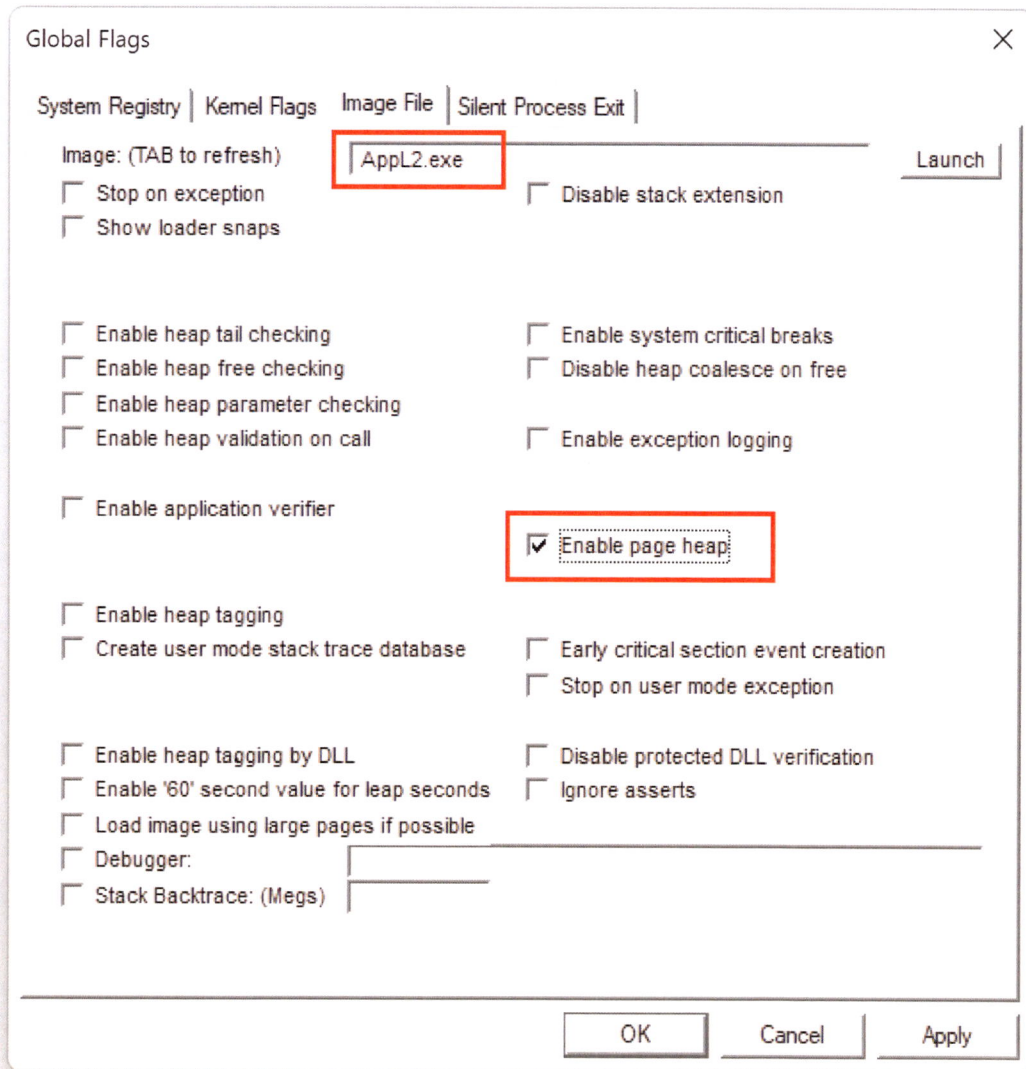

If page heap is enabled, heap entries are created at the end of pages with the next page after the allocated buffer is made inaccessible (reserved), as shown in the picture below:

298`31da8000                                    298`31da9000

| unused | allocated buffer | reserved page |

Subsequent buffer overwrite triggers invalid memory exception, and we can see the exact point of corruption during heap allocation or free instead of heap diagnostics done later. Please also see Debugging.TV episode 0x26 for information about underwrites.

8.   Page heap recommendation was implemented, and the new run of the *AppL2* application resulted in the collection of *AppL2.exe.928.dmp*. We load this dump in WinDbg:

```
Microsoft (R) Windows Debugger Version 10.0.25877.1004 AMD64
Copyright (c) Microsoft Corporation. All rights reserved.


Loading Dump File [C:\AWMDA-Dumps\Process\x64\AppL2.exe.928.dmp]
User Mini Dump File with Full Memory: Only application data is available


************* Path validation summary **************
Response                        Time (ms)     Location
Deferred                                      srv*
OK                                            C:\AWMDA-Dumps\Symbols
Symbol search path is: srv*;C:\AWMDA-Dumps\Symbols
Executable search path is:
Windows 10 Version 18362 MP (2 procs) Free x64
Product: WinNt, suite: SingleUserTS Personal
Edition build lab: 18362.1.amd64fre.19h1_release.190318-1202
Machine Name:
Debug session time: Fri Nov  1 09:50:12.000 2019 (UTC + 1:00)
System Uptime: 0 days 0:19:45.096
Process Uptime: 0 days 0:00:13.000
........
This dump file has an exception of interest stored in it.
The stored exception information can be accessed via .ecxr.
(3a0.25a8): Access violation - code c0000005 (first/second chance not available)
For analysis of this file, run !analyze -v
ntdll!NtWaitForMultipleObjects+0x14:
00007ffe`fd2dcc24 c3              ret
```

Note: We see a different exception in this dump: access violation, c0000005.

9.   We provide application symbols and source code path to WinDbg before our next analysis steps:

```
0:001> .logappend C:\AWMDA-Dumps\Process\x64\AppL2.log
Opened log file 'C:\AWMDA-Dumps\Process\x64\AppL2.log'


0:001> .sympath+ C:\AWMDA-Dumps\Symbols
Symbol search path is: srv*;C:\AWMDA-Dumps\Symbols
Expanded Symbol search path is:
cache*;SRV*https://msdl.microsoft.com/download/symbols;c:\awmda-dumps\symbols


************* Path validation summary **************
Response                        Time (ms)     Location
Deferred                                      srv*
OK                                            C:\AWMDA-Dumps\Symbols


0:001> .srcpath+ C:\AWMDA-Dumps\Source
Source search path is: SRV*;C:\AWMDA-Dumps\Source


************* Path validation summary **************
Response                        Time (ms)     Location
Deferred                                      SRV*
OK                                            C:\AWMDA-Dumps\Source


0:001> .reload
........
```

10.   We get the following stack trace which shows exception processing possibly originating in the *thread_one* function from the *AppL2* module:

```
0:001> kL
 # Child-SP          RetAddr           Call Site
00 0000009a`5b7fe348 00007ffe`fb097ff7 ntdll!NtWaitForMultipleObjects+0x14
01 0000009a`5b7fe350 00007ffe`fb097ede KERNELBASE!WaitForMultipleObjectsEx+0x107
02 0000009a`5b7fe650 00007ffe`fbd371fb KERNELBASE!WaitForMultipleObjects+0xe
03 0000009a`5b7fe690 00007ffe`fbd36ca8 kernel32!WerpReportFaultInternal+0x51b
04 0000009a`5b7fe7b0 00007ffe`fb13f988 kernel32!WerpReportFault+0xac
05 0000009a`5b7fe7f0 00007ffe`fd2e4af2 KERNELBASE!UnhandledExceptionFilter+0x3b8
06 0000009a`5b7fe910 00007ffe`fd2cc6e6 ntdll!RtlUserThreadStart$filt$0+0xa2
07 0000009a`5b7fe950 00007ffe`fd2e120f ntdll!_C_specific_handler+0x96
08 0000009a`5b7fe9c0 00007ffe`fd2aa299 ntdll!RtlpExecuteHandlerForException+0xf
09 0000009a`5b7fe9f0 00007ffe`fd2dfe7e ntdll!RtlDispatchException+0x219
0a 0000009a`5b7ff100 00007ff6`dbe9142f ntdll!KiUserExceptionDispatch+0x2e
0b 0000009a`5b7ff8a0 00007ff6`dbe91ef5 AppL2!thread_one+0x3f
0c 0000009a`5b7ff910 00007ff6`dbe91e0b AppL2!std::_Invoker_functor::_Call<void (__cdecl*)(void)>+0x15
0d 0000009a`5b7ff940 00007ff6`dbe91a84 AppL2!std::invoke<void (__cdecl*)(void)>+0x1b
0e 0000009a`5b7ff970 00007ff6`dbe99c58 AppL2!std::thread::_Invoke<std::tuple<void (__cdecl*)(void)>,0>+0x64
0f 0000009a`5b7ff9c0 00007ffe`fbce7bd4 AppL2!thread_start<unsigned int (__cdecl*)(void *),1>+0x50
10 0000009a`5b7ff9f0 00007ffe`fd2acee1 kernel32!BaseThreadInitThunk+0x14
11 0000009a`5b7ffa20 00000000`00000000 ntdll!RtlUserThreadStart+0x21
```

11.   Let's now check the output of the **!analyze -v** command:

```
0:001> !analyze -v
*******************************************************************************
*                                                                             *
*                        Exception Analysis                                   *
*                                                                             *
*******************************************************************************

KEY_VALUES_STRING: 1

    Key  : AV.Fault
    Value: Write

    Key  : Analysis.CPU.mSec
    Value: 624

    Key  : Analysis.DebugAnalysisManager
    Value: Create

    Key  : Analysis.Elapsed.mSec
    Value: 1046

    Key  : Analysis.Init.CPU.mSec
    Value: 1077

    Key  : Analysis.Init.Elapsed.mSec
    Value: 201966

    Key  : Analysis.Memory.CommitPeak.Mb
    Value: 79

    Key  : Timeline.OS.Boot.DeltaSec
    Value: 1185

    Key  : Timeline.Process.Start.DeltaSec
    Value: 13

    Key  : WER.OS.Branch
    Value: 19h1_release

    Key  : WER.OS.Timestamp
    Value: 2019-03-18T12:02:00Z

    Key  : WER.OS.Version
    Value: 10.0.18362.1

    Key  : WER.Process.Version
    Value: 2.0.0.1

FILE_IN_CAB:  AppL2.exe.928.dmp

NTGLOBALFLAG:  2000000

PROCESS_BAM_CURRENT_THROTTLED: 0

PROCESS_BAM_PREVIOUS_THROTTLED: 0

APPLICATION_VERIFIER_FLAGS:  0
```

```
APPLICATION_VERIFIER_LOADED: 1

CONTEXT:  (.ecxr)
rax=00007ff6dbead6b0 rbx=0000029831d48fd0 rcx=000000000000002e
rdx=d0d0d0d0d0d0d0d0 rsi=00007ff6dbead6d0 rdi=0000029831da9000
rip=00007ff6dbe9142f rsp=0000009a5b7ff8a0 rbp=0000000000000000
 r8=0000000000000000  r9=0000000000000000 r10=0000029831da8fe0
r11=0000009a5b7ff810 r12=0000000000000000 r13=0000000000000000
r14=0000000000000000 r15=0000000000000000
iopl=0         nv up ei pl nz na po nc
cs=0033  ss=002b  ds=002b  es=002b  fs=0053  gs=002b             efl=00010206
AppL2!thread_one+0x3f:
00007ff6`dbe9142f f3a4           rep movs byte ptr [rdi],byte ptr [rsi]
Resetting default scope

EXCEPTION_RECORD:  (.exr -1)
ExceptionAddress: 00007ff6dbe9142f (AppL2!thread_one+0x000000000000003f)
   ExceptionCode: c0000005 (Access violation)
   ExceptionFlags: 00000000
NumberParameters: 2
   Parameter[0]: 0000000000000001
   Parameter[1]: 0000029831da9000
Attempt to write to address 0000029831da9000

PROCESS_NAME:  AppL2.exe

WRITE_ADDRESS:  0000029831da9000

ERROR_CODE: (NTSTATUS) 0xc0000005 - The instruction at 0x%p referenced memory at 0x%p. The memory could not be %s.

EXCEPTION_CODE_STR:  c0000005

EXCEPTION_PARAMETER1:  0000000000000001

EXCEPTION_PARAMETER2:  0000029831da9000

STACK_TEXT:
0000009a`5b7ff8a0 00007ff6`dbe91ef5     : 00000298`31d46ff0 00000000`00000000 00000000`00000000 00007ff6`dbe91de5 : AppL2!thread_one+0x3f
0000009a`5b7ff910 00007ff6`dbe91e0b     : 00000298`31d46ff0 00000000`00000000 00000000`00000000 00007ffe`fb0b62d5 : AppL2!std::_Invoker_functor::_Call<void
(__cdecl*)(void)>+0x15
0000009a`5b7ff940 00007ff6`dbe91a84     : 00000298`31d46ff0 00000298`31d46ff0 00000000`00000001 00007ff6`dbe9d02e : AppL2!std::invoke<void
(__cdecl*)(void)>+0x1b
0000009a`5b7ff970 00007ff6`dbe99c58     : 00000298`31d46ff0 00000000`00000000 00000000`00000000 00000000`00000000 : AppL2!std::thread::_Invoke<std::tuple<void
(__cdecl*)(void)>,0>+0x64
0000009a`5b7ff9c0 00007ffe`fbce7bd4     : 00000000`00000000 00000000`00000000 00000000`00000000 00000000`00000000 : AppL2!thread_start<unsigned int
(__cdecl*)(void *),1>+0x50
0000009a`5b7ff9f0 00007ffe`fd2acee1     : 00000000`00000000 00000000`00000000 00000000`00000000 00000000`00000000 : kernel32!BaseThreadInitThunk+0x14
0000009a`5b7ffa20 00000000`00000000     : 00000000`00000000 00000000`00000000 00000000`00000000 00000000`00000000 : ntdll!RtlUserThreadStart+0x21


STACK_COMMAND:  ~1s; .ecxr ; kb

FAULTING_SOURCE_LINE:  C:\AWMDA-Examples\AppL2\AppL2.cpp

FAULTING_SOURCE_FILE:  C:\AWMDA-Examples\AppL2\AppL2.cpp

FAULTING_SOURCE_LINE_NUMBER:  18

FAULTING_SOURCE_CODE:
    14:     while (true)
    15:     {
    16:             auto p = new wchar_t[10];
    17:
>   18:             memcpy(p, str, sizeof(str));
    19:
    20:             std::this_thread::sleep_for(std::chrono::milliseconds(100));
    21:
    22:             delete[] p;
    23:     }


SYMBOL_NAME:  AppL2!thread_one+3f

MODULE_NAME: AppL2

IMAGE_NAME:  AppL2.exe

FAILURE_BUCKET_ID:  INVALID_POINTER_WRITE_AVRF_c0000005_AppL2.exe!thread_one

OS_VERSION:  10.0.18362.1

BUILDLAB_STR:  19h1_release

OSPLATFORM_TYPE:  x64

OSNAME:  Windows 10

IMAGE_VERSION:  2.0.0.1

FAILURE_ID_HASH:  {899c6275-bd56-1ca2-dcdc-82ccc32d6b7d}

Followup:     MachineOwner
---------
```

Note: In addition to exception information that shows an invalid write operation to the 0000029831da9000 address, there is also a source code reference.

12.   We can manually double-check this analysis by setting the frame for the *thread_one* function (using **/c** option to make it current for the stack trace and **/r** to show possible register values):

```
0:001> kc
 # Call Site
00 ntdll!NtWaitForMultipleObjects
01 KERNELBASE!WaitForMultipleObjectsEx
02 KERNELBASE!WaitForMultipleObjects
03 kernel32!WerpReportFaultInternal
04 kernel32!WerpReportFault
05 KERNELBASE!UnhandledExceptionFilter
06 ntdll!RtlUserThreadStart$filt$0
07 ntdll!_C_specific_handler
08 ntdll!RtlpExecuteHandlerForException
09 ntdll!RtlDispatchException
0a ntdll!KiUserExceptionDispatch
0b AppL2!thread_one
0c AppL2!std::_Invoker_functor::_Call<void (__cdecl*)(void)>
0d AppL2!std::invoke<void (__cdecl*)(void)>
0e AppL2!std::thread::_Invoke<std::tuple<void (__cdecl*)(void)>,0>
0f AppL2!thread_start<unsigned int (__cdecl*)(void *),1>
10 kernel32!BaseThreadInitThunk
11 ntdll!RtlUserThreadStart
```

```
0:001> .frame /r /c b
0b 0000009a`5b7ff8a0 00007ff6`dbe91ef5 AppL2!thread_one+0x3f [C:\AWMDA-Examples\AppL2\AppL2.cpp @ 18]
rax=000000000000005b rbx=0000029831d48fd0 rcx=0000000000000003
rdx=0000009a5b7fe748 rsi=00007ff6dbead6d0 rdi=0000029831da9000
rip=00007ff6dbe9142f rsp=0000009a5b7ff8a0 rbp=0000000000000000
 r8=0000000000000000  r9=00000000ffffffff r10=0000000000000000
r11=0000009a5b7fdaf0 r12=0000000000000000 r13=0000000000000000
r14=0000000000000000 r15=0000000000000000
iopl=0         nv up ei pl zr na po nc
cs=0033  ss=002b  ds=002b  es=002b  fs=0053  gs=002b                efl=00000246
AppL2!thread_one+0x3f:
00007ff6`dbe9142f f3a4            rep movs byte ptr [rdi],byte ptr [rsi]
```

```
0:001> kL
  *** Stack trace for last set context - .thread/.cxr resets it
 # Child-SP          RetAddr           Call Site
0b 0000009a`5b7ff8a0 00007ff6`dbe91ef5 AppL2!thread_one+0x3f
0c 0000009a`5b7ff910 00007ff6`dbe91e0b AppL2!std::_Invoker_functor::_Call<void (__cdecl*)(void)>+0x15
0d 0000009a`5b7ff940 00007ff6`dbe91a84 AppL2!std::invoke<void (__cdecl*)(void)>+0x1b
0e 0000009a`5b7ff970 00007ff6`dbe99c58 AppL2!std::thread::_Invoke<std::tuple<void (__cdecl*)(void)>,0>+0x64
0f 0000009a`5b7ff9c0 00007ffe`fbce7bd4 AppL2!thread_start<unsigned int (__cdecl*)(void *),1>+0x50
10 0000009a`5b7ff9f0 00007ffe`fd2acee1 kernel32!BaseThreadInitThunk+0x14
11 0000009a`5b7ffa20 00000000`00000000 ntdll!RtlUserThreadStart+0x21
```

13.   Let's check the region of memory the invalid write pointer **0000029831da9000** belongs to:

```
0:001> !address 0000029831da9000


Mapping file section regions...
Mapping module regions...
Mapping PEB regions...
Mapping TEB and stack regions...
Mapping heap regions...
Mapping page heap regions...
Mapping other regions...
Mapping stack trace database regions...
Mapping activation context regions...
```

```
Usage:                  <unknown>
Base Address:           00000298`31da9000
End Address:            00000298`31daa000
Region Size:            00000000`00001000 (   4.000 kB)
State:                  00002000            MEM_RESERVE
Protect:                <info not present at the target>
Type:                   00020000            MEM_PRIVATE
Allocation Base:        00000298`31b30000
Allocation Protect:     00000001            PAGE_NOACCESS


Content source: 0 (invalid), length: 1000
```

Note: We see that it belongs to a single reserved page that doesn't have physical memory committed to it. Since it is also the start of that page, let's look at the previous byte's region properties:

```
0:001> !address 0000029831da9000-1

Usage:                  <unknown>
Base Address:           00000298`31da8000
End Address:            00000298`31da9000
Region Size:            00000000`00001000 (   4.000 kB)
State:                  00001000            MEM_COMMIT
Protect:                00000004            PAGE_READWRITE
Type:                   00020000            MEM_PRIVATE
Allocation Base:        00000298`31b30000
Allocation Protect:     00000001            PAGE_NOACCESS


Content source: 1 (target), length: 1
```

Note: We see that this is also a single page, but it is committed. Let's dump memory contents around the page boundary where we have an invalid write operation:

```
0:001> dc 0000029831da9000-50
00000298`31da8fb0  00000014 00000000 00001000 00000000  ................
00000298`31da8fc0  00000000 00000000 00000000 00000000  ................
00000298`31da8fd0  30358ea0 00000298 00000000 dcbabbbb  ..50............
00000298`31da8fe0  00650048 006c006c 0020006f 00720043  H.e.l.l.o. .C.r.
00000298`31da8ff0  00730061 00210068 00480020 006c0065  a.s.h.!. .H.e.l.
00000298`31da9000  ???????? ???????? ???????? ????????  ????????????????
00000298`31da9010  ???????? ???????? ???????? ????????  ????????????????
00000298`31da9020  ???????? ???????? ???????? ????????  ????????????????
```

14.   Since we identified the buffer overwrite, we now double-check other threads to see if there is something anomalous there as well:

```
0:001> ~*kL

  0  Id: 3a0.2544 Suspend: 1 Teb: 0000009a`5b4e8000 Unfrozen
 # Child-SP          RetAddr           Call Site
00 0000009a`5b6ffc28 00007ffe`fb078ba3 ntdll!NtWaitForSingleObject+0x14
01 0000009a`5b6ffc30 00007ff6`dbe93623 KERNELBASE!WaitForSingleObjectEx+0x93
02 0000009a`5b6ffcd0 00007ff6`dbe913af AppL2!_Thrd_join+0x1f
03 0000009a`5b6ffd00 00007ff6`dbe9159a AppL2!std::thread::join+0x5f
04 0000009a`5b6ffd60 00007ff6`dbe94060 AppL2!wmain+0x4a
05 (Inline Function) --------`-------- AppL2!invoke_main+0x22
06 0000009a`5b6ffdd0 00007ffe`fbce7bd4 AppL2!__scrt_common_main_seh+0x10c
07 0000009a`5b6ffe10 00007ffe`fd2acee1 kernel32!BaseThreadInitThunk+0x14
08 0000009a`5b6ffe40 00000000`00000000 ntdll!RtlUserThreadStart+0x21
```

```
#  1  Id: 3a0.25a8 Suspend: 0 Teb: 0000009a`5b4ea000 Unfrozen
 # Child-SP          RetAddr           Call Site
00 0000009a`5b7fe348 00007ffe`fb097ff7 ntdll!NtWaitForMultipleObjects+0x14
01 0000009a`5b7fe350 00007ffe`fb097ede KERNELBASE!WaitForMultipleObjectsEx+0x107
02 0000009a`5b7fe650 00007ffe`fbd371fb KERNELBASE!WaitForMultipleObjects+0xe
03 0000009a`5b7fe690 00007ffe`fbd36ca8 kernel32!WerpReportFaultInternal+0x51b
04 0000009a`5b7fe7b0 00007ffe`fb13f988 kernel32!WerpReportFault+0xac
05 0000009a`5b7fe7f0 00007ffe`fd2e4af2 KERNELBASE!UnhandledExceptionFilter+0x3b8
06 0000009a`5b7fe910 00007ffe`fd2cc6e6 ntdll!RtlUserThreadStart$filt$0+0xa2
07 0000009a`5b7fe950 00007ffe`fd2e120f ntdll!_C_specific_handler+0x96
08 0000009a`5b7fe9c0 00007ffe`fd2aa299 ntdll!RtlpExecuteHandlerForException+0xf
09 0000009a`5b7fe9f0 00007ffe`fd2dfe7e ntdll!RtlDispatchException+0x219
0a 0000009a`5b7ff100 00007ff6`dbe9142f ntdll!KiUserExceptionDispatch+0x2e
0b 0000009a`5b7ff8a0 00007ff6`dbe91ef5 AppL2!thread_one+0x3f
0c 0000009a`5b7ff910 00007ff6`dbe91e0b AppL2!std::_Invoker_functor::_Call<void (__cdecl*)(void)>+0x15
0d 0000009a`5b7ff940 00007ff6`dbe91a84 AppL2!std::invoke<void (__cdecl*)(void)>+0x1b
0e 0000009a`5b7ff970 00007ff6`dbe99c58 AppL2!std::thread::_Invoke<std::tuple<void (__cdecl*)(void)>,0>+0x64
0f 0000009a`5b7ff9c0 00007ffe`fbce7bd4 AppL2!thread_start<unsigned int (__cdecl*)(void *),1>+0x50
10 0000009a`5b7ff9f0 00007ffe`fd2acee1 kernel32!BaseThreadInitThunk+0x14
11 0000009a`5b7ffa20 00000000`00000000 ntdll!RtlUserThreadStart+0x21

   2  Id: 3a0.1f64 Suspend: 1 Teb: 0000009a`5b4ec000 Unfrozen
 # Child-SP          RetAddr           Call Site
00 0000009a`5b8fe6c8 00007ffe`fb086931 ntdll!NtDelayExecution+0x14
01 0000009a`5b8fe6d0 00007ffe`fbd36c93 KERNELBASE!SleepEx+0xa1
02 0000009a`5b8fe770 00007ffe`fb13f988 kernel32!WerpReportFault+0x97
03 0000009a`5b8fe7b0 00007ffe`fd2e4af2 KERNELBASE!UnhandledExceptionFilter+0x3b8
04 0000009a`5b8fe8d0 00007ffe`fd2cc6e6 ntdll!RtlUserThreadStart$filt$0+0xa2
05 0000009a`5b8fe910 00007ffe`fd2e120f ntdll!_C_specific_handler+0x96
06 0000009a`5b8fe980 00007ffe`fd2aa299 ntdll!RtlpExecuteHandlerForException+0xf
07 0000009a`5b8fe9b0 00007ffe`fd2dfe7e ntdll!RtlDispatchException+0x219
08 0000009a`5b8ff0c0 00007ff6`dbe914df ntdll!KiUserExceptionDispatch+0x2e
09 0000009a`5b8ff860 00007ff6`dbe91ef5 AppL2!thread_two+0x3f
0a 0000009a`5b8ff8d0 00007ff6`dbe91e0b AppL2!std::_Invoker_functor::_Call<void (__cdecl*)(void)>+0x15
0b 0000009a`5b8ff900 00007ff6`dbe91a84 AppL2!std::invoke<void (__cdecl*)(void)>+0x1b
0c 0000009a`5b8ff930 00007ff6`dbe99c58 AppL2!std::thread::_Invoke<std::tuple<void (__cdecl*)(void)>,0>+0x64
0d 0000009a`5b8ff980 00007ffe`fbce7bd4 AppL2!thread_start<unsigned int (__cdecl*)(void *),1>+0x50
0e 0000009a`5b8ff9b0 00007ffe`fd2acee1 kernel32!BaseThreadInitThunk+0x14
0f 0000009a`5b8ff9e0 00000000`00000000 ntdll!RtlUserThreadStart+0x21

   3  Id: 3a0.2704 Suspend: 1 Teb: 0000009a`5b4ee000 Unfrozen
 # Child-SP          RetAddr           Call Site
00 0000009a`5b9ffa78 00007ffe`fd274060 ntdll!NtWaitForWorkViaWorkerFactory+0x14
01 0000009a`5b9ffa80 00007ffe`fbce7bd4 ntdll!TppWorkerThread+0x300
02 0000009a`5b9ffe40 00007ffe`fd2acee1 kernel32!BaseThreadInitThunk+0x14
03 0000009a`5b9ffe70 00000000`00000000 ntdll!RtlUserThreadStart+0x21

   4  Id: 3a0.26a0 Suspend: 1 Teb: 0000009a`5b4f0000 Unfrozen
 # Child-SP          RetAddr           Call Site
00 0000009a`5baff6a8 00007ffe`fd274060 ntdll!NtWaitForWorkViaWorkerFactory+0x14
01 0000009a`5baff6b0 00007ffe`fbce7bd4 ntdll!TppWorkerThread+0x300
02 0000009a`5baffa70 00007ffe`fd2acee1 kernel32!BaseThreadInitThunk+0x14
03 0000009a`5baffaa0 00000000`00000000 ntdll!RtlUserThreadStart+0x21
```

Note: We see similar exception processing in thread #2.

15.   To see what happened in another thread, we switch to it and do the similar frame analysis that we did for thread #1:

```
0:001> ~2s
ntdll!NtDelayExecution+0x14:
00007ffe`fd2dc754 c3              ret
```

```
0:002> .frame /c /r 9
09 0000009a`5b8ff860 00007ff6`dbe91ef5 AppL2!thread_two+0x3f [C:\AWMDA-Examples\AppL2\AppL2.cpp @ 32]
rax=0000000000000034 rbx=0000029831d4cfd0 rcx=0000000000000000
rdx=0000009a5b8fe6f0 rsi=00007ff6dbead6d0 rdi=0000029831db1000
rip=00007ff6dbe914df rsp=0000009a5b8ff860 rbp=0000000000000000
 r8=0000000000000008  r9=0000009a5b8fe470 r10=00000298303302c0
r11=000002983035a930 r12=0000000000000000 r13=0000000000000000
r14=0000000000000000 r15=0000000000000000
iopl=0         nv up ei pl zr na po nc
cs=0033  ss=002b  ds=002b  es=002b  fs=0053  gs=002b          efl=00000246
AppL2!thread_two+0x3f:
00007ff6`dbe914df f3a4              rep movs byte ptr [rdi],byte ptr [rsi]

0:002> kL
 *** Stack trace for last set context - .thread/.cxr resets it
 # Child-SP          RetAddr           Call Site
09 0000009a`5b8ff860 00007ff6`dbe91ef5 AppL2!thread_two+0x3f
0a 0000009a`5b8ff8d0 00007ff6`dbe91e0b AppL2!std::_Invoker_functor::_Call<void (__cdecl*)(void)>+0x15
0b 0000009a`5b8ff900 00007ff6`dbe91a84 AppL2!std::invoke<void (__cdecl*)(void)>+0x1b
0c 0000009a`5b8ff930 00007ff6`dbe99c58 AppL2!std::thread::_Invoke<std::tuple<void (__cdecl*)(void)>,0>+0x64
0d 0000009a`5b8ff980 00007ffe`fbce7bd4 AppL2!thread_start<unsigned int (__cdecl*)(void *),1>+0x50
0e 0000009a`5b8ff9b0 00007ffe`fd2acee1 kernel32!BaseThreadInitThunk+0x14
0f 0000009a`5b8ff9e0 00000000`00000000 ntdll!RtlUserThreadStart+0x21

0:002> dc 0000029831db1000-50
00000298`31db0fb0  00000014 00000000 00001000 00000000  ...............
00000298`31db0fc0  00000000 00000000 00000000 00000000  ...............
00000298`31db0fd0  3035a8b0 00000298 00000000 dcbabbbb  ..50...........
00000298`31db0fe0  00650048 006c006c 0020006f 00720043  H.e.l.l.o. .C.r.
00000298`31db0ff0  00730061 00210068 00480020 006c0065  a.s.h.!. .H.e.l.
00000298`31db1000  ???????? ???????? ???????? ????????  ????????????????
00000298`31db1010  ???????? ???????? ???????? ????????  ????????????????
00000298`31db1020  ???????? ???????? ???????? ????????  ????????????????
```

Note: We see a similar buffer overwrite for a different buffer, and if we set up the source code path correctly WinDbg would open the source code window and point to the exact location if we type the **.cxr** command:

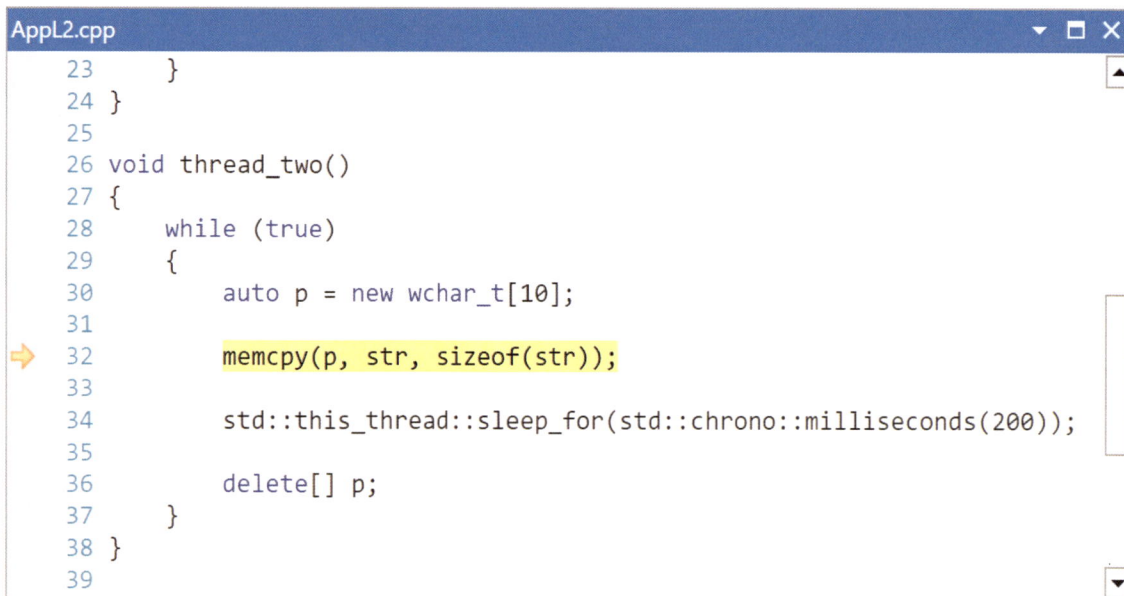

```
AppL2.cpp                                                       ▼ □ ✕
   23      }
   24  }
   25
   26  void thread_two()
   27  {
   28      while (true)
   29      {
   30          auto p = new wchar_t[10];
   31
⇨ 32          memcpy(p, str, sizeof(str));
   33
   34          std::this_thread::sleep_for(std::chrono::milliseconds(200));
   35
   36          delete[] p;
   37      }
   38  }
   39
```

16.   We close logging before exiting WinDbg:

```
0:002> .logclose
Closing open log file C:\AWMDA-Dumps\Process\x64\AppL2.log
```

Exercise P8

- **Goal:** Learn how to recognize CPU spikes, invalid pointers, disassemble code, and reconstruct stack trace

- **Patterns:** Wild Code; Active Thread; Spiking Thread; NULL Pointer (Code); Truncated Stack Trace; Stored Exception

- \AWMDA-Dumps\Exercise-P8-Analysis-process-dump-AppM-64.pdf

Exercise P8: Analysis of an application process dump (AppM, 64-bit)

Goal: Learn how to recognize CPU spikes, invalid pointers, disassemble code, and reconstruct stack trace.

Patterns: Wild Code; Active Thread; Spiking Thread; NULL Pointer (Code); Truncated Stack Trace; Stored Exception.

1.   Launch WinDbg.

2.   Open \AWMDA-Dumps\Process\x64\AppM.exe.9192.dmp.

3.   We get the dump file loaded:

```
Microsoft (R) Windows Debugger Version 10.0.25877.1004 AMD64
Copyright (c) Microsoft Corporation. All rights reserved.


Loading Dump File [C:\AWMDA-Dumps\Process\x64\AppM.exe.9192.dmp]
User Mini Dump File with Full Memory: Only application data is available


************* Path validation summary **************
Response                        Time (ms)      Location
Deferred                                       srv*
OK                                             C:\AWMDA-Dumps\Symbols
Symbol search path is: srv*;C:\AWMDA-Dumps\Symbols
Executable search path is:
Windows 10 Version 18362 MP (2 procs) Free x64
Product: WinNt, suite: SingleUserTS Personal
Edition build lab: 18362.1.amd64fre.19h1_release.190318-1202
Machine Name:
Debug session time: Sun Nov  3 21:32:21.000 2019 (UTC + 1:00)
System Uptime: 0 days 0:30:06.518
Process Uptime: 0 days 0:01:01.000
.......
This dump file has an exception of interest stored in it.
The stored exception information can be accessed via .ecxr.
(23e8.2794): Access violation - code c0000005 (first/second chance not available)
For analysis of this file, run !analyze -v
ntdll!NtWaitForMultipleObjects+0x14:
00007ffe`fd2dcc24 c3              ret
```

4.   Open a log file using **.logopen** command, set up source code path (**.srcpath+**), and load application symbols (**.sympath+** and **.reload**):

```
0:004> .logopen C:\AWMDA-Dumps\Process\x64\AppM.log
Opened log file 'C:\AWMDA-Dumps\Process\x64\AppM.log'

0:004> .srcpath+ C:\AWMDA-Dumps\Source
Source search path is: C:\AWMDA-Dumps\Source

************* Path validation summary **************
Response                        Time (ms)      Location
OK                                             C:\AWMDA-Dumps\Source
```

```
0:004> .sympath+ C:\AWMDA-Dumps\Symbols
Symbol search path is: srv*;C:\AWMDA-Dumps\Symbols
Expanded Symbol search path is:
cache*;SRV*https://msdl.microsoft.com/download/symbols;c:\awmda-dumps\symbols

************* Path validation summary **************
Response                        Time (ms)      Location
Deferred                                       srv*
OK                                             C:\AWMDA-Dumps\Symbols

0:004> .reload
............
```

5.   Type the **kL** command to verify the correctness of the stack trace for the current thread #4 (source code thread names are mapped to different ordinal thread numbers in the dump file):

```
0:004> kL
# Child-SP          RetAddr           Call Site
00 0000002c`b74fe548 00007ffe`fb097ff7 ntdll!NtWaitForMultipleObjects+0x14
01 0000002c`b74fe550 00007ffe`fb097ede KERNELBASE!WaitForMultipleObjectsEx+0x107
02 0000002c`b74fe850 00007ffe`fbd371fb KERNELBASE!WaitForMultipleObjects+0xe
03 0000002c`b74fe890 00007ffe`fbd36ca8 kernel32!WerpReportFaultInternal+0x51b
04 0000002c`b74fe9b0 00007ffe`fb13f988 kernel32!WerpReportFault+0xac
05 0000002c`b74fe9f0 00007ffe`fd2e4af2 KERNELBASE!UnhandledExceptionFilter+0x3b8
06 0000002c`b74feb10 00007ffe`fd2cc6e6 ntdll!RtlUserThreadStart$filt$0+0xa2
07 0000002c`b74feb50 00007ffe`fd2e120f ntdll!_C_specific_handler+0x96
08 0000002c`b74febc0 00007ffe`fd2aa299 ntdll!RtlpExecuteHandlerForException+0xf
09 0000002c`b74febf0 00007ffe`fd2dfe7e ntdll!RtlDispatchException+0x219
0a 0000002c`b74ff300 00007ff6`380c1366 ntdll!KiUserExceptionDispatch+0x2e
*** WARNING: Unable to verify checksum for AppM.exe
0b 0000002c`b74ffaa0 00007ff6`380c1db5 AppM!thread_one+0x16
0c 0000002c`b74ffac0 00007ff6`380c1a9b AppM!std::_Invoker_functor::_Call<void (__cdecl*)(void)>+0x15
0d 0000002c`b74ffaf0 00007ff6`380c1874 AppM!std::invoke<void (__cdecl*)(void)>+0x1b
0e 0000002c`b74ffb20 00007ff6`380c9ac8 AppM!std::thread::_Invoke<std::tuple<void (__cdecl*)(void)>,0>+0x64
0f 0000002c`b74ffb70 00007ffe`fbce7bd4 AppM!thread_start<unsigned int (__cdecl*)(void *),1>+0x50
10 0000002c`b74ffba0 00007ffe`fd2acee1 kernel32!BaseThreadInitThunk+0x14
11 0000002c`b74ffbd0 00000000`00000000 ntdll!RtlUserThreadStart+0x21
```

Note: We have a stored exception, and the **.ecxr** command may show us the thread stack prior to exception processing :

```
This dump file has an exception of interest stored in it.
The stored exception information can be accessed via .ecxr.
(23e8.2794): Access violation - code c0000005 (first/second chance not available)
```

```
0:004> ~4
.  4  Id: 23e8.2794 Suspend: 0 Teb: 0000002c`b6c73000 Unfrozen
       Start: AppM!thread_start<unsigned int (__cdecl*)(void *),1> (00007ff6`380c9a78)
       Priority: 0  Priority class: 32  Affinity: 3
```

```
0:004> .ecxr
rax=f123456789abcdef rbx=0000018ed15cbcb0 rcx=0000018ed15cbc90
rdx=0000000000000004 rsi=0000000000000000 rdi=0000000000000000
rip=00007ff6380c1366 rsp=0000002cb74ffaa0 rbp=0000000000000000
 r8=0000002cb74ffb28  r9=0000002cb74ffb00 r10=000049d48a79d3a2
r11=0000002cb74ffae0 r12=0000000000000000 r13=0000000000000000
r14=0000000000000000 r15=0000000000000000
iopl=0         nv up ei pl nz na po nc
cs=0033  ss=002b  ds=002b  es=002b  fs=0053  gs=002b              efl=00010206
AppM!thread_one+0x16:
00007ff6`380c1366 c70001000000    mov     dword ptr [rax],1 ds:f1234567`89abcdef=????????
```

```
0:004> kL
 *** Stack trace for last set context - .thread/.cxr resets it
 # Child-SP          RetAddr           Call Site
00 0000002c`b74ffaa0 00007ff6`380c1db5 AppM!thread_one+0x16
01 0000002c`b74ffac0 00007ff6`380c1a9b AppM!std::_Invoker_functor::_Call<void (__cdecl*)(void)>+0x15
02 0000002c`b74ffaf0 00007ff6`380c1874 AppM!std::invoke<void (__cdecl*)(void)>+0x1b
03 0000002c`b74ffb20 00007ff6`380c9ac8 AppM!std::thread::_Invoke<std::tuple<void (__cdecl*)(void)>,0>+0x64
04 0000002c`b74ffb70 00007ffe`fbce7bd4 AppM!thread_start<unsigned int (__cdecl*)(void *),1>+0x50
05 0000002c`b74ffba0 00007ffe`fd2acee1 kernel32!BaseThreadInitThunk+0x14
06 0000002c`b74ffbd0 00000000`00000000 ntdll!RtlUserThreadStart+0x21
```

Note: We see a memory access violation through the invalid pointer f1234567`89abcdef.

```
0:004> !address f1234567`89abcdef


Mapping file section regions...
Mapping module regions...
Mapping PEB regions...
Mapping TEB and stack regions...
Mapping heap regions...
Mapping page heap regions...
Mapping other regions...
Mapping stack trace database regions...
Mapping activation context regions...
Address f123456789abcdef could not be mapped in any of the available regions
```

Note: Since we previously set up the source code path WinDbg shows a window with highlighted problem source code statement:

```
AppM.cpp                                                          ▼ □ ✕
     1 // AppM - Models invalid pointers for data and code, NULL code pointer
     2 // Copyright (c) 2011-2019 Software Diagnostics Technology and Service
     3 // GNU GENERAL PUBLIC LICENSE
     4 // http://www.gnu.org/licenses/gpl-3.0.txt
     5
     6 #include <thread>
     7 #include <chrono>
     8
     9 void thread_one()
    10 {
    11     int* p{ reinterpret_cast<int*>(0xF123456789ABCDEF) };
    12
 ⇨  13     *p = 1;
    14 }
    15
    16 void thread_two()
    17 {
    18     void (*p)() {};
    19
    20     (*p)();
    21 }
```

6.   Because of the *0:004>* prompt, we know there are several threads, and we check their stack traces:

```
0:004> ~*kL

   0  Id: 23e8.730 Suspend: 1 Teb: 0000002c`b6c67000 Unfrozen
 # Child-SP          RetAddr           Call Site
00 0000002c`b6eff4f8 00007ffe`fb086931 ntdll!NtDelayExecution+0x14
01 0000002c`b6eff500 00007ff6`380c3510 KERNELBASE!SleepEx+0xa1
02 0000002c`b6eff5a0 00007ff6`380c1965 AppM!_Thrd_sleep+0x3c
03 0000002c`b6eff5f0 00007ff6`380c167d
AppM!std::this_thread::sleep_until<std::chrono::steady_clock,std::chrono::duration<__int64,std::ratio<1,1000000000> >
>+0x65
04 0000002c`b6eff650 00007ff6`380c1485 AppM!std::this_thread::sleep_for<int,std::ratio<3600,1> >+0x2d
05 0000002c`b6eff690 00007ff6`380c3ed0 AppM!wmain+0xa5
06 (Inline Function) --------`-------- AppM!invoke_main+0x22
07 0000002c`b6eff720 00007ffe`fbce7bd4 AppM!__scrt_common_main_seh+0x10c
08 0000002c`b6eff760 00007ffe`fd2acee1 kernel32!BaseThreadInitThunk+0x14
09 0000002c`b6eff790 00000000`00000000 ntdll!RtlUserThreadStart+0x21

   1  Id: 23e8.6c0 Suspend: 1 Teb: 0000002c`b6c69000 Unfrozen
 # Child-SP          RetAddr           Call Site
00 0000002c`b6fff6a8 00007ff6`380c1db5 AppM!thread_four+0x2
01 0000002c`b6fff6b0 00007ff6`380c1a9b AppM!std::_Invoker_functor::_Call<void (__cdecl*)(void)>+0x15
02 0000002c`b6fff6e0 00007ff6`380c1874 AppM!std::invoke<void (__cdecl*)(void)>+0x1b
03 0000002c`b6fff710 00007ff6`380c9ac8 AppM!std::thread::_Invoke<std::tuple<void (__cdecl*)(void)>,0>+0x64
04 0000002c`b6fff760 00007ffe`fbce7bd4 AppM!thread_start<unsigned int (__cdecl*)(void *),1>+0x50
05 0000002c`b6fff790 00007ffe`fd2acee1 kernel32!BaseThreadInitThunk+0x14
06 0000002c`b6fff7c0 00000000`00000000 ntdll!RtlUserThreadStart+0x21

   2  Id: 23e8.cfc Suspend: 1 Teb: 0000002c`b6c6f000 Unfrozen
 # Child-SP          RetAddr           Call Site
00 0000002c`b72fe6c8 00007ffe`fb086931 ntdll!NtDelayExecution+0x14
01 0000002c`b72fe6d0 00007ffe`fbd36c93 KERNELBASE!SleepEx+0xa1
02 0000002c`b72fe770 00007ffe`fb13f988 kernel32!WerpReportFault+0x97
03 0000002c`b72fe7b0 00007ffe`fd2e4af2 KERNELBASE!UnhandledExceptionFilter+0x3b8
04 0000002c`b72fe8d0 00007ffe`fd2cc6e6 ntdll!RtlUserThreadStart$filt$0+0xa2
05 0000002c`b72fe910 00007ffe`fd2e120f ntdll!_C_specific_handler+0x96
06 0000002c`b72fe980 00007ffe`fd2aa299 ntdll!RtlpExecuteHandlerForException+0xf
07 0000002c`b72fe9b0 00007ffe`fd2dfe7e ntdll!RtlDispatchException+0x219
08 0000002c`b72ff0c0 0000018e`d15ccbf0 ntdll!KiUserExceptionDispatch+0x2e
09 0000002c`b72ff878 00007ff6`380c13c1 0x0000018e`d15ccbf0
0a 0000002c`b72ff880 00007ff6`380c1db5 AppM!thread_three+0x21
0b 0000002c`b72ff8c0 00007ff6`380c1a9b AppM!std::_Invoker_functor::_Call<void (__cdecl*)(void)>+0x15
0c 0000002c`b72ff8f0 00007ff6`380c1874 AppM!std::invoke<void (__cdecl*)(void)>+0x1b
0d 0000002c`b72ff920 00007ff6`380c9ac8 AppM!std::thread::_Invoke<std::tuple<void (__cdecl*)(void)>,0>+0x64
0e 0000002c`b72ff970 00007ffe`fbce7bd4 AppM!thread_start<unsigned int (__cdecl*)(void *),1>+0x50
0f 0000002c`b72ff9a0 00007ffe`fd2acee1 kernel32!BaseThreadInitThunk+0x14
10 0000002c`b72ff9d0 00000000`00000000 ntdll!RtlUserThreadStart+0x21

   3  Id: 23e8.293c Suspend: 1 Teb: 0000002c`b6c71000 Unfrozen
 # Child-SP          RetAddr           Call Site
00 0000002c`b73fe548 00007ffe`fb086931 ntdll!NtDelayExecution+0x14
01 0000002c`b73fe550 00007ffe`fbd36c93 KERNELBASE!SleepEx+0xa1
02 0000002c`b73fe5f0 00007ffe`fb13f988 kernel32!WerpReportFault+0x97
03 0000002c`b73fe630 00007ffe`fd2e4af2 KERNELBASE!UnhandledExceptionFilter+0x3b8
04 0000002c`b73fe750 00007ffe`fd2cc6e6 ntdll!RtlUserThreadStart$filt$0+0xa2
05 0000002c`b73fe790 00007ffe`fd2e120f ntdll!_C_specific_handler+0x96
06 0000002c`b73fe800 00007ffe`fd2aa299 ntdll!RtlpExecuteHandlerForException+0xf
07 0000002c`b73fe830 00007ffe`fd2dfe7e ntdll!RtlDispatchException+0x219
08 0000002c`b73fef40 00000000`00000000 ntdll!KiUserExceptionDispatch+0x2e

 #  4  Id: 23e8.2794 Suspend: 0 Teb: 0000002c`b6c73000 Unfrozen
 # Child-SP          RetAddr           Call Site
00 0000002c`b74fe548 00007ffe`fb097ff7 ntdll!NtWaitForMultipleObjects+0x14
01 0000002c`b74fe550 00007ffe`fb097ede KERNELBASE!WaitForMultipleObjectsEx+0x107
02 0000002c`b74fe850 00007ffe`fbd371fb KERNELBASE!WaitForMultipleObjects+0xe
03 0000002c`b74fe890 00007ffe`fbd36ca8 kernel32!WerpReportFaultInternal+0x51b
04 0000002c`b74fe9b0 00007ffe`fb13f988 kernel32!WerpReportFault+0xac
05 0000002c`b74fe9f0 00007ffe`fd2e4af2 KERNELBASE!UnhandledExceptionFilter+0x3b8
06 0000002c`b74feb10 00007ffe`fd2cc6e6 ntdll!RtlUserThreadStart$filt$0+0xa2
07 0000002c`b74feb50 00007ffe`fd2e120f ntdll!_C_specific_handler+0x96
08 0000002c`b74febc0 00007ffe`fd2aa299 ntdll!RtlpExecuteHandlerForException+0xf
09 0000002c`b74febf0 00007ffe`fd2dfe7e ntdll!RtlDispatchException+0x219
0a 0000002c`b74ff300 00007ff6`380c1366 ntdll!KiUserExceptionDispatch+0x2e
```

133

```
0b 0000002c`b74ffaa0 00007ff6`380c1db5 AppM!thread_one+0x16
0c 0000002c`b74ffac0 00007ff6`380c1a9b AppM!std::_Invoker_functor::_Call<void (__cdecl*)(void)>+0x15
0d 0000002c`b74ffaf0 00007ff6`380c1874 AppM!std::invoke<void (__cdecl*)(void)>+0x1b
0e 0000002c`b74ffb20 00007ff6`380c9ac8 AppM!std::thread::_Invoke<std::tuple<void (__cdecl*)(void)>,0>+0x64
0f 0000002c`b74ffb70 00007ffe`fbce7bd4 AppM!thread_start<unsigned int (__cdecl*)(void *),1>+0x50
10 0000002c`b74ffba0 00007ffe`fd2acee1 kernel32!BaseThreadInitThunk+0x14
11 0000002c`b74ffbd0 00000000`00000000 ntdll!RtlUserThreadStart+0x21
```

Note: We see thread #1 is not waiting, and the top function on the stack trace is *AppM* code ***thread_four***. Threads #2 and #3 have exception processing code (in addition to already analyzed thread #4). We also notice raw code pointer 0x00000210`49ab0f50 in the 2nd stack trace. Thread #3 stack trace looks truncated as we only see the exception processing part. We now look at each thread separately.

7.   We now switch to thread #1:

```
0:004> ~1s
AppM!thread_four+0x2:
00007ff6`380c13d2 33c0              xor     eax,eax
```

```
0:001> kL
 # Child-SP          RetAddr           Call Site
00 0000002c`b6fff6a8 00007ff6`380c1db5 AppM!thread_four+0x2
01 0000002c`b6fff6b0 00007ff6`380c1a9b AppM!std::_Invoker_functor::_Call<void (__cdecl*)(void)>+0x15
02 0000002c`b6fff6e0 00007ff6`380c1874 AppM!std::invoke<void (__cdecl*)(void)>+0x1b
03 0000002c`b6fff710 00007ff6`380c9ac8 AppM!std::thread::_Invoke<std::tuple<void (__cdecl*)(void)>,0>+0x64
04 0000002c`b6fff760 00007ffe`fbce7bd4 AppM!thread_start<unsigned int (__cdecl*)(void *),1>+0x50
05 0000002c`b6fff790 00007ffe`fd2acee1 kernel32!BaseThreadInitThunk+0x14
06 0000002c`b6fff7c0 00000000`00000000 ntdll!RtlUserThreadStart+0x21
```

Note: If we disassemble code, we see a code jump instruction back to the start of disassembly, so perhaps the code was spinning (looping) and, indeed, with source code path available, WinDbg shows another window with highlighted while loop:

```
0:001> u 00007ff6`380c13d2
AppM!thread_four+0x2 [C:\AWMDA-Examples\AppM\AppM.cpp @ 32]:
00007ff6`380c13d2 33c0              xor     eax,eax
00007ff6`380c13d4 83f801            cmp     eax,1
00007ff6`380c13d7 7402              je      AppM!thread_four+0xb (00007ff6`380c13db)
00007ff6`380c13d9 ebf7              jmp     AppM!thread_four+0x2 (00007ff6`380c13d2)
00007ff6`380c13db c3                ret
00007ff6`380c13dc cc                int     3
00007ff6`380c13dd cc                int     3
00007ff6`380c13de cc                int     3
```

```
AppM.cpp                                          ▾ ☐ ✕
  21 }
  22
  23 void thread_three()
  24 {
  25     void (*p)() = reinterpret_cast<void (*)()>(new char[1024]);
  26
  27     (*p)();
  28 }
  29
  30 void thread_four()
  31 {
⇨ 32     while (true);
  33 }
  34
  35 int wmain(int argc, wchar_t* argv[])
  36 {
  37     std::thread t4(thread_four);
  38
  39     std::this_thread::sleep_for(std::chrono::minutes(1));
  40
  41     std::thread t3(thread_three);
  42     std::thread t2(thread_two);
```

We check CPU consumption (**!runaway** command):

```
0:001> !runaway f
User Mode Time
  Thread       Time
    1:6c0      0 days 0:00:59.421
    4:2794     0 days 0:00:00.000
    3:293c     0 days 0:00:00.000
    2:cfc      0 days 0:00:00.000
    0:730      0 days 0:00:00.000
Kernel Mode Time
  Thread       Time
    1:6c0      0 days 0:00:00.015
    4:2794     0 days 0:00:00.000
    3:293c     0 days 0:00:00.000
    2:cfc      0 days 0:00:00.000
    0:730      0 days 0:00:00.000
Elapsed Time
  Thread       Time
    0:730      0 days 0:01:00.377
    1:6c0      0 days 0:01:00.098
    2:cfc      0 days 0:00:00.095
    3:293c     0 days 0:00:00.095
    4:2794     0 days 0:00:00.095
```

Note: We see the thread had spent almost all time accumulating CPU since its creation. It is clearly a CPU spike in *AppM*.

8.   Now we check thread #2:

```
0:001> ~2s
ntdll!NtDelayExecution+0x14:
00007ffe`fd2dc754 c3                    ret
```

135

```
0:002> kL
 # Child-SP          RetAddr           Call Site
00 0000002c`b72fe6c8 00007ffe`fb086931 ntdll!NtDelayExecution+0x14
01 0000002c`b72fe6d0 00007ffe`fbd36c93 KERNELBASE!SleepEx+0xa1
02 0000002c`b72fe770 00007ffe`fb13f988 kernel32!WerpReportFault+0x97
03 0000002c`b72fe7b0 00007ffe`fd2e4af2 KERNELBASE!UnhandledExceptionFilter+0x3b8
04 0000002c`b72fe8d0 00007ffe`fd2cc6e6 ntdll!RtlUserThreadStart$filt$0+0xa2
05 0000002c`b72fe910 00007ffe`fd2e120f ntdll!_C_specific_handler+0x96
06 0000002c`b72fe980 00007ffe`fd2aa299 ntdll!RtlpExecuteHandlerForException+0xf
07 0000002c`b72fe9b0 00007ffe`fd2dfe7e ntdll!RtlDispatchException+0x219
08 0000002c`b72ff0c0 0000018e`d15ccbf0 ntdll!KiUserExceptionDispatch+0x2e
09 0000002c`b72ff878 00007ff6`380c13c1 0x0000018e`d15ccbf0
0a 0000002c`b72ff880 00007ff6`380c1db5 AppM!thread_three+0x21
0b 0000002c`b72ff8c0 00007ff6`380c1a9b AppM!std::_Invoker_functor::_Call<void (__cdecl*)(void)>+0x15
0c 0000002c`b72ff8f0 00007ff6`380c1874 AppM!std::invoke<void (__cdecl*)(void)>+0x1b
0d 0000002c`b72ff920 00007ff6`380c9ac8 AppM!std::thread::_Invoke<std::tuple<void (__cdecl*)(void)>,0>+0x64
0e 0000002c`b72ff970 00007ffe`fbce7bd4 AppM!thread_start<unsigned int (__cdecl*)(void *),1>+0x50
0f 0000002c`b72ff9a0 00007ffe`fd2acee1 kernel32!BaseThreadInitThunk+0x14
10 0000002c`b72ff9d0 00000000`00000000 ntdll!RtlUserThreadStart+0x21

0:002> u 0000018e`d15ccbf0
0000018e`d15ccbf0 50              push    rax
0000018e`d15ccbf1 015cd18e        add     dword ptr [rcx+rdx*8-72h],ebx
0000018e`d15ccbf5 0100            add     dword ptr [rax],eax
0000018e`d15ccbf7 00a0be5cd18e    add     byte ptr [rax-712EA342h],ah
0000018e`d15ccbfd 0100            add     dword ptr [rax],eax
0000018e`d15ccbff 0000            add     byte ptr [rax],al
0000018e`d15ccc01 0000            add     byte ptr [rax],al
0000018e`d15ccc03 0000            add     byte ptr [rax],al

0:002> .frame /c /r 9
09 0000002c`b72ff878 00007ff6`380c13c1 0x0000018e`d15ccbf0
rax=0000000000000034 rbx=0000018ed15cbbe0 rcx=0000000000000000
rdx=0000002cb72fe6f0 rsi=0000000000000000 rdi=0000000000000000
rip=0000018ed15ccbf0 rsp=0000002cb72ff878 rbp=0000000000000000
 r8=00007ff6380c13c1  r9=00007ff6380e3084 r10=00007ff6380e3084
r11=0000000000000001 r12=0000000000000000 r13=0000000000000000
r14=0000000000000000 r15=0000000000000000
iopl=0         nv up ei pl zr na po nc
cs=0033  ss=002b  ds=002b  es=002b  fs=0053  gs=002b             efl=00000246
0000018e`d15ccbf0 50              push    rax
```

Note: We see that the faulting instruction looks normal (the subsequent instructions look rather wild). Nevertheless, we have an exception. Let's disassemble its return address backward:

```
0:002> kL
 *** Stack trace for last set context - .thread/.cxr resets it
 # Child-SP          RetAddr           Call Site
09 0000002c`b72ff878 00007ff6`380c13c1 0x0000018e`d15ccbf0
0a 0000002c`b72ff880 00007ff6`380c1db5 AppM!thread_three+0x21
0b 0000002c`b72ff8c0 00007ff6`380c1a9b AppM!std::_Invoker_functor::_Call<void (__cdecl*)(void)>+0x15
0c 0000002c`b72ff8f0 00007ff6`380c1874 AppM!std::invoke<void (__cdecl*)(void)>+0x1b
0d 0000002c`b72ff920 00007ff6`380c9ac8 AppM!std::thread::_Invoke<std::tuple<void (__cdecl*)(void)>,0>+0x64
0e 0000002c`b72ff970 00007ffe`fbce7bd4 AppM!thread_start<unsigned int (__cdecl*)(void *),1>+0x50
0f 0000002c`b72ff9a0 00007ffe`fd2acee1 kernel32!BaseThreadInitThunk+0x14
10 0000002c`b72ff9d0 00000000`00000000 ntdll!RtlUserThreadStart+0x21

0:002> ub 00007ff6`380c13c1
AppM!thread_two+0x1f:
00007ff6`380c139f cc              int     3
AppM!thread_three [C:\AWMDA-Examples\AppM\AppM.cpp @ 24]:
00007ff6`380c13a0 4883ec38        sub     rsp,38h
00007ff6`380c13a4 b900040000      mov     ecx,400h
00007ff6`380c13a9 e82a290000      call    AppM!operator new[] (00007ff6`380c3cd8)
00007ff6`380c13ae 4889442420      mov     qword ptr [rsp+20h],rax
```

```
00007ff6`380c13b3 488b442420          mov     rax,qword ptr [rsp+20h]
00007ff6`380c13b8 4889442428          mov     qword ptr [rsp+28h],rax
00007ff6`380c13bd ff542428            call    qword ptr [rsp+28h]
```

Note: We see the *operator new[]* heap allocation function was called (the result was returned in the RAX register) prior to the *call* instruction that transferred execution to address 0x0000018e`d15ccbf0. Therefore, we expect that that address belongs to a heap region. Indeed, this is the case:

```
0:002> !address 0x0000018e`d15ccbf0

Usage:               Heap
Base Address:        0000018e`d15c0000
End Address:         0000018e`d15ce000
Region Size:         00000000`0000e000 (  56.000 kB)
State:               00001000          MEM_COMMIT
Protect:             00000004          PAGE_READWRITE
Type:                00020000          MEM_PRIVATE
Allocation Base:     0000018e`d15c0000
Allocation Protect:  00000004          PAGE_READWRITE
More info:           heap owning the address: !heap 0x18ed15c0000
More info:           heap segment
More info:           heap entry containing the address: !heap -x 0x18ed15ccbf0


Content source: 1 (target), length: 1410
```

Note: The address is a non-executable (PAGE_READWRITE) address, so this is why there was an exception.

9.   Now we check thread #3:

```
0:002> ~3s
ntdll!NtDelayExecution+0x14:
00007ffe`fd2dc754 c3                  ret

0:003> kL
 # Child-SP          RetAddr           Call Site
00 0000002c`b73fe548 00007ffe`fb086931 ntdll!NtDelayExecution+0x14
01 0000002c`b73fe550 00007ffe`fbd36c93 KERNELBASE!SleepEx+0xa1
02 0000002c`b73fe5f0 00007ffe`fb13f988 kernel32!WerpReportFault+0x97
03 0000002c`b73fe630 00007ffe`fd2e4af2 KERNELBASE!UnhandledExceptionFilter+0x3b8
04 0000002c`b73fe750 00007ffe`fd2cc6e6 ntdll!RtlUserThreadStart$filt$0+0xa2
05 0000002c`b73fe790 00007ffe`fd2e120f ntdll!_C_specific_handler+0x96
06 0000002c`b73fe800 00007ffe`fd2aa299 ntdll!RtlpExecuteHandlerForException+0xf
07 0000002c`b73fe830 00007ffe`fd2dfe7e ntdll!RtlDispatchException+0x219
08 0000002c`b73fef40 00000000`00000000 ntdll!KiUserExceptionDispatch+0x2e
```

Note: We see a truncated stack trace since there is nothing past exception processing functions. This may be because we have the 0 return address, so WinDbg stopped there. We set the exception context to the stack value 0000002c`b73fef40:

```
0:003> .cxr 0000002c`b73fef40
rax=0000018ed15cbc40 rbx=0000018ed15cbc60 rcx=0000018ed15cbc40
rdx=0000000000000004 rsi=0000000000000000 rdi=0000000000000000
rip=0000000000000000 rsp=0000002cb73ff6e8 rbp=0000000000000000
 r8=0000002cb73ff798  r9=0000002cb73ff770 r10=000049d48a79d3a2
r11=0000002cb73ff750 r12=0000000000000000 r13=0000000000000000
r14=0000000000000000 r15=0000000000000000
iopl=0         nv up ei pl nz na po nc
```

```
cs=0033  ss=002b  ds=002b  es=002b  fs=0053  gs=002b            efl=00010206
00000000`00000000 ??                ???
```

```
0:003> kL
 *** Stack trace for last set context - .thread/.cxr resets it
 # Child-SP          RetAddr           Call Site
00 0000002c`b73ff6e8 00007ff6`380c1391 0x0
01 0000002c`b73ff6f0 00007ff6`380c1db5 AppM!thread_two+0x11
02 0000002c`b73ff730 00007ff6`380c1a9b AppM!std::_Invoker_functor::_Call<void (__cdecl*)(void)>+0x15
03 0000002c`b73ff760 00007ff6`380c1874 AppM!std::invoke<void (__cdecl*)(void)>+0x1b
04 0000002c`b73ff790 00007ff6`380c9ac8 AppM!std::thread::_Invoke<std::tuple<void (__cdecl*)(void)>,0>+0x64
05 0000002c`b73ff7e0 00007ffe`fbce7bd4 AppM!thread_start<unsigned int (__cdecl*)(void *),1>+0x50
06 0000002c`b73ff810 00007ffe`fd2acee1 kernel32!BaseThreadInitThunk+0x14
07 0000002c`b73ff840 00000000`00000000 ntdll!RtlUserThreadStart+0x21
```

Note: To double check that the code indeed called 0 address, we disassemble the return address backward:

```
0:003> ub 00007ff6`380c1391
AppM!thread_one+0x2b:
00007ff6`380c137b cc              int     3
00007ff6`380c137c cc              int     3
00007ff6`380c137d cc              int     3
00007ff6`380c137e cc              int     3
00007ff6`380c137f cc              int     3
AppM!thread_two [C:\AWMDA-Examples\AppM\AppM.cpp @ 17]:
00007ff6`380c1380 4883ec38        sub     rsp,38h
00007ff6`380c1384 48c744242000000000 mov   qword ptr [rsp+20h],0
00007ff6`380c138d ff542420        call    qword ptr [rsp+20h]
```

10.   We close logging before exiting WinDbg:

```
0:003> .logclose
Closing open log file C:\AWMDA-Dumps\Process\x64\AppM.log
```

Exercise P9

◉ **Goal:** Learn how to recognize critical section waits and deadlocks, dump raw stack data, and see hidden exceptions

◉ **Patterns:** Deadlock (Critical Sections); Hidden Exception (User Space)

◉ \AWMDA-Dumps\Exercise-P9-Analysis-process-dump-AppN-64.pdf

Exercise P9: Analysis of an application process dump (AppN, 64-bit)

Goal: Learn how to recognize critical section waits and deadlocks, dump raw stack data, and see hidden exceptions.

Patterns: Deadlock (Critical Sections); Hidden Exception (User Space).

1.   Launch WinDbg.

2.   Open \AWMDA-Dumps\Process\x64\AppN.DMP.

3.   We get the dump file loaded:

```
Microsoft (R) Windows Debugger Version 10.0.25877.1004 AMD64
Copyright (c) Microsoft Corporation. All rights reserved.


Loading Dump File [C:\AWMDA-Dumps\Process\x64\AppN.DMP]
User Mini Dump File with Full Memory: Only application data is available


************* Path validation summary **************
Response                      Time (ms)     Location
Deferred                                    srv*
OK                                          C:\AWMDA-Dumps\Symbols
Symbol search path is: srv*;C:\AWMDA-Dumps\Symbols
Executable search path is:
Windows 10 Version 18362 MP (2 procs) Free x64
Product: WinNt, suite: SingleUserTS Personal
Edition build lab: 18362.1.amd64fre.19h1_release.190318-1202
Machine Name:
Debug session time: Sun Nov  3 21:40:24.000 2019 (UTC + 1:00)
System Uptime: 0 days 0:40:48.805
Process Uptime: 0 days 0:06:18.000
........
For analysis of this file, run !analyze -v
ntdll!NtWaitForSingleObject+0x14:
00007ffe`fd2dc154 c3              ret
```

4.   Open a log file using the **.logopen** command:

```
0:000> .logopen C:\AWMDA-Dumps\Process\x64\AppN.log
Opened log file 'C:\AWMDA-Dumps\Process\x64\AppN.log'
```

Note: In this exercise, we don't want to load *AppN* symbols because we want to model a 3rd party application hang where we don't have access to symbol files. However, source code and PDB exist in the usual locations, so that you can try with a symbol file as a homework exercise. Since the symbol file path was specified in the previous exercises, we reset it:

```
0:000> .symfix

0:000> .sympath
Symbol search path is: srv*
Expanded Symbol search path is: cache*;SRV*https://msdl.microsoft.com/download/symbols
```

```
************* Path validation summary **************
Response                        Time (ms)   Location
Deferred                                    srv*
```

5.   Type the ~*k command to verify the correctness of all stack traces:

```
0:000> ~*k

.  0  Id: 2b0.1c80 Suspend: 0 Teb: 00000031`4d19c000 Unfrozen
 # Child-SP          RetAddr           Call Site
00 00000031`4d2ffad8 00007ffe`fb078ba3 ntdll!NtWaitForSingleObject+0x14
*** WARNING: Unable to verify checksum for AppN.exe
01 00000031`4d2ffae0 00007ff7`5e9934c3 KERNELBASE!WaitForSingleObjectEx+0x93
02 00000031`4d2ffb80 00007ff7`5e99124f AppN+0x34c3
03 00000031`4d2ffbb0 00007ff7`5e9913f3 AppN+0x124f
04 00000031`4d2ffc10 00007ff7`5e993ef8 AppN+0x13f3
05 00000031`4d2ffc80 00007ffe`fbce7bd4 AppN+0x3ef8
06 00000031`4d2ffcc0 00007ffe`fd2acee1 kernel32!BaseThreadInitThunk+0x14
07 00000031`4d2ffcf0 00000000`00000000 ntdll!RtlUserThreadStart+0x21

   1  Id: 2b0.2ab0 Suspend: 0 Teb: 00000031`4d19e000 Unfrozen
 # Child-SP          RetAddr           Call Site
00 00000031`4d3ff468 00007ffe`fd247619 ntdll!NtWaitForAlertByThreadId+0x14
01 00000031`4d3ff470 00007ffe`fd2474d2 ntdll!RtlpWaitOnAddressWithTimeout+0x81
02 00000031`4d3ff4a0 00007ffe`fd2472fd ntdll!RtlpWaitOnAddress+0xae
03 00000031`4d3ff510 00007ffe`fd25b5f6 ntdll!RtlpWaitOnCriticalSection+0xfd
04 00000031`4d3ff5f0 00007ffe`fd25b440 ntdll!RtlpEnterCriticalSectionContended+0x1a6
05 00000031`4d3ff650 00007ff7`5e9912f1 ntdll!RtlEnterCriticalSection+0x40
06 00000031`4d3ff680 00007ff7`5e991d75 AppN+0x12f1
07 00000031`4d3ff6d0 00007ff7`5e991c8b AppN+0x1d75
08 00000031`4d3ff700 00007ff7`5e991904 AppN+0x1c8b
09 00000031`4d3ff730 00007ff7`5e999ae8 AppN+0x1904
0a 00000031`4d3ff780 00007ffe`fbce7bd4 AppN+0x9ae8
0b 00000031`4d3ff7b0 00007ffe`fd2acee1 kernel32!BaseThreadInitThunk+0x14
0c 00000031`4d3ff7e0 00000000`00000000 ntdll!RtlUserThreadStart+0x21

   2  Id: 2b0.257c Suspend: 0 Teb: 00000031`4d1a4000 Unfrozen
 # Child-SP          RetAddr           Call Site
00 00000031`4d6ff668 00007ffe`fd247619 ntdll!NtWaitForAlertByThreadId+0x14
01 00000031`4d6ff670 00007ffe`fd2474d2 ntdll!RtlpWaitOnAddressWithTimeout+0x81
02 00000031`4d6ff6a0 00007ffe`fd2472fd ntdll!RtlpWaitOnAddress+0xae
03 00000031`4d6ff710 00007ffe`fd25b5f6 ntdll!RtlpWaitOnCriticalSection+0xfd
04 00000031`4d6ff7f0 00007ffe`fd25b440 ntdll!RtlpEnterCriticalSectionContended+0x1a6
05 00000031`4d6ff850 00007ff7`5e99132e ntdll!RtlEnterCriticalSection+0x40
06 00000031`4d6ff880 00007ff7`5e991d75 AppN+0x132e
07 00000031`4d6ff8c0 00007ff7`5e991c8b AppN+0x1d75
08 00000031`4d6ff8f0 00007ff7`5e991904 AppN+0x1c8b
09 00000031`4d6ff920 00007ff7`5e999ae8 AppN+0x1904
0a 00000031`4d6ff970 00007ffe`fbce7bd4 AppN+0x9ae8
0b 00000031`4d6ff9a0 00007ffe`fd2acee1 kernel32!BaseThreadInitThunk+0x14
0c 00000031`4d6ff9d0 00000000`00000000 ntdll!RtlUserThreadStart+0x21

   3  Id: 2b0.1c10 Suspend: 0 Teb: 00000031`4d1a6000 Unfrozen
 # Child-SP          RetAddr           Call Site
00 00000031`4d4ff9f8 00007ffe`fd274060 ntdll!NtWaitForWorkViaWorkerFactory+0x14
01 00000031`4d4ffa00 00007ffe`fbce7bd4 ntdll!TppWorkerThread+0x300
02 00000031`4d4ffdc0 00007ffe`fd2acee1 kernel32!BaseThreadInitThunk+0x14
03 00000031`4d4ffdf0 00000000`00000000 ntdll!RtlUserThreadStart+0x21
```

Note: We see that threads #1 and #2 tried to enter a critical section and were waiting for its availability. So we suspect a critical section deadlock where both threads are waiting for each other.

6.   Let's see what the **!analyze -v -hang** command tells us:

```
0:000> !analyze -v -hang
*******************************************************************************
*                                                                             *
*                        Exception Analysis                                   *
*                                                                             *
*******************************************************************************

KEY_VALUES_STRING: 1

    Key  : Analysis.CPU.mSec
    Value: 562

    Key  : Analysis.DebugAnalysisManager
    Value: Create

    Key  : Analysis.Elapsed.mSec
    Value: 552

    Key  : Analysis.Init.CPU.mSec
    Value: 1374

    Key  : Analysis.Init.Elapsed.mSec
    Value: 330375

    Key  : Analysis.Memory.CommitPeak.Mb
    Value: 233

    Key  : Timeline.OS.Boot.DeltaSec
    Value: 2448

    Key  : Timeline.Process.Start.DeltaSec
    Value: 378

    Key  : WER.OS.Branch
    Value: 19h1_release

    Key  : WER.OS.Timestamp
    Value: 2019-03-18T12:02:00Z

    Key  : WER.OS.Version
    Value: 10.0.18362.1

    Key  : WER.Process.Version
    Value: 2.0.0.1


FILE_IN_CAB:  AppN.DMP

NTGLOBALFLAG:  0

PROCESS_BAM_CURRENT_THROTTLED:  0

PROCESS_BAM_PREVIOUS_THROTTLED:  0

APPLICATION_VERIFIER_FLAGS:  0

CONTEXT:  (.cxr;r)
rax=0000000000000004 rbx=0000000000000000 rcx=00000000000000a8
rdx=0000000000000000 rsi=0000000000000000 rdi=00000000000000a8
rip=00007ffefd2dc154 rsp=000000314d2ffad8 rbp=0000000000000000
 r8=000000314d2ff598  r9=0000000000000000 r10=0000000000000000
r11=0000000000000246 r12=0000000000000000 r13=0000000000000000
r14=00000000000000a8 r15=0000000000000000
iopl=0         nv up ei pl zr na po nc
cs=0033  ss=002b  ds=002b  es=002b  fs=0053  gs=002b             efl=00000246
ntdll!NtWaitForSingleObject+0x14:
00007ffe`fd2dc154 c3              ret

EXCEPTION_RECORD:  (.exr -1)
ExceptionAddress: 0000000000000000
   ExceptionCode: 80000003 (Break instruction exception)
  ExceptionFlags: 00000000
NumberParameters: 0

FAULTING_THREAD:  00001c80

PROCESS_NAME:  AppN.exe

WATSON_BKT_EVENT:  AppHang

BLOCKING_THREAD:  0000000000001c80

ERROR_CODE: (NTSTATUS) 0xcfffffff - <Unable to get error code text>

EXCEPTION_CODE_STR:  cfffffff

DERIVED_WAIT_CHAIN:

Dl Eid Cid    WaitType
```

142

```
-- --- ------ ------------------------
  0   2b0.1c80 (null)

WAIT_CHAIN_COMMAND:  ~0s;k;;

STACK_TEXT:
00000031`4d2ffad8 00007ffe`fb078ba3 : 0000048f`23e75532 00000000`00000000 00000000`00000000 00000000`00000000 : ntdll!NtWaitForSingleObject+0x14
00000031`4d2ffae0 00007ff7`5e9934c3 : 00000000`00000000 000001ef`8ceb5870 00000000`00000000 00000000`000000a8 : KERNELBASE!WaitForSingleObjectEx+0x93
00000031`4d2ffb80 00007ff7`5e99124f : 00000031`4d2ffc58 000001ef`8ceb1930 00000000`0000257c 00007ff7`5e9914dd : AppN+0x34c3
00000031`4d2ffbb0 00007ff7`5e9913f3 : 00000031`4d2ffc58 00007ff7`5e991310 00000000`0002625a 01d59286`09e07b9f : AppN+0x124f
00000031`4d2ffc10 00007ff7`5e993ef8 : 00000000`00000001 000001ef`8ceb1930 00000000`00000000 00000000`00000000 : AppN+0x13f3
00000031`4d2ffc80 00007ffe`fbce7bd4 : 00000000`00000000 00000000`00000000 00000000`00000000 00000000`00000000 : AppN+0x3ef8
00000031`4d2ffcc0 00007ffe`fd2acee1 : 00000000`00000000 00000000`00000000 00000000`00000000 00000000`00000000 : kernel32!BaseThreadInitThunk+0x14
00000031`4d2ffcf0 00000000`00000000 : 00000000`00000000 00000000`00000000 00000000`00000000 00000000`00000000 : ntdll!RtlUserThreadStart+0x21


STACK_COMMAND:  ~0s ; .cxr ; kb

SYMBOL_NAME:  appn+0x34c3

MODULE_NAME:  AppN

IMAGE_NAME:  AppN.exe

FAILURE_BUCKET_ID:  APPLICATION_HANG_cfffffff_AppN.exe+0x34c3

OS_VERSION:  10.0.18362.1

BUILDLAB_STR:  19h1_release

OSPLATFORM_TYPE:  x64

OSNAME:  Windows 10

IMAGE_VERSION:  2.0.0.1

FAILURE_ID_HASH:  {d80fb71d-1fd2-3183-d980-2d16966e459c}

Followup:   MachineOwner
---------
```

Note: We see that WinDbg wasn't able to recognize the possible problem with critical sections in this manual dump. It detects that the application was hung but shows the first thread stack trace. So let's explore other threads.

7.   When a thread enters a critical section, it becomes "locked." We can get a list of all locked critical sections by using the **!cs -l -o -s** command:

```
0:000> !cs -l -o -s
---------------------------------------
DebugInfo          = 0x00007ffefd3a3e00
Critical section   = 0x00007ff75e9b26d8 (AppN+0x226D8)
LOCKED
LockCount          = 0x1
WaiterWoken        = No
OwningThread       = 0x0000000000002ab0
RecursionCount     = 0x1
LockSemaphore      = 0xFFFFFFFF
SpinCount          = 0x00000000020007d0
OwningThread DbgId = ~1s
OwningThread Stack =
         Child-SP          RetAddr           : Args to Child                                                              : Call Site
         00000031`4d3ff468 00007ffe`fd247619 : 00000031`4d3ff4f0 00000031`4d3ff498 00000000`00000000 00007ff7`5e99cebe : ntdll!NtWaitForAlertByThreadId+0x14
         00000031`4d3ff470 00007ffe`fd2474d2 : 00000000`00000000 00000000`00000000 00000000`00000000 00000031`4d3ff558 00007ff7`5e9b2708 :
ntdll!RtlpWaitOnAddressWithTimeout+0x81
         00000031`4d3ff4a0 00007ffe`fd2472fd : 00007ff7`5e9b2700 00000000`00001722 00000000`00000000 000001e2`d2cc5734 : ntdll!RtlpWaitOnAddress+0xae
         00000031`4d3ff510 00007ffe`fd25b5f6 : 00000031`4d3ff608 00007ff7`5e991781 00000000`fffffffa 000001e2`d2cc5734 :
ntdll!RtlpWaitOnCriticalSection+0xfd
         00000031`4d3ff5f0 00007ffe`fd25b440 : 00000031`4d3ff6b0 00000031`4d3ff700 000001ef`8ceac170 000001e2`d124d0f0 :
ntdll!RtlpEnterCriticalSectionContended+0x1a6
         00000031`4d3ff650 00007ff7`5e9912f1 : 00000031`4d3ff6b0 00000031`4d3ff6a0 ffffffff`ffffffff 00000000`00000002 : ntdll!RtlEnterCriticalSection+0x40
         00000031`4d3ff680 00007ff7`5e991d75 : 000001ef`8ceb3150 00000000`00000000 00000000`00000000 00007ff7`5e991c65 : AppN+0x12f1
         00000031`4d3ff6d0 00007ff7`5e991c8b : 000001ef`8ceb3150 00000000`00000000 00000000`00000000 00007ffe`fb0b62d5 : AppN+0x1d75
         00000031`4d3ff700 00007ff7`5e991904 : 000001ef`8ceb3150 000001ef`8ceb3150 00000000`00000001 00007ff7`5e99cebe : AppN+0x1c8b
         00000031`4d3ff730 00007ff7`5e999ae8 : 000001ef`8ceb3150 00000000`00000000 00000000`00000000 00000000`00000000 : AppN+0x1904
         00000031`4d3ff780 00007ffe`fbce7bd4 : 00000000`00000000 00000000`00000000 00000000`00000000 00000000`00000000 : AppN+0x9ae8
         00000031`4d3ff7b0 00007ffe`fd2acee1 : 00000000`00000000 00000000`00000000 00000000`00000000 00000000`00000000 : kernel32!BaseThreadInitThunk+0x14
         00000031`4d3ff7e0 00000000`00000000 : 00000000`00000000 00000000`00000000 00000000`00000000 00000000`00000000 : ntdll!RtlUserThreadStart+0x21
ntdll!RtlpStackTraceDataBase is NULL. Probably the stack traces are not enabled.
---------------------------------------
DebugInfo          = 0x00007ffefd3a3e30
Critical section   = 0x00007ff75e9b2700 (AppN+0x22700)
LOCKED
LockCount          = 0x1
WaiterWoken        = No
OwningThread       = 0x000000000000257c
RecursionCount     = 0x1
LockSemaphore      = 0xFFFFFFFF
SpinCount          = 0x00000000020007d0
OwningThread DbgId = ~2s
OwningThread Stack =
         Child-SP          RetAddr           : Args to Child                                                              : Call Site
         00000031`4d6ff668 00007ffe`fd247619 : 00000000`00000001 00000000`00000008 00000000`0000007c 000001ef`8ceb6800 : ntdll!NtWaitForAlertByThreadId+0x14
```

143

```
        00000031`4d6ff670 00007ffe`fd2474d2 : 00000000`00000000 00000000`00000000 00000031`4d6ff758 00007ff7`5e9b26e0 :
ntdll!RtlpWaitOnAddressWithTimeout+0x81
        00000031`4d6ff6a0 00007ffe`fd2472fd : 00007ff7`5e9b26d8 00000000`00001722 00000000`00000000 00000000`00000000 : ntdll!RtlpWaitOnAddress+0xae
        00000031`4d6ff710 00007ffe`fd25b5f6 : 000001ef`8cea0000 00007ffe`fd27babb 00000000`fffffffa 00000000`0000000a :
ntdll!RtlpWaitOnCriticalSection+0xfd
        00000031`4d6ff7f0 00007ffe`fd25b440 : 00000000`00000000 00000000`00000000 000001ef`8ceb6060 00000000`00000000 :
ntdll!RtlpEnterCriticalSectionContended+0x1a6
        00000031`4d6ff850 00007ff7`5e99132e : 00000000`00000000 00000000`00000000 00000000`00000000 00000000`00000000 : ntdll!RtlEnterCriticalSection+0x40
        00000031`4d6ff880 00007ff7`5e991d75 : 000001ef`8ceb5870 00000000`00000000 000001ef`8ceb6810 00007ff7`5e991c65 : AppN+0x132e
        00000031`4d6ff8c0 00007ff7`5e991c8b : 000001ef`8ceb5870 00000000`00000031`4d6ff900 00000004`00000004 000001ef`8ceb6810 : AppN+0x1d75
        00000031`4d6ff8f0 00007ff7`5e991904 : 000001ef`8ceb5870 000001ef`8ceb5870 00000000`00000000 00007ff7`5e99c597 : AppN+0x1c8b
        00000031`4d6ff920 00007ff7`5e999ae8 : 000001ef`8ceb5870 00000000`00000000 00000000`00000000 00000000`00000000 : AppN+0x1904
        00000031`4d6ff970 00007ffe`fbce7bd4 : 00000000`00000000 00000000`00000000 00000000`00000000 00000000`00000000 : AppN+0x9ae8
        00000031`4d6ff9a0 00007ffe`fd2acee1 : 00000000`00000000 00000000`00000000 00000000`00000000 00000000`00000000 : kernel32!BaseThreadInitThunk+0x14
        00000031`4d6ff9d0 00000000`00000000 : 00000000`00000000 00000000`00000000 00000000`00000000 00000000`00000000 : ntdll!RtlUserThreadStart+0x21
ntdll!RtlpStackTraceDataBase is NULL. Probably the stack traces are not enabled.
```

Note: Concise summary of the command output: thread #1 owns (entered successfully and locked it) the critical section (CS) 0x00007ff75e9b26d8 (CS1), and thread #2 owns CS 0x00007ff75e9b2700 (CS2). If we see that thread #1 tried to enter CS2 and simultaneously thread #2 tried to enter CS1, then we prove a deadlock.

8.   Let's see which critical section thread #1 was trying to enter:

```
0:000> ~1s
ntdll!NtWaitForAlertByThreadId+0x14:
00007ffe`fd2dfa04 c3              ret

0:001> k
 # Child-SP          RetAddr           Call Site
00 00000031`4d3ff468 00007ffe`fd247619 ntdll!NtWaitForAlertByThreadId+0x14
01 00000031`4d3ff470 00007ffe`fd2474d2 ntdll!RtlpWaitOnAddressWithTimeout+0x81
02 00000031`4d3ff4a0 00007ffe`fd2472fd ntdll!RtlpWaitOnAddress+0xae
03 00000031`4d3ff510 00007ffe`fd25b5f6 ntdll!RtlpWaitOnCriticalSection+0xfd
04 00000031`4d3ff5f0 00007ffe`fd25b440 ntdll!RtlpEnterCriticalSectionContended+0x1a6
05 00000031`4d3ff650 00007ff7`5e9912f1 ntdll!RtlEnterCriticalSection+0x40
06 00000031`4d3ff680 00007ff7`5e991d75 AppN+0x12f1
07 00000031`4d3ff6d0 00007ff7`5e991c8b AppN+0x1d75
08 00000031`4d3ff700 00007ff7`5e991904 AppN+0x1c8b
09 00000031`4d3ff730 00007ff7`5e999ae8 AppN+0x1904
0a 00000031`4d3ff780 00007ffe`fbce7bd4 AppN+0x9ae8
0b 00000031`4d3ff7b0 00007ffe`fd2acee1 kernel32!BaseThreadInitThunk+0x14
0c 00000031`4d3ff7e0 00000000`00000000 ntdll!RtlUserThreadStart+0x21

0:001> ub 00007ff7`5e9912f1
AppN+0x12c5:
00007ff7`5e9912c5 c744242002000000 mov     dword ptr [rsp+20h],2
00007ff7`5e9912cd 488d542420       lea     rdx,[rsp+20h]
00007ff7`5e9912d2 488d4c2430       lea     rcx,[rsp+30h]
00007ff7`5e9912d7 e8b4010000       call    AppN+0x1490 (00007ff7`5e991490)
00007ff7`5e9912dc 488bc8           mov     rcx,rax
00007ff7`5e9912df e8cc010000       call    AppN+0x14b0 (00007ff7`5e9914b0)
00007ff7`5e9912e4 488d0d15140200   lea     rcx,[AppN+0x22700 (00007ff7`5e9b2700)]
00007ff7`5e9912eb ff150f2d0100     call    qword ptr [AppN+0x14000 (00007ff7`5e9a4000)]

0:001> dps 00007ff7`5e9a4000 L1
00007ff7`5e9a4000  00007ffe`fd25b400 ntdll!RtlEnterCriticalSection
```

Note: The trick here (for x64 code) is to check what parameter was passed to the *RtlEnterCriticalSection* function by unassembling the return address. If we see the pattern above (*rcx, call*) we get 00007ff7`5e9b2700 which is CS2. On x64 Windows platforms RCX register is used to pass the first function parameter. Please don't forget to remove or add ` from address when searching: 64-bit addresses have the form 00007ff75e9b2700 or 00007ff7`5e9b2700 in the command output.

9.   Let's see which critical section thread #2 was trying to enter:

```
0:001> ~2s
ntdll!NtWaitForAlertByThreadId+0x14:
00007ffe`fd2dfa04 c3              ret


0:002> k
 # Child-SP          RetAddr           Call Site
00 00000031`4d6ff668 00007ffe`fd247619 ntdll!NtWaitForAlertByThreadId+0x14
01 00000031`4d6ff670 00007ffe`fd2474d2 ntdll!RtlpWaitOnAddressWithTimeout+0x81
02 00000031`4d6ff6a0 00007ffe`fd2472fd ntdll!RtlpWaitOnAddress+0xae
03 00000031`4d6ff710 00007ffe`fd25b5f6 ntdll!RtlpWaitOnCriticalSection+0xfd
04 00000031`4d6ff7f0 00007ffe`fd25b440 ntdll!RtlpEnterCriticalSectionContended+0x1a6
05 00000031`4d6ff850 00007ff7`5e99132e ntdll!RtlEnterCriticalSection+0x40
06 00000031`4d6ff880 00007ff7`5e991d75 AppN+0x132e
07 00000031`4d6ff8c0 00007ff7`5e991c8b AppN+0x1d75
08 00000031`4d6ff8f0 00007ff7`5e991904 AppN+0x1c8b
09 00000031`4d6ff920 00007ff7`5e999ae8 AppN+0x1904
0a 00000031`4d6ff970 00007ffe`fbce7bd4 AppN+0x9ae8
0b 00000031`4d6ff9a0 00007ffe`fd2acee1 kernel32!BaseThreadInitThunk+0x14
0c 00000031`4d6ff9d0 00000000`00000000 ntdll!RtlUserThreadStart+0x21


0:002> ub 00007ff7`5e99132e
AppN+0x130d:
00007ff7`5e99130d cc              int     3
00007ff7`5e99130e cc              int     3
00007ff7`5e99130f cc              int     3
00007ff7`5e991310 4883ec38        sub     rsp,38h
00007ff7`5e991314 488d0de5130200  lea     rcx,[AppN+0x22700 (00007ff7`5e9b2700)]
00007ff7`5e99131b ff15df2c0100    call    qword ptr [AppN+0x14000 (00007ff7`5e9a4000)]
00007ff7`5e991321 488d0ddb130200  lea     rcx,[AppN+0x226d8 (00007ff7`5e9b26d8)]
00007ff7`5e991328 ff15d22c0100    call    qword ptr [AppN+0x14000 (00007ff7`5e9a4000)]


0:002> dps 00007ff7`5e9a4000 L1
00007ff7`5e9a4000  00007ffe`fd25b400 ntdll!RtlEnterCriticalSection
```

Note: When we check with the output, we see that 00007ff7`5e9b26d8 is CS1. So we see that T1 owned CS1 but tried to enter CS2. T2 owned CS2 but tried to enter CS1.

10.   Have we found a root cause already? Perhaps there was a hidden exception that *AppN* was able to catch, process, and dismiss itself. However, such exceptions can lead to accumulated corruption and application hangs. In order to find any hidden exceptions, we search for exception processing signs in raw stack data. The general procedure is outlined here:

   a.   Get stack region bounds (**!teb** command);
   b.   Dump all memory between bounds and show possible symbols (**dps *<StackLimit> <StackBase>*** command);
   c.   Search for exception processing functions;
   d.   Try to change the exception context based on values below exception processing function symbols.

```
0:002> ~1s
ntdll!NtWaitForAlertByThreadId+0x14:
00007ffe`fd2dfa04 c3              ret
```

```
0:001> !teb
TEB at 000000314d19e000
    ExceptionList:          0000000000000000
    StackBase:              000000314d400000
    StackLimit:             000000314d3fc000
    SubSystemTib:           0000000000000000
    FiberData:              0000000000001e00
    ArbitraryUserPointer:   0000000000000000
    Self:                   000000314d19e000
    EnvironmentPointer:     0000000000000000
    ClientId:               00000000000002b0 . 0000000000002ab0
    RpcHandle:              0000000000000000
    Tls Storage:            000001ef8ceb45b0
    PEB Address:            000000314d19b000
    LastErrorValue:         187
    LastStatusValue:        c000000d
    Count Owned Locks:      0
    HardErrorMode:          0

0:001> dps 000000314d3fc000 000000314d400000
00000031`4d3fc000  00000000`00000000
00000031`4d3fc008  00000000`00000000
00000031`4d3fc010  00000000`00000000
00000031`4d3fc018  00000000`00000000
00000031`4d3fc020  00000000`00000000
00000031`4d3fc028  00000000`00000000
00000031`4d3fc030  00000000`00000000
00000031`4d3fc038  00000000`00000000
00000031`4d3fc040  00000000`00000000
00000031`4d3fc048  00000000`00000000
00000031`4d3fc050  00000000`00000000
00000031`4d3fc058  00000000`00000000
00000031`4d3fc060  00000000`00000000
00000031`4d3fc068  00000000`00000000
00000031`4d3fc070  00000000`00000000
00000031`4d3fc078  00000000`00000000
00000031`4d3fc080  00000000`00000000
00000031`4d3fc088  00000000`00000000
00000031`4d3fc090  00000000`00000000
[...]
00000031`4d3feee8  00000000`00000000
00000031`4d3feef0  00000000`00000000
00000031`4d3feef8  00007ffe`fd2dfe7e ntdll!KiUserExceptionDispatch+0x2e
00000031`4d3fef00  000001ef`00000001
00000031`4d3fef08  00000031`00001f80
00000031`4d3fef10  000001ef`8ceac170
00000031`4d3fef18  00000000`00000000
00000031`4d3fef20  00000000`00000000
00000031`4d3fef28  00000000`00000004
00000031`4d3fef30  00001f80`0010005f
00000031`4d3fef38  0053002b`002b0033
00000031`4d3fef40  00010206`002b002b
00000031`4d3fef48  00000000`00000000
00000031`4d3fef50  00000000`00000000
00000031`4d3fef58  00000000`00000000
00000031`4d3fef60  00000000`00000000
00000031`4d3fef68  00000000`00000000
00000031`4d3fef70  00000000`00000000
00000031`4d3fef78  00000000`00000000
00000031`4d3fef80  00007ff7`5e9b26d8 AppN+0x226d8
```

```
00000031`4d3fef88    00000000`00000000
00000031`4d3fef90    000001ef`8ceac170
00000031`4d3fef98    00000031`4d3ff680
00000031`4d3fefa0    00000000`00000000
00000031`4d3fefa8    00000000`00000000
[...]
00000031`4d3fffc8    00000000`00000000
00000031`4d3fffd0    00000000`00000000
00000031`4d3fffd8    00000000`00000000
00000031`4d3fffe0    00000000`00000000
00000031`4d3fffe8    00000000`00000000
00000031`4d3ffff0    00000000`00000000
00000031`4d3ffff8    00000000`00000000
00000031`4d400000    ????????`????????

0:001> .cxr 00000031`4d3fef00
rax=0000000000000000 rbx=000001ef8ceac170 rcx=00007ff75e9b26d8
rdx=0000000000000000 rsi=0000000000000000 rdi=0000000000000000
rip=00007ff75e9912af rsp=000000314d3ff680 rbp=0000000000000000
 r8=000000314d3ff738  r9=0000000000000002 r10=0000000000000000
r11=0000000000000246 r12=0000000000000000 r13=0000000000000000
r14=0000000000000000 r15=0000000000000000
iopl=0         nv up ei pl nz na po nc
cs=0033  ss=002b  ds=002b  es=002b  fs=0053  gs=002b            efl=00010206
AppN+0x12af:
00007ff7`5e9912af c70000000000    mov     dword ptr [rax],0 ds:00000000`00000000=????????

0:001> k
 *** Stack trace for last set context - .thread/.cxr resets it
 # Child-SP          RetAddr           Call Site
00 00000031`4d3ff680 00007ff7`5e991d75 AppN+0x12af
01 00000031`4d3ff6d0 00007ff7`5e991c8b AppN+0x1d75
02 00000031`4d3ff700 00007ff7`5e991904 AppN+0x1c8b
03 00000031`4d3ff730 00007ff7`5e999ae8 AppN+0x1904
04 00000031`4d3ff780 00007ffe`fbce7bd4 AppN+0x9ae8
05 00000031`4d3ff7b0 00007ffe`fd2acee1 kernel32!BaseThreadInitThunk+0x14
06 00000031`4d3ff7e0 00000000`00000000 ntdll!RtlUserThreadStart+0x21
```

Note: We see that *AppN* had a NULL pointer access violation. Perhaps it was crashing previously, and in the new version, a developer added a bit of code to mask that annoyance.

11.   We close logging before exiting WinDbg:

```
0:001> .logclose
Closing open log file C:\AWMDA-Dumps\Process\x64\AppN.log
```

Deadlock

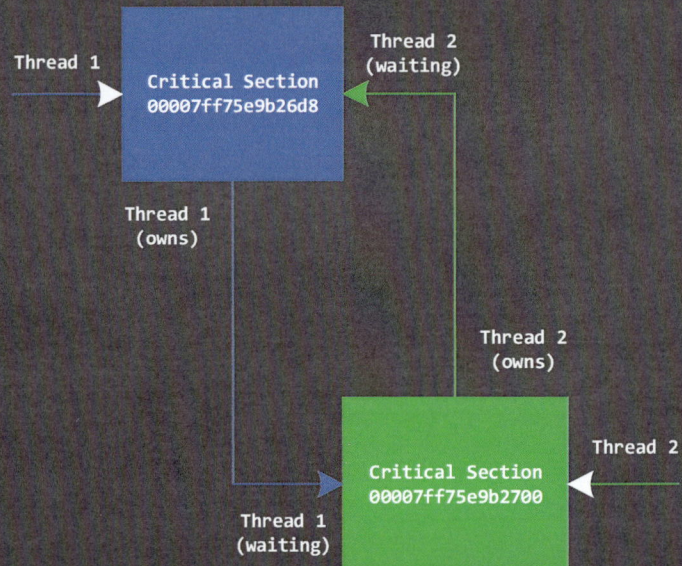

This diagram depicts the critical section deadlock from Exercise P9.

Exercise P10

- **Goal:** Learn how to recognize application heap problems, buffer and stack overflow patterns, and analyze raw stack data

- **Patterns:** Double Free (Process Heap); Local Buffer Overflow (User Space); Stack Overflow (User Mode)

- \AWMDA-Dumps\Exercise-P10-Analysis-process-dump-AppO-64.pdf

Exercise P10: Analysis of an application process dump (AppO, 64-bit)

Goal: Learn how to recognize application heap problems, buffer and stack overflow patterns, and analyze raw stack data.

Patterns: Double Free (Process Heap); Local Buffer Overflow (User Space); Stack Overflow (User Mode).

1.   Launch WinDbg.

2.   Open \AWMDA-Dumps\Process\x64\AppO.exe.7392.dmp.

3.   We get the dump file loaded:

```
Microsoft (R) Windows Debugger Version 10.0.25877.1004 AMD64
Copyright (c) Microsoft Corporation. All rights reserved.


Loading Dump File [C:\AWMDA-Dumps\Process\x64\AppO.exe.7392.dmp]
User Mini Dump File with Full Memory: Only application data is available


************* Path validation summary **************
Response                      Time (ms)      Location
Deferred                                     srv*
Symbol search path is: srv*
Executable search path is:
Windows 10 Version 18362 MP (2 procs) Free x64
Product: WinNt, suite: SingleUserTS Personal
Edition build lab: 18362.1.amd64fre.19h1_release.190318-1202
Machine Name:
Debug session time: Mon Nov 11 23:18:53.000 2019 (UTC + 1:00)
System Uptime: 0 days 0:40:46.237
Process Uptime: 0 days 0:00:02.000
........
```
```
This dump file has an exception of interest stored in it.
The stored exception information can be accessed via .ecxr.
(1ce0.628): Stack overflow - code c00000fd (first/second chance not available)
```
```
For analysis of this file, run !analyze -v
*** WARNING: Unable to verify checksum for AppO.exe
AppO+0x140b:
00007ff7`2cac140b e8e0ffffff      call    AppO+0x13f0 (00007ff7`2cac13f0)
```

4.   Open a log file using **.logopen** command:

```
0:003> .logopen C:\AWMDA-Dumps\Process\x64\AppO.log
Opened log file 'C:\AWMDA-Dumps\Process\x64\AppO.log'
```

Note: In this exercise, we don't load *AppO* symbols because we want to model a 3rd party application crash where we don't have access to symbol files. However, source code and PDB exist in the usual locations, so that you can try with a symbol file as a homework exercise.

5.   Type the ~*k command to verify the correctness of all stack traces (the output for thread #3 was truncated for visual clarity):

```
0:003> ~*k

   0  Id: 1ce0.2ba8 Suspend: 1 Teb: 00000024`1fbde000 Unfrozen
 # Child-SP          RetAddr               Call Site
00 00000024`1f9ef908 00007fff`ce6a8ba3 ntdll!NtWaitForSingleObject+0x14
01 00000024`1f9ef910 00007ff7`2cac3323 KERNELBASE!WaitForSingleObjectEx+0x93
02 00000024`1f9ef9b0 00007ff7`2cac13af App0+0x3323
03 00000024`1f9ef9e0 00007ff7`2cac15ad App0+0x13af
04 00000024`1f9efa40 00007ff7`2cac3d28 App0+0x15ad
05 00000024`1f9efab0 00007fff`cf787bd4 App0+0x3d28
06 00000024`1f9efaf0 00007fff`d0aacee1 kernel32!BaseThreadInitThunk+0x14
07 00000024`1f9efb20 00000000`00000000 ntdll!RtlUserThreadStart+0x21

   1  Id: 1ce0.28b4 Suspend: 1 Teb: 00000024`1fbe0000 Unfrozen
 # Child-SP          RetAddr               Call Site
00 00000024`1fcfe398 00007fff`d0b1cd25 ntdll!NtSetInformationProcess+0x14
01 00000024`1fcfe3a0 00007fff`d0b1c13f ntdll!WerpSetProcessFaultInformation+0x31
02 00000024`1fcfe3d0 00007fff`d0b1bbcb ntdll!RtlReportExceptionHelper+0x6f
03 00000024`1fcfe4a0 00007fff`d0b392a3 ntdll!RtlReportException+0x9b
04 00000024`1fcfe520 00007fff`d0acc6e6 ntdll!RtlReportFatalFailure$filt$0+0x33
05 00000024`1fcfe550 00007fff`d0ae120f ntdll!_C_specific_handler+0x96
06 00000024`1fcfe5c0 00007fff`d0aaa299 ntdll!RtlpExecuteHandlerForException+0xf
07 00000024`1fcfe5f0 00007fff`d0aaa053 ntdll!RtlDispatchException+0x219
08 00000024`1fcfed00 00007fff`d0b39269 ntdll!RtlRaiseException+0x153
09 00000024`1fcff570 00007fff`d0b39233 ntdll!RtlReportFatalFailure+0x9
0a 00000024`1fcff5c0 00007fff`d0b41622 ntdll!RtlReportCriticalFailure+0x97
0b 00000024`1fcff6b0 00007fff`d0b4192a ntdll!RtlpHeapHandleError+0x12
0c 00000024`1fcff6e0 00007fff`d0b4a8e9 ntdll!RtlpHpHeapHandleError+0x7a
0d 00000024`1fcff710 00007fff`d0a8088d ntdll!RtlpLogHeapFailure+0x45
0e 00000024`1fcff740 00007fff`d0a7fc11 ntdll!RtlpFreeHeapInternal+0x80d
0f 00000024`1fcff7f0 00007ff7`2cacbfb8 ntdll!RtlFreeHeap+0x51
10 00000024`1fcff830 00007ff7`2cac155b App0+0xbfb8
11 00000024`1fcff860 00007ff7`2cac1d15 App0+0x155b
12 00000024`1fcff8b0 00007ff7`2cac1a8b App0+0x1d15
13 00000024`1fcff8e0 00007ff7`2cac18e5 App0+0x1a8b
14 00000024`1fcff910 00007ff7`2cac9958 App0+0x18e5
15 00000024`1fcff960 00007fff`cf787bd4 App0+0x9958
16 00000024`1fcff990 00007fff`d0aacee1 kernel32!BaseThreadInitThunk+0x14
17 00000024`1fcff9c0 00000000`00000000 ntdll!RtlUserThreadStart+0x21

   2  Id: 1ce0.188c Suspend: 1 Teb: 00000024`1fbe2000 Unfrozen
 # Child-SP          RetAddr               Call Site
00 00000024`1fdfdd08 00007fff`d0b1c851 ntdll!NtOpenEvent+0x14
01 00000024`1fdfdd10 00007fff`d0b1c5c0 ntdll!WaitForWerSvc+0x59
02 00000024`1fdfdd80 00007fff`d0b1bad7 ntdll!SendMessageToWERService+0x84
03 00000024`1fdfdee0 00007fff`cf7d70af ntdll!ReportExceptionInternal+0xe3
04 00000024`1fdfea50 00007fff`cf7d6ca8 kernel32!WerpReportFaultInternal+0x3cf
05 00000024`1fdfeb70 00007fff`ce76f988 kernel32!WerpReportFault+0xac
06 00000024`1fdfebb0 00007fff`d0ae4af2 KERNELBASE!UnhandledExceptionFilter+0x3b8
07 00000024`1fdfecd0 00007fff`d0acc6e6 ntdll!RtlUserThreadStart$filt$0+0xa2
08 00000024`1fdfed10 00007fff`d0ae120f ntdll!_C_specific_handler+0x96
09 00000024`1fdfed80 00007fff`d0aaa299 ntdll!RtlpExecuteHandlerForException+0xf
0a 00000024`1fdfedb0 00007fff`d0adfe7e ntdll!RtlDispatchException+0x219
0b 00000024`1fdff4c0 00007ff7`2cac14cb ntdll!KiUserExceptionDispatch+0x2e
0c 00000024`1fdffc48 43206f6c`6c654820 App0+0x14cb
0d 00000024`1fdffc50 65482021`68736172 0x43206f6c`6c654820
```

```
0e 00000024`1fdffc58 73617243`206f6c6c 0x65482021`68736172
0f 00000024`1fdffc60 00000000`00002168 0x73617243`206f6c6c
10 00000024`1fdffc68 00007ff7`2cacc348 0x2168
11 00000024`1fdffc70 00007ff7`2cac1d9c App0+0xc348
12 00000024`1fdffca0 00007ff7`2cac1a65 App0+0x1d9c
13 00000024`1fdffcd0 00007ff7`2cac18e5 App0+0x1a65
14 00000024`1fdffd10 00007ff7`2cac9958 App0+0x18e5
15 00000024`1fdffd60 00007fff`cf787bd4 App0+0x9958
16 00000024`1fdffd90 00007fff`d0aacee1 kernel32!BaseThreadInitThunk+0x14
17 00000024`1fdffdc0 00000000`00000000 ntdll!RtlUserThreadStart+0x21

#  3  Id: 1ce0.628 Suspend: 0 Teb: 00000024`1fbe4000 Unfrozen
 # Child-SP          RetAddr           Call Site
00 00000024`1fe04000 00007ff7`2cac1410 App0+0x140b
01 00000024`1fe04030 00007ff7`2cac1410 App0+0x1410
02 00000024`1fe04060 00007ff7`2cac1410 App0+0x1410
03 00000024`1fe04090 00007ff7`2cac1410 App0+0x1410
04 00000024`1fe040c0 00007ff7`2cac1410 App0+0x1410
05 00000024`1fe040f0 00007ff7`2cac1410 App0+0x1410
06 00000024`1fe04120 00007ff7`2cac1410 App0+0x1410
07 00000024`1fe04150 00007ff7`2cac1410 App0+0x1410
08 00000024`1fe04180 00007ff7`2cac1410 App0+0x1410
09 00000024`1fe041b0 00007ff7`2cac1410 App0+0x1410
0a 00000024`1fe041e0 00007ff7`2cac1410 App0+0x1410
0b 00000024`1fe04210 00007ff7`2cac1410 App0+0x1410
0c 00000024`1fe04240 00007ff7`2cac1410 App0+0x1410
0d 00000024`1fe04270 00007ff7`2cac1410 App0+0x1410
0e 00000024`1fe042a0 00007ff7`2cac1410 App0+0x1410
0f 00000024`1fe042d0 00007ff7`2cac1410 App0+0x1410
10 00000024`1fe04300 00007ff7`2cac1410 App0+0x1410
[...]
e7 00000024`1fe06b50 00007ff7`2cac1410 App0+0x1410
e8 00000024`1fe06b80 00007ff7`2cac1410 App0+0x1410
e9 00000024`1fe06bb0 00007ff7`2cac1410 App0+0x1410
ea 00000024`1fe06be0 00007ff7`2cac1410 App0+0x1410
eb 00000024`1fe06c10 00007ff7`2cac1410 App0+0x1410
ec 00000024`1fe06c40 00007ff7`2cac1410 App0+0x1410
ed 00000024`1fe06c70 00007ff7`2cac1410 App0+0x1410
ee 00000024`1fe06ca0 00007ff7`2cac1410 App0+0x1410
ef 00000024`1fe06cd0 00007ff7`2cac1410 App0+0x1410
f0 00000024`1fe06d00 00007ff7`2cac1410 App0+0x1410
f1 00000024`1fe06d30 00007ff7`2cac1410 App0+0x1410
f2 00000024`1fe06d60 00007ff7`2cac1410 App0+0x1410
f3 00000024`1fe06d90 00007ff7`2cac1410 App0+0x1410
f4 00000024`1fe06dc0 00007ff7`2cac1410 App0+0x1410
f5 00000024`1fe06df0 00007ff7`2cac1410 App0+0x1410
f6 00000024`1fe06e20 00007ff7`2cac1410 App0+0x1410
f7 00000024`1fe06e50 00007ff7`2cac1410 App0+0x1410
f8 00000024`1fe06e80 00007ff7`2cac1410 App0+0x1410
f9 00000024`1fe06eb0 00007ff7`2cac1410 App0+0x1410
fa 00000024`1fe06ee0 00007ff7`2cac1410 App0+0x1410
fb 00000024`1fe06f10 00007ff7`2cac1410 App0+0x1410
fc 00000024`1fe06f40 00007ff7`2cac1410 App0+0x1410
fd 00000024`1fe06f70 00007ff7`2cac1410 App0+0x1410
fe 00000024`1fe06fa0 00007ff7`2cac1410 App0+0x1410
ff 00000024`1fe06fd0 00007ff7`2cac1410 App0+0x1410

 4  Id: 1ce0.2a08 Suspend: 1 Teb: 00000024`1fbe6000 Unfrozen
 # Child-SP          RetAddr           Call Site
00 00000024`1ffffeb8 00000000`00000000 ntdll!RtlUserThreadStart
```

Note: Thread #1 shows a heap failure pattern. It is, in fact, a double free as seen from the output of the heap verification command:

```
0:003> !heap -s -v

********************************************************************************
                          NT HEAP STATS BELOW
********************************************************************************
*************************************************************
*                                                           *
*                  HEAP ERROR DETECTED                      *
*                                                           *
*************************************************************

Details:

Heap address:  000001b7e7070000
Error address: 000001b7e7085250
Error type: HEAP_FAILURE_BLOCK_NOT_BUSY
Details:    The caller performed an operation (such as a free
            or a size check) that is illegal on a free block.
Follow-up:  Check the error's stack trace to find the culprit.


Stack trace:
Stack trace at 0x00007fffd0ba2848
    00007fffd0b4a8e9: ntdll!RtlpLogHeapFailure+0x45
    00007fffd0a8088d: ntdll!RtlpFreeHeapInternal+0x80d
    00007fffd0a7fc11: ntdll!RtlFreeHeap+0x51
    00007ff72cacbfb8: App0+0xbfb8
    00007ff72cac155b: App0+0x155b
    00007ff72cac1d15: App0+0x1d15
    00007ff72cac1a8b: App0+0x1a8b
    00007ff72cac18e5: App0+0x18e5
    00007ff72cac9958: App0+0x9958
    00007fffcf787bd4: kernel32!BaseThreadInitThunk+0x14
    00007fffd0aacee1: ntdll!RtlUserThreadStart+0x21

LFH Key                   : 0x2fb3049446c85c22
Termination on corruption : ENABLED
          Heap     Flags   Reserv  Commit  Virt   Free  List   UCR  Virt  Lock  Fast
                            (k)     (k)     (k)    (k) length      blocks cont. heap
-------------------------------------------------------------------------------------
.000001b7e7070000 00000002   1072    100   1020     2     3     1     0      0  LFH
.000001b7e6f70000 00008000     64      4     64     2     1     1     0      0
.000001b7e7300000 00001002    112     32     60     6     2     1     0      0  LFH
-------------------------------------------------------------------------------------
```

Thread #2 has ASCII-like data across stack trace. We try to make sense of it using the **da** *<address>* command:

```
0:003> ~2s
ntdll!NtOpenEvent+0x14:
00007fff`d0adc8d4 c3              ret

0:002> .frame /c 0c
0c 00000024`1fdffc48 43206f6c`6c654820 App0+0x14cb
rax=0000000000000000 rbx=000001b7e707c320 rcx=0000000000000000
rdx=0000000000000000 rsi=216873617243206f rdi=6c6c654820216873
rip=00007ff72cac14cb rsp=000000241fdffc48 rbp=0000000000000000
```

153

```
        r8=0000000000000000  r9=0000000000000000 r10=0000000000000000
        r11=0000000000000000 r12=0000000000000000 r13=0000000000000000
        r14=0000000000000000 r15=0000000000000000
        iopl=0         nv up ei pl zr na po nc
        cs=0033  ss=002b  ds=002b  es=002b  fs=0053  gs=002b          efl=00000246
        AppO+0x14cb:
        00007ff7`2cac14cb c3              ret
```

```
0:002> k
   *** Stack trace for last set context - .thread/.cxr resets it
 # Child-SP          RetAddr           Call Site
0c 00000024`1fdffc48 43206f6c`6c654820 AppO+0x14cb
0d 00000024`1fdffc50 65482021`68736172 0x43206f6c`6c654820
0e 00000024`1fdffc58 73617243`206f6c6c 0x65482021`68736172
0f 00000024`1fdffc60 00000000`00002168 0x73617243`206f6c6c
10 00000024`1fdffc68 00007ff7`2cacc348 0x2168
11 00000024`1fdffc70 00007ff7`2cac1d9c AppO+0xc348
12 00000024`1fdffca0 00007ff7`2cac1a65 AppO+0x1d9c
13 00000024`1fdffcd0 00007ff7`2cac18e5 AppO+0x1a65
14 00000024`1fdffd10 00007ff7`2cac9958 AppO+0x18e5
15 00000024`1fdffd60 00007fff`cf787bd4 AppO+0x9958
16 00000024`1fdffd90 00007fff`d0aacee1 kernel32!BaseThreadInitThunk+0x14
17 00000024`1fdffdc0 00000000`00000000 ntdll!RtlUserThreadStart+0x21
```

```
0:002> da 00000024`1fdffc50
00000024`1fdffc50  "rash! Hello Crash!"
```

Such ASCII or UNICODE data is usually a sign of famous stack buffer overflows.

Thread #3 has all signs of stack overflow when a function calls itself recursively until it hits stack memory limits and generates an exception.

6.   Let's find the bottom of the stack trace of thread #3 in the raw stack dump (we try to find the repeated pattern of AppO+0x1410 from the end of the output):

```
0:002> ~3s
AppO+0x140b:
00007ff7`2cac140b e8e0ffffff       call    AppO+0x13f0 (00007ff7`2cac13f0)
```

```
0:003> !teb
TEB at 000000241fbe4000
    ExceptionList:        0000000000000000
    StackBase:            000000241ff00000
    StackLimit:           000000241fe01000
    SubSystemTib:         0000000000000000
    FiberData:            0000000000001e00
    ArbitraryUserPointer: 0000000000000000
    Self:                 000000241fbe4000
    EnvironmentPointer:   0000000000000000
    ClientId:             0000000000001ce0 . 0000000000000628
    RpcHandle:            0000000000000000
    Tls Storage:          000001b7e7084550
    PEB Address:          000000241fbdd000
    LastErrorValue:       87
    LastStatusValue:      c000000d
    Count Owned Locks:    0
    HardErrorMode:        0
```

```
0:003> dps 000000241fe01000 000000241ff00000
[...]
00000024`1feff4e8  00007ff7`2cac1410  App0+0x1410
00000024`1feff4f0  00000000`000000fe
00000024`1feff4f8  00000000`00000000
00000024`1feff500  00000000`00000000
00000024`1feff508  00000000`00000000
00000024`1feff510  00000000`00000000
00000024`1feff518  00007ff7`2cac1410  App0+0x1410
00000024`1feff520  00000000`000003d0
00000024`1feff528  00000000`00000000
00000024`1feff530  00000000`00000000
00000024`1feff538  00000000`00000000
00000024`1feff540  00000000`000000c1
00000024`1feff548  00007ff7`2cac1410  App0+0x1410
00000024`1feff550  00000000`00000000
00000024`1feff558  00000000`00000000
00000024`1feff560  00000000`fe0000fe
00000024`1feff568  00000000`00000000
00000024`1feff570  00000000`0e00000e
00000024`1feff578  00007ff7`2cac1410  App0+0x1410
00000024`1feff580  00000000`00000000
00000024`1feff588  00000000`00000000
00000024`1feff590  00000000`00000000
00000024`1feff598  00000000`00000000
00000024`1feff5a0  00000000`00000000
00000024`1feff5a8  00007ff7`2cac1410  App0+0x1410
00000024`1feff5b0  00000000`00000000
00000024`1feff5b8  00000000`00000008
00000024`1feff5c0  00000000`0000003d
00000024`1feff5c8  00000000`000003d0
00000024`1feff5d0  000001b7`e7070000
00000024`1feff5d8  00007ff7`2cac1410  App0+0x1410
00000024`1feff5e0  000001b7`e7070000
00000024`1feff5e8  00000000`0000000a
00000024`1feff5f0  00000000`000003c8
00000024`1feff5f8  00000000`000003d0
00000024`1feff600  000001b7`e7070518
00000024`1feff608  00007ff7`2cac1410  App0+0x1410
00000024`1feff610  000001b7`e7085ff0
00000024`1feff618  00000000`00000000
00000024`1feff620  00000000`00000000
00000024`1feff628  00000000`00000000
00000024`1feff630  00000000`00000000
00000024`1feff638  00007ff7`2cac1410  App0+0x1410
00000024`1feff640  00000000`00000000
00000024`1feff648  00000000`00000000
00000024`1feff650  00000000`00000000
00000024`1feff658  00007ff7`2cacc348  App0+0xc348
00000024`1feff660  00000000`00000000
00000024`1feff668  00007ff7`2cac1410  App0+0x1410
00000024`1feff670  00000000`00000000
00000024`1feff678  00000000`00000000
00000024`1feff680  00000024`1feff700
00000024`1feff688  00007ff7`2cac1d9c  App0+0x1d9c
00000024`1feff690  00000024`1feff708
00000024`1feff698  00007ff7`2cac1d15  App0+0x1d15
00000024`1feff6a0  000001b7`e7083190
00000024`1feff6a8  00000000`00000000
00000024`1feff6b0  000001b7`e7085ff0
```

```
00000024`1feff6b8  00007ff7`2cac1a65  App0+0x1a65
00000024`1feff6c0  00000024`1feff728
00000024`1feff6c8  00007ff7`2cac1a8b  App0+0x1a8b
00000024`1feff6d0  000001b7`e7083190
00000024`1feff6d8  00000024`1feff6e0
00000024`1feff6e0  00000004`00000004
00000024`1feff6e8  000001b7`e7085ff0
00000024`1feff6f0  00007ff7`2cae26b0  App0+0x226b0
00000024`1feff6f8  00007ff7`2cac18e5  App0+0x18e5
00000024`1feff700  000001b7`e7083190
00000024`1feff708  000001b7`e7083190
00000024`1feff710  00000000`00000000
00000024`1feff718  00007ff7`2cacc407  App0+0xc407
00000024`1feff720  00000000`00000057
00000024`1feff728  000001b7`e7083190
00000024`1feff730  000001b7`e7083190
00000024`1feff738  00000000`00000005
00000024`1feff740  000001b7`e707c380
00000024`1feff748  00007ff7`2cac9958  App0+0x9958
00000024`1feff750  000001b7`e7083190
00000024`1feff758  00000000`00000000
00000024`1feff760  00000000`00000000
00000024`1feff768  00000000`00000000
00000024`1feff770  00000000`00000000
00000024`1feff778  00007fff`cf787bd4  kernel32!BaseThreadInitThunk+0x14
00000024`1feff780  00000000`00000000
00000024`1feff788  00000000`00000000
00000024`1feff790  00000000`00000000
00000024`1feff798  00000000`00000000
00000024`1feff7a0  00000000`00000000
00000024`1feff7a8  00007fff`d0aacee1  ntdll!RtlUserThreadStart+0x21
00000024`1feff7b0  00000000`00000000
00000024`1feff7b8  00000000`00000000
[...]
00000024`1fefffa0  00000000`00000000
00000024`1fefffa8  00000000`00000000
00000024`1fefffb0  00000000`00000000
00000024`1fefffb8  00000000`00000000
00000024`1fefffc0  00000000`00000000
00000024`1fefffc8  00000000`00000000
00000024`1fefffd0  00000000`00000000
00000024`1fefffd8  00000000`00000000
00000024`1fefffe0  00000000`00000000
00000024`1fefffe8  00000000`00000000
00000024`1feffff0  00000000`00000000
00000024`1feffff8  00000000`00000000
00000024`1ff00000  ????????`????????
```

Note: We can find one of the addresses and use the following form of the **k** command to get the bottom of the stack trace (manual stack trace reconstruction). If some addresses do not work or give malformed stack traces, we can try other similar or nearby addresses:

```
0:003> kL=00000024`1feff518
 # Child-SP          RetAddr           Call Site
00 00000024`1feff518 00000000`000000c1 App0+0x140b
01 00000024`1feff548 00007ff7`2cac1410 0xc1
02 00000024`1feff550 00007ff7`2cac1410 App0+0x1410
03 00000024`1feff580 00007ff7`2cac1410 App0+0x1410
04 00000024`1feff5b0 00007ff7`2cac1410 App0+0x1410
```

```
05 00000024`1feff5e0 00007ff7`2cac1410 App0+0x1410
06 00000024`1feff610 00007ff7`2cac1410 App0+0x1410
07 00000024`1feff640 00007ff7`2cac1410 App0+0x1410
08 00000024`1feff670 00007ff7`2cac1d15 App0+0x1410
09 00000024`1feff6a0 00007ff7`2cac1a8b App0+0x1d15
0a 00000024`1feff6d0 00007ff7`2cac18e5 App0+0x1a8b
0b 00000024`1feff700 00007ff7`2cac9958 App0+0x18e5
0c 00000024`1feff750 00007fff`cf787bd4 App0+0x9958
0d 00000024`1feff780 00007fff`d0aacee1 kernel32!BaseThreadInitThunk+0x14
0e 00000024`1feff7b0 00000000`00000000 ntdll!RtlUserThreadStart+0x21


0:003> kL=00000024`1feff520
 # Child-SP          RetAddr           Call Site
00 00000024`1feff520 00007ff7`2cac1410 App0+0x140b
01 00000024`1feff550 00007ff7`2cac1410 App0+0x1410
02 00000024`1feff580 00007ff7`2cac1410 App0+0x1410
03 00000024`1feff5b0 00007ff7`2cac1410 App0+0x1410
04 00000024`1feff5e0 00007ff7`2cac1410 App0+0x1410
05 00000024`1feff610 00007ff7`2cac1410 App0+0x1410
06 00000024`1feff640 00007ff7`2cac1410 App0+0x1410
07 00000024`1feff670 00007ff7`2cac1d15 App0+0x1410
08 00000024`1feff6a0 00007ff7`2cac1a8b App0+0x1d15
09 00000024`1feff6d0 00007ff7`2cac18e5 App0+0x1a8b
0a 00000024`1feff700 00007ff7`2cac9958 App0+0x18e5
0b 00000024`1feff750 00007fff`cf787bd4 App0+0x9958
0c 00000024`1feff780 00007fff`d0aacee1 kernel32!BaseThreadInitThunk+0x14
0d 00000024`1feff7b0 00000000`00000000 ntdll!RtlUserThreadStart+0x21
```

7.   Another option is to increase the number of frames to show:

```
0:003> .kframes 0xffff
Default stack trace depth is 0n65535 frames


0:003> k
 # Child-SP          RetAddr            Call Site
00 00000024`1fe04000 00007ff7`2cac1410  App0+0x140b
01 00000024`1fe04030 00007ff7`2cac1410  App0+0x1410
02 00000024`1fe04060 00007ff7`2cac1410  App0+0x1410
03 00000024`1fe04090 00007ff7`2cac1410  App0+0x1410
04 00000024`1fe040c0 00007ff7`2cac1410  App0+0x1410
05 00000024`1fe040f0 00007ff7`2cac1410  App0+0x1410
...
53cc 00000024`1feff640 00007ff7`2cac1410  App0+0x1410
53cd 00000024`1feff670 00007ff7`2cac1d15  App0+0x1410
53ce 00000024`1feff6a0 00007ff7`2cac1a8b  App0+0x1d15
53cf 00000024`1feff6d0 00007ff7`2cac18e5  App0+0x1a8b
53d0 00000024`1feff700 00007ff7`2cac9958  App0+0x18e5
53d1 00000024`1feff750 00007fff`cf787bd4  App0+0x9958
53d2 00000024`1feff780 00007fff`d0aacee1  kernel32!BaseThreadInitThunk+0x14
53d3 00000024`1feff7b0 00000000`00000000  ntdll!RtlUserThreadStart+0x21
```

8.   We close logging before exiting WinDbg:

```
0:003> .logclose
Closing open log file C:\AWMDA-Dumps\Process\x64\App0.log
```

Exercise P11

- **Goal:** Learn how to analyze exception patterns, raw stacks, and execution residue

- **Patterns:** Divide by Zero (User Mode); C++ Exception; Execution Residue (Unmanaged Space, User)

- \AWMDA-Dumps\Exercise-P11-Analysis-process-dump-AppP-64.pdf

© 2023 Software Diagnostics Services

158

Exercise P11: Analysis of an application process dump (AppP, 64-bit)

Goal: Learn how to analyze various exception patterns, raw stacks, and execution residue.

Patterns: Divide by Zero (User Mode); C++ Exception; Execution Residue (Unmanaged Space, User).

1. Launch WinDbg.

2. Open \AWMDA-Dumps\Process\x64\AppP.exe.7628.dmp.

3. We get the dump file loaded:

```
Microsoft (R) Windows Debugger Version 10.0.25877.1004 AMD64
Copyright (c) Microsoft Corporation. All rights reserved.


Loading Dump File [C:\AWMDA-Dumps\Process\x64\AppP.exe.7628.dmp]
User Mini Dump File with Full Memory: Only application data is available


************* Path validation summary **************
Response                     Time (ms)     Location
Deferred                                   srv*
Symbol search path is: srv*
Executable search path is:
Windows 10 Version 18362 MP (2 procs) Free x64
Product: WinNt, suite: SingleUserTS Personal
Edition build lab: 18362.1.amd64fre.19h1_release.190318-1202
Machine Name:
Debug session time: Wed Nov 13 21:11:14.000 2019 (UTC + 1:00)
System Uptime: 0 days 0:03:24.494
Process Uptime: 0 days 0:00:04.000
........
This dump file has an exception of interest stored in it.
The stored exception information can be accessed via .ecxr.
(1dcc.1f18): Security check failure or stack buffer overrun - code c0000409 (first/second
chance not available)
Subcode: 0x7 FAST_FAIL_FATAL_APP_EXIT
For analysis of this file, run !analyze -v
*** WARNING: Unable to verify checksum for AppP.exe
AppP!abort+0x35:
00007ff6`3b5aa07d cd29          int        29h
```

4. Open a log file using the **.logopen** command and specify application symbols (**.sympath+** and **.reload** commands):

```
0:002> .logopen C:\AWMDA-Dumps\Process\x64\AppP.log
Opened log file 'C:\AWMDA-Dumps\Process\x64\AppP.log'

0:002> .sympath+ C:\AWMDA-Dumps\Symbols
Symbol search path is: srv*;C:\AWMDA-Dumps\Symbols
Expanded Symbol search path is:
cache*;SRV*https://msdl.microsoft.com/download/symbols;c:\awmda-dumps\symbols


************* Path validation summary **************
```

```
Response                        Time (ms)    Location
Deferred                                     srv*
OK                                           C:\AWMDA-Dumps\Symbols
*** WARNING: Unable to verify checksum for AppP.exe
```

```
0:002> .reload
```
```
........
*** WARNING: Unable to verify checksum for AppP.exe
```

5.   Type the ~*kL command to verify the correctness of all stack traces:

```
0:002> ~*kL
```

```
   0  Id: 1dcc.1dec Suspend: 1 Teb: 000000b6`d3771000 Unfrozen
 # Child-SP          RetAddr           Call Site
00 000000b6`d35ff6c8 00007ffa`57278ba3 ntdll!NtWaitForSingleObject+0x14
01 000000b6`d35ff6d0 00007ff6`3b5a3523 KERNELBASE!WaitForSingleObjectEx+0x93
02 000000b6`d35ff770 00007ff6`3b5a13af AppP!_Thrd_join+0x1f
03 000000b6`d35ff7a0 00007ff6`3b5a168c AppP!std::thread::join+0x5f
04 000000b6`d35ff800 00007ff6`3b5a3f84 AppP!wmain+0x5c
05 (Inline Function) --------`-------- AppP!invoke_main+0x22
06 000000b6`d35ff880 00007ffa`583e7bd4 AppP!__scrt_common_main_seh+0x10c
07 000000b6`d35ff8c0 00007ffa`5a02ced1 kernel32!BaseThreadInitThunk+0x14
08 000000b6`d35ff8f0 00000000`00000000 ntdll!RtlUserThreadStart+0x21

   1  Id: 1dcc.1b5c Suspend: 1 Teb: 000000b6`d3773000 Unfrozen
 # Child-SP          RetAddr           Call Site
00 000000b6`d38fe9c8 00007ffa`5a064af2 KERNELBASE!UnhandledExceptionFilter
01 000000b6`d38fe9d0 00007ffa`5a04c6d6 ntdll!RtlUserThreadStart$filt$0+0xa2
02 000000b6`d38fea10 00007ffa`5a0611ff ntdll!_C_specific_handler+0x96
03 000000b6`d38fea80 00007ffa`5a02a289 ntdll!RtlpExecuteHandlerForException+0xf
04 000000b6`d38feab0 00007ffa`5a05fe6e ntdll!RtlDispatchException+0x219
05 000000b6`d38ff1c0 00007ff6`3b5a1621 ntdll!KiUserExceptionDispatch+0x2e
06 000000b6`d38ff950 00007ff6`3b5a1f15 AppP!thread_three+0x11
07 000000b6`d38ff970 00007ff6`3b5a1e9b AppP!std::_Invoker_functor::_Call<void (__cdecl*)(void)>+0x15
08 000000b6`d38ff9a0 00007ff6`3b5a1b64 AppP!std::invoke<void (__cdecl*)(void)>+0x1b
09 000000b6`d38ff9d0 00007ff6`3b5a9b48 AppP!std::thread::_Invoke<std::tuple<void (__cdecl*)(void)>,0>+0x64
0a 000000b6`d38ffa20 00007ffa`583e7bd4 AppP!thread_start<unsigned int (__cdecl*)(void *),1>+0x50
0b 000000b6`d38ffa50 00007ffa`5a02ced1 kernel32!BaseThreadInitThunk+0x14
0c 000000b6`d38ffa80 00000000`00000000 ntdll!RtlUserThreadStart+0x21

#  2  Id: 1dcc.1f18 Suspend: 0 Teb: 000000b6`d3775000 Unfrozen
 # Child-SP          RetAddr           Call Site
00 000000b6`d39fe6f0 00007ff6`3b5a9d23 AppP!abort+0x35
01 000000b6`d39fe720 00007ff6`3b5a7867 AppP!terminate+0x1f
02 000000b6`d39fe750 00007ff6`3b5a84d5 AppP!FindHandler<__FrameHandler4>+0x523
03 000000b6`d39fe930 00007ff6`3b5a585d AppP!__InternalCxxFrameHandler<__FrameHandler4>+0x281
04 000000b6`d39fe9d0 00007ff6`3b5b31c8 AppP!__CxxFrameHandler4+0xa9
05 000000b6`d39fea40 00007ffa`5a0611ff AppP!__GSHandlerCheck_EH4+0x64
06 000000b6`d39fea70 00007ffa`5a02a289 ntdll!RtlpExecuteHandlerForException+0xf
07 000000b6`d39feaa0 00007ffa`5a02a043 ntdll!RtlDispatchException+0x219
08 000000b6`d39ff1b0 00007ffa`5727a839 ntdll!RtlRaiseException+0x153
09 000000b6`d39ffa20 00007ff6`3b5a59bc KERNELBASE!RaiseException+0x69
0a 000000b6`d39ffb00 00007ff6`3b5a15fd AppP!_CxxThrowException+0x90
0b 000000b6`d39ffb60 00007ff6`3b5a1f15 AppP!thread_two+0x1d
0c 000000b6`d39ffba0 00007ff6`3b5a1e9b AppP!std::_Invoker_functor::_Call<void (__cdecl*)(void)>+0x15
0d 000000b6`d39ffbd0 00007ff6`3b5a1b64 AppP!std::invoke<void (__cdecl*)(void)>+0x1b
0e 000000b6`d39ffc00 00007ff6`3b5a9b48 AppP!std::thread::_Invoke<std::tuple<void (__cdecl*)(void)>,0>+0x64
0f 000000b6`d39ffc50 00007ffa`583e7bd4 AppP!thread_start<unsigned int (__cdecl*)(void *),1>+0x50
10 000000b6`d39ffc80 00007ffa`5a02ced1 kernel32!BaseThreadInitThunk+0x14
11 000000b6`d39ffcb0 00000000`00000000 ntdll!RtlUserThreadStart+0x21

   3  Id: 1dcc.1b20 Suspend: 1 Teb: 000000b6`d3777000 Unfrozen
 # Child-SP          RetAddr           Call Site
00 000000b6`d3aff878 00007ffa`57286931 ntdll!NtDelayExecution+0x14
01 000000b6`d3aff880 00007ff6`3b5a35a8 KERNELBASE!SleepEx+0xa1
02 000000b6`d3aff920 00007ff6`3b5a1a55 AppP!_Thrd_sleep+0x3c
03 000000b6`d3aff970 00007ff6`3b5a179d
AppP!std::this_thread::sleep_until<std::chrono::steady_clock,std::chrono::duration<__int64,std::ratio<1,1000000000> >
>+0x65
```

160

```
04 000000b6`d3aff9d0 00007ff6`3b5a15bb AppP!std::this_thread::sleep_for<int,std::ratio<3600,1> >+0x2d
05 000000b6`d3affa10 00007ff6`3b5a1f15 AppP!thread_one+0x5b
06 000000b6`d3affad0 00007ff6`3b5a1e9b AppP!std::_Invoker_functor::_Call<void (__cdecl*)(void)>+0x15
07 000000b6`d3affb00 00007ff6`3b5a1b64 AppP!std::invoke<void (__cdecl*)(void)>+0x1b
08 000000b6`d3affb30 00007ff6`3b5a9b48 AppP!std::thread::_Invoke<std::tuple<void (__cdecl*)(void)>,0>+0x64
09 000000b6`d3affb80 00007ffa`583e7bd4 AppP!thread_start<unsigned int (__cdecl*)(void *),1>+0x50
0a 000000b6`d3affbb0 00007ffa`5a02ced1 kernel32!BaseThreadInitThunk+0x14
0b 000000b6`d3affbe0 00000000`00000000 ntdll!RtlUserThreadStart+0x21

   4  Id: 1dcc.1314 Suspend: 1 Teb: 000000b6`d3779000 Unfrozen
 # Child-SP          RetAddr           Call Site
00 000000b6`d3bff648 00007ffa`59ff1a86 ntdll!NtReleaseWorkerFactoryWorker+0x14
01 000000b6`d3bff650 00007ffa`59ff3155 ntdll!TpPostTask+0x15e
02 000000b6`d3bff680 00007ffa`59ff0842 ntdll!TppWorkCallbackPrologRelease+0x1c9
03 000000b6`d3bff6e0 00007ffa`59ff4634 ntdll!TppWorkpExecuteCallback+0x52
04 000000b6`d3bff730 00007ffa`583e7bd4 ntdll!TppWorkerThread+0x8d4
05 000000b6`d3bffaf0 00007ffa`5a02ced1 kernel32!BaseThreadInitThunk+0x14
06 000000b6`d3bffb20 00000000`00000000 ntdll!RtlUserThreadStart+0x21

   5  Id: 1dcc.710 Suspend: 1 Teb: 000000b6`d377b000 Unfrozen
 # Child-SP          RetAddr           Call Site
00 000000b6`d3cfff38 00000000`00000000 ntdll!RtlUserThreadStart
```

Note: We see threads #1 and #2 have the exception processing code. The presence of _Cxx on one of the stack traces suggests a C++ exception.

6.   Let's see that the **!analyze -v** command says:

```
0:002> !analyze -v
*******************************************************************************
*                                                                             *
*                        Exception Analysis                                   *
*                                                                             *
*******************************************************************************

KEY_VALUES_STRING: 1

    Key  : Analysis.CPU.mSec
    Value: 765

    Key  : Analysis.DebugAnalysisManager
    Value: Create

    Key  : Analysis.Elapsed.mSec
    Value: 1486

    Key  : Analysis.Init.CPU.mSec
    Value: 374

    Key  : Analysis.Init.Elapsed.mSec
    Value: 106753

    Key  : Analysis.Memory.CommitPeak.Mb
    Value: 75

    Key  : FailFast.Name
    Value: FATAL_APP_EXIT

    Key  : FailFast.Type
    Value: 7

    Key  : Timeline.OS.Boot.DeltaSec
    Value: 204

    Key  : Timeline.Process.Start.DeltaSec
    Value: 4

    Key  : WER.OS.Branch
    Value: 19h1_release

    Key  : WER.OS.Timestamp
    Value: 2019-03-18T12:02:00Z

    Key  : WER.OS.Version
    Value: 10.0.18362.1

    Key  : WER.Process.Version
    Value: 2.0.0.1

FILE_IN_CAB:  AppP.exe.7628.dmp

NTGLOBALFLAG:  400

PROCESS_BAM_CURRENT_THROTTLED: 0
```

```
PROCESS_BAM_PREVIOUS_THROTTLED: 0

APPLICATION_VERIFIER_FLAGS:  0

CONTEXT:  (.ecxr)
rax=0000000000000001 rbx=000000b6d39ffa40 rcx=0000000000000007
rdx=000000b6d39fe700 rsi=000000b6d39ff030 rdi=0000000000000000
rip=00007ff63b5aa07d rsp=000000b6d39fe6f0 rbp=000000b6d39fe850
 r8=000000b6d39fe6f0  r9=000000b6d39fe6f8 r10=0000000000000012
r11=000000b6d39fe6e8 r12=0000000000000000 r13=000000b6d39ff1f0
r14=000000b6d39fea10 r15=000000b6d39fea40
iopl=0         nv up ei pl nz na pe nc
cs=0033  ss=002b  es=002b  fs=0053  gs=002b             efl=00000202
AppP!abort+0x35:
00007ff6`3b5aa07d cd29            int     29h
Resetting default scope

EXCEPTION_RECORD:  (.exr -1)
ExceptionAddress: 00007ff63b5aa07d (AppP!abort+0x0000000000000035)
   ExceptionCode: c0000409 (Security check failure or stack buffer overrun)
  ExceptionFlags: 00000001
NumberParameters: 1
   Parameter[0]: 0000000000000007
Subcode: 0x7 FAST_FAIL_FATAL_APP_EXIT

PROCESS_NAME:  AppP.exe

ERROR_CODE: (NTSTATUS) 0xc0000409 - The system detected an overrun of a stack-based buffer in this application. This overrun could potentially allow a
malicious user to gain control of this application.

EXCEPTION_CODE_STR:  c0000409

EXCEPTION_PARAMETER1:  0000000000000007

FAULTING_THREAD:  00001f18

STACK_TEXT:
000000b6`d39fe6f0 00007ff6`3b5a9d23     : 000000b6`d39ffa40 000000b6`d39ff030 00000000`00000000 00000000`00000000 : AppP!abort+0x35
000000b6`d39fe720 00007ff6`3b5a7867     : 000000b6`d39ffa40 000000b6`d39ff030 000000b6`d39ffa40 000000b6`d39fea10 : AppP!terminate+0x1f
000000b6`d39fe750 00007ff6`3b5a84d5     : 00000000`000000bb 00007ffa`57261edb 00000000`00000001 000000b6`d39ffa40 : AppP!FindHandler<__FrameHandler4>+0x523
000000b6`d39fe930 00007ff6`3b5a585d     : 00007ff6`3b5a0000 000000b6`d39ffa40 000000b6`d39ff1f0 000000b6`d39ff030 : AppP!__InternalCxxFrameHandler<__FrameHandler4>+0x281
000000b6`d39fe9d0 00007ff6`3b5b31c8     : 000000b6`d39ffc00 00007ff6`3b5be410 000000b6`d39ffa40 000000b6`d39ffc00 : AppP!__CxxFrameHandler4+0xa9
000000b6`d39fea40 00007ffa`5a0611ff     : 00000000`00000000 000000b6`d39fefe0 000000b6`d39ffa40 00000000`00000001 : AppP!__GSHandlerCheck_EH4+0x64
000000b6`d39fea70 00007ffa`5a02a289     : 000000b6`00000001 00007ff6`3b5a0000 00000000`00000000 00007ff6`3b5c3138 : ntdll!RtlpExecuteHandlerForException+0xf
000000b6`d39feaa0 00007ffa`5a02a043     : 80000000`00000000 00007ffa`59fc0000 00000000`00000000 00007ffa`5a12e81c : ntdll!RtlDispatchException+0x219
000000b6`d39ff1b0 00007ff6`5727a839     : 00000000`00000800 00007ff6`3b5bf678 000000b6`d39ffb80 00000000`00000009 : ntdll!RtlRaiseException+0x153
000000b6`d39ffa20 00007ff6`3b5a59bc     : 00002406`808f568e 00000000`0000001d 00000000`00000000 00000000`00000000 : KERNELBASE!RaiseException+0x69
000000b6`d39ffb00 00007ff6`3b5a15fd     : ffffffff`ffffffff 00007ffa`5724ddbe 000001c0`5b0eb510 00000000`00000000 : AppP!_CxxThrowException+0x90
000000b6`d39ffb60 00007ff6`3b5a1f15     : 000001c0`5b0eba30 00000000`00000000 00000000`00000000 00007ff6`3b5a1e75 : AppP!thread_two+0x1d
000000b6`d39ffba0 00007ff6`3b5a1e9b     : 000001c0`5b0eba30 00000000`00000000 00000000`00000000 00007ffa`572b62d5 : AppP!std::_Invoker_functor::_Call<void
(__cdecl*)(void)>+0x15
000000b6`d39ffbd0 00007ff6`3b5a1b64     : 000001c0`5b0eba30 000001c0`5b0eba30 00000000`00000001 00007ff6`3b5acf9e : AppP!std::invoke<void
(__cdecl*)(void)>+0x1b
000000b6`d39ffc00 00007ff6`3b5a9b48     : 000001c0`5b0eba30 00000000`00000000 00000000`00000000 00000000`00000000 : AppP!std::thread::_Invoke<std::tuple<void
(__cdecl*)(void)>,0>+0x64
000000b6`d39ffc50 00007ffa`583e7bd4     : 00000000`00000000 00000000`00000000 00000000`00000000 00000000`00000000 : AppP!thread_start<unsigned int
(__cdecl*)(void *),1>+0x50
000000b6`d39ffc80 00007ffa`5a02ced1     : 00000000`00000000 00000000`00000000 00000000`00000000 00000000`00000000 : kernel32!BaseThreadInitThunk+0x14
000000b6`d39ffcb0 00000000`00000000     : 00000000`00000000 00000000`00000000 00000000`00000000 00000000`00000000 : ntdll!RtlUserThreadStart+0x21


STACK_COMMAND:  ~2s ; .cxr ; kb

FAULTING_SOURCE_LINE:  minkernel\crts\ucrt\src\appcrt\startup\abort.cpp

FAULTING_SOURCE_FILE:  minkernel\crts\ucrt\src\appcrt\startup\abort.cpp

FAULTING_SOURCE_LINE_NUMBER:  77

FAULTING_SOURCE_CODE:
No source found for 'minkernel\crts\ucrt\src\appcrt\startup\abort.cpp'


SYMBOL_NAME:  appp!abort+35

MODULE_NAME:  AppP

IMAGE_NAME:  AppP.exe

FAILURE_BUCKET_ID:  FAIL_FAST_FATAL_APP_EXIT_c0000409_AppP.exe!abort

OS_VERSION:  10.0.18362.1

BUILDLAB_STR:  19h1_release

OSPLATFORM_TYPE:  x64

OSNAME:  Windows 10

IMAGE_VERSION:  2.0.0.1

FAILURE_ID_HASH:  {fc3ea540-6a94-d5a9-c49b-b4a140fd659a}

Followup:     MachineOwner
---------
```

Note: Probably due to the *abort* function, WinDbg is unable to get exception context and record correctly. Because of that, the reported 0xc0000409 code may be incorrect too. So we need to navigate through threads manually.

7.   Let's first check thread #1:

```
0:002> ~1s
KERNELBASE!UnhandledExceptionFilter:
00007ffa`5733f490 48895c2410      mov     qword ptr [rsp+10h],rbx ss:000000b6`d38fe9d8=00007ff63b5b3302

0:001> kL
 # Child-SP          RetAddr           Call Site
00 000000b6`d38fe9c8 00007ffa`5a064af2 KERNELBASE!UnhandledExceptionFilter
01 000000b6`d38fe9d0 00007ffa`5a04c6d6 ntdll!RtlUserThreadStart$filt$0+0xa2
02 000000b6`d38fea10 00007ffa`5a0611ff ntdll!_C_specific_handler+0x96
03 000000b6`d38fea80 00007ffa`5a02a289 ntdll!RtlpExecuteHandlerForException+0xf
04 000000b6`d38feab0 00007ffa`5a05fe6e ntdll!RtlDispatchException+0x219
05 000000b6`d38ff1c0 00007ff6`3b5a1621 ntdll!KiUserExceptionDispatch+0x2e
06 000000b6`d38ff950 00007ff6`3b5a1f15 AppP!thread_three+0x11
07 000000b6`d38ff970 00007ff6`3b5a1e9b AppP!std::_Invoker_functor::_Call<void (__cdecl*)(void)>+0x15
08 000000b6`d38ff9a0 00007ff6`3b5a1b64 AppP!std::invoke<void (__cdecl*)(void)>+0x1b
09 000000b6`d38ff9d0 00007ff6`3b5a9b48 AppP!std::thread::_Invoke<std::tuple<void (__cdecl*)(void)>,0>+0x64
0a 000000b6`d38ffa20 00007ffa`583e7bd4 AppP!thread_start<unsigned int (__cdecl*)(void *),1>+0x50
0b 000000b6`d38ffa50 00007ffa`5a02ced1 kernel32!BaseThreadInitThunk+0x14
0c 000000b6`d38ffa80 00000000`00000000 ntdll!RtlUserThreadStart+0x21
```

Note: The thread is non-waiting (active) and was probably caught during fault reporting of an exception. We can get exception context here either by using the **.frame /c 6** or the **.cxr** command with the RSP pointer value 000000b6`d38ff1c0:

```
0:001> .cxr 000000b6`d38ff1c0
rax=0000000000000001 rbx=000001c05b0eb570 rcx=000001c05b0eb200
rdx=0000000000000000 rsi=0000000000000000 rdi=0000000000000000
rip=00007ff63b5a1621 rsp=000000b6d38ff950 rbp=0000000000000000
 r8=000000b6d38ff9d8  r9=0000000000000002 r10=0000000000000000
r11=0000000000000246 r12=0000000000000000 r13=0000000000000000
r14=0000000000000000 r15=0000000000000000
iopl=0         nv up ei pl nz na po nc
cs=0033  ss=002b  ds=002b  es=002b  fs=0053  gs=002b             efl=00010206
AppP!thread_three+0x11:
00007ff6`3b5a1621 f73c24                  idiv    eax,dword ptr [rsp] ss:000000b6`d38ff950=00000000
```

```
0:001> kL
  *** Stack trace for last set context - .thread/.cxr resets it
 # Child-SP          RetAddr           Call Site
00 000000b6`d38ff950 00007ff6`3b5a1f15 AppP!thread_three+0x11
01 000000b6`d38ff970 00007ff6`3b5a1e9b AppP!std::_Invoker_functor::_Call<void (__cdecl*)(void)>+0x15
02 000000b6`d38ff9a0 00007ff6`3b5a1b64 AppP!std::invoke<void (__cdecl*)(void)>+0x1b
03 000000b6`d38ff9d0 00007ff6`3b5a9b48 AppP!std::thread::_Invoke<std::tuple<void (__cdecl*)(void)>,0>+0x64
04 000000b6`d38ffa20 00007ffa`583e7bd4 AppP!thread_start<unsigned int (__cdecl*)(void *),1>+0x50
05 000000b6`d38ffa50 00007ffa`5a02ced1 kernel32!BaseThreadInitThunk+0x14
06 000000b6`d38ffa80 00000000`00000000 ntdll!RtlUserThreadStart+0x21
```

Note: We see the *idiv* instruction (**i**nteger **div**ide). So divide by zero happened in this thread. The way to double-check that the **.cxr** command was fed the correct context pointer is to verify *efl* and *cs, ss, ds, es, fs, gs* values. They should be similar to the ones highlighted in green above. For example, an incorrect pointer may show some zero and random values and the stack trace is incorrect as a result:

```
0:001> .cxr 000000b6`d38feab0
rax=0000000000000033 rbx=00cb00ca00000011 rcx=00010206002b0740
rdx=00c700c600c500c4 rsi=00d700d600d500d4 rdi=000000000000007f
rip=00ff00fe00fd00fc rsp=0000000000000011 rbp=000000000000007f
 r8=00df00de00dd0000  r9=0000000000000011 r10=00e700e600e500e4
r11=0000000000000000 r12=000000b6d38ffb00 r13=0000000000000000
r14=0000000000000000 r15=0000000000000000
iopl=0         nv up di ng nz na pe nc
cs=0000  ss=00a1  ds=0000  es=0000  fs=0000  gs=0001          efl=00a300a2
00ff00fe`00fd00fc ??                 ???
```

```
0:001> k
  *** Stack trace for last set context - .thread/.cxr resets it
 # Child-SP          RetAddr           Call Site
00 00000000`00000011 00000000`00000000 0x00ff00fe`00fd00fc
```

Note: To reverse accidentally set context, we can use the **.cxr** command without any parameters:

```
0:001> .cxr
Resetting default scope
```

```
0:001> kc
 # Call Site
00 KERNELBASE!UnhandledExceptionFilter
01 ntdll!RtlUserThreadStart$filt$0
02 ntdll!_C_specific_handler
03 ntdll!RtlpExecuteHandlerForException
04 ntdll!RtlDispatchException
05 ntdll!KiUserExceptionDispatch
06 AppP!thread_three
07 AppP!std::_Invoker_functor::_Call<void (__cdecl*)(void)>
08 AppP!std::invoke<void (__cdecl*)(void)>
09 AppP!std::thread::_Invoke<std::tuple<void (__cdecl*)(void)>,0>
0a AppP!thread_start<unsigned int (__cdecl*)(void *),1>
0b kernel32!BaseThreadInitThunk
0c ntdll!RtlUserThreadStart
```

8.   Now we switch to thread #2:

```
0:001> ~2s
AppP!abort+0x35:
00007ff6`3b5aa07d cd29              int     29h
```

```
0:002> kL
 # Child-SP          RetAddr           Call Site
00 000000b6`d39fe6f0 00007ff6`3b5a9d23 AppP!abort+0x35
01 000000b6`d39fe720 00007ff6`3b5a7867 AppP!terminate+0x1f
02 000000b6`d39fe750 00007ff6`3b5a84d5 AppP!FindHandler<__FrameHandler4>+0x523
03 000000b6`d39fe930 00007ff6`3b5a585d AppP!__InternalCxxFrameHandler<__FrameHandler4>+0x281
04 000000b6`d39fe9d0 00007ff6`3b5b31c8 AppP!__CxxFrameHandler4+0xa9
05 000000b6`d39fea40 00007ffa`5a0611ff AppP!__GSHandlerCheck_EH4+0x64
06 000000b6`d39fea70 00007ffa`5a02a289 ntdll!RtlpExecuteHandlerForException+0xf
07 000000b6`d39feaa0 00007ffa`5a02a043 ntdll!RtlDispatchException+0x219
08 000000b6`d39ff1b0 00007ff6`5727a839 ntdll!RtlRaiseException+0x153
09 000000b6`d39ffa20 00007ff6`3b5a59bc KERNELBASE!RaiseException+0x69
0a 000000b6`d39ffb00 00007ff6`3b5a15fd AppP!_CxxThrowException+0x90
0b 000000b6`d39ffb60 00007ff6`3b5a1f15 AppP!thread_two+0x1d
0c 000000b6`d39ffba0 00007ff6`3b5a1e9b AppP!std::_Invoker_functor::_Call<void (__cdecl*)(void)>+0x15
0d 000000b6`d39ffbd0 00007ff6`3b5a1b64 AppP!std::invoke<void (__cdecl*)(void)>+0x1b
0e 000000b6`d39ffc00 00007ff6`3b5a9b48 AppP!std::thread::_Invoke<std::tuple<void (__cdecl*)(void)>,0>+0x64
0f 000000b6`d39ffc50 00007ffa`583e7bd4 AppP!thread_start<unsigned int (__cdecl*)(void *),1>+0x50
10 000000b6`d39ffc80 00007ffa`5a02ced1 kernel32!BaseThreadInitThunk+0x14
11 000000b6`d39ffcb0 00000000`00000000 ntdll!RtlUserThreadStart+0x21
```

Note: We check the code called _CxxThrowException:

```
0:002> ub 00007ff6`3b5a15fd
AppP!thread_one+0x7d:
00007ff6`3b5a15dd cc                int    3
00007ff6`3b5a15de cc                int    3
00007ff6`3b5a15df cc                int    3
AppP!thread_two [C:\AWMDA-Examples\AppP\AppP.cpp @ 34]:
00007ff6`3b5a15e0 4883ec38          sub    rsp,38h
00007ff6`3b5a15e4 c744242078563412  mov    dword ptr [rsp+20h],12345678h
00007ff6`3b5a15ec 488d1585e00100    lea    rdx,[AppP!TI1H (00007ff6`3b5bf678)]
00007ff6`3b5a15f3 488d4c2420        lea    rcx,[rsp+20h]
00007ff6`3b5a15f8 e82f430000        call   AppP!_CxxThrowException (00007ff6`3b5a592c)
```

Note: We see that the first parameter (via RCX) can be traced to the 12345678 value of exception, which can be double-checked in the C++ code of *AppP* at the end of this book.

9.   Let's now investigate the raw stack for thread #3 (the output of the **dps** command is truncated here for clarity):

```
0:002> ~3s
ntdll!NtDelayExecution+0x14:
00007ffa`5a05c744 c3                ret

0:003> !teb
TEB at 000000b6d3777000
    ExceptionList:        0000000000000000
    StackBase:            000000b6d3b00000
    StackLimit:           000000b6d3aff000
    SubSystemTib:         0000000000000000
    FiberData:            0000000000001e00
    ArbitraryUserPointer: 0000000000000000
    Self:                 000000b6d3777000
    EnvironmentPointer:   0000000000000000
    ClientId:             0000000000001dcc . 0000000000001b20
    RpcHandle:            0000000000000000
    Tls Storage:          000001c05b0f0370
    PEB Address:          000000b6d3770000
    LastErrorValue:       187
    LastStatusValue:      c000000d
    Count Owned Locks:    0
    HardErrorMode:        0

0:003> dps 000000b6d3aff000 000000b6d3b00000
000000b6`d3aff000  00000000`00000000
000000b6`d3aff008  00000000`00000000
000000b6`d3aff010  00000000`00000000
000000b6`d3aff018  00000000`00000000
000000b6`d3aff020  00000000`00000000
[...]
000000b6`d3aff6b0  000000b6`d3affb38
000000b6`d3aff6b8  000000b6`00000000
000000b6`d3aff6c0  000001c0`5b0eb270
000000b6`d3aff6c8  00007ff6`3b5a1762 AppP!strcat_s<60>+0x22 [C:\Program Files (x86)\Windows
Kits\10\Include\10.0.18362.0\ucrt\string.h @ 79]
000000b6`d3aff6d0  000000b6`d3affb38
000000b6`d3aff6d8  000000b6`d3aff810
000000b6`d3aff6e0  00000000`00000200
```

```
000000b6`d3aff6e8  000000b6`d3aff900
000000b6`d3aff6f0  00000000`00000001
000000b6`d3aff6f8  00007ff6`3b5a14e7 AppP!bar+0xf7 [C:\AWMDA-Examples\AppP\AppP.cpp @ 18]
000000b6`d3aff700  000000b6`d3aff720
000000b6`d3aff708  00007ff6`3b5bd6b4 AppP!__log_F_inv_qword+0x814
000000b6`d3aff710  00007ffa`5a1252f0 ntdll!LdrpWorkQueue
000000b6`d3aff718  000000b6`d3aff801
000000b6`d3aff720  74736572`65746e49
000000b6`d3aff728  61746164`20676e69
000000b6`d3aff730  6d206e65`76452021
000000b6`d3aff738  65746e69`2065726f
000000b6`d3aff740  20676e69`74736572
000000b6`d3aff748  00000021`61746164
000000b6`d3aff750  00000000`00000000
000000b6`d3aff758  00007ffa`00000000
000000b6`d3aff760  00000000`00000000
000000b6`d3aff768  00000000`00000000
000000b6`d3aff770  00000000`00000000
000000b6`d3aff778  00000000`00000000
000000b6`d3aff780  00000000`00000000
000000b6`d3aff788  00000000`00000000
000000b6`d3aff790  00000000`00000000
000000b6`d3aff798  00000000`00000000
000000b6`d3aff7a0  00000000`00000000
000000b6`d3aff7a8  00000000`00000000
000000b6`d3aff7b0  00000000`00000000
000000b6`d3aff7b8  00000000`00000000
000000b6`d3aff7c0  00007ff6`00000000
000000b6`d3aff7c8  000001c0`5b0efe80
000000b6`d3aff7d0  00000000`00000000
000000b6`d3aff7d8  00000000`00000000
000000b6`d3aff7e0  00000000`00000000
000000b6`d3aff7e8  00000000`00000000
[...]
000000b6`d3afffd0  00000000`00000000
000000b6`d3afffd8  00000000`00000000
000000b6`d3afffe0  00000000`00000000
000000b6`d3afffe8  00000000`00000000
000000b6`d3affff0  00000000`00000000
000000b6`d3affff8  00000000`00000000
000000b6`d3b00000  ????????`????????
```

Note: We see a fragment of ASCII and examine it using the **da** command (**du** for UNICODE fragments):

```
0:003> da /c 0n256 000000b6`d3aff720
000000b6`d3aff720  "Interesting data! Even more interesting data!"
```

Note: If you see any address like this, you can examine its probable string content:

```
0:003> ~1s
KERNELBASE!UnhandledExceptionFilter:
00007ffa`5733f490 48895c2410      mov     qword ptr [rsp+10h],rbx
ss:000000b6`d38fe9d8=00007ff63b5b3302

0:001> !teb
TEB at 000000b6d3773000
    ExceptionList:        0000000000000000
    StackBase:            000000b6d3900000
```

```
     StackLimit:           000000b6d38fe000
     SubSystemTib:         0000000000000000
     FiberData:            0000000000001e00
     ArbitraryUserPointer: 0000000000000000
     Self:                 000000b6d3773000
     EnvironmentPointer:   0000000000000000
     ClientId:             0000000000001dcc . 0000000000001b5c
     RpcHandle:            0000000000000000
     Tls Storage:          000001c05b0f0250
     PEB Address:          000000b6d3770000
     LastErrorValue:       187
     LastStatusValue:      c000000d
     Count Owned Locks:    0
     HardErrorMode:        0

0:001> dps 000000b6d38fe000 000000b6d3900000
[...]
000000b6`d38ff870  00007ff6`3b5b74f0 AppP!`string'
[...]


0:001> dc 00007ff6`3b5b74f0
00007ff6`3b5b74f0  00700061 002d0069 0073006d 0077002d  a.p.i.-.m.s.-.w.
00007ff6`3b5b7500  006e0069 0061002d 00700070 006f006d  i.n.-.a.p.p.m.o.
00007ff6`3b5b7510  00650064 002d006c 00750072 0074006e  d.e.l.-.r.u.n.t.
00007ff6`3b5b7520  006d0069 002d0065 0031006c 0031002d  i.m.e.-.l.1.-.1.
00007ff6`3b5b7530  0032002d 00000000 00730075 00720065  -.2.....u.s.e.r.
00007ff6`3b5b7540  00320033 00000000 00780065 002d0074  3.2.....e.x.t.-.
00007ff6`3b5b7550  0073006d 0000002d 00000006 00000010  m.s.-...........
00007ff6`3b5b7560  00000001 00000010 00000001 00000010  ................

0:001> du /c 0n256 00007ff6`3b5b74f0
00007ff6`3b5b74f0  "api-ms-win-appmodel-runtime-l1-1-2"
```

Note: You can use commands **dpp**, **dpa**, and **dpu** on any memory range to get symbolic, ASCII, and UNICODE representation of the second column, for example (the output is truncated for clarity):

```
0:001> dpa 000000b6d38fe000 000000b6d3900000
[...]
000000b6`d38ff100  00007ffa`5847acd8 ".{."
000000b6`d38ff108  00007ffa`59fc0000 "MZ."
000000b6`d38ff110  00007ffa`5a12e9f0 "..."
000000b6`d38ff118  00007ffa`58134568 "H.{.H.D$0H.C.H.D$(H..H..t8........G...u*H..H..H."
000000b6`d38ff120  000000b6`d38ff190 ""
000000b6`d38ff128  000001c0`5b090750 "csm.."
000000b6`d38ff130  00007ffa`58134ff0 "@SH.. H..."..H..H.. [..L"
000000b6`d38ff138  00000000`19930520
000000b6`d38ff140  00000000`00000000
000000b6`d38ff148  000001c0`5b090750 "csm.."
000000b6`d38ff150  000001c0`5b090820 "hd.X.."
000000b6`d38ff158  00007ffa`59ffbabb "H..H.E.H....\...L.m.eH..%0"
000000b6`d38ff160  00007ffa`581b4650 "P..[.."
000000b6`d38ff168  00007ffa`58134db9 "H.'"
000000b6`d38ff170  00002406`809f4efe
000000b6`d38ff178  00007ffa`581a68c8 ""
000000b6`d38ff180  00000000`00000000
000000b6`d38ff188  00000000`00000000
000000b6`d38ff190  00000000`00000000
000000b6`d38ff198  00000000`00000000
```

```
000000b6`d38ff1a0  00000000`00000000
000000b6`d38ff1a8  00000000`00000000
000000b6`d38ff1b0  00000000`00000000
000000b6`d38ff1b8  00007ffa`5a05fe6e  "..t.H..3..T.....H..H...."
000000b6`d38ff1c0  00000000`00000000
000000b6`d38ff1c8  00000000`00000004
000000b6`d38ff1d0  000001c0`5b0eb570  ""
000000b6`d38ff1d8  000000b6`d38ff288  ""
000000b6`d38ff1e0  00007ffa`581a68c8  ""
000000b6`d38ff1e8  00007ffa`58120000  "MZ."
000000b6`d38ff1f0  00001f80`0010005f
000000b6`d38ff1f8  0053002b`002b0033
000000b6`d38ff200  00010206`002b002b
000000b6`d38ff208  00000000`00000000
000000b6`d38ff210  00000000`00000000
000000b6`d38ff218  00000000`00000000
000000b6`d38ff220  00000000`00000000
000000b6`d38ff228  00000000`00000000
[...]
```

Note: We see PE header ASCII signatures ("MZ") and can examine associated module information because pointers to PE headers are pointers to the loaded modules:

```
0:001> !lmi 00007ffa`58120000
Loaded Module Info: [00007ffa`58120000]
         Module: msvcrt
   Base Address: 00007ffa58120000
     Image Name: msvcrt.dll
   Machine Type: 34404 (X64)
     Time Stamp: f5bdefd7 (This is a reproducible build file hash, not a true timestamp)
           Size: 9e000
       CheckSum: a591e
Characteristics: 2022
Debug Data Dirs: Type   Size    VA   Pointer
            CODEVIEW    23, 823bc,    813bc RSDS - GUID: {1FEA8DB6-B57F-5FBF-A935-E090243420D0}
              Age: 1, Pdb: msvcrt.pdb
                POGO   3c4, 823e0,    813e0 [Data not mapped]
               REPRO    24, 827a4,    817a4 Reproducible build[Data not mapped]
     Image Type: MEMORY   - Image read successfully from loaded memory.
    Symbol Type: PDB      - Symbols loaded successfully from image header.
             C:\ProgramData\dbg\sym\msvcrt.pdb\1FEA8DB6B57F5FBFA935E090243420D01\msvcrt.pdb
    Load Report: public symbols , not source indexed
             C:\ProgramData\dbg\sym\msvcrt.pdb\1FEA8DB6B57F5FBFA935E090243420D01\msvcrt.pdb

0:001> !lmi 00007ff6`3b5a0000
Loaded Module Info: [00007ff6`3b5a0000]
         Module: AppP
   Base Address: 00007ff63b5a0000
     Image Name: AppP.exe
   Machine Type: 34404 (X64)
     Time Stamp: 5dcb22ca Tue Nov 12 21:23:22 2019
           Size: 28000
       CheckSum: 0
Characteristics: 22
Debug Data Dirs: Type   Size    VA   Pointer
            CODEVIEW    44, 1decc,    1cccc RSDS - GUID: {ECC2E0E9-C0E7-44B3-B5F9-0CF5F29213FF}
              Age: 1, Pdb: C:\AWMDA-Examples\AppP\x64\Release\AppP.pdb
          VC_FEATURE    14, 1df10,    1cd10 [Data not mapped]
                POGO   354, 1df24,    1cd24 [Data not mapped]
```

168

```
         ILTCG      0,     0,       0 [Debug data not mapped]
Image Type: MEMORY     - Image read successfully from loaded memory.
Symbol Type: PDB       - Symbols loaded successfully from image header.
          C:\ProgramData\dbg\sym\AppP.pdb\ECC2E0E9C0E744B3B5F90CF5F29213FF1\AppP.pdb
  Compiler: Linker - front end [0.0 bld 0] - back end [14.23 bld 28106]
Load Report: private symbols & lines, not source indexed
          C:\ProgramData\dbg\sym\AppP.pdb\ECC2E0E9C0E744B3B5F90CF5F29213FF1\AppP.pdb
```

Note: It is possible to do triple and even more levels of dereferencing (the **dpp** command does only two levels). Please see the reprinted *Triple Dereference* article at the end of this book, and the *Extended Windows Memory Dump Analysis* training teaches how to write an extension that does an arbitrary number of dereferences.

10.   We close logging before exiting WinDbg:

```
0:001> .logclose
Closing open log file C:\AWMDA-Dumps\Process\x64\AppP.log
```

Exercise P12

- **Goal:** Learn how to analyze managed space

- **Patterns:** Platform-Specific Debugger; CLR Thread; JIT Code (.NET); Managed Code Exception; Managed Stack Trace

- \AWMDA-Dumps\Exercise-P12-Analysis-process-dump-AppR2-64.pdf

Exercise P12: Analysis of an application process dump (AppR2, 64-bit)

Goal: Learn how to analyze managed space.

Patterns: Platform-Specific Debugger; CLR Thread; JIT Code (.NET); Managed Code Exception; Managed Stack Trace.

1.   Launch WinDbg.

2.   Open \AWMDA-Dumps\Process\x64\AppR2.exe.2816.dmp.

3.   We get the dump file loaded:

```
Microsoft (R) Windows Debugger Version 10.0.25877.1004 AMD64
Copyright (c) Microsoft Corporation. All rights reserved.

Loading Dump File [C:\AWMDA-Dumps\Process\x64\AppR2.exe.2816.dmp]
User Mini Dump File with Full Memory: Only application data is available

************* Path validation summary **************
Response                     Time (ms)     Location
Deferred                                   srv*
Symbol search path is: srv*
Executable search path is:
Windows 10 Version 22000 MP (2 procs) Free x64
Product: WinNt, suite: SingleUserTS Personal
Edition build lab: 22000.1.amd64fre.co_release.210604-1628
Machine Name:
Debug session time: Sat Nov 27 12:24:02.000 2021 (UTC + 1:00)
System Uptime: 0 days 0:05:25.898
Process Uptime: 0 days 0:02:46.000
.....................................................
...............................................
Loading unloaded module list
..
This dump file has an exception of interest stored in it.
The stored exception information can be accessed via .ecxr.
(b00.27c4): Access violation - code c0000005 (first/second chance not available)
For analysis of this file, run !analyze -v
ntdll!NtWaitForMultipleObjects+0x14:
00007ffd`70403eb4 c3               ret
```

Note: AppR2 shows this dialog on Windows 11 when launched:

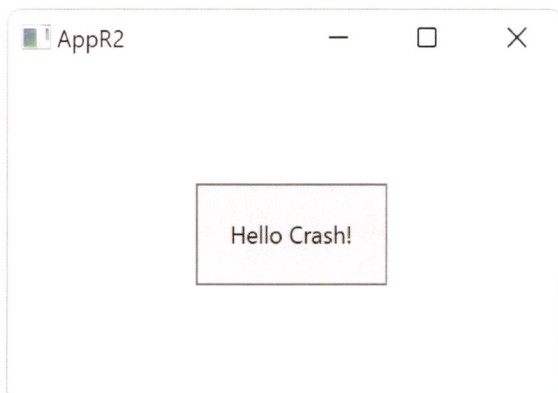

When we click on a button, it crashes, and if the *LocalDumps* registry key is set up[2], the crash dump is saved.

4.   Open a log file using the **.logopen** command:

```
0:000> .logopen C:\AWMDA-Dumps\Process\x64\AppR2.log
Opened log file 'C:\AWMDA-Dumps\Process\x64\AppR2.log'
```

5.   Type the ~*k command to verify the correctness of all stack traces:

```
0:000> ~*kL
```

```
.  0  Id: b00.27c4 Suspend: 0 Teb: 00000003`1ed0a000 Unfrozen
 # Child-SP          RetAddr           Call Site
00 00000003`1ef7b808 00007ffd`6dbcf9f0 ntdll!NtWaitForMultipleObjects+0x14
01 00000003`1ef7b810 00007ffd`6dbcf8ee KERNELBASE!WaitForMultipleObjectsEx+0xf0
02 00000003`1ef7bb00 00007ffd`6e25ef97 KERNELBASE!WaitForMultipleObjects+0xe
03 00000003`1ef7bb40 00007ffd`6e25e9d6 kernel32!WerpReportFaultInternal+0x587
04 00000003`1ef7bc60 00007ffd`6dcc24d3 kernel32!WerpReportFault+0xbe
05 00000003`1ef7bca0 00007ffd`7040a36c KERNELBASE!UnhandledExceptionFilter+0x3e3
06 00000003`1ef7bdc0 00007ffd`703f3626 ntdll!RtlUserThreadStart$filt$0+0xac
07 00000003`1ef7be00 00007ffd`704082ff ntdll!_C_specific_handler+0x96
08 00000003`1ef7be70 00007ffd`70395a0a ntdll!RtlpExecuteHandlerForException+0xf
09 00000003`1ef7bea0 00007ffd`70392cd3 ntdll!RtlDispatchException+0x25a
0a 00000003`1ef7c5f0 00007ffd`6dbc466c ntdll!RtlRaiseException+0x163
0b 00000003`1ef7cdd0 00007ffd`22e3b6f9 KERNELBASE!RaiseException+0x6c
0c 00000003`1ef7ceb0 00007ffd`22e3b72b coreclr!NakedThrowHelper2+0x9
0d 00000003`1ef7cee0 00007ffd`22e3b735 coreclr!NakedThrowHelper_RspAligned+0x1e
0e 00000003`1ef7d408 00007ffc`c3c6f8e9 coreclr!NakedThrowHelper_FixRsp+0x5
0f 00000003`1ef7d410 00007ffc`c3ad85c3 0x00007ffc`c3c6f8e9
10 00000003`1ef7d450 00007ffc`c3ad7cc4 0x00007ffc`c3ad85c3
11 00000003`1ef7d510 00007ffd`217f88d7 0x00007ffc`c3ad7cc4
12 00000003`1ef7d570 00007ffd`216dd0a0 PresentationFramework+0xbb88d7
13 00000003`1ef7d5b0 00007ffd`217f9350 PresentationFramework+0xa9d0a0
14 00000003`1ef7d5f0 00000000`5c933702 PresentationFramework+0xbb9350
15 00000003`1ef7d630 00000000`5c958522 PresentationCore+0x403702
16 00000003`1ef7d670 00007ffc`c3ad52f3 PresentationCore+0x428522
17 00000003`1ef7d6b0 00007ffc`c3ad85c3 0x00007ffc`c3ad52f3
18 00000003`1ef7d6f0 00000000`5c9416f9 0x00007ffc`c3ad85c3
19 00000003`1ef7d7b0 00000000`5c93344a PresentationCore+0x4116f9
1a 00000003`1ef7d820 00000000`5c958522 PresentationCore+0x40344a
1b 00000003`1ef7d860 00007ffc`c3ad52f3 PresentationCore+0x428522
1c 00000003`1ef7d8a0 00007ffc`c3ad85c3 0x00007ffc`c3ad52f3
1d 00000003`1ef7d8e0 00007ffc`c3ad7cc4 0x00007ffc`c3ad85c3
1e 00000003`1ef7d9a0 00007ffc`c3adfc11 0x00007ffc`c3ad7cc4
1f 00000003`1ef7da00 00007ffc`c3ae885d 0x00007ffc`c3adfc11
20 00000003`1ef7da40 00007ffc`c3c41e81 0x00007ffc`c3ae885d
21 00000003`1ef7db00 00007ffc`c3c4a9b4 0x00007ffc`c3c41e81
22 00000003`1ef7db50 00007ffc`c3ae18a4 0x00007ffc`c3c4a9b4
23 00000003`1ef7dc80 00007ffc`c3ae1026 0x00007ffc`c3ae18a4
24 00000003`1ef7dd20 00007ffc`c3ae0b7d 0x00007ffc`c3ae1026
25 00000003`1ef7dd90 00007ffc`c3ae0a86 0x00007ffc`c3ae0b7d
26 00000003`1ef7de20 00007ffc`c3ad90f7 0x00007ffc`c3ae0a86
27 00000003`1ef7de70 00007ffc`c3ad8f25 0x00007ffc`c3ad90f7
28 00000003`1ef7ded0 00007ffc`c3ae06fc 0x00007ffc`c3ad8f25
29 00000003`1ef7df20 00007ffc`c3adfff7 0x00007ffc`c3ae06fc
2a 00000003`1ef7dfb0 00007ffc`c32cd892 0x00007ffc`c3adfff7
2b 00000003`1ef7e0b0 00007ffd`6ea11c4c 0x00007ffc`c32cd892
2c 00000003`1ef7e130 00007ffd`6ea10ea6 user32!UserCallWinProcCheckWow+0x33c
2d 00000003`1ef7e2a0 00007ffc`c371039b user32!DispatchMessageWorker+0x2a6
2e 00000003`1ef7e320 00007ffd`234d7f03 0x00007ffc`c371039b
2f 00000003`1ef7e3e0 00007ffd`234d53e1 WindowsBase+0x197f03
30 00000003`1ef7e470 00007ffd`234d538e WindowsBase+0x1953e1
```

[2] Collecting User-Mode Dumps https://docs.microsoft.com/en-us/windows/win32/wer/collecting-user-mode-dumps

```
31 00000003`1ef7e4a0 00007ffd`2140dfdc     WindowsBase+0x19538e
32 00000003`1ef7e4d0 00007ffd`2140c63d     PresentationFramework+0x7cdfdc
33 00000003`1ef7e500 00007ffd`214095cc     PresentationFramework+0x7cc63d
34 00000003`1ef7e550 00007ffc`c32b619e     PresentationFramework+0x7c95cc
35 00000003`1ef7e580 00007ffd`22e3a793     0x00007ffc`c32b619e
36 00000003`1ef7e5d0 00007ffd`22d258fa     coreclr!CallDescrWorkerInternal+0x83
37 00000003`1ef7e610 00007ffd`22d1fc7f     coreclr!MethodDescCallSite::CallTargetWorker+0x3d2
38 (Inline Function) --------`--------     coreclr!MethodDescCallSite::Call+0xb
39 00000003`1ef7e7a0 00007ffd`22d1fa4a     coreclr!RunMainInternal+0x11f
3a 00000003`1ef7e8d0 00007ffd`22d1f7a9     coreclr!RunMain+0xd2
3b 00000003`1ef7e980 00007ffd`22d20108     coreclr!Assembly::ExecuteMainMethod+0x1cd
3c 00000003`1ef7ed10 00007ffd`22d15112     coreclr!CorHost2::ExecuteAssembly+0x1c8
3d 00000003`1ef7ee80 00007ffd`26362993     coreclr!coreclr_execute_assembly+0xe2
3e (Inline Function) --------`--------     hostpolicy!coreclr_t::execute_assembly+0x27
3f 00000003`1ef7ef20 00007ffd`26362c07     hostpolicy!run_app_for_context+0x3d3
40 00000003`1ef7f0b0 00007ffd`2636354e     hostpolicy!run_app+0x37
41 00000003`1ef7f0f0 00007ffd`263c3d95     hostpolicy!corehost_main+0xfe
42 00000003`1ef7f2a0 00007ffd`263c6f48     hostfxr!execute_app+0x21d
43 (Inline Function) --------`--------     hostfxr!?A0xe58ccfba::read_config_and_execute+0x10a
44 00000003`1ef7f390 00007ffd`263c59b8     hostfxr!fx_muxer_t::handle_exec_host_command+0x214
45 00000003`1ef7f480 00007ffd`263c21a9     hostfxr!fx_muxer_t::execute+0x20c
*** WARNING: Unable to verify checksum for AppR2.exe
46 00000003`1ef7f5b0 00007ff7`902adc1c     hostfxr!hostfxr_main_startupinfo+0x89
47 00000003`1ef7f6b0 00007ff7`902adf81     AppR2_exe!exe_start+0x604
48 00000003`1ef7f8a0 00007ff7`902af4f8     AppR2_exe!wmain+0x129
49 (Inline Function) --------`--------     AppR2_exe!invoke_main+0x22
4a 00000003`1ef7fa10 00007ffd`6e2054e0     AppR2_exe!__scrt_common_main_seh+0x10c
4b 00000003`1ef7fa50 00007ffd`7036485b     kernel32!BaseThreadInitThunk+0x10
4c 00000003`1ef7fa80 00000000`00000000     ntdll!RtlUserThreadStart+0x2b

   1  Id: b00.21e0 Suspend: 0 Teb: 00000003`1ed12000 Unfrozen
 # Child-SP          RetAddr               Call Site
00 00000003`1f57f168 00007ffd`6dbcf9f0     ntdll!NtWaitForMultipleObjects+0x14
01 00000003`1f57f170 00007ffd`6dbcf8ee     KERNELBASE!WaitForMultipleObjectsEx+0xf0
02 00000003`1f57f460 00007ffd`22dd8afa     KERNELBASE!WaitForMultipleObjects+0xe
03 00000003`1f57f4a0 00007ffd`22dd8733     coreclr!IpcStream::DiagnosticsIpc::Poll+0x132
04 00000003`1f57f520 00007ffd`22dd8452     coreclr!IpcStreamFactory::GetNextAvailableStream+0x2bb
05 00000003`1f57f7f0 00007ffd`6e2054e0     coreclr!DiagnosticServer::DiagnosticsServerThread+0x92
06 00000003`1f57f8b0 00007ffd`7036485b     kernel32!BaseThreadInitThunk+0x10
07 00000003`1f57f8e0 00000000`00000000     ntdll!RtlUserThreadStart+0x2b

   2  Id: b00.119c Suspend: 0 Teb: 00000003`1ed14000 Unfrozen
 # Child-SP          RetAddr               Call Site
00 00000003`1f6ff848 00007ffd`6dbcf9f0     ntdll!NtWaitForMultipleObjects+0x14
01 00000003`1f6ff850 00007ffd`22dd907d     KERNELBASE!WaitForMultipleObjectsEx+0xf0
02 00000003`1f6ffb40 00007ffd`22dd8f8d     coreclr!DebuggerRCThread::MainLoop+0xe9
03 00000003`1f6ffc00 00007ffd`22dd90ce     coreclr!DebuggerRCThread::ThreadProc+0x139
04 00000003`1f6ffc60 00007ffd`6e2054e0     coreclr!DebuggerRCThread::ThreadProcStatic+0x3e
05 00000003`1f6ffc90 00007ffd`7036485b     kernel32!BaseThreadInitThunk+0x10
06 00000003`1f6ffcc0 00000000`00000000     ntdll!RtlUserThreadStart+0x2b

   3  Id: b00.bc0 Suspend: 0 Teb: 00000003`1ed16000 Unfrozen ""
 # Child-SP          RetAddr               Call Site
00 00000003`1f87fa18 00007ffd`6dbc292e     ntdll!NtWaitForSingleObject+0x14
01 00000003`1f87fa20 00007ffd`22d6a4b0     KERNELBASE!WaitForSingleObjectEx+0x8e
02 (Inline Function) --------`--------     coreclr!CLREventWaitHelper2+0x6
03 00000003`1f87fac0 00007ffd`22d67435     coreclr!CLREventWaitHelper+0x20
04 (Inline Function) --------`--------     coreclr!CLREventBase::WaitEx+0x10
05 (Inline Function) --------`--------     coreclr!CLREventBase::Wait+0x10
06 00000003`1f87fb20 00007ffd`22d66f5a     coreclr!FinalizerThread::WaitForFinalizerEvent+0x21
07 00000003`1f87fb60 00007ffd`22d3d593     coreclr!FinalizerThread::FinalizerThreadWorker+0x3a
08 (Inline Function) --------`--------     coreclr!ManagedThreadBase_DispatchInner+0xd
09 00000003`1f87fb90 00007ffd`22d3d477     coreclr!ManagedThreadBase_DispatchMiddle+0x8f
0a 00000003`1f87fca0 00007ffd`22dd834e     coreclr!ManagedThreadBase_DispatchOuter+0xb3
0b (Inline Function) --------`--------     coreclr!ManagedThreadBase_NoADTransition+0x28
0c (Inline Function) --------`--------     coreclr!ManagedThreadBase::FinalizerBase+0x28
0d 00000003`1f87fd50 00007ffd`6e2054e0     coreclr!FinalizerThread::FinalizerThreadStart+0x9e
```

```
0e 00000003`1f87fe60 00007ffd`7036485b     kernel32!BaseThreadInitThunk+0x10
0f 00000003`1f87fe90 00000000`00000000     ntdll!RtlUserThreadStart+0x2b

   4  Id: b00.1598 Suspend: 0 Teb: 00000003`1ed18000 Unfrozen ""
 # Child-SP          RetAddr               Call Site
00 00000003`1eb3fa58 00007ffd`703bb4c3     ntdll!NtDelayExecution+0x14
01 00000003`1eb3fa60 00007ffd`6dbcb281     ntdll!RtlDelayExecution+0x43
02 00000003`1eb3fa90 00007ffd`22d3c8d5     KERNELBASE!SleepEx+0x71
03 00000003`1eb3fb10 00007ffd`22d3c860     coreclr!ThreadpoolMgr::TimerThreadFire+0x71
04 00000003`1eb3fbb0 00007ffd`6e2054e0     coreclr!ThreadpoolMgr::TimerThreadStart+0x90
05 00000003`1eb3fbe0 00007ffd`7036485b     kernel32!BaseThreadInitThunk+0x10
06 00000003`1eb3fc10 00000000`00000000     ntdll!RtlUserThreadStart+0x2b

   5  Id: b00.1eb4 Suspend: 0 Teb: 00000003`1ed20000 Unfrozen
 # Child-SP          RetAddr               Call Site
00 00000003`1fb7fd98 00007ffd`6dbc292e     ntdll!NtWaitForSingleObject+0x14
01 00000003`1fb7fda0 00007ffd`20130b26     KERNELBASE!WaitForSingleObjectEx+0x8e
02 00000003`1fb7fe40 00007ffd`20131013     wpfgfx_cor3!CPartitionManager::GetWork+0x196
03 00000003`1fb7fe90 00007ffd`20130d73     wpfgfx_cor3!CPartitionThread::Run+0x23
04 00000003`1fb7fec0 00007ffd`6e2054e0     wpfgfx_cor3!CPartitionThread::ThreadMain+0x23
05 00000003`1fb7fef0 00007ffd`7036485b     kernel32!BaseThreadInitThunk+0x10
06 00000003`1fb7ff20 00000000`00000000     ntdll!RtlUserThreadStart+0x2b

   6  Id: b00.1b88 Suspend: 0 Teb: 00000003`1ed22000 Unfrozen
 # Child-SP          RetAddr               Call Site
00 00000003`1fcff928 00007ffd`70376b4f     ntdll!NtWaitForWorkViaWorkerFactory+0x14
01 00000003`1fcff930 00007ffd`6e2054e0     ntdll!TppWorkerThread+0x2df
02 00000003`1fcffc20 00007ffd`7036485b     kernel32!BaseThreadInitThunk+0x10
03 00000003`1fcffc50 00000000`00000000     ntdll!RtlUserThreadStart+0x2b

   7  Id: b00.1ec4 Suspend: 0 Teb: 00000003`1ed24000 Unfrozen
 # Child-SP          RetAddr               Call Site
00 00000003`1fe7f988 00007ffd`70376b4f     ntdll!NtWaitForWorkViaWorkerFactory+0x14
01 00000003`1fe7f990 00007ffd`6e2054e0     ntdll!TppWorkerThread+0x2df
02 00000003`1fe7fc80 00007ffd`7036485b     kernel32!BaseThreadInitThunk+0x10
03 00000003`1fe7fcb0 00000000`00000000     ntdll!RtlUserThreadStart+0x2b

   8  Id: b00.1f2c Suspend: 0 Teb: 00000003`1ed26000 Unfrozen ""
 # Child-SP          RetAddr               Call Site
00 00000003`1ffff5b8 00007ffd`6ea1d1ee     win32u!NtUserMsgWaitForMultipleObjectsEx+0x14
01 00000003`1ffff5c0 00007ffd`1f8074a1     user32!RealMsgWaitForMultipleObjectsEx+0x1e
02 00000003`1ffff600 00007ffd`1f8078b9     PenIMC_cor3!CPimcContext::GetPenEvent+0xb1
03 00000003`1ffff6c0 00007ffc`c3aa2794     PenIMC_cor3!GetPenEvent+0x69
04 00000003`1ffff710 00000000`5caf1151     0x00007ffc`c3aa2794
05 00000003`1ffff810 00007ffd`220abf7f     PresentationCore+0x5c1151
06 00000003`1ffff8d0 00007ffd`220b5520
System_Private_CoreLib!System.Threading.ThreadHelper.ThreadStart_Context(System.Object)$##60025B9+0x2f
07 00000003`1ffff900 00007ffd`220ac08b
System_Private_CoreLib!System.Threading.ExecutionContext.RunInternal(System.Threading.ExecutionContext,
System.Threading.ContextCallback, System.Object)$##6002787+0x80
08 00000003`1ffff970 00007ffd`22e3a793
System_Private_CoreLib!System.Threading.ThreadHelper.ThreadStart()$##60025BC+0x2b
09 00000003`1ffff9b0 00007ffd`22d258fa     coreclr!CallDescrWorkerInternal+0x83
0a 00000003`1ffff9f0 00007ffd`22e280ac     coreclr!MethodDescCallSite::CallTargetWorker+0x3d2
0b 00000003`1ffffb80 00007ffd`22d3d593     coreclr!ThreadNative::KickOffThread_Worker+0x10c
0c (Inline Function) --------`--------     coreclr!ManagedThreadBase_DispatchInner+0xd
0d 00000003`1ffffce0 00007ffd`22d3d477     coreclr!ManagedThreadBase_DispatchMiddle+0x8f
0e 00000003`1ffffdf0 00007ffd`22dd9f41     coreclr!ManagedThreadBase_DispatchOuter+0xb3
0f (Inline Function) --------`--------     coreclr!ManagedThreadBase_FullTransition+0x28
10 (Inline Function) --------`--------     coreclr!ManagedThreadBase::KickOff+0x28
11 00000003`1ffffea0 00007ffd`6e2054e0     coreclr!ThreadNative::KickOffThread+0x81
12 00000003`1fffff00 00007ffd`7036485b     kernel32!BaseThreadInitThunk+0x10
13 00000003`1fffff30 00000000`00000000     ntdll!RtlUserThreadStart+0x2b

   9  Id: b00.1d3c Suspend: 0 Teb: 00000003`1ed2a000 Unfrozen
 # Child-SP          RetAddr               Call Site
00 00000003`202ff508 00007ffd`70376b4f     ntdll!NtWaitForWorkViaWorkerFactory+0x14
```

```
01 00000003`202ff510 00007ffd`6e2054e0    ntdll!TppWorkerThread+0x2df
02 00000003`202ff800 00007ffd`7036485b    kernel32!BaseThreadInitThunk+0x10
03 00000003`202ff830 00000000`00000000    ntdll!RtlUserThreadStart+0x2b

  10  Id: b00.1d38 Suspend: 0 Teb: 00000003`1ed2c000 Unfrozen
 # Child-SP          RetAddr               Call Site
00 00000003`2047f478 00007ffd`70376b4f    ntdll!NtWaitForWorkViaWorkerFactory+0x14
01 00000003`2047f480 00007ffd`6e2054e0    ntdll!TppWorkerThread+0x2df
02 00000003`2047f770 00007ffd`7036485b    kernel32!BaseThreadInitThunk+0x10
03 00000003`2047f7a0 00000000`00000000    ntdll!RtlUserThreadStart+0x2b

  11  Id: b00.1abc Suspend: 0 Teb: 00000003`1ed2e000 Unfrozen
 # Child-SP          RetAddr               Call Site
00 00000003`205ff8b8 00007ffd`6ea2464e    win32u!NtUserGetMessage+0x14
01 00000003`205ff8c0 00007ffd`6e34d118    user32!GetMessageW+0x2e
02 00000003`205ff920 00007ffd`6e34d050    combase!CDllHost::STAWorkerLoop+0x64
03 00000003`205ff9a0 00007ffd`6e3023bc    combase!CDllHost::WorkerThread+0xd4
04 00000003`205ff9e0 00007ffd`6e302339    combase!CRpcThread::WorkerLoop+0x58
05 00000003`205ffa50 00007ffd`6e2054e0    combase!CRpcThreadCache::RpcWorkerThreadEntry+0x29
06 00000003`205ffa80 00007ffd`7036485b    kernel32!BaseThreadInitThunk+0x10
07 00000003`205ffab0 00000000`00000000    ntdll!RtlUserThreadStart+0x2b

  12  Id: b00.1928 Suspend: 0 Teb: 00000003`1ed32000 Unfrozen ""
 # Child-SP          RetAddr               Call Site
00 00000003`208ffbb8 00007ffd`6ea1d1ee    win32u!NtUserMsgWaitForMultipleObjectsEx+0x14
01 00000003`208ffbc0 00007ffd`1f7ac45a    user32!RealMsgWaitForMultipleObjectsEx+0x1e
02 00000003`208ffc00 00007ffd`6fb6dfb4    wisp!CServiceModule::WispInputThreadProc+0x34a
03 00000003`208ffcc0 00007ffd`6fb6e08c    msvcrt!_callthreadstartex+0x28
04 00000003`208ffcf0 00007ffd`6e2054e0    msvcrt!_threadstartex+0x7c
05 00000003`208ffd20 00007ffd`7036485b    kernel32!BaseThreadInitThunk+0x10
06 00000003`208ffd50 00000000`00000000    ntdll!RtlUserThreadStart+0x2b

  13  Id: b00.3b8 Suspend: 0 Teb: 00000003`1ed36000 Unfrozen
 # Child-SP          RetAddr               Call Site
00 00000003`20bffa28 00007ffd`6ea1d1ee    win32u!NtUserMsgWaitForMultipleObjectsEx+0x14
01 00000003`20bffa30 00007ffd`1f80b254    user32!RealMsgWaitForMultipleObjectsEx+0x1e
02 00000003`20bffa70 00007ffd`6e2054e0    PenIMC_cor3!CPimcManager::HookThreadProc+0x74
03 00000003`20bffb00 00007ffd`7036485b    kernel32!BaseThreadInitThunk+0x10
04 00000003`20bffb30 00000000`00000000    ntdll!RtlUserThreadStart+0x2b

  14  Id: b00.14fc Suspend: 0 Teb: 00000003`1ed56000 Unfrozen ""
 # Child-SP          RetAddr               Call Site
00 00000003`1f0ff6f8 00007ffd`6dbd0913    ntdll!NtRemoveIoCompletion+0x14
01 00000003`1f0ff700 00007ffd`22d73a38    KERNELBASE!GetQueuedCompletionStatus+0x53
02 00000003`1f0ff760 00007ffd`22d73993    coreclr!CLRLifoSemaphore::WaitForSignal+0x30
03 00000003`1f0ff7a0 00007ffd`22d732ad    coreclr!CLRLifoSemaphore::Wait+0x113
04 00000003`1f0ff7e0 00007ffd`6e2054e0    coreclr!ThreadpoolMgr::WorkerThreadStart+0x27d
05 00000003`1f0ff8e0 00007ffd`7036485b    kernel32!BaseThreadInitThunk+0x10
06 00000003`1f0ff910 00000000`00000000    ntdll!RtlUserThreadStart+0x2b

  15  Id: b00.284c Suspend: 0 Teb: 00000003`1ed5a000 Unfrozen ""
 # Child-SP          RetAddr               Call Site
00 00000003`1f27faf8 00007ffd`6dbd0913    ntdll!NtRemoveIoCompletion+0x14
01 00000003`1f27fb00 00007ffd`22d73a38    KERNELBASE!GetQueuedCompletionStatus+0x53
02 00000003`1f27fb60 00007ffd`22d73993    coreclr!CLRLifoSemaphore::WaitForSignal+0x30
03 00000003`1f27fba0 00007ffd`22d732ad    coreclr!CLRLifoSemaphore::Wait+0x113
04 00000003`1f27fbe0 00007ffd`6e2054e0    coreclr!ThreadpoolMgr::WorkerThreadStart+0x27d
05 00000003`1f27fce0 00007ffd`7036485b    kernel32!BaseThreadInitThunk+0x10
06 00000003`1f27fd10 00000000`00000000    ntdll!RtlUserThreadStart+0x2b

  16  Id: b00.2b2c Suspend: 0 Teb: 00000003`1ed5c000 Unfrozen ""
 # Child-SP          RetAddr               Call Site
00 00000003`1eb7f548 00007ffd`6dbc292e    ntdll!NtWaitForSingleObject+0x14
01 00000003`1eb7f550 00007ffd`22d72cdf    KERNELBASE!WaitForSingleObjectEx+0x8e
02 (Inline Function) --------`--------    coreclr!GateThreadTimer::Wait+0x15
03 00000003`1eb7f5f0 00007ffd`6e2054e0    coreclr!ThreadpoolMgr::GateThreadStart+0x1ef
04 00000003`1eb7f750 00007ffd`7036485b    kernel32!BaseThreadInitThunk+0x10
```

```
05 00000003`1eb7f780 00000000`00000000      ntdll!RtlUserThreadStart+0x2b

  17  Id: b00.2b34 Suspend: 0 Teb: 00000003`1ed5e000 Unfrozen
# Child-SP          RetAddr               Call Site
00 00000003`1f3ff258 00007ffd`6dbcf9f0      ntdll!NtWaitForMultipleObjects+0x14
01 00000003`1f3ff260 00007ffd`6e302748      KERNELBASE!WaitForMultipleObjectsEx+0xf0
02 00000003`1f3ff550 00007ffd`6e3025ba      combase!WaitCoalesced+0xa4
03 00000003`1f3ff7e0 00007ffd`6e3023bc      combase!CROIDTable::WorkerThreadLoop+0x5a
04 00000003`1f3ff830 00007ffd`6e302339      combase!CRpcThread::WorkerLoop+0x58
05 00000003`1f3ff8a0 00007ffd`6e2054e0      combase!CRpcThreadCache::RpcWorkerThreadEntry+0x29
06 00000003`1f3ff8d0 00007ffd`7036485b      kernel32!BaseThreadInitThunk+0x10
07 00000003`1f3ff900 00000000`00000000      ntdll!RtlUserThreadStart+0x2b

  18  Id: b00.1de8 Suspend: 0 Teb: 00000003`1ed60000 Unfrozen
# Child-SP          RetAddr               Call Site
00 00000003`1f9ff748 00007ffd`6dbcf9f0      ntdll!NtWaitForMultipleObjects+0x14
01 00000003`1f9ff750 00007ffd`6e302748      KERNELBASE!WaitForMultipleObjectsEx+0xf0
02 00000003`1f9ffa40 00007ffd`6e302481      combase!WaitCoalesced+0xa4
03 00000003`1f9ffcd0 00007ffd`6e302339      combase!CRpcThread::WorkerLoop+0x11d
04 00000003`1f9ffd40 00007ffd`6e2054e0      combase!CRpcThreadCache::RpcWorkerThreadEntry+0x29
05 00000003`1f9ffd70 00007ffd`7036485b      kernel32!BaseThreadInitThunk+0x10
06 00000003`1f9ffda0 00000000`00000000      ntdll!RtlUserThreadStart+0x2b
```

Note: We see that threads #0 - #4, #8, #14 - #16 have the coreclr module on their stack traces (the previous versions of .NET Framework used **clr** and **mscorwks** modules). We also see signs of software exception (in red) and exception stack trace #0, with signs of managed code exception processing (in yellow). Finally, the stack trace fragment from our *AppR2* module is shown in green.

6.   Let's see what the **!analyze -v** command says:

```
0:000> !analyze -v
*******************************************************************************
*                                                                             *
*                        Exception Analysis                                   *
*                                                                             *
*******************************************************************************

!ip2md 7ffcc3c6f8e9

MethodDesc:      00007ffcc384c900
Method Name:         AppR2.MainWindow.Button_Click(System.Object, System.Windows.RoutedEventArgs)
Class:               00007ffcc3839448
MethodTable:         00007ffcc384c9e0
mdToken:             0000000006000005
Module:              00007ffcc3352750
IsJitted:            yes
Current CodeAddr:    00007ffcc3c6f8b0
Version History:
  ILCodeVersion:     0000000000000000
  ReJIT ID:          0
  IL Addr:           0000016dfc54209c
     CodeAddr:          00007ffcc3c6f8b0  (MinOptJitted)
     NativeCodeVersion: 0000000000000000

KEY_VALUES_STRING: 1

    Key  : AV.Dereference
    Value: NullPtr

    Key  : AV.Fault
    Value: Write

    Key  : Analysis.CPU.mSec
    Value: 5093

    Key  : Analysis.DebugAnalysisManager
    Value: Create

    Key  : Analysis.Elapsed.mSec
    Value: 9288

    Key  : Analysis.Init.CPU.mSec
    Value: 406

    Key  : Analysis.Init.Elapsed.mSec
    Value: 170073

    Key  : Analysis.Memory.CommitPeak.Mb
    Value: 229

    Key  : CLR.Engine
```

```
    Value: CORECLR

    Key  : CLR.Version
    Value: 5.0.1021.41214

    Key  : Timeline.OS.Boot.DeltaSec
    Value: 325

    Key  : Timeline.Process.Start.DeltaSec
    Value: 166

    Key  : WER.OS.Branch
    Value: co_release

    Key  : WER.OS.Timestamp
    Value: 2021-06-04T16:28:00Z

    Key  : WER.OS.Version
    Value: 10.0.22000.1

    Key  : WER.Process.Version
    Value: 1.0.0.0


FILE_IN_CAB: AppR2.exe.2816.dmp

NTGLOBALFLAG:  400

PROCESS_BAM_CURRENT_THROTTLED: 0

PROCESS_BAM_PREVIOUS_THROTTLED: 0

APPLICATION_VERIFIER_FLAGS:  0

CONTEXT:  (.ecxr)
rax=0000000000820014 rbx=0000016d80081ec8 rcx=00000007fff9fffe
rdx=00007ffcc384c900 rsi=0000016d80145f40 rdi=0000016d80142e18
rip=00007ffd6dbc466c rsp=000000031ef7cdd0 rbp=000000031ef7d440
 r8=00007ffcc3c40020  r9=0000000c0000000c r10=00007ffcc3c6f8f8
r11=0000000100000001 r12=0000016d801425e0 r13=0000016d80081ec8
r14=0000000000000000 r15=0000016d80142e30
iopl=0         nv up ei pl nz na po nc
cs=0033  ss=002b  ds=002b  es=002b  fs=0053  gs=002b             efl=00000206
KERNELBASE!RaiseException+0x6c:
00007ffd`6dbc466c 0f1f440000      nop     dword ptr [rax+rax]
Resetting default scope

EXCEPTION_RECORD:  (.exr -1)
ExceptionAddress: 00007ffcc3c6f8e9
   ExceptionCode: c0000005 (Access violation)
  ExceptionFlags: 00000080
NumberParameters: 2
   Parameter[0]: 0000000000000001
   Parameter[1]: 0000000000000000
Attempt to write to address 0000000000000000

PROCESS_NAME:  AppR2.exe

WRITE_ADDRESS:  0000000000000000

ERROR_CODE: (NTSTATUS) 0xc0000005 - The instruction at 0x%p referenced memory at 0x%p. The memory could not be %s.

EXCEPTION_CODE_STR:  c0000005

EXCEPTION_PARAMETER1:  0000000000000001

EXCEPTION_PARAMETER2:  0000000000000000

STACK_TEXT:
00000003`1ef7cdd0 00007ffd`22e3b6f9     : 00000000`00000000 00000000`00000000 00000000`00000000 00000000`00000000 : KERNELBASE!RaiseException+0x6c
00000003`1ef7ceb0 00007ffd`22e3b72b     : 00000000`00000000 00000000`00000000 00000000`00001085 00000040`14622002 : coreclr!NakedThrowHelper2+0x9
00000003`1ef7cee0 00007ffd`22e3b735     : 00007ffc`c3c6f8e9 0000016d`80145f40 0000016d`80081ec8 00000000`00000000 : coreclr!NakedThrowHelper_RspAligned+0x1e
00000003`1ef7d408 00007ffc`c3c6f8e9     : 0000016d`80145f40 0000016d`80081ec8 00000000`00000000 0000016d`801425e0 : coreclr!NakedThrowHelper_FixRsp+0x5
00000003`1ef7d410 00007ffc`c3ad85c3     : 0000016d`8005e288 0000016d`80081ec8 0000016d`80145f40 00000000`00000000 : AppR2!AppR2.MainWindow.Button_Click+0x39
00000003`1ef7d450 00007ffc`c3ad7cc4     : 00000000`00000000 00000000`00000000 00000000`00000000 00000003`5c950cb5 : PresentationCore!System.Windows.EventRoute.InvokeHandlersImpl+0x143
00000003`1ef7d510 00007ffd`217f88d7     : 0000016d`80081ec8 0000016d`80145f40 0000016d`80081ec8 00000003`1ef7d490 : PresentationCore!System.Windows.UIElement.RaiseEventImpl+0xf4
00000003`1ef7d570 00007ffd`216dd0a0     : 0000016d`80081ec8 0000016d`fabbe820 0000016d`800f6b98 00000003`1ef7d490 : PresentationFramework!System.Windows.Controls.Primitives.ButtonBase.OnClick+0x37
00000003`1ef7d5b0 00007ffd`217f9350     : 0000016d`80081ec8 00000003`00000130 00000003`1ef7d4c0 : PresentationFramework!System.Windows.Controls.Button.OnClick+0x50
00000003`1ef7d5f0 00000000`5c933702     : 0000016d`80081ec8 0000016d`801425e0 00007ffc`c396c6f8 00000000`00000001 : PresentationFramework!System.Windows.Controls.Primitives.ButtonBase.OnMouseLeftButtonUp+0xa0
00000003`1ef7d630 00000000`5c958522     : 0000016d`80081ec8 0000016d`801425e0 0000016d`801425e0 00000000`00000001 : PresentationCore!System.Windows.UIElement.OnMouseLeftButtonUpThunk+0x62
00000003`1ef7d670 00007ffc`c3ad52f3     : 0000016d`801425e0 0000016d`80081ec8 00000000`00000000 : PresentationCore!System.Windows.Input.MouseButtonEventArgs.InvokeEventHandler+0x22
00000003`1ef7d6b0 00007ffc`c3ad85c3     : 0000016d`801425e0 00000000`00000000 0000016d`80081ec8 0000016d`80137ff0 : PresentationCore!System.Windows.RoutedEventArgs.InvokeHandler+0x33
00000003`1ef7d6f0 00000000`5c9416f9     : 0000016d`80081ec8 0000016d`801425e0 00007ffc`c396c6f8 00000000`00000000 : PresentationCore!System.Windows.EventRoute.InvokeHandlersImpl+0x143
00000003`1ef7d7b0 00000000`5c93344a     : 0000016d`80081ec8 0000016d`801425e0 0000016d`801425e0 00000000`00000000 : PresentationCore!System.Windows.UIElement.ReRaiseEventAs+0x169
00000003`1ef7d820 00000000`5c958522     : 0000016d`80081ec8 0000016d`801425e0 0000016d`80081ec8 00000000`00000000 : PresentationCore!System.Windows.UIElement.OnMouseUpThunk+0xba
00000003`1ef7d860 00007ffc`c3ad52f3     : 0000016d`80069ab0 00000000`00000001 0000016d`80081ec8 00000000`00000000 : PresentationCore!System.Windows.Input.MouseButtonEventArgs.InvokeEventHandler+0x22
00000003`1ef7d8a0 00007ffc`c3ad85c3     : 0000016d`801425e0 00007ffc`c3ad3b7f 00000000`00000000 0000016d`8005e288 : PresentationCore!System.Windows.RoutedEventArgs.InvokeHandler+0x33
00000003`1ef7d8e0 00007ffc`c3ad7cc4     : 00000000`00000000 00000000`00000000 00000000`00000000 00000000`00000000 : PresentationCore!System.Windows.EventRoute.InvokeHandlersImpl+0x143
00000003`1ef7d9a0 00007ffc`c3adfc11     : 0000016d`80081ec8 0000016d`801425e0 0000016d`801086c8 0000016d`8005f208 : PresentationCore!System.Windows.UIElement.RaiseEventImpl+0xf4
00000003`1ef7da00 00007ffc`c3ae885d     : 0000016d`801425e0 0000016d`801425e0 0000016d`801086c8 0000016d`80141080 : PresentationCore!System.Windows.UIElement.RaiseTrustedEvent+0x31
00000003`1ef7da40 00007ffc`c3c41e81     : 00007ffc`c3638240 00000000`00000000 0000016d`fabbe820 0000016d`800ce828 : PresentationCore!System.Windows.Input.InputManager.ProcessStagingArea+0x45d
00000003`1ef7db00 00007ffc`c3c4a9b4     : 0000016d`801425e0 00000000`00000000 00000000`00000000 00000000`00000000 : PresentationCore!System.Windows.Input.InputProviderSite.ReportInput+0x61
00000003`1ef7db50 00007ffc`c3ae18a4     : 0000016d`800ce0c0 00000000`000104d0 00000000`00000000 00000003`0004d28e : PresentationCore!System.Windows.Interop.HwndMouseInputProvider.ReportInput+0x444
00000003`1ef7dc80 00007ffc`c3ae1026     : 0000016d`800ce0c0 00000000`000104d0 0000016d`00000202 00000000`00000000 : PresentationCore!System.Windows.Interop.HwndMouseInputProvider.FilterMessage+0x344
00000003`1ef7dd20 00007ffc`c3ae0b7d     : 00000000`00000000 00000003`1ef7dd70 00007ffc`c3bb8548 00007ffd`22ff4c4d : PresentationCore!System.Windows.Interop.HwndSource.InputFilterMessage+0xb6
00000003`1ef7dd90 00007ffc`c3ae0a86     : 00000000`00000000 00007ffc`c3bb8548 0000016d`ff1f3b50 00007ffd`22ff68d7 : WindowsBase!MS.Win32.HwndWrapper.WndProc+0xbd
00000003`1ef7de20 00007ffc`c3ad90f7     : 00000000`000304ac 00000000`00000000 0000016d`ff1fe4f0 00000000`0000000a : WindowsBase!MS.Win32.HwndSubclass.DispatcherCallbackOperation+0x86
00000003`1ef7de70 00007ffc`c3ad8f25     : 0000016d`80017140 00007ffc`c3ad8e45 00007ffc`c333ab38 00007ffc`c3bd26a0 : WindowsBase!System.Windows.Threading.ExceptionWrapper.InternalRealCall+0x107
00000003`1ef7ded0 00007ffc`c3ae06fc     : 0000016d`80017058 0000016d`80017140 00000000`00000202 00007ffc`c3ad2049 : WindowsBase!System.Windows.Threading.ExceptionWrapper.TryCatchWhen+0x35
```

177

```
00000003`1ef7df20 00007ffc`c3adfff7  : 00007ffc`c3bb8548 00000000`00000000 ffffffff`ffffd8f0 0000016d`fabbe820 : WindowsBase!System.Windows.Threading.Dispatcher.LegacyInvokeImpl+0x1bc
00000003`1ef7dfb0 00007ffc`c32cd892  : 0000016d`8010aac0 00007ffd`6ea01da6 00000003`1ef7e1a8 00007ffd`6ea24b65 : WindowsBase!MS.Win32.HwndSubclass.SubclassWndProc+0x277
00000003`1ef7e0b0 00007ffd`6ea11c4c  : 00000003`1ef7e168 00007ffd`22d83aca 00000000`00000001 00000000`00000000 : 0x00007ffc`c32cd892
00000003`1ef7e130 00007ffd`6ea10ea6  : 00000003`1ef7e3d0 00007ffc`c3173484 00000000`000104d0 00000000`00000202 : user32!UserCallWinProcCheckWow+0x33c
00000003`1ef7e2a0 00007ffc`c371039b  : 00007ffc`c3173484 00000003`1ef7e710 00000003`1ef7e420 00000000`00000001 : user32!DispatchMessageWorker+0x2a6
00000003`1ef7e320 00007ffd`234d7f03  : 0000016d`80039998 00000003`1ef7e420 00000000`00000000 00000000`00000000 : 0x00007ffc`c371039b
00000003`1ef7e3e0 00007ffd`234d53e1  : 00000003`1ef7e660 00007ffd`22d582ae 00000003`1ef7e710 00000000`00000000 : WindowsBase!System.Windows.Threading.Dispatcher.PushFrameImpl+0xc3
00000003`1ef7e470 00007ffd`234d538e  : 0000016d`800541d0 0000016d`80039998 0000016d`80039848 00000000`00000001 : WindowsBase!System.Windows.Threading.Dispatcher.PushFrame+0x41
00000003`1ef7e4a0 00007ffd`2140dfdc  : 0000016d`8000ded8 00000000`00000000 00000000`00000130 00000003`1ef7dcf0 : WindowsBase!System.Windows.Threading.Dispatcher.Run+0x3e
00000003`1ef7e4d0 00007ffd`2140c63d  : 0000016d`8000ded8 00000000`00000000 00000000`00000130 00000003`1ef7dcf0 : PresentationFramework!System.Windows.Application.RunDispatcher+0x1c
00000003`1ef7e500 00007ffd`214095cc  : 0000016d`8000ded8 00000000`00000000 0000016d`fcf16530 00000000`00000008 : PresentationFramework!System.Windows.Application.RunInternal+0x15d
00000003`1ef7e550 00007ffc`c32b619e  : 0000016d`8000ded8 0000016d`80053950 0000016d`fcf16530 00000000`00000008 : PresentationFramework!System.Windows.Application.Run+0x2c
00000003`1ef7e580 00007ffd`22e3a793  : 00000003`1ef7e9c0 00000003`1ef7e8a0 00007ffd`22da65c8 00000000`00000001 : AppR2!AppR2.App.Main+0x5e
00000003`1ef7e5d0 00007ffd`22d258fa  : 00000003`1ef7e660 00007ffd`22d582ae 00000003`1ef7e710 00000000`00000000 : coreclr!CallDescrWorkerInternal+0x83
00000003`1ef7e610 00007ffd`22d1fc7f  : 00000003`1ef7e8f8 00000000`00000001 00000000`00000130 00000000`000000b2 : coreclr!MethodDescCallSite::CallTargetWorker+0x3d2
00000003`1ef7e7a0 00007ffd`22d1fa4a  : 00000000`00000000 00000000`00000000 00000000`00000001 00000003`1ef7ed38 : coreclr!RunMainInternal+0x11f
00000003`1ef7e8d0 00007ffd`22d1f7a9  : 0000016d`fabbe820 00000003`00000001 0000016d`fabbe820 00000003`1ef7ecb8 : coreclr!RunMain+0xd2
00000003`1ef7e980 00007ffd`22d20108  : 00000000`00000000 00000000`00000130 00000000`00000130 00007ffc`c3353990 : coreclr!Assembly::ExecuteMainMethod+0x1cd
00000003`1ef7ed10 00007ffd`22d15112  : 0000016d`fc6bec50 00000000`00000001 00000000`00000001 00000000`00000000 : coreclr!CorHost2::ExecuteAssembly+0x1c8
00000003`1ef7ee80 00007ffd`26362993  : 0000016d`fabb5780 0000016d`fab0da10 0000016d`fc5dda10 0000016d`fab0da10 : coreclr!coreclr_execute_assembly+0xe2
00000003`1ef7ef20 00007ffd`26362c07  : 0000016d`fab04ba8 0000016d`fab04ba0 00000003`2639bce0 0000016d`fab04ba8 : hostpolicy!run_app_for_context+0x3d3
00000003`1ef7f0b0 00007ffd`2636354e  : 00000000`00000000 00000000`00000000 00000000`00000000 00000003`1ef7f1f0 00000000`00000000 : hostpolicy!run_app+0x37
00000003`1ef7f0f0 00007ffd`263c3d95  : 00000000`00000000 00000000`00000000 00000000`00000000 0000016d`faafb670 : hostpolicy!corehost_main+0xfe
00000003`1ef7f2a0 00007ffd`263c6f48  : 0000016d`fab0dd10 00000000`00000000 00000000`00000000 00000000`00000000 : hostfxr!execute_app+0x21d
00000003`1ef7f390 00007ffd`263c59b8  : 00000003`1ef7f5f0 00000003`1ef7f561 00000003`1ef7f610 00000000`00000000 : hostfxr!fx_muxer_t::handle_exec_host_command+0x214
00000003`1ef7f480 00007ffd`263c21a9  : 00000003`1ef7f610 0000016d`fab043e0 00000000`00000001 00007ffd`6df4218b : hostfxr!fx_muxer_t::execute+0x20c
00000003`1ef7f5b0 00007ff7`902adc1c  : 00000000`00000000 0000016d`fab043e0 00000000`00000008 00007ffd`263c2bc0 : hostfxr!hostfxr_main_startupinfo+0x89
00000003`1ef7f6b0 00007ff7`902adf81  : 00007ff7`902b80a0 00000000`00000007 00000000`00000000 000000000`0000005b : AppR2_exe!exe_start+0x604
00000003`1ef7f8a0 00007ff7`902af4f8  : 00000000`00000000 00007ff7`902af579 0000016d`fab04ba0 00000000`00000000 : AppR2_exe!wmain+0x129
00000003`1ef7fa10 00007ffd`6e2054e0  : 00000000`00000000 00000000`00000000 00000000`00000000 00000000`00000000 : AppR2_exe!__scrt_common_main_seh+0x10c
00000003`1ef7fa50 00007ffd`7036485b  : 00000000`00000000 00000000`00000000 00000000`00000000 00000000`00000000 : kernel32!BaseThreadInitThunk+0x10
00000003`1ef7fa80 00000000`00000000  : 00000000`00000000 00000000`00000000 00000000`00000000 00000000`00000000 : ntdll!RtlUserThreadStart+0x2b
```

```
STACK_COMMAND:  ~0s; .ecxr ; kb

SYMBOL_NAME:  AppR2!AppR2.MainWindow.Button_Click+39

MODULE_NAME: AppR2

IMAGE_NAME:  AppR2.dll

FAILURE_BUCKET_ID:  NULL_POINTER_WRITE_c0000005_AppR2.dll!AppR2.MainWindow.Button_Click

OS_VERSION:  10.0.22000.1

BUILDLAB_STR:  co_release

OSPLATFORM_TYPE:  x64

OSNAME:  Windows 10

IMAGE_VERSION:  1.0.0.0

FAILURE_ID_HASH:  {fbc6af11-bc49-860d-9fac-6159c73acd0e}

Followup:     MachineOwner
---------
```

Note: We see the unmanaged NULL pointer exception (in red), and the stack trace shows only unmanaged code. We also see information about the managed method (in green) that looks like a method from the managed stack trace we see later. But we don't see managed .NET Core exception in the output.

Note: If we opened the dump using the x86 version of WinDbg instead or chose *X86 Target architecture* in WinDbg when opening a dump file, we would have seen these messages (in blue) because WinDbg requires SOS extension DLL having the same bitness as the process memory dump (x64), so 32-bit WinDbg is not able to load 64-bit extension DLL:

```
0:000> !analyze -v
*******************************************************************
*                                                                 *
*                      Exception Analysis                         *
*                                                                 *
*******************************************************************

SOS does not support the current target architecture 'x64' (0x8664). A 32 bit target may require a 32 bit debugger or vice versa. In general, try to use the
same bitness for the debugger and target process.
SOS does not support the current target architecture 'x64' (0x8664). A 32 bit target may require a 32 bit debugger or vice versa. In general, try to use the
same bitness for the debugger and target process.
SOS does not support the current target architecture 'x64' (0x8664). A 32 bit target may require a 32 bit debugger or vice versa. In general, try to use the
same bitness for the debugger and target process.

KEY_VALUES_STRING: 1

    Key  : AV.Dereference
    Value: NullPtr

    Key  : AV.Fault
    Value: Write

    Key  : Analysis.CPU.mSec
    Value: 2280

    Key  : Analysis.Elapsed.mSec
    Value: 5631
```

```
    Key  : Analysis.IO.Other.Mb
    Value: 0

    Key  : Analysis.IO.Read.Mb
    Value: 1

    Key  : Analysis.IO.Write.Mb
    Value: 0

    Key  : Analysis.Init.CPU.mSec
    Value: 405

    Key  : Analysis.Init.Elapsed.mSec
    Value: 7889

    Key  : Analysis.Memory.CommitPeak.Mb
    Value: 177

    Key  : CLR.Engine
    Value: CORECLR

    Key  : CLR.Version
    Value: 5.0.1021.41214

    Key  : Failure.Bucket
    Value: BITNESS_MISMATCH_X64_NULL_POINTER_WRITE_c0000005_coreclr.dll!NakedThrowHelper2

    Key  : Failure.Hash
    Value: {f566558b-c6d6-352c-a5e9-a7aba649e443}

    Key  : Timeline.OS.Boot.DeltaSec
    Value: 325

    Key  : Timeline.Process.Start.DeltaSec
    Value: 166

    Key  : WER.OS.Branch
    Value: co_release

    Key  : WER.OS.Version
    Value: 10.0.22000.1

    Key  : WER.Process.Version
    Value: 1.0.0.0


FILE_IN_CAB:  AppR2.exe.2816.dmp

NTGLOBALFLAG:  400

PROCESS_BAM_CURRENT_THROTTLED: 0

PROCESS_BAM_PREVIOUS_THROTTLED: 0

APPLICATION_VERIFIER_FLAGS:  0

CONTEXT:  (.ecxr)
rax=0000000000820014 rbx=0000016d80081ec8 rcx=00000007fff9fffe
rdx=00007ffcc384c900 rsi=0000016d80145f40 rdi=0000016d80142e18
rip=00007ffd6dbc466c rsp=000000031ef7cdd0 rbp=000000031ef7d440
 r8=00007ffcc3c40020  r9=0000000c0000000c r10=00007ffcc3c6f8f8
r11=0000000100000001 r12=0000016d801425e0 r13=0000016d80081ec8
r14=0000000000000000 r15=0000016d80142e30
iopl=0         nv up ei pl nz na po nc
cs=0033  ss=002b  ds=002b  es=002b  fs=0053  gs=002b             efl=00000206
KERNELBASE!RaiseException+0x6c:
00007ffd`6dbc466c 0f1f440000      nop     dword ptr [rax+rax]
Resetting default scope

EXCEPTION_RECORD:  (.exr -1)
ExceptionAddress: 00007ffcc3c6f8e9
   ExceptionCode: c0000005 (Access violation)
  ExceptionFlags: 00000080
NumberParameters: 2
   Parameter[0]: 0000000000000001
   Parameter[1]: 0000000000000000
Attempt to write to address 0000000000000000

PROCESS_NAME:  AppR2.exe

WRITE_ADDRESS:  0000000000000000

ERROR_CODE: (NTSTATUS) 0xc0000005 - The instruction at 0x%p referenced memory at 0x%p. The memory could not be %s.

EXCEPTION_CODE_STR:  c0000005

EXCEPTION_PARAMETER1:  0000000000000001

EXCEPTION_PARAMETER2:  0000000000000000

STACK_TEXT:
00000003`1ef7cdd0 00007ffd`22e3b6f9     : 00000000`00000000 00000000`00000000 00000000`00000000 00000000`00000000 : KERNELBASE!RaiseException+0x6c
00000003`1ef7ceb0 00007ffd`22e3b72b     : 00000000`00000000 00000000`00000000 00000000`00001085 00000040`14622002 : coreclr!NakedThrowHelper2+0x9
00000003`1ef7cee0 00007ffd`22e3b735     : 00007ffc`c3c6f8e9 0000016d`80145f40 0000016d`80081ec8 00000000`00000000 : coreclr!NakedThrowHelper_RspAligned+0x1e
00000003`1ef7d408 00007ffc`c3c6f8e9     : 0000016d`80145f40 0000016d`80081ec8 00000000`00000000 0000016d`801425e0 : coreclr!NakedThrowHelper_FixRsp+0x5
00000003`1ef7d410 00007ffc`c3ad85c3     : 0000016d`8005e288 0000016d`80081ec8 0000016d`80145f40 00000000`00000000 : 0x00007ffc`c3c6f8e9
00000003`1ef7d450 00007ffc`c3ad7cc4     : 00000000`00000000 00000000`00000000 00000000`00000000 5c950cb5`00000000 : 0x00007ffc`c3ad85c3
00000003`1ef7d510 00007ffd`217f88d7     : 0000016d`80081ec8 0000016d`80145f40 0000016d`80081ec8 00000003`1ef7d490 : 0x00007ffc`c3ad7cc4
00000003`1ef7d570 00007ffd`216dd0a0     : 0000016d`80081ec8 0000016d`fabbe820 0000016d`800f6b98 00000003`1ef7d490 : PresentationFramework+0xbb88d7
```
179

```
00000003`1ef7d5b0 00007ffd`217f9350 : 0000016d`80081ec8 00000003`1ef7e348 00000000`00000130 00000003`1ef7d4c0 : PresentationFramework+0xa9d0a0
00000003`1ef7d5f0 00000000`5c933702 : 0000016d`80081ec8 0000016d`801425e0 00007ffc`c396c6f8 00000000`00000001 : PresentationFramework+0xbb9350
00000003`1ef7d630 00000000`5c958522 : 0000016d`80081ec8 0000016d`801425e0 0000016d`801425e0 00000000`00000001 : PresentationCore+0x403702
00000003`1ef7d670 00007ffc`c3ad52f3 : 00000000`00000000 00000000`00000000 0000016d`80081ec8 00000000`00000000 : PresentationCore+0x428522
00000003`1ef7d6b0 00007ffc`c3ad85c3 : 0000016d`801425e0 00000000`00000000 0000016d`80081ec8 0000016d`80137ff0 : 0x00007ffc`c3ad52f3
00000003`1ef7d6f0 00000000`5c9416f9 : 00000000`00000000 00000000`00000000 00000000`00000000 00000000`00000000 : 0x00007ffc`c3ad85c3
00000003`1ef7d7b0 00000000`5c958522 : 0000016d`80081ec8 0000016d`801425e0 00007ffc`c396c6f8 00000000`00000000 : PresentationCore+0x4116f9
00000003`1ef7d820 00000000`5c958522 : 0000016d`80081ec8 0000016d`801425e0 0000016d`801425e0 00000000`00000000 : PresentationCore+0x40344a
00000003`1ef7d860 00007ffc`c3ad52f3 : 0000016d`80069ab0 00000000`00000001 0000016d`80081ec8 00000000`00000000 : PresentationCore+0x428522
00000003`1ef7d8a0 00007ffc`c3ad85c3 : 0000016d`801425e0 00007ffc`c3ad3b7f 00000000`00000000 0000016d`8005e288 : 0x00007ffc`c3ad52f3
00000003`1ef7d8e0 00007ffc`c3ad7cc4 : 00000000`00000000 00000000`00000000 00000000`00000000 00000000`00000000 : 0x00007ffc`c3ad85c3
00000003`1ef7d9a0 00007ffc`c3adfc11 : 0000016d`80081ec8 0000016d`801425e0 0000016d`801086c8 0000016d`8005f208 : 0x00007ffc`c3ad7cc4
00000003`1ef7da00 000104d0`000104d0 : 0000016d`801425e0 0000016d`801086c8 0000016d`80141080 00000000`00000000 : 0x00007ffc`c3adfc11
00000003`1ef7da40 00007ffc`c3c41e81 : 00007ffc`c3638240 00000000`00000000 0000016d`fabbe820 0000016d`800ce828 : 0x00007ffc`c3ae885d
00000003`1ef7db00 00007ffc`c3c4a9b4 : 00000000`00000000 00000000`00000000 00000000`00000000 00000000`00000000 : 0x00007ffc`c3c41e81
00000003`1ef7db50 00007ffc`c3ae18a4 : 0000016d`800ce0c0 000104d0`00000000 00000000`00000000 00000003`0004d28e : 0x00007ffc`c3c4a9b4
00000003`1ef7dc80 00007ffc`c3ae1026 : 0000016d`800ce0c0 00000000`000104d0 00000000`00000202 00000000`00000000 : 0x00007ffc`c3ae18a4
00000003`1ef7dd20 00007ffc`c3ae0b7d : 00000000`00000000 00000003`1ef7dd70 00007ffc`c3bb8548 00007ffd`22ff4c4d : 0x00007ffc`c3ae1026
00000003`1ef7dd90 00007ffc`c3ae0a86 : 00000000`00000000 00007ffc`c3bb8548 00007ffd`ff1f3b50 00007ffd`22ff68d7 : 0x00007ffc`c3ae0b7d
00000003`1ef7de20 00007ffc`c3ad90f7 : 00000000`000304ac 00000000`00000000 0000016d`ff1fe4f0 00000000`0000000a : 0x00007ffc`c3ae0a86
00000003`1ef7de70 00007ffc`c3ad8f25 : 0000016d`80017140 00007ffc`c3ad8e45 00007ffc`c333ab38 00007ffc`c3bd26a0 : 0x00007ffc`c3ad90f7
00000003`1ef7ded0 00007ffc`c3ae06fc : 0000016d`80017058 0000016d`80017140 00000000`00000202 00007ffc`c3ad2049 : 0x00007ffc`c3ad8f25
00000003`1ef7df20 00007ffc`c3adfff7 : 00007ffc`c3bb8548 00000000`00000000 ffffffff`ffffd8f0 0000016d`fabbe820 : 0x00007ffc`c3ae06fc
00000003`1ef7dfb0 00007ffc`c32cd892 : 0000016d`8010aac0 00007ffd`6ea01da6 00000003`1ef7e1a8 00007ffd`6ea24b65 : 0x00007ffc`c3adfff7
00000003`1ef7e0b0 00007ffd`6ea11c4c : 00000003`1ef7e168 00007ffd`22d83aca 00000000`00000001 00000000`00000000 : 0x00007ffc`c32cd892
00000003`1ef7e130 00007ffd`6ea10ea6 : 00000003`1ef7e3d0 00007ffc`c3173484 00000000`000104d0 00000000`00000202 : user32!UserCallWinProcCheckWow+0x33c
00000003`1ef7e2a0 00007ffc`c371039b : 00007ffc`c3173484 00000003`1ef7e710 00000003`1ef7e420 00000000`00000001 : user32!DispatchMessageWorker+0x2a6
00000003`1ef7e320 00007ffd`234d7f03 : 0000016d`80039998 00000003`1ef7e420 0000016d`80081ec8 00000000`00000000 : 0x00007ffc`c371039b
00000003`1ef7e3e0 00007ffd`234d53e1 : 0000016d`80017140 0000016d`800541d0 0000016d`80039848 00000000`00000000 : WindowsBase+0x197f03
00000003`1ef7e470 00007ffd`234d538e : 0000016d`800541d0 0000016d`80039998 0000016d`80039848 00000000`00000001 : WindowsBase+0x1953e1
00000003`1ef7e4a0 00007ffd`2140dfdc : 0000016d`8000ded8 00000000`00000000 00000000`00000130 00000003`1ef7dcf0 : WindowsBase+0x19538e
00000003`1ef7e4d0 00007ffd`2140c63d : 0000016d`8000ded8 00000000`00000000 00000000`00000130 00000003`1ef7dcf0 : PresentationFramework+0x7cdfdc
00000003`1ef7e500 00007ffd`214095cc : 0000016d`8000ded8 00000000`00000000 0000016d`fcf16530 00000000`00000008 : PresentationFramework+0x7cc63d
00000003`1ef7e550 00007ffd`22e3a793 : 0000016d`8000ded8 0000016d`80053950 0000016d`fcf16530 00000000`00000008 : PresentationFramework+0x7c95cc
00000003`1ef7e580 00007ffd`22d258fa : 00000003`1ef7e9c0 00000003`1ef7e8a0 00007ffd`22da65c8 00000000`00000001 : 0x00007ffc`c32b619e
00000003`1ef7e5d0 00007ffd`22d1fc7f : 00000003`1ef7e660 00007ffd`22d582ae 00000003`1ef7e710 00000000`00000000 : coreclr!CallDescrWorkerInternal+0x83
00000003`1ef7e610 00007ffd`22d1fc7f : 00007ffc`1ef7e8f8 00000000`00000001 00000000`00000130 00000000`000000b2 :
coreclr!MethodDescCallSite::CallTargetWorker+0x3d2
00000003`1ef7e7a0 00007ffd`22d1fa4a : 00000000`00000000 00000000`00000000 00000000`00000001 00000003`1ef7ed38 : coreclr!RunMainInternal+0x11f
00000003`1ef7e8d0 00007ffd`22d1f7a9 : 0000016d`fabbe820 00000003`00000001 0000016d`fabbe820 00007ffc`c3ecb8 : coreclr!RunMain+0xd2
00000003`1ef7e980 00007ffd`22d20108 : 00000000`00000000 00000000`00000130 00000000`00000130 00007ffc`c3353990 : coreclr!Assembly::ExecuteMainMethod+0x1cd
00000003`1ef7ed10 00007ffd`22d15112 : 0000016d`fc6bec50 00000000`00000001 00000000`00000001 00000000`00000000 : coreclr!CorHost2::ExecuteAssembly+0x1c8
00000003`1ef7ee80 00007ffd`26362993 : 0000016d`fabb5780 0000016d`fab0da10 00007ffc`fc5dda10 0000016d`fab0da10 : coreclr!coreclr_execute_assembly+0xe2
00000003`1ef7ef20 00007ffd`26362c07 : 0000016d`fab04ba8 0000016d`fab04ba0 00007ffd`2639bce0 0000016d`fab04ba8 : hostpolicy!run_app_for_context+0x3d3
00000003`1ef7f0b0 00007ffd`2636354e : 00000000`00000000 00000000`00000000 00000003`1ef7f1f0 00000000`00000000 : hostpolicy!run_app+0x37
00000003`1ef7f0f0 00007ffd`263c3d95 : 00000000`00000000 00000000`00000000 00000000`00000000 0000016d`faafb670 : hostpolicy!corehost_main+0xfe
00000003`1ef7f2a0 00007ffd`263c6f48 : 0000016d`fab0dd10 00000000`00000000 00000000`00000000 00000000`00000000 : hostfxr!execute_app+0x21d
00000003`1ef7f390 00007ffd`263c59b8 : 00000003`1ef7f5f0 00000003`1ef7f561 00000003`1ef7f610 00000000`00000000 :
hostfxr!fx_muxer_t::handle_exec_host_command+0x214
00000003`1ef7f480 00007ffd`263c21a9 : 00000003`1ef7f610 0000016d`fab043e0 00000000`00000001 00007ffd`6df4218b : hostfxr!fx_muxer_t::execute+0x20c
00000003`1ef7f5b0 00007ff7`902adc1c : 00000000`00000008 0000016d`fab043e0 00000000`00000008 00007ffd`263c2bc0 : hostfxr!hostfxr_main_startupinfo+0x89
00000003`1ef7f6b0 00007ff7`902adf81 : 00007ff7`902b80a0 00000000`00000007 00000000`00000000 00000000`0000005b : AppR2_exe!exe_start+0x604
00000003`1ef7f8a0 00007ff7`902af4f8 : 00000000`00000000 00007ff7`902af579 0000016d`fab04ba0 00000000`00000000 : AppR2_exe!wmain+0x129
00000003`1ef7fa10 00007ffd`6e2054e0 : 00000000`00000000 00000000`00000000 00000000`00000000 00000000`00000000 : AppR2_exe!__scrt_common_main_seh+0x10c
00000003`1ef7fa50 00007ffd`7036485b : 00000000`00000000 00000000`00000000 00000000`00000000 00000000`00000000 : kernel32!BaseThreadInitThunk+0x10
00000003`1ef7fa80 00000000`00000000 : 00000000`00000000 00000000`00000000 00000000`00000000 00000000`00000000 : ntdll!RtlUserThreadStart+0x2b
```

STACK_COMMAND: ~0s; .ecxr ; kb

FAULTING_SOURCE_LINE: D:\workspace_work\1\s\src\coreclr\src\vm\amd64\RedirectedHandledJITCase.asm

FAULTING_SOURCE_FILE: D:\workspace_work\1\s\src\coreclr\src\vm\amd64\RedirectedHandledJITCase.asm

FAULTING_SOURCE_LINE_NUMBER: 228

FAULTING_SOURCE_CODE:
No source found for 'D:\workspace_work\1\s\src\coreclr\src\vm\amd64\RedirectedHandledJITCase.asm'

SYMBOL_NAME: coreclr!NakedThrowHelper2+9

MODULE_NAME: coreclr

IMAGE_NAME: coreclr.dll

FAILURE_BUCKET_ID: BITNESS_MISMATCH_X64_NULL_POINTER_WRITE_c0000005_coreclr.dll!NakedThrowHelper2

OS_VERSION: 10.0.22000.1

BUILDLAB_STR: co_release

OSPLATFORM_TYPE: x64

OSNAME: Windows 10

IMAGE_VERSION: 5.0.1021.41214

FAILURE_ID_HASH: {f566558b-c6d6-352c-a5e9-a7aba649e443}

Followup: MachineOwner
----

7.   We now check the version of .NET Core used when *AppR2* was running:

```
0:000> lmv m coreclr
Browse full module list
start             end               module name
00007ffd`22cf0000 00007ffd`231ff000   coreclr    (private pdb symbols)
C:\ProgramData\dbg\sym\coreclr.pdb\9921B9E0569B4C178EEA6D77C48041D31\coreclr.pdb
    Loaded symbol image file: coreclr.dll
    Image path: C:\Program Files\dotnet\shared\Microsoft.NETCore.App\5.0.10\coreclr.dll
    Image name: coreclr.dll
    Browse all global symbols  functions  data
    Timestamp:        Thu Aug 12 22:18:15 2021 (61159017)
    CheckSum:         004FA99F
    ImageSize:        0050F000
    File version:     5.0.1021.41214
    Product version:  5.0.1021.41214
    File flags:       0 (Mask 3F)
    File OS:          4 Unknown Win32
    File type:        0.0 Unknown
    File date:        00000000.00000000
    Translations:     0409.04b0
    Information from resource tables:
        CompanyName:      Microsoft Corporation
        ProductName:      Microsoft® .NET
        InternalName:     CoreCLR.dll
        OriginalFilename: CoreCLR.dll
        ProductVersion:   5,0,1021,41214 @Commit: e1825b4928afa9455cc51e1de2b2e66c8be3018d
        FileVersion:      5,0,1021,41214 @Commit: e1825b4928afa9455cc51e1de2b2e66c8be3018d
        FileDescription:  Microsoft .NET Runtime
        LegalCopyright:   © Microsoft Corporation. All rights reserved.
        Comments:         Flavor=Retail
```

8.   We can see the list of loaded WinDbg extensions by using the **.chain** command:

```
0:000> .chain
Extension DLL search Path:
[...]
Extension DLL chain:
    Ext: image 10.0.22550.1002, API 1.0.0,
        [path: C:\Program Files\WindowsApps\Microsoft.WinDbg_1.2202.7001.0_neutral__8wekyb3d8bbwe\amd64\winext\ext.dll]
    sos: image 6.0.257301+27172ce4d05e8a3b0ffdefd65f073d40a1b1fe54, API 2.0.0, built Tue Nov 23 22:21:39 2021
        [path: C:\Program Files\WindowsApps\Microsoft.WinDbg_1.2202.7001.0_neutral__8wekyb3d8bbwe\amd64\winext\sos\sos.dll]
    CLRComposition: image 10.0.22549.1000, API 0.0.0,
        [path: C:\Program Files\WindowsApps\Microsoft.WinDbg_1.2202.7001.0_neutral__8wekyb3d8bbwe\amd64\winext\CLRComposition.dll]
    dbghelp: image 10.0.22549.1000, API 10.0.6,
        [path: C:\Program Files\WindowsApps\Microsoft.WinDbg_1.2202.7001.0_neutral__8wekyb3d8bbwe\amd64\dbghelp.dll]
    exts: image 10.0.22549.1000, API 1.0.0,
        [path: C:\Program Files\WindowsApps\Microsoft.WinDbg_1.2202.7001.0_neutral__8wekyb3d8bbwe\amd64\WINXP\exts.dll]
    uext: image 10.0.22549.1000, API 1.0.0,
        [path: C:\Program Files\WindowsApps\Microsoft.WinDbg_1.2202.7001.0_neutral__8wekyb3d8bbwe\amd64\winext\uext.dll]
    ntsdexts: image 10.0.22550.1002, API 1.0.0,
        [path: C:\Program Files\WindowsApps\Microsoft.WinDbg_1.2202.7001.0_neutral__8wekyb3d8bbwe\amd64\WINXP\ntsdexts.dll]
```

9.   We now try the **!pe** command (**!PrintException**):

```
0:000> !pe
Exception object: 0000016d80145f70
Exception type:   System.NullReferenceException
Message:          Object reference not set to an instance of an object.
InnerException:   <none>
StackTrace (generated):
    SP               IP               Function
    000000031EF7D410 00007FFCC3C6F8E9 AppR2!AppR2.MainWindow.Button_Click(System.Object, System.Windows.RoutedEventArgs)+0x39
    000000031EF7D450 00007FFCC3AD85C3 PresentationCore!System.Windows.EventRoute.InvokeHandlersImpl(System.Object, System.Windows.RoutedEventArgs,
Boolean)+0x143
    000000031EF7D510 00007FFCC3AD7CC4 PresentationCore!System.Windows.UIElement.RaiseEventImpl(System.Windows.DependencyObject,
System.Windows.RoutedEventArgs)+0xf4
    000000031EF7D570 00007FFD217F88D7 PresentationFramework!System.Windows.Controls.Primitives.ButtonBase.OnClick()+0x37
    000000031EF7D5B0 00007FFD216DD0A0 PresentationFramework!System.Windows.Controls.Button.OnClick()+0x50
```

181

```
          000000031EF7D5F0 00007FFD217F9350
PresentationFramework!System.Windows.Controls.Primitives.ButtonBase.OnMouseLeftButtonUp(System.Windows.Input.MouseButtonEventArgs)+0xa0
          000000031EF7D630 000000005C933702 PresentationCore!System.Windows.UIElement.OnMouseLeftButtonUpThunk(System.Object,
System.Windows.Input.MouseButtonEventArgs)+0x62
          000000031EF7D670 000000005C958522 PresentationCore!System.Windows.Input.MouseButtonEventArgs.InvokeEventHandler(System.Delegate, System.Object)+0x22
          000000031EF7D6B0 00007FFCC3AD52F3 PresentationCore!System.Windows.RoutedEventArgs.InvokeHandler(System.Delegate, System.Object)+0x33
          000000031EF7D6F0 00007FFCC3AD85C3 PresentationCore!System.Windows.EventRoute.InvokeHandlersImpl(System.Object, System.Windows.RoutedEventArgs,
Boolean)+0x143
          000000031EF7D7B0 000000005C9416F9 PresentationCore!System.Windows.UIElement.ReRaiseEventAs(System.Windows.DependencyObject,
System.Windows.RoutedEventArgs, System.Windows.RoutedEvent)+0x169
          000000031EF7D820 000000005C93344A PresentationCore!System.Windows.UIElement.OnMouseUpThunk(System.Object, System.Windows.Input.MouseButtonEventArgs)+0xba
          000000031EF7D860 000000005C958522 PresentationCore!System.Windows.Input.MouseButtonEventArgs.InvokeEventHandler(System.Delegate, System.Object)+0x22
          000000031EF7D8A0 00007FFCC3AD52F3 PresentationCore!System.Windows.RoutedEventArgs.InvokeHandler(System.Delegate, System.Object)+0x33
          000000031EF7D8E0 00007FFCC3AD85C3 PresentationCore!System.Windows.EventRoute.InvokeHandlersImpl(System.Object, System.Windows.RoutedEventArgs,
Boolean)+0x143
          000000031EF7D9A0 00007FFCC3AD7CC4 PresentationCore!System.Windows.UIElement.RaiseEventImpl(System.Windows.DependencyObject,
System.Windows.RoutedEventArgs)+0xf4
          000000031EF7DA00 00007FFCC3ADFC11 PresentationCore!System.Windows.UIElement.RaiseTrustedEvent(System.Windows.RoutedEventArgs)+0x31
          000000031EF7DA40 00007FFCC3AE885D PresentationCore!System.Windows.Input.InputManager.ProcessStagingArea()+0x45d
          000000031EF7DB00 00007FFCC3C41E81 PresentationCore!System.Windows.Input.InputProviderSite.ReportInput(System.Windows.Input.InputReport)+0x61
          000000031EF7DB50 00007FFCC3C4A9B4 PresentationCore!System.Windows.Interop.HwndMouseInputProvider.ReportInput(IntPtr, System.Windows.Input.InputMode,
Int32, System.Windows.Input.RawMouseActions, Int32, Int32, Int32)+0x444
          000000031EF7DC80 00007FFCC3AE18A4 PresentationCore!System.Windows.Interop.HwndMouseInputProvider.FilterMessage(IntPtr, MS.Internal.Interop.WindowMessage,
IntPtr, IntPtr, Boolean ByRef)+0x344
          000000031EF7DD20 00007FFCC3AE1026 PresentationCore!System.Windows.Interop.HwndSource.InputFilterMessage(IntPtr, Int32, IntPtr, IntPtr, Boolean ByRef)+0xb6
          000000031EF7DD90 00007FFCC3AE0B7D WindowsBase!MS.Win32.HwndWrapper.WndProc(IntPtr, Int32, IntPtr, IntPtr, Boolean ByRef)+0xbd
          000000031EF7DE20 00007FFCC3AE0A86 WindowsBase!MS.Win32.HwndSubclass.DispatcherCallbackOperation(System.Object)+0x86
          000000031EF7DE70 00007FFCC3AD90F7 WindowsBase!System.Windows.Threading.ExceptionWrapper.InternalRealCall(System.Delegate, System.Object, Int32)+0x107
          000000031EF7DED0 00007FFCC3AD8F25 WindowsBase!System.Windows.Threading.ExceptionWrapper.TryCatchWhen(System.Object, System.Delegate, System.Object, Int32,
System.Delegate)+0x35
          000000031EF7DF20 00007FFCC3AE06FC WindowsBase!System.Windows.Threading.Dispatcher.LegacyInvokeImpl(System.Windows.Threading.DispatcherPriority,
System.TimeSpan, System.Delegate, System.Object, Int32)+0x1bc
          000000031EF7DFB0 00007FFCC3ADFFF7 WindowsBase!MS.Win32.HwndSubclass.SubclassWndProc(IntPtr, Int32, IntPtr, IntPtr)+0x277
          000000031EF7E320 0000000000000001 WindowsBase!MS.Win32.UnsafeNativeMethods.DispatchMessage(System.Windows.Interop.MSG ByRef)+0x2
          000000031EF7E3E0 00007FFD234D7F03 WindowsBase!System.Windows.Threading.Dispatcher.PushFrameImpl(System.Windows.Threading.DispatcherFrame)+0xc3
          000000031EF7E470 00007FFD234D53E1 WindowsBase!System.Windows.Threading.Dispatcher.PushFrame(System.Windows.Threading.DispatcherFrame)+0x41
          000000031EF7E4A0 00007FFD234D538E WindowsBase!System.Windows.Threading.Dispatcher.Run()+0x3e
          000000031EF7E4D0 00007FFD2140DFDC PresentationFramework!System.Windows.Application.RunDispatcher(System.Object)+0x1c
          000000031EF7E500 00007FFD2140C63D PresentationFramework!System.Windows.Application.RunInternal(System.Windows.Window)+0x15d
          000000031EF7E550 00007FFD214095CC PresentationFramework!System.Windows.Application.Run()+0x2c
          000000031EF7E580 00007FFCC32B619E AppR2!AppR2.App.Main()+0x5e


StackTraceString: <none>
HResult: 80004003
```

10.   To get managed stack trace for the current thread, we can use the **!CLRStack** SOS extension command:

```
0:000> !CLRStack
OS Thread Id: 0x27c4 (0)
        Child SP               IP Call Site
000000031EF7CF10 00007ffd70403eb4 [FaultingExceptionFrame: 000000031ef7cf10]
000000031EF7D410 00007ffcc3c6f8e9 AppR2.MainWindow.Button_Click(System.Object, System.Windows.RoutedEventArgs)
000000031EF7D450 00007ffcc3ad85c3 System.Windows.EventRoute.InvokeHandlersImpl(System.Object, System.Windows.RoutedEventArgs, Boolean)
000000031EF7D510 00007ffcc3ad7cc4 System.Windows.UIElement.RaiseEventImpl(System.Windows.DependencyObject, System.Windows.RoutedEventArgs)
000000031EF7D570 00007ffd217f88d7 System.Windows.Controls.Primitives.ButtonBase.OnClick()
000000031EF7D5B0 00007ffd216dd0a0 System.Windows.Controls.Button.OnClick()
000000031EF7D5F0 00007ffd217f9350 System.Windows.Controls.Primitives.ButtonBase.OnMouseLeftButtonUp(System.Windows.Input.MouseButtonEventArgs)
000000031EF7D630 000000005c933702 System.Windows.UIElement.OnMouseLeftButtonUpThunk(System.Object, System.Windows.Input.MouseButtonEventArgs)
000000031EF7D670 000000005c958522 System.Windows.Input.MouseButtonEventArgs.InvokeEventHandler(System.Delegate, System.Object)
000000031EF7D6B0 00007ffcc3ad52f3 System.Windows.RoutedEventArgs.InvokeHandler(System.Delegate, System.Object)
000000031EF7D6F0 00007ffcc3ad85c3 System.Windows.EventRoute.InvokeHandlersImpl(System.Object, System.Windows.RoutedEventArgs, Boolean)
000000031EF7D7B0 000000005c9416f9 System.Windows.UIElement.ReRaiseEventAs(System.Windows.DependencyObject, System.Windows.RoutedEventArgs,
System.Windows.RoutedEvent)
000000031EF7D820 000000005c93344a System.Windows.UIElement.OnMouseUpThunk(System.Object, System.Windows.Input.MouseButtonEventArgs)
000000031EF7D860 000000005c958522 System.Windows.Input.MouseButtonEventArgs.InvokeEventHandler(System.Delegate, System.Object)
000000031EF7D8A0 00007ffcc3ad52f3 System.Windows.RoutedEventArgs.InvokeHandler(System.Delegate, System.Object)
000000031EF7D8E0 00007ffcc3ad85c3 System.Windows.EventRoute.InvokeHandlersImpl(System.Object, System.Windows.RoutedEventArgs, Boolean)
000000031EF7D9A0 00007ffcc3ad7cc4 System.Windows.UIElement.RaiseEventImpl(System.Windows.DependencyObject, System.Windows.RoutedEventArgs)
000000031EF7DA00 00007ffcc3adfc11 System.Windows.UIElement.RaiseTrustedEvent(System.Windows.RoutedEventArgs)
000000031EF7DA40 00007ffcc3ae885d System.Windows.Input.InputManager.ProcessStagingArea()
000000031EF7DB00 00007ffcc3c41e81 System.Windows.Input.InputProviderSite.ReportInput(System.Windows.Input.InputReport)
000000031EF7DB50 00007ffcc3c4a9b4 System.Windows.Interop.HwndMouseInputProvider.ReportInput(IntPtr, System.Windows.Input.InputMode, Int32,
System.Windows.Input.RawMouseActions, Int32, Int32, Int32)
000000031EF7DC80 00007ffcc3ae18a4 System.Windows.Interop.HwndMouseInputProvider.FilterMessage(IntPtr, MS.Internal.Interop.WindowMessage, IntPtr, IntPtr,
Boolean ByRef)
000000031EF7DD20 00007ffcc3ae1026 System.Windows.Interop.HwndSource.InputFilterMessage(IntPtr, Int32, IntPtr, IntPtr, Boolean ByRef)
000000031EF7DD90 00007ffcc3ae0b7d MS.Win32.HwndWrapper.WndProc(IntPtr, Int32, IntPtr, IntPtr, Boolean ByRef)
000000031EF7DE20 00007ffcc3ae0a86 MS.Win32.HwndSubclass.DispatcherCallbackOperation(System.Object)
000000031EF7DE70 00007ffcc3ad90f7 System.Windows.Threading.ExceptionWrapper.InternalRealCall(System.Delegate, System.Object, Int32)
000000031EF7DED0 00007ffcc3ad8f25 System.Windows.Threading.ExceptionWrapper.TryCatchWhen(System.Object, System.Delegate, System.Object, Int32,
System.Delegate)
000000031EF7DF20 00007ffcc3ae06fc System.Windows.Threading.Dispatcher.LegacyInvokeImpl(System.Windows.Threading.DispatcherPriority, System.TimeSpan,
System.Delegate, System.Object, Int32)
000000031EF7DFB0 00007ffcc3adfff7 MS.Win32.HwndSubclass.SubclassWndProc(IntPtr, Int32, IntPtr, IntPtr)
000000031EF7E0B0 00007ffcc32cd892 ILStubClass.IL_STUB_ReversePInvoke(Int64, Int32, Int64, Int64)
000000031EF7E348 00007ffd6ea11c4c [InlinedCallFrame: 000000031ef7e348] MS.Win32.UnsafeNativeMethods.DispatchMessage(System.Windows.Interop.MSG ByRef)
000000031EF7E348 00007ffcc371039b [InlinedCallFrame: 000000031ef7e348] MS.Win32.UnsafeNativeMethods.DispatchMessage(System.Windows.Interop.MSG ByRef)
000000031EF7E320 00007ffcc371039b ILStubClass.IL_STUB_PInvoke(System.Windows.Interop.MSG ByRef)
000000031EF7E3E0 00007ffd234d7f03 System.Windows.Threading.Dispatcher.PushFrameImpl(System.Windows.Threading.DispatcherFrame)
000000031EF7E470 00007ffd234d53e1 System.Windows.Threading.Dispatcher.PushFrame(System.Windows.Threading.DispatcherFrame)
000000031EF7E4A0 00007ffd234d538e System.Windows.Threading.Dispatcher.Run()
000000031EF7E4D0 00007ffd2140dfdc System.Windows.Application.RunDispatcher(System.Object)
000000031EF7E500 00007ffd2140c63d System.Windows.Application.RunInternal(System.Windows.Window)
000000031EF7E550 00007ffd214095cc System.Windows.Application.Run()
000000031EF7E580 00007ffcc32b619e AppR2.App.Main()
```

Note: We can also reconstruct stack frames from JIT code addresses using the **!IP2MD** SOS extension command, for example (we get methods that correspond to names in the output of the **!analyze -v** command above, highlighted in yellow now):

```
0:000> kL
# Child-SP          RetAddr           Call Site
[..]
2b 00000003`1ef7e0b0 00007ffd`6ea11c4c    0x00007ffc`c32cd892
2c 00000003`1ef7e130 00007ffd`6ea10ea6    user32!UserCallWinProcCheckWow+0x33c
2d 00000003`1ef7e2a0 00007ffc`c371039b    user32!DispatchMessageWorker+0x2a6
2e 00000003`1ef7e320 00007ffd`234d7f03    0x00007ffc`c371039b
[...]

0:000> !IP2MD 0x00007ffc`c32cd892
MethodDesc:     00007ffcc3647a18
Method Name:            ILStubClass.IL_STUB_ReversePInvoke(Int64, Int32, Int64, Int64)
Class:                  00007ffcc35adf70
MethodTable:            00007ffcc35adfe8
mdToken:                0000000006000000
Module:                 00007ffcc3584f60
IsJitted:               yes
Current CodeAddr:       00007ffcc32cd840
Version History:
  ILCodeVersion:        0000000000000000
  ReJIT ID:             0
  IL Addr:              0000000000000000
     CodeAddr:             00007ffcc32cd840  (Optimized)
     NativeCodeVersion:  0000000000000000

0:000> !IP2MD 0x00007ffc`c371039b
MethodDesc:     00007ffcc37e8870
Method Name:            ILStubClass.IL_STUB_PInvoke(System.Windows.Interop.MSG ByRef)
Class:                  00007ffcc35adf70
MethodTable:            00007ffcc35adfe8
mdToken:                0000000006000000
Module:                 00007ffcc3584f60
IsJitted:               yes
Current CodeAddr:       00007ffcc3710320
Version History:
  ILCodeVersion:        0000000000000000
  ReJIT ID:             0
  IL Addr:              0000000000000000
     CodeAddr:             00007ffcc3710320  (Optimized)
     NativeCodeVersion:  0000000000000000
```

11.   We close logging before exiting WinDbg:

```
0:000> .logclose
Closing open log file C:\AWMDA-Dumps\Process\x64\AppR2.log
```

Exercise P13

- **Goal:** Learn how to analyze the 32-bit process saved as a 64-bit process memory dump

- **Patterns:** Virtualized Process (WOW64); Message Box; Debugger Bug; Rough Stack Trace (Unmanaged Space)

- \AWMDA-Dumps\Exercise-P13-Analysis-process-dump-AppA-WOW64.pdf

Exercise P13: Analysis of an application process dump (AppA, WOW64)

Goal: Learn how to analyze the 32-bit process saved as a 64-bit process memory dump.

Patterns: Virtualized Process (WOW64); Message Box; Debugger Bug; Rough Stack Trace (Unmanaged Space).

1. Launch WinDbg.

2. Open \AWMDA-Dumps\Process\x86\WOW64\AppA.DMP

3. We get the dump file loaded:

```
Microsoft (R) Windows Debugger Version 10.0.25877.1004 AMD64
Copyright (c) Microsoft Corporation. All rights reserved.


Loading Dump File [C:\AWMDA-Dumps\Process\x86\WOW64\AppA.DMP]
User Mini Dump File with Full Memory: Only application data is available


************* Path validation summary **************
Response                        Time (ms)       Location
Deferred                                        srv*
Symbol search path is: srv*
Executable search path is:
Windows 10 Version 18362 MP (2 procs) Free x64
Product: WinNt, suite: SingleUserTS Personal
Edition build lab: 18362.1.amd64fre.19h1_release.190318-1202
Machine Name:
Debug session time: Sat Nov 16 22:28:22.000 2019 (UTC + 1:00)
System Uptime: 0 days 0:38:04.247
Process Uptime: 0 days 0:00:23.000
.................................
For analysis of this file, run !analyze -v
wow64cpu!CpupSyscallStub+0xc:
00000000`77281cbc c3              ret
```

Note: *wow64cpu!CpupSyscallStub* function shows that we have a 32-bit process saved as a 64-bit dump.

4. Open a log file using the **.logopen** command:

```
0:000> .logopen C:\AWMDA-Dumps\Process\x86\WOW64\AppA.log
Opened log file 'C:\AWMDA-Dumps\Process\x86\WOW64\AppA.log'
```

5. Type the **~*k** command to verify the correctness of all stack traces:

```
0:000> ~*k

.  0  Id: 22fc.aec Suspend: 0 Teb: 00000000`00559000 Unfrozen
 # Child-SP          RetAddr           Call Site
00 00000000`0065ebd8 00000000`77281b1d wow64cpu!CpupSyscallStub+0xc
01 00000000`0065ebe0 00000000`77281199 wow64cpu!Thunk0ArgReloadState+0x5
02 00000000`0065ec90 00007ffa`59d7c77a wow64cpu!BTCpuSimulate+0x9
03 00000000`0065ecd0 00007ffa`59d7c637 wow64!RunCpuSimulation+0xa
04 00000000`0065ed00 00007ffa`5a093fb3 wow64!Wow64LdrpInitialize+0x127
05 00000000`0065efb0 00007ffa`5a081db5 ntdll!LdrpInitializeProcess+0x186b
```

```
06 00000000`0065f3f0 00007ffa`5a031853 ntdll!_LdrpInitialize+0x50549
07 00000000`0065f490 00007ffa`5a0317fe ntdll!LdrpInitialize+0x3b
08 00000000`0065f4c0 00000000`00000000 ntdll!LdrInitializeThunk+0xe

   1  Id: 22fc.f70 Suspend: 0 Teb: 00000000`0055c000 Unfrozen
 # Child-SP          RetAddr          Call Site
00 00000000`007ce688 00007ffa`59d7acee ntdll!NtWaitForWorkViaWorkerFactory+0x14
01 00000000`007ce690 00007ffa`59d77123 wow64!whNtWaitForWorkViaWorkerFactory+0x11e
02 00000000`007ce720 00000000`77281783 wow64!Wow64SystemServiceEx+0x153
03 00000000`007cefe0 00000000`77281199 wow64cpu!ServiceNoTurbo+0xb
04 00000000`007cf090 00007ffa`59d7c77a wow64cpu!BTCpuSimulate+0x9
05 00000000`007cf0d0 00007ffa`59d7c637 wow64!RunCpuSimulation+0xa
06 00000000`007cf100 00007ffa`5a03196b wow64!Wow64LdrpInitialize+0x127
07 00000000`007cf3b0 00007ffa`5a031853 ntdll!_LdrpInitialize+0xff
08 00000000`007cf450 00007ffa`5a0317fe ntdll!LdrpInitialize+0x3b
09 00000000`007cf480 00000000`00000000 ntdll!LdrInitializeThunk+0xe

   2  Id: 22fc.2ac4 Suspend: 0 Teb: 00000000`0055f000 Unfrozen
 # Child-SP          RetAddr          Call Site
00 00000000`0080e7a8 00007ffa`59d7acee ntdll!NtWaitForWorkViaWorkerFactory+0x14
01 00000000`0080e7b0 00007ffa`59d77123 wow64!whNtWaitForWorkViaWorkerFactory+0x11e
02 00000000`0080e840 00000000`77281783 wow64!Wow64SystemServiceEx+0x153
03 00000000`0080f100 00000000`77281199 wow64cpu!ServiceNoTurbo+0xb
04 00000000`0080f1b0 00007ffa`59d7c77a wow64cpu!BTCpuSimulate+0x9
05 00000000`0080f1f0 00007ffa`59d7c637 wow64!RunCpuSimulation+0xa
06 00000000`0080f220 00007ffa`5a03196b wow64!Wow64LdrpInitialize+0x127
07 00000000`0080f4d0 00007ffa`5a031853 ntdll!_LdrpInitialize+0xff
08 00000000`0080f570 00007ffa`5a0317fe ntdll!LdrpInitialize+0x3b
09 00000000`0080f5a0 00000000`00000000 ntdll!LdrInitializeThunk+0xe

   3  Id: 22fc.221c Suspend: 0 Teb: 00000000`00562000 Unfrozen
 # Child-SP          RetAddr          Call Site
00 00000000`0084f178 00000000`77281b99 wow64cpu!CpupSyscallStub+0xc
01 00000000`0084f180 00000000`77281199 wow64cpu!Thunk2ArgNSpNSpReloadState+0xc
02 00000000`0084f230 00007ffa`59d7c77a wow64cpu!BTCpuSimulate+0x9
03 00000000`0084f270 00007ffa`59d7c637 wow64!RunCpuSimulation+0xa
04 00000000`0084f2a0 00007ffa`5a03196b wow64!Wow64LdrpInitialize+0x127
05 00000000`0084f550 00007ffa`5a031853 ntdll!_LdrpInitialize+0xff
06 00000000`0084f5f0 00007ffa`5a0317fe ntdll!LdrpInitialize+0x3b
07 00000000`0084f620 00000000`00000000 ntdll!LdrInitializeThunk+0xe

   4  Id: 22fc.2a8c Suspend: 0 Teb: 00000000`00565000 Unfrozen
 # Child-SP          RetAddr          Call Site
00 00000000`0089f0d8 00000000`77281b99 wow64cpu!CpupSyscallStub+0xc
01 00000000`0089f0e0 00000000`77281199 wow64cpu!Thunk2ArgNSpNSpReloadState+0xc
02 00000000`0089f190 00007ffa`59d7c77a wow64cpu!BTCpuSimulate+0x9
03 00000000`0089f1d0 00007ffa`59d7c637 wow64!RunCpuSimulation+0xa
04 00000000`0089f200 00007ffa`5a03196b wow64!Wow64LdrpInitialize+0x127
05 00000000`0089f4b0 00007ffa`5a031853 ntdll!_LdrpInitialize+0xff
06 00000000`0089f550 00007ffa`5a0317fe ntdll!LdrpInitialize+0x3b
07 00000000`0089f580 00000000`00000000 ntdll!LdrInitializeThunk+0xe

   5  Id: 22fc.2b9c Suspend: 0 Teb: 00000000`00568000 Unfrozen
 # Child-SP          RetAddr          Call Site
00 00000000`008deb98 00000000`77281b99 wow64cpu!CpupSyscallStub+0xc
01 00000000`008deba0 00000000`77281199 wow64cpu!Thunk2ArgNSpNSpReloadState+0xc
02 00000000`008dec50 00007ffa`59d7c77a wow64cpu!BTCpuSimulate+0x9
03 00000000`008dec90 00007ffa`59d7c637 wow64!RunCpuSimulation+0xa
04 00000000`008decc0 00007ffa`5a03196b wow64!Wow64LdrpInitialize+0x127
05 00000000`008def70 00007ffa`5a031853 ntdll!_LdrpInitialize+0xff
```

```
06 00000000`008df010 00007ffa`5a0317fe ntdll!LdrpInitialize+0x3b
07 00000000`008df040 00000000`00000000 ntdll!LdrInitializeThunk+0xe

   6  Id: 22fc.2554 Suspend: 0 Teb: 00000000`0056b000 Unfrozen
 # Child-SP          RetAddr           Call Site
00 00000000`0093eb38 00000000`77281c7b wow64cpu!CpupSyscallStub+0xc
01 00000000`0093eb40 00000000`77281199 wow64cpu!Thunk0Arg+0x5
02 00000000`0093ebf0 00007ffa`59d7c77a wow64cpu!BTCpuSimulate+0x9
03 00000000`0093ec30 00007ffa`59d7c637 wow64!RunCpuSimulation+0xa
04 00000000`0093ec60 00007ffa`5a03196b wow64!Wow64LdrpInitialize+0x127
05 00000000`0093ef10 00007ffa`5a031853 ntdll!_LdrpInitialize+0xff
06 00000000`0093efb0 00007ffa`5a0317fe ntdll!LdrpInitialize+0x3b
07 00000000`0093efe0 00000000`00000000 ntdll!LdrInitializeThunk+0xe

   7  Id: 22fc.14e0 Suspend: 0 Teb: 00000000`0056e000 Unfrozen
 # Child-SP          RetAddr           Call Site
00 00000000`0097f298 00000000`77281b99 wow64cpu!CpupSyscallStub+0xc
01 00000000`0097f2a0 00000000`77281199 wow64cpu!Thunk2ArgNSpNSpReloadState+0xc
02 00000000`0097f350 00007ffa`59d7c77a wow64cpu!BTCpuSimulate+0x9
03 00000000`0097f390 00007ffa`59d7c637 wow64!RunCpuSimulation+0xa
04 00000000`0097f3c0 00007ffa`5a03196b wow64!Wow64LdrpInitialize+0x127
05 00000000`0097f670 00007ffa`5a031853 ntdll!_LdrpInitialize+0xff
06 00000000`0097f710 00007ffa`5a0317fe ntdll!LdrpInitialize+0x3b
07 00000000`0097f740 00000000`00000000 ntdll!LdrInitializeThunk+0xe

   8  Id: 22fc.2060 Suspend: 0 Teb: 00000000`00571000 Unfrozen
 # Child-SP          RetAddr           Call Site
00 00000000`02a5f018 00000000`77281b99 wow64cpu!CpupSyscallStub+0xc
01 00000000`02a5f020 00000000`77281199 wow64cpu!Thunk2ArgNSpNSpReloadState+0xc
02 00000000`02a5f0d0 00007ffa`59d7c77a wow64cpu!BTCpuSimulate+0x9
03 00000000`02a5f110 00007ffa`59d7c637 wow64!RunCpuSimulation+0xa
04 00000000`02a5f140 00007ffa`5a03196b wow64!Wow64LdrpInitialize+0x127
05 00000000`02a5f3f0 00007ffa`5a031853 ntdll!_LdrpInitialize+0xff
06 00000000`02a5f490 00007ffa`5a0317fe ntdll!LdrpInitialize+0x3b
07 00000000`02a5f4c0 00000000`00000000 ntdll!LdrInitializeThunk+0xe
```

Note: All stack traces have *wow64** modules.

6.   Let's now switch to x86 32-stack traces by changing the effective processor architecture:

```
0:000> .effmach x86
Effective machine: x86 compatible (x86)

0:000:x86> .reload
.....................
```

Note: The prompt has changed to include x86.

7.   Let's now check all stack traces again:

```
0:000:x86> ~*kL


.  0  Id: 22fc.aec Suspend: 0 Teb: 00559000 Unfrozen
 # ChildEBP RetAddr
00 0075fb5c 76cde279 ntdll_77290000!NtWaitForSingleObject+0xc
01 0075fbd0 749cb211 KERNELBASE!WaitForSingleObjectEx+0x99
02 0075fbe8 008f1411 msvcp140!_Thrd_join+0x11
```

```
WARNING: Stack unwind information not available. Following frames may be wrong.
03 0075fc4c 008f1a4d AppA+0x1411
04 0075fc94 761a6359 AppA+0x1a4d
05 0075fca4 772f7b74 kernel32!BaseThreadInitThunk+0x19
06 0075fd00 772f7b44 ntdll_77290000!__RtlUserThreadStart+0x2f
07 0075fd10 00000000 ntdll_77290000!_RtlUserThreadStart+0x1b

   1  Id: 22fc.f70 Suspend: 0 Teb: 0055c000 Unfrozen
 # ChildEBP RetAddr
00 00c7fd84 772e66ef ntdll_77290000!NtWaitForWorkViaWorkerFactory+0xc
01 00c7ff40 761a6359 ntdll_77290000!TppWorkerThread+0x33f
02 00c7ff50 772f7b74 kernel32!BaseThreadInitThunk+0x19
03 00c7ffac 772f7b44 ntdll_77290000!__RtlUserThreadStart+0x2f
04 00c7ffbc 00000000 ntdll_77290000!_RtlUserThreadStart+0x1b

   2  Id: 22fc.2ac4 Suspend: 0 Teb: 0055f000 Unfrozen
 # ChildEBP RetAddr
00 00d7f85c 772e66ef ntdll_77290000!NtWaitForWorkViaWorkerFactory+0xc
01 00d7fa18 761a6359 ntdll_77290000!TppWorkerThread+0x33f
02 00d7fa28 772f7b74 kernel32!BaseThreadInitThunk+0x19
03 00d7fa84 772f7b44 ntdll_77290000!__RtlUserThreadStart+0x2f
04 00d7fa94 00000000 ntdll_77290000!_RtlUserThreadStart+0x1b

   3  Id: 22fc.221c Suspend: 0 Teb: 00562000 Unfrozen
 # ChildEBP RetAddr
00 0261fd08 76cee83f ntdll_77290000!NtDelayExecution+0xc
01 0261fd70 76cee7cf KERNELBASE!SleepEx+0x5f
02 0261fd80 749cb284 KERNELBASE!Sleep+0xf
03 0261fda4 008f17c9 msvcp140!_Thrd_sleep+0x34
WARNING: Stack unwind information not available. Following frames may be wrong.
04 0261fde8 008f1092 AppA+0x17c9
05 0261fe10 008f181a AppA+0x1092
06 0261fe2c 7573248f AppA+0x181a
07 0261fe64 761a6359 ucrtbase!thread_start<unsigned int (__stdcall*)(void *),1>+0x3f
08 0261fe74 772f7b74 kernel32!BaseThreadInitThunk+0x19
09 0261fed0 772f7b44 ntdll_77290000!__RtlUserThreadStart+0x2f
0a 0261fee0 00000000 ntdll_77290000!_RtlUserThreadStart+0x1b

   4  Id: 22fc.2a8c Suspend: 0 Teb: 00565000 Unfrozen
 # ChildEBP RetAddr
00 0271f7d8 76cee83f ntdll_77290000!NtDelayExecution+0xc
01 0271f840 76cee7cf KERNELBASE!SleepEx+0x5f
02 0271f850 749cb284 KERNELBASE!Sleep+0xf
03 0271f874 008f17c9 msvcp140!_Thrd_sleep+0x34
WARNING: Stack unwind information not available. Following frames may be wrong.
04 0271f8b8 008f1122 AppA+0x17c9
05 0271f8e4 008f181a AppA+0x1122
06 0271f900 7573248f AppA+0x181a
07 0271f938 761a6359 ucrtbase!thread_start<unsigned int (__stdcall*)(void *),1>+0x3f
08 0271f948 772f7b74 kernel32!BaseThreadInitThunk+0x19
09 0271f9a4 772f7b44 ntdll_77290000!__RtlUserThreadStart+0x2f
0a 0271f9b4 00000000 ntdll_77290000!_RtlUserThreadStart+0x1b

   5  Id: 22fc.2b9c Suspend: 0 Teb: 00568000 Unfrozen
 # ChildEBP RetAddr
00 0281fa48 76cee83f ntdll_77290000!NtDelayExecution+0xc
01 0281fab0 76cee7cf KERNELBASE!SleepEx+0x5f
02 0281fac0 749cb284 KERNELBASE!Sleep+0xf
03 0281fae4 008f17c9 msvcp140!_Thrd_sleep+0x34
WARNING: Stack unwind information not available. Following frames may be wrong.
```

```
04 0281fb28 008f11b2 AppA+0x17c9
05 0281fb54 008f181a AppA+0x11b2
06 0281fb70 7573248f AppA+0x181a
07 0281fba8 761a6359 ucrtbase!thread_start<unsigned int (__stdcall*)(void *),1>+0x3f
08 0281fbb8 772f7b74 kernel32!BaseThreadInitThunk+0x19
09 0281fc14 772f7b44 ntdll_77290000!__RtlUserThreadStart+0x2f
0a 0281fc24 00000000 ntdll_77290000!_RtlUserThreadStart+0x1b

   6  Id: 22fc.2554 Suspend: 0 Teb: 0056b000 Unfrozen
 # ChildEBP RetAddr
00 0291f9e8 7645b8f3 win32u!NtUserWaitMessage+0xc
01 0291fa28 7645b7e4 user32!DialogBox2+0x102
02 0291fa58 764a182b user32!InternalDialogBox+0xd9
03 0291fb24 764a06c7 user32!SoftModalMessageBox+0x72b
04 0291fc80 764a10a5 user32!MessageBoxWorker+0x2ca
05 0291fd0c 764a10ea user32!MessageBoxTimeoutW+0x165
06 0291fd2c 6d703ddb user32!MessageBoxW+0x1a
07 0291fd70 008f11e4 apphelp!MbHook_MessageBoxW+0x2b
WARNING: Stack unwind information not available. Following frames may be wrong.
08 0291fdac 008f181a AppA+0x11e4
09 0291fdc8 7573248f AppA+0x181a
0a 0291fe00 761a6359 ucrtbase!thread_start<unsigned int (__stdcall*)(void *),1>+0x3f
0b 0291fe10 772f7b74 kernel32!BaseThreadInitThunk+0x19
0c 0291fe6c 772f7b44 ntdll_77290000!__RtlUserThreadStart+0x2f
0d 0291fe7c 00000000 ntdll_77290000!_RtlUserThreadStart+0x1b

   7  Id: 22fc.14e0 Suspend: 0 Teb: 0056e000 Unfrozen
 # ChildEBP RetAddr
00 02a1f6f0 76cee83f ntdll_77290000!NtDelayExecution+0xc
01 02a1f758 76cee7cf KERNELBASE!SleepEx+0x5f
02 02a1f768 749cb284 KERNELBASE!Sleep+0xf
03 02a1f78c 008f17c9 msvcp140!_Thrd_sleep+0x34
WARNING: Stack unwind information not available. Following frames may be wrong.
04 02a1f7d0 008f11b2 AppA+0x17c9
05 02a1f7fc 008f181a AppA+0x11b2
06 02a1f818 7573248f AppA+0x181a
07 02a1f850 761a6359 ucrtbase!thread_start<unsigned int (__stdcall*)(void *),1>+0x3f
08 02a1f860 772f7b74 kernel32!BaseThreadInitThunk+0x19
09 02a1f8bc 772f7b44 ntdll_77290000!__RtlUserThreadStart+0x2f
0a 02a1f8cc 00000000 ntdll_77290000!_RtlUserThreadStart+0x1b

   8  Id: 22fc.2060 Suspend: 0 Teb: 00571000 Unfrozen
 # ChildEBP RetAddr
00 02b5f808 76cee83f ntdll_77290000!NtDelayExecution+0xc
01 02b5f870 76cee7cf KERNELBASE!SleepEx+0x5f
02 02b5f880 749cb284 KERNELBASE!Sleep+0xf
03 02b5f8a4 008f17c9 msvcp140!_Thrd_sleep+0x34
WARNING: Stack unwind information not available. Following frames may be wrong.
04 02b5f8e8 008f11b2 AppA+0x17c9
05 02b5f910 008f181a AppA+0x11b2
06 02b5f92c 7573248f AppA+0x181a
07 02b5f964 761a6359 ucrtbase!thread_start<unsigned int (__stdcall*)(void *),1>+0x3f
08 02b5f974 772f7b74 kernel32!BaseThreadInitThunk+0x19
09 02b5f9d0 772f7b44 ntdll_77290000!__RtlUserThreadStart+0x2f
0a 02b5f9e0 00000000 ntdll_77290000!_RtlUserThreadStart+0x1b
```

Note: One of the previous WinDbg versions couldn't get them correctly:

```
.  0  Id: 22fc.aec Suspend: 0 Teb: 00559000 Unfrozen
 # ChildEBP RetAddr
00 0075fbd0 00000000     wow64cpu!CpupSyscallStub+0xc

   1  Id: 22fc.f70 Suspend: 0 Teb: 0055c000 Unfrozen
 # ChildEBP RetAddr
WARNING: Frame IP not in any known module. Following frames may be wrong.
00 007ce684 59d7acee     0x5a05fa54
01 00c7ff40 761a6359     0x59d7acee
02 00c7ff50 772f7b74     kernel32!BaseThreadInitThunk+0x19
03 00c7ffac 772f7b44     ntdll_77290000!__RtlUserThreadStart+0x2f
04 00c7ffbc 00000000     ntdll_77290000!_RtlUserThreadStart+0x1b

   2  Id: 22fc.2ac4 Suspend: 0 Teb: 0055f000 Unfrozen
 # ChildEBP RetAddr
WARNING: Frame IP not in any known module. Following frames may be wrong.
00 0080e7a4 59d7acee     0x5a05fa54
01 00d7fa18 761a6359     0x59d7acee
02 00d7fa28 772f7b74     kernel32!BaseThreadInitThunk+0x19
03 00d7fa84 772f7b44     ntdll_77290000!__RtlUserThreadStart+0x2f
04 00d7fa94 00000000     ntdll_77290000!_RtlUserThreadStart+0x1b

   3  Id: 22fc.221c Suspend: 0 Teb: 00562000 Unfrozen
 # ChildEBP RetAddr
00 0261fd70 00000000     wow64cpu!CpupSyscallStub+0xc

   4  Id: 22fc.2a8c Suspend: 0 Teb: 00565000 Unfrozen
 # ChildEBP RetAddr
00 0271f840 00000000     wow64cpu!CpupSyscallStub+0xc

   5  Id: 22fc.2b9c Suspend: 0 Teb: 00568000 Unfrozen
 # ChildEBP RetAddr
00 0281fab0 00000000     wow64cpu!CpupSyscallStub+0xc

   6  Id: 22fc.2554 Suspend: 0 Teb: 0056b000 Unfrozen
 # ChildEBP RetAddr
00 0291fa28 00000000     wow64cpu!CpupSyscallStub+0xc

   7  Id: 22fc.14e0 Suspend: 0 Teb: 0056e000 Unfrozen
 # ChildEBP RetAddr
00 02a1f758 00000000     wow64cpu!CpupSyscallStub+0xc

   8  Id: 22fc.2060 Suspend: 0 Teb: 00571000 Unfrozen
 # ChildEBP RetAddr
00 02b5f870 00000000     wow64cpu!CpupSyscallStub+0xc
```

8.   In our case, suppose we still get them incorrectly, so we try to reconstruct the 6th 32-bit stack trace after checking 32-bit raw stack data:

```
0:000:x86> .effmach AMD64
Effective machine: x64 (AMD64)

0:000> ~6s
wow64cpu!CpupSyscallStub+0xc:
00000000`77281cbc c3              ret
```

190

```
0:006> .effmach x86
Effective machine: x86 compatible (x86)

0:006:x86> !teb
Wow64 TEB32 at 0056d000
    ExceptionList:        0291fd60
    StackBase:            02920000
    StackLimit:           0291c000
    SubSystemTib:         00000000
    FiberData:            00001e00
    ArbitraryUserPointer: 00000000
    Self:                 0056d000
    EnvironmentPointer:   00000000
    ClientId:             000022fc . 00002554
    RpcHandle:            00000000
    Tls Storage:          009eb360
    PEB Address:          00558000
    LastErrorValue:       0
    LastStatusValue:      c0000034
    Count Owned Locks:    0
    HardErrorMode:        0


Wow64 TEB at 0056b000
    ExceptionList:        0056d000
    StackBase:            0093fd20
    StackLimit:           00938000
    SubSystemTib:         00000000
    FiberData:            00001e00
    ArbitraryUserPointer: 00000000
    Self:                 0056b000
    EnvironmentPointer:   00000000
    ClientId:             000022fc . 00002554
    RpcHandle:            00000000
    Tls Storage:          00000000
    PEB Address:          00557000
    LastErrorValue:       0
    LastStatusValue:      0
    Count Owned Locks:    0
    HardErrorMode:        0

0:006:x86> dpS 0291c000 02920000
 772eb783 ntdll_77290000!RtlpFindEntry+0x23
 772cc630 ntdll_77290000!RtlpAllocateHeap+0xc10
 772cd17f ntdll_77290000!RtlpAllocateHeap+0x175f
 77307520 ntdll_77290000!bsearch+0x60
 772c9a20 ntdll_77290000!RtlpFindUnicodeStringInSection+0x200
 77309f80 ntdll_77290000!_except_handler4
 772cb02f ntdll_77290000!RtlpAllocateHeapInternal+0x22f
 772cd4df ntdll_77290000!RtlGetFullPathName_Ustr+0x2cf
 772cd4f9 ntdll_77290000!RtlGetFullPathName_Ustr+0x2e9
 772cadee ntdll_77290000!RtlAllocateHeap+0x3e
 772cadee ntdll_77290000!RtlAllocateHeap+0x3e
 772cab32 ntdll_77290000!RtlpDosPathNameToRelativeNtPathName+0x252
 772cabc3 ntdll_77290000!RtlpDosPathNameToRelativeNtPathName+0x2e3
 77291070 ntdll_77290000!RtlpDosDevicesPrefix
 77290052 ntdll_77290000!LdrpMscoreeDllName <PERF> (ntdll_77290000+0x52)
 772eb783 ntdll_77290000!RtlpFindEntry+0x23
 772ce780 ntdll_77290000!RtlpFreeHeap+0xb10
 772ce9f9 ntdll_77290000!RtlpFreeHeap+0xd89
 77309f80 ntdll_77290000!_except_handler4
 77316cdb ntdll_77290000!RtlpFreeHeapInternal+0x783
```

191

```
77316d02  ntdll_77290000!RtlpFreeHeapInternal+0x7aa
773020ac  ntdll_77290000!NtOpenFile+0xc
772cdc16  ntdll_77290000!RtlFreeHeap+0x46
772bd47e  ntdll_77290000!LdrpMapResourceFile+0xf1
76420000  user32!pfnClientA <PERF> (user32+0x0)
76420000  user32!pfnClientA <PERF> (user32+0x0)
772bd362  ntdll_77290000!LdrpSetAlternateResourceModuleHandle+0x274
773ae798  ntdll_77290000!MuiCacheSWRLock
772bd241  ntdll_77290000!LdrpSetAlternateResourceModuleHandle+0x153
76420000  user32!pfnClientA <PERF> (user32+0x0)
77309f80  ntdll_77290000!_except_handler4
772c11c0  ntdll_77290000!LdrLoadAlternateResourceModuleEx+0x4b0
76420000  user32!pfnClientA <PERF> (user32+0x0)
77307520  ntdll_77290000!bsearch+0x60
772c98cb  ntdll_77290000!RtlpFindUnicodeStringInSection+0xab
772c9a20  ntdll_77290000!RtlpFindUnicodeStringInSection+0x200
772c98cb  ntdll_77290000!RtlpFindUnicodeStringInSection+0xab
772c9a20  ntdll_77290000!RtlpFindUnicodeStringInSection+0x200
772c93ea  ntdll_77290000!RtlFindActivationContextSectionString+0x1ba
772c8f15  ntdll_77290000!sxsisol_SearchActCtxForDllName+0x95
772c8f73  ntdll_77290000!sxsisol_SearchActCtxForDllName+0xf3
77298d98  ntdll_77290000!`string'
77307520  ntdll_77290000!bsearch+0x60
772c8c7e  ntdll_77290000!RtlDosApplyFileIsolationRedirection_Ustr+0x35e
772c8cf9  ntdll_77290000!RtlDosApplyFileIsolationRedirection_Ustr+0x3d9
77298bd8  ntdll_77290000!`string'
772c8f73  ntdll_77290000!sxsisol_SearchActCtxForDllName+0xf3
77298d98  ntdll_77290000!`string'
77291060  ntdll_77290000!LdrpDefaultExtension
77309f80  ntdll_77290000!_except_handler4
772c62d3  ntdll_77290000!LdrpPreprocessDllName+0x283
772c62e2  ntdll_77290000!LdrpPreprocessDllName+0x292
745d00f0  CoreMessaging!`dynamic initializer for 'Cn::Context::s_lockType'' <PERF> (CoreMessaging+0xf0)
772cb095  ntdll_77290000!RtlpAllocateHeapInternal+0x295
773ae584  ntdll_77290000!LdrpModuleDatatableLock
772c62d3  ntdll_77290000!LdrpPreprocessDllName+0x283
772c549b  ntdll_77290000!RtlEqualUnicodeString+0x5b
7497bac8  oleacc!MemStreamWrite_GUID+0x7
772c5334  ntdll_77290000!LdrpFindLoadedDllByName+0x174
773adb40  ntdll_77290000!LdrpHashTable+0xa0
772eb783  ntdll_77290000!RtlpFindEntry+0x23
772cff3f  ntdll_77290000!RtlpInsertFreeBlock+0x11f
772d7f0a  ntdll_77290000!RtlIntegerToChar+0x8a
772d3c97  ntdll_77290000!ApiSetpSearchForApiSet+0xb7
772c5c37  ntdll_77290000!RtlAppendUnicodeToString+0x57
77309f80  ntdll_77290000!_except_handler4
772c62d3  ntdll_77290000!LdrpPreprocessDllName+0x283
772c62e2  ntdll_77290000!LdrpPreprocessDllName+0x292
7ffe0030  SharedUserData+0x30
77309f80  ntdll_77290000!_except_handler4
772eb783  ntdll_77290000!RtlpFindEntry+0x23
772cc630  ntdll_77290000!RtlpAllocateHeap+0xc10
772cd17f  ntdll_77290000!RtlpAllocateHeap+0x175f
772c98cb  ntdll_77290000!RtlpFindUnicodeStringInSection+0xab
772c549b  ntdll_77290000!RtlEqualUnicodeString+0x5b
772c5334  ntdll_77290000!LdrpFindLoadedDllByName+0x174
773ae584  ntdll_77290000!LdrpModuleDatatableLock
773adb20  ntdll_77290000!LdrpHashTable+0x80
772c5154  ntdll_77290000!LdrpFastpthReloadedDll+0xc2
773ae584  ntdll_77290000!LdrpModuleDatatableLock
772c810c  ntdll_77290000!RtlDeactivateActivationContextUnsafeFast+0x9c
772c4ef6  ntdll_77290000!LdrpLoadDllInternal+0x3a
77309f80  ntdll_77290000!_except_handler4
772d4086  ntdll_77290000!LdrpLoadForwardedDll+0x10e
772d40f8  ntdll_77290000!LdrpLoadForwardedDll+0x180
772d4092  ntdll_77290000!LdrpLoadForwardedDll+0x11a
76a2304c  win32u!NtGdiCreateCompatibleBitmap+0xc
```

```
74e8634e gdi32full!CreateCompatibleBitmap+0x11e
74e8636c gdi32full!CreateCompatibleBitmap+0x13c
764200e8 user32!pfnClientA <PERF> (user32+0xe8)
772cadee ntdll_77290000!RtlAllocateHeap+0x3e
772cadee ntdll_77290000!RtlAllocateHeap+0x3e
764cfa08 user32!ext-ms-win-edputil-policy-l1-1-0_NULL_THUNK_DATA_DLA <PERF> (user32+0xafa08)
772cb1e1 ntdll_77290000!RtlpAllocateHeapInternal+0x3e1
772c0b34 ntdll_77290000!LdrpLoadResourceFromAlternativeModule+0x234
772cadee ntdll_77290000!RtlAllocateHeap+0x3e
772cadee ntdll_77290000!RtlAllocateHeap+0x3e
764689ac user32!CopyDibHdr+0x2db
6d6b9fcb apphelp!SE_GetProcAddressForCaller+0x2ab
6d70e820 apphelp!g_EngineLock
6d6b9fe3 apphelp!SE_GetProcAddressForCaller+0x2c3
77309f80 ntdll_77290000!_except_handler4
74e00000 gdi32full!ShapingLibraryInternal::ScriptProperties <PERF> (gdi32full+0x0)
74e000f8 gdi32full!ShapingLibraryInternal::ScriptProperties <PERF> (gdi32full+0xf8)
772bbf5b ntdll_77290000!RtlImageDirectoryEntryToData+0x1b
74f2f4c0 gdi32full!mscms_NULL_THUNK_DATA_DLB+0x10
74e00000 gdi32full!ShapingLibraryInternal::ScriptProperties <PERF> (gdi32full+0x0)
74aed292 gdi32!ext-ms-win-gdi-wcs-l1-1-0_NULL_THUNK_DATA_DLN+0x31e
772b639d ntdll_77290000!LdrpGetProcedureAddress+0x55
74e00000 gdi32full!ShapingLibraryInternal::ScriptProperties <PERF> (gdi32full+0x0)
74f304c4 gdi32full!mscms_NULL_THUNK_DATA_DLB+0x1014
74f31478 gdi32full!mscms_NULL_THUNK_DATA_DLB+0x1fc8
74afd098 gdi32!_imp__GetViewportOrgEx
772eb783 ntdll_77290000!RtlpFindEntry+0x23
772cc630 ntdll_77290000!RtlpAllocateHeap+0xc10
772cd17f ntdll_77290000!RtlpAllocateHeap+0x175f
74afd000 gdi32!_imp__RectVisible
772c3e10 ntdll_77290000!LdrpHandleProtectedDelayload+0x3e0
74ae0000 gdi32!_load_config_used <PERF> (gdi32+0x0)
772c3cd9 ntdll_77290000!LdrpHandleProtectedDelayload+0x2a9
76d7c230 KERNELBASE!DelayLoadFailureHook
6d6b9d20 apphelp!SE_GetProcAddressForCaller
74afd098 gdi32!_imp__GetViewportOrgEx
772eb783 ntdll_77290000!RtlpFindEntry+0x23
772ce780 ntdll_77290000!RtlpFreeHeap+0xb10
772ce9f9 ntdll_77290000!RtlpFreeHeap+0xd89
7643da62 user32!Scale3232+0xa2
7643d9c0 user32!Scale3232
77309f80 ntdll_77290000!_except_handler4
77316cdb ntdll_77290000!RtlpFreeHeapInternal+0x783
77316d02 ntdll_77290000!RtlpFreeHeapInternal+0x7aa
7643f39b user32!SmartStretchDIBits+0x1e7
772cdc16 ntdll_77290000!RtlFreeHeap+0x46
772eb783 ntdll_77290000!RtlpFindEntry+0x23
772ce780 ntdll_77290000!RtlpFreeHeap+0xb10
772ce9f9 ntdll_77290000!RtlpFreeHeap+0xd89
764c2f88 user32!gcsHdc
77309f80 ntdll_77290000!_except_handler4
77316cdb ntdll_77290000!RtlpFreeHeapInternal+0x783
77316d02 ntdll_77290000!RtlpFreeHeapInternal+0x7aa
74f37c80 gdi32full!ListCachedColorSpace
74e8ea7e gdi32full!IcmReleaseCachedColorSpace+0x2e
74f37c60 gdi32full!semColorSpaceCache
76a22dcc win32u!NtGdiDeleteObjectApp+0xc
74ae393f gdi32!InternalDeleteObject+0x29f
76a2357c win32u!NtUserSetCursorIconData+0xc
7644f3b4 user32!_SetCursorIconData+0x52
7644f3cc user32!_SetCursorIconData+0x6a
76441c9f user32!CopyIcoCur+0x34e
76441b0e user32!CopyIcoCur+0x1bd
772eb783 ntdll_77290000!RtlpFindEntry+0x23
772ccca0 ntdll_77290000!RtlpAllocateHeap+0x1280
772cd17f ntdll_77290000!RtlpAllocateHeap+0x175f
772cd17f ntdll_77290000!RtlpAllocateHeap+0x175f
```

```
764447e9 user32!_GetWindowLong+0xe9
76a22c0c win32u!NtUserMessageCall+0xc
76447a2d user32!RealDefWindowProcWorker+0x2cd
76447a3b user32!RealDefWindowProcWorker+0x2db
76449945 user32!SetWindowLongW+0x15
77307520 ntdll_77290000!bsearch+0x60
772c98cb ntdll_77290000!RtlpFindUnicodeStringInSection+0xab
772c9a20 ntdll_77290000!RtlpFindUnicodeStringInSection+0x200
772c93ea ntdll_77290000!RtlFindActivationContextSectionString+0x1ba
772c8f15 ntdll_77290000!sxsisol_SearchActCtxForDllName+0x95
772c8f73 ntdll_77290000!sxsisol_SearchActCtxForDllName+0xf3
772cb095 ntdll_77290000!RtlpAllocateHeapInternal+0x295
772cd4df ntdll_77290000!RtlGetFullPathName_Ustr+0x2cf
772cd4f9 ntdll_77290000!RtlGetFullPathName_Ustr+0x2e9
772cadee ntdll_77290000!RtlAllocateHeap+0x3e
772cadee ntdll_77290000!RtlAllocateHeap+0x3e
772cab32 ntdll_77290000!RtlpDosPathNameToRelativeNtPathName+0x252
772cabc3 ntdll_77290000!RtlpDosPathNameToRelativeNtPathName+0x2e3
77291070 ntdll_77290000!RtlpDosDevicesPrefix
77290040 ntdll_77290000!LdrpMscoreeDllName <PERF> (ntdll_77290000+0x40)
772cb095 ntdll_77290000!RtlpAllocateHeapInternal+0x295
772cd4df ntdll_77290000!RtlGetFullPathName_Ustr+0x2cf
772cd4f9 ntdll_77290000!RtlGetFullPathName_Ustr+0x2e9
772cadee ntdll_77290000!RtlAllocateHeap+0x3e
772cadee ntdll_77290000!RtlAllocateHeap+0x3e
772cab32 ntdll_77290000!RtlpDosPathNameToRelativeNtPathName+0x252
772cabc3 ntdll_77290000!RtlpDosPathNameToRelativeNtPathName+0x2e3
77291070 ntdll_77290000!RtlpDosDevicesPrefix
77290040 ntdll_77290000!LdrpMscoreeDllName <PERF> (ntdll_77290000+0x40)
77307520 ntdll_77290000!bsearch+0x60
74e94811 gdi32full!COtlsClient::GetCache+0x51
764446a7 user32!GetWindowLongW+0x127
74ccc520 msctf!UIWndProc
74e94811 gdi32full!COtlsClient::GetCache+0x51
76466660 user32!_except_handler4
74ccc97d msctf!CIMEUIWindowHandler::ImeUINotifyHandler+0x1d
74e94695 gdi32full!COtlsClient::FreeMem+0x25
74e94670 gdi32full!COtlsClient::FreeMem
74e953a3 gdi32full!otlPairPosLookup::apply+0x163
772c810c ntdll_77290000!RtlDeactivateActivationContextUnsafeFast+0x9c
772d43c0 ntdll_77290000!RtlActivateActivationContextUnsafeFast+0x70
74e94f6d gdi32full!ApplyLookup+0x34d
74e94811 gdi32full!COtlsClient::GetCache+0x51
74e946d7 gdi32full!CUspShapingClient::FreeMem+0x37
74e94695 gdi32full!COtlsClient::FreeMem+0x25
74e94670 gdi32full!COtlsClient::FreeMem
74e93b86 gdi32full!ApplyFeatures+0xf36
74e93b99 gdi32full!ApplyFeatures+0xf49
7646474b user32!_InternalCallWinProc+0x2b
74e8d4b2 gdi32full!COtlsClient::ReleaseOtlTable+0x82
74e908e0 gdi32full!COtlsClient::GetVariationAxisValues
74e8d4f0 gdi32full!CUspShapingFont::ReleaseFontTable
74e946a0 gdi32full!CUspShapingClient::FreeMem
74e946d7 gdi32full!CUspShapingClient::FreeMem+0x37
74e919a9 gdi32full!GenericEngineGetGlyphPositions+0xe59
74e919bc gdi32full!GenericEngineGetGlyphPositions+0xe6c
746c6664 CoreUIComponents!IRemoteTextInputState$R::Reflection__get_InputPaneTryHide+0x4
76440004 user32!InternalCreateDialog+0xa04
74e02dec gdi32full!COtlsClient::`vftable'
74ea1b2c gdi32full!bBatchTextOut+0x28c
74ea1863 gdi32full!ExtTextOutWImpl+0x5d3
74f37d40 gdi32full!semLocal
74e86e65 gdi32full!GetTextMetricsW+0x1b5
74ae52f4 gdi32!ExtTextOutW+0x34
74ea9ede gdi32full!CUspShapingDrawingSurface::GenericGlyphOut+0x14c
74ea9efd gdi32full!CUspShapingDrawingSurface::GenericGlyphOut+0x16b
74ea1975 gdi32full!bBatchTextOut+0xd5
```

```
76a22f1c win32u!NtGdiExtTextOutW+0xc
76a2329c win32u!NtGdiTransformPoints+0xc
74ea9b82 gdi32full!DPToLPInternal+0xe3
74ea9d79 gdi32full!CUspShapingDrawingSurface::DrawGlyphs+0x79
74ea9d00 gdi32full!CUspShapingDrawingSurface::DrawGlyphs
74ae4812 gdi32!SetBkMode+0x22
74ea9cea gdi32full!GenericEngineDrawGlyphs+0x5a
74ea9c90 gdi32full!GenericEngineDrawGlyphs
74eaa1a2 gdi32full!ShlTextOut+0x222
74ea9c90 gdi32full!GenericEngineDrawGlyphs
74eaa1c1 gdi32full!ShlTextOut+0x241
74eaa1d4 gdi32full!ShlTextOut+0x254
74e07018 gdi32full!CUspShapingClient::`vftable'
74e02de8 gdi32full!CUspShapingDrawingSurface::`vftable'
746c6664 CoreUIComponents!IRemoteTextInputState$R::Reflection__get_InputPaneTryHide+0x4
746c6664 CoreUIComponents!IRemoteTextInputState$R::Reflection__get_InputPaneTryHide+0x4
746c6664 CoreUIComponents!IRemoteTextInputState$R::Reflection__get_InputPaneTryHide+0x4
74e06fec gdi32full!CUspShapingFont::`vftable'
746c6664 CoreUIComponents!IRemoteTextInputState$R::Reflection__get_InputPaneTryHide+0x4
74ea97e6 gdi32full!ScriptTextOut+0x186
74ea956a gdi32full!InternalStringOut+0xca
74ea9472 gdi32full!ScriptStringOut+0x512
74ea9485 gdi32full!ScriptStringOut+0x525
74ae5a28 gdi32!GetTextExtentPointWStub+0x28
76466660 user32!_except_handler4
76449109 user32!DefWindowProcWorker+0x39
7644684f user32!DefDlgProcWorker+0x26f
74e8d5a8 gdi32full!UspAcquireTempAlloc+0x98
74e84a8a gdi32full!LpkStringAnalyse+0xad
74e84a97 gdi32full!LpkStringAnalyse+0xba
74f0b853 gdi32full!LpkInternalPSMTextOut+0xa9
74e9ad78 gdi32full!SetViewportOrgEx+0xc8
74f0b87f gdi32full!LpkInternalPSMTextOut+0xd5
74ae56a8 gdi32!SetViewportOrgExStub+0x28
76459bd4 user32!DrawStateW+0x134
76459bf1 user32!DrawStateW+0x151
764c2f88 user32!gcsHdc
74e8806e gdi32full!SetTextColorImpl+0xfe
74ebf696 gdi32full!IntersectClipRectImpl+0xa6
7647ef1c user32!xxxBNDrawText+0x347
7647dcd0 user32!BNMultiDraw
76459a80 user32!FillRect+0x50
74e88454 gdi32full!SelectObjectImpl+0x254
772c810c ntdll_77290000!RtlDeactivateActivationContextUnsafeFast+0x9c
76a22c0c win32u!NtUserMessageCall+0xc
76447a2d user32!RealDefWindowProcWorker+0x2cd
76447a3b user32!RealDefWindowProcWorker+0x2db
7644701d user32!UserCallDlgProcCheckWow+0x1ed
7644713b user32!UserCallDlgProcCheckWow+0x30b
7644702c user32!UserCallDlgProcCheckWow+0x1fc
76447694 user32!DefWindowProcW+0x214
764476a5 user32!DefWindowProcW+0x225
7649fd70 user32!MB_DlgProc
76466660 user32!_except_handler4
76466660 user32!_except_handler4
76446785 user32!DefDlgProcWorker+0x1a5
76446793 user32!DefDlgProcWorker+0x1b3
772c810c ntdll_77290000!RtlDeactivateActivationContextUnsafeFast+0x9c
764465c8 user32!DefDlgProcW+0x48
7646474b user32!_InternalCallWinProc+0x2b
773182d0 ntdll_77290000!NtdllDialogWndProc_W
764460bc user32!UserCallWinProcCheckWow+0x3ac
76446361 user32!UserCallWinProcCheckWow+0x651
764460e0 user32!UserCallWinProcCheckWow+0x3d0
764446a7 user32!GetWindowLongW+0x127
76445f0b user32!UserCallWinProcCheckWow+0x1fb
76446361 user32!UserCallWinProcCheckWow+0x651
```

```
773182d0 ntdll_77290000!NtdllDialogWndProc_W
76466660 user32!_except_handler4
76445c5a user32!DispatchClientMessage+0xea
773182d0 ntdll_77290000!NtdllDialogWndProc_W
77318430 ntdll_77290000!NtdllDispatchMessage_W
76446361 user32!UserCallWinProcCheckWow+0x651
76466660 user32!_except_handler4
7644e62f user32!__fnDWORD+0x3f
77301dac ntdll_77290000!NtCallbackReturn+0xc
7644e647 user32!__fnDWORD+0x57
773041cd ntdll_77290000!KiUserCallbackDispatcher+0x4d
77304100 ntdll_77290000!KiUserCallbackExceptionHandler
773182d0 ntdll_77290000!NtdllDialogWndProc_W
77318430 ntdll_77290000!NtdllDispatchMessage_W
76a22bac win32u!NtUserPeekMessage+0xc
7644c4ee user32!_PeekMessage+0x2e
7644520e user32!DispatchMessageWorker+0x20e
74ccc520 msctf!UIWndProc
7644c460 user32!PeekMessageW+0x160
76a22c5c win32u!NtUserWaitMessage+0xc
7645b8f3 user32!DialogBox2+0x102
7645b7e4 user32!InternalDialogBox+0xd9
764a17cb user32!SoftModalMessageBox+0x6cb
76420000 user32!pfnClientA <PERF> (user32+0x0)
764a182b user32!SoftModalMessageBox+0x72b
7649fd70 user32!MB_DlgProc
008f31be AppA!`string'+0x2
77304100 ntdll_77290000!KiUserCallbackExceptionHandler
76a23bac win32u!NtUserModifyUserStartupInfoFlags+0xc
764a06c7 user32!MessageBoxWorker+0x2ca
008f31bc AppA!`string'
7730391c ntdll_77290000!NtTestAlert+0xc
76427ed4 user32!SEBbuttons+0x4
77290000 ntdll_77290000!LdrpMscoreeDllName <PERF> (ntdll_77290000+0x0)
77309f80 ntdll_77290000!_except_handler4
773021ac ntdll_77290000!NtContinue+0xc
772e1c29 ntdll_77290000!LdrInitializeThunk+0x29
77290000 ntdll_77290000!LdrpMscoreeDllName <PERF> (ntdll_77290000+0x0)
75732450 ucrtbase!thread_start<unsigned int (__stdcall*)(void *),1>
773042c0 ntdll_77290000!RtlUserThreadStart
008f31bc AppA!`string'
764a0f70 user32!MessageBoxTimeoutW+0x30
764a10a5 user32!MessageBoxTimeoutW+0x165
764a10d0 user32!MessageBoxW
008f31bc AppA!`string'
008f31b0 AppA!`string'
764a10ea user32!MessageBoxW+0x1a
008f31bc AppA!`string'
008f31b0 AppA!`string'
6d703ddb apphelp!MbHook_MessageBoxW+0x2b
008f31bc AppA!`string'
008f31b0 AppA!`string'
6d6c8840 apphelp!_except_handler4
008f11e4 AppA!thread_D+0x24 [C:\AWMDA-Examples\AppA\AppA.cpp @ 39]
008f31bc AppA!`string'
008f31b0 AppA!`string'
772f01c9 ntdll_77290000!RtlSetLastWin32Error+0x39
76cceb70 KERNELBASE!FlsGetValue
008f181a AppA!std::thread::_Invoke<std::tuple<void (__cdecl*)(void)>,0>+0x2a [C:\Program Files
(x86)\Microsoft Visual Studio\2019\Professional\VC\Tools\MSVC\14.23.28105\include\thread @ 41]
008f17f0 AppA!std::thread::_Invoke<std::tuple<void (__cdecl*)(void)>,0> [C:\Program Files
(x86)\Microsoft Visual Studio\2019\Professional\VC\Tools\MSVC\14.23.28105\include\thread @ 36]
008f2c80 AppA!_ltod3+0xe0
7573248f ucrtbase!thread_start<unsigned int (__stdcall*)(void *),1>+0x3f
75732450 ucrtbase!thread_start<unsigned int (__stdcall*)(void *),1>
75732450 ucrtbase!thread_start<unsigned int (__stdcall*)(void *),1>
7574e5c0 ucrtbase!_except_handler4
```

```
761a6359 kernel32!BaseThreadInitThunk+0x19
761a6340 kernel32!BaseThreadInitThunk
772f7b74 ntdll_77290000!__RtlUserThreadStart+0x2f
77309f80 ntdll_77290000!_except_handler4
772f7b44 ntdll_77290000!_RtlUserThreadStart+0x1b
77318f1a ntdll_77290000!FinalExceptionHandlerPad42
75732450 ucrtbase!thread_start<unsigned int (__stdcall*)(void *),1>

0:006:x86> ub 764a10ea
user32!MessageBoxW+0x3:
764a10d3 8bec            mov     ebp,esp
764a10d5 6aff            push    0FFFFFFFFh
764a10d7 6a00            push    0
764a10d9 ff7514          push    dword ptr [ebp+14h]
764a10dc ff7510          push    dword ptr [ebp+10h]
764a10df ff750c          push    dword ptr [ebp+0Ch]
764a10e2 ff7508          push    dword ptr [ebp+8]
764a10e5 e856feffff      call    user32!MessageBoxTimeoutW (764a0f40)

0:006:x86> .effmach AMD64
Effective machine: x64 (AMD64)

0:006> !teb
Wow64 TEB32 at 000000000056d000
    ExceptionList:        000000000291fd60
    StackBase:            0000000002920000
    StackLimit:           000000000291c000
    SubSystemTib:         0000000000000000
    FiberData:            0000000000001e00
    ArbitraryUserPointer: 0000000000000000
    Self:                 000000000056d000
    EnvironmentPointer:   0000000000000000
    ClientId:             0000000000022fc . 0000000000002554
    RpcHandle:            0000000000000000
    Tls Storage:          00000000009eb360
    PEB Address:          0000000000558000
    LastErrorValue:       0
    LastStatusValue:      c0000034
    Count Owned Locks:    0
    HardErrorMode:        0


Wow64 TEB at 000000000056b000
    ExceptionList:        000000000056d000
    StackBase:            000000000093fd20
    StackLimit:           0000000000938000
    SubSystemTib:         0000000000000000
    FiberData:            0000000000001e00
    ArbitraryUserPointer: 0000000000000000
    Self:                 000000000056b000
    EnvironmentPointer:   0000000000000000
    ClientId:             0000000000022fc . 0000000000002554
    RpcHandle:            0000000000000000
    Tls Storage:          0000000000000000
    PEB Address:          0000000000557000
    LastErrorValue:       0
    LastStatusValue:      0
    Count Owned Locks:    0
    HardErrorMode:        0
```

```
0:006> dt ntdll!_TEB 000000000056b000
   +0x000 NtTib            : _NT_TIB
   +0x038 EnvironmentPointer : (null)
   +0x040 ClientId         : _CLIENT_ID
   +0x050 ActiveRpcHandle  : (null)
   +0x058 ThreadLocalStoragePointer : (null)
   +0x060 ProcessEnvironmentBlock : 0x00000000`00557000 _PEB
   +0x068 LastErrorValue   : 0
   +0x06c CountOfOwnedCriticalSections : 0
   +0x070 CsrClientThread  : (null)
   +0x078 Win32ThreadInfo  : 0x00000000`00002554 Void
   +0x080 User32Reserved   : [26] 0
   +0x0e8 UserReserved     : [5] 0
   +0x100 WOW32Reserved    : (null)
   +0x108 CurrentLocale    : 0x1809
   +0x10c FpSoftwareStatusRegister : 0
   +0x110 ReservedForDebuggerInstrumentation : [16] (null)
   +0x190 SystemReserved1  : [30] (null)
   +0x280 PlaceholderCompatibilityMode : 0 ''
   +0x281 PlaceholderHydrationAlwaysExplicit : 0 ''
   +0x282 PlaceholderReserved : [10]  ""
   +0x28c ProxiedProcessId : 0
   +0x290 _ActivationStack : _ACTIVATION_CONTEXT_STACK
   +0x2b8 WorkingOnBehalfTicket : [8]  ""
   +0x2c0 ExceptionCode    : 0n0
   +0x2c4 Padding0         : [4]  ""
   +0x2c8 ActivationContextStackPointer : (null)
   +0x2d0 InstrumentationCallbackSp : 0
   +0x2d8 InstrumentationCallbackPreviousPc : 0
   +0x2e0 InstrumentationCallbackPreviousSp : 0
   +0x2e8 TxFsContext      : 0xfffe
   +0x2ec InstrumentationCallbackDisabled : 0 ''
   +0x2ed UnalignedLoadStoreExceptions : 0 ''
   +0x2ee Padding1         : [2]  ""
   +0x2f0 GdiTebBatch      : _GDI_TEB_BATCH
   +0x7d8 RealClientId     : _CLIENT_ID
   +0x7e8 GdiCachedProcessHandle : (null)
   +0x7f0 GdiClientPID     : 0
   +0x7f4 GdiClientTID     : 0
   +0x7f8 GdiThreadLocalInfo : (null)
   +0x800 Win32ClientInfo  : [62] 0x388
   +0x9f0 glDispatchTable  : [233] (null)
   +0x1138 glReserved1     : [29] 0
   +0x1220 glReserved2     : (null)
   +0x1228 glSectionInfo   : (null)
   +0x1230 glSection       : (null)
   +0x1238 glTable         : (null)
   +0x1240 glCurrentRC     : (null)
   +0x1248 glContext       : (null)
   +0x1250 LastStatusValue : 0
   +0x1254 Padding2        : [4]  ""
   +0x1258 StaticUnicodeString : _UNICODE_STRING ""
   +0x1268 StaticUnicodeBuffer : [261]  ""
   +0x1472 Padding3        : [6]  ""
   +0x1478 DeallocationStack : 0x00000000`00900000 Void
   +0x1480 TlsSlots        : [64] (null)
   +0x1680 TlsLinks        : _LIST_ENTRY [ 0x00000000`00000000 - 0x00000000`00000000 ]
   +0x1690 Vdm             : (null)
   +0x1698 ReservedForNtRpc : (null)
   +0x16a0 DbgSsReserved   : [2] (null)
```

```
+0x16b0 HardErrorMode      : 0
+0x16b4 Padding4           : [4]  ""
+0x16b8 Instrumentation    : [11] (null)
+0x1710 ActivityId         : _GUID {00000000-0000-0000-0000-000000000000}
+0x1720 SubProcessTag      : (null)
+0x1728 PerflibData        : (null)
+0x1730 EtwTraceData       : (null)
+0x1738 WinSockData        : (null)
+0x1740 GdiBatchCount      : 0
+0x1744 CurrentIdealProcessor : _PROCESSOR_NUMBER
+0x1744 IdealProcessorValue : 0x1010000
+0x1744 ReservedPad0       : 0 ''
+0x1745 ReservedPad1       : 0 ''
+0x1746 ReservedPad2       : 0x1 ''
+0x1747 IdealProcessor     : 0x1 ''
+0x1748 GuaranteedStackBytes : 0
+0x174c Padding5           : [4]  ""
+0x1750 ReservedForPerf    : (null)
+0x1758 ReservedForOle     : (null)
+0x1760 WaitingOnLoaderLock : 0
+0x1764 Padding6           : [4]  ""
+0x1768 SavedPriorityState : (null)
+0x1770 ReservedForCodeCoverage : 0
+0x1778 ThreadPoolData     : (null)
+0x1780 TlsExpansionSlots  : (null)
+0x1788 DeallocationBStore : (null)
+0x1790 BStoreLimit        : (null)
+0x1798 MuiGeneration      : 0
+0x179c IsImpersonating    : 0
+0x17a0 NlsCache           : (null)
+0x17a8 pShimData          : (null)
+0x17b0 HeapData           : 0
+0x17b4 Padding7           : [4]  ""
+0x17b8 CurrentTransactionHandle : (null)
+0x17c0 ActiveFrame        : (null)
+0x17c8 FlsData            : (null)
+0x17d0 PreferredLanguages : (null)
+0x17d8 UserPrefLanguages  : (null)
+0x17e0 MergedPrefLanguages : (null)
+0x17e8 MuiImpersonation   : 0
+0x17ec CrossTebFlags      : 0
+0x17ec SpareCrossTebBits  : 0y0000000000000000 (0)
+0x17ee SameTebFlags       : 0
+0x17ee SafeThunkCall      : 0y0
+0x17ee InDebugPrint       : 0y0
+0x17ee HasFiberData       : 0y0
+0x17ee SkipThreadAttach   : 0y0
+0x17ee WerInShipAssertCode : 0y0
+0x17ee RanProcessInit     : 0y0
+0x17ee ClonedThread       : 0y0
+0x17ee SuppressDebugMsg   : 0y0
+0x17ee DisableUserStackWalk : 0y0
+0x17ee RtlExceptionAttached : 0y0
+0x17ee InitialThread      : 0y0
+0x17ee SessionAware       : 0y0
+0x17ee LoadOwner          : 0y0
+0x17ee LoaderWorker       : 0y0
+0x17ee SkipLoaderInit     : 0y0
+0x17ee SpareSameTebBits   : 0y0
+0x17f0 TxnScopeEnterCallback : (null)
```

```
+0x17f8 TxnScopeExitCallback : (null)
+0x1800 TxnScopeContext   : (null)
+0x1808 LockCount         : 0
+0x180c WowTebOffset      : 0n8192
+0x1810 ResourceRetValue  : (null)
+0x1818 ReservedForWdf    : (null)
+0x1820 ReservedForCrt    : 0
+0x1828 EffectiveContainerId : _GUID {00000000-0000-0000-0000-000000000000}
```

Note: The second slot contains an address of the 32-bit thread context structure with CPU register values we need:

```
0:006> dp 000000000056b000+0x1480+8
00000000`0056c488  00000000`0093fd20 00000000`00000000
00000000`0056c498  00000000`00000000 00000000`00000000
00000000`0056c4a8  00000000`00000000 00000000`00000000
00000000`0056c4b8  00000000`00000000 00000000`00000000
00000000`0056c4c8  00000000`00000000 00000000`00558480
00000000`0056c4d8  00000000`00000000 00000000`00000000
00000000`0056c4e8  00000000`00000000 00000000`00000000
00000000`0056c4f8  00000000`00000000 00000000`00000000

0:006> dd 00000000`0093fd20
00000000`0093fd20  014c0002 0001003f 00000000 00000000
00000000`0093fd30  00000000 00000000 00000000 00000000
00000000`0093fd40  0000027f 00000000 0000ffff 00000000
00000000`0093fd50  00000000 00000000 00000000 0291f908
00000000`0093fd60  00000000 77304180 00000000 00000000
00000000`0093fd70  00000000 00000000 00000000 00000000
00000000`0093fd80  00000000 00000000 00000000 00000000
00000000`0093fd90  00000000 00000000 00000000 00000000
```

Note: We need to use the 32-bit _CONTEXT structure, so we use the *WinTypes* module if the *AppA* module is not listed:

```
0:006> dt *!_CONTEXT
          ntdll!_CONTEXT
          VCRUNTIME140!_CONTEXT
          msvcp140!_CONTEXT
          combase!_CONTEXT
          WinTypes!_CONTEXT

0:006> dt WinTypes!_CONTEXT 00000000`0093fd20+4
   +0x000 ContextFlags    : 0x1003f
   +0x004 Dr0             : 0
   +0x008 Dr1             : 0
   +0x00c Dr2             : 0
   +0x010 Dr3             : 0
   +0x014 Dr6             : 0
   +0x018 Dr7             : 0
   +0x01c FloatSave       : _FLOATING_SAVE_AREA
   +0x08c SegGs           : 0x2b
   +0x090 SegFs           : 0x53
   +0x094 SegEs           : 0x2b
   +0x098 SegDs           : 0x2b
   +0x09c Edi             : 0
   +0x0a0 Esi             : 0
   +0x0a4 Ebx             : 0x40646
   +0x0a8 Edx             : 0
   +0x0ac Ecx             : 0
```

```
+0x0b0 Eax              : 0
+0x0b4 Ebp              : 0x291fa28
+0x0b8 Eip              : 0x76a22c5c
+0x0bc SegCs            : 0x23
+0x0c0 EFlags           : 0x202
+0x0c4 Esp              : 0x291f9ec
+0x0c8 SegSs            : 0x2b
+0x0cc ExtendedRegisters : [512]  "???"
```

```
0:006> .effmach x86
Effective machine: x86 compatible (x86)
```

```
0:006:x86> .reload
...................................
```

```
************* Symbol Loading Error Summary **************
Module name            Error
SharedUserData         No error - symbol load deferred

You can troubleshoot most symbol related issues by turning on symbol loading diagnostics (!sym
noisy) and repeating the command that caused symbols to be loaded.
You should also verify that your symbol search path (.sympath) is correct.
```

```
0:006:x86> k=0x291fa28 0x291f9ec 0x76a22c5c
# ChildEBP RetAddr
00 0291f9e8 7645b8f3     win32u!NtUserWaitMessage+0xc
01 0291fa28 7645b7e4     user32!DialogBox2+0x102
02 0291fa58 764a182b     user32!InternalDialogBox+0xd9
03 0291fb24 764a06c7     user32!SoftModalMessageBox+0x72b
04 0291fc80 764a10a5     user32!MessageBoxWorker+0x2ca
05 0291fd0c 764a10ea     user32!MessageBoxTimeoutW+0x165
06 0291fd2c 6d703ddb     user32!MessageBoxW+0x1a
*** WARNING: Unable to verify checksum for AppA.exe
07 0291fd70 008f11e4     apphelp!MbHook_MessageBoxW+0x2b
WARNING: Stack unwind information not available. Following frames may be wrong.
08 0291fdac 008f181a     AppA+0x11e4
09 0291fdc8 7573248f     AppA+0x181a
0a 0291fe00 761a6359     ucrtbase!thread_start<unsigned int (__stdcall*)(void *),1>+0x3f
0b 0291fe10 772f7b74     kernel32!BaseThreadInitThunk+0x19
0c 0291fe6c 772f7b44     ntdll_77290000!__RtlUserThreadStart+0x2f
0d 0291fe7c 00000000     ntdll_77290000!_RtlUserThreadStart+0x1b
```

9.   We now dump the stack trace lines with parameters (the **kv** command) and inspect the *MessageBoxW*
function parameters (2nd and 3rd parameters) using the **du** command (because the function is a UNICODE variant of
MessageBox, use the **da** command for the ASCII variant such as *MessageBoxA*):

```
0:006:x86> kv=0x291fa28 0x291f9ec 0x76a22c5c
# ChildEBP RetAddr      Args to Child
00 0291f9e8 7645b8f3     00000000 00000000 00000000 win32u!NtUserWaitMessage+0xc (FPO: [0,0,0])
01 0291fa28 7645b7e4     00000000 00000000 00000000 user32!DialogBox2+0x102 (FPO: [Non-Fpo])
02 0291fa58 764a182b     00000000 7649fd70 0291fc98 user32!InternalDialogBox+0xd9 (FPO: [Non-Fpo])
03 0291fb24 764a06c7     0291fc98 008f31bc 00000000 user32!SoftModalMessageBox+0x72b (FPO: [1,41,4])
04 0291fc80 764a10a5     00000000 764a10d0 009bbb30 user32!MessageBoxWorker+0x2ca (FPO: [Non-Fpo])
05 0291fd0c 764a10ea     00000000 008f31bc 008f31b0 user32!MessageBoxTimeoutW+0x165 (FPO: [6,29,4])
06 0291fd2c 6d703ddb     00000000 008f31bc 008f31b0 user32!MessageBoxW+0x1a (FPO: [Non-Fpo])
07 0291fd70 008f11e4     00000000 008f31bc 008f31b0 apphelp!MbHook_MessageBoxW+0x2b (FPO: [Non-Fpo])
WARNING: Stack unwind information not available. Following frames may be wrong.
08 0291fdac 008f181a     14b16ffb 008f17f0 0291fdf0 AppA+0x11e4
09 0291fdc8 7573248f     009c6ed0 280a0f23 75732450 AppA+0x181a
0a 0291fe00 761a6359     009bbb30 761a6340 0291fe6c ucrtbase!thread_start<unsigned int (__stdcall*)(void *),1>+0x3f (FPO: [Non-Fpo])
0b 0291fe10 772f7b74     009bbb30 4fcd0992 00000000 kernel32!BaseThreadInitThunk+0x19 (FPO: [Non-Fpo])
0c 0291fe6c 772f7b44     ffffffff 77318f1a 00000000 ntdll_77290000!__RtlUserThreadStart+0x2f (FPO: [SEH])
0d 0291fe7c 00000000     75732450 009bbb30 00000000 ntdll_77290000!_RtlUserThreadStart+0x1b (FPO: [Non-Fpo])
```

```
0:006:x86> du 008f31bc
008f31bc  "Message"

0:006:x86> du 008f31b0
008f31b0  "Error"
```

Note: We can also use the **!sw** command from the *wow64exts* extension for switching between modes (there's also the the **!k** command for the combined stack trace):

```
0:006:x86> .load wow64exts

0:006:x86> !sw
Switched to Host mode

0:000:x86> !k
Walking Native Stack...
 # Child-SP          RetAddr             Call Site
00 00000000`0065ebd8 00000000`77281b1d  wow64cpu!CpupSyscallStub+0xc
01 00000000`0065ebe0 00000000`77281199  wow64cpu!Thunk0ArgReloadState+0x5
02 00000000`0065ec90 00007ffa`59d7c77a  wow64cpu!BTCpuSimulate+0x9
03 00000000`0065ecd0 00007ffa`59d7c637  wow64!RunCpuSimulation+0xa
04 00000000`0065ed00 00007ffa`5a093fb3  wow64!Wow64LdrpInitialize+0x127
05 00000000`0065efb0 00007ffa`5a081db5  ntdll!LdrpInitializeProcess+0x186b
06 00000000`0065f3f0 00007ffa`5a031853  ntdll!_LdrpInitialize+0x50549
07 00000000`0065f490 00007ffa`5a0317fe  ntdll!LdrpInitialize+0x3b
08 00000000`0065f4c0 00000000`00000000  ntdll!LdrInitializeThunk+0xe
Walking Guest (WoW) Stack...
 # ChildEBP RetAddr
00 0075fb5c 76cde279    ntdll_77290000!NtWaitForSingleObject+0xc
01 0075fbd0 749cb211    KERNELBASE!WaitForSingleObjectEx+0x99
02 0075fbe8 008f1411    msvcp140!_Thrd_join+0x11
[d:\agent\_work\3\s\src\vctools\crt\crtw32\stdcpp\thr\cthread.c @ 48]
03 (Inline) --------    AppA!std::thread::join+0x2b [C:\Program Files (x86)\Microsoft Visual
Studio\2019\Professional\VC\Tools\MSVC\14.23.28105\include\thread @ 113]
04 0075fc4c 008f1a4d    AppA!wmain+0x1b1 [C:\AWMDA-Examples\AppA\AppA.cpp @ 68]
05 (Inline) --------    AppA!invoke_main+0x1c
[d:\agent\_work\4\s\src\vctools\crt\vcstartup\src\startup\exe_common.inl @ 90]
06 0075fc94 761a6359    AppA!__scrt_common_main_seh+0xfa
[d:\agent\_work\4\s\src\vctools\crt\vcstartup\src\startup\exe_common.inl @ 288]
07 0075fca4 772f7b74    kernel32!BaseThreadInitThunk+0x19
08 0075fd00 772f7b44    ntdll_77290000!__RtlUserThreadStart+0x2f
09 0075fd10 00000000    ntdll_77290000!_RtlUserThreadStart+0x1b

0:006> !sw
Switched to Guest (WoW) mode
```

10.   We close logging before exiting WinDbg:

```
0:006:x86> .logclose
Closing open log file C:\AWMDA-Dumps\Process\x86\WOW64\AppA.log
```

Exercise P14

- ◎ **Goal:** Learn how to analyze process memory leaks

- ◎ **Patterns:** Thread Age; Memory Leak (Process Heap)

- ◎ \AWMDA-Dumps\Exercise-P14-Analysis-process-dump-AppS-64.pdf

Exercise P14: Analysis of an application process dump (AppS, 64-bit)

Goal: Learn how to analyze memory leaks.

Patterns: Thread Age; Memory Leak (Process Heap).

1.   Launch WinDbg.

2.   Open \AWMDA-Dumps\Process\x64\AppS.DMP

3.   We get the dump file loaded:

```
Microsoft (R) Windows Debugger Version 10.0.25877.1004 AMD64
Copyright (c) Microsoft Corporation. All rights reserved.


Loading Dump File [C:\AWMDA-Dumps\Process\x64\AppS.DMP]
User Mini Dump File with Full Memory: Only application data is available


************* Path validation summary **************
Response                        Time (ms)     Location
Deferred                                      srv*
Symbol search path is: srv*
Executable search path is:
Windows 10 Version 18362 MP (2 procs) Free x64
Product: WinNt, suite: SingleUserTS Personal
Edition build lab: 18362.1.amd64fre.19h1_release.190318-1202
Machine Name:
Debug session time: Sat Nov 23 17:00:19.000 2019 (UTC + 1:00)
System Uptime: 0 days 2:01:52.255
Process Uptime: 0 days 0:03:42.000
.......
For analysis of this file, run !analyze -v
ntdll!NtWaitForSingleObject+0x14:
00007ff9`ff8dc144 c3              ret
```

4.   Open a log file using the **.logopen** command:

```
0:000> .logopen C:\AWMDA-Dumps\Process\x64\AppS.log
Opened log file 'C:\AWMDA-Dumps\Process\x64\AppS.log'
```

5.   *AppS* was reported to consuming more memory than usual 100Mb:

```
🖥️ Task Manager                                    —    □    ✕

File  Options  View

Processes  Performance  App history  Start-up  Users  Details  Services

Name                      PID    Status      Username     CPU  Commit size    ⌃
🔳 ApplicationFrameHos... 6120   Running     Training     00      17,624 K
🔳 AppS.exe               9988   Running     Training     00   1,062,256 K
🔳 browser_broker.exe     6332   Running     Training     00       1,652 K
⬛ cmd.exe                2292   Running     Training     00       2,756 K
⬛ conhost.exe            940    Running     Training     00       7,488 K
⬛ conhost.exe            9292   Running     Training     00       7,244 K
🔳 csrss.exe             420    Running     SYSTEM       00       1,688 K
🔳 csrss.exe             500    Running     SYSTEM       00       1,756 K
📝 ctfmon.exe            6884   Running     Training     00       9,300 K
🔳 dllhost.exe           3696   Running     SYSTEM       00       3,848 K
🔳 dllhost.exe           3568   Running     Training     00       1,876 K
🔳 dllhost.exe           6480   Running     Training     00       4,596 K
🔳 dwm.exe               368    Running     DWM-1        00     361,416 K
📁 explorer.exe          5088   Running     Training     00      95,000 K
🔳 fontdrvhost.exe       768    Running     UMFD-0       00       1,424 K
🔳 gflags.exe            3104   Running     Training     00       2,064 K
🔳 LocalBridge.exe       9336   Running     Training     00      29,664 K
🔳 lsass.exe             584    Running     SYSTEM       00       6,740 K
🔳 Microsoft.Photos.exe  5660   Suspended   Training     00      48,880 K
🌐 MicrosoftEdge.exe     1008   Suspended   Training     00      23,324 K
🌐 MicrosoftEdgeCP.exe   6644   Suspended   Training     00       5,684 K
🔳 MicrosoftEdgeSH.exe   6620   Suspended   Training     00       3,820 K
🔳 msdtc.exe             4112   Running     NETWORK ...  00       2,884 K   ⌄
<                                                              >

⌃ Fewer details                                          End task
```

6.   Type the **~*k** command to verify the correctness of all stack traces:

```
0:000> ~*k

.  0  Id: 2704.27d4 Suspend: 0 Teb: 00000053`8e5a6000 Unfrozen
 # Child-SP          RetAddr           Call Site
00 00000053`8e6ff798 00007ff9`fc8b8ba3 ntdll!NtWaitForSingleObject+0x14
*** WARNING: Unable to verify checksum for AppS.exe
01 00000053`8e6ff7a0 00007ff7`1c50498f KERNELBASE!WaitForSingleObjectEx+0x93
02 00000053`8e6ff840 00007ff7`1c5017ef AppS+0x498f
03 00000053`8e6ff870 00007ff7`1c501afc AppS+0x17ef
04 00000053`8e6ff8d0 00007ff7`1c5052fc AppS+0x1afc
05 00000053`8e6ff950 00007ff9`fdc57bd4 AppS+0x52fc
06 00000053`8e6ff990 00007ff9`ff8aced1 kernel32!BaseThreadInitThunk+0x14
07 00000053`8e6ff9c0 00000000`00000000 ntdll!RtlUserThreadStart+0x21
```

```
   1  Id: 2704.1ba8 Suspend: 0 Teb: 00000053`8e5a8000 Unfrozen
 # Child-SP          RetAddr           Call Site
00 00000053`8e7ff488 00007ff9`fc8c6931 ntdll!NtDelayExecution+0x14
01 00000053`8e7ff490 00007ff7`1c504a14 KERNELBASE!SleepEx+0xa1
02 00000053`8e7ff530 00007ff7`1c5025c5 AppS+0x4a14
03 00000053`8e7ff580 00007ff7`1c50209d AppS+0x25c5
04 00000053`8e7ff5e0 00007ff7`1c501a93 AppS+0x209d
05 00000053`8e7ff620 00007ff7`1c5031e5 AppS+0x1a93
06 00000053`8e7ff660 00007ff7`1c502fbb AppS+0x31e5
07 00000053`8e7ff690 00007ff7`1c502714 AppS+0x2fbb
08 00000053`8e7ff6c0 00007ff7`1c50aee8 AppS+0x2714
09 00000053`8e7ff710 00007ff9`fdc57bd4 AppS+0xaee8
0a 00000053`8e7ff740 00007ff9`ff8aced1 kernel32!BaseThreadInitThunk+0x14
0b 00000053`8e7ff770 00000000`00000000 ntdll!RtlUserThreadStart+0x21

   2  Id: 2704.784 Suspend: 0 Teb: 00000053`8e5aa000 Unfrozen
 # Child-SP          RetAddr           Call Site
00 00000053`8e8ff508 00007ff9`fc8c6931 ntdll!NtDelayExecution+0x14
01 00000053`8e8ff510 00007ff7`1c504a14 KERNELBASE!SleepEx+0xa1
02 00000053`8e8ff5b0 00007ff7`1c5025c5 AppS+0x4a14
03 00000053`8e8ff600 00007ff7`1c50209d AppS+0x25c5
04 00000053`8e8ff660 00007ff7`1c501a93 AppS+0x209d
05 00000053`8e8ff6a0 00007ff7`1c5031e5 AppS+0x1a93
06 00000053`8e8ff6e0 00007ff7`1c502fbb AppS+0x31e5
07 00000053`8e8ff710 00007ff7`1c502714 AppS+0x2fbb
08 00000053`8e8ff740 00007ff7`1c50aee8 AppS+0x2714
09 00000053`8e8ff790 00007ff9`fdc57bd4 AppS+0xaee8
0a 00000053`8e8ff7c0 00007ff9`ff8aced1 kernel32!BaseThreadInitThunk+0x14
0b 00000053`8e8ff7f0 00000000`00000000 ntdll!RtlUserThreadStart+0x21

   3  Id: 2704.1f98 Suspend: 0 Teb: 00000053`8e5ac000 Unfrozen
 # Child-SP          RetAddr           Call Site
00 00000053`8e9ff938 00007ff9`fc8c6931 ntdll!NtDelayExecution+0x14
01 00000053`8e9ff940 00007ff7`1c504a14 KERNELBASE!SleepEx+0xa1
02 00000053`8e9ff9e0 00007ff7`1c5025c5 AppS+0x4a14
03 00000053`8e9ffa30 00007ff7`1c50209d AppS+0x25c5
04 00000053`8e9ffa90 00007ff7`1c5019de AppS+0x209d
05 00000053`8e9ffad0 00007ff7`1c501a39 AppS+0x19de
06 00000053`8e9ffba0 00007ff7`1c501a49 AppS+0x1a39
07 00000053`8e9ffbd0 00007ff7`1c5031e5 AppS+0x1a49
08 00000053`8e9ffc10 00007ff7`1c502fbb AppS+0x31e5
09 00000053`8e9ffc40 00007ff7`1c502714 AppS+0x2fbb
0a 00000053`8e9ffc70 00007ff7`1c50aee8 AppS+0x2714
0b 00000053`8e9ffcc0 00007ff9`fdc57bd4 AppS+0xaee8
0c 00000053`8e9ffcf0 00007ff9`ff8aced1 kernel32!BaseThreadInitThunk+0x14
0d 00000053`8e9ffd20 00000000`00000000 ntdll!RtlUserThreadStart+0x21
```

7. Let's check CPU consumption:

```
0:000> !runaway f
User Mode Time
  Thread       Time
   3:1f98      0 days 0:02:32.125
   2:784       0 days 0:00:00.000
   1:1ba8      0 days 0:00:00.000
   0:27d4      0 days 0:00:00.000
 Kernel Mode Time
  Thread       Time
   3:1f98      0 days 0:00:05.281
```

```
   1:1ba8       0 days 0:00:00.015
   2:784        0 days 0:00:00.000
   0:27d4       0 days 0:00:00.000
 Elapsed Time
  Thread        Time
   0:27d4       0 days 0:03:41.858
   1:1ba8       0 days 0:03:41.697
   2:784        0 days 0:03:41.697
   3:1f98       0 days 0:03:41.697
```

Note: We see thread #3 had accumulated more than 50% of the time since its creation.

8.   Because it was reported that the application was growing in size, and its memory dump is unusually large (~1Gb), we suspect a process heap memory leak. We check its heap statistics using the the **!heap -s** command:

```
0:000> !heap -s

*******************************************************************************
                             NT HEAP STATS BELOW
*******************************************************************************
NtGlobalFlag enables following debugging aids for new heaps:
    stack back traces
LFH Key                 : 0x6be8329b1783ab99
Termination on corruption : ENABLED
          Heap     Flags   Reserv  Commit  Virt   Free  List   UCR  Virt Lock  Fast
                             (k)     (k)    (k)    (k) length       blocks cont. heap
-------------------------------------------------------------------------------------
0000024ea09e0000 08000002 1068636 1051532 1068584  15804    78    70    1       0   LFH
0000024e9ef80000 08008000      64       4      64      2     1     1    0       0
0000024ea0910000 08001002     112      32      60      6     2     1    0       0   LFH
-------------------------------------------------------------------------------------
```

Note: We see that one heap `0000024ea09e0000` is very large. If such a problem occurs, one of the troubleshooting steps is to enable **user mode stack trace database** to include all stack traces from threads that were using heap allocation functions. It is usually done by using *gflags.exe* from Debugging Tools for Windows. We used the x64 version because the process was 64-bit. It is also called Global Flags (X64) in the Windows Kits menu. There is also a separate version for x86. This procedure had already been done for this application:

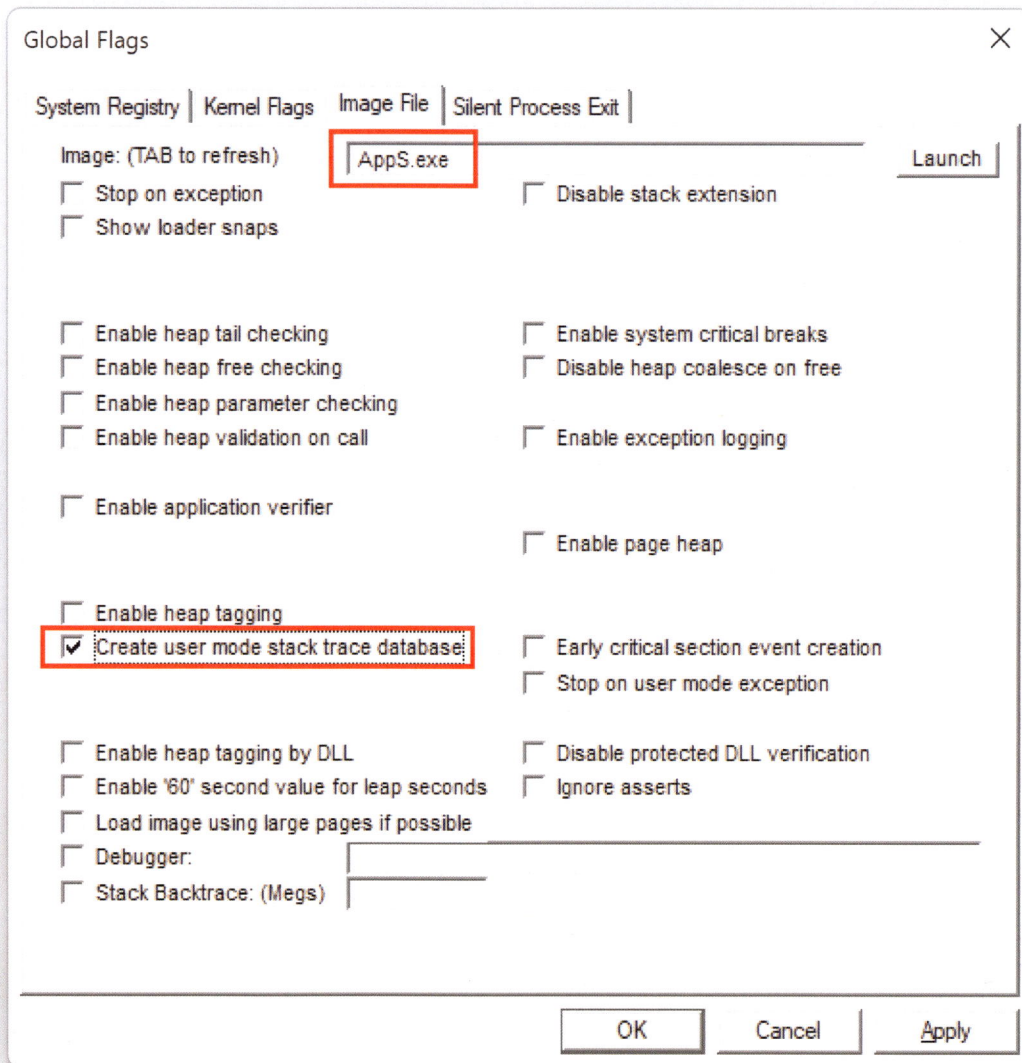

Note: We can always verify such flags in a dump using **!gflag** command:

```
0:000> !gflag
Current NtGlobalFlag contents: 0x00001000
    ust - Create user mode stack trace database
```

Note: You may also notice "stack back traces" in the output of the **!heap -s** command above.

9.   The following command lists heap segments and their entries:

```
0:000> !heap -h 0000024ea09e0000
HEAPEXT: Unable to get address of ntdll!RtlpHeapInvalidBadAddress.
Index   Address   Name       Debugging options enabled
  1:    24ea09e0000
    Segment at 0000024ea09e0000 to 0000024ea0adf000 (000f0000 bytes committed)
    Segment at 0000024ea1290000 to 0000024ea138f000 (000c9000 bytes committed)
    Segment at 0000024ea1390000 to 0000024ea158f000 (001d6000 bytes committed)
    Segment at 0000024ea1590000 to 0000024ea198f000 (003ee000 bytes committed)
    Segment at 0000024ea1990000 to 0000024ea218f000 (007db000 bytes committed)
    Segment at 0000024ea2190000 to 0000024ea315f000 (00fb5000 bytes committed)
    Segment at 0000024ea3160000 to 0000024ea412f000 (00fb5000 bytes committed)
```

```
Segment at 0000024ea4130000 to 0000024ea50ff000 (00fb5000 bytes committed)
Segment at 0000024ea5100000 to 0000024ea60cf000 (00fb5000 bytes committed)
Segment at 0000024ea60d0000 to 0000024ea709f000 (00fb5000 bytes committed)
Segment at 0000024ea70a0000 to 0000024ea806f000 (00fb5000 bytes committed)
Segment at 0000024ea8070000 to 0000024ea903f000 (00fb5000 bytes committed)
Segment at 0000024ea9040000 to 0000024eaa00f000 (00fb5000 bytes committed)
Segment at 0000024eaa010000 to 0000024eaafdf000 (00fb5000 bytes committed)
Segment at 0000024eaafe0000 to 0000024eabfaf000 (00fb5000 bytes committed)
Segment at 0000024eabfb0000 to 0000024eacf7f000 (00fb5000 bytes committed)
Segment at 0000024eacf80000 to 0000024eadf4f000 (00fb5000 bytes committed)
Segment at 0000024eadf50000 to 0000024eaef1f000 (00fb5000 bytes committed)
Segment at 0000024eaef20000 to 0000024eafeef000 (00fb5000 bytes committed)
Segment at 0000024eafef0000 to 0000024eb0ebf000 (00fb5000 bytes committed)
Segment at 0000024eb0ec0000 to 0000024eb1e8f000 (00fb5000 bytes committed)
Segment at 0000024eb1e90000 to 0000024eb2e5f000 (00fb5000 bytes committed)
Segment at 0000024eb2e60000 to 0000024eb3e2f000 (00fb5000 bytes committed)
Segment at 0000024eb3e30000 to 0000024eb4dff000 (00fb5000 bytes committed)
Segment at 0000024eb4e00000 to 0000024eb5dcf000 (00fb5000 bytes committed)
Segment at 0000024eb5dd0000 to 0000024eb6d9f000 (00fb5000 bytes committed)
Segment at 0000024eb6da0000 to 0000024eb7d6f000 (00fb5000 bytes committed)
Segment at 0000024eb7d70000 to 0000024eb8d3f000 (00fb5000 bytes committed)
Segment at 0000024eb8d40000 to 0000024eb9d0f000 (00fb5000 bytes committed)
Segment at 0000024eb9d10000 to 0000024ebacdf000 (00fb5000 bytes committed)
Segment at 0000024ebace0000 to 0000024ebbcaf000 (00fb5000 bytes committed)
Segment at 0000024ebbcb0000 to 0000024ebcc7f000 (00fb5000 bytes committed)
Segment at 0000024ebcc80000 to 0000024ebdc4f000 (00fb5000 bytes committed)
Segment at 0000024ebdc50000 to 0000024ebec1f000 (00fb5000 bytes committed)
Segment at 0000024ebec20000 to 0000024ebfbef000 (00fb5000 bytes committed)
Segment at 0000024ebfbf0000 to 0000024ec0bbf000 (00fb5000 bytes committed)
Segment at 0000024ec0bc0000 to 0000024ec1b8f000 (00fb5000 bytes committed)
Segment at 0000024ec1b90000 to 0000024ec2b5f000 (00fb5000 bytes committed)
Segment at 0000024ec2b60000 to 0000024ec3b2f000 (00fb5000 bytes committed)
Segment at 0000024ec3b30000 to 0000024ec4aff000 (00fb5000 bytes committed)
Segment at 0000024ec4b00000 to 0000024ec5acf000 (00fb5000 bytes committed)
Segment at 0000024ec5ad0000 to 0000024ec6a9f000 (00fb5000 bytes committed)
Segment at 0000024ec6aa0000 to 0000024ec7a6f000 (00fb5000 bytes committed)
Segment at 0000024ec7a70000 to 0000024ec8a3f000 (00fb5000 bytes committed)
Segment at 0000024ec8a40000 to 0000024ec9a0f000 (00fb5000 bytes committed)
Segment at 0000024ec9a10000 to 0000024eca9df000 (00fb5000 bytes committed)
Segment at 0000024eca9e0000 to 0000024ecb9af000 (00fb5000 bytes committed)
Segment at 0000024ecb9b0000 to 0000024ecc97f000 (00fb5000 bytes committed)
Segment at 0000024ecc980000 to 0000024ecd94f000 (00fb5000 bytes committed)
Segment at 0000024ecd950000 to 0000024ece91f000 (00fb5000 bytes committed)
Segment at 0000024ece920000 to 0000024ecf8ef000 (00fb5000 bytes committed)
Segment at 0000024ecf8f0000 to 0000024ed08bf000 (00fb5000 bytes committed)
Segment at 0000024ed08c0000 to 0000024ed188f000 (00fb5000 bytes committed)
Segment at 0000024ed1890000 to 0000024ed285f000 (00fb5000 bytes committed)
Segment at 0000024ed2860000 to 0000024ed382f000 (00fb5000 bytes committed)
Segment at 0000024ed3830000 to 0000024ed47ff000 (00fb5000 bytes committed)
Segment at 0000024ed4800000 to 0000024ed57cf000 (00fb5000 bytes committed)
Segment at 0000024ed57d0000 to 0000024ed679f000 (00fb5000 bytes committed)
Segment at 0000024ed67a0000 to 0000024ed776f000 (00fb5000 bytes committed)
Segment at 0000024ed7770000 to 0000024ed873f000 (00fb5000 bytes committed)
Segment at 0000024ed8740000 to 0000024ed970f000 (00fb5000 bytes committed)
Segment at 0000024ed9710000 to 0000024eda6df000 (00fb5000 bytes committed)
Segment at 0000024eda6e0000 to 0000024edb6af000 (00fb5000 bytes committed)
Segment at 0000024edb6b0000 to 0000024edc67f000 (00fb5000 bytes committed)
Segment at 0000024edc680000 to 0000024edd64f000 (00fb5000 bytes committed)
Segment at 0000024edd650000 to 0000024ede61f000 (00fb5000 bytes committed)
Segment at 0000024ede620000 to 0000024edf5ef000 (00fb5000 bytes committed)
```

```
Segment at 0000024edf5f0000 to 0000024ee05bf000 (00fb5000 bytes committed)
Segment at 0000024ee05c0000 to 0000024ee158f000 (00fb5000 bytes committed)
Segment at 0000024ee1590000 to 0000024ee255f000 (00649000 bytes committed)
Flags:              08000002
ForceFlags:         00000000
Granularity:        16 bytes
Segment Reserve:    413d0000
Segment Commit:     00002000
DeCommit Block Thres: 00000400
DeCommit Total Thres: 00001000
Total Free Size:    000f6f2f
Max. Allocation Size: 00007ffffffdefff
Lock Variable at:   0000024ea09e02c0
Next TagIndex:      0000
Maximum TagIndex:   0000
Tag Entries:        00000000
PsuedoTag Entries:  00000000
Virtual Alloc List: 24ea09e0110
    0000024ea0ae3000: 007a1227 [commited 7a2000, unused dd9] - busy (b), tail fill
Uncommitted ranges: 24ea09e00f0
FreeList[ 00 ] at 0000024ea09e0150: 0000024ea3108010 . 0000024ea09ed180   (78 blocks)

Heap entries for Segment00 in Heap 0000024ea09e0000
            address: psize . size  flags   state (requested size)
    0000024ea09e0000: 00000 . 00740 [101] - busy (73f)
    0000024ea09e0740: 00740 . 00060 [101] - busy (30)
    0000024ea09e07a0: 00060 . 00080 [101] - busy (4a)
    0000024ea09e0820: 00080 . 00030 [101] - busy (8)
    0000024ea09e0850: 00030 . 00130 [101] - busy (100)
    0000024ea09e0980: 00130 . 00200 [101] - busy (1d8)
    0000024ea09e0b80: 00200 . 00200 [101] - busy (1d8)
    0000024ea09e0d80: 00200 . 00070 [101] - busy (48)
    0000024ea09e0df0: 00070 . 00030 [101] - busy (4)
    0000024ea09e0e20: 00030 . 00040 [101] - busy (10)
    0000024ea09e0e60: 00040 . 00130 [101] - busy (100)
    0000024ea09e0f90: 00130 . 00130 [101] - busy (100)
    0000024ea09e10c0: 00130 . 00c30 [101] - busy (bfe)
    0000024ea09e1cf0: 00c30 . 00750 [101] - busy (71e)
    0000024ea09e2440: 00750 . 00070 [101] - busy (3c)
    0000024ea09e24b0: 00070 . 00060 [101] - busy (30)
    0000024ea09e2510: 00060 . 00090 [101] - busy (62)
    0000024ea09e25a0: 00090 . 00150 [101] - busy (120)
    0000024ea09e26f0: 00150 . 00080 [101] - busy (50)
    0000024ea09e2770: 00080 . 00150 [101] - busy (120)
    0000024ea09e28c0: 00150 . 00080 [101] - busy (50)
    0000024ea09e2940: 00080 . 00260 [101] - busy (238)
    0000024ea09e2ba0: 00260 . 000b0 [101] - busy (88)
    0000024ea09e2c50: 000b0 . 00060 [101] - busy (30)
    0000024ea09e2cb0: 00060 . 00150 [101] - busy (120)
    0000024ea09e2e00: 00150 . 00080 [101] - busy (50)
    0000024ea09e2e80: 00080 . 00070 [101] - busy (42)
    0000024ea09e2ef0: 00070 . 00200 [101] - busy (1d8)
    0000024ea09e30f0: 00200 . 00070 [101] - busy (48)
    0000024ea09e3160: 00070 . 00040 [101] - busy (10)
    0000024ea09e31a0: 00040 . 00060 [101] - busy (30)
    0000024ea09e3200: 00060 . 00050 [101] - busy (20)
    0000024ea09e3250: 00050 . 00080 [101] - busy (50)
    0000024ea09e32d0: 00080 . 00060 [101] - busy (30)
    0000024ea09e3330: 00060 . 00030 [101] - busy (8)
    0000024ea09e3360: 00030 . 00150 [101] - busy (120)
```

```
0000024ea09e34b0: 00150 . 00080 [101] - busy (50)
0000024ea09e3530: 00080 . 00070 [101] - busy (46)
0000024ea09e35a0: 00070 . 00030 [101] - busy (4)
0000024ea09e35d0: 00030 . 00020 [100]
0000024ea09e35f0: 00020 . 00070 [101] - busy (42)
0000024ea09e3660: 00070 . 00050 [101] - busy (20)
0000024ea09e36b0: 00050 . 00430 [101] - busy (400)
0000024ea09e3ae0: 00430 . 00430 [101] - busy (400)
0000024ea09e3f10: 00430 . 00080 [101] - busy (50)
0000024ea09e3f90: 00080 . 00080 [101] - busy (50)
0000024ea09e4010: 00080 . 00090 [101] - busy (68)
0000024ea09e40a0: 00090 . 00060 [101] - busy (30)
0000024ea09e4100: 00060 . 00130 [101] - busy (100)
0000024ea09e4230: 00130 . 00130 [101] - busy (100)
0000024ea09e4360: 00130 . 00130 [101] - busy (100)
0000024ea09e4490: 00130 . 00130 [101] - busy (100)
0000024ea09e45c0: 00130 . 00120 [101] - busy (f0)
0000024ea09e46e0: 00120 . 00190 [101] - busy (168)
0000024ea09e4870: 00190 . 00130 [101] - busy (108)
0000024ea09e49a0: 00130 . 00060 [101] - busy (30)
0000024ea09e4a00: 00060 . 00060 [101] - busy (30)
0000024ea09e4a60: 00060 . 00060 [101] - busy (30)
0000024ea09e4ac0: 00060 . 00060 [101] - busy (30)
0000024ea09e4b20: 00060 . 00060 [101] - busy (30)
0000024ea09e4b80: 00060 . 00060 [101] - busy (30)
0000024ea09e4be0: 00060 . 00060 [101] - busy (30)
0000024ea09e4c40: 00060 . 00060 [101] - busy (30)
0000024ea09e4ca0: 00060 . 00060 [101] - busy (30)
0000024ea09e4d00: 00060 . 00060 [101] - busy (30)
0000024ea09e4d60: 00060 . 00060 [101] - busy (30)
0000024ea09e4dc0: 00060 . 00060 [101] - busy (30)
0000024ea09e4e20: 00060 . 00810 [101] - busy (80f) Internal
0000024ea09e5630: 00810 . 01cb0 [101] - busy (1caf) Internal
0000024ea09e72e0: 01cb0 . 003f0 [101] - busy (3c8)
0000024ea09e76d0: 003f0 . 01230 [101] - busy (1200)
0000024ea09e8900: 01230 . 00830 [101] - busy (800) Internal
0000024ea09e9130: 00830 . 00420 [101] - busy (3f0) Internal
0000024ea09e9550: 00420 . 01030 [101] - busy (1000) Internal
0000024ea09ea580: 01030 . 01030 [101] - busy (1000) Internal
0000024ea09eb5b0: 01030 . 00250 [101] - busy (228)
0000024ea09eb800: 00250 . 00130 [101] - busy (100)
0000024ea09eb930: 00130 . 00170 [101] - busy (140)
0000024ea09ebaa0: 00170 . 00070 [101] - busy (3e)
0000024ea09ebb10: 00070 . 00080 [101] - busy (4e)
0000024ea09ebb90: 00080 . 00090 [101] - busy (62)
0000024ea09ebc20: 00090 . 000a0 [101] - busy (78)
0000024ea09ebcc0: 000a0 . 00090 [101] - busy (62)
0000024ea09ebd50: 00090 . 00070 [101] - busy (3a)
0000024ea09ebdc0: 00070 . 00070 [101] - busy (48)
0000024ea09ebe30: 00070 . 00090 [101] - busy (64)
0000024ea09ebec0: 00090 . 00090 [101] - busy (62)
0000024ea09ebf50: 00090 . 00080 [101] - busy (50)
0000024ea09ebfd0: 00080 . 00050 [101] - busy (1a)
0000024ea09ec020: 00050 . 00080 [101] - busy (54)
0000024ea09ec0a0: 00080 . 00070 [101] - busy (3c)
0000024ea09ec110: 00070 . 00070 [101] - busy (42)
0000024ea09ec180: 00070 . 00050 [101] - busy (1c)
0000024ea09ec1d0: 00050 . 001a0 [101] - busy (174)
0000024ea09ec370: 001a0 . 000b0 [101] - busy (7c)
0000024ea09ec420: 000b0 . 00070 [101] - busy (3a)
```

```
0000024ea09ec490: 00070 . 000d0 [101] - busy (94)
0000024ea09ec560: 000d0 . 004a0 [101] - busy (470)
0000024ea09eca00: 004a0 . 00050 [101] - busy (28)
0000024ea09eca50: 00050 . 00050 [101] - busy (28)
0000024ea09ecaa0: 00050 . 00030 [101] - busy (8)
0000024ea09ecad0: 00030 . 00050 [101] - busy (28)
0000024ea09ecb20: 00050 . 00080 [101] - busy (50)
0000024ea09ecba0: 00080 . 000b0 [101] - busy (88)
0000024ea09ecc50: 000b0 . 003f0 [101] - busy (3c8)
0000024ea09ed040: 003f0 . 00080 [101] - busy (50)
0000024ea09ed0c0: 00080 . 000b0 [101] - busy (88)
0000024ea09ed170: 000b0 . 00020 [100]
0000024ea09ed190: 00020 . 00050 [101] - busy (24)
0000024ea09ed1e0: 00050 . 00070 [101] - busy (3c)
0000024ea09ed250: 00070 . 00080 [101] - busy (52)
0000024ea09ed2d0: 00080 . 00070 [101] - busy (3c)
0000024ea09ed340: 00070 . 00100 [101] - busy (d6)
0000024ea09ed440: 00100 . 00050 [101] - busy (28)
0000024ea09ed490: 00050 . 00050 [101] - busy (1e)
0000024ea09ed4e0: 00050 . 00080 [101] - busy (4e)
0000024ea09ed560: 00080 . 00080 [101] - busy (4c)
0000024ea09ed5e0: 00080 . 00080 [101] - busy (54)
0000024ea09ed660: 00080 . 00050 [101] - busy (24)
0000024ea09ed6b0: 00050 . 00050 [101] - busy (24)
0000024ea09ed700: 00050 . 01030 [101] - busy (1000)
0000024ea09ee730: 01030 . 003f0 [101] - busy (3c8)
0000024ea09eeb20: 003f0 . 00140 [100]
0000024ea09eec60: 00140 . 00150 [101] - busy (120)
0000024ea09eedb0: 00150 . 01030 [101] - busy (1000) Internal
0000024ea09efde0: 01030 . 000c0 [101] - busy (88)
0000024ea09efea0: 000c0 . 00050 [101] - busy (20)
0000024ea09efef0: 00050 . 00100 [100]
0000024ea09efff0: 00100 . 00150 [101] - busy (120)
0000024ea09f0140: 00150 . 00070 [101] - busy (3e)
0000024ea09f01b0: 00070 . 000e0 [100]
0000024ea09f0290: 000e0 . 00050 [101] - busy (20)
0000024ea09f02e0: 00050 . 00100 [100]
0000024ea09f03e0: 00100 . 00150 [101] - busy (120)
0000024ea09f0530: 00150 . 00070 [101] - busy (3e)
0000024ea09f05a0: 00070 . 001a0 [100]
0000024ea09f0740: 001a0 . 00070 [101] - busy (48)
0000024ea09f07b0: 00070 . 00040 [101] - busy (18)
0000024ea09f07f0: 00040 . 00040 [101] - busy (18)
0000024ea09f0830: 00040 . 00040 [101] - busy (18)
0000024ea09f0870: 00040 . 00040 [101] - busy (18)
0000024ea09f08b0: 00040 . 003f0 [101] - busy (3c8)
0000024ea09f0ca0: 003f0 . 00410 [101] - busy (3e8)
0000024ea09f10b0: 00410 . 00410 [101] - busy (3e8)
0000024ea09f14c0: 00410 . 00410 [101] - busy (3e8)
0000024ea09f18d0: 00410 . 00410 [101] - busy (3e8)
0000024ea09f1ce0: 00410 . 00410 [101] - busy (3e8)
0000024ea09f20f0: 00410 . 00410 [101] - busy (3e8)
0000024ea09f2500: 00410 . 00410 [101] - busy (3e8)
0000024ea09f2910: 00410 . 00410 [101] - busy (3e8)
0000024ea09f2d20: 00410 . 00410 [101] - busy (3e8)
0000024ea09f3130: 00410 . 00410 [101] - busy (3e8)
0000024ea09f3540: 00410 . 00410 [101] - busy (3e8)
0000024ea09f3950: 00410 . 00410 [101] - busy (3e8)
0000024ea09f3d60: 00410 . 00410 [101] - busy (3e8)
0000024ea09f4170: 00410 . 00410 [101] - busy (3e8)
```

```
0000024ea09f4580: 00410 . 00410 [101] - busy (3e8)
0000024ea09f4990: 00410 . 00410 [101] - busy (3e8)
0000024ea09f4da0: 00410 . 00410 [101] - busy (3e8)
0000024ea09f51b0: 00410 . 04030 [101] - busy (4000) Internal
0000024ea09f91e0: 04030 . 08030 [101] - busy (8000) Internal
0000024ea0a01210: 08030 . 003c0 [100]
0000024ea0a015d0: 003c0 . 08030 [101] - busy (8000) Internal
0000024ea0a09600: 08030 . 003c0 [100]
0000024ea0a099c0: 003c0 . 08030 [101] - busy (8000) Internal
0000024ea0a119f0: 08030 . 08030 [101] - busy (8000) Internal
0000024ea0a19a20: 08030 . 08030 [101] - busy (8000) Internal
0000024ea0a21a50: 08030 . 08030 [101] - busy (8000) Internal
0000024ea0a29a80: 08030 . 08030 [101] - busy (8000) Internal
0000024ea0a31ab0: 08030 . 41550 [101] - busy (41520) Internal
0000024ea0a73000: 41550 . 10030 [101] - busy (10000) Internal
0000024ea0a83030: 10030 . 20030 [101] - busy (20000) Internal
0000024ea0aa3060: 20030 . 20030 [101] - busy (20000) Internal
0000024ea0ac3090: 20030 . 00420 [101] - busy (3f0) Internal
0000024ea0ac34b0: 00420 . 00420 [101] - busy (3f0) Internal
0000024ea0ac38d0: 00420 . 00420 [101] - busy (3f0) Internal
0000024ea0ac3cf0: 00420 . 00420 [101] - busy (3f0) Internal
0000024ea0ac4110: 00420 . 00420 [101] - busy (3f0) Internal
0000024ea0ac4530: 00420 . 00420 [101] - busy (3f0) Internal
0000024ea0ac4950: 00420 . 00420 [101] - busy (3f0) Internal
0000024ea0ac4d70: 00420 . 00420 [101] - busy (3f0) Internal
0000024ea0ac5190: 00420 . 00420 [101] - busy (3f0) Internal
0000024ea0ac55b0: 00420 . 00420 [101] - busy (3f0) Internal
0000024ea0ac59d0: 00420 . 00420 [101] - busy (3f0) Internal
0000024ea0ac5df0: 00420 . 00420 [101] - busy (3f0) Internal
0000024ea0ac6210: 00420 . 00420 [101] - busy (3f0) Internal
0000024ea0ac6630: 00420 . 00420 [101] - busy (3f0) Internal
0000024ea0ac6a50: 00420 . 00420 [101] - busy (3f0) Internal
0000024ea0ac6e70: 00420 . 00420 [101] - busy (3f0) Internal
0000024ea0ac7290: 00420 . 00420 [101] - busy (3f0) Internal
0000024ea0ac76b0: 00420 . 00420 [101] - busy (3f0) Internal
0000024ea0ac7ad0: 00420 . 00420 [101] - busy (3f0) Internal
0000024ea0ac7ef0: 00420 . 00420 [101] - busy (3f0) Internal
0000024ea0ac8310: 00420 . 00420 [101] - busy (3f0) Internal
0000024ea0ac8730: 00420 . 00420 [101] - busy (3f0) Internal
0000024ea0ac8b50: 00420 . 00420 [101] - busy (3f0) Internal
0000024ea0ac8f70: 00420 . 00420 [101] - busy (3f0) Internal
0000024ea0ac9390: 00420 . 00420 [101] - busy (3f0) Internal
0000024ea0ac97b0: 00420 . 00420 [101] - busy (3f0) Internal
0000024ea0ac9bd0: 00420 . 00420 [101] - busy (3f0) Internal
0000024ea0ac9ff0: 00420 . 00420 [101] - busy (3f0) Internal
[...]
0000024ee115a000: 42000 . 42000 [101] - busy (41fd0) Internal
0000024ee119c000: 42000 . 42000 [101] - busy (41fd0) Internal
0000024ee11de000: 42000 . 42000 [101] - busy (41fd0) Internal
0000024ee1220000: 42000 . 42000 [101] - busy (41fd0) Internal
0000024ee1262000: 42000 . 42000 [101] - busy (41fd0) Internal
0000024ee12a4000: 42000 . 42000 [101] - busy (41fd0) Internal
0000024ee12e6000: 42000 . 42000 [101] - busy (41fd0) Internal
0000024ee1328000: 42000 . 42000 [101] - busy (41fd0) Internal
0000024ee136a000: 42000 . 42000 [101] - busy (41fd0) Internal
0000024ee13ac000: 42000 . 42000 [101] - busy (41fd0) Internal
0000024ee13ee000: 42000 . 42000 [101] - busy (41fd0) Internal
0000024ee1430000: 42000 . 42000 [101] - busy (41fd0) Internal
0000024ee1472000: 42000 . 42000 [101] - busy (41fd0) Internal
0000024ee14b4000: 42000 . 42000 [101] - busy (41fd0) Internal
```

```
             0000024ee14f6000: 42000 . 42000 [101] - busy (41fd0) Internal
             0000024ee1538000: 42000 . 3cfc0 [100]
             0000024ee1574fc0: 3cfc0 . 00040 [111] - busy (3d)
             0000024ee1575000:      0001a000      - uncommitted bytes.
         Heap entries for Segment69 in Heap 0000024ea09e0000
                  address: psize . size  flags   state (requested size)
             0000024ee1590000: 00000 . 00070 [101] - busy (6f)
             0000024ee1590070: 00070 . 41f90 [101] - busy (41f60) Internal
             0000024ee15d2000: 41f90 . 42000 [101] - busy (41fd0) Internal
             0000024ee1614000: 42000 . 42000 [101] - busy (41fd0) Internal
             0000024ee1656000: 42000 . 42000 [101] - busy (41fd0) Internal
             0000024ee1698000: 42000 . 00420 [101] - busy (3f0) Internal
             0000024ee1698420: 00420 . 41be0 [101] - busy (41bb0) Internal
             0000024ee16da000: 41be0 . 42000 [101] - busy (41fd0) Internal
             0000024ee171c000: 42000 . 42000 [101] - busy (41fd0) Internal
             0000024ee175e000: 42000 . 42000 [101] - busy (41fd0) Internal
             0000024ee17a0000: 42000 . 42000 [101] - busy (41fd0) Internal
             0000024ee17e2000: 42000 . 42000 [101] - busy (41fd0) Internal
             0000024ee1824000: 42000 . 42000 [101] - busy (41fd0) Internal
             0000024ee1866000: 42000 . 42000 [101] - busy (41fd0) Internal
             0000024ee18a8000: 42000 . 42000 [101] - busy (41fd0) Internal
             0000024ee18ea000: 42000 . 42000 [101] - busy (41fd0) Internal
             0000024ee192c000: 42000 . 42000 [101] - busy (41fd0) Internal
             0000024ee196e000: 42000 . 42000 [101] - busy (41fd0) Internal
             0000024ee19b0000: 42000 . 42000 [101] - busy (41fd0) Internal
             0000024ee19f2000: 42000 . 42000 [101] - busy (41fd0) Internal
             0000024ee1a34000: 42000 . 42000 [101] - busy (41fd0) Internal
             0000024ee1a76000: 42000 . 00420 [101] - busy (3f0) Internal
             0000024ee1a76420: 00420 . 41be0 [101] - busy (41bb0) Internal
             0000024ee1ab8000: 41be0 . 42000 [101] - busy (41fd0) Internal
             0000024ee1afa000: 42000 . 42000 [101] - busy (41fd0) Internal
             0000024ee1b3c000: 42000 . 42000 [101] - busy (41fd0) Internal
             0000024ee1b7e000: 42000 . 42000 [101] - busy (41fd0) Internal
             0000024ee1bc0000: 42000 . 18fc0 [100]
             0000024ee1bd8fc0: 18fc0 . 00040 [111] - busy (3d)
             0000024ee1bd9000:      00986000      - uncommitted bytes.
```

Note: We see many uniform trace entries and dump one of them:

```
0:000> dp 0000024ee192c000
0000024e`e192c000   00000000`00000000 423a742e`449c19c3
0000024e`e192c010   0000024e`a080c030 0000024e`a3108010
0000024e`e192c020   00000000`00000000 05020030`00000001
0000024e`e192c030   0000024e`e1698310 003a742d`f7000ef9
0000024e`e192c040   f0e0d0c0`0fd00112 0000024e`6cf86bc9
0000024e`e192c050   00000000`000000ff 0000024e`e192c060
0000024e`e192c060   ffffffff`ffffffff ffffffff`ffffffff
0000024e`e192c070   ffffffff`ffffffff ffffffff`ffffffff
```

Note: The 3rd 64-bit (QWORD) value is a pointer to information, including allocation stack trace:

```
0:000> dps 0000024e`a080c030 L20
0000024e`a080c030   0000024e`a08089b0
0000024e`a080c038   00000014`31886398
0000024e`a080c040   00007ff9`ff92ff83 ntdll!RtlpCallInterceptRoutine+0x3f
0000024e`a080c048   00007ff9`ff8f5db5 ntdll!RtlpReAllocateHeapInternal+0x73075
0000024e`a080c050   00007ff9`ff882d0a ntdll!RtlReAllocateHeap+0x5a
0000024e`a080c058   00007ff9`ff8585a4 ntdll!RtlpAllocateUserBlockFromHeap+0xf8
```

```
0000024e`a080c060   00007ff9`ff858433 ntdll!RtlpAllocateUserBlock+0x10b
0000024e`a080c068   00007ff9`ff87cb26 ntdll!RtlpLowFragHeapAllocFromContext+0x8c6
0000024e`a080c070   00007ff9`ff87ba17 ntdll!RtlpAllocateHeapInternal+0x127
0000024e`a080c078   00007ff7`1c50e9f4 AppS+0xe9f4
0000024e`a080c080   00007ff7`1c5050bb AppS+0x50bb
0000024e`a080c088   00007ff7`1c502018 AppS+0x2018
0000024e`a080c090   00007ff7`1c501fb0 AppS+0x1fb0
0000024e`a080c098   00007ff7`1c501908 AppS+0x1908
0000024e`a080c0a0   00007ff7`1c501a39 AppS+0x1a39
0000024e`a080c0a8   00007ff7`1c501a49 AppS+0x1a49
0000024e`a080c0b0   00007ff7`1c5031e5 AppS+0x31e5
0000024e`a080c0b8   00007ff7`1c502fbb AppS+0x2fbb
0000024e`a080c0c0   00007ff7`1c502714 AppS+0x2714
0000024e`a080c0c8   00007ff7`1c50aee8 AppS+0xaee8
0000024e`a080c0d0   00007ff9`fdc57bd4 kernel32!BaseThreadInitThunk+0x14
0000024e`a080c0d8   00007ff9`ff8aced1 ntdll!RtlUserThreadStart+0x21
0000024e`a080c0e0   00000000`00000000
0000024e`a080c0e8   00000000`00000000
0000024e`a080c0f0   00000000`00000000
0000024e`a080c0f8   00000000`00000000
0000024e`a080c100   00000000`00000000
0000024e`a080c108   00000000`00000000
0000024e`a080c110   00000000`00000000
0000024e`a080c118   00000000`00000000
0000024e`a080c120   00000000`00000000
0000024e`a080c128   00000000`00000000
```

Note: We can also check statistics for heap block size block distribution and inspect entries from the most prevalent (the latter can time consuming, and we can get entries from the log we opened at the beginning of this exercise since the output doesn't fit into the WinDbg command window).

Note: The following **exts** extension command works WinDbg (**!heap -l** may also detect leaked blocks):

```
0:000> !heap -s -h 0000024ea09e0000
Walking the heap 0000024ea09e0000
.........................................................
 0: Heap 0000024ea09e0000
   Flags            08000002 - HEAP_GROWABLE
   Reserved memory in segments            1068584 (k)
   Commited memory in segments            1051524 (k)
   Virtual bytes (correction for large UCR) 1058832 (k)
   Free space                               15804 (k) (78 blocks)
   External fragmentation          1% (78 free blocks)
   Virtual address fragmentation   0% (70 uncommited ranges)
   Virtual blocks  1 - total 7816 KBytes
   Lock contention 0
   Segments        1

   Low fragmentation heap    0000024e9ef90000
       Metadata usage    269312 bytes
       Statistics:
           Segments created        3936
           Segments deleted           0
           Segments reused            0
       Block cache:
           4:        2048 bytes (     1,     0)
           5:        4096 bytes (     3,     0)
           7:       16384 bytes (     1,     0)
```

215

```
           8:         32768 bytes (       7,       0)
           9:         65536 bytes (       1,       0)
          10:        131072 bytes (       4,       0)
          11:        262144 bytes (    3919,       0)


      Buckets info:
  Size   Blocks  Seg  Empty  Aff    Distribution
  -------------------------------------------------
    96      102    3      0   0  (3-102,0-0)
   128       31    1      0   0  (1-31,0-0)
  1040  1000069 3932      0   0  (3932-1000069,0-0)
  -------------------------------------------------


                    Default heap    Front heap      Unused bytes
   Range (bytes)    Busy   Free     Busy   Free    Total  Average
  -----------------------------------------------------------------
       0 -   1024    259     11       97     36    10463       29
    1024 -   2048    285      1   999983     86 40012819       40
    2048 -   3072      2      0        0      0        2        1
    3072 -   4096      1      0        0      0       50       50
    4096 -   5120      2      0        0      0       96       48
    7168 -   8192      1      0        0      0        1        1
   89088 -  90112      0      1        0      0        0        0
  101376 - 102400      0      1        0      0        0        0
  248832 - 249856      0     64        0      0        0        0
  523264 - 524288      1      0        0      0        0        0
  -----------------------------------------------------------------
   Total            551     78  1000080    122 40023431       39
```

`0:000> !heap -s -h 0000024ea09e0000 -d 0n1040`

```
0: Heap 0000024ea09e0000
   Flags            08000002 - HEAP_GROWABLE
   Low fragmentation heap    0000024e9ef90000
      Metadata usage    269312 bytes
      Statistics:
          Segments created        3936
          Segments deleted           0
          Segments reused            0
      Block cache:
           4:          2048 bytes (       1,       0)
           5:          4096 bytes (       3,       0)
           7:         16384 bytes (       1,       0)
           8:         32768 bytes (       7,       0)
           9:         65536 bytes (       1,       0)
          10:        131072 bytes (       4,       0)
          11:        262144 bytes (    3919,       0)

      Buckets info:
  Size   Blocks  Seg  Empty  Aff    Distribution
  -------------------------------------------------
    96      102    3      0   0  (3-102,0-0)
   128       31    1      0   0  (1-31,0-0)
  1040  1000069 3932      0   0  (3932-1000069,0-0)
  -------------------------------------------------
0: Segment 0000024ea09e0000
   Signature:               0xffeeffee
   Flags:                   0x00000000
   Range:                   0x0000024ea09e0000 - 0x0000024ea0adf000
   Reserved memory (KBytes):    1020
   Committed memory (KBytes):   960
   LargestUnCommittedRange: 0x0000000000000000
   Number of pages:         255
   Uncommitted pages:       15
   Uncommitted ranges:      1
Sub-segment 0000024ea09e9180
   User blocks:      0x0000024ea09e8930
   Block size:       0x60
```

216

```
   Block count:        20
   Free blocks:        0
   Size index:         5
   Affinity index:     0
   Lock mask:          0x1
   Flags:              0x0
Sub-segment 0000024ea09e91c0
   User blocks:        0x0000024ea09e9580
   Block size:         0x60
   Block count:        41
   Free blocks:        0
   Size index:         5
   Affinity index:     0
   Lock mask:          0x1
   Flags:              0x0
Sub-segment 0000024ea09e9200
   User blocks:        0x0000024ea09ea5b0
   Block size:         0x60
   Block count:        41
   Free blocks:        14
   Size index:         5
   Affinity index:     0
   Lock mask:          0x7
   Flags:              0x0
Sub-segment 0000024ea09e9240
   User blocks:        0x0000024ea09eede0
   Block size:         0x80
   Block count:        31
   Free blocks:        22
   Size index:         7
   Affinity index:     0
   Lock mask:          0x7
   Flags:              0x0
0000024ea09f0ca0  0000024ea09f0cd0  0000024ea09e0000  0000024ea09e0000   410   3f0   28  busy
0000024ea09f10b0  0000024ea09f10e0  0000024ea09e0000  0000024ea09e0000   410   410   28  busy
0000024ea09f14c0  0000024ea09f14f0  0000024ea09e0000  0000024ea09e0000   410   410   28  busy
0000024ea09f18d0  0000024ea09f1900  0000024ea09e0000  0000024ea09e0000   410   410   28  busy
0000024ea09f1ce0  0000024ea09f1d10  0000024ea09e0000  0000024ea09e0000   410   410   28  busy
0000024ea09f20f0  0000024ea09f2120  0000024ea09e0000  0000024ea09e0000   410   410   28  busy
0000024ea09f2500  0000024ea09f2530  0000024ea09e0000  0000024ea09e0000   410   410   28  busy
0000024ea09f2910  0000024ea09f2940  0000024ea09e0000  0000024ea09e0000   410   410   28  busy
0000024ea09f2d20  0000024ea09f2d50  0000024ea09e0000  0000024ea09e0000   410   410   28  busy
0000024ea09f3130  0000024ea09f3160  0000024ea09e0000  0000024ea09e0000   410   410   28  busy
0000024ea09f3540  0000024ea09f3570  0000024ea09e0000  0000024ea09e0000   410   410   28  busy
0000024ea09f3950  0000024ea09f3980  0000024ea09e0000  0000024ea09e0000   410   410   28  busy
0000024ea09f3d60  0000024ea09f3d90  0000024ea09e0000  0000024ea09e0000   410   410   28  busy
0000024ea09f4170  0000024ea09f41a0  0000024ea09e0000  0000024ea09e0000   410   410   28  busy
0000024ea09f4580  0000024ea09f45b0  0000024ea09e0000  0000024ea09e0000   410   410   28  busy
0000024ea09f4990  0000024ea09f49c0  0000024ea09e0000  0000024ea09e0000   410   410   28  busy
0000024ea09f4da0  0000024ea09f4dd0  0000024ea09e0000  0000024ea09e0000   410   410   28  busy
Sub-segment 0000024ea09e9280
   User blocks:        0x0000024ea09f51e0
   Block size:         0x410
   Block count:        15
   Free blocks:        0
   Size index:         64
   Affinity index:     0
   Lock mask:          0x1
   Flags:              0x0
0000024ea09f5220  0000024ea09f5250  0000024ea09e0000  0000024ea09e9280   410   -   28  LFH;busy
0000024ea09f5630  0000024ea09f5660  0000024ea09e0000  0000024ea09e9280   410   -   28  LFH;busy
0000024ea09f5a40  0000024ea09f5a70  0000024ea09e0000  0000024ea09e9280   410   -   28  LFH;busy
0000024ea09f5e50  0000024ea09f5e80  0000024ea09e0000  0000024ea09e9280   410   -   28  LFH;busy
0000024ea09f6260  0000024ea09f6290  0000024ea09e0000  0000024ea09e9280   410   -   28  LFH;busy
0000024ea09f6670  0000024ea09f66a0  0000024ea09e0000  0000024ea09e9280   410   -   28  LFH;busy
0000024ea09f6a80  0000024ea09f6ab0  0000024ea09e0000  0000024ea09e9280   410   -   28  LFH;busy
0000024ea09f6e90  0000024ea09f6ec0  0000024ea09e0000  0000024ea09e9280   410   -   28  LFH;busy
0000024ea09f72a0  0000024ea09f72d0  0000024ea09e0000  0000024ea09e9280   410   -   28  LFH;busy
0000024ea09f76b0  0000024ea09f76e0  0000024ea09e0000  0000024ea09e9280   410   -   28  LFH;busy
0000024ea09f7ac0  0000024ea09f7af0  0000024ea09e0000  0000024ea09e9280   410   -   28  LFH;busy
0000024ea09f7ed0  0000024ea09f7f00  0000024ea09e0000  0000024ea09e9280   410   -   28  LFH;busy
0000024ea09f82e0  0000024ea09f8310  0000024ea09e0000  0000024ea09e9280   410   -   28  LFH;busy
0000024ea09f86f0  0000024ea09f8720  0000024ea09e0000  0000024ea09e9280   410   -   28  LFH;busy
0000024ea09f8b00  0000024ea09f8b30  0000024ea09e0000  0000024ea09e9280   410   -   28  LFH;busy
Sub-segment 0000024ea09e92c0
```

```
User blocks:        0x0000024ea09f9210
Block size:         0x410
Block count:        31
Free blocks:        0
Size index:         64
Affinity index:     0
Lock mask:          0x1
Flags:              0x0
0000024ea09f9250  0000024ea09f9280  0000024ea09e0000  0000024ea09e92c0      410      -      28   LFH;busy
0000024ea09f9660  0000024ea09f9690  0000024ea09e0000  0000024ea09e92c0      410      -      28   LFH;busy
0000024ea09f9a70  0000024ea09f9aa0  0000024ea09e0000  0000024ea09e92c0      410      -      28   LFH;busy
0000024ea09f9e80  0000024ea09f9eb0  0000024ea09e0000  0000024ea09e92c0      410      -      28   LFH;busy
0000024ea09fa290  0000024ea09fa2c0  0000024ea09e0000  0000024ea09e92c0      410      -      28   LFH;busy
0000024ea09fa6a0  0000024ea09fa6d0  0000024ea09e0000  0000024ea09e92c0      410      -      28   LFH;busy
0000024ea09faab0  0000024ea09faae0  0000024ea09e0000  0000024ea09e92c0      410      -      28   LFH;busy
0000024ea09faec0  0000024ea09faef0  0000024ea09e0000  0000024ea09e92c0      410      -      28   LFH;busy
0000024ea09fb2d0  0000024ea09fb300  0000024ea09e0000  0000024ea09e92c0      410      -      28   LFH;busy
0000024ea09fb6e0  0000024ea09fb710  0000024ea09e0000  0000024ea09e92c0      410      -      28   LFH;busy
0000024ea09fbaf0  0000024ea09fbb20  0000024ea09e0000  0000024ea09e92c0      410      -      28   LFH;busy
0000024ea09fbf00  0000024ea09fbf30  0000024ea09e0000  0000024ea09e92c0      410      -      28   LFH;busy
0000024ea09fc310  0000024ea09fc340  0000024ea09e0000  0000024ea09e92c0      410      -      28   LFH;busy
0000024ea09fc720  0000024ea09fc750  0000024ea09e0000  0000024ea09e92c0      410      -      28   LFH;busy
0000024ea09fcb30  0000024ea09fcb60  0000024ea09e0000  0000024ea09e92c0      410      -      28   LFH;busy
0000024ea09fcf40  0000024ea09fcf70  0000024ea09e0000  0000024ea09e92c0      410      -      28   LFH;busy
0000024ea09fd350  0000024ea09fd380  0000024ea09e0000  0000024ea09e92c0      410      -      28   LFH;busy
0000024ea09fd760  0000024ea09fd790  0000024ea09e0000  0000024ea09e92c0      410      -      28   LFH;busy
0000024ea09fdb70  0000024ea09fdba0  0000024ea09e0000  0000024ea09e92c0      410      -      28   LFH;busy
```

```
0:000> dp 0000024ea09fdb70
0000024e`a09fdb70  00000000`00000000 c2001200`5982562e
0000024e`a09fdb80  0000024e`a080bb70 00000000`00000000
0000024e`a09fdb90  00000000`00000000 05020028`00000001
0000024e`a09fdba0  00000000`00000000 00000000`00000000
0000024e`a09fdbb0  00000000`00000000 00000000`00000000
0000024e`a09fdbc0  00000000`00000000 00000000`00000000
0000024e`a09fdbd0  00000000`00000000 00000000`00000000
0000024e`a09fdbe0  00000000`00000000 00000000`00000000
```

```
0:000> dps 0000024e`a080bb70 L20
0000024e`a080bb70  00000000`00000000
0000024e`a080bb78  0000000f`33e58de0
0000024e`a080bb80  00007ff9`ff92ff83 ntdll!RtlpCallInterceptRoutine+0x3f
0000024e`a080bb88  00007ff9`ff8f441b ntdll!RtlpAllocateHeapInternal+0x78b2b
0000024e`a080bb90  00007ff7`1c50e9f4 AppS+0xe9f4
0000024e`a080bb98  00007ff7`1c5050bb AppS+0x50bb
0000024e`a080bba0  00007ff7`1c502018 AppS+0x2018
0000024e`a080bba8  00007ff7`1c501fb0 AppS+0x1fb0
0000024e`a080bbb0  00007ff7`1c501908 AppS+0x1908
0000024e`a080bbb8  00007ff7`1c501a39 AppS+0x1a39
0000024e`a080bbc0  00007ff7`1c501a49 AppS+0x1a49
0000024e`a080bbc8  00007ff7`1c5031e5 AppS+0x31e5
0000024e`a080bbd0  00007ff7`1c502fbb AppS+0x2fbb
0000024e`a080bbd8  00007ff7`1c502714 AppS+0x2714
0000024e`a080bbe0  00007ff7`1c50aee8 AppS+0xaee8
0000024e`a080bbe8  00007ff9`fdc57bd4 kernel32!BaseThreadInitThunk+0x14
0000024e`a080bbf0  00007ff9`ff8aced1 ntdll!RtlUserThreadStart+0x21
0000024e`a080bbf8  00000000`00000000
0000024e`a080bc00  00000000`00000000
0000024e`a080bc08  00000000`00000000
0000024e`a080bc10  00000000`00000000
0000024e`a080bc18  00000000`00000000
0000024e`a080bc20  00000000`00000000
0000024e`a080bc28  00000000`00000000
0000024e`a080bc30  00000000`00000000
0000024e`a080bc38  00000000`00000000
```

```
0000024e`a080bc40  00000000`00000000
0000024e`a080bc48  00000000`00000000
0000024e`a080bc50  00000000`00000000
0000024e`a080bc58  00000000`00000000
0000024e`a080bc60  00000000`00000000
0000024e`a080bc68  00000000`00000000
```

10.   Let's now load application symbols:

```
0:000> .sympath+ C:\AWMDA-Dumps\Symbols
Symbol search path is: srv*;C:\AWMDA-Dumps\Symbols
Expanded Symbol search path is:
cache*;SRV*https://msdl.microsoft.com/download/symbols;c:\awmda-dumps\symbols

************ Path validation summary **************
Response                         Time (ms)    Location
Deferred                                      srv*
OK                                            C:\AWMDA-Dumps\Symbols

0:000> .reload
.......
```

11.   We check a stack trace to see if symbols were loaded correctly:

```
0:000> kL
# Child-SP          RetAddr           Call Site
00 00000053`8e6ff798 00007ff9`fc8b8ba3 ntdll!NtWaitForSingleObject+0x14
*** WARNING: Unable to verify checksum for AppS.exe
01 00000053`8e6ff7a0 00007ff7`1c50498f KERNELBASE!WaitForSingleObjectEx+0x93
02 00000053`8e6ff840 00007ff7`1c5017ef AppS!_Thrd_join+0x1f
03 00000053`8e6ff870 00007ff7`1c501afc AppS!std::thread::join+0x5f
04 00000053`8e6ff8d0 00007ff7`1c5052fc AppS!wmain+0x5c
05 (Inline Function) --------`-------- AppS!invoke_main+0x22
06 00000053`8e6ff950 00007ff9`fdc57bd4 AppS!__scrt_common_main_seh+0x10c
07 00000053`8e6ff990 00007ff9`ff8aced1 kernel32!BaseThreadInitThunk+0x14
08 00000053`8e6ff9c0 00000000`00000000 ntdll!RtlUserThreadStart+0x21
```

12.   Now we repeat the previous heap entry commands:

```
0:000> dps 0000024e`a080c030 L20
0000024e`a080c030  0000024e`a08089b0
0000024e`a080c038  00000014`31886398
0000024e`a080c040  00007ff9`ff92ff83 ntdll!RtlpCallInterceptRoutine+0x3f
0000024e`a080c048  00007ff9`ff8f5db5 ntdll!RtlpReAllocateHeapInternal+0x73075
0000024e`a080c050  00007ff9`ff882d0a ntdll!RtlReAllocateHeap+0x5a
0000024e`a080c058  00007ff9`ff8585a4 ntdll!RtlAllocateUserBlockFromHeap+0xf8
0000024e`a080c060  00007ff9`ff858433 ntdll!RtlAllocateUserBlock+0x10b
0000024e`a080c068  00007ff9`ff87cb26 ntdll!RtlpLowFragHeapAllocFromContext+0x8c6
0000024e`a080c070  00007ff9`ff87ba17 ntdll!RtlpAllocateHeapInternal+0x127
0000024e`a080c078  00007ff7`1c50e9f4 AppS!_malloc_base+0x44 [minkernel\crts\ucrt\src\appcrt\heap\malloc_base.cpp @ 34]
0000024e`a080c080  00007ff7`1c5050bb AppS!operator new+0x1f [d:\agent\_work\3\s\src\vctools\crt\vcstartup\src\heap\new_scalar.cpp @ 35]
0000024e`a080c088  00007ff7`1c502018 AppS!<lambda_f42620142e15e7a022a268c8eed3c9cb>::operator()<enum std::byte *>+0x38 [C:\AWMDA-
Examples\AppS\AppS.cpp @ 21]
0000024e`a080c090  00007ff7`1c501fb0 AppS!std::for_each<std::_Vector_iterator<std::_Vector_val<std::_Simple_types<enum std::byte *> >
>,<lambda_f42620142e15e7a022a268c8eed3c9cb> >+0x70 [C:\Program Files (x86)\Microsoft Visual
Studio\2019\Professional\VC\Tools\MSVC\14.23.28105\include\algorithm @ 85]
0000024e`a080c098  00007ff7`1c501908 AppS!bar+0xd8 [C:\AWMDA-Examples\AppS\AppS.cpp @ 24]
0000024e`a080c0a0  00007ff7`1c501a39 AppS!foo+0x9 [C:\AWMDA-Examples\AppS\AppS.cpp @ 37]
0000024e`a080c0a8  00007ff7`1c501a49 AppS!thread_one+0x9 [C:\AWMDA-Examples\AppS\AppS.cpp @ 42]
0000024e`a080c0b0  00007ff7`1c5031e5 AppS!std::_Invoker_functor::_Call<void (__cdecl*)(void)>+0x15 [C:\Program Files (x86)\Microsoft
Visual Studio\2019\Professional\VC\Tools\MSVC\14.23.28105\include\type_traits @ 1571]
0000024e`a080c0b8  00007ff7`1c502fbb AppS!std::invoke<void (__cdecl*)(void)>+0x1b [C:\Program Files (x86)\Microsoft Visual
Studio\2019\Professional\VC\Tools\MSVC\14.23.28105\include\type_traits @ 1571]
0000024e`a080c0c0  00007ff7`1c502714 AppS!std::thread::_Invoke<std::tuple<void (__cdecl*)(void)>,0>+0x64 [C:\Program Files
(x86)\Microsoft Visual Studio\2019\Professional\VC\Tools\MSVC\14.23.28105\include\thread @ 40]
0000024e`a080c0c8  00007ff7`1c50aee8 AppS!thread_start<unsigned int (__cdecl*)(void *),1>+0x50
[minkernel\crts\ucrt\src\appcrt\startup\thread.cpp @ 97]
```

219

```
0000024e`a080c0d0  00007ff9`fdc57bd4  kernel32!BaseThreadInitThunk+0x14
0000024e`a080c0d8  00007ff9`ff8aced1  ntdll!RtlUserThreadStart+0x21
0000024e`a080c0e0  00000000`00000000
0000024e`a080c0e8  00000000`00000000
0000024e`a080c0f0  00000000`00000000
0000024e`a080c0f8  00000000`00000000
0000024e`a080c100  00000000`00000000
0000024e`a080c108  00000000`00000000
0000024e`a080c110  00000000`00000000
0000024e`a080c118  00000000`00000000
0000024e`a080c120  00000000`00000000
0000024e`a080c128  00000000`00000000
```

Note: Now, we see *AppS* stack traces allocating from the heap. For large heap size allocations, the picture and the analysis approach are different. Please refer to a reprinted case study and the **!address** command examples at the end of this book.

13.   We close logging before exiting WinDbg:

```
0:000> .logclose
Closing open log file C:\AWMDA-Dumps\Process\x64\AppS.log
```

Parameters and Locals

Debugging TV Frames episode 0x18

There were previous requests to include commands for parameter and local variable inspection, so I made this a free session for everyone. Please check the slides and recording for Debugging TV Frames episode 0x18: www.debugging.tv.

Symbol Types

- Exported and imported names

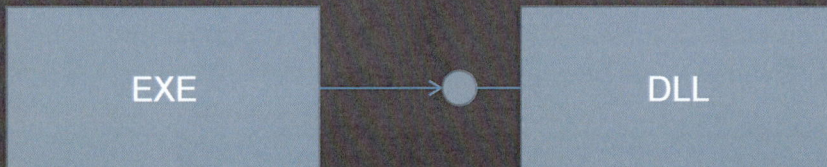

EXE	→ ● —	DLL

- Function and variable names

- Data types

Before we proceed with the last 6 exercises, I'd like to say that there are different types of symbols. First, there are the so-called exported names used for dynamic linking. A typical example is exported functions from *user32.dll*, such as *GetMessageA* and *GetMessageW*. The other types are function or variable names and data types like structure definitions.

Exercise P15

- **Goal:** Learn how to navigate function parameters in cases of reduced symbolic information in 32-bit process memory dumps

- **Patterns:** Reduced Symbolic Information

- \AWMDA-Dumps\Exercise-P15-Analysis-process-dump-notepad-32.pdf

Exercise P15: Analysis of an application process dump (notepad, 32-bit)

Goal: Learn how to navigate function parameters in cases of reduced symbolic information in 32-bit process memory dumps.

Patterns: Reduced Symbolic Information.

1.   Launch WinDbg.

2.   Open \AWMDA-Dumps\Process\x86\notepad.DMP

3.   We get the dump file loaded:

```
Microsoft (R) Windows Debugger Version 10.0.25877.1004 AMD64
Copyright (c) Microsoft Corporation. All rights reserved.


Loading Dump File [C:\AWMDA-Dumps\Process\x86\notepad.DMP]
User Mini Dump File with Full Memory: Only application data is available


************* Path validation summary **************
Response                        Time (ms)     Location
Deferred                                      srv*
Symbol search path is: srv*
Executable search path is:
Windows 10 Version 18362 MP (2 procs) Free x86 compatible
Product: WinNt, suite: SingleUserTS Personal
Edition build lab: 18362.239.x86fre.19h1_release_svc_prod1.190628-1641
Machine Name:
Debug session time: Thu Sep  5 07:40:03.000 2019 (UTC + 1:00)
System Uptime: 0 days 0:06:41.506
Process Uptime: 0 days 0:01:00.000
.................................................
For analysis of this file, run !analyze -v
eax=00000001 ebx=00910000 ecx=00000000 edx=00000000 esi=02d9faac edi=00910000
eip=75962bfc esp=02d9fa40 ebp=02d9fa78 iopl=0         nv up ei pl nz ac po nc
cs=0023  ss=002b  ds=002b  es=002b  fs=0053  gs=002b            efl=00000212
win32u!NtUserGetMessage+0xc:
75962bfc c21000          ret     10h
```

4. Open the previous log file using the **.logappend** command:

```
0:000> .logappend C:\AWMDA-Dumps\Process\x86\notepad.log
Opened log file 'C:\AWMDA-Dumps\Process\x86\notepad.log'
```

5.   Type the **kb** command to verify the correctness of the stack trace:

```
0:000> kb
 # ChildEBP RetAddr  Args to Child
00 02d9fa3c 7570ec70 02d9faac 00000000 00000000 win32u!NtUserGetMessage+0xc
01 02d9fa78 0091c486 02d9faac 00000000 00000000 user32!GetMessageW+0x30
02 02d9faf4 0092fa00 00910000 00000000 033333ca notepad!WinMain+0x1a3
03 02d9fb84 75896359 02f33000 75896340 02d9fbf0 notepad!__mainCRTStartup+0x146
04 02d9fb94 77c37b74 02f33000 2d76afff 00000000 kernel32!BaseThreadInitThunk+0x19
```

```
05 02d9fbf0 77c37b44 ffffffff 77c58f26 00000000 ntdll!__RtlUserThreadStart+0x2f
06 02d9fc00 00000000 0092f8b0 02f33000 00000000 ntdll!_RtlUserThreadStart+0x1b
```

6.   Discover available *notepad* module symbols (**x** command):

```
0:000> x notepad!*
0092c869          notepad!InitializeTelemetryDataPoints (void)
00919eb0
notepad!wistd::__function::__func<<lambda_4b29d149b8821cfbae4eba16ce6a2849>,bool __stdcall(void
*,unsigned int,void *,unsigned int,unsigned int)>::__clone (void)
0091a3f9          notepad!ShowOpenSaveDialog (void)
0092d69b          notepad!StringLengthWorkerW (void)
[...]
0091c2e3          notepad!WinMain (_WinMain@16)
[...]
009330dc          notepad!_imp__GetMessageW = <no type information>
[...]
0091e4f1          notepad!InsertDateTime (<no parameter info>)
00919cb5          notepad!wil::details::WriteResultString<unsigned short const *> (<no
parameter info>)
00932ca8          notepad!g_WarbirdPaintInitTime = <no type information>
00933420          notepad!api-ms-win-shcore-scaling-l1-1-1_NULL_THUNK_DATA = <no type
information>

0:000> dt notepad!*
[...]
```

Note: We don't see any data types – only imported (*_imp_*) and global functions.

7.   Inspect *WinMain* parameters based on Microsoft Docs description (https://docs.microsoft.com/en-us/windows/win32/api/winbase/nf-winbase-winmain):

```
int __clrcall WinMain(
  HINSTANCE hInstance,
  HINSTANCE hPrevInstance,
  LPSTR     lpCmdLine,
  int       nShowCmd
);
```

```
0:000> kb
 # ChildEBP RetAddr  Args to Child
00 02d9fa3c 7570ec70 02d9faac 00000000 00000000 win32u!NtUserGetMessage+0xc
01 02d9fa78 0091c486 02d9faac 00000000 00000000 user32!GetMessageW+0x30
02 02d9faf4 0092fa00 00910000 00000000 033333ca notepad!WinMain+0x1a3
03 02d9fb84 75896359 02f33000 75896340 02d9fbf0 notepad!__mainCRTStartup+0x146
04 02d9fb94 77c37b74 02f33000 2d76afff 00000000 kernel32!BaseThreadInitThunk+0x19
05 02d9fbf0 77c37b44 ffffffff 77c58f26 00000000 ntdll!__RtlUserThreadStart+0x2f
06 02d9fc00 00000000 0092f8b0 02f33000 00000000 ntdll!_RtlUserThreadStart+0x1b
```

```
0:000> dc 00910000
00910000  00905a4d 00000003 00000004 0000ffff  MZ..............
00910010  000000b8 00000000 00000040 00000000  ........@.......
00910020  00000000 00000000 00000000 00000000  ................
00910030  00000000 00000000 00000000 000000f0  ................
00910040  0eba1f0e cd09b400 4c01b821 685421cd  ........!..L.!Th
00910050  70207369 72676f72 63206d61 6f6e6e61  is program canno
00910060  65622074 6e757220 206e6920 20534f44  t be run in DOS
00910070  65646f6d 0a0d0d2e 00000024 00000000  mode....$.......
```

```
0:000> da 033333ca
033333ca  ""

0:000> du 033333ca
033333ca  ""

0:000> dc 033333ca
033333ca  00000000 115d0000 a4437b9a 00000800  ......]..{C.....
033333da  00000000 00000000 00000000 00000000  ................
033333ea  00000000 00000000 00000000 00000000  ................
033333fa  00000000 00000000 00000000 00000000  ................
0333340a  00000000 00000000 00000000 00000000  ................
0333341a  00000000 00000000 00000000 00000000  ................
0333342a  00000000 00000000 00000000 00000000  ................
0333343a  89200000 00000334 00000000 00000000  .. .4...........
```

Note: The first parameter is the address of a notepad module, and the third parameter is an empty command line.

8.   Inspect *GetMessageW* parameters based on Microsoft Docs descriptions (https://docs.microsoft.com/en-us/windows/win32/api/winuser/nf-winuser-getmessagew):

```
BOOL GetMessageW(
  LPMSG lpMsg,
  HWND  hWnd,
  UINT  wMsgFilterMin,
  UINT  wMsgFilterMax
);
```

(https://docs.microsoft.com/windows/desktop/api/winuser/ns-winuser-msg)

```
typedef struct tagMSG {
  HWND    hwnd;
  UINT    message;
  WPARAM  wParam;
  LPARAM  lParam;
  DWORD   time;
  POINT   pt;
  DWORD   lPrivate;
} MSG, *PMSG, *NPMSG, *LPMSG;
```

```
0:000> kb
 # ChildEBP RetAddr  Args to Child
00 02d9fa3c 7570ec70 02d9faac 00000000 00000000 win32u!NtUserGetMessage+0xc
01 02d9fa78 0091c486 02d9faac 00000000 00000000 user32!GetMessageW+0x30
02 02d9faf4 0092fa00 00910000 00000000 033333ca notepad!WinMain+0x1a3
03 02d9fb84 75896359 02f33000 75896340 02d9fbf0 notepad!__mainCRTStartup+0x146
04 02d9fb94 77c37b74 02f33000 2d76afff 00000000 kernel32!BaseThreadInitThunk+0x19
05 02d9fbf0 77c37b44 ffffffff 77c58f26 00000000 ntdll!__RtlUserThreadStart+0x2f
06 02d9fc00 00000000 0092f8b0 02f33000 00000000 ntdll!_RtlUserThreadStart+0x1b
```

```
0:000> dc 02d9faac
02d9faac  0002079a 000002a3 00000000 00000000  ................
02d9fabc  00055e15 00000519 000001de 02d9fae8  .^..............
02d9facc  7550e8bc 00000000 033333c8 75574078  ..Pu.....33.x@Wu
02d9fadc  032d1290 032d05b8 00930601 02d9fb00  ..-...-.........
02d9faec  b74b9e0d 00000000 02d9fb84 0092fa00  ..K.............
02d9fafc  00910000 00000000 033333ca 00000001  .........33.....
02d9fb0c  b74b9f15 0092f8b0 0092f8b0 02f33000  ..K..........0..
02d9fb1c  00000044 03331cf2 03331cd2 03331c92  D.....3...3...3.
```

```
04ebf990   00000401 00000001 00000000 00000000   ................
```

Note: The last received window message 0x2a3 was directed to a window with a 0x2079a window handle and had a mouse pointer at (0x519, 0x1de).

9.   We close logging before exiting WinDbg:

```
0:000> .logclose
Closing open log file C:\AWMDA-Dumps\Process\x86\notepad.log
```

Exercise P16

- **Goal:** Learn how to navigate function parameters in x64 process memory dumps

- **Patterns:** False Function Parameters; Injected Symbols

- \AWMDA-Dumps\Exercise-P16-Analysis-process-dump-notepad-64.pdf

Exercise P16: Analysis of an application process dump (notepad, 64-bit)

Goal: Learn how to navigate function parameters in x64 process memory dumps.

Patterns: False Function Parameters; Injected Symbols.

1. Launch WinDbg.

2. Open \AWMDA-Dumps\Process\x64\notepad.DMP

3. We get the dump file loaded:

```
Microsoft (R) Windows Debugger Version 10.0.25877.1004 AMD64
Copyright (c) Microsoft Corporation. All rights reserved.


Loading Dump File [C:\AWMDA-Dumps\Process\x64\notepad.DMP]
User Mini Dump File with Full Memory: Only application data is available


************ Path validation summary **************
Response                     Time (ms)      Location
Deferred                                    srv*
Symbol search path is: srv*
Executable search path is:
Windows 10 Version 18362 MP (2 procs) Free x64
Product: WinNt, suite: SingleUserTS Personal
Edition build lab: 18362.1.amd64fre.19h1_release.190318-1202
Machine Name:
Debug session time: Thu Sep  5 07:37:05.000 2019 (UTC + 1:00)
System Uptime: 0 days 0:03:43.584
Process Uptime: 0 days 0:02:07.000
.........................................
For analysis of this file, run !analyze -v
win32u!NtUserGetMessage+0x14:
00007ffe`dad31164 c3              ret
```

4. Open the previous log file using the **.logappend** command:

```
0:000> .logappend C:\AWMDA-Dumps\Process\x64\notepad.log
Opened log file 'C:\AWMDA-Dumps\Process\x64\notepad.log'
```

5. Type the **kv** command to verify the correctness of the stack trace:

```
0:000> kv
 # Child-SP          RetAddr           : Args to Child                                                           : Call Site
00 000000a1`c2ccf988 00007ffe`dc19477d : 00000000`00007f48 00000000`0001e327 000019ee`00000000 00007ff7`00000001 : win32u!NtUserGetMessage+0x14
01 000000a1`c2ccf990 00007ff7`437da3d3 : 00007ff7`437d0000 00000000`0006038b 00000000`00000000 00000000`00000000 : user32!GetMessageW+0x2d
02 000000a1`c2ccf9f0 00007ff7`437f02b7 : 00000221`19ac3390 00000221`19ac3392 00000000`00000000 00000000`00000000 : notepad!WinMain+0x293
03 000000a1`c2ccfac0 00007ffe`dc557bd4 : 00000000`00000000 00000000`00000000 00000000`00000000 00000000`00000000 : notepad!__mainCRTStartup+0x19f
04 000000a1`c2ccfb80 00007ffe`ddc6cee1 : 00000000`00000000 00000000`00000000 00000000`00000000 00000000`00000000 : kernel32!BaseThreadInitThunk+0x14
05 000000a1`c2ccfbb0 00000000`00000000 : 00000000`00000000 00000000`00000000 00000000`00000000 00000000`00000000 : ntdll!RtlUserThreadStart+0x21
```

Note: Most parameters are absent because they are passed by registers, and the values you see are taken from whatever values are on the thread raw stack region.

6.   Recover the first *hInstance WinMain* parameter from the disassembly of the return address:

```
int __clrcall WinMain(
  HINSTANCE hInstance,
  HINSTANCE hPrevInstance,
  LPSTR     lpCmdLine,
  int       nShowCmd
);
```

```
0:000> ub 00007ff7`437f02b7
notepad!__mainCRTStartup+0x177:
00007ff7`437f028f f644247c01     test    byte ptr [rsp+7Ch],1
00007ff7`437f0294 0fb7842480000000 movzx  eax,word ptr [rsp+80h]
00007ff7`437f029c 41b90a000000   mov     r9d,0Ah
00007ff7`437f02a2 440f45c8       cmovne  r9d,eax
00007ff7`437f02a6 4c8bc3         mov     r8,rbx
00007ff7`437f02a9 33d2           xor     edx,edx
00007ff7`437f02ab 488d0d4efdfdff lea     rcx,[notepad!TlgWrite <PERF> (notepad+0x0) (00007ff7`437d0000)]
00007ff7`437f02b2 e8899efeff     call    notepad!WinMain (00007ff7`437da140)
```

```
0:000> dc 00007ff7`437d0000
00007ff7`437d0000  00905a4d 00000003 00000004 0000ffff  MZ..............
00007ff7`437d0010  000000b8 00000000 00000040 00000000  ........@.......
00007ff7`437d0020  00000000 00000000 00000000 00000000  ................
00007ff7`437d0030  00000000 00000000 00000000 000000f8  ................
00007ff7`437d0040  0eba1f0e cd09b400 4c01b821 685421cd  ........!..L.!Th
00007ff7`437d0050  70207369 72676f72 63206d61 6f6e6e61  is program canno
00007ff7`437d0060  65622074 6e757220 206e6920 20534f44  t be run in DOS
00007ff7`437d0070  65646f6d 0a0d0d2e 00000024 00000000  mode....$.......
```

```
0:000> !lmi 00007ff7`437d0000
Loaded Module Info: [00007ff7`437d0000]
        Module: notepad
  Base Address: 00007ff7437d0000
    Image Name: notepad.exe
  Machine Type: 34404 (X64)
    Time Stamp: 9e7797dd (This is a reproducible build file hash, not a true timestamp)
          Size: 32000
      CheckSum: 34590
Characteristics: 22
Debug Data Dirs: Type  Size       VA  Pointer
          CODEVIEW    24, 26ec8,   258c8 RSDS - GUID: {48F76637-AE64-DAE8-764C-8F9F4B27AEA5}
              Age: 1, Pdb: notepad.pdb
             POGO    3ac, 26eec,   258ec [Data not mapped]
             REPRO    24, 27298,   25c98 Reproducible build[Data not mapped]
    Image Type: MEMORY    - Image read successfully from loaded memory.
   Symbol Type: PDB       - Symbols loaded successfully from image header.

C:\ProgramData\dbg\sym\notepad.pdb\48F76637AE64DAE8764C8F9F4B27AEA51\notepad.pdb
    Load Report: public symbols , not source indexed

C:\ProgramData\dbg\sym\notepad.pdb\48F76637AE64DAE8764C8F9F4B27AEA51\notepad.pdb
```

7.   Inspect the first *GetMessageW* parameter based on the disassembly of a return address:

```
0:000> k
 # Child-SP          RetAddr             Call Site
00 000000a1`c2ccf988 00007ffe`dc19477d win32u!NtUserGetMessage+0x14
01 000000a1`c2ccf990 00007ff7`437da3d3 user32!GetMessageW+0x2d
02 000000a1`c2ccf9f0 00007ff7`437f02b7 notepad!WinMain+0x293
03 000000a1`c2ccfac0 00007ffe`dc557bd4 notepad!__mainCRTStartup+0x19f
04 000000a1`c2ccfb80 00007ffe`ddc6cee1 kernel32!BaseThreadInitThunk+0x14
05 000000a1`c2ccfbb0 00000000`00000000 ntdll!RtlUserThreadStart+0x21


0:000> ub 00007ff7`437da3d3
notepad!WinMain+0x271:
00007ff7`437da3b1 ff1589850100    call    qword ptr [notepad!_imp_TranslateMessage (00007ff7`437f2940)]
00007ff7`437da3b7 488d4de7        lea     rcx,[rbp-19h]
00007ff7`437da3bb ff1587850100    call    qword ptr [notepad!_imp_DispatchMessageW (00007ff7`437f2948)]
00007ff7`437da3c1 4533c9          xor     r9d,r9d
00007ff7`437da3c4 488d4de7        lea     rcx,[rbp-19h]
00007ff7`437da3c8 4533c0          xor     r8d,r8d
00007ff7`437da3cb 33d2            xor     edx,edx
00007ff7`437da3cd ff1555850100    call    qword ptr [notepad!_imp_GetMessageW (00007ff7`437f2928)]
```

Note: Because the address of the *MSG* structure is located at RBP-0x19, we need to find out the value of RBP at that time. Usually, the value of such a register is stable throughout the function assembly language code and used to address function parameters and local variables. So we try to get it from the **.frame /c** command output:

```
0:000> .frame /c 2
02 000000a1`c2ccf9f0 00007ff7`437f02b7     notepad!WinMain+0x293
rax=0000000000001009 rbx=000000000006038b rcx=000000a1c2ccfa40
rdx=0000000000000000 rsi=0000000000000000 rdi=00007ff7437d0000
rip=00007ff7437da3d3 rsp=000000a1c2ccf9f0 rbp=000000a1c2ccfa59
 r8=0000000000000080  r9=0000000000010412 r10=0000000000010412
r11=1151005044840000 r12=0000000000000000 r13=0000000000000000
r14=00007ff7437d0000 r15=0000000000000001
iopl=0         nv up ei pl zr na po nc
cs=0033  ss=002b  ds=002b  es=002b  fs=0053  gs=002b             efl=00000246
notepad!WinMain+0x293:
00007ff7`437da3d3 85c0            test    eax,eax


0:000> ? rbp-19
Evaluate expression: 694757947968 = 000000a1`c2ccfa40


0:000> dp 000000a1`c2ccfa40
000000a1`c2ccfa40  00000000`00000000 00000000`00000113
000000a1`c2ccfa50  00000000`00007f48 00007ffe`dc4166d0
000000a1`c2ccfa60  00000461`0001e327 00000000`0000006a
000000a1`c2ccfa70  4d58714d`e29eb67a 0b627ee8`de4698a5
000000a1`c2ccfa80  00007b20`14b53ed5 00007ffe`ddb2a643
000000a1`c2ccfa90  00000000`00000000 00007ff7`437f3180
000000a1`c2ccfaa0  00000000`00000000 00000000`00000000
000000a1`c2ccfab0  00000000`00000000 00007ff7`437f02b7
```

Note: We see a possible message structure with 0x113 as a window message and (0x461, 0x6a) as a mouse pointer value. Some structure fields are DWORD and some QWORD, so we double-check with the **dc** command (DWORD values):

```
typedef struct tagMSG {
    HWND    hwnd;                    // QWORD, 8 bytes
    UINT    message;                // DWORD, 4 bytes + 4-byte padding
    WPARAM  wParam;                 // QWORD
    LPARAM  lParam;                 // QWORD
    DWORD   time;                   // DWORD
    POINT   pt;
    DWORD   lPrivate;
} MSG, *PMSG, *NPMSG, *LPMSG;
```

```
0:000> dc 000000a1`c2ccfa40
000000a1`c2ccfa40  00000000 00000000 00000113 00000000  ................
000000a1`c2ccfa50  00007f48 00000000 dc4166d0 00007ffe  H........fA.....
000000a1`c2ccfa60  0001e327 00000461 0000006a 00000000  '...a...j.......
000000a1`c2ccfa70  e29eb67a 4d58714d de4698a5 0b627ee8  z...MqXM..F..~b.
000000a1`c2ccfa80  14b53ed5 00007b20 ddb2a643 00007ffe  .>.. {..C.......
000000a1`c2ccfa90  00000000 00000000 437f3180 00007ff7  .........1.C....
000000a1`c2ccfaa0  00000000 00000000 00000000 00000000  ................
000000a1`c2ccfab0  00000000 00000000 437f02b7 00007ff7  ...........C....
```

Note: To double-check our findings, we try to get the value of RBP explicitly without relying on the **.frame** command. We first disassemble *WinMain* to find out what the value RBP got initially before calling *GetMessageW*:

```
0:000> .cxr
Resetting default scope
```

```
0:000> k
 # Child-SP          RetAddr           Call Site
00 000000a1`c2ccf988 00007ffe`dc19477d win32u!NtUserGetMessage+0x14
01 000000a1`c2ccf990 00007ff7`437da3d3 user32!GetMessageW+0x2d
02 000000a1`c2ccf9f0 00007ff7`437f02b7 notepad!WinMain+0x293
03 000000a1`c2ccfac0 00007ffe`dc557bd4 notepad!__mainCRTStartup+0x19f
04 000000a1`c2ccfb80 00007ffe`ddc6cee1 kernel32!BaseThreadInitThunk+0x14
05 000000a1`c2ccfbb0 00000000`00000000 ntdll!RtlUserThreadStart+0x21
```

```
0:000> u WinMain
notepad!WinMain:
00007ff7`437da140 48895c2410      mov     qword ptr [rsp+10h],rbx
00007ff7`437da145 4889742418      mov     qword ptr [rsp+18h],rsi
00007ff7`437da14a 55              push    rbp
00007ff7`437da14b 57              push    rdi
00007ff7`437da14c 4154            push    r12
00007ff7`437da14e 4156            push    r14
00007ff7`437da150 4157            push    r15
00007ff7`437da152 488d6c24c9      lea     rbp,[rsp-37h]
```

Note: We see that the value of RBP comes from RSP, the stack pointer register. At the time of entering *WinMain*, it had the value pointing to the return address (00007ff7`437f02b7) of the function that called *WinMain* (__mainCRTStartup), then 5 8-byte values were subtracted (push instructions):

```
0:000> dps 000000a1`c2ccf9f0 L20
000000a1`c2ccf9f0  00007ff7`437d0000 notepad!TlgWrite <PERF> (notepad+0x0)
000000a1`c2ccf9f8  00000000`0006038b
000000a1`c2ccfa00  00000000`00000000
```

```
000000a1`c2ccfa08   00000000`00000000
000000a1`c2ccfa10   00000000`00000740
000000a1`c2ccfa18   00000221`00000000
000000a1`c2ccfa20   00000000`00000000
000000a1`c2ccfa28   00007ff7`437f0670 notepad!onexit+0x28
000000a1`c2ccfa30   00000000`00000000
000000a1`c2ccfa38   00000003`00000000
000000a1`c2ccfa40   00000000`00000000
000000a1`c2ccfa48   00000000`00000113
000000a1`c2ccfa50   00000000`00007f48
000000a1`c2ccfa58   00007ffe`dc4166d0 msctf!CThreadInputMgr::TimerProc
000000a1`c2ccfa60   00000461`0001e327
000000a1`c2ccfa68   00000000`0000006a
000000a1`c2ccfa70   4d58714d`e29eb67a
000000a1`c2ccfa78   0b627ee8`de4698a5
000000a1`c2ccfa80   00007b20`14b53ed5
000000a1`c2ccfa88   00007ffe`ddb2a643 msvcrt!initterm+0x43
000000a1`c2ccfa90   00000000`00000000
000000a1`c2ccfa98   00007ff7`437f3180 notepad!_xi_z
000000a1`c2ccfaa0   00000000`00000000
000000a1`c2ccfaa8   00000000`00000000
000000a1`c2ccfab0   00000000`00000000
000000a1`c2ccfab8   00007ff7`437f02b7 notepad!__mainCRTStartup+0x19f
000000a1`c2ccfac0   00000221`19ac3390
000000a1`c2ccfac8   00000221`19ac3392
000000a1`c2ccfad0   00000000`00000000
000000a1`c2ccfad8   00000000`00000000
000000a1`c2ccfae0   00000000`00000000
000000a1`c2ccfae8   00000221`19ac3392
```

```
0:000> ? 000000a1`c2ccfab8 - 5*8 - 37
Evaluate expression: 694757947993 = 000000a1`c2ccfa59
```

Note: We got the same RBP value 000000a1`c2ccfa59 as we got from the output .frame command. Also, note that the *MSG* symbol is not available:

```
0:000> dt MSG 000000a1`c2ccfa40
Symbol MSG not found.
```

8.   Now download the *TestWER* package from this address: http://support.citrix.com/article/CTX111901 or use existing symbols from the *\AWMDA-Dumps\TestWER\x64* folder. We try to inject *MSG* definition from other symbol files that contain it.

9.   Add *TestWER64* symbol path:

```
0:000> .sympath+ C:\AWMDA-Dumps\TestWER\x64
Symbol search path is: srv*;C:\AWMDA-Dumps\TestWER\x64
Expanded Symbol search path is:
cache*;SRV*https://msdl.microsoft.com/download/symbols;c:\awmda-dumps\testwer\x64

************ Path validation summary **************
Response                     Time (ms)    Location
Deferred                                  srv*
OK                                        C:\AWMDA-Dumps\TestWER\x64
```

233

10.   Find a place to load the *TestWER64* module (shown in a small font for clarity):

```
0:000> !address
```

```
Mapping file section regions...
Mapping module regions...
Mapping PEB regions...
Mapping TEB and stack regions...
Mapping heap regions...
Mapping page heap regions...
Mapping other regions...
Mapping stack trace database regions...
Mapping activation context regions...
```

	BaseAddress	EndAddress+1	RegionSize	Type	State	Protect	Usage	
+	0`00000000	0`198d0000	0`198d0000		MEM_FREE	PAGE_NOACCESS	Free	
+	0`198d0000	0`198d1000	0`00001000	MEM_PRIVATE	MEM_COMMIT	PAGE_READWRITE	<unknown>	[2.........J....]
+	0`198d1000	0`198e0000	0`0000f000		MEM_FREE	PAGE_NOACCESS	Free	
+	0`198e0000	0`198e1000	0`00001000	MEM_PRIVATE	MEM_COMMIT	PAGE_READWRITE	<unknown>	[0.........J....]
+	0`198e1000	0`7ffe0000	0`666ff000		MEM_FREE	PAGE_NOACCESS	Free	
+	0`7ffe0000	0`7ffe1000	0`00001000	MEM_PRIVATE	MEM_COMMIT	PAGE_READONLY	Other	[User Shared Data]
+	0`7ffe1000	0`7ffef000	0`0000e000		MEM_FREE	PAGE_NOACCESS	Free	
+	0`7ffef000	0`7fff0000	0`00001000	MEM_PRIVATE	MEM_COMMIT	PAGE_READONLY	<unknown>	[.........Z...M6.]
+	0`7fff0000	a1`c2c50000	a1`42c60000		MEM_FREE	PAGE_NOACCESS	Free	
+	a1`c2c50000	a1`c2cbc000	0`0006c000	MEM_PRIVATE	MEM_RESERVE		Stack	[~0; 740.750]
	a1`c2cbc000	a1`c2cbf000	0`00003000	MEM_PRIVATE	MEM_COMMIT	PAGE_READWRITE|PAGE_GUARD	Stack	[~0; 740.750]
	<u>a1`c2cbf000</u>	a1`c2cd0000	0`00011000	MEM_PRIVATE	MEM_COMMIT	PAGE_READWRITE	Stack	[~0; 740.750]
+	a1`c2cd0000	a1`c2e00000	0`00130000		MEM_FREE	PAGE_NOACCESS	Free	
+	a1`c2e00000	a1`c2f93000	0`00193000	MEM_PRIVATE	MEM_RESERVE		<unknown>	
	a1`c2f93000	a1`c2f94000	0`00001000	MEM_PRIVATE	MEM_COMMIT	PAGE_READWRITE	PEB	[740]
	a1`c2f94000	a1`c2f96000	0`00002000	MEM_PRIVATE	MEM_COMMIT	PAGE_READWRITE	TEB	[~0; 740.750]
	a1`c2f96000	a1`c2f9a000	0`00004000	MEM_PRIVATE	MEM_RESERVE		<unknown>	
	a1`c2f9a000	a1`c2f9c000	0`00002000	MEM_PRIVATE	MEM_COMMIT	PAGE_READWRITE	TEB	[~1; 740.770]
	a1`c2f9c000	a1`c2f9e000	0`00002000	MEM_PRIVATE	MEM_RESERVE		<unknown>	
	a1`c2f9e000	a1`c2fa0000	0`00002000	MEM_PRIVATE	MEM_COMMIT	PAGE_READWRITE	TEB	[~2; 740.7e0]
	a1`c2fa0000	a1`c3000000	0`00060000	MEM_PRIVATE	MEM_RESERVE		<unknown>	
+	a1`c3000000	a1`c306c000	0`0006c000	MEM_PRIVATE	MEM_RESERVE		Stack	[~1; 740.770]
	a1`c306c000	a1`c306f000	0`00003000	MEM_PRIVATE	MEM_COMMIT	PAGE_READWRITE|PAGE_GUARD	Stack	[~1; 740.770]
	a1`c306f000	a1`c3080000	0`00011000	MEM_PRIVATE	MEM_COMMIT	PAGE_READWRITE	Stack	[~1; 740.770]
+	a1`c3080000	a1`c3100000	0`00080000		MEM_FREE	PAGE_NOACCESS	Free	
+	a1`c3100000	a1`c316c000	0`0006c000	MEM_PRIVATE	MEM_RESERVE		Stack	[~2; 740.7e0]
	a1`c316c000	a1`c316f000	0`00003000	MEM_PRIVATE	MEM_COMMIT	PAGE_READWRITE|PAGE_GUARD	Stack	[~2; 740.7e0]
	a1`c316f000	a1`c3180000	0`00011000	MEM_PRIVATE	MEM_COMMIT	PAGE_READWRITE	Stack	[~2; 740.7e0]
+	a1`c3180000	221`198d0000	17f`56750000		MEM_FREE	PAGE_NOACCESS	Free	

```
[...]
```

```
0:000> .reload /f /i C:\AWMDA-Dumps\TestWER\x64\TestWER64.exe= a1`c2cbf000
```

```
0:000> lm
start             end               module name
000000a1`c2cbf000 000000a1`c2d06000 TestWER64    (private pdb symbols)  C:\ProgramData\dbg\sym\TestWER64.pdb\CB8F1BD7357D4A28958CA8B394CA24881\TestWER64.pdb
00007ff7`437d0000 00007ff7`43802000 notepad      (deferred)
00007ffe`b0ae0000 00007ffe`b0bb7000 efswrt       (deferred)
00007ffe`c67e0000 00007ffe`c6a65000 comctl32     (deferred)
00007ffe`c9300000 00007ffe`c939e000 TextInputFramework   (deferred)
00007ffe`cbd70000 00007ffe`cbe82000 MrmCoreR     (deferred)
00007ffe`cdb70000 00007ffe`cdbd5000 oleacc       (deferred)
00007ffe`d2d80000 00007ffe`d2d9b000 mpr          (deferred)
00007ffe`d3280000 00007ffe`d3526000 iertutil     (deferred)
00007ffe`d5fb0000 00007ffe`d6103000 WinTypes     (deferred)
00007ffe`d6110000 00007ffe`d643a000 CoreUIComponents    (deferred)
00007ffe`d8590000 00007ffe`d8664000 CoreMessaging (deferred)
00007ffe`d89f0000 00007ffe`d8a89000 uxtheme      (deferred)
00007ffe`d8ac0000 00007ffe`d8d1a000 twinapi_appcore     (deferred)
00007ffe`d8e10000 00007ffe`d8e39000 rmclient     (deferred)
00007ffe`d9b60000 00007ffe`d9b91000 ntmarta      (deferred)
00007ffe`daad0000 00007ffe`daae0000 umpdc        (deferred)
00007ffe`daae0000 00007ffe`dab2a000 powrprof     (deferred)
00007ffe`dab30000 00007ffe`dab41000 kernel_appcore      (deferred)
00007ffe`dab70000 00007ffe`dab8f000 profapi      (deferred)
00007ffe`dab90000 00007ffe`dad24000 gdi32full    (deferred)
00007ffe`dad30000 00007ffe`dad51000 win32u       (pdb symbols)  C:\ProgramData\dbg\sym\win32u.pdb\BC2E49ABE46D2E93B278B4DECFCA62A81\win32u.pdb
00007ffe`dae40000 00007ffe`dae8a000 cfgmgr32     (deferred)
00007ffe`dae90000 00007ffe`daf10000 bcryptPrimitives    (deferred)
00007ffe`daf10000 00007ffe`db00a000 ucrtbase     (deferred)
00007ffe`db010000 00007ffe`db2b3000 KERNELBASE   (deferred)
00007ffe`db2c0000 00007ffe`db35e000 msvcp_win    (deferred)
00007ffe`db360000 00007ffe`db377000 cryptsp      (deferred)
00007ffe`db3e0000 00007ffe`dbb5e000 windows_storage     (deferred)
00007ffe`dbe70000 00007ffe`dbec2000 shlwapi      (deferred)
00007ffe`dbf60000 00007ffe`dc080000 rpcrt4       (deferred)
00007ffe`dc170000 00007ffe`dc303000 user32       (pdb symbols)  C:\ProgramData\dbg\sym\user32.pdb\BC4CC7CC9A33B8A66AEA91BFB0D5FCAA1\user32.pdb
00007ffe`dc400000 00007ffe`dc536000 msctf        (deferred)
00007ffe`dc540000 00007ffe`dc5f2000 kernel32     (deferred)
00007ffe`dca80000 00007ffe`dcb29000 SHCore       (deferred)
00007ffe`dcb40000 00007ffe`dcbe2000 clbcatq      (deferred)
00007ffe`dcbf0000 00007ffe`dcc16000 gdi32        (deferred)
00007ffe`dcc20000 00007ffe`dccc3000 advapi32     (deferred)
00007ffe`dce80000 00007ffe`dd565000 shell32      (deferred)
00007ffe`dd570000 00007ffe`dd634000 oleaut32     (deferred)
```

```
00007ffe`dd710000 00007ffe`dd7a7000   sechost    (deferred)
00007ffe`dd7b0000 00007ffe`ddae6000   combase    (deferred)
00007ffe`ddaf0000 00007ffe`ddb8e000   msvcrt     (deferred)
00007ffe`ddb90000 00007ffe`ddbbe000   imm32      (deferred)
00007ffe`ddc00000 00007ffe`dddf0000   ntdll      (pdb symbols)        C:\ProgramData\dbg\sym\ntdll.pdb\27A66DD3103F6B2E03B27D315F1A8AF31\ntdll.pdb
```

11.   We examine the *MSG* structure now:

```
0:000> dt -r MSG 000000a1`c2ccfa40
TestWER64!MSG
   +0x000 hwnd                 : (null)
   +0x008 message              : 0x113
   +0x010 wParam               : 0x7f48
   +0x018 lParam               : 0n140732593694416
   +0x020 time                 : 0x1e327
   +0x024 pt                   : tagPOINT
      +0x000 x                    : 0n1121
      +0x004 y                    : 0n106
```

12.   We close logging before exiting WinDbg:

```
0:000> .logclose
Closing open log file C:\AWMDA-Dumps\Process\x64\notepad.log
```

235

Exercise P17

- **Goal:** Learn how to navigate object wait chains in 32-bit memory dumps saved with ProcDump

- **Patterns:** Embedded Comments; Wait Chain (General); No Data Types; Deadlock (Mixed Objects, User Space)

- \AWMDA-Dumps\Exercise-P17-Analysis-process-dump-AppQ-32.pdf

Exercise P17: Analysis of an application process dump (AppQ, 32-bit)

Goal: Learn how to navigate object wait chains in 32-bit memory dumps saved with ProcDump.

Patterns: Embedded Comments; Wait Chain (General), Deadlock (Mixed Object, User Space).

1.   Launch WinDbg.

2.   Open \AWMDA-Dumps\Process\x86\AppQ.exe_191117_150657.dmp

3.   We get the dump file loaded:

```
Microsoft (R) Windows Debugger Version 10.0.25877.1004 AMD64
Copyright (c) Microsoft Corporation. All rights reserved.


Loading Dump File [C:\AWMDA-Dumps\Process\x86\AppQ.exe_191117_150657.dmp]
User Mini Dump File with Full Memory: Only application data is available

Comment: '
*** procdump.exe  -ma 1628
*** Manual dump'

************* Path validation summary **************
Response                     Time (ms)     Location
Deferred                                   srv*
Symbol search path is: srv*
Executable search path is:
Windows 10 Version 18362 MP (2 procs) Free x86 compatible
Product: WinNt, suite: SingleUserTS Personal
Edition build lab: 18362.239.x86fre.19h1_release_svc_prod1.190628-1641
Machine Name:
Debug session time: Sun Nov 17 16:06:57.000 2019 (UTC + 1:00)
System Uptime: 0 days 0:35:00.946
Process Uptime: 0 days 0:03:37.000
...........................
For analysis of this file, run !analyze -v
eax=00000000 ebx=003711d0 ecx=00000000 edx=00000000 esi=00000000 edi=000002a4
eip=778f1d9c esp=00cff528 ebp=00cff598 iopl=0         nv up ei pl nz na pe nc
cs=0023  ss=002b  ds=002b  es=002b  fs=0053  gs=002b            efl=00000206
ntdll!NtWaitForSingleObject+0xc:
778f1d9c c20c00          ret     0Ch
```

4.   We now open a log file:

```
0:000> .logopen C:\AWMDA-Dumps\Process\x86\AppQ.log
Opened log file 'C:\AWMDA-Dumps\Process\x86\AppQ.log'
```

5.   The application process was reported hanging (frozen), and we now try the default analysis command for hangs:

```
0:000> !analyze -v -hang
*******************************************************************
*                                                                 *
*                      Exception Analysis                         *
*                                                                 *
*******************************************************************


KEY_VALUES_STRING: 1

    Key  : Analysis.CPU.mSec
    Value: 7843

    Key  : Analysis.DebugAnalysisManager
    Value: Create

    Key  : Analysis.Elapsed.mSec
    Value: 7949

    Key  : Analysis.Init.CPU.mSec
    Value: 624

    Key  : Analysis.Init.Elapsed.mSec
    Value: 53676

    Key  : Analysis.Memory.CommitPeak.Mb
    Value: 73

    Key  : Timeline.OS.Boot.DeltaSec
    Value: 2100

    Key  : Timeline.Process.Start.DeltaSec
    Value: 217

    Key  : WER.BlockedOn
    Value: MissingThread

    Key  : WER.OS.Branch
    Value: 19h1_release_svc_prod1

    Key  : WER.OS.Timestamp
    Value: 2019-06-28T16:41:00Z

    Key  : WER.OS.Version
    Value: 10.0.18362.239

    Key  : WER.Process.Version
    Value: 2.0.0.1


FILE_IN_CAB:  AppQ.exe_191117_150657.dmp

COMMENT:
*** procdump.exe  -ma 1628
*** Manual dump
```

```
APPLICATION_VERIFIER_FLAGS:  0

CONTEXT:  (.cxr;r)
eax=00000000 ebx=003711d0 ecx=00000000 edx=00000000 esi=00000000 edi=000002a4
eip=778f1d9c esp=00cff528 ebp=00cff598 iopl=0         nv up ei pl nz na pe nc
cs=0023  ss=002b  ds=002b  es=002b  fs=0053  gs=002b          efl=00000206
ntdll!NtWaitForSingleObject+0xc:
778f1d9c c20c00          ret     0Ch

EXCEPTION_RECORD:  (.exr -1)
ExceptionAddress: 00000000
   ExceptionCode: 80000003 (Break instruction exception)
  ExceptionFlags: 00000000
NumberParameters: 0

FAULTING_THREAD:  000021dc

PROCESS_NAME:  AppQ.exe

WATSON_BKT_EVENT:  AppHang

BLOCKING_THREAD:  000021dc

ERROR_CODE: (NTSTATUS) 0xcfffffff - <Unable to get error code text>

EXCEPTION_CODE_STR:  cfffffff

DERIVED_WAIT_CHAIN:

Dl Eid Cid      WaitType
-- --- ------- ---------------------------
   0   65c.648 Thread Handle          -->
   1   65c.2328 Thread Handle          -->
   2   65c.21dc Thread Handle

WAIT_CHAIN_COMMAND:  ~0s;k;;~1s;k;;~2s;k;;

STACK_TEXT:
0386fba8 7646bad3      00000003 0386fd74 00000000 ntdll!NtWaitForMultipleObjects+0xc
0386fd3c 7646b988      00000003 0386fd74 00000001 KERNELBASE!WaitForMultipleObjectsEx+0x133
0386fd58 00371445      00000003 0386fd74 00000001 KERNELBASE!WaitForMultipleObjects+0x18
WARNING: Stack unwind information not available. Following frames may be wrong.
0386fd84 76dc6359      00000000 76dc6340 0386fdf0 AppQ+0x1445
0386fd94 778e7b74      00000000 ecb19264 00000000 kernel32!BaseThreadInitThunk+0x19
0386fdf0 778e7b44      ffffffff 77908f28 00000000 ntdll!__RtlUserThreadStart+0x2f
0386fe00 00000000      003713b0 00000000 00000000 ntdll!_RtlUserThreadStart+0x1b


STACK_COMMAND:  ~2s ; .cxr ; kb

SYMBOL_NAME:  appq+1445

MODULE_NAME: AppQ

IMAGE_NAME:  AppQ.exe

FAILURE_BUCKET_ID:  APPLICATION_HANG_BlockedOn_MissingThread_cfffffff_AppQ.exe!Unknown

OS_VERSION:  10.0.18362.239
```

```
BUILDLAB_STR:  19h1_release_svc_prod1

OSPLATFORM_TYPE:  x86

OSNAME:  Windows 10

IMAGE_VERSION:  2.0.0.1

FAILURE_ID_HASH:  {1ee698f1-9c0d-bf25-1f4f-9394728a17a2}

Followup:     MachineOwner
---------
```

Note: We see WinDbg found a wait chain (DERIVED_WAIT_CHAIN): thread #0 is waiting for thread #1, and the latter is waiting for thread #2. From the stack trace, thread #2 appears waiting for multiple objects (*WaitForMultipleObjects*), and some of them no longer exist (DEFAULT_BUCKET_ID).

6. Let's switch to **BLOCKING_THREAD** (we can use ~~ to switch to a particular TID):

```
0:000> ~~[000021dc]s
eax=00000000 ebx=00000000 ecx=00000000 edx=00000000 esi=00000003 edi=00000003
eip=778f232c esp=0386fbac ebp=0386fd3c iopl=0         nv up ei pl nz na pe nc
cs=0023  ss=002b  ds=002b  es=002b  fs=0053  gs=002b          efl=00000206
ntdll!NtWaitForMultipleObjects+0xc:
778f232c c21400          ret     14h
```

```
0:002> kb
 # ChildEBP RetAddr  Args to Child
00 0386fba8 7646bad3 00000003 0386fd74 00000000 ntdll!NtWaitForMultipleObjects+0xc
01 0386fd3c 7646b988 00000003 0386fd74 00000001 KERNELBASE!WaitForMultipleObjectsEx+0x133
02 0386fd58 00371445 00000003 0386fd74 00000001 KERNELBASE!WaitForMultipleObjects+0x18
WARNING: Stack unwind information not available. Following frames may be wrong.
03 0386fd84 76dc6359 00000000 76dc6340 0386fdf0 AppQ+0x1445
04 0386fd94 778e7b74 00000000 ecb19264 00000000 kernel32!BaseThreadInitThunk+0x19
05 0386fdf0 778e7b44 ffffffff 77908f28 00000000 ntdll!__RtlUserThreadStart+0x2f
06 0386fe00 00000000 003713b0 00000000 00000000 ntdll!_RtlUserThreadStart+0x1b
```

Note: The meaning of the first 3 parameters for *WaitForMultipleObjects* can be found in Microsoft Docs (https://docs.microsoft.com/en-us/windows/win32/api/synchapi/nf-synchapi-waitformultipleobjects):

```
DWORD WaitForMultipleObjects(
  DWORD          nCount,
  const HANDLE  *lpHandles,
  BOOL           bWaitAll,
  DWORD          dwMilliseconds
);
```

To see all 4 parameters we need to dump raw stack (we then see the timeout was specified as -1 (0xFFFFFFFF), INFINITE):

```
0:002> dps 0386fd58
0386fd58  0386fd84
0386fd5c  00371445 AppQ+0x1445
0386fd60  00000003
0386fd64  0386fd74
0386fd68  00000001
```

```
0386fd6c  ffffffff
0386fd70  000002ac
0386fd74  000002b0
0386fd78  000002b4
0386fd7c  000002b8
0386fd80  bfbcabb6
0386fd84  0386fd94
0386fd88  76dc6359 kernel32!BaseThreadInitThunk+0x19
0386fd8c  00000000
0386fd90  76dc6340 kernel32!BaseThreadInitThunk
0386fd94  0386fdf0
0386fd98  778e7b74 ntdll!__RtlUserThreadStart+0x2f
0386fd9c  00000000
0386fda0  ecb19264
0386fda4  00000000
0386fda8  00000000
0386fdac  00000000
0386fdb0  00000000
0386fdb4  00000000
0386fdb8  00000000
0386fdbc  00000000
0386fdc0  00000000
0386fdc4  00000000
0386fdc8  00000000
0386fdcc  00000000
0386fdd0  00000000
0386fdd4  00000000
```

7.   We now check the object array of 3 handles the thread was waiting for:

```
0:002> dp 0386fd74 L3
0386fd74  000002b0 000002b4 000002b8

0:002> !handle 2b0 ff
Handle 000002b0
  Type            Thread
  Attributes      0
  GrantedAccess   0x1fffff:
        Delete,ReadControl,WriteDac,WriteOwner,Synch

Terminate,Suspend,Alert,GetContext,SetContext,SetInfo,QueryInfo,SetToken,Impersonate,DirectImpe
rsonate
  HandleCount     2
  PointerCount    65537
  Name            <none>
  Object specific information
    Thread Id   65c.2064
    Priority    10
    Base Priority 0

0:002> ~~[2064]s
            ^ Illegal thread error in '~~[2064]s'

0:002> !handle 2b4 ff
Handle 000002b4
  Type            Thread
  Attributes      0
  GrantedAccess   0x1fffff:
        Delete,ReadControl,WriteDac,WriteOwner,Synch
```

241

```
Terminate,Suspend,Alert,GetContext,SetContext,SetInfo,QueryInfo,SetToken,Impersonate,DirectImpe
rsonate
    HandleCount        2
    PointerCount       65537
    Name               <none>
    Object specific information
       Thread Id   65c.d00
       Priority    11
       Base Priority 0


0:002> ~~[d00]s
            ^ Illegal thread error in '~~[d00]s'


0:002> !handle 2b8 ff
Handle 000002b8
  Type               Thread
  Attributes         0
  GrantedAccess      0x1fffff:
        Delete,ReadControl,WriteDac,WriteOwner,Synch

Terminate,Suspend,Alert,GetContext,SetContext,SetInfo,QueryInfo,SetToken,Impersonate,DirectImpe
rsonate
    HandleCount        3
    PointerCount       131058
    Name               <none>
    Object specific information
       Thread Id   65c.1e88
       Priority    10
       Base Priority 0


0:002> ~~[1e88]s
eax=003714a0 ebx=000002ac ecx=00000000 edx=00000000 esi=00000000 edi=000002ac
eip=778f1d9c esp=0515f854 ebp=0515f8c4 iopl=0         nv up ei pl nz na po nc
cs=0023  ss=002b  ds=002b  es=002b  fs=0053  gs=002b            efl=00000202
ntdll!NtWaitForSingleObject+0xc:
778f1d9c c20c00          ret     0Ch


0:003> kb
 # ChildEBP RetAddr  Args to Child
00 0515f850 7645e2c9 000002ac 00000000 00000000 ntdll!NtWaitForSingleObject+0xc
01 0515f8c4 7645e222 000002ac ffffffff 00000000 KERNELBASE!WaitForSingleObjectEx+0x99
02 0515f8d8 003714af 000002ac ffffffff 0515f8f8 KERNELBASE!WaitForSingleObject+0x12
WARNING: Stack unwind information not available. Following frames may be wrong.
03 0515f8e8 76dc6359 000002ac 76dc6340 0515f954 AppQ+0x14af
04 0515f8f8 778e7b74 000002ac ea2296c0 00000000 kernel32!BaseThreadInitThunk+0x19
05 0515f954 778e7b44 ffffffff 77908f28 00000000 ntdll!__RtlUserThreadStart+0x2f
06 0515f964 00000000 003714a0 000002ac 00000000 ntdll!_RtlUserThreadStart+0x1b


0:003> !handle 2ac ff
Handle 000002ac
  Type               Event
  Attributes         0
  GrantedAccess      0x1f0003:
        Delete,ReadControl,WriteDac,WriteOwner,Synch
        QueryState,ModifyState
    HandleCount        2
    PointerCount       65538
    Name               <none>
    Object specific information
```

```
Event Type Auto Reset
Event is Waiting
```

Note: We see that thread #2 was waiting for 2 threads that were no longer available (possibly terminated and signaled) and also waiting for thread #3, which was also waiting for an event object. Unfortunately, events do not have owners.

8.   We can search for event handles on other raw stacks and make an intelligent guess if this looks like a local variable (sometimes, we may even be lucky if we see a call residue to *CreateEvent,* but not in our case). We check, for example, the raw stack for thread #2 (we use **~e** to execute any command for thread #2):

```
0:003> ~2e !teb
TEB at 00bd7000
error InitTypeRead( TEB )...

0:003> dt *!_TEB
        WinTypes!_TEB
        combase!_TEB

0:003> dt WinTypes_TEB
   +0x000 NtTib : _NT_TIB
   +0x01c EnvironmentPointer : Ptr32 Void
   +0x020 ClientId         : _CLIENT_ID
   +0x028 ActiveRpcHandle  : Ptr32 Void
   +0x02c ThreadLocalStoragePointer : Ptr32 Void
   +0x030 ProcessEnvironmentBlock : Ptr32 _PEB
   +0x034 LastErrorValue   : Uint4B
   +0x038 CountOfOwnedCriticalSections : Uint4B
   +0x03c CsrClientThread  : Ptr32 Void
   +0x040 Win32ThreadInfo  : Ptr32 Void
   +0x044 User32Reserved   : [26] Uint4B
   +0x0ac UserReserved     : [5] Uint4B
   +0x0c0 WOW32Reserved    : Ptr32 Void
   +0x0c4 CurrentLocale    : Uint4B
   +0x0c8 FpSoftwareStatusRegister : Uint4B
   +0x0cc ReservedForDebuggerInstrumentation : [16] Ptr32 Void
   +0x10c SystemReserved1  : [26] Ptr32 Void
   +0x174 PlaceholderCompatibilityMode : Char
   +0x175 PlaceholderHydrationAlwaysExplicit : UChar
   +0x176 PlaceholderReserved : [10] Char
   +0x180 ProxiedProcessId : Uint4B
   +0x184 _ActivationStack : _ACTIVATION_CONTEXT_STACK
   +0x19c WorkingOnBehalfTicket : [8] UChar
   +0x1a4 ExceptionCode    : Int4B
   +0x1a8 ActivationContextStackPointer : Ptr32 _ACTIVATION_CONTEXT_STACK
   +0x1ac InstrumentationCallbackSp : Uint4B
   +0x1b0 InstrumentationCallbackPreviousPc : Uint4B
   +0x1b4 InstrumentationCallbackPreviousSp : Uint4B
   +0x1b8 InstrumentationCallbackDisabled : UChar
   +0x1b9 SpareBytes       : [23] UChar
   +0x1d0 TxFsContext      : Uint4B
   +0x1d4 GdiTebBatch      : _GDI_TEB_BATCH
   +0x6b4 RealClientId     : _CLIENT_ID
   +0x6bc GdiCachedProcessHandle : Ptr32 Void
   +0x6c0 GdiClientPID     : Uint4B
   +0x6c4 GdiClientTID     : Uint4B
   +0x6c8 GdiThreadLocalInfo : Ptr32 Void
   +0x6cc Win32ClientInfo  : [62] Uint4B
```

```
+0x7c4 glDispatchTable      : [233] Ptr32 Void
+0xb68 glReserved1          : [29] Uint4B
+0xbdc glReserved2          : Ptr32 Void
+0xbe0 glSectionInfo        : Ptr32 Void
+0xbe4 glSection            : Ptr32 Void
+0xbe8 glTable              : Ptr32 Void
+0xbec glCurrentRC          : Ptr32 Void
+0xbf0 glContext            : Ptr32 Void
+0xbf4 LastStatusValue      : Uint4B
+0xbf8 StaticUnicodeString  : _UNICODE_STRING
+0xc00 StaticUnicodeBuffer  : [261] Wchar
+0xe0c DeallocationStack    : Ptr32 Void
+0xe10 TlsSlots             : [64] Ptr32 Void
+0xf10 TlsLinks             : _LIST_ENTRY
+0xf18 Vdm                  : Ptr32 Void
+0xf1c ReservedForNtRpc     : Ptr32 Void
+0xf20 DbgSsReserved        : [2] Ptr32 Void
+0xf28 HardErrorMode        : Uint4B
+0xf2c Instrumentation      : [9] Ptr32 Void
+0xf50 ActivityId           : _GUID
+0xf60 SubProcessTag        : Ptr32 Void
+0xf64 PerflibData          : Ptr32 Void
+0xf68 EtwTraceData         : Ptr32 Void
+0xf6c WinSockData          : Ptr32 Void
+0xf70 GdiBatchCount        : Uint4B
+0xf74 CurrentIdealProcessor : _PROCESSOR_NUMBER
+0xf74 IdealProcessorValue  : Uint4B
+0xf74 ReservedPad0         : UChar
+0xf75 ReservedPad1         : UChar
+0xf76 ReservedPad2         : UChar
+0xf77 IdealProcessor       : UChar
+0xf78 GuaranteedStackBytes : Uint4B
+0xf7c ReservedForPerf      : Ptr32 Void
+0xf80 ReservedForOle       : Ptr32 Void
+0xf84 WaitingOnLoaderLock  : Uint4B
+0xf88 SavedPriorityState   : Ptr32 Void
+0xf8c ReservedForCodeCoverage : Uint4B
+0xf90 ThreadPoolData       : Ptr32 Void
+0xf94 TlsExpansionSlots    : Ptr32 Ptr32 Void
+0xf98 MuiGeneration        : Uint4B
+0xf9c IsImpersonating      : Uint4B
+0xfa0 NlsCache             : Ptr32 Void
+0xfa4 pShimData            : Ptr32 Void
+0xfa8 HeapData             : Uint4B
+0xfac CurrentTransactionHandle : Ptr32 Void
+0xfb0 ActiveFrame          : Ptr32 _TEB_ACTIVE_FRAME
+0xfb4 FlsData              : Ptr32 Void
+0xfb8 PreferredLanguages   : Ptr32 Void
+0xfbc UserPrefLanguages    : Ptr32 Void
+0xfc0 MergedPrefLanguages  : Ptr32 Void
+0xfc4 MuiImpersonation     : Uint4B
+0xfc8 CrossTebFlags        : Uint2B
+0xfc8 SpareCrossTebBits    : Pos 0, 16 Bits
+0xfca SameTebFlags         : Uint2B
+0xfca SafeThunkCall        : Pos 0, 1 Bit
+0xfca InDebugPrint         : Pos 1, 1 Bit
+0xfca HasFiberData         : Pos 2, 1 Bit
+0xfca SkipThreadAttach     : Pos 3, 1 Bit
+0xfca WerInShipAssertCode  : Pos 4, 1 Bit
+0xfca RanProcessInit       : Pos 5, 1 Bit
```

```
    +0xfca ClonedThread      : Pos 6, 1 Bit
    +0xfca SuppressDebugMsg  : Pos 7, 1 Bit
    +0xfca DisableUserStackWalk : Pos 8, 1 Bit
    +0xfca RtlExceptionAttached : Pos 9, 1 Bit
    +0xfca InitialThread     : Pos 10, 1 Bit
    +0xfca SessionAware      : Pos 11, 1 Bit
    +0xfca LoadOwner         : Pos 12, 1 Bit
    +0xfca LoaderWorker      : Pos 13, 1 Bit
    +0xfca SkipLoaderInit    : Pos 14, 1 Bit
    +0xfca SpareSameTebBits  : Pos 15, 1 Bit
    +0xfcc TxnScopeEnterCallback : Ptr32 Void
    +0xfd0 TxnScopeExitCallback : Ptr32 Void
    +0xfd4 TxnScopeContext   : Ptr32 Void
    +0xfd8 LockCount         : Uint4B
    +0xfdc WowTebOffset      : Int4B
    +0xfe0 ResourceRetValue  : Ptr32 Void
    +0xfe4 ReservedForWdf    : Ptr32 Void
    +0xfe8 ReservedForCrt    : Uint8B
    +0xff0 EffectiveContainerId : _GUID
[...]

0:003> dt _NT_TIB 00bd7000
combase!_NT_TIB
    +0x000 ExceptionList     : 0x0386fd2c _EXCEPTION_REGISTRATION_RECORD
    +0x004 StackBase         : 0x03870000 Void
    +0x008 StackLimit        : 0x0386f000 Void
    +0x00c SubSystemTib      : (null)
    +0x010 FiberData         : 0x00001e00 Void
    +0x010 Version           : 0x1e00
    +0x014 ArbitraryUserPointer : (null)
    +0x018 Self              : 0x00bd7000 _NT_TIB
```

Note: If no modules have the required data structure definition, we can force symbols from other modules (**.reload /f**), get it from a different process memory dump that belongs to a different build or even processor architecture. For example, in our case, the x64 notepad memory dump has the _TEB_ structure definition:

```
0:000> dt _NT_TIB
ntdll!_NT_TIB
    +0x000 ExceptionList     : Ptr64 _EXCEPTION_REGISTRATION_RECORD
    +0x008 StackBase         : Ptr64 Void
    +0x010 StackLimit        : Ptr64 Void
    +0x018 SubSystemTib      : Ptr64 Void
    +0x020 FiberData         : Ptr64 Void
    +0x020 Version           : Uint4B
    +0x028 ArbitraryUserPointer : Ptr64 Void
    +0x030 Self              : Ptr64 _NT_TIB
```

From this 64-bit structure layout, we can infer the corresponding 32-bit structure.

Since we identified stack region boundaries, we can search for the handle **2ac**:

```
0:003> s-d 0x0386f000 0x03870000 2ac
0386fa80  000002ac 00000000 00000000 00000000   ................
0386fb1c  000002ac 00000000 0000065c 00001e88   ........\.......
0386fd70  000002ac 000002b0 000002b4 000002b8   ................
```

Note: The last occurrence of the handle value makes sense since the next 3 values look like saved handle values we found previously:

245

```
0:003> dps 0386fd70-10
0386fd60  00000003
0386fd64  0386fd74
0386fd68  00000001
0386fd6c  ffffffff
0386fd70  000002ac
0386fd74  000002b0
0386fd78  000002b4
0386fd7c  000002b8
0386fd80  bfbcabb6
0386fd84  0386fd94
0386fd88  76dc6359 kernel32!BaseThreadInitThunk+0x19
0386fd8c  00000000
0386fd90  76dc6340 kernel32!BaseThreadInitThunk
0386fd94  0386fdf0
0386fd98  778e7b74 ntdll!__RtlUserThreadStart+0x2f
0386fd9c  00000000
0386fda0  ecb19264
0386fda4  00000000
0386fda8  00000000
0386fdac  00000000
0386fdb0  00000000
0386fdb4  00000000
0386fdb8  00000000
0386fdbc  00000000
0386fdc0  00000000
0386fdc4  00000000
0386fdc8  00000000
0386fdcc  00000000
0386fdd0  00000000
0386fdd4  00000000
0386fdd8  0386fda0
0386fddc  00000000
```

Note: If thread #2 is the owner of the event and is waiting for thread #3, which is waiting for the event, then we identified a deadlock.

9.   Let's also dump all thread stacks to see whether we missed anything:

```
0:003> ~*kb

#  0  Id: 65c.648 Suspend: 0 Teb: 00bcb000 Unfrozen
 # ChildEBP RetAddr  Args to Child
00 00cff524 7645e2c9 000002a4 00000000 00000000 ntdll!NtWaitForSingleObject+0xc
01 00cff598 7645e222 000002a4 ffffffff 00000000 KERNELBASE!WaitForSingleObjectEx+0x99
02 00cff5ac 00371378 000002a4 ffffffff 000002a4 KERNELBASE!WaitForSingleObject+0x12
WARNING: Stack unwind information not available. Following frames may be wrong.
03 00cff5c0 00371239 00001388 00008003 00008003 AppQ+0x1378
04 00cff61c 765a46cb 00040154 00000111 00008003 AppQ+0x1239
05 00cff648 765860bc 003711d0 00040154 00000111 user32!_InternalCallWinProc+0x2b
06 00cff72c 7658520e 003711d0 00000000 00000111 user32!UserCallWinProcCheckWow+0x3ac
07 00cff7a0 76584fd0 00000111 00cff7dc 003710a7 user32!DispatchMessageWorker+0x20e
08 00cff7ac 003710a7 00cff7bc 000706cd 00040154 user32!DispatchMessageW+0x10
09 00cff7dc 00371681 00370000 00000000 00f41ca0 AppQ+0x10a7
0a 00cff828 76dc6359 00bc8000 76dc6340 00cff894 AppQ+0x1681
0b 00cff838 778e7b74 00bc8000 eff89700 00000000 kernel32!BaseThreadInitThunk+0x19
0c 00cff894 778e7b44 ffffffff 77908f28 00000000 ntdll!__RtlUserThreadStart+0x2f
0d 00cff8a4 00000000 00371705 00bc8000 00000000 ntdll!_RtlUserThreadStart+0x1b

  1  Id: 65c.2328 Suspend: 0 Teb: 00bd4000 Unfrozen
```

246

```
 # ChildEBP RetAddr  Args to Child
00 0372f9cc 7645e2c9 000002a8 00000000 00000000 ntdll!NtWaitForSingleObject+0xc
01 0372fa40 7645e222 000002a8 ffffffff 00000000 KERNELBASE!WaitForSingleObjectEx+0x99
02 0372fa54 003713a8 000002a8 ffffffff 000002a8 KERNELBASE!WaitForSingleObject+0x12
WARNING: Stack unwind information not available. Following frames may be wrong.
03 0372fa68 76dc6359 00000000 76dc6340 0372fad4 AppQ+0x13a8
04 0372fa78 778e7b74 00000000 ec459540 00000000 kernel32!BaseThreadInitThunk+0x19
05 0372fad4 778e7b44 ffffffff 77908f28 00000000 ntdll!__RtlUserThreadStart+0x2f
06 0372fae4 00000000 00371380 00000000 00000000 ntdll!_RtlUserThreadStart+0x1b

   2  Id: 65c.21dc Suspend: 0 Teb: 00bd7000 Unfrozen
 # ChildEBP RetAddr  Args to Child
00 0386fba8 7646bad3 00000003 0386fd74 00000000 ntdll!NtWaitForMultipleObjects+0xc
01 0386fd3c 7646b988 00000003 0386fd74 00000001 KERNELBASE!WaitForMultipleObjectsEx+0x133
02 0386fd58 00371445 00000003 0386fd74 00000001 KERNELBASE!WaitForMultipleObjects+0x18
WARNING: Stack unwind information not available. Following frames may be wrong.
03 0386fd84 76dc6359 00000000 76dc6340 0386fdf0 AppQ+0x1445
04 0386fd94 778e7b74 00000000 ecb19264 00000000 kernel32!BaseThreadInitThunk+0x19
05 0386fdf0 778e7b44 ffffffff 77908f28 00000000 ntdll!__RtlUserThreadStart+0x2f
06 0386fe00 00000000 003713b0 00000000 00000000 ntdll!_RtlUserThreadStart+0x1b

   3  Id: 65c.1e88 Suspend: 0 Teb: 00be0000 Unfrozen
 # ChildEBP RetAddr  Args to Child
00 0515f850 7645e2c9 000002ac 00000000 00000000 ntdll!NtWaitForSingleObject+0xc
01 0515f8c4 7645e222 000002ac ffffffff 00000000 KERNELBASE!WaitForSingleObjectEx+0x99
02 0515f8d8 003714af 000002ac ffffffff 0515f8f8 KERNELBASE!WaitForSingleObject+0x12
WARNING: Stack unwind information not available. Following frames may be wrong.
03 0515f8e8 76dc6359 000002ac 76dc6340 0515f954 AppQ+0x14af
04 0515f8f8 778e7b74 000002ac ea2296c0 00000000 kernel32!BaseThreadInitThunk+0x19
05 0515f954 778e7b44 ffffffff 77908f28 00000000 ntdll!__RtlUserThreadStart+0x2f
06 0515f964 00000000 003714a0 000002ac 00000000 ntdll!_RtlUserThreadStart+0x1b

   4  Id: 65c.168c Suspend: 0 Teb: 00be3000 Unfrozen
 # ChildEBP RetAddr  Args to Child
00 0396f93c 778d66ef 000001e4 00f889f8 00000010 ntdll!NtWaitForWorkViaWorkerFactory+0xc
01 0396faf8 76dc6359 00f754f0 76dc6340 0396fb64 ntdll!TppWorkerThread+0x33f
02 0396fb08 778e7b74 00f754f0 eca194f0 00000000 kernel32!BaseThreadInitThunk+0x19
03 0396fb64 778e7b44 ffffffff 77908f28 00000000 ntdll!__RtlUserThreadStart+0x2f
04 0396fb74 00000000 778d63b0 00f754f0 00000000 ntdll!_RtlUserThreadStart+0x1b

   5  Id: 65c.138 Suspend: 0 Teb: 00be6000 Unfrozen
 # ChildEBP RetAddr  Args to Child
00 03aaf974 778d66ef 000001e4 00f75618 00000010 ntdll!NtWaitForWorkViaWorkerFactory+0xc
01 03aafb30 76dc6359 00f754f0 76dc6340 03aafb9c ntdll!TppWorkerThread+0x33f
02 03aafb40 778e7b74 00f754f0 ec9d9408 00000000 kernel32!BaseThreadInitThunk+0x19
03 03aafb9c 778e7b44 ffffffff 77908f28 00000000 ntdll!__RtlUserThreadStart+0x2f
04 03aafbac 00000000 778d63b0 00f754f0 00000000 ntdll!_RtlUserThreadStart+0x1b
```

10.   We close logging before exiting WinDbg:

```
0:003> .logclose
Closing open log file C:\AWMDA-Dumps\Process\x86\AppQ.log
```

Exercise P18

- **Goal:** Learn how to navigate object wait chains in 64-bit memory dumps saved with ProcDump

- **Patterns:** Not My Thread; Blocked Thread (Software); Main Thread; Passive Thread (User Space); Coincidental Symbolic Information

- \AWMDA-Dumps\Exercise-P18-Analysis-process-dump-AppQ-64.pdf

Exercise P18: Analysis of an application process dump (AppQ, 64-bit)

Goal: Learn how to navigate object wait chains in 64-bit memory dumps saved with ProcDump.

Patterns: Not My Thread; Blocked Thread (Software); Main Thread; Passive Thread (User Space); Coincidental Symbolic Information.

1.   Launch WinDbg.

2.   Open \AWMDA-Dumps\Process\x64\AppQ.exe_191119_083619.dmp

3.   We get the dump file loaded:

```
Microsoft (R) Windows Debugger Version 10.0.25877.1004 AMD64
Copyright (c) Microsoft Corporation. All rights reserved.


Loading Dump File [C:\AWMDA-Dumps\Process\x64\AppQ.exe_191119_083619.dmp]
User Mini Dump File with Full Memory: Only application data is available

Comment: '
*** procdump.exe  -ma 9700
*** Manual dump'

************* Path validation summary **************
Response                      Time (ms)      Location
Deferred                                     srv*
Symbol search path is: srv*
Executable search path is:
Windows 10 Version 18362 MP (2 procs) Free x64
Product: WinNt, suite: SingleUserTS Personal
Edition build lab: 18362.1.amd64fre.19h1_release.190318-1202
Machine Name:
Debug session time: Tue Nov 19 09:36:19.000 2019 (UTC + 1:00)
System Uptime: 0 days 0:41:24.571
Process Uptime: 0 days 0:03:26.000
............................
For analysis of this file, run !analyze -v
ntdll!NtWaitForSingleObject+0x14:
00007ff9`ff8dc144 c3              ret
```

4.   We now open a log file:

```
0:000> .logopen C:\AWMDA-Dumps\Process\x64\AppQ.log
Opened log file 'C:\AWMDA-Dumps\Process\x64\AppQ.log'
```

5.   The application process was reported hanging (frozen), and we now try the default analysis command for hangs:

```
0:000> !analyze -v -hang
***************************************************************************
*                                                                         *
*                         Exception Analysis                              *
*                                                                         *
***************************************************************************


KEY_VALUES_STRING: 1

    Key  : Analysis.CPU.mSec
    Value: 421

    Key  : Analysis.Elapsed.mSec
    Value: 1777

    Key  : Analysis.IO.Other.Mb
    Value: 0

    Key  : Analysis.IO.Read.Mb
    Value: 1

    Key  : Analysis.IO.Write.Mb
    Value: 0

    Key  : Analysis.Init.CPU.mSec
    Value: 218

    Key  : Analysis.Init.Elapsed.mSec
    Value: 1539066

    Key  : Analysis.Memory.CommitPeak.Mb
    Value: 94

    Key  : Failure.Bucket
    Value: APPLICATION_HANG_cfffffff_AppQ.exe!Unknown

    Key  : Failure.Hash
    Value: {245dfb12-f521-0b0e-492d-89dac4b89e14}

    Key  : Timeline.OS.Boot.DeltaSec
    Value: 2484

    Key  : Timeline.Process.Start.DeltaSec
    Value: 206

    Key  : WER.OS.Branch
    Value: 19h1_release

    Key  : WER.OS.Version
    Value: 10.0.18362.1

    Key  : WER.Process.Version
    Value: 2.0.0.1


FILE_IN_CAB:  AppQ.exe_191119_083619.dmp

COMMENT:
*** procdump.exe  -ma 9700
*** Manual dump

NTGLOBALFLAG:  400

PROCESS_BAM_CURRENT_THROTTLED: 0

PROCESS_BAM_PREVIOUS_THROTTLED: 0

APPLICATION_VERIFIER_FLAGS:  0

CONTEXT:  (.cxr;r)
.cxr;r
rax=0000000000000004 rbx=0000000000000000 rcx=0000000000000258
rdx=0000000000000000 rsi=0000000000000000 rdi=0000000000000258
rip=00007ff9ff8dc144 rsp=000000e60c3afa28 rbp=0000000000000000
 r8=000000e60c3afb00  r9=0000000000000000 r10=00000000000f05d8
r11=0000000000000200 r12=0000000000000111 r13=00000000000f05d8
r14=0000000000000258 r15=0000000000000000
iopl=0         nv up ei pl zr na po nc
cs=0033  ss=002b  ds=002b  es=002b  fs=0053  gs=002b             efl=00000246
ntdll!NtWaitForSingleObject+0x14:
00007ff9`ff8dc144 c3              ret

EXCEPTION_RECORD:  (.exr -1)
.exr -1
ExceptionAddress: 0000000000000000
   ExceptionCode: 80000003 (Break instruction exception)
  ExceptionFlags: 00000000
NumberParameters: 0

FAULTING_THREAD:  000008ac

PROCESS_NAME:  AppQ.exe
```

```
WATSON_BKT_EVENT:  AppHang

BLOCKING_THREAD:  00000000000008ac

ERROR_CODE: (NTSTATUS) 0xcfffffff - <Unable to get error code text>

EXCEPTION_CODE_STR:  cfffffff

DERIVED_WAIT_CHAIN:

Dl Eid Cid     WaitType
-- --- ------- -------------------------
   0  25e4.8ac (null)

WAIT_CHAIN_COMMAND:  ~0s;k;;

STACK_TEXT:
000000e6`0c3afa28 00007ff9`fc8b8ba3 : 00000000`00000000 00000000`000000a1 0000d2ab`9e7d656d 00000000`00000001 : ntdll!NtWaitForSingleObject+0x14
000000e6`0c3afa30 00007ff7`afd414ee : 00000000`00000001 00007ff9`fdf06274 00007ff9`00000000 00000000`00000258 : KERNELBASE!WaitForSingleObjectEx+0x93
000000e6`0c3afad0 00007ff7`afd41338 : 00000000`00000001 00000000`00000000 00000000`80006010 00000000`000000a1 : AppQ+0x14ee
000000e6`0c3afb20 00007ff9`fdf063ed : 00000000`000f05d8 00000000`00000111 00000000`00008003 00000000`00000000 : AppQ+0x1338
000000e6`0c3afbe0 00007ff9`fdf05de2 : 0000023d`62b0ee00 00007ff7`afd412a0 00000000`000f05d8 000000e6`0c3afe18 : user32!UserCallWinProcCheckWow+0x2bd
000000e6`0c3afd70 00007ff7`afd410df : 00007ff7`afd412a0 00000000`00000001 00000000`00000000 00000000`00000000 : user32!DispatchMessageWorker+0x1e2
000000e6`0c3afdf0 00007ff7`afd418ce : 00007ff7`afd40000 00000000`00000000 0000023d`625722cc 00000000`00000001 : AppQ+0x10df
000000e6`0c3afe60 00007ff9`fdc57bd4 : 00000000`00000000 00000000`00000000 00000000`00000000 00000000`00000000 : AppQ+0x18ce
000000e6`0c3afea0 00007ff9`ff8aced1 : 00000000`00000000 00000000`00000000 00000000`00000000 00000000`00000000 : kernel32!BaseThreadInitThunk+0x14
000000e6`0c3afed0 00000000`00000000 : 00000000`00000000 00000000`00000000 00000000`00000000 00000000`00000000 : ntdll!RtlUserThreadStart+0x21

STACK_COMMAND:  ~0s ; .cxr ; kb

SYMBOL_NAME:  appq+14ee

MODULE_NAME: AppQ

IMAGE_NAME:  AppQ.exe

FAILURE_BUCKET_ID:  APPLICATION_HANG_cfffffff_AppQ.exe!Unknown

OS_VERSION:  10.0.18362.1

BUILDLAB_STR:  19h1_release

OSPLATFORM_TYPE:  x64

OSNAME:  Windows 10

IMAGE_VERSION:  2.0.0.1

FAILURE_ID_HASH:  {245dfb12-f521-0b0e-492d-89dac4b89e14}

Followup:     MachineOwner
---------
```

Note: We see that WinDbg wasn't able to identify a wait chain like it was done in the previous exercise P17.

6.   Let's list stack traces for all threads:

```
0:000> ~*k

.  0  Id: 25e4.8ac Suspend: 0 Teb: 000000e6`0c44a000 Unfrozen
 # Child-SP          RetAddr           Call Site
00 000000e6`0c3afa28 00007ff9`fc8b8ba3 ntdll!NtWaitForSingleObject+0x14
01 000000e6`0c3afa30 00007ff7`afd414ee KERNELBASE!WaitForSingleObjectEx+0x93
02 000000e6`0c3afad0 00007ff7`afd41338 AppQ+0x14ee
03 000000e6`0c3afb20 00007ff9`fdf063ed AppQ+0x1338
04 000000e6`0c3afbe0 00007ff9`fdf05de2 user32!UserCallWinProcCheckWow+0x2bd
05 000000e6`0c3afd70 00007ff7`afd410df user32!DispatchMessageWorker+0x1e2
06 000000e6`0c3afdf0 00007ff7`afd418ce AppQ+0x10df
07 000000e6`0c3afe60 00007ff9`fdc57bd4 AppQ+0x18ce
08 000000e6`0c3afea0 00007ff9`ff8aced1 kernel32!BaseThreadInitThunk+0x14
09 000000e6`0c3afed0 00000000`00000000 ntdll!RtlUserThreadStart+0x21

   1  Id: 25e4.25f8 Suspend: 0 Teb: 000000e6`0c450000 Unfrozen
 # Child-SP          RetAddr           Call Site
00 000000e6`0c8ff968 00007ff9`fc8b8ba3 ntdll!NtWaitForSingleObject+0x14
01 000000e6`0c8ff970 00007ff7`afd41543 KERNELBASE!WaitForSingleObjectEx+0x93
02 000000e6`0c8ffa10 00007ff9`fdc57bd4 AppQ+0x1543
03 000000e6`0c8ffa60 00007ff9`ff8aced1 kernel32!BaseThreadInitThunk+0x14
04 000000e6`0c8ffa90 00000000`00000000 ntdll!RtlUserThreadStart+0x21
```

```
   2  Id: 25e4.25e0 Suspend: 0 Teb: 000000e6`0c452000 Unfrozen
 # Child-SP          RetAddr           Call Site
00 000000e6`0c9ffaf8 00007ff9`fc8d7ff7 ntdll!NtWaitForMultipleObjects+0x14
01 000000e6`0c9ffb00 00007ff9`fc8d7ede KERNELBASE!WaitForMultipleObjectsEx+0x107
02 000000e6`0c9ffe00 00007ff7`afd41634 KERNELBASE!WaitForMultipleObjects+0xe
03 000000e6`0c9ffe40 00007ff9`fdc57bd4 AppQ+0x1634
04 000000e6`0c9ffeb0 00007ff9`ff8aced1 kernel32!BaseThreadInitThunk+0x14
05 000000e6`0c9ffee0 00000000`00000000 ntdll!RtlUserThreadStart+0x21

   3  Id: 25e4.1180 Suspend: 0 Teb: 000000e6`0c458000 Unfrozen
 # Child-SP          RetAddr           Call Site
00 000000e6`0ccffda8 00007ff9`fc8b8ba3 ntdll!NtWaitForSingleObject+0x14
01 000000e6`0ccffdb0 00007ff7`afd416a9 KERNELBASE!WaitForSingleObjectEx+0x93
02 000000e6`0ccffe50 00007ff9`fdc57bd4 AppQ+0x16a9
03 000000e6`0ccffe80 00007ff9`ff8aced1 kernel32!BaseThreadInitThunk+0x14
04 000000e6`0ccffeb0 00000000`00000000 ntdll!RtlUserThreadStart+0x21

   4  Id: 25e4.26a8 Suspend: 0 Teb: 000000e6`0c45a000 Unfrozen
 # Child-SP          RetAddr           Call Site
00 000000e6`0caff7b8 00007ff9`ff874060 ntdll!NtWaitForWorkViaWorkerFactory+0x14
01 000000e6`0caff7c0 00007ff9`fdc57bd4 ntdll!TppWorkerThread+0x300
02 000000e6`0caffb80 00007ff9`ff8aced1 kernel32!BaseThreadInitThunk+0x14
03 000000e6`0caffbb0 00000000`00000000 ntdll!RtlUserThreadStart+0x21

   5  Id: 25e4.1c60 Suspend: 0 Teb: 000000e6`0c45c000 Unfrozen
 # Child-SP          RetAddr           Call Site
00 000000e6`0cbff4b8 00007ff9`ff874060 ntdll!NtWaitForWorkViaWorkerFactory+0x14
01 000000e6`0cbff4c0 00007ff9`fdc57bd4 ntdll!TppWorkerThread+0x300
02 000000e6`0cbff880 00007ff9`ff8aced1 kernel32!BaseThreadInitThunk+0x14
03 000000e6`0cbff8b0 00000000`00000000 ntdll!RtlUserThreadStart+0x21
```

Note: We see a couple of worker threads (#4, #5) that are usually added at runtime, the main thread or passive thread #0 that is blocked on waiting, and blocked waiting threads #1 - #3. We now try to untangle the waiting chain manually, and it may be easy since we already have hindsight from the previous exercise P17.

7.   We switch thread #2, which is waiting for multiple objects. Because it is impossible to guess or get the right parameters from x64 stack traces due to a different calling convention, we have to use disassembly:

```
0:000> ~2s
ntdll!NtWaitForMultipleObjects+0x14:
00007ff9`ff8dcc14 c3              ret
```

```
0:002> kb
 # RetAddr           : Args to Child                                                                              : Call Site
00 00007ff9`fc8d7ff7 : 00000000`00000000 00000000`00000000 00000000`00000000 00000000`00000000 : ntdll!NtWaitForMultipleObjects+0x14
01 00007ff9`fc8d7ede : 00000000`00000000 00000000`00000000 00000000`00000000 00000000`00000000 : KERNELBASE!WaitForMultipleObjectsEx+0x107
02 00007ff7`afd41634 : 00000000`00000000 00000000`00000000 00000000`00000000 00000000`00000000 : KERNELBASE!WaitForMultipleObjects+0xe
03 00007ff9`fdc57bd4 : 00000000`00000000 00000000`00000000 00000000`00000000 00000000`00000000 : AppQ+0x1634
04 00007ff9`ff8aced1 : 00000000`00000000 00000000`00000000 00000000`00000000 00000000`00000000 : kernel32!BaseThreadInitThunk+0x14
05 00000000`00000000 : 00000000`00000000 00000000`00000000 00000000`00000000 00000000`00000000 : ntdll!RtlUserThreadStart+0x21
```

```
0:002> ub 00007ff7`afd41634
AppQ+0x160a:
00007ff7`afd4160a b908000000      mov     ecx,8
00007ff7`afd4160f 486bc902        imul    rcx,rcx,2
00007ff7`afd41613 4889440c38      mov     qword ptr [rsp+rcx+38h],rax
00007ff7`afd41618 41b9ffffffff    mov     r9d,0FFFFFFFFh
00007ff7`afd4161e 41b801000000    mov     r8d,1
00007ff7`afd41624 488d542438      lea     rdx,[rsp+38h]
```

```
00007ff7`afd41629 b903000000        mov     ecx,3
00007ff7`afd4162e ff15cca90000      call    qword ptr [AppQ+0xc000 (00007ff7`afd4c000)]
```

Note: We see that all 4 parameters are quite nicely passed via 4 registers. We need to find the handle buffer address: RSP+0x38. We can take the value of RSP pointing to the return address, see what operation was done on RSP at the beginning of the function that includes AppQ+0x1634 address (the **uf** command, unassemble function) and add 0x38:

```
0:002> uf AppQ+0x1634
AppQ+0x1550:
00007ff7`afd41550 48894c2408          mov     qword ptr [rsp+8],rcx
00007ff7`afd41555 4883ec68            sub     rsp,68h
00007ff7`afd41559 488b05a83a0100      mov     rax,qword ptr [AppQ+0x15008 (00007ff7`afd55008)]
00007ff7`afd41560 4833c4              xor     rax,rsp
00007ff7`afd41563 4889442450          mov     qword ptr [rsp+50h],rax
00007ff7`afd41568 4533c9              xor     r9d,r9d
00007ff7`afd4156b 4533c0              xor     r8d,r8d
00007ff7`afd4156e 33d2                xor     edx,edx
00007ff7`afd41570 33c9                xor     ecx,ecx
00007ff7`afd41572 ff1598aa0000        call    qword ptr [AppQ+0xc010 (00007ff7`afd4c010)]
00007ff7`afd41578 4889442430          mov     qword ptr [rsp+30h],rax
00007ff7`afd4157d 48c744242800000000  mov     qword ptr [rsp+28h],0
00007ff7`afd41586 c744242000000000    mov     dword ptr [rsp+20h],0
00007ff7`afd4158e 4533c9              xor     r9d,r9d
00007ff7`afd41591 4c8d05b8000000      lea     r8,[AppQ+0x1650 (00007ff7`afd41650)]
00007ff7`afd41598 33d2                xor     edx,edx
00007ff7`afd4159a 33c9                xor     ecx,ecx
00007ff7`afd4159c ff157eaa0000        call    qword ptr [AppQ+0xc020 (00007ff7`afd4c020)]
00007ff7`afd415a2 b908000000          mov     ecx,8
00007ff7`afd415a7 486bc900            imul    rcx,rcx,0
00007ff7`afd415ab 4889440c38          mov     qword ptr [rsp+rcx+38h],rax
00007ff7`afd415b0 48c744242800000000  mov     qword ptr [rsp+28h],0
00007ff7`afd415b9 c744242000000000    mov     dword ptr [rsp+20h],0
00007ff7`afd415c1 4533c9              xor     r9d,r9d
00007ff7`afd415c4 4c8d05a5000000      lea     r8,[AppQ+0x1670 (00007ff7`afd41670)]
00007ff7`afd415cb 33d2                xor     edx,edx
00007ff7`afd415cd 33c9                xor     ecx,ecx
00007ff7`afd415cf ff154baa0000        call    qword ptr [AppQ+0xc020 (00007ff7`afd4c020)]
00007ff7`afd415d5 b908000000          mov     ecx,8
00007ff7`afd415da 486bc901            imul    rcx,rcx,1
00007ff7`afd415de 4889440c38          mov     qword ptr [rsp+rcx+38h],rax
00007ff7`afd415e3 48c744242800000000  mov     qword ptr [rsp+28h],0
00007ff7`afd415ec c744242000000000    mov     dword ptr [rsp+20h],0
00007ff7`afd415f4 4c8b4c2430          mov     r9,qword ptr [rsp+30h]
00007ff7`afd415f9 4c8d0590000000      lea     r8,[AppQ+0x1690 (00007ff7`afd41690)]
00007ff7`afd41600 33d2                xor     edx,edx
00007ff7`afd41602 33c9                xor     ecx,ecx
00007ff7`afd41604 ff1516aa0000        call    qword ptr [AppQ+0xc020 (00007ff7`afd4c020)]
00007ff7`afd4160a b908000000          mov     ecx,8
00007ff7`afd4160f 486bc902            imul    rcx,rcx,2
00007ff7`afd41613 4889440c38          mov     qword ptr [rsp+rcx+38h],rax
00007ff7`afd41618 41b9ffffffff        mov     r9d,0FFFFFFFFh
00007ff7`afd4161e 41b801000000        mov     r8d,1
00007ff7`afd41624 488d542438          lea     rdx,[rsp+38h]
00007ff7`afd41629 b903000000          mov     ecx,3
00007ff7`afd4162e ff15cca90000        call    qword ptr [AppQ+0xc000 (00007ff7`afd4c000)]
00007ff7`afd41634 488b4c2450          mov     rcx,qword ptr [rsp+50h]
00007ff7`afd41639 4833cc              xor     rcx,rsp
```

253

```
00007ff7`afd4163c e87f000000          call     AppQ+0x16c0 (00007ff7`afd416c0)
00007ff7`afd41641 4883c468          add      rsp,68h
00007ff7`afd41645 c3               ret
```

```
0:002> k
 # Child-SP          RetAddr           Call Site
00 000000e6`0c9ffaf8 00007ff9`fc8d7ff7 ntdll!NtWaitForMultipleObjects+0x14
01 000000e6`0c9ffb00 00007ff9`fc8d7ede KERNELBASE!WaitForMultipleObjectsEx+0x107
02 000000e6`0c9ffe00 00007ff7`afd41634 KERNELBASE!WaitForMultipleObjects+0xe
03 000000e6`0c9ffe40 00007ff9`fdc57bd4 AppQ+0x1634
04 000000e6`0c9ffeb0 00007ff9`ff8aced1 kernel32!BaseThreadInitThunk+0x14
05 000000e6`0c9ffee0 00000000`00000000 ntdll!RtlUserThreadStart+0x21
```

```
0:002> dps 000000e6`0c9ffe40
000000e6`0c9ffe40  00000000`00000000
000000e6`0c9ffe48  00000000`00000000
000000e6`0c9ffe50  00000000`00000000
000000e6`0c9ffe58  00000000`00000000
000000e6`0c9ffe60  00000000`00000000
000000e6`0c9ffe68  00000000`00000000
000000e6`0c9ffe70  00000000`00000254
000000e6`0c9ffe78  00000000`00000260
000000e6`0c9ffe80  00000000`00000264
000000e6`0c9ffe88  00000000`00000268
000000e6`0c9ffe90  00006356`1acef2c5
000000e6`0c9ffe98  00000000`00000000
000000e6`0c9ffea0  00000000`00000000
000000e6`0c9ffea8  00007ff9`fdc57bd4 kernel32!BaseThreadInitThunk+0x14
000000e6`0c9ffeb0  00000000`00000000
000000e6`0c9ffeb8  00000000`00000000
```

```
0:002> ? 000000e6`0c9ffea8  - 68 + 38
Evaluate expression: 988054290040 = 000000e6`0c9ffe78
```

```
0:002> dps 000000e6`0c9ffe78 L3
000000e6`0c9ffe78  00000000`00000260
000000e6`0c9ffe80  00000000`00000264
000000e6`0c9ffe88  00000000`00000268
```

8.   We now inspect handles 0x260, 0x264, 0x268 like we did in the previous exercise P17:

```
0:002> !handle 0x260 f
Handle 0000000000000260
  Type            Thread
  Attributes      0
  GrantedAccess   0x1fffff:
        Delete,ReadControl,WriteDac,WriteOwner,Synch
Terminate,Suspend,Alert,GetContext,SetContext,SetInfo,QueryInfo,SetToken,Impersonate,DirectImpe
rsonate
  HandleCount     2
  PointerCount    65538
  Name            <none>
  Object specific information
    Thread Id   25e4.25ac
    Priority    10
    Base Priority 0
```

254

```
0:002> !handle 0x264 f
Handle 0000000000000264
  Type            Thread
  Attributes      0
  GrantedAccess   0x1fffff:
        Delete,ReadControl,WriteDac,WriteOwner,Synch

Terminate,Suspend,Alert,GetContext,SetContext,SetInfo,QueryInfo,SetToken,Impersonate,DirectImpe
rsonate
  HandleCount     2
  PointerCount    65538
  Name            <none>
  Object specific information
    Thread Id    25e4.15c8
    Priority     10
    Base Priority 0

0:002> !handle 0x268 f
Handle 0000000000000268
  Type            Thread
  Attributes      0
  GrantedAccess   0x1fffff:
        Delete,ReadControl,WriteDac,WriteOwner,Synch

Terminate,Suspend,Alert,GetContext,SetContext,SetInfo,QueryInfo,SetToken,Impersonate,DirectImpe
rsonate
  HandleCount     3
  PointerCount    131066
  Name            <none>
  Object specific information
    Thread Id    25e4.1180
    Priority     10
    Base Priority 0

0:002> ~~[25ac]s
           ^ Illegal thread error in '~~[25ac]s'

0:002> ~~[15c8]s
           ^ Illegal thread error in '~~[15c8]s'

0:002> ~~[1180]s
ntdll!NtWaitForSingleObject+0x14:
00007ff9`ff8dc144 c3              ret

0:003> k
 # Child-SP          RetAddr           Call Site
00 000000e6`0ccffda8 00007ff9`fc8b8ba3 ntdll!NtWaitForSingleObject+0x14
01 000000e6`0ccffdb0 00007ff7`afd416a9 KERNELBASE!WaitForSingleObjectEx+0x93
02 000000e6`0ccffe50 00007ff9`fdc57bd4 AppQ+0x16a9
03 000000e6`0ccffe80 00007ff9`ff8aced1 kernel32!BaseThreadInitThunk+0x14
04 000000e6`0ccffeb0 00000000`00000000 ntdll!RtlUserThreadStart+0x21
```

9.   We found that one of the handles points to another thread waiting for another handle. Let's find out its value via disassembling again:

```
0:003> ub 00007ff7`afd416a9
AppQ+0x168d:
00007ff7`afd4168d cc              int     3
00007ff7`afd4168e cc              int     3
```

```
00007ff7`afd4168f cc                      int     3
00007ff7`afd41690 48894c2408              mov     qword ptr [rsp+8],rcx
00007ff7`afd41695 4883ec28                sub     rsp,28h
00007ff7`afd41699 baffffffff              mov     edx,0FFFFFFFFh
00007ff7`afd4169e 488b4c2430              mov     rcx,qword ptr [rsp+30h]
00007ff7`afd416a3 ff155fa90000            call    qword ptr [AppQ+0xc008 (00007ff7`afd4c008)]

0:003> uf AppQ+0x16a9
AppQ+0x1690:
00007ff7`afd41690 48894c2408              mov     qword ptr [rsp+8],rcx
00007ff7`afd41695 4883ec28                sub     rsp,28h
00007ff7`afd41699 baffffffff              mov     edx,0FFFFFFFFh
00007ff7`afd4169e 488b4c2430              mov     rcx,qword ptr [rsp+30h]
00007ff7`afd416a3 ff155fa90000            call    qword ptr [AppQ+0xc008 (00007ff7`afd4c008)]
00007ff7`afd416a9 4883c428                add     rsp,28h
00007ff7`afd416ad c3                      ret

0:003> dps 000000e6`0ccffe50
000000e6`0ccffe50  00000000`00000000
000000e6`0ccffe58  00000000`00000000
000000e6`0ccffe60  00000000`00000000
000000e6`0ccffe68  00000000`00000254
000000e6`0ccffe70  00000000`00000000
000000e6`0ccffe78  00007ff9`fdc57bd4 kernel32!BaseThreadInitThunk+0x14
000000e6`0ccffe80  00000000`00000254
000000e6`0ccffe88  00000000`00000000
000000e6`0ccffe90  00000000`00000000
000000e6`0ccffe98  00000000`00000000
000000e6`0ccffea0  00000000`00000000
000000e6`0ccffea8  00007ff9`ff8aced1 ntdll!RtlUserThreadStart+0x21
000000e6`0ccffeb0  00000000`00000000
000000e6`0ccffeb8  00000000`00000000
000000e6`0ccffec0  00000000`00000000
000000e6`0ccffec8  00000000`00000000

0:003> dps 000000e6`0ccffe78 - 28 + 30 L1
000000e6`0ccffe80  00000000`00000254
```

Note: You may have noticed the same handle value on the thread #2 raw stack above when we investigated multiple object wait. Perhaps it was simply stored there as a variable:

```
0:002> dps 000000e6`0c9ffe40
000000e6`0c9ffe40  00000000`00000000
000000e6`0c9ffe48  00000000`00000000
000000e6`0c9ffe50  00000000`00000000
000000e6`0c9ffe58  00000000`00000000
000000e6`0c9ffe60  00000000`00000000
000000e6`0c9ffe68  00000000`00000000
000000e6`0c9ffe70  00000000`00000254
000000e6`0c9ffe78  00000000`00000260
000000e6`0c9ffe80  00000000`00000264
000000e6`0c9ffe88  00000000`00000268
000000e6`0c9ffe90  00006356`1acef2c5
000000e6`0c9ffe98  00000000`00000000
000000e6`0c9ffea0  00000000`00000000
000000e6`0c9ffea8  00007ff9`fdc57bd4 kernel32!BaseThreadInitThunk+0x14
000000e6`0c9ffeb0  00000000`00000000
000000e6`0c9ffeb8  00000000`00000000
```

10.   One last note for this exercise. Often symbolic references such as function return addresses found on raw stack regions may be coincidental, just their addresses happening to be in proximity to some other function name. So we should always do a backward disassembly to see if we have a real call that resulted in the saved return address:

```
0:003> !teb
TEB at 000000e60c458000
    ExceptionList:         0000000000000000
    StackBase:             000000e60cd00000
    StackLimit:            000000e60ccff000
    SubSystemTib:          0000000000000000
    FiberData:             0000000000001e00
    ArbitraryUserPointer:  0000000000000000
    Self:                  000000e60c458000
    EnvironmentPointer:    0000000000000000
    ClientId:              00000000000025e4 . 0000000000001180
    RpcHandle:             0000000000000000
    Tls Storage:           0000023d625c9970
    PEB Address:           000000e60c449000
    LastErrorValue:        0
    LastStatusValue:       c000000d
    Count Owned Locks:     0
    HardErrorMode:         0

0:003> dps 000000e60ccff000 000000e60cd00000
000000e6`0ccff000  00000000`00000000
000000e6`0ccff008  00000000`00000000
000000e6`0ccff010  00000000`00000000
000000e6`0ccff018  00000000`00000000
[...]
000000e6`0ccff770  00000000`00000000
000000e6`0ccff778  00007ff9`ff000718 advapi32!AdvapiInitRoutines+0x8
000000e6`0ccff780  00000000`00000004
[...]

0:003> ub 00007ff9`ff000718
                           ^ Unable to find valid previous instruction for 'ub
00007ff9`ff000718'

0:003> u 00007ff9`ff000718
advapi32!AdvapiInitRoutines+0x8:
00007ff9`ff000718 0f0000          sldt    word ptr [rax]
00007ff9`ff00071b 0000            add     byte ptr [rax],al
00007ff9`ff00071d 0000            add     byte ptr [rax],al
00007ff9`ff00071f 0000            add     byte ptr [rax],al
00007ff9`ff000721 4efb            sti
00007ff9`ff000723 fe              ???
00007ff9`ff000724 f9              stc
00007ff9`ff000725 7f00            jg      advapi32!AdvapiInitRoutines+0x17 (00007ff9`ff000727)
```

Note: We see not only a difficulty in finding *call* instructions, but the forward code after the "return address" doesn't make sense and is even invalid.

11.   We close logging before exiting WinDbg:

```
0:003> .logclose
Closing open log file C:\AWMDA-Dumps\Process\x64\AppQ.log
```

257

Exercise P19

- **Goal:** Learn how to analyze process handle leaks

- **Patterns:** Active Space; Handle Leak

- \AWMDA-Dumps\Exercise-P19-Analysis-process-dump-AppT-64.pdf

Exercise P19: Analysis of an application process dump (AppT, 64-bit)

Goal: Learn how to analyze process handle leaks.

Patterns: Active Space; Handle Leak.

1.   Launch WinDbg.

2.   Open \AWMDA-Dumps\Process\x64\AppT.DMP

3.   We get the dump file loaded:

```
Microsoft (R) Windows Debugger Version 10.0.25877.1004 AMD64
Copyright (c) Microsoft Corporation. All rights reserved.


Loading Dump File [C:\AWMDA-Dumps\Process\x64\AppT.DMP]
User Mini Dump File with Full Memory: Only application data is available


************* Path validation summary **************
Response                        Time (ms)      Location
Deferred                                       srv*
Symbol search path is: srv*
Executable search path is:
Windows 10 Version 18362 MP (2 procs) Free x64
Product: WinNt, suite: SingleUserTS Personal
Edition build lab: 18362.1.amd64fre.19h1_release.190318-1202
Machine Name:
Debug session time: Sat Nov 23 15:30:46.000 2019 (UTC + 1:00)
System Uptime: 0 days 1:50:53.230
Process Uptime: 0 days 0:22:02.000
........
For analysis of this file, run !analyze -v
ntdll!NtWaitForSingleObject+0x14:
00007ff9`ff8dc144 c3              ret
```

4.   Open a log file using the **.logopen** command:

```
0:000> .logopen C:\AWMDA-Dumps\Process\x64\AppT.log
Opened log file 'C:\AWMDA-Dumps\Process\x64\AppT.log'
```

5.   It was reported that *AppT* consumed a very large number of handles:

```
Task Manager                                              —    □    ×
File  Options  View

Processes  Performance  App history  Start-up  Users  Details  Services

Name                    PID    Status      Username    CPU  Memory (ac...  Handles  U/
ApplicationFrameHos...  6120   Running     Training     00     2,780 K         537  Di
AppT.exe                1212   Running     Training     00    39,912 K     123,499  Di
backgroundTaskHost....  576    Suspended   Training     00         0 K         318  Di
backgroundTaskHost....  3436   Suspended   Training     00         0 K       1,224  Di
backgroundTaskHost....  1428   Suspended   Training     00         0 K         292  Di
browser_broker.exe      6332   Running     Training     00       408 K         137  Di
cmd.exe                 2292   Running     Training     00       176 K          75  Nc
conhost.exe             940    Running     Training     00       408 K         256  Nc
conhost.exe             8896   Running     Training     00     6,024 K         208  Di
csrss.exe               420    Running     SYSTEM       00       520 K         550  Nc
csrss.exe               500    Running     SYSTEM       00       556 K         500  Nc
ctfmon.exe              6884   Running     Training     00     4,024 K         442  Di
dllhost.exe             3696   Running     SYSTEM       00     1,228 K         259  Nc
dllhost.exe             3568   Running     Training     00       856 K         139  Di
dllhost.exe             6480   Running     Training     00     1,496 K         264  Di
dwm.exe                 368    Running     DWM-1        00    52,396 K       1,033  Di
explorer.exe            5088   Running     Training     02    36,888 K       2,962  Di
fontdrvhost.exe         768    Running     UMFD-0       00       244 K          32  Di
gflags.exe              3424   Running     Training     00       812 K         146  Nc
LocalBridge.exe         9336   Running     Training     00     8,224 K         483  Di
lsass.exe               584    Running     SYSTEM       00     4,016 K       1,428  Nc
Microsoft.Photos.exe    5660   Suspended   Training     00         0 K         810  Di
MicrosoftEdge.exe       1008   Suspended   Training     00         0 K         874  Di

<    Fewer details                                              End task
```

6.   Type the ~*k command to verify the correctness of all stack traces:

```
0:000> ~*k

.  0  Id: 4bc.2144 Suspend: 0 Teb: 00000086`b3785000 Unfrozen
 # Child-SP          RetAddr           Call Site
00 00000086`b35bfa18 00007ff9`f2911838 ntdll!NtWaitForSingleObject+0x14
01 00000086`b35bfa20 00007ff9`fc8b8ba3 verifier!AVrfpNtWaitForSingleObject+0x38
02 00000086`b35bfa50 00007ff9`f2911602 KERNELBASE!WaitForSingleObjectEx+0x93
03 00000086`b35bfaf0 00007ff9`f2911688 verifier!AVrfpWaitForSingleObjectExCommon+0x9a
04 00000086`b35bfb20 00007ff9`f2911602 verifier!AVrfpKernelbaseWaitForSingleObjectEx+0x18
05 00000086`b35bfb60 00007ff9`f2911665 verifier!AVrfpWaitForSingleObjectExCommon+0x9a
*** WARNING: Unable to verify checksum for AppT.exe
06 00000086`b35bfb90 00007ff6`098d496f verifier!AVrfpKernel32WaitForSingleObjectEx+0x25
07 00000086`b35bfbd0 00007ff6`098d17ef AppT+0x496f
08 00000086`b35bfc00 00007ff6`098d1abc AppT+0x17ef
09 00000086`b35bfc60 00007ff6`098d52d4 AppT+0x1abc
0a 00000086`b35bfce0 00007ff9`fdc57bd4 AppT+0x52d4
```

```
0b 00000086`b35bfd20 00007ff9`ff8aced1 kernel32!BaseThreadInitThunk+0x14
0c 00000086`b35bfd50 00000000`00000000 ntdll!RtlUserThreadStart+0x21


   1  Id: 4bc.131c Suspend: 0 Teb: 00000086`b3787000 Unfrozen
 # Child-SP          RetAddr               Call Site
00 00000086`b38ff538 00007ff9`fc8c6931 ntdll!NtDelayExecution+0x14
01 00000086`b38ff540 00007ff6`098d49f4 KERNELBASE!SleepEx+0xa1
02 00000086`b38ff5e0 00007ff6`098d25a5 AppT+0x49f4
03 00000086`b38ff630 00007ff6`098d207d AppT+0x25a5
04 00000086`b38ff690 00007ff6`098d1a53 AppT+0x207d
05 00000086`b38ff6d0 00007ff6`098d31c5 AppT+0x1a53
06 00000086`b38ff710 00007ff6`098d2f9b AppT+0x31c5
07 00000086`b38ff740 00007ff6`098d26f4 AppT+0x2f9b
08 00000086`b38ff770 00007ff6`098daeb8 AppT+0x26f4
09 00000086`b38ff7c0 00007ff9`f290e684 AppT+0xaeb8
0a 00000086`b38ff7f0 00007ff9`fdc57bd4 verifier!AVrfpStandardThreadFunction+0x44
0b 00000086`b38ff830 00007ff9`ff8aced1 kernel32!BaseThreadInitThunk+0x14
0c 00000086`b38ff860 00000000`00000000 ntdll!RtlUserThreadStart+0x21


   2  Id: 4bc.230c Suspend: 0 Teb: 00000086`b3789000 Unfrozen
 # Child-SP          RetAddr               Call Site
00 00000086`b39ffc08 00007ff9`fc8c6931 ntdll!NtDelayExecution+0x14
01 00000086`b39ffc10 00007ff6`098d49f4 KERNELBASE!SleepEx+0xa1
02 00000086`b39ffcb0 00007ff6`098d25a5 AppT+0x49f4
03 00000086`b39ffd00 00007ff6`098d207d AppT+0x25a5
04 00000086`b39ffd60 00007ff6`098d1a53 AppT+0x207d
05 00000086`b39ffda0 00007ff6`098d31c5 AppT+0x1a53
06 00000086`b39ffde0 00007ff6`098d2f9b AppT+0x31c5
07 00000086`b39ffe10 00007ff6`098d26f4 AppT+0x2f9b
08 00000086`b39ffe40 00007ff6`098daeb8 AppT+0x26f4
09 00000086`b39ffe90 00007ff9`f290e684 AppT+0xaeb8
0a 00000086`b39ffec0 00007ff9`fdc57bd4 verifier!AVrfpStandardThreadFunction+0x44
0b 00000086`b39fff00 00007ff9`ff8aced1 kernel32!BaseThreadInitThunk+0x14
0c 00000086`b39fff30 00000000`00000000 ntdll!RtlUserThreadStart+0x21


   3  Id: 4bc.c50 Suspend: 0 Teb: 00000086`b378b000 Unfrozen
 # Child-SP          RetAddr               Call Site
00 00000086`b3aff918 00007ff9`fc8c6931 ntdll!NtDelayExecution+0x14
01 00000086`b3aff920 00007ff6`098d49f4 KERNELBASE!SleepEx+0xa1
02 00000086`b3aff9c0 00007ff6`098d25a5 AppT+0x49f4
03 00000086`b3affa10 00007ff6`098d207d AppT+0x25a5
04 00000086`b3affa70 00007ff6`098d19a4 AppT+0x207d
05 00000086`b3affab0 00007ff6`098d19f9 AppT+0x19a4
06 00000086`b3affb70 00007ff6`098d1a09 AppT+0x19f9
07 00000086`b3affba0 00007ff6`098d31c5 AppT+0x1a09
08 00000086`b3affbe0 00007ff6`098d2f9b AppT+0x31c5
09 00000086`b3affc10 00007ff6`098d26f4 AppT+0x2f9b
0a 00000086`b3affc40 00007ff6`098daeb8 AppT+0x26f4
0b 00000086`b3affc90 00007ff9`f290e684 AppT+0xaeb8
0c 00000086`b3affcc0 00007ff9`fdc57bd4 verifier!AVrfpStandardThreadFunction+0x44
0d 00000086`b3affd00 00007ff9`ff8aced1 kernel32!BaseThreadInitThunk+0x14
0e 00000086`b3affd30 00000000`00000000 ntdll!RtlUserThreadStart+0x21
```

Note: We see that *AppT* was instrumented by the *Application Verifier*. It is also visible when we check *gflags*:

```
0:000> !gflag
Current NtGlobalFlag contents: 0x02000100
    vrf - Enable application verifier
    hpa - Place heap allocations at ends of pages
```

7.   Let's check CPU consumption:

```
0:000> !runaway f
User Mode Time
  Thread       Time
   3:c50       0 days 0:00:24.750
   0:2144      0 days 0:00:00.015
   2:230c      0 days 0:00:00.000
   1:131c      0 days 0:00:00.000
 Kernel Mode Time
  Thread       Time
   3:c50       0 days 0:09:31.640
   0:2144      0 days 0:00:00.015
   2:230c      0 days 0:00:00.000
   1:131c      0 days 0:00:00.000
 Elapsed Time
  Thread       Time
   0:2144      0 days 0:22:01.595
   1:131c      0 days 0:22:01.408
   2:230c      0 days 0:22:01.408
   3:c50       0 days 0:22:01.408
```

Note: We see thread #3 had accumulated almost 50% of the time since its creation. But it consumed much more in kernel space than in user space. Perhaps, this correlates with the handle leak we saw in the screenshot above.

8.   We check the handles:

```
0:000> !handle
Handle 0000000000000004
  Type            Event
Handle 0000000000000008
  Type            Key
Handle 000000000000000c
  Type            File
Handle 0000000000000010
  Type            File
Handle 0000000000000014
  Type            File
Handle 0000000000000018
  Type            Event
Handle 000000000000001c
  Type            Event
Handle 0000000000000020
  Type            WaitCompletionPacket
Handle 0000000000000024
  Type            IoCompletion
Handle 0000000000000028
  Type            TpWorkerFactory
Handle 000000000000002c
  Type            IRTimer
Handle 0000000000000030
  Type            WaitCompletionPacket
Handle 0000000000000034
  Type            IRTimer
Handle 0000000000000038
  Type            WaitCompletionPacket
Handle 000000000000003c
```

262

```
   Type
Handle 0000000000000040
   Type
Handle 0000000000000044
   Type
Handle 0000000000000048
   Type                Directory
Handle 000000000000004c
   Type                File
Handle 0000000000000050
   Type                Event
Handle 0000000000000054
   Type                Event
Handle 0000000000000058
   Type                File
Handle 000000000000005c
   Type                Semaphore
Handle 0000000000000060
   Type                Semaphore
Handle 0000000000000064
   Type                File
Handle 0000000000000068
   Type                File
Handle 000000000000006c
   Type                File
Handle 0000000000000070
   Type                File
Handle 0000000000000074
   Type                File
Handle 0000000000000078
   Type                File
Handle 000000000000007c
   Type                File
Handle 0000000000000080
   Type                File
Handle 0000000000000084
   Type                File
Handle 0000000000000088
   Type                File
Handle 000000000000008c
   Type                File
Handle 0000000000000090
   Type                Semaphore
Handle 0000000000000094
   Type                Semaphore
Handle 0000000000000098
   Type
Handle 000000000000009c
   Type                File
Handle 00000000000000a0
   Type                File
Handle 00000000000000a4
   Type                File
Handle 00000000000000a8
   Type                File
Handle 00000000000000ac
   Type                ALPC Port
Handle 00000000000000b0
   Type                File
Handle 00000000000000b4
```

```
    Type                File
Handle 00000000000000b8
    Type                File
Handle 00000000000000bc
    Type                File
Handle 00000000000000c0
    Type                File
Handle 00000000000000c4
    Type                File
Handle 00000000000000c8
    Type
Handle 00000000000000cc
    Type
Handle 00000000000000d0
    Type
Handle 00000000000000d4
    Type                File
Handle 00000000000000d8
    Type
Handle 00000000000000dc
    Type                File
Handle 00000000000000e0
    Type                File
Handle 00000000000000e4
    Type                IoCompletion
Handle 00000000000000e8
    Type                TpWorkerFactory
Handle 00000000000000ec
    Type                IRTimer
Handle 00000000000000f0
    Type                WaitCompletionPacket
Handle 00000000000000f4
    Type                IRTimer
Handle 00000000000000f8
    Type                WaitCompletionPacket
Handle 00000000000000fc
    Type                Key
Handle 0000000000000100
    Type                Thread
Handle 0000000000000104
    Type                Thread
Handle 0000000000000108
    Type                Thread
Handle 000000000000010c
    Type                File
Handle 0000000000000110
    Type                File
Handle 0000000000000114
    Type                File
Handle 0000000000000118
    Type                File
Handle 000000000000011c
    Type                File
Handle 0000000000000120
    Type                File
Handle 0000000000000124
    Type                File
Handle 0000000000000128
    Type                File
Handle 000000000000012c
```

```
         Type                File
Handle 0000000000000130
         Type                File
Handle 0000000000000134
         Type                File
Handle 0000000000000138
         Type                File
Handle 000000000000013c
         Type                File
Handle 0000000000000140
         Type                File
Handle 0000000000000144
         Type                File
Handle 0000000000000148
         Type                File
Handle 000000000000014c
         Type                File
Handle 0000000000000150
         Type                File
Handle 0000000000000154
         Type                File
Handle 0000000000000158
         Type                File
Handle 000000000000015c
         Type                File
Handle 0000000000000160
         Type                File
Handle 0000000000000164
         Type                File
Handle 0000000000000168
         Type                File
Handle 000000000000016c
         Type                File
Handle 0000000000000170
         Type                File
Handle 0000000000000174
         Type                File
Handle 0000000000000178
         Type                File
Handle 000000000000017c
         Type                File
Handle 0000000000000180
         Type                File
Handle 0000000000000184
         Type                File
Handle 0000000000000188
         Type                File
Handle 000000000000018c
         Type                File
Handle 0000000000000190
         Type                File
Handle 0000000000000194
         Type                File
Handle 0000000000000198
         Type                File
Handle 000000000000019c
         Type                File
Handle 00000000000001a0
         Type                File
Handle 00000000000001a4
```

```
     Type            File
Handle 00000000000001a8
     Type            File
Handle 00000000000001ac
     Type            File
Handle 00000000000001b0
     Type            File
Handle 00000000000001b4
     Type            File
Handle 00000000000001b8
     Type            File
Handle 00000000000001bc
     Type            File
Handle 00000000000001c0
     Type            File
Handle 00000000000001c4
     Type            File
Handle 00000000000001c8
     Type            File
Handle 00000000000001cc
     Type            File
Handle 00000000000001d0
     Type            File
Handle 00000000000001d4
     Type            File
Handle 00000000000001d8
     Type            File
Handle 00000000000001dc
     Type            File
Handle 00000000000001e0
     Type            File
Handle 00000000000001e4
     Type            File
Handle 00000000000001e8
     Type            File
Handle 00000000000001ec
     Type            File
Handle 00000000000001f0
     Type            File
[...]
Handle 00000000000790fc
     Type            File
Handle 0000000000079100
     Type            File
Handle 0000000000079104
     Type            File
Handle 0000000000079108
     Type            File
Handle 000000000007910c
     Type            File
Handle 0000000000079110
     Type            File
Handle 0000000000079114
     Type            File
Handle 0000000000079118
     Type            File
Handle 000000000007911c
     Type            File
Handle 0000000000079120
     Type            File
```

```
Handle 0000000000079124
    Type              File
Handle 0000000000079128
    Type              File
Handle 000000000007912c
    Type              File
Handle 0000000000079130
    Type              File
Handle 0000000000079134
    Type              File
Handle 0000000000079138
    Type              File
Handle 000000000007913c
    Type              File
123499 Handles
Type                  Count
None                  12
Event                 5
File                  123462
Directory             1
Semaphore             4
Key                   2
Thread                3
IoCompletion          2
TpWorkerFactory       2
ALPC Port             1
WaitCompletionPacket  5
```

Note: We see a very large number of file handles. To trace handle creation to modules and functions, we can enable Application Verifier in *gflags.exe*. It was already done before the process memory dump was saved:

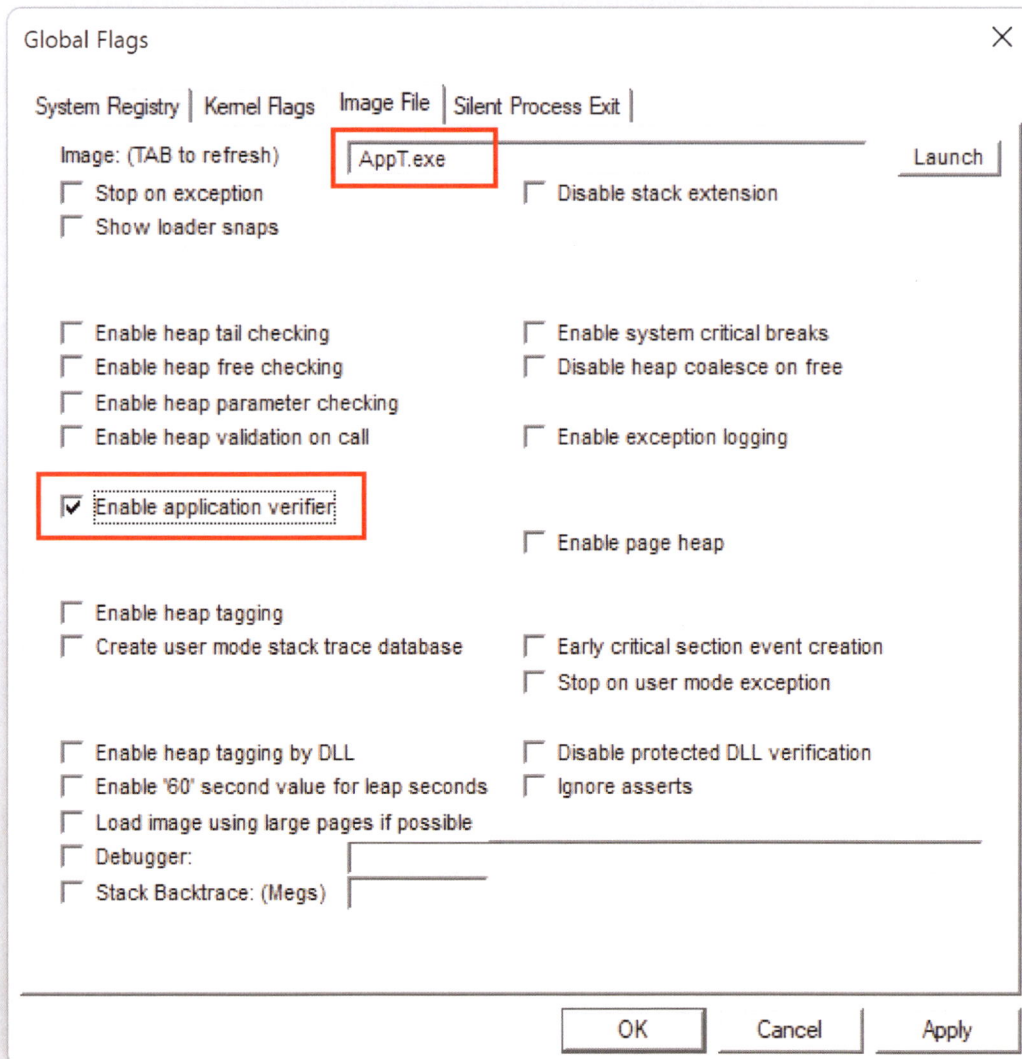

9.   The following command lists stack traces for handle creation (the output doesn't fit into the WinDbg command window, so we need to inspect the log file we opened at the beginning of this exercise):

```
0:000> !htrace
--------------------------------------
Handle = 0x000000000007913c - OPEN
Thread ID = 0x0000000000000c50, Process ID = 0x00000000000004bc

0x00007ff9ff8dcb64: ntdll!NtCreateFile+0x0000000000000014
0x00007ff9f290cacb: verifier!AVrfpNtCreateFile+0x00000000000000db
0x00007ff9fc8a45e4: KERNELBASE!CreateFileInternal+0x00000000000002f4
0x00007ff9fc8a42d6: KERNELBASE!CreateFileW+0x0000000000000066
0x00007ff9f290cf8a: verifier!AVrfpCreateFileWCommon+0x0000000000000142
0x00007ff9f290d09a: verifier!AVrfpKernelbaseCreateFileW+0x000000000000004a
0x00007ff9f290cf8a: verifier!AVrfpCreateFileWCommon+0x0000000000000142
0x00007ff9f290d038: verifier!AVrfpKernel32CreateFileW+0x0000000000000058
0x00007ff6098d2002: AppT+0x0000000000002002
0x00007ff6098d1f70: AppT+0x0000000000001f70
0x00007ff6098d1905: AppT+0x0000000000001905
0x00007ff6098d19f9: AppT+0x00000000000019f9
0x00007ff6098d1a09: AppT+0x0000000000001a09
--------------------------------------
```

```
Handle = 0x0000000000079138 - OPEN
Thread ID = 0x0000000000000c50, Process ID = 0x00000000000004bc

0x00007ff9ff8dcb64: ntdll!NtCreateFile+0x0000000000000014
0x00007ff9f290cacb: verifier!AVrfpNtCreateFile+0x00000000000000db
0x00007ff9fc8a45e4: KERNELBASE!CreateFileInternal+0x00000000000002f4
0x00007ff9fc8a42d6: KERNELBASE!CreateFileW+0x0000000000000066
0x00007ff9f290cf8a: verifier!AVrfpCreateFileWCommon+0x0000000000000142
0x00007ff9f290d09a: verifier!AVrfpKernelbaseCreateFileW+0x000000000000004a
0x00007ff9f290cf8a: verifier!AVrfpCreateFileWCommon+0x0000000000000142
0x00007ff9f290d038: verifier!AVrfpKernel32CreateFileW+0x0000000000000058
0x00007ff6098d2002: AppT+0x0000000000002002
0x00007ff6098d1f70: AppT+0x0000000000001f70
0x00007ff6098d1905: AppT+0x0000000000001905
0x00007ff6098d19f9: AppT+0x00000000000019f9
0x00007ff6098d1a09: AppT+0x0000000000001a09
-------------------------------------
Handle = 0x0000000000079134 - OPEN
Thread ID = 0x0000000000000c50, Process ID = 0x00000000000004bc

0x00007ff9ff8dcb64: ntdll!NtCreateFile+0x0000000000000014
0x00007ff9f290cacb: verifier!AVrfpNtCreateFile+0x00000000000000db
0x00007ff9fc8a45e4: KERNELBASE!CreateFileInternal+0x00000000000002f4
0x00007ff9fc8a42d6: KERNELBASE!CreateFileW+0x0000000000000066
0x00007ff9f290cf8a: verifier!AVrfpCreateFileWCommon+0x0000000000000142
0x00007ff9f290d09a: verifier!AVrfpKernelbaseCreateFileW+0x000000000000004a
0x00007ff9f290cf8a: verifier!AVrfpCreateFileWCommon+0x0000000000000142
0x00007ff9f290d038: verifier!AVrfpKernel32CreateFileW+0x0000000000000058
0x00007ff6098d2002: AppT+0x0000000000002002
0x00007ff6098d1f70: AppT+0x0000000000001f70
0x00007ff6098d1905: AppT+0x0000000000001905
0x00007ff6098d19f9: AppT+0x00000000000019f9
0x00007ff6098d1a09: AppT+0x0000000000001a09
-------------------------------------
[...]
Handle = 0x0000000000075108 - OPEN
Thread ID = 0x0000000000000c50, Process ID = 0x00000000000004bc

0x00007ff9ff8dcb64: ntdll!NtCreateFile+0x0000000000000014
0x00007ff9f290cacb: verifier!AVrfpNtCreateFile+0x00000000000000db
0x00007ff9fc8a45e4: KERNELBASE!CreateFileInternal+0x00000000000002f4
0x00007ff9fc8a42d6: KERNELBASE!CreateFileW+0x0000000000000066
0x00007ff9f290cf8a: verifier!AVrfpCreateFileWCommon+0x0000000000000142
0x00007ff9f290d09a: verifier!AVrfpKernelbaseCreateFileW+0x000000000000004a
0x00007ff9f290cf8a: verifier!AVrfpCreateFileWCommon+0x0000000000000142
0x00007ff9f290d038: verifier!AVrfpKernel32CreateFileW+0x0000000000000058
0x00007ff6098d2002: AppT+0x0000000000002002
0x00007ff6098d1f70: AppT+0x0000000000001f70
0x00007ff6098d1905: AppT+0x0000000000001905
0x00007ff6098d19f9: AppT+0x00000000000019f9
0x00007ff6098d1a09: AppT+0x0000000000001a09
-------------------------------------
Handle = 0x0000000000075104 - OPEN
Thread ID = 0x0000000000000c50, Process ID = 0x00000000000004bc

0x00007ff9ff8dcb64: ntdll!NtCreateFile+0x0000000000000014
0x00007ff9f290cacb: verifier!AVrfpNtCreateFile+0x00000000000000db
0x00007ff9fc8a45e4: KERNELBASE!CreateFileInternal+0x00000000000002f4
0x00007ff9fc8a42d6: KERNELBASE!CreateFileW+0x0000000000000066
0x00007ff9f290cf8a: verifier!AVrfpCreateFileWCommon+0x0000000000000142
```

```
0x00007ff9f290d09a: verifier!AVrfpKernelbaseCreateFileW+0x000000000000004a
0x00007ff9f290cf8a: verifier!AVrfpCreateFileWCommon+0x0000000000000142
0x00007ff9f290d038: verifier!AVrfpKernel32CreateFileW+0x0000000000000058
0x00007ff6098d2002: AppT+0x0000000000002002
0x00007ff6098d1f70: AppT+0x0000000000001f70
0x00007ff6098d1905: AppT+0x0000000000001905
0x00007ff6098d19f9: AppT+0x00000000000019f9
0x00007ff6098d1a09: AppT+0x0000000000001a09
--------------------------------------
Handle = 0x0000000000075100 - OPEN
Thread ID = 0x0000000000000c50, Process ID = 0x00000000000004bc

0x00007ff9ff8dcb64: ntdll!NtCreateFile+0x0000000000000014
0x00007ff9f290cacb: verifier!AVrfpNtCreateFile+0x00000000000000db
0x00007ff9fc8a45e4: KERNELBASE!CreateFileInternal+0x00000000000002f4
0x00007ff9fc8a42d6: KERNELBASE!CreateFileW+0x0000000000000066
0x00007ff9f290cf8a: verifier!AVrfpCreateFileWCommon+0x0000000000000142
0x00007ff9f290d09a: verifier!AVrfpKernelbaseCreateFileW+0x000000000000004a
0x00007ff9f290cf8a: verifier!AVrfpCreateFileWCommon+0x0000000000000142
0x00007ff9f290d038: verifier!AVrfpKernel32CreateFileW+0x0000000000000058
```

```
0x00007ff6098d2002: AppT+0x0000000000002002
0x00007ff6098d1f70: AppT+0x0000000000001f70
0x00007ff6098d1905: AppT+0x0000000000001905
0x00007ff6098d19f9: AppT+0x00000000000019f9
0x00007ff6098d1a09: AppT+0x0000000000001a09
```

```
--------------------------------------
Parsed 0x1000 stack traces.
Dumped 0x1000 stack traces.
```

10.   Let's now load application symbols:

```
0:000> .sympath+ C:\AWMDA-Dumps\Symbols
Symbol search path is: srv*;C:\AWMDA-Dumps\Symbols
Expanded Symbol search path is:
cache*;SRV*https://msdl.microsoft.com/download/symbols;c:\awmda-dumps\symbols

************* Path validation summary **************
Response                     Time (ms)     Location
Deferred                                   srv*
OK                                         C:\AWMDA-Dumps\Symbols

0:000> .reload
.......
```

11.   We check a stack trace to see if symbols were loaded correctly:

```
0:000> kL
# Child-SP          RetAddr           Call Site
00 00000086`b35bfa18 00007ff9`f2911838 ntdll!NtWaitForSingleObject+0x14
01 00000086`b35bfa20 00007ff9`fc8b8ba3 verifier!AVrfpNtWaitForSingleObject+0x38
02 00000086`b35bfa50 00007ff9`f2911602 KERNELBASE!WaitForSingleObjectEx+0x93
03 00000086`b35bfaf0 00007ff9`f2911688 verifier!AVrfpWaitForSingleObjectExCommon+0x9a
04 00000086`b35bfb20 00007ff9`f2911602 verifier!AVrfpKernelbaseWaitForSingleObjectEx+0x18
05 00000086`b35bfb60 00007ff9`f2911665 verifier!AVrfpWaitForSingleObjectExCommon+0x9a
*** WARNING: Unable to verify checksum for AppT.exe
06 00000086`b35bfb90 00007ff6`098d496f verifier!AVrfpKernel32WaitForSingleObjectEx+0x25
07 00000086`b35bfbd0 00007ff6`098d17ef AppT!_Thrd_join+0x1f
08 00000086`b35bfc00 00007ff6`098d1abc AppT!std::thread::join+0x5f
```

```
09 00000086`b35bfc60 00007ff6`098d52d4 AppT!wmain+0x5c
0a (Inline Function) --------`-------- AppT!invoke_main+0x22
0b 00000086`b35bfce0 00007ff9`fdc57bd4 AppT!__scrt_common_main_seh+0x10c
0c 00000086`b35bfd20 00007ff9`ff8aced1 kernel32!BaseThreadInitThunk+0x14
0d 00000086`b35bfd50 00000000`00000000 ntdll!RtlUserThreadStart+0x21
```

12.   Now we repeat the previous the **!htrace** command:

```
0:000> !htrace
---------------------------------------
Handle = 0x000000000007913c - OPEN
Thread ID = 0x0000000000000c50, Process ID = 0x00000000000004bc

0x00007ff9ff8dcb64: ntdll!NtCreateFile+0x0000000000000014
0x00007ff9f290cacb: verifier!AVrfpNtCreateFile+0x00000000000000db
0x00007ff9fc8a45e4: KERNELBASE!CreateFileInternal+0x00000000000002f4
0x00007ff9fc8a42d6: KERNELBASE!CreateFileW+0x0000000000000066
0x00007ff9f290cf8a: verifier!AVrfpCreateFileWCommon+0x0000000000000142
0x00007ff9f290d09a: verifier!AVrfpKernelbaseCreateFileW+0x000000000000004a
0x00007ff9f290cf8a: verifier!AVrfpCreateFileWCommon+0x0000000000000142
0x00007ff9f290d038: verifier!AVrfpKernel32CreateFileW+0x0000000000000058
0x00007ff6098d2002: AppT!<lambda_c052d1644f2ebc862a362f9ae27dd1b1>::operator()<void *>+0x0000000000000062
0x00007ff6098d1f70: AppT!std::for_each<std::_Vector_iterator<std::_Vector_val<std::_Simple_types<void *>
> >,<lambda_c052d1644f2ebc862a362f9ae27dd1b1> >+0x0000000000000070
0x00007ff6098d1905: AppT!bar+0x00000000000000d5
0x00007ff6098d19f9: AppT!foo+0x0000000000000009
0x00007ff6098d1a09: AppT!thread_one+0x0000000000000009
---------------------------------------
Handle = 0x0000000000079138 - OPEN
Thread ID = 0x0000000000000c50, Process ID = 0x00000000000004bc

0x00007ff9ff8dcb64: ntdll!NtCreateFile+0x0000000000000014
0x00007ff9f290cacb: verifier!AVrfpNtCreateFile+0x00000000000000db
0x00007ff9fc8a45e4: KERNELBASE!CreateFileInternal+0x00000000000002f4
0x00007ff9fc8a42d6: KERNELBASE!CreateFileW+0x0000000000000066
0x00007ff9f290cf8a: verifier!AVrfpCreateFileWCommon+0x0000000000000142
0x00007ff9f290d09a: verifier!AVrfpKernelbaseCreateFileW+0x000000000000004a
0x00007ff9f290cf8a: verifier!AVrfpCreateFileWCommon+0x0000000000000142
0x00007ff9f290d038: verifier!AVrfpKernel32CreateFileW+0x0000000000000058
0x00007ff6098d2002: AppT!<lambda_c052d1644f2ebc862a362f9ae27dd1b1>::operator()<void *>+0x0000000000000062
0x00007ff6098d1f70: AppT!std::for_each<std::_Vector_iterator<std::_Vector_val<std::_Simple_types<void *>
> >,<lambda_c052d1644f2ebc862a362f9ae27dd1b1> >+0x0000000000000070
0x00007ff6098d1905: AppT!bar+0x00000000000000d5
0x00007ff6098d19f9: AppT!foo+0x0000000000000009
0x00007ff6098d1a09: AppT!thread_one+0x0000000000000009
---------------------------------------
Handle = 0x0000000000079134 - OPEN
Thread ID = 0x0000000000000c50, Process ID = 0x00000000000004bc

0x00007ff9ff8dcb64: ntdll!NtCreateFile+0x0000000000000014
0x00007ff9f290cacb: verifier!AVrfpNtCreateFile+0x00000000000000db
0x00007ff9fc8a45e4: KERNELBASE!CreateFileInternal+0x00000000000002f4
0x00007ff9fc8a42d6: KERNELBASE!CreateFileW+0x0000000000000066
0x00007ff9f290cf8a: verifier!AVrfpCreateFileWCommon+0x0000000000000142
0x00007ff9f290d09a: verifier!AVrfpKernelbaseCreateFileW+0x000000000000004a
0x00007ff9f290cf8a: verifier!AVrfpCreateFileWCommon+0x0000000000000142
0x00007ff9f290d038: verifier!AVrfpKernel32CreateFileW+0x0000000000000058
0x00007ff6098d2002: AppT!<lambda_c052d1644f2ebc862a362f9ae27dd1b1>::operator()<void *>+0x0000000000000062
0x00007ff6098d1f70: AppT!std::for_each<std::_Vector_iterator<std::_Vector_val<std::_Simple_types<void *>
> >,<lambda_c052d1644f2ebc862a362f9ae27dd1b1> >+0x0000000000000070
0x00007ff6098d1905: AppT!bar+0x00000000000000d5
0x00007ff6098d19f9: AppT!foo+0x0000000000000009
0x00007ff6098d1a09: AppT!thread_one+0x0000000000000009
---------------------------------------
[...]
```

```
Handle = 0x0000000000075108 - OPEN
Thread ID = 0x0000000000000c50, Process ID = 0x00000000000004bc

0x00007ff9ff8dcb64: ntdll!NtCreateFile+0x0000000000000014
0x00007ff9f290cacb: verifier!AVrfpNtCreateFile+0x00000000000000db
0x00007ff9fc8a45e4: KERNELBASE!CreateFileInternal+0x00000000000002f4
0x00007ff9fc8a42d6: KERNELBASE!CreateFileW+0x0000000000000066
0x00007ff9f290cf8a: verifier!AVrfpCreateFileWCommon+0x0000000000000142
0x00007ff9f290d09a: verifier!AVrfpKernelbaseCreateFileW+0x000000000000004a
0x00007ff9f290cf8a: verifier!AVrfpCreateFileWCommon+0x0000000000000142
0x00007ff9f290d038: verifier!AVrfpKernel32CreateFileW+0x0000000000000058
0x00007ff6098d2002: AppT!<lambda_c052d1644f2ebc862a362f9ae27dd1b1>::operator()<void *>+0x0000000000000062
0x00007ff6098d1f70: AppT!std::for_each<std::_Vector_iterator<std::_Vector_val<std::_Simple_types<void *>
> >,<lambda_c052d1644f2ebc862a362f9ae27dd1b1> >+0x0000000000000070
0x00007ff6098d1905: AppT!bar+0x00000000000000d5
0x00007ff6098d19f9: AppT!foo+0x0000000000000009
0x00007ff6098d1a09: AppT!thread_one+0x0000000000000009
--------------------------------------
Handle = 0x0000000000075104 - OPEN
Thread ID = 0x0000000000000c50, Process ID = 0x00000000000004bc

0x00007ff9ff8dcb64: ntdll!NtCreateFile+0x0000000000000014
0x00007ff9f290cacb: verifier!AVrfpNtCreateFile+0x00000000000000db
0x00007ff9fc8a45e4: KERNELBASE!CreateFileInternal+0x00000000000002f4
0x00007ff9fc8a42d6: KERNELBASE!CreateFileW+0x0000000000000066
0x00007ff9f290cf8a: verifier!AVrfpCreateFileWCommon+0x0000000000000142
0x00007ff9f290d09a: verifier!AVrfpKernelbaseCreateFileW+0x000000000000004a
0x00007ff9f290cf8a: verifier!AVrfpCreateFileWCommon+0x0000000000000142
0x00007ff9f290d038: verifier!AVrfpKernel32CreateFileW+0x0000000000000058
0x00007ff6098d2002: AppT!<lambda_c052d1644f2ebc862a362f9ae27dd1b1>::operator()<void *>+0x0000000000000062
0x00007ff6098d1f70: AppT!std::for_each<std::_Vector_iterator<std::_Vector_val<std::_Simple_types<void *>
> >,<lambda_c052d1644f2ebc862a362f9ae27dd1b1> >+0x0000000000000070
0x00007ff6098d1905: AppT!bar+0x00000000000000d5
0x00007ff6098d19f9: AppT!foo+0x0000000000000009
0x00007ff6098d1a09: AppT!thread_one+0x0000000000000009
--------------------------------------
Handle = 0x0000000000075100 - OPEN
Thread ID = 0x0000000000000c50, Process ID = 0x00000000000004bc

0x00007ff9ff8dcb64: ntdll!NtCreateFile+0x0000000000000014
0x00007ff9f290cacb: verifier!AVrfpNtCreateFile+0x00000000000000db
0x00007ff9fc8a45e4: KERNELBASE!CreateFileInternal+0x00000000000002f4
0x00007ff9fc8a42d6: KERNELBASE!CreateFileW+0x0000000000000066
0x00007ff9f290cf8a: verifier!AVrfpCreateFileWCommon+0x0000000000000142
0x00007ff9f290d09a: verifier!AVrfpKernelbaseCreateFileW+0x000000000000004a
0x00007ff9f290cf8a: verifier!AVrfpCreateFileWCommon+0x0000000000000142
0x00007ff9f290d038: verifier!AVrfpKernel32CreateFileW+0x0000000000000058
0x00007ff6098d2002: AppT!<lambda_c052d1644f2ebc862a362f9ae27dd1b1>::operator()<void *>+0x0000000000000062
0x00007ff6098d1f70: AppT!std::for_each<std::_Vector_iterator<std::_Vector_val<std::_Simple_types<void *>
> >,<lambda_c052d1644f2ebc862a362f9ae27dd1b1> >+0x0000000000000070
0x00007ff6098d1905: AppT!bar+0x00000000000000d5
0x00007ff6098d19f9: AppT!foo+0x0000000000000009
0x00007ff6098d1a09: AppT!thread_one+0x0000000000000009

--------------------------------------
Parsed 0x1000 stack traces.
Dumped 0x1000 stack traces.
```

Note: Now, we see *AppT* stack traces creating the file handles.

13.   We close logging before exiting WinDbg:

```
0:000> .logclose
Closing open log file C:\AWMDA-Dumps\Process\x64\AppT.log
```

Exercise P20

- **Goal:** Learn how to analyze service memory dumps

- **Patterns:** Input Thread; Blocking Module

- \AWMDA-Dumps\Exercise-P20-Analysis-process-dump-ServiceA-64.pdf

Exercise P20: Analysis of a service process dump (ServiceA, 64-bit)

Goal: Learn how to analyze service memory dumps.

Patterns: Input Thread; Blocking Module.

1.   Launch WinDbg.

2.   Open \AWMDA-Dumps\Process\x64\ServiceA.DMP

3.   We get the dump file loaded:

```
Microsoft (R) Windows Debugger Version 10.0.25877.1004 AMD64
Copyright (c) Microsoft Corporation. All rights reserved.


Loading Dump File [C:\AWMDA-Dumps\Process\x64\ServiceA.DMP]
User Mini Dump File with Full Memory: Only application data is available


************* Path validation summary **************
Response                        Time (ms)     Location
Deferred                                      srv*
Symbol search path is: srv*
Executable search path is:
Windows 10 Version 22000 MP (2 procs) Free x64
Product: WinNt, suite: SingleUserTS Personal
Edition build lab: 22000.1.amd64fre.co_release.210604-1628
Machine Name:
Debug session time: Tue May 10 00:41:02.000 2022 (UTC + 1:00)
System Uptime: 0 days 0:50:13.113
Process Uptime: 0 days 0:01:58.000
...............
For analysis of this file, run !analyze -v
ntdll!NtWaitForSingleObject+0x14:
00007ffe`715237d4 c3              ret
```

4.   Open a log file using the **.logopen** command:

```
0:000> .logopen C:\AWMDA-Dumps\Process\x64\ServiceA.log
Opened log file 'C:\AWMDA-Dumps\Process\x64\ServiceA.log'
```

5.   Since it was reported that several client applications were not able to communicate with the *ServiceA* process, we look at its stack traces:

```
0:000> ~*kL

.  0  Id: 1910.2340 Suspend: 0 Teb: 0000003e`b2957000 Unfrozen
 # Child-SP          RetAddr               Call Site
00 0000003e`b278f758 00007ffe`6ee22a4e     ntdll!NtWaitForSingleObject+0x14
01 0000003e`b278f760 00007ffe`700b44a1     KERNELBASE!WaitForSingleObjectEx+0x8e
02 0000003e`b278f800 00007ffe`700b3d5b     sechost!ScSendResponseReceiveControls+0x149
03 0000003e`b278f940 00007ffe`700b3760     sechost!ScDispatcherLoop+0x14b
04 0000003e`b278fa80 00007ff6`9ef21042     sechost!StartServiceCtrlDispatcherW+0x70
05 0000003e`b278fab0 00007ff6`9ef2160a     ServiceA!wWinMain+0x42
```

```
06 (Inline Function) --------`--------       ServiceA!invoke_main+0x21
07 0000003e`b278fb10 00007ffe`6f3d54e0       ServiceA!__scrt_common_main_seh+0x106
08 0000003e`b278fb50 00007ffe`7148485b       kernel32!BaseThreadInitThunk+0x10
09 0000003e`b278fb80 00000000`00000000       ntdll!RtlUserThreadStart+0x2b

   1  Id: 1910.1648 Suspend: 0 Teb: 0000003e`b295d000 Unfrozen
 # Child-SP          RetAddr               Call Site
00 0000003e`b2cff988 00007ffe`6ee22a4e       ntdll!NtWaitForSingleObject+0x14
01 0000003e`b2cff990 00007ff6`9ef21227       KERNELBASE!WaitForSingleObjectEx+0x8e
02 0000003e`b2cffa30 00007ffe`700c9e12       ServiceA!ServiceMain+0x1c7
03 0000003e`b2cffac0 00007ffe`6f3d54e0       sechost!ScSvcctrlThreadW+0x32
04 0000003e`b2cffaf0 00007ffe`7148485b       kernel32!BaseThreadInitThunk+0x10
05 0000003e`b2cffb20 00000000`00000000       ntdll!RtlUserThreadStart+0x2b

   2  Id: 1910.2464 Suspend: 0 Teb: 0000003e`b295f000 Unfrozen
 # Child-SP          RetAddr               Call Site
00 0000003e`b2dff368 00007ffe`702164cc       win32u!NtUserWaitMessage+0x14
01 0000003e`b2dff370 00007ffe`7023924b       user32!DialogBox2+0x254
02 0000003e`b2dff410 00007ffe`7025d346       user32!InternalDialogBox+0x14b
03 0000003e`b2dff470 00007ffe`7025bc91       user32!SoftModalMessageBox+0x836
04 0000003e`b2dff5b0 00007ffe`7025ca78       user32!MessageBoxWorker+0x341
05 0000003e`b2dff760 00007ffe`7025cafe       user32!MessageBoxTimeoutW+0x198
06 0000003e`b2dff860 00007ff6`9ef213db       user32!MessageBoxW+0x4e
07 0000003e`b2dff8a0 00007ffe`6f3d54e0       ServiceA!ThreadProcA+0x2b
08 0000003e`b2dff8d0 00007ffe`7148485b       kernel32!BaseThreadInitThunk+0x10
09 0000003e`b2dff900 00000000`00000000       ntdll!RtlUserThreadStart+0x2b
```

Note: We immediately spot a thread waiting for user input blocking the session 0 process since it is not interacting with a desktop.

6.   We close logging before exiting WinDbg:

```
0:000> .logclose
Closing open log file C:\AWMDA-Dumps\Process\x64\ServiceA.log
```

Exercise P21

- **Goal:** Learn how to analyze memory dumps from Rust processes

- **Patterns:** Language-Specific Subtrace (Rust)

- \AWMDA-Dumps\Exercise-P21-Analysis-process-dump-rusty.pdf

Exercise P21: Analysis of a Rust process dump (Rusty, 64-bit)

Goal: Learn how to analyze memory dumps from Rust processes.

Patterns: Language-Specific Subtrace (Rust).

1.   Launch WinDbg.

2.   Open \AWMDA-Dumps\Process\x64\rusty.DMP

3.   We get the dump file loaded:

```
Microsoft (R) Windows Debugger Version 10.0.25877.1004 AMD64
Copyright (c) Microsoft Corporation. All rights reserved.


Loading Dump File [C:\AWMDA-Dumps\Process\x64\rusty.DMP]
User Mini Dump File with Full Memory: Only application data is available


************* Path validation summary **************
Response                      Time (ms)     Location
Deferred                                    srv*
Symbol search path is: srv*
Executable search path is:
Windows 10 Version 22000 MP (2 procs) Free x64
Product: WinNt, suite: SingleUserTS Personal
Edition build lab: 22000.1.amd64fre.co_release.210604-1628
Debug session time: Wed Jul 26 22:09:35.000 2023 (UTC + 1:00)
System Uptime: 0 days 0:30:23.442
Process Uptime: 0 days 0:00:17.000
.....................
For analysis of this file, run !analyze -v
win32u!NtUserWaitMessage+0x14:
00007ffd`48df14d4 c3              ret
```

4.   Open a log file using the **.logopen** command:

```
0:000> .logopen C:\AWMDA-Dumps\Process\x64\rusty.log
Opened log file 'C:\AWMDA-Dumps\Process\x64\rusty.log'
```

5.   Let's check stack traces:

```
0:000> ~*kL

.  0  Id: 2320.1a70 Suspend: 0 Teb: 00000029`a7924000 Unfrozen
 # Child-SP          RetAddr               Call Site
00 00000029`a77df558 00007ffd`4a7e64cc     win32u!NtUserWaitMessage+0x14
01 00000029`a77df560 00007ffd`4a80924b     user32!DialogBox2+0x254
02 00000029`a77df600 00007ffd`4a82d346     user32!InternalDialogBox+0x14b
03 00000029`a77df660 00007ffd`4a82bc91     user32!SoftModalMessageBox+0x836
04 00000029`a77df7a0 00007ffd`4a82ca78     user32!MessageBoxWorker+0x341
05 00000029`a77df950 00007ffd`4a82cafe     user32!MessageBoxTimeoutW+0x198
06 00000029`a77dfa50 00007ff6`e2211117     user32!MessageBoxW+0x4e
07 00000029`a77dfa90 00007ff6`e22110c9     rusty+0x1117
```

```
08 00000029`a77dfad0 00007ff6`e2211129      rusty+0x10c9
09 00000029`a77dfb00 00007ff6`e22111c6      rusty+0x1129
0a 00000029`a77dfb30 00007ff6`e2211017      rusty+0x11c6
0b 00000029`a77dfb60 00007ff6`e221118c      rusty+0x1017
0c 00000029`a77dfba0 00007ff6`e22167ab      rusty+0x118c
0d 00000029`a77dfbd0 00007ff6`e2211170      rusty+0x67ab
0e 00000029`a77dfc60 00007ff6`e2211146      rusty+0x1170
0f 00000029`a77dfca0 00007ff6`e22282d4      rusty+0x1146
10 00000029`a77dfcd0 00007ffd`4a2654e0      rusty+0x182d4
11 00000029`a77dfd10 00007ffd`4af8485b      kernel32!BaseThreadInitThunk+0x10
12 00000029`a77dfd40 00000000`00000000      ntdll!RtlUserThreadStart+0x2b

    1  Id: 2320.c34 Suspend: 0 Teb: 00000029`a7926000 Unfrozen
 # Child-SP          RetAddr               Call Site
00 00000029`a7aff808 00007ffd`4af96c2f      ntdll!NtWaitForWorkViaWorkerFactory+0x14
01 00000029`a7aff810 00007ffd`4a2654e0      ntdll!TppWorkerThread+0x2df
02 00000029`a7affb00 00007ffd`4af8485b      kernel32!BaseThreadInitThunk+0x10
03 00000029`a7affb30 00000000`00000000      ntdll!RtlUserThreadStart+0x2b

    2  Id: 2320.d10 Suspend: 0 Teb: 00000029`a7928000 Unfrozen
 # Child-SP          RetAddr               Call Site
00 00000029`a7bff9e8 00007ffd`4af96c2f      ntdll!NtWaitForWorkViaWorkerFactory+0x14
01 00000029`a7bff9f0 00007ffd`4a2654e0      ntdll!TppWorkerThread+0x2df
02 00000029`a7bffce0 00007ffd`4af8485b      kernel32!BaseThreadInitThunk+0x10
03 00000029`a7bffd10 00000000`00000000      ntdll!RtlUserThreadStart+0x2b
```

6. Let's apply symbols, if any:

```
0:000> .sympath+ C:\AWMDA-Dumps\Symbols
Symbol search path is: srv*;C:\AWMDA-Dumps\Symbols
Expanded Symbol search path is:
cache*;SRV*https://msdl.microsoft.com/download/symbols;c:\awmda-dumps\symbols

************* Path validation summary **************
Response                        Time (ms)     Location
Deferred                                      srv*
OK                                            C:\AWMDA-Dumps\Symbols


0:000> kL
# Child-SP          RetAddr               Call Site
00 00000029`a77df558 00007ffd`4a7e64cc      win32u!NtUserWaitMessage+0x14
01 00000029`a77df560 00007ffd`4a80924b      user32!DialogBox2+0x254
02 00000029`a77df600 00007ffd`4a82d346      user32!InternalDialogBox+0x14b
03 00000029`a77df660 00007ffd`4a82bc91      user32!SoftModalMessageBox+0x836
04 00000029`a77df7a0 00007ffd`4a82ca78      user32!MessageBoxWorker+0x341
05 00000029`a77df950 00007ffd`4a82cafe      user32!MessageBoxTimeoutW+0x198
06 00000029`a77dfa50 00007ff6`e2211117      user32!MessageBoxW+0x4e
07 00000029`a77dfa90 00007ff6`e22110c9      rusty!rusty::bar+0x47
08 00000029`a77dfad0 00007ff6`e2211129      rusty!rusty::foo+0x9
09 00000029`a77dfb00 00007ff6`e22111c6      rusty!rusty::main+0x9
0a 00000029`a77dfb30 00007ff6`e2211017      rusty!core::ops::function::FnOnce::call_once<void
(*)(),tuple$<> >+0x6
0b 00000029`a77dfb60 00007ff6`e221118c
rusty!std::sys_common::backtrace::__rust_begin_short_backtrace<void (*)(),tuple$<> >+0x17
0c 00000029`a77dfba0 00007ff6`e22167ab      rusty!std::rt::lang_start::closure$0<tuple$<> >+0xc
0d (Inline Function) --------`--------
rusty!core::ops::function::impls::impl$2::call_once+0xb
0e (Inline Function) --------`--------     rusty!std::panicking::try::do_call+0xb
0f (Inline Function) --------`--------     rusty!std::panicking::try+0xb
10 (Inline Function) --------`--------     rusty!std::panic::catch_unwind+0xb
```

```
11 (Inline Function) --------`--------        rusty!std::rt::lang_start_internal::closure$2+0xb
12 (Inline Function) --------`--------        rusty!std::panicking::try::do_call+0xb
13 (Inline Function) --------`--------        rusty!std::panicking::try+0xb
14 (Inline Function) --------`--------        rusty!std::panic::catch_unwind+0xb
15 00000029`a77dfbd0 00007ff6`e2211170        rusty!std::rt::lang_start_internal+0x2b
16 00000029`a77dfc60 00007ff6`e2211146        rusty!std::rt::lang_start<tuple$<> >+0x20
17 00000029`a77dfca0 00007ff6`e22282d4        rusty!main+0x16
18 (Inline Function) --------`--------        rusty!invoke_main+0x22
19 00000029`a77dfcd0 00007ffd`4a2654e0        rusty!__scrt_common_main_seh+0x10c
1a 00000029`a77dfd10 00007ffd`4af8485b        kernel32!BaseThreadInitThunk+0x10
1b 00000029`a77dfd40 00000000`00000000        ntdll!RtlUserThreadStart+0x2b
```

Note: We see Rust source code stack trace (in blue) with its own *main* function distinct from the process *main* function (in green). To get symbolic references for Rust functions instead of mangled names you need to enable debug info in the *Cargo.toml* file:

```
[profile.release]
opt-level = 0
debug = 1
```

7.   We close logging before exiting WinDbg:

```
0:000> .logclose
Closing open log file C:\AWMDA-Dumps\Process\x64\rusty.log
```

Pattern Links

Spiking Thread
C++ Exception
Divide by Zero (User Mode)
Dynamic Memory Corruption (Process Heap)
Execution Residue (Unmanaged Space, User)
Invalid Pointer (General)
Manual Dump (Process)
Managed Stack Trace
Not My Version (Software)
NULL Pointer (Code)
Stack Trace Collection (Unmanaged Space)
Environment Hint
Unknown Component
Virtualized Process (WOW64)
False Function Parameters
Reduced Symbolic Information
Stored Exception
Instrumentation Information
JIT Code (.NET)
Embedded Comment
Deadlock (Mixed Object, User Space)
Blocked Thread (Software)
Passive Thread (User Space)
Rough Stack Trace (Unmanaged Space)
Memory Leak (Process Heap)

CLR Thread
Deadlock (Critical Sections)
Double Free (Process Heap)
Exception Stack Trace
Hidden Exception (User Space)
Local Buffer Overflow (User Space)
Managed Code Exception
Multiple Exceptions (User Mode)
NULL Pointer (Data)
Stack Trace
Stack Overflow (User Mode)
Wild Code
Wait Chain (Critical Sections)
Message Box
Injected Symbols
Truncated Stack Trace
Incorrect Stack Trace
Active Thread
Thread Age
Wait Chain (General)
Not My Thread
Main Thread
Coincidental Symbolic Information
Platform-Specific Debugger
Language-Specific Subtrace (Rust)

Active Space
Debugger Bug
Exception Module
Blocking Module
Last Error Collection
Handle Leak
Input Thread

Here are links to analysis pattern descriptions and additional examples:

http://www.dumpanalysis.org/blog/index.php/crash-dump-analysis-patterns/

Also available in **Memory Dump Analysis Anthology** volumes and **Encyclopedia of Crash Dump Analysis Patterns**.

Pattern Classification

Space/Mode
Hooksware
DLL Link Patterns
Contention Patterns
Stack Trace Patterns
Exception Patterns
Module Patterns
Thread Patterns
Dynamic Memory Corruption Patterns
.NET / CLR / Managed Space Patterns
Falsity and Coincidence Patterns
Hidden Artifact Patterns
Frame Patterns

Memory dump type
Wait Chain Patterns
Insufficient Memory Patterns
Stack Overflow Patterns
Symbol Patterns
Meta-Memory Dump Patterns
Optimization Patterns
Process Patterns
Deadlock and Livelock Patterns
Executive Resource Patterns
RPC, LPC and ALPC Patterns
Pointer Patterns
CPU Consumption Patterns

Ongoing classification links can be found https://www.dumpanalysis.org/memory-dump-analysis-pattern-classification and in the **Encyclopedia of Crash Dump Analysis Patterns**.

Pattern Case Studies

More than 70 multiple pattern case studies:

http://www.dumpanalysis.org/blog/index.php/pattern-cooperation/

Pattern Interaction chapters in
Memory Dump Analysis Anthology

Online link: http://www.dumpanalysis.org/blog/index.php/pattern-cooperation/

Additional Resources

- ◉ WinDbg Help / WinDbg.org (quick links)
- ◉ DumpAnalysis.org / SoftwareDiagnostics.Institute / PatternDiagnostics.com
- ◉ Debugging.TV / YouTube.com/DebuggingTV / YouTube.com/PatternDiagnostics
- ◉ Windows Internals, 6th ed. (Chapter 14. Crash Dump Analysis), 7th ed.
- ◉ Advanced Windows Debugging
- ◉ Inside Windows Debugging
- ◉ Principles of Memory Dump Analysis
- ◉ Windows Debugging Notebook: Essential User Space WinDbg Commands
- ◉ Encyclopedia of Crash Dump Analysis Patterns, 3rd edition
- ◉ Memory Dump Analysis Anthology (Diagnomicon)

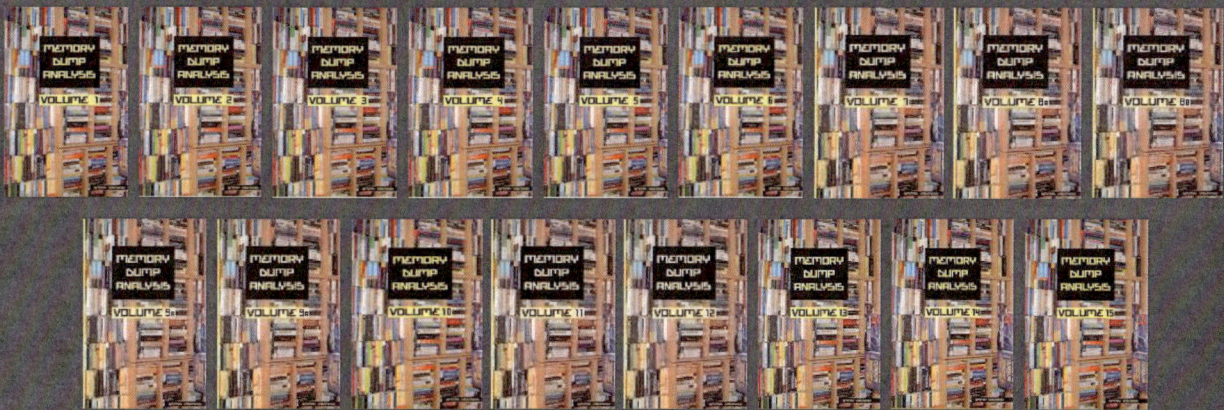

© 2023 Software Diagnostics Services

Additional learning and reference resources:

WinDbg quick links
http://WinDbg.org

Software Diagnostics Institute
http://www.dumpanalysis.org

Debugging.TV
http://debugging.tv

Pattern Diagnostics Seminars
https://www.youtube.com/PatternDiagnostics

Software Diagnostics Services
http://www.patterndiagnostics.com

Principles of Memory Dump Analysis
http://www.dumpanalysis.org/principles-memory-dump-analysis-book

Windows Debugging Notebook: Essential User Space WinDbg Commands
http://www.dumpanalysis.org/Forthcoming+Windows+Debugging+Notebook

Encyclopedia of Crash Dump Analysis Patterns, 3rd edition
http://www.dumpanalysis.org/encyclopedia-crash-dump-analysis-patterns

Memory Dump Analysis Anthology (Diagnomicon)
http://www.dumpanalysis.org/advanced-software-debugging-reference

Further Training Courses

- Accelerated Windows Memory Dump Analysis, 6th Edition, Part 2

- Practical Foundations of Windows Debugging, Disassembling, Reversing, 2nd Edition

- Advanced Windows Memory Dump Analysis with Data Structures, 4th Edition, Revised

- Accelerated .NET Core Memory Dump Analysis, Revised Edition

- Accelerated Windows Malware Analysis with Memory Dumps, 3rd Edition

- Accelerated Disassembly, Reconstruction and Reversing, 2nd Revised Edition

- Accelerated Windows Debugging[4], 3rd Edition

- Extended Windows Memory Dump Analysis

- Accelerated Windows API for Software Diagnostics

Additional training courses are available in PDF format:

Accelerated Windows Memory Dump Analysis, 6th Edition, Part 2
https://www.patterndiagnostics.com/accelerated-windows-memory-dump-analysis-book-part2

Practical Foundations of Windows Debugging, Disassembling, Reversing, 2nd Edition
https://www.patterndiagnostics.com/practical-foundations-windows-debugging-disassembling-reversing

Advanced Windows Memory Dump Analysis with Data Structures, 4th Edition, Revised
https://www.patterndiagnostics.com/advanced-windows-memory-dump-analysis-book

Accelerated .NET Core Memory Dump Analysis, Revised Edition
https://www.patterndiagnostics.com/accelerated-net-memory-dump-analysis-book

Accelerated Windows Malware Analysis with Memory Dumps, 3rd Edition
https://www.patterndiagnostics.com/accelerated-windows-malware-analysis-book

Accelerated Disassembly, Reconstruction and Reversing, 2nd Revised Edition
https://www.patterndiagnostics.com/accelerated-disassembly-reconstruction-reversing-book

Accelerated Windows Debugging[4], 3rd Edition

https://www.patterndiagnostics.com/accelerated-windows-debugging-book

Extended Windows Memory Dump Analysis

https://www.patterndiagnostics.com/extended-windows-memory-dump-analysis-book

Accelerated Windows API for Software Diagnostics

https://www.patterndiagnostics.com/accelerated-windows-api-book

Application Source Code

AppA

```
// AppA - Models MessageBox memory dump analysis pattern
// Copyright (c) 2011 - 2019 Software Diagnostics Technology and Services
// GNU GENERAL PUBLIC LICENSE
// http://www.gnu.org/licenses/gpl-3.0.txt

#include <windows.h>
#include <thread>
#include <chrono>

void thread_A()
{
      while (true)
      {
            std::this_thread::sleep_for(std::chrono::seconds('A'));
      }
}

void thread_B()
{
      while (true)
      {
            std::this_thread::sleep_for(std::chrono::seconds('B'));
      }
}

void thread_C()
{
      while (true)
      {
            std::this_thread::sleep_for(std::chrono::seconds('C'));
      }
}

void thread_D()
{
      while (true)
      {
            MessageBox(NULL, L"Message", L"Error", MB_OK);
            std::this_thread::sleep_for(std::chrono::seconds('D'));
      }
}

void thread_E()
{
      while (true)
      {
            std::this_thread::sleep_for(std::chrono::seconds('C'));
      }
}

void thread_F()
{
      while (true)
      {
            std::this_thread::sleep_for(std::chrono::seconds('C'));
      }
```

```
}

int wmain(int argc, wchar_t* argv[])
{
        std::thread tA(thread_A);
        std::thread tB(thread_B);
        std::thread tC(thread_C);
        std::thread tD(thread_D);
        std::thread tE(thread_E);
        std::thread tF(thread_F);

        tA.join();
        tB.join();
        tC.join();
        tD.join();
        tE.join();
        tF.join();

        std::this_thread::sleep_for(std::chrono::hours(1));
        return 0;
}
```

```cpp
// AppK - Models multiple exceptions in user mode
// Copyright (c) 2011-2019 Software Diagnostics Technology and Services
// GNU GENERAL PUBLIC LICENSE
// http://www.gnu.org/licenses/gpl-3.0.txt

#include <windows.h>
#include <process.h>

void thread_one(void*)
{
	int one{ 1 };

	*(int*)nullptr = 0;
}

void thread_two(void*)
{
	int two{ 2 };

	*(int*)nullptr = 0;
}

int wmain(int argc, wchar_t* argv[])
{
	_beginthread(thread_two, 0, nullptr);
	_beginthread(thread_one, 0, nullptr);

	DebugBreak();

	return 0;
}
```

AppL

```cpp
// AppL - Models process heap memory corruption
// Copyright (c) 2011-2019 Software Diagnostics Technology and Services
// GNU GENERAL PUBLIC LICENSE
// http://www.gnu.org/licenses/gpl-3.0.txt

#include <windows.h>
#include <process.h>

void thread_one(void*)
{
        auto p = new short [100];
        *(p - 4) = '11';
        delete[] p;
}

void thread_two(void*)
{
        auto p = new short [100];
        *(p - 4) = '22';
        delete[] p;
}

int wmain(int argc, wchar_t* argv[])
{
        _beginthread(thread_two, 0, nullptr);
        _beginthread(thread_one, 0, nullptr);

        Sleep(INFINITE);
        return 0;
}
```

AppL2

```cpp
// AppL2 - Models process heap memory corruption via buffer overflow
// Copyright (c) 2011-2019 Software Diagnostics Technology and Services
// GNU GENERAL PUBLIC LICENSE
// http://www.gnu.org/licenses/gpl-3.0.txt

#include <thread>
#include <chrono>
#include <string>

const wchar_t str[] = L"Hello Crash! Hello Crash! Hello Crash!";

void thread_one()
{
     while (true)
     {
          auto p = new wchar_t[10];

          memcpy(p, str, sizeof(str));

          std::this_thread::sleep_for(std::chrono::milliseconds(100));

          delete[] p;
     }
}

void thread_two()
{
     while (true)
     {
          auto p = new wchar_t[10];

          memcpy(p, str, sizeof(str));

          std::this_thread::sleep_for(std::chrono::milliseconds(200));

          delete[] p;
     }
}

int wmain(int argc, wchar_t* argv[])
{
     std::thread t1(thread_one);
     std::thread t2(thread_two);

     t1.join();
     t2.join();

     std::this_thread::sleep_for(std::chrono::hours(1));
     return 0;
}
```

AppM

```
// AppM - Models invalid pointers for data and code, NULL code pointer, wild pointers and code,
spiking thread
// Copyright (c) 2011-2019 Software Diagnostics Technology and Services
// GNU GENERAL PUBLIC LICENSE
// http://www.gnu.org/licenses/gpl-3.0.txt

#include <thread>
#include <chrono>

void thread_one()
{
	int* p{ reinterpret_cast<int*>(0xF123456789ABCDEF) };

	*p = 1;
}

void thread_two()
{
	void (*p)() {};

	(*p)();
}

void thread_three()
{
	void (*p)() = reinterpret_cast<void (*)()>(new char[1024]);

	(*p)();
}

void thread_four()
{
	while (true);
}

int wmain(int argc, wchar_t* argv[])
{
	std::thread t4(thread_four);

	std::this_thread::sleep_for(std::chrono::minutes(1));

	std::thread t3(thread_three);
	std::thread t2(thread_two);
	std::thread t1(thread_one);

	std::this_thread::sleep_for(std::chrono::hours(1));
	return 0;
}
```

```
// AppN - Models hidden exception and critical section deadlock
// Copyright (c) 2011-2019 Software Diagnostics Technology and Services
// GNU GENERAL PUBLIC LICENSE
// http://www.gnu.org/licenses/gpl-3.0.txt

#include <windows.h>
#include <thread>
#include <chrono>

CRITICAL_SECTION cs1;
CRITICAL_SECTION cs2;

void thread_one()
{
        int* p{};

        try
        {
                EnterCriticalSection(&cs1);
                *p = 0;
                LeaveCriticalSection(&cs1);
        }
        catch (...)
        {
        }

        std::this_thread::sleep_for(std::chrono::seconds(2));

        EnterCriticalSection(&cs2);
        LeaveCriticalSection(&cs2);
}

void thread_two()
{
        EnterCriticalSection(&cs2);
        EnterCriticalSection(&cs1);

        std::this_thread::sleep_for(std::chrono::seconds(3));

        LeaveCriticalSection(&cs1);
        LeaveCriticalSection(&cs2);
}

int wmain(int argc, wchar_t* argv[]) {
        InitializeCriticalSection(&cs1);
        InitializeCriticalSection(&cs2);

        std::thread t1(thread_one);
        std::this_thread::sleep_for(std::chrono::seconds(1));
        std::thread t2(thread_two);

        t1.join();
        t2.join();
        std::this_thread::sleep_for(std::chrono::minutes(1));
        return 0;
}
```

```cpp
// AppO - Models stack overflow, local buffer overflow, and double free patterns
// Copyright (c) 2011-2019 Software Diagnostics Technology and Services
// GNU GENERAL PUBLIC LICENSE
// http://www.gnu.org/licenses/gpl-3.0.txt

#include <thread>
#include <chrono>

void thread_one()
{
      static int i{};
      ++i;
      while (i)
      {
            thread_one();
      }
}

void bar()
{
      char buffer[200] = "Hello Crash! Hello Crash! Hello Crash! Hello Crash! Hello Crash!
Hello Crash! Hello Crash! Hello Crash! Hello Crash! Hello Crash!";

      memcpy(buffer+strlen(buffer), buffer, strlen(buffer));
}

void foo()
{
      bar();
}

void thread_two()
{
      foo();
}

void do_smth(char* p)
{
      delete[] p;
}

void thread_three()
{
      auto* p = new char[100];

      do_smth(p);

      delete[] p;
}

int wmain(int argc, wchar_t* argv[])
{
      std::thread t3(thread_three);
      std::thread t2(thread_two);
      std::thread t1(thread_one);
```

```cpp
    t1.join();
    t2.join();
    t3.join();

    std::this_thread::sleep_for(std::chrono::hours(1));
    return 0;
}
```

AppP

```cpp
// AppP - Models execution residue (ASCII, UNICODE), C++ exception, divide by zero
// Copyright (c) 2011-2019 Software Diagnostics Technology and Services
// GNU GENERAL PUBLIC LICENSE
// http://www.gnu.org/licenses/gpl-3.0.txt

#include <thread>
#include <chrono>

void bar()
{
        char buffer1[100] = "";
        char buffer[60] = "Interesting data! Even more interesting data";
        char buffer2[100] = "";
        wchar_t buffer3[60] = L"Interesting data! Even more interesting data!";
        char buffer4[100] = "";

        strcat_s(buffer, "!");
}

void foo()
{
        char buffer[100] = "";
        bar();
}

void thread_one()
{
        char buffer[100] = "";
        foo();
        std::this_thread::sleep_for(std::chrono::hours(1));
}

void thread_two()
{
        throw 0x12345678;
}

void thread_three()
{
        int j = 0;
        int i = 1 / j;
}

int wmain(int argc, wchar_t* argv[])
{
        std::thread t3(thread_three);
        std::thread t2(thread_two);
        std::thread t1(thread_one);

        t1.join();
        t2.join();
        t3.join();

        std::this_thread::sleep_for(std::chrono::hours(1));
        return 0;
}
```

AppR2

```csharp
using System;
using System.Collections.Generic;
using System.Linq;
using System.Text;
using System.Threading.Tasks;
using System.Windows;
using System.Windows.Controls;
using System.Windows.Data;
using System.Windows.Documents;
using System.Windows.Input;
using System.Windows.Media;
using System.Windows.Media.Imaging;
using System.Windows.Navigation;
using System.Windows.Shapes;

namespace AppR2
{
    /// <summary>
    /// Interaction logic for MainWindow.xaml
    /// </summary>
    public partial class MainWindow : Window
    {
        public MainWindow()
        {
            InitializeComponent();
        }

        private void Button_Click(System.Object sender, System.Windows.RoutedEventArgs e)
        {
            unsafe
            {
                int* p = (int*)0;
                *p = 1;
            }
        }
    }
}
```

AppS

```cpp
// AppS - Models memory leak (process heap)
// Copyright (c) 2011 - 2019 Software Diagnostics Technology and Services
// GNU GENERAL PUBLIC LICENSE
// http://www.gnu.org/licenses/gpl-3.0.txt

#include <thread>
#include <chrono>
#include <vector>
#include <algorithm>

void bar()
{
        std::vector<std::byte*> data;

        data.resize(1000000);

        std::for_each(data.begin(), data.end(),
            [](auto& elem)
            {
                    for (int j = 0; j < 100000; ++j);
                    new std::byte[1000]; // Forgot to assign...
            });

        std::this_thread::sleep_for(std::chrono::minutes(1)); // One minute work...

        for (const auto& elem : data)
        {
                delete[] elem; // We think we release memory after work...
        }

        std::this_thread::sleep_for(std::chrono::hours(1));
}

void foo()
{
        bar();
}

void thread_one()
{
        foo();
        std::this_thread::sleep_for(std::chrono::hours(1));
}

void thread_two()
{
        std::this_thread::sleep_for(std::chrono::hours(1));
}

void thread_three()
{
        std::this_thread::sleep_for(std::chrono::hours(1));
}
```

```
int wmain(int argc, wchar_t* argv[])
{
        std::thread t3(thread_three);
        std::thread t2(thread_two);
        std::thread t1(thread_one);

        t3.join();
        t2.join();
        t1.join();

        std::this_thread::sleep_for(std::chrono::hours(1));
        return 0;
}
```

AppQ

```cpp
// AppQ - Illustrates Wait Chain memory dump analysis pattern
// Copyright (c) 2013 - 2019 Software Diagnostics Services
// GNU GENERAL PUBLIC LICENSE
// http://www.gnu.org/licenses/gpl-3.0.txt

#include "framework.h"
#include "AppQ.h"

#define MAX_LOADSTRING 100

// Global Variables:
HINSTANCE hInst;                                // current instance
WCHAR szTitle[MAX_LOADSTRING];                  // The title bar text
WCHAR szWindowClass[MAX_LOADSTRING];            // the main window class name

// Forward declarations of functions included in this code module:
ATOM                MyRegisterClass(HINSTANCE hInstance);
BOOL                InitInstance(HINSTANCE, int);
LRESULT CALLBACK    WndProc(HWND, UINT, WPARAM, LPARAM);
INT_PTR CALLBACK    About(HWND, UINT, WPARAM, LPARAM);
void                StartModeling();

int APIENTRY wWinMain(_In_ HINSTANCE hInstance,
                     _In_opt_ HINSTANCE hPrevInstance,
                     _In_ LPWSTR     lpCmdLine,
                     _In_ int        nCmdShow)
{
    UNREFERENCED_PARAMETER(hPrevInstance);
    UNREFERENCED_PARAMETER(lpCmdLine);

    // TODO: Place code here.

    // Initialize global strings
    LoadStringW(hInstance, IDS_APP_TITLE, szTitle, MAX_LOADSTRING);
    LoadStringW(hInstance, IDC_APPQ, szWindowClass, MAX_LOADSTRING);
    MyRegisterClass(hInstance);

    // Perform application initialization:
    if (!InitInstance (hInstance, nCmdShow))
    {
        return FALSE;
    }

    HACCEL hAccelTable = LoadAccelerators(hInstance, MAKEINTRESOURCE(IDC_APPQ));

    MSG msg;

    // Main message loop:
    while (GetMessage(&msg, nullptr, 0, 0))
    {
        if (!TranslateAccelerator(msg.hwnd, hAccelTable, &msg))
        {
            TranslateMessage(&msg);
            DispatchMessage(&msg);
        }
    }
```

```
    return (int) msg.wParam;
}

//
//  FUNCTION: MyRegisterClass()
//
//  PURPOSE: Registers the window class.
//
ATOM MyRegisterClass(HINSTANCE hInstance)
{
    WNDCLASSEXW wcex;

    wcex.cbSize = sizeof(WNDCLASSEX);

    wcex.style          = CS_HREDRAW | CS_VREDRAW;
    wcex.lpfnWndProc    = WndProc;
    wcex.cbClsExtra     = 0;
    wcex.cbWndExtra     = 0;
    wcex.hInstance      = hInstance;
    wcex.hIcon          = LoadIcon(hInstance, MAKEINTRESOURCE(IDI_APPQ));
    wcex.hCursor        = LoadCursor(nullptr, IDC_ARROW);
    wcex.hbrBackground  = (HBRUSH)(COLOR_WINDOW+1);
    wcex.lpszMenuName   = MAKEINTRESOURCEW(IDC_APPQ);
    wcex.lpszClassName  = szWindowClass;
    wcex.hIconSm        = LoadIcon(wcex.hInstance, MAKEINTRESOURCE(IDI_SMALL));

    return RegisterClassExW(&wcex);
}

//
//   FUNCTION: InitInstance(HINSTANCE, int)
//
//   PURPOSE: Saves instance handle and creates main window
//
//   COMMENTS:
//
//        In this function, we save the instance handle in a global variable and
//        create and display the main program window.
//
BOOL InitInstance(HINSTANCE hInstance, int nCmdShow)
{
   hInst = hInstance; // Store instance handle in our global variable

   HWND hWnd = CreateWindowW(szWindowClass, szTitle, WS_OVERLAPPEDWINDOW,
      CW_USEDEFAULT, 0, CW_USEDEFAULT, 0, nullptr, nullptr, hInstance, nullptr);

   if (!hWnd)
   {
      return FALSE;
   }

   ShowWindow(hWnd, nCmdShow);
   UpdateWindow(hWnd);

   return TRUE;
}

//
//  FUNCTION: WndProc(HWND, UINT, WPARAM, LPARAM)
```
303

```
//
//   PURPOSE: Processes messages for the main window.
//
//   WM_COMMAND  - process the application menu
//   WM_PAINT    - Paint the main window
//   WM_DESTROY  - post a quit message and return
//
//
LRESULT CALLBACK WndProc(HWND hWnd, UINT message, WPARAM wParam, LPARAM lParam)
{
    switch (message)
    {
    case WM_COMMAND:
        {
            int wmId = LOWORD(wParam);
            // Parse the menu selections:
            switch (wmId)
            {
            case ID_FILE_START:
                StartModeling();
                break;
            case IDM_ABOUT:
                DialogBox(hInst, MAKEINTRESOURCE(IDD_ABOUTBOX), hWnd, About);
                break;
            case IDM_EXIT:
                DestroyWindow(hWnd);
                break;
            default:
                return DefWindowProc(hWnd, message, wParam, lParam);
            }
        }
        break;
    case WM_PAINT:
        {
            PAINTSTRUCT ps;
            HDC hdc = BeginPaint(hWnd, &ps);
            // TODO: Add any drawing code that uses hdc here...
            EndPaint(hWnd, &ps);
        }
        break;
    case WM_DESTROY:
        PostQuitMessage(0);
        break;
    default:
        return DefWindowProc(hWnd, message, wParam, lParam);
    }
    return 0;
}

// Message handler for about box.
INT_PTR CALLBACK About(HWND hDlg, UINT message, WPARAM wParam, LPARAM lParam)
{
    UNREFERENCED_PARAMETER(lParam);
    switch (message)
    {
    case WM_INITDIALOG:
        return (INT_PTR)TRUE;

    case WM_COMMAND:
        if (LOWORD(wParam) == IDOK || LOWORD(wParam) == IDCANCEL)
```

```
                {
                    EndDialog(hDlg, LOWORD(wParam));
                    return (INT_PTR)TRUE;
                }
            break;
        }
        return (INT_PTR)FALSE;
}

DWORD WINAPI ThreadProcAB(LPVOID);
DWORD WINAPI ThreadProcBCDE(LPVOID);
DWORD WINAPI ThreadProcC(LPVOID);
DWORD WINAPI ThreadProcD(LPVOID);
DWORD WINAPI ThreadProcE(LPVOID);

void StartModeling(void)
{
        HANDLE hThread = CreateThread(NULL, 0, ThreadProcAB, NULL, 0, NULL);

        WaitForSingleObject(hThread, INFINITE);
}

DWORD WINAPI ThreadProcAB(LPVOID)
{
        HANDLE hThread = CreateThread(NULL, 0, ThreadProcBCDE, NULL, 0, NULL);

        return WaitForSingleObject(hThread, INFINITE);
}

DWORD WINAPI ThreadProcBCDE(LPVOID)
{
        HANDLE hThreads[3];

        HANDLE hEvent = CreateEvent(NULL, FALSE, FALSE, NULL);

        hThreads[0] = CreateThread(NULL, 0, ThreadProcC, NULL, 0, NULL);
        hThreads[1] = CreateThread(NULL, 0, ThreadProcD, NULL, 0, NULL);
        hThreads[2] = CreateThread(NULL, 0, ThreadProcE, hEvent, 0, NULL);

        return WaitForMultipleObjects(3, hThreads, TRUE, INFINITE);
}

DWORD WINAPI ThreadProcC(LPVOID)
{
        Sleep(1000);
        return 0;
}

DWORD WINAPI ThreadProcD(LPVOID)
{
        Sleep(2000);
        return 0;
}

DWORD WINAPI ThreadProcE(LPVOID hEvent)
{
        return WaitForSingleObject((HANDLE)hEvent, INFINITE);
}
```

AppT

```cpp
// AppT - Models handle leak
// Copyright (c) 2019 Software Diagnostics Technology and Services
// GNU GENERAL PUBLIC LICENSE
// http://www.gnu.org/licenses/gpl-3.0.txt

#include <windows.h>

#include <thread>
#include <chrono>
#include <vector>
#include <algorithm>

void bar()
{
	std::vector<HANDLE> data;

	data.resize(123456);

	std::for_each(data.begin(), data.end(),
		[](auto& elem)
		{
			for (int j = 0; j < 100000; ++j);
			::CreateFile(L"AppT.txt", GENERIC_READ, FILE_SHARE_READ,
				nullptr, OPEN_ALWAYS, FILE_ATTRIBUTE_NORMAL, nullptr); // Forgot to
assign...
		});

	std::this_thread::sleep_for(std::chrono::minutes(1)); // One minute work...

	for (const auto& elem : data)
	{
		::CloseHandle(elem); // We think we close handles after work...
	}

	std::this_thread::sleep_for(std::chrono::hours(1));
}

void foo()
{
	bar();
}

void thread_one()
{
	foo();
	std::this_thread::sleep_for(std::chrono::hours(1));
}

void thread_two()
{
	std::this_thread::sleep_for(std::chrono::hours(1));
}

void thread_three()
{
	std::this_thread::sleep_for(std::chrono::hours(1));
```

```
}

int wmain(int argc, wchar_t* argv[])
{
        std::thread t3(thread_three);
        std::thread t2(thread_two);
        std::thread t1(thread_one);

        t3.join();
        t2.join();
        t1.join();

        std::this_thread::sleep_for(std::chrono::hours(1));
        return 0;
}
```

ServiceA

```cpp
// ServiceA - Models Input Thread and Blocking Module memory analysis patterns
// Copyright (c) 2022 Software Diagnostics Technology and Services
// GNU GENERAL PUBLIC LICENSE
// http://www.gnu.org/licenses/gpl-3.0.txt

#include <windows.h>
#include <thread>

static WCHAR s_ServiceName[] = L"ServiceA";
static const DWORD WAIT_HINT = 2000;
static SERVICE_STATUS_HANDLE s_hServiceStatus;
static HANDLE s_hServiceEvent;
static DWORD s_dwServiceState;

static void WINAPI ServiceHandler(DWORD dwControl, DWORD dwEventType, LPVOID lpEventData,
LPVOID lpContext);
static void WINAPI ServiceMain(DWORD dwArgc, LPWSTR *lpszArgv);

static bool NotifySCM(DWORD dwState, DWORD dwWin32ExitCode, DWORD dwServiceSpecificExitCode,
DWORD dwProgress, DWORD dwWaitHint = WAIT_HINT);

static bool ServiceInit();
static bool ServiceRun();
static bool ServiceShutdown();

int WINAPI wWinMain(_In_ HINSTANCE hInstance, _In_opt_ HINSTANCE hPrevInstance, _In_ LPWSTR
lpCmdLine, _In_ int nCmdShow)
{
        SERVICE_TABLE_ENTRY ServiceTable[] =
        {
                { s_ServiceName, (LPSERVICE_MAIN_FUNCTION)ServiceMain },
                { nullptr, nullptr }
        };

        if (!::StartServiceCtrlDispatcher(ServiceTable))
        {
                return -1;
        }

        return 0;
}

static void WINAPI ServiceMain(DWORD dwArgc, LPWSTR *lpszArgv)
{
        s_hServiceStatus = ::RegisterServiceCtrlHandlerEx(s_ServiceName,
(LPHANDLER_FUNCTION_EX)ServiceHandler, nullptr);

        if (!s_hServiceStatus)
        {
                return;
        }

        ::NotifySCM(SERVICE_START_PENDING, 0, 0, 1);

        if (!ServiceInit())
        {
```

```cpp
            NotifySCM(SERVICE_STOPPED, ERROR_SERVICE_SPECIFIC_ERROR, ::GetLastError(), 0);
            return;
        }

        NotifySCM(SERVICE_START_PENDING, 0, 0, 2);

        s_hServiceEvent = ::CreateEvent(nullptr, true, false, nullptr);

        if (!s_hServiceEvent)
        {
            NotifySCM(SERVICE_STOPPED, ::GetLastError(), 0, 0);
            return;
        }

        NotifySCM(SERVICE_START_PENDING, 0, 0, 3);

        if (!ServiceRun())
        {
            NotifySCM(SERVICE_STOPPED, ERROR_SERVICE_SPECIFIC_ERROR, ::GetLastError(), 0);
            return;
        }

        NotifySCM(SERVICE_RUNNING, 0, 0, 0);

        WaitForSingleObject(s_hServiceEvent, INFINITE);

        NotifySCM(SERVICE_STOP_PENDING, 0, 0, 1, WAIT_HINT*10);

        ServiceShutdown();

        NotifySCM(SERVICE_STOPPED, 0, 0, 0);
}

static void WINAPI ServiceHandler(DWORD dwControl, DWORD dwEventType, LPVOID lpEventData,
LPVOID lpContext)
{
        switch (dwControl)
        {
            case SERVICE_CONTROL_STOP:
            {
                NotifySCM(SERVICE_STOP_PENDING, 0, 0, 1);
                ::SetEvent(s_hServiceEvent);
                break;
            }

            case SERVICE_CONTROL_INTERROGATE:
            {
                NotifySCM(s_dwServiceState, 0, 0, 1);
                break;
            }

            case SERVICE_CONTROL_SHUTDOWN:
            {
                NotifySCM(SERVICE_STOP_PENDING, 0, 0, 1);
                SetEvent(s_hServiceEvent);
                break;
            }
        }
}
```

```cpp
static bool NotifySCM(DWORD dwState, DWORD dwWin32ExitCode, DWORD dwServiceSpecificExitCode,
DWORD dwProgress, DWORD dwWaitHint)
{
    if (dwServiceSpecificExitCode)
    {
    }

    SERVICE_STATUS serviceStatus;

    serviceStatus.dwServiceType = SERVICE_WIN32_OWN_PROCESS;
    serviceStatus.dwCurrentState = s_dwServiceState = dwState;
    serviceStatus.dwControlsAccepted = SERVICE_ACCEPT_STOP | SERVICE_ACCEPT_SHUTDOWN;
    serviceStatus.dwWin32ExitCode = dwWin32ExitCode;
    serviceStatus.dwServiceSpecificExitCode = dwServiceSpecificExitCode;
    serviceStatus.dwCheckPoint = dwProgress;
    serviceStatus.dwWaitHint = dwWaitHint;

    return ::SetServiceStatus(s_hServiceStatus, &serviceStatus);
}

bool ServiceInit()
{
    return true;
}

DWORD WINAPI ThreadProcA(LPVOID)
{
    Sleep(5000);
    MessageBox(NULL, L"Error Text", L"Error Caption", MB_OK | MB_SETFOREGROUND);
    return 0;
}

bool ServiceRun()
{
    CreateThread(NULL, 0, ThreadProcA, NULL, 0, NULL);
    return true;
}

bool ServiceShutdown()
{
    return true;
}

// for debug build
int wmain(int argc, wchar_t* argv[])
{
    return 0;
}
```

Rusty

```rust
// Rusty - Models Stack Trace and Message Box patterns
// Copyright (c) 2023 Software Diagnostics Technology and Services
// GNU GENERAL PUBLIC LICENSE
// http://www.gnu.org/licenses/gpl-3.0.txt

use windows_sys::{
    core::*, Win32::UI::WindowsAndMessaging::*
  };

fn foo()
{
  bar();
}

fn bar()
{
  unsafe {
    MessageBoxW(0, w!("Hello Windows API!"), w!("From Rust"), MB_OK);
  }
}

fn main() {
  foo();
}
```

Selected Q&A

Questions and answers added in the 5.5 version:

Q. How does WinDbg know or relate to the PDB file? For example, I have two versions of the same process, v1 and v2. When analyzing the v2 dump, I added the path of PDBs for both v1 and v2. How does WinDbg map the symbols in that case?

A. Currently, it looks at symbol file GUID information in Debug Data Directory from the PE header in the loaded module and matches that with GUID information stored in the PDB file:

```
0:000> lmv m win32u
Browse full module list
start             end               module name
00007ffe`dad30000 00007ffe`dad51000  win32u     (pdb symbols)
C:\ProgramData\dbg\sym\win32u.pdb\BC2E49ABE46D2E93B278B4DECFCA62A81\win32u.pdb
    Loaded symbol image file: win32u.dll
    Image path: C:\Windows\System32\win32u.dll
    Image name: win32u.dll
    Browse all global symbols  functions  data
    Image was built with /Brepro flag.
    Timestamp:        5343F4FB (This is a reproducible build file hash, not a timestamp)
    CheckSum:         00023FD6
    ImageSize:        00021000
    File version:     10.0.18362.329
    Product version:  10.0.18362.329
    File flags:       0 (Mask 3F)
    File OS:          40004 NT Win32
    File type:        1.0 App
    File date:        00000000.00000000
    Translations:     0409.04b0
    Information from resource tables:
        CompanyName:      Microsoft Corporation
        ProductName:      Microsoft® Windows® Operating System
        InternalName:     Win32u
        OriginalFilename: Win32u.DLL
        ProductVersion:   10.0.18362.329
        FileVersion:      10.0.18362.329 (WinBuild.160101.0800)
        FileDescription:  Win32u
        LegalCopyright:   © Microsoft Corporation. All rights reserved.

0:000> !lmi win32u
Loaded Module Info: [win32u]
         Module: win32u
   Base Address: 00007ffedad30000
     Image Name: win32u.dll
   Machine Type: 34404 (X64)
     Time Stamp: 5343f4fb (This is a reproducible build file hash, not a true timestamp)
           Size: 21000
       CheckSum: 23fd6
Characteristics: 2022
Debug Data Dirs: Type  Size      VA  Pointer
           CODEVIEW    23,  ca04,    bc04 RSDS - GUID: {BC2E49AB-E46D-2E93-B278-B4DECFCA62A8}
               Age: 1, Pdb: win32u.pdb
              POGO    100,  ca28,    bc28 [Data not mapped]
             REPRO     24,  cb28,    bd28 Reproducible build[Data not mapped]
     Image Type: MEMORY   - Image read successfully from loaded memory.
    Symbol Type: PDB      - Symbols loaded successfully from image header.
                 C:\ProgramData\dbg\sym\win32u.pdb\BC2E49ABE46D2E93B278B4DECFCA62A81\win32u.pdb
    Load Report: public symbols , not source indexed
```

```
0:000> !dh win32u

File Type: DLL
FILE HEADER VALUES
    8664 machine (X64)
       6 number of sections
5343F4FB time date stamp Tue Apr  8 14:09:15 2014

       0 file pointer to symbol table
       0 number of symbols
      F0 size of optional header
    2022 characteristics
            Executable
            App can handle >2gb addresses
            DLL


OPTIONAL HEADER VALUES
     20B magic #
   14.15 linker version
    9E00 size of code
   12C00 size of initialized data
       0 size of uninitialized data
       0 address of entry point
    1000 base of code
         ----- new -----
00007ffedad30000 image base
    1000 section alignment
     200 file alignment
       2 subsystem (Windows GUI)
   10.00 operating system version
   10.00 image version
   10.00 subsystem version
   21000 size of image
     400 size of headers
   23FD6 checksum
0000000000040000 size of stack reserve
0000000000001000 size of stack commit
0000000000100000 size of heap reserve
0000000000001000 size of heap commit
    4160  DLL characteristics
            High entropy VA supported
            Dynamic base
            NX compatible
            Guard
    DF00 [    B3A0] address [size] of Export Directory
       0 [       0] address [size] of Import Directory
   1F000 [     3D8] address [size] of Resource Directory
   1B000 [    3B04] address [size] of Exception Directory
   1CA00 [    2730] address [size] of Security Directory
   20000 [      14] address [size] of Base Relocation Directory
    C9B0 [      54] address [size] of Debug Directory
       0 [       0] address [size] of Description Directory
       0 [       0] address [size] of Special Directory
       0 [       0] address [size] of Thread Storage Directory
    B000 [     108] address [size] of Load Configuration Directory
       0 [       0] address [size] of Bound Import Directory
       0 [       0] address [size] of Import Address Table Directory
       0 [       0] address [size] of Delay Import Directory
```

316

```
       0 [        0] address [size] of COR20 Header Directory
       0 [        0] address [size] of Reserved Directory


SECTION HEADER #1
   .text name
   9D82 virtual size
   1000 virtual address
   9E00 size of raw data
    400 file pointer to raw data
      0 file pointer to relocation table
      0 file pointer to line numbers
      0 number of relocations
      0 number of line numbers
60000020 flags
         Code
         (no align specified)
         Execute Read


SECTION HEADER #2
   .rdata name
   E2A0 virtual size
   B000 virtual address
   E400 size of raw data
   A200 file pointer to raw data
      0 file pointer to relocation table
      0 file pointer to line numbers
      0 number of relocations
      0 number of line numbers
40000040 flags
         Initialized Data
         (no align specified)
         Read Only


Debug Directories(3)
        Type        Size    Address  Pointer
        cv           23      ca04     bc04    Format: RSDS, guid, 1, win32u.pdb
        (   13)      100      ca28     bc28
        (   16)       24      cb28     bd28


SECTION HEADER #3
   .data name
    580 virtual size
  1A000 virtual address
    200 size of raw data
  18600 file pointer to raw data
      0 file pointer to relocation table
      0 file pointer to line numbers
      0 number of relocations
      0 number of line numbers
C0000040 flags
         Initialized Data
         (no align specified)
         Read Write


SECTION HEADER #4
   .pdata name
   3B04 virtual size
  1B000 virtual address
```

```
       3C00 size of raw data
      18800 file pointer to raw data
          0 file pointer to relocation table
          0 file pointer to line numbers
          0 number of relocations
          0 number of line numbers
   40000040 flags
            Initialized Data
            (no align specified)
            Read Only


SECTION HEADER #5
    .rsrc name
        3D8 virtual size
      1F000 virtual address
        400 size of raw data
      1C400 file pointer to raw data
          0 file pointer to relocation table
          0 file pointer to line numbers
          0 number of relocations
          0 number of line numbers
   40000040 flags
            Initialized Data
            (no align specified)
            Read Only


SECTION HEADER #6
   .reloc name
         14 virtual size
      20000 virtual address
        200 size of raw data
      1C800 file pointer to raw data
          0 file pointer to relocation table
          0 file pointer to line numbers
          0 number of relocations
          0 number of line numbers
   42000040 flags
            Initialized Data
            Discardable
            (no align specified)
            Read Only
```

```
0:000> dc 00007ffedad30000 + ca04
00007ffe`dad3ca04  53445352 bc2e49ab 2e93e46d deb478b2  RSDS.I..m....x..
00007ffe`dad3ca14  a862cacf 00000001 336e6977 702e7532  ..b.....win32u.p
00007ffe`dad3ca24  00006264 4c544347 00001000 00000020  db..GCTL.... ...
00007ffe`dad3ca34  7865742e 6e6d2474 00000000 00001020  .text$mn.... ...
00007ffe`dad3ca44  00009d62 7865742e 6e6d2474 00303024  b....text$mn$00.
00007ffe`dad3ca54  0000b000 00000108 6164722e 62246174  .........rdata$b
00007ffe`dad3ca64  00006372 0000b108 00000010 6330302e  rc...........00c
00007ffe`dad3ca74  00006766 0000b118 00001898 6966672e  fg...........gfi
```

Q. Do we have any place where WinDbg saves PDB files in the cache? I have faced a problem where if I load the PDB once and after that remove the symbol path, WinDbg still prints the thread output with mapped symbols.

A. You can see it from the output of the **lm** command:

```
0:000> lm m win32u
Browse full module list
start               end                     module name
00007ffe`dad30000   00007ffe`dad51000           win32u              (pdb    symbols)
C:\ProgramData\dbg\sym\win32u.pdb\BC2E49ABE46D2E93B278B4DECFCA62A81\win32u.pdb
```

Q. What does Child-SP correspond to in the **k** command output?

A. This address points to the stack region fragment that corresponds to the current frame, including the stored return address of the caller:

```
0:000> k
 # Child-SP          RetAddr             Call Site
00 000000a1`c2ccf988 00007ffe`dc19477d   win32u!NtUserGetMessage+0x14
01 000000a1`c2ccf990 00007ff7`437da3d3   user32!GetMessageW+0x2d
02 000000a1`c2ccf9f0 00007ff7`437f02b7   notepad!WinMain+0x293
03 000000a1`c2ccfac0 00007ffe`dc557bd4   notepad!__mainCRTStartup+0x19f
04 000000a1`c2ccfb80 00007ffe`ddc6cee1   kernel32!BaseThreadInitThunk+0x14
05 000000a1`c2ccfbb0 00000000`00000000   ntdll!RtlUserThreadStart+0x21
```

```
0:000> dps 000000a1`c2ccf990-8
000000a1`c2ccf988  00007ffe`dc19477d user32!GetMessageW+0x2d
000000a1`c2ccf990  00000000`00007f48
000000a1`c2ccf998  00000000`0001e327
000000a1`c2ccf9a0  000019ee`00000000
000000a1`c2ccf9a8  00007ff7`00000001
000000a1`c2ccf9b0  00000000`00000001
000000a1`c2ccf9b8  00007ff7`437d0000 notepad!TlgWrite <PERF> (notepad+0x0)
000000a1`c2ccf9c0  00000000`00000001
000000a1`c2ccf9c8  00007ff7`437d0000 notepad!TlgWrite <PERF> (notepad+0x0)
000000a1`c2ccf9d0  00000000`00000000
000000a1`c2ccf9d8  00000000`00000000
000000a1`c2ccf9e0  00000000`0006038b
000000a1`c2ccf9e8  00007ff7`437da3d3 notepad!WinMain+0x293
000000a1`c2ccf9f0  00007ff7`437d0000 notepad!TlgWrite <PERF> (notepad+0x0)
000000a1`c2ccf9f8  00000000`0006038b
000000a1`c2ccfa00  00000000`00000000
```

Q. Does the module name in **!analyze -v** output have any significance?

A. It makes sense for automated tools. However, it is usually either the top current stack trace module or the one that caused the exception. However, there may be several exceptions in different modules, but only one is reported.

Q. How does **!analyze -v** identify the exception or bugcheck details? How can I write a command myself to get the exception output? I want to understand the Failure Bucket ID published by **!analyze -v** command.

A. Since I'm not a developer of the WinDbg **analyze** extension, I can only guess that it combines exception class and code with the module name and corresponding function name from the stack trace. You can find the sequence of commands to get this information from the STACK_COMMAND key in the output.

Q. What does "Affinity: 3" mean in the **!uniqstack** command output?

A. It is a bitmask that shows on which CPUs this thread is allowed to be scheduled. 3 here corresponds to 11 in binary, an all 2 VM CPUs. The mask I see on my laptop with 4 cores and 8 logical processors is "Affinity: ff."

Q. When we have multiple exceptions in threads, how do we know which thread caused the exception first?

A. There may be hints. For example, one thread that got it first may progress further in exception processing on the stack trace. Also, in the kernel and complete memory dumps, there may be further hints, such as **Thread Waiting Time** analysis pattern:

https://www.dumpanalysis.org/blog/index.php/2007/07/22/crash-dump-analysis-patterns-part-19/.

Q. Why do we have a checksum warning for *AppK.exe* when running the **k** command?

A. I think this is because the module information doesn't have a *CheckSum* value compared to other system modules:

```
0:000> !lmi AppK
Loaded Module Info: [appk]
         Module: AppK
   Base Address: 00007ff794980000
     Image Name: AppK.exe
   Machine Type: 34404 (X64)
     Time Stamp: 5d93d8ca Tue Oct  1 23:52:58 2019
           Size: 1b000
       CheckSum: 0
Characteristics: 22
Debug Data Dirs: Type  Size     VA  Pointer
            CODEVIEW    44, 133b8,   125b8 RSDS - GUID: {44C94F62-4BB3-475F-957D-CEB0B6E2F211}
              Age: 1, Pdb: C:\AWMDA-Examples\AppK\x64\Release\AppK.pdb
          VC_FEATURE    14, 133fc,   125fc [Data not mapped]
                POGO   2b8, 13410,   12610 [Data not mapped]
     Image Type: MEMORY   - Image read successfully from loaded memory.
    Symbol Type: PDB      - Symbols loaded successfully from image header.
                 C:\ProgramData\dbg\sym\AppK.pdb\44C94F624BB3475F957DCEB0B6E2F2111\AppK.pdb
       Compiler: Resource - front end [0.0 bld 0] - back end [14.22 bld 27905]
    Load Report: private symbols & lines, not source indexed
                 C:\ProgramData\dbg\sym\AppK.pdb\44C94F624BB3475F957DCEB0B6E2F2111\AppK.pdb

0:000> !lmi kernel32
Loaded Module Info: [kernel32]
         Module: kernel32
   Base Address: 00007ffefbcd0000
     Image Name: kernel32.dll
   Machine Type: 34404 (X64)
     Time Stamp: d0cecc10 (This is a reproducible build file hash, not a true timestamp)
           Size: b2000
       CheckSum: bbbc4
Characteristics: 2022
Debug Data Dirs: Type  Size     VA  Pointer
            CODEVIEW    25, 88200,   86e00 RSDS - GUID: {5A77DE8C-E8D5-8731-F0EA-38F1C92F48D8}
              Age: 1, Pdb: kernel32.pdb
```

```
            POGO   4ec, 88228,   86e28 [Data not mapped]
            REPRO   24, 88714,   87314 Reproducible build[Data not mapped]
  Image Type: MEMORY   - Image read successfully from loaded memory.
  Symbol Type: PDB     - Symbols loaded successfully from image header.
```

C:\ProgramData\dbg\sym\kernel32.pdb\5A77DE8CE8D58731F0EA38F1C92F48D81\kernel32.pdb
    Load Report: public symbols , not source indexed

C:\ProgramData\dbg\sym\kernel32.pdb\5A77DE8CE8D58731F0EA38F1C92F48D81\kernel32.pdb

Q. If threads are waiting, why is the state still showing as suspended and unfrozen?

A. Most threads are waiting to be scheduled to run because there are only a few CPUs to run them simultaneously. Even waiting threads can be suspended if there is an exception and OS decides to freeze the remaining threads to preserve the process state. The thread that executes the exception processing code may still be running. The process threads are also suspended if a debugger breaks in or is non-invasively attached. However, frozen and unfrozen states are meaningful only if a debugger is attached, which can freeze and unfreeze threads while controlling the process, for example, to allow only some threads to continue running. In the example below, thread 0 is not suspended because it is processing the exception and waiting from the *WerFault.exe* process:

```
0:000> ~*kL

.  0  Id: 2124.2150 Suspend: 0 Teb: 00000032`b52cf000 Unfrozen
 # Child-SP          RetAddr               Call Site
00 00000032`b51fe788 00007ffe`fb097ff7     ntdll!NtWaitForMultipleObjects+0x14
01 00000032`b51fe790 00007ffe`fb097ede     KERNELBASE!WaitForMultipleObjectsEx+0x107
02 00000032`b51fea90 00007ffe`fbd371fb     KERNELBASE!WaitForMultipleObjects+0xe
03 00000032`b51fead0 00007ffe`fbd36ca8     kernel32!WerpReportFaultInternal+0x51b
04 00000032`b51febf0 00007ffe`fb13f988     kernel32!WerpReportFault+0xac
05 00000032`b51fec30 00007ffe`fd2e4af2     KERNELBASE!UnhandledExceptionFilter+0x3b8
06 00000032`b51fed50 00007ffe`fd2cc6e6     ntdll!RtlUserThreadStart$filt$0+0xa2
07 00000032`b51fed90 00007ffe`fd2e120f     ntdll!_C_specific_handler+0x96
08 00000032`b51fee00 00007ffe`fd2aa299     ntdll!RtlpExecuteHandlerForException+0xf
09 00000032`b51fee30 00007ffe`fd2dfe7e     ntdll!RtlDispatchException+0x219
0a 00000032`b51ff540 00007ffe`fb1002b2     ntdll!KiUserExceptionDispatch+0x2e
0b 00000032`b51ffcd8 00007ff7`94981075     KERNELBASE!wil::details::DebugBreak+0x2
0c 00000032`b51ffce0 00007ff7`9498126c     AppK!wmain+0x35
0d (Inline Function) --------`--------     AppK!invoke_main+0x22
0e 00000032`b51ffd10 00007ffe`fbce7bd4     AppK!__scrt_common_main_seh+0x10c
0f 00000032`b51ffd50 00007ffe`fd2acee1     kernel32!BaseThreadInitThunk+0x14
10 00000032`b51ffd80 00000000`00000000     ntdll!RtlUserThreadStart+0x21

   1  Id: 2124.1e4c Suspend: 1 Teb: 00000032`b52d1000 Unfrozen
 # Child-SP          RetAddr               Call Site
00 00000032`b54feb88 00007ffe`fb086931     ntdll!NtDelayExecution+0x14
01 00000032`b54feb90 00007ffe`fbd36c93     KERNELBASE!SleepEx+0xa1
02 00000032`b54fec30 00007ffe`fb13f988     kernel32!WerpReportFault+0x97
03 00000032`b54fec70 00007ffe`fd2e4af2     KERNELBASE!UnhandledExceptionFilter+0x3b8
04 00000032`b54fed90 00007ffe`fd2cc6e6     ntdll!RtlUserThreadStart$filt$0+0xa2
05 00000032`b54fedd0 00007ffe`fd2e120f     ntdll!_C_specific_handler+0x96
06 00000032`b54fee40 00007ffe`fd2aa299     ntdll!RtlpExecuteHandlerForException+0xf
07 00000032`b54fee70 00007ffe`fd2dfe7e     ntdll!RtlDispatchException+0x219
08 00000032`b54ff580 00007ff7`94981030     ntdll!KiUserExceptionDispatch+0x2e
09 00000032`b54ffd20 00007ff7`94982888     AppK!thread_two+0x10
0a 00000032`b54ffd40 00007ffe`fbce7bd4     AppK!thread_start<void (__cdecl*)(void *),0>+0x50
```

321

```
0b 00000032`b54ffd70 00007ffe`fd2acee1       kernel32!BaseThreadInitThunk+0x14
0c 00000032`b54ffda0 00000000`00000000       ntdll!RtlUserThreadStart+0x21

    2  Id: 2124.1ce0 Suspend: 1 Teb: 00000032`b52d3000 Unfrozen
 # Child-SP          RetAddr               Call Site
00 00000032`b55fe8c8 00007ffe`fb086931       ntdll!NtDelayExecution+0x14
01 00000032`b55fe8d0 00007ffe`fbd36c93       KERNELBASE!SleepEx+0xa1
02 00000032`b55fe970 00007ffe`fb13f988       kernel32!WerpReportFault+0x97
03 00000032`b55fe9b0 00007ffe`fd2e4af2       KERNELBASE!UnhandledExceptionFilter+0x3b8
04 00000032`b55fead0 00007ffe`fd2cc6e6       ntdll!RtlUserThreadStart$filt$0+0xa2
05 00000032`b55feb10 00007ffe`fd2e120f       ntdll!_C_specific_handler+0x96
06 00000032`b55feb80 00007ffe`fd2aa299       ntdll!RtlpExecuteHandlerForException+0xf
07 00000032`b55febb0 00007ffe`fd2dfe7e       ntdll!RtlDispatchException+0x219
08 00000032`b55ff2c0 00007ff7`94981010       ntdll!KiUserExceptionDispatch+0x2e
09 00000032`b55ffa40 00007ff7`94982888       AppK!thread_one+0x10
0a 00000032`b55ffa60 00007ffe`fbce7bd4       AppK!thread_start<void (__cdecl*)(void *),0>+0x50
0b 00000032`b55ffa90 00007ffe`fd2acee1       kernel32!BaseThreadInitThunk+0x14
0c 00000032`b55ffac0 00000000`00000000       ntdll!RtlUserThreadStart+0x21

    3  Id: 2124.11ac Suspend: 1 Teb: 00000032`b52d5000 Unfrozen
 # Child-SP          RetAddr               Call Site
00 00000032`b56ff728 00007ffe`fd274060       ntdll!NtWaitForWorkViaWorkerFactory+0x14
01 00000032`b56ff730 00007ffe`fbce7bd4       ntdll!TppWorkerThread+0x300
02 00000032`b56ffaf0 00007ffe`fd2acee1       kernel32!BaseThreadInitThunk+0x14
03 00000032`b56ffb20 00000000`00000000       ntdll!RtlUserThreadStart+0x21

    4  Id: 2124.1fc0 Suspend: 1 Teb: 00000032`b52d7000 Unfrozen
 # Child-SP          RetAddr               Call Site
00 00000032`b57ff868 00007ffe`fd274060       ntdll!NtWaitForWorkViaWorkerFactory+0x14
01 00000032`b57ff870 00007ffe`fbce7bd4       ntdll!TppWorkerThread+0x300
02 00000032`b57ffc30 00007ffe`fd2acee1       kernel32!BaseThreadInitThunk+0x14
03 00000032`b57ffc60 00000000`00000000       ntdll!RtlUserThreadStart+0x21
```

Q. In which scenarios should we use this command: **dps** *stacklimit stackbase*?

A. We use this to check hints from past thread execution behavior that may have left useful traces of saved return addresses with symbolic references.

Q. k= some address ... when to use this command?

A. We use this command to guide WinDbg in stack trace reconstruction. Please see the selected usage examples and analysis patterns:

Incorrect Stack Trace https://www.dumpanalysis.org/blog/index.php/2007/04/03/crash-dump-analysis-patterns-part-11/

Reconstructing stack trace manually
https://www.dumpanalysis.org/blog/index.php/2007/07/25/reconstructing-stack-trace-manually/

Wild code and partial stack reconstruction
https://www.dumpanalysis.org/blog/index.php/2009/09/04/wild-code-and-partial-stack-reconstruction/

Empty Stack Trace https://www.dumpanalysis.org/blog/index.php/2011/12/12/crash-dump-analysis-patterns-part-161/

Lateral damage, stack overflow and execution residue: pattern cooperation

Q. When to use **dc** or **dp** or **dd** command and **dps** commands or **dpp**? What are the criteria?

A. It all depends on how you want to format your memory data: as byte characters simultaneously with 4-byte values (**dc**), as memory addresses (**dp**), as 8-byte values (**dq**), as 4-byte values (**dd**), 2-byte values (**dw**), as byte values (**db**), as memory addresses with corresponding symbolic references (**dps**), or memory addresses pointing to memory addresses with corresponding symbolic references (**dpp**).

Q. When an application crashes, does the RIP register always point to the crashed location?

A. If you mean when we open the dump file, sometimes, yes, if the dump was saved at that location. However, the memory dump may be saved later during exception processing, and in that case, the current thread RIP value is different.

Q. How to increase the disassembly lines in the output of **u** and **ub** commands?

A. You can specify the number of lines as a parameter:

```
0:000> ub 00007ff7`437da3d3
notepad!WinMain+0x271:
00007ff7`437da3b1 ff1589850100    call    qword ptr [notepad!_imp_TranslateMessage
(00007ff7`437f2940)]
00007ff7`437da3b7 488d4de7        lea     rcx,[rbp-19h]
00007ff7`437da3bb ff1587850100    call    qword ptr [notepad!_imp_DispatchMessageW
(00007ff7`437f2948)]
00007ff7`437da3c1 4533c9          xor     r9d,r9d
00007ff7`437da3c4 488d4de7        lea     rcx,[rbp-19h]
00007ff7`437da3c8 4533c0          xor     r8d,r8d
00007ff7`437da3cb 33d2            xor     edx,edx
00007ff7`437da3cd ff1555850100    call    qword ptr [notepad!_imp_GetMessageW
(00007ff7`437f2928)]

0:000> ub 00007ff7`437da3d3 L20
notepad!WinMain+0x20a:
00007ff7`437da34a 4533c9          xor     r9d,r9d
00007ff7`437da34d 4533c0          xor     r8d,r8d
00007ff7`437da350 ba01800000      mov     edx,8001h
00007ff7`437da355 ff15ed840100    call    qword ptr [notepad!_imp_PostMessageW
(00007ff7`437f2848)]
00007ff7`437da35b 488b1576200200  mov     rdx,qword ptr [notepad!hGlobalAccel
(00007ff7`437fc3d8)]
00007ff7`437da362 4c8d45e7        lea     r8,[rbp-19h]
00007ff7`437da366 488b0d0b300200  mov     rcx,qword ptr [notepad!hwndNP (00007ff7`437fd378)]
00007ff7`437da36d ff15bd850100    call    qword ptr [notepad!_imp_TranslateAcceleratorW
(00007ff7`437f2930)]
00007ff7`437da373 85c0            test    eax,eax
00007ff7`437da375 754a            jne     notepad!WinMain+0x281 (00007ff7`437da3c1)
00007ff7`437da377 488b0de22f0200  mov     rcx,qword ptr [notepad!hDlgFind (00007ff7`437fd360)]
```
323

```
00007ff7`437da37e 4885c9              test    rcx,rcx
00007ff7`437da381 740e                je      notepad!WinMain+0x251 (00007ff7`437da391)
00007ff7`437da383 488d55e7            lea     rdx,[rbp-19h]
00007ff7`437da387 ff15ab850100        call    qword ptr [notepad!_imp_IsDialogMessageW
(00007ff7`437f2938)]
00007ff7`437da38d 85c0                test    eax,eax
00007ff7`437da38f 7530                jne     notepad!WinMain+0x281 (00007ff7`437da3c1)
00007ff7`437da391 488b1538200200      mov     rdx,qword ptr [notepad!hAccel (00007ff7`437fc3d0)]
00007ff7`437da398 4c8d45e7            lea     r8,[rbp-19h]
00007ff7`437da39c 488b0dd52f0200      mov     rcx,qword ptr [notepad!hwndNP (00007ff7`437fd378)]
00007ff7`437da3a3 ff1587850100        call    qword ptr [notepad!_imp_TranslateAcceleratorW
(00007ff7`437f2930)]
00007ff7`437da3a9 85c0                test    eax,eax
00007ff7`437da3ab 7514                jne     notepad!WinMain+0x281 (00007ff7`437da3c1)
00007ff7`437da3ad 488d4de7            lea     rcx,[rbp-19h]
00007ff7`437da3b1 ff1589850100        call    qword ptr [notepad!_imp_TranslateMessage
(00007ff7`437f2940)]
00007ff7`437da3b7 488d4de7            lea     rcx,[rbp-19h]
00007ff7`437da3bb ff1587850100        call    qword ptr [notepad!_imp_DispatchMessageW
(00007ff7`437f2948)]
00007ff7`437da3c1 4533c9              xor     r9d,r9d
00007ff7`437da3c4 488d4de7            lea     rcx,[rbp-19h]
00007ff7`437da3c8 4533c0              xor     r8d,r8d
00007ff7`437da3cb 33d2                xor     edx,edx
00007ff7`437da3cd ff1555850100        call    qword ptr [notepad!_imp_GetMessageW
(00007ff7`437f2928)]
```

Q. What should we do when there are no matching symbols?

A. You can force their load using **.reload /f /i** *module_name* command.

Q. Can we know the file name and path using the file handle?

A. In process memory dumps, this is usually not possible unless that information is saved in the dump file. If the file handle is found on the raw stack region, the nearby data may point to ASCII or UNICODE strings if that information was not overwritten in the past. So you can dump memory contents in ASCII and UNICODE formats using **dpa** and **dpu** commands and do a memory search for strings using **s-sa** and **s-su** commands. It is usually possible in the kernel and complete memory dumps:

https://www.dumpanalysis.org/blog/index.php/2008/05/30/who-opened-that-file/.

Questions and answers from the earlier versions of this training course:

Q. What's the difference between **.symfix .reload** and **.loadby sos mscorwks**?

A. .symfix and **.reload** are necessary to specify the Microsoft symbol file server and then reload symbol files to update stack traces if necessary. In exercise P12, we have seen that there is no need to use **.loadby,** and we only need to pay attention to .NET Framework version and unload and load appropriate *sos.dll* manually.

Q. Is this type of hooking/modifying modules that is used by virus scanners to monitor access?

A. Yes, you can use **!chkimg** to detect such modifications in user space, and they are used by 3rd party modules to enable value-added services. Please refer to the **Hooksware** page for various case studies:

https://www.dumpanalysis.org/blog/index.php/2008/08/10/hooksware/

Q. Do you have a good reference for integer problems?

A. The only case study I have is about data alignment:

https://www.dumpanalysis.org/blog/index.php/2008/10/06/crash-dump-analysis-patterns-part-76/

Q. Is it possible to get a handle table from process dumps? I tried it, but **!handle 0 0** doesn't work.

A. Yes, it is possible, but it depends on how the dump was saved; for example, *userdump.exe* saves handle information but without specific details such as file names and paths:

```
0:000> !handle
Handle 0000000000000004
  Type              Directory
Handle 0000000000000008
  Type              File
Handle 000000000000000c
  Type              File
Handle 0000000000000010
  Type              Key
Handle 0000000000000014
  Type              ALPC Port
Handle 0000000000000018
  Type              Mutant
Handle 000000000000001c
  Type              Key
Handle 0000000000000020
  Type              Event
Handle 0000000000000024
  Type              Key
Handle 000000000000002c
  Type              Event
Handle 0000000000000030
  Type              WindowStation
Handle 0000000000000034
  Type              Desktop
Handle 0000000000000038
  Type              WindowStation
```

```
Handle 0000000000000080
    Type            Event
Handle 0000000000000084
    Type            Event
Handle 0000000000000088
    Type            Event
Handle 000000000000008c
    Type            Event
Handle 0000000000000090
    Type            Event
Handle 0000000000000094
    Type            Event
Handle 0000000000000098
    Type            Directory
Handle 000000000000009c
    Type            Event
Handle 00000000000000a0
    Type            Event
Handle 00000000000000a4
    Type            File
Handle 00000000000000a8
    Type            Key
Handle 00000000000000ac
    Type            Key
Handle 00000000000000b0
    Type            Key
Handle 00000000000000b4
    Type            Key
Handle 00000000000000c0
    Type            File
Handle 00000000000000c4
    Type            ALPC Port
Handle 00000000000000c8
    Type            Mutant
30 Handles
Type                Count
None                2
Event               10
File                4
Directory           2
Mutant              2
WindowStation       2
Key                 7
Desktop             1

0:000> !handle 000000000000000c ff
Handle 000000000000000c
    Type            File
    Attributes      0
    GrantedAccess   0x100020:
        Synch
        Execute/Traverse
    HandleCount     2
    PointerCount    3
    No object specific information available
```

ProcDump saves thread information, such as shown in exercises P17 – P19.

Q. I've heard a number of times that I should use the x64 version of WinDbg to open x64 dumps and x86 WinDbg to open x86 dumps. It looks like this is not quite required. Is there any restriction or rule on opening or taking dumps with the correct version of WinDbg?

A. What you should have in mind is that it is easier to analyze process memory dumps of 32-bit processes if they are saved by 32-bit tools. Then you don't need to switch to the x86 context where not all extension commands would work correctly.

Q. WinDbg appears to have many commands. Do you have a list of "most useful" commands and what they do? We can go through the exercises and extract the commands and then look in the help files, but a quick list could be very nice if you have one.

A. Please check the book "Windows Debugging Notebook: Essential User Space WinDbg Commands":

https://www.dumpanalysis.org/Forthcoming+Windows+Debugging+Notebook

Also, the first print issue of Debugged! MZ/PE magazine has an extensive command-to-pattern table:

https://www.amazon.com/Debugged-MZ-PE-Practicing-Engineers-ebook/dp/B01034WL9U/

Q. Is a return address related to the function on the same line or to the previous function on the next line?

A. It is related to the function on the next line where the execution resumes upon the return:

```
0:000> k
Child-SP          RetAddr           Call Site
00000000`0027f738 00000000`76d6c95e user32!NtUserGetMessage+0xa
00000000`0027f740 00000000`ff751064 user32!GetMessageW+0x34
00000000`0027f770 00000000`ff75133c notepad!WinMain+0x182
00000000`0027f7f0 00000000`76c4f33d notepad!DisplayNonGenuineDlgWorker+0x2da
00000000`0027f8b0 00000000`771e2cc1 kernel32!BaseThreadInitThunk+0xd
00000000`0027f8e0 00000000`00000000 ntdll!RtlUserThreadStart+0x1d


0:000> ub 00000000`ff751064
notepad!WinMain+0xf5:
00000000`ff751046 ff1544b40000    call    qword ptr [notepad!_imp_SetWinEventHook
(00000000`ff75c490)]
00000000`ff75104c 488bd8          mov     rbx,rax
00000000`ff75104f eb00            jmp     notepad!WinMain+0x16f (00000000`ff751051)
00000000`ff751051 488d4c2440      lea     rcx,[rsp+40h]
00000000`ff751056 4533c9          xor     r9d,r9d
00000000`ff751059 4533c0          xor     r8d,r8d
00000000`ff75105c 33d2            xor     edx,edx
00000000`ff75105e ff1524b40000    call    qword ptr [notepad!_imp_GetMessageW
(00000000`ff75c488)]
```

Q. Is there a way to load custom symbol paths into WinDbg that it will load by default? The idea would be to load our company's symbol files into a standard location, and then WinDbg could always access those symbol files.

A. Yes, it is possible to specify symbols paths in File \ Symbol File Path... and then do File \ Save Workspace.

Q. Why do we still see incorrect symbols warning message during **!analyze –v** after **.symfix** and **.reload**?

A. Sometimes, extension commands need private symbols. This usually happens if Microsoft changes public symbols but doesn't update extension commands.

Q. What is the difference between user and kernel space addresses on x64?

A. Please see the examples in this article:

https://www.dumpanalysis.org/blog/index.php/category/dictionary-of-debugging/8/

Q. Is there a command to clear the screen like tcsh ^L or cls in *cmd.exe*?

A. Yes, there is such a command: **.cls**

Q. Regarding stack traces, what does the ChildEBP stand for, and what dictates its order? Is there any particular reason why ChildEBP seems to count down in address instead of up? Or is that just a design consideration?

A. These are memory address values from the stack region. The stack grows down, so are ChildEBP addresses. Each address points to the saved EBP register value that belonged to the execution of the previous stack frame, followed by the saved return address and call parameters, if any. We can check this for the first few values:

```
0:001> kL
  *** Stack trace for last set context - .thread/.cxr resets it
ChildEBP RetAddr
0070f98c 77ad2d07 ntdll!RtlpCoalesceFreeBlocks+0x268
0070fa84 77ad2bf2 ntdll!RtlpFreeHeap+0x1f4
0070faa4 752914d1 ntdll!RtlFreeHeap+0x142
0070fab8 010b11f0 kernel32!HeapFree+0x14
0070faf8 010b1274 ApplicationL!free+0x6e
0070fb30 010b1310 ApplicationL!_callthreadstart+0x1b
0070fb38 75293677 ApplicationL!_threadstart+0x76
0070fb44 77ad9f02 kernel32!BaseThreadInitThunk+0xe
0070fb84 77ad9ed5 ntdll!__RtlUserThreadStart+0x70
0070fb9c 00000000 ntdll!_RtlUserThreadStart+0x1b

0:001> dps 0070f98c
0070f98c  0070fa84
0070f990  77ad2d07 ntdll!RtlpFreeHeap+0x1f4
0070f994  00740000
0070f998  007416b8
0070f99c  0070fa54
0070f9a0  00000000
0070f9a4  77e972c0
0070f9a8  00000000
0070f9ac  00740000
0070f9b0  007416c0
0070f9b4  00000000
0070f9b8  007422b0
0070f9bc  00000000
0070f9c0  00000029
0070f9c4  77b10ae5 ntdll!_except_handler4
```

```
0070f9c8  0000000e
0070f9cc  7534974f kernel32!$$VProc_ImageExportDirectory+0xa027
0070f9d0  0000019b
0070f9d4  75280000 kernel32!_imp__DebugBreak <PERF> (kernel32+0x0)
0070f9d8  00740000
0070f9dc  00740150
0070f9e0  29000029
0070f9e4  007400c4
0070f9e8  a60001a7
0070f9ec  00000000
0070f9f0  9a00019b
0070f9f4  00000000
0070f9f8  0000007f
0070f9fc  fffffffe
0070fa00  a60001a7
0070fa04  00000003
0070fa08  00000001

0:001> dps 0070fa84
0070fa84  0070faa4
0070fa88  77ad2bf2 ntdll!RtlFreeHeap+0x142
0070fa8c  007416b8
0070fa90  007416c0
0070fa94  007416c0
0070fa98  00000000
0070fa9c  00741280
0070faa0  007416b8
0070faa4  0070fab8
0070faa8  752914d1 kernel32!HeapFree+0x14
0070faac  00740000
0070fab0  00000000
0070fab4  007416c0
0070fab8  0070faf8
0070fabc  010b11f0 ApplicationL!free+0x6e [f:\dd\vctools\crt_bld\self_x86\crt\src\free.c @ 110]
0070fac0  00740000
0070fac4  00000000
0070fac8  007416c0
0070facc  1551789b
0070fad0  00000000
0070fad4  00000000
0070fad8  00741280
0070fadc  00000000
0070fae0  0070facc
0070fae4  0070f528
0070fae8  0070fb20
0070faec  010b2330 ApplicationL!_except_handler4
0070faf0  142a1103
0070faf4  fffffffe
0070faf8  0070fb30
0070fafc  010b1274 ApplicationL!_callthreadstart+0x1b
[f:\dd\vctools\crt_bld\self_x86\crt\src\thread.c @ 293]
0070fb00  007416c0
```

Q. What does the "deferred module" mean? Is it because the symbols for that module were not loaded?

A. It means the loading and applying symbol files was deferred because no references from such modules had been encountered during the execution of WinDbg commands:

```
0:000> lm
start    end      module name
00b90000 00bb8000 notepad    (deferred)
733a0000 733e1000 winspool   (deferred)
74d00000 74e94000 comctl32   (deferred)
750f0000 7512f000 uxtheme    (deferred)
75f70000 7602f000 advapi32   (deferred)
76100000 7614b000 gdi32      (deferred)
76150000 76228000 kernel32   (deferred)
76260000 76d2e000 shell32    (deferred)
76d60000 76e27000 msctf      (deferred)
76e30000 76ef3000 rpcrt4     (deferred)
76f00000 76f8c000 oleaut32   (deferred)
76f90000 76fae000 imm32      (deferred)
77000000 7707d000 usp10      (deferred)
772a0000 7733e000 user32     (deferred)
77390000 7743a000 msvcrt     (deferred)
77440000 77584000 ole32      (deferred)
776c0000 777de000 ntdll      (pdb symbols)
c:\mss\ntdll.pdb\C0A498F0036E4D4FB5CBF69005B0F9242\ntdll.pdb
77800000 77809000 lpk        (deferred)
77810000 77865000 shlwapi    (deferred)
77880000 778f4000 comdlg32   (deferred)

0:000> k
ChildEBP RetAddr
0024f9a0 772c199a ntdll!KiFastSystemCallRet
0024f9a4 772c19cd user32!NtUserGetMessage+0xc
0024f9c0 00b9149c user32!GetMessageW+0x33
0024fa00 00b91971 notepad!WinMain+0xec
0024fa90 76193833 notepad!_initterm_e+0x1a1
0024fa9c 776fa9bd kernel32!BaseThreadInitThunk+0xe
0024fadc 00000000 ntdll!_RtlUserThreadStart+0x23

0:000> lm
start    end      module name
00b90000 00bb8000 notepad    (pdb symbols)
c:\mss\notepad.pdb\A38D071FFAAF48F598510A34C7441E632\notepad.pdb
733a0000 733e1000 winspool   (deferred)
74d00000 74e94000 comctl32   (deferred)
750f0000 7512f000 uxtheme    (deferred)
75f70000 7602f000 advapi32   (deferred)
76100000 7614b000 gdi32      (deferred)
76150000 76228000 kernel32   (pdb symbols)
c:\mss\kernel32.pdb\04B9D5F57B154AA2BDBAB7946947DC4F2\kernel32.pdb
76260000 76d2e000 shell32    (deferred)
76d60000 76e27000 msctf      (deferred)
76e30000 76ef3000 rpcrt4     (deferred)
76f00000 76f8c000 oleaut32   (deferred)
76f90000 76fae000 imm32      (deferred)
77000000 7707d000 usp10      (deferred)
772a0000 7733e000 user32     (pdb symbols)
c:\mss\user32.pdb\211E0AFAB60349CAA056BBDF0BFABC862\user32.pdb
77390000 7743a000 msvcrt     (deferred)
77440000 77584000 ole32      (deferred)
776c0000 777de000 ntdll      (pdb symbols)
c:\mss\ntdll.pdb\C0A498F0036E4D4FB5CBF69005B0F9242\ntdll.pdb
77800000 77809000 lpk        (deferred)
77810000 77865000 shlwapi    (deferred)
77880000 778f4000 comdlg32   (deferred)
```

We can enable loading all symbols by changing this symbol engine option:

```
0:000> .symopt-4
Symbol options are 0x30233:
  0x00000001 - SYMOPT_CASE_INSENSITIVE
  0x00000002 - SYMOPT_UNDNAME
  0x00000010 - SYMOPT_LOAD_LINES
  0x00000020 - SYMOPT_OMAP_FIND_NEAREST
  0x00000200 - SYMOPT_FAIL_CRITICAL_ERRORS
  0x00010000 - SYMOPT_AUTO_PUBLICS
  0x00020000 - SYMOPT_NO_IMAGE_SEARCH

0:000> lm
start    end       module name
00b90000 00bb8000   notepad    (pdb symbols)
c:\mss\notepad.pdb\A38D071FFAAF48F598510A34C7441E632\notepad.pdb
733a0000 733e1000   winspool   (pdb symbols)
c:\mss\winspool.pdb\269416BE07D444DBA4FBE4CC0D54CD1F1\winspool.pdb
74d00000 74e94000   comctl32   (pdb symbols)
c:\mss\comctl32.pdb\21E9875AABA84F2B8684918034532B032\comctl32.pdb
750f0000 7512f000   uxtheme    (pdb symbols)
c:\mss\UxTheme.pdb\7785CC6B21A548F9813607AF098FDC802\UxTheme.pdb
75f70000 7602f000   advapi32   (pdb symbols)
c:\mss\advapi32.pdb\19D721512AA34917998058CB02F5E5F92\advapi32.pdb
76100000 7614b000   gdi32      (pdb symbols)
c:\mss\gdi32.pdb\E577982B8C2B46FAB6643BE7E4F8B5802\gdi32.pdb
76150000 76228000   kernel32   (pdb symbols)
c:\mss\kernel32.pdb\04B9D5F57B154AA2BDBAB7946947DC4F2\kernel32.pdb
76260000 76d2e000   shell32    (pdb symbols)
c:\mss\shell32.pdb\8BA1535FFD254B96B351C1BABA3264AF2\shell32.pdb
76d60000 76e27000   msctf      (pdb symbols)
c:\mss\msctf.pdb\1377BE94C653479BA027ADFEF2014B032\msctf.pdb
76e30000 76ef3000   rpcrt4     (pdb symbols)
c:\mss\rpcrt4.pdb\F4D03C747491485FA6118AC629DE03932\rpcrt4.pdb
76f00000 76f8c000   oleaut32   (pdb symbols)
c:\mss\oleaut32.pdb\9C2CE2B52D9740CE80BC19F9F840C70E2\oleaut32.pdb
76f90000 76fae000   imm32      (pdb symbols)
c:\mss\imm32.pdb\F08E00C515AF488C9D89C9EFFED71E292\imm32.pdb
77000000 7707d000   usp10      (pdb symbols)
c:\mss\usp10.pdb\676B6AF372034FB1A49400E8A5BAA1522\usp10.pdb
772a0000 7733e000   user32     (pdb symbols)
c:\mss\user32.pdb\211E0AFAB60349CAA056BBDF0BFABC862\user32.pdb
77390000 7743a000   msvcrt     (pdb symbols)
c:\mss\msvcrt.pdb\8A24BF4B1A05412FB0312AD4CB7867042\msvcrt.pdb
77440000 77584000   ole32      (pdb symbols)
c:\mss\ole32.pdb\DE10A65FA3FE400D97D24EAFF32FC08E2\ole32.pdb
776c0000 777de000   ntdll      (pdb symbols)
c:\mss\ntdll.pdb\C0A498F0036E4D4FB5CBF69005B0F9242\ntdll.pdb
77800000 77809000   lpk        (pdb symbols)
c:\mss\lpk.pdb\7C176ABDDBD54AE6B2B51399AFDBEE952\lpk.pdb
77810000 77865000   shlwapi    (pdb symbols)
c:\mss\shlwapi.pdb\7D3C64434A3248EA958A1352DAE70CC52\shlwapi.pdb
77880000 778f4000   comdlg32   (pdb symbols)
c:\mss\comdlg32.pdb\0A186B22C5294AA7A85FD86BC02EB3922\comdlg32.pdb
```

Q. Are user exceptions always stored at the same address?

```
EXCEPTION_RECORD:  ffffffff -- (.exr 0xffffffffffffffff)
```

It looks like some exercises point to the same exception record.

A. It is just the command **.exr -1** that shows the most recent exception (perhaps the address is not available for this command, and it needs to find it during its execution):

```
0:001> .exr 0xffffffffffffffff
ExceptionAddress: 77ad3b30 (ntdll!RtlpCoalesceFreeBlocks+0x00000268)
   ExceptionCode: c0000005 (Access violation)
  ExceptionFlags: 00000000
NumberParameters: 2
   Parameter[0]: 00000000
   Parameter[1]: 00000003
Attempt to read from address 00000003

0:001> .exr -1
ExceptionAddress: 77ad3b30 (ntdll!RtlpCoalesceFreeBlocks+0x00000268)
   ExceptionCode: c0000005 (Access violation)
  ExceptionFlags: 00000000
NumberParameters: 2
   Parameter[0]: 00000000
   Parameter[1]: 00000003
Attempt to read from address 00000003
```

Q. What is an exception_record? Is exception_record == context? Can you please clarify what "CONTEXT" is exactly?

A. An exception record contains an exception description, whereas a context structure contains the processor register snapshot at the time of the exception:

```
0:001> dt _EXCEPTION_RECORD
ApplicationL!_EXCEPTION_RECORD
   +0x000 ExceptionCode    : Uint4B
   +0x004 ExceptionFlags   : Uint4B
   +0x008 ExceptionRecord  : Ptr32 _EXCEPTION_RECORD
   +0x00c ExceptionAddress : Ptr32 Void
   +0x010 NumberParameters : Uint4B
   +0x014 ExceptionInformation : [15] Uint4B


0:001> dt _CONTEXT
ApplicationL!_CONTEXT
   +0x000 ContextFlags     : Uint4B
   +0x004 Dr0              : Uint4B
   +0x008 Dr1              : Uint4B
   +0x00c Dr2              : Uint4B
   +0x010 Dr3              : Uint4B
   +0x014 Dr6              : Uint4B
   +0x018 Dr7              : Uint4B
   +0x01c FloatSave        : _FLOATING_SAVE_AREA
   +0x08c SegGs            : Uint4B
   +0x090 SegFs            : Uint4B
   +0x094 SegEs            : Uint4B
   +0x098 SegDs            : Uint4B
   +0x09c Edi              : Uint4B
```

```
    +0x0a0 Esi                 : Uint4B
    +0x0a4 Ebx                 : Uint4B
    +0x0a8 Edx                 : Uint4B
    +0x0ac Ecx                 : Uint4B
    +0x0b0 Eax                 : Uint4B
    +0x0b4 Ebp                 : Uint4B
    +0x0b8 Eip                 : Uint4B
    +0x0bc SegCs               : Uint4B
    +0x0c0 EFlags              : Uint4B
    +0x0c4 Esp                 : Uint4B
    +0x0c8 SegSs               : Uint4B
    +0x0cc ExtendedRegisters : [512] Uchar
```

Q. So, is there only one exception record for a process? How can one identify an exception record from the raw stack?

A. There can be many exception records **per thread**. You can either try to get _EXCEPTION_POINTERS structure from *UnhandledExceptionFilter* or play with nearby function parameters:

```
0:001> kv
ChildEBP RetAddr  Args to Child
0070f2e0 770d0bdd 00000002 0070f330 00000001 ntdll!NtWaitForMultipleObjects+0x15 (FPO: [5,0,0])
0070f37c 7529162d 0070f330 0070f3a4 00000000 KERNELBASE!WaitForMultipleObjectsEx+0x100 (FPO:
[Non-Fpo])
0070f3c4 75291921 00000002 7efde000 00000000
kernel32!WaitForMultipleObjectsExImplementation+0xe0 (FPO: [Non-Fpo])
0070f3e0 752b9b2d 00000002 0070f414 00000000 kernel32!WaitForMultipleObjects+0x18 (FPO: [Non-
Fpo])
0070f44c 752b9bca 0070f52c 00000001 00000001 kernel32!WerpReportFaultInternal+0x186 (FPO: [Non-
Fpo])
0070f460 752b98f8 0070f52c 00000001 0070f4fc kernel32!WerpReportFault+0x70 (FPO: [Non-Fpo])
0070f470 752b9875 0070f52c 00000001 154fde2b kernel32!BasepReportFault+0x20 (FPO: [Non-Fpo])
0070f4fc 77b10df7 00000000 77b10cd4 00000000 kernel32!UnhandledExceptionFilter+0x1af (FPO:
[Non-Fpo])
0070f504 77b10cd4 00000000 0070fb84 77acc550 ntdll!__RtlUserThreadStart+0x62 (FPO: [SEH])
0070f518 77b10b71 00000000 00000000 00000000 ntdll!_EH4_CallFilterFunc+0x12 (FPO: [Uses EBP]
[0,0,4])
0070f540 77ae6ac9 fffffffe 0070fb74 0070f67c ntdll!_except_handler4+0x8e (FPO: [Non-Fpo])
0070f564 77ae6a9b 0070f62c 0070fb74 0070f67c ntdll!ExecuteHandler2+0x26
0070f614 77ab010f 0170f62c 0070f67c 0070f62c ntdll!ExecuteHandler+0x24
0070f614 77ad3b30 0170f62c 0070f67c 0070f62c ntdll!KiUserExceptionDispatcher+0xf (FPO: [2,0,0])
(CONTEXT @ 0070f67c)
0070f98c 77ad2d07 00740000 007416b8 0070fa54 ntdll!RtlpCoalesceFreeBlocks+0x268 (FPO: [Non-
Fpo])
0070fa84 77ad2bf2 007416b8 007416c0 007416c0 ntdll!RtlpFreeHeap+0x1f4 (FPO: [Non-Fpo])
0070faa4 752914d1 00740000 00000000 007416c0 ntdll!RtlFreeHeap+0x142 (FPO: [Non-Fpo])
0070fab8 010b11f0 00740000 00000000 007416c0 kernel32!HeapFree+0x14 (FPO: [Non-Fpo])
0070faf8 010b1274 007416c0 15517953 00000000 ApplicationL!free+0x6e (FPO: [Non-Fpo]) (CONV:
cdecl) [f:\dd\vctools\crt_bld\self_x86\crt\src\free.c @ 110]
0070fb30 010b1310 0070fb44 75293677 00741280 ApplicationL!_callthreadstart+0x1b (FPO: [Non-
Fpo]) (CONV: cdecl) [f:\dd\vctools\crt_bld\self_x86\crt\src\thread.c @ 293]
0070fb38 75293677 00741280 0070fb84 77ad9f02 ApplicationL!_threadstart+0x76 (FPO: [Non-Fpo])
(CONV: stdcall) [f:\dd\vctools\crt_bld\self_x86\crt\src\thread.c @ 275]
0070fb44 77ad9f02 00741280 77e973c0 00000000 kernel32!BaseThreadInitThunk+0xe (FPO: [Non-Fpo])
0070fb84 77ad9ed5 010b129a 00741280 ffffffff ntdll!__RtlUserThreadStart+0x70 (FPO: [Non-Fpo])
0070fb9c 00000000 010b129a 00741280 00000000 ntdll!_RtlUserThreadStart+0x1b (FPO: [Non-Fpo])
```

```
0:001> dt _EXCEPTION_POINTERS 0070f52c
ApplicationL!_EXCEPTION_POINTERS
   +0x000 ExceptionRecord : 0x0070f62c _EXCEPTION_RECORD
   +0x004 ContextRecord  : 0x0070f67c _CONTEXT

0:001> .exr 0070f62c
ExceptionAddress: 77ad3b30 (ntdll!RtlpCoalesceFreeBlocks+0x00000268)
   ExceptionCode: c0000005 (Access violation)
  ExceptionFlags: 00000000
NumberParameters: 2
   Parameter[0]: 00000000
   Parameter[1]: 00000003
Attempt to read from address 00000003

0:001> .cxr 0070f67c
eax=00740f30 ebx=007416b8 ecx=ffffffff edx=00000a00 esi=00740f28 edi=00740000
eip=77ad3b30 esp=0070f964 ebp=0070f98c iopl=0         nv up ei pl zr na pe nc
cs=0023  ss=002b  ds=002b  es=002b  fs=0053  gs=002b            efl=00010246
ntdll!RtlpCoalesceFreeBlocks+0x268:
77ad3b30 8b4904          mov     ecx,dword ptr [ecx+4] ds:002b:00000003=????????
```

There is another viewing command too:

```
0:001> .exptr 0070f52c

----- Exception record at 0070f62c:
ExceptionAddress: 77ad3b30 (ntdll!RtlpCoalesceFreeBlocks+0x00000268)
   ExceptionCode: c0000005 (Access violation)
  ExceptionFlags: 00000000
NumberParameters: 2
   Parameter[0]: 00000000
   Parameter[1]: 00000003
Attempt to read from address 00000003

----- Context record at 0070f67c:
eax=00740f30 ebx=007416b8 ecx=ffffffff edx=00000a00 esi=00740f28 edi=00740000
eip=77ad3b30 esp=0070f964 ebp=0070f98c iopl=0         nv up ei pl zr na pe nc
cs=0023  ss=002b  ds=002b  es=002b  fs=0053  gs=002b            efl=00010246
ntdll!RtlpCoalesceFreeBlocks+0x268:
77ad3b30 8b4904          mov     ecx,dword ptr [ecx+4] ds:002b:00000003=????????
```

When looking at raw stack data, we can get them from nearby exception processing function residue:

```
[...]
0070f584  0070f62c
0070f588  0070fb74
0070f58c  77ae6a3d ntdll!RtlDispatchException+0x127
0070f590  0070f62c
0070f594  0070fb74
0070f598  0070f67c
0070f59c  0070f600
0070f5a0  77b10ae5 ntdll!_except_handler4
0070f5a4  00740000
0070f5a8  0070f62c
0070f5ac  00740f28
0070f5b0  00000000
0070f5b4  00000000
0070f5b8  00000000
0070f5bc  00000000
0070f5c0  00000000
```

```
0070f5c4  00000000
0070f5c8  00000000
0070f5cc  00000000
0070f5d0  00000000
0070f5d4  00000000
0070f5d8  00000000
0070f5dc  00000000
0070f5e0  00000000
0070f5e4  00000000
0070f5e8  00000000
0070f5ec  00000000
0070f5f0  00000000
0070f5f4  00000000
0070f5f8  00000000
0070f5fc  00000000
0070f600  00000000
0070f604  0000000d
0070f608  00710000
0070f60c  0070e000
0070f610  00000000
0070f614  0070f98c
0070f618  77ab010f ntdll!KiUserExceptionDispatcher+0xf
0070f61c  0170f62c
0070f620  0070f67c
0070f624  0070f62c
0070f628  0070f67c
0070f62c  c0000005
0070f630  00000000
0070f634  00000000
[...]
```

Sometimes we can spot **0001003f**, and its address can be the beginning of a context record:

```
[...]
0070f668  00000000
0070f66c  00000000
0070f670  00000000
0070f674  00000000
0070f678  00000000
0070f67c  0001003f
0070f680  00000000
0070f684  00000000
0070f688  00000000
0070f68c  00000000
0070f690  00000000
0070f694  00000000
0070f698  0000027f
0070f69c  00000000
0070f6a0  0000ffff
0070f6a4  00000000
0070f6a8  00000000
0070f6ac  00000000
0070f6b0  00000000
0070f6b4  00000000
0070f6b8  00000000
0070f6bc  00000000
0070f6c0  00000000
0070f6c4  00000000
0070f6c8  00000000
```

```
0070f6cc   00000000
0070f6d0   00000000
0070f6d4   00000000
0070f6d8   00000000
0070f6dc   00000000
0070f6e0   00000000
0070f6e4   00000000
0070f6e8   00000000
0070f6ec   00000000
0070f6f0   00000000
0070f6f4   00000000
0070f6f8   00000000
0070f6fc   00000000
0070f700   00000000
0070f704   00000001
0070f708   0000002b
0070f70c   00000053
0070f710   0000002b
0070f714   0000002b
0070f718   00740000
0070f71c   00740f28
0070f720   007416b8
0070f724   00000a00
0070f728   ffffffff
0070f72c   00740f30
0070f730   0070f98c
0070f734   77ad3b30 ntdll!RtlpCoalesceFreeBlocks+0x268
0070f738   00000023
0070f73c   00010246
0070f740   0070f964
0070f744   0000002b
0070f748   0000027f
0070f74c   00000000
0070f750   00000000
0070f754   00000000
0070f758   00000000
0070f75c   00000000
0070f760   00001f80
0070f764   0000ffff
0070f768   00000000
0070f76c   00000000
[...]
```

Q. I don't get error text descriptions (**!error** 0xc0000374). Could this have to do with my system being 32-bit?

A. Yes, the error description text might not be available on a crash dump analysis system. WinDbg calls an API that translates an error code to the corresponding description text.

Q. Is there a way to determine in a memory dump whether **gflags** were enabled on an application?

A. Yes, there is a command for this:

```
0:000> !gflag
Current NtGlobalFlag contents: 0x00001000
    ust - Create user mode stack trace database
```

Q. 3 out of the 5 threads in a process memory dump have exceptions. How come the process didn't catch and die on the first exception?

A. This is because exception threads were reporting faults to WER, and WER dialogs were waiting for user input.

Q. Would **!locks** help in deadlock and wait chain diagnosis? Is it the same as the **!cs -l -o -s** command?

A. In the past, the **!locks** command stopped working, so I started recommending the **!cs** variant. Now, it is working again, but **!cs** gives more details for wait chain analysis, so we use it in this training.

```
0:000> !locks

CritSec ApplicationN!cs1+0 at 000000013fd7ef08
WaiterWoken        No
LockCount          1
RecursionCount     1
OwningThread       66c
EntryCount         0
ContentionCount    1
*** Locked

CritSec ApplicationN!cs2+0 at 000000013fd7eee0
WaiterWoken        No
LockCount          1
RecursionCount     1
OwningThread       a88
EntryCount         0
ContentionCount    1
*** Locked

Scanned 39 critical sections
```

Q. Are critical sections a system resource? How are they defined?

A. Usually, such resources are defined using system synchronization primitives such as events and semaphores:

```
0:000> dt _RTL_CRITICAL_SECTION
ntdll!_RTL_CRITICAL_SECTION
   +0x000 DebugInfo        : Ptr64 _RTL_CRITICAL_SECTION_DEBUG
   +0x008 LockCount        : Int4B
   +0x00c RecursionCount   : Int4B
   +0x010 OwningThread     : Ptr64 Void
   +0x018 LockSemaphore    : Ptr64 Void
   +0x020 SpinCount        : Uint8B
```

Q. Is there an easier way to get 64-bit function arguments?

A. You can try the **!stack** command from this extension:
https://www.codemachine.com/downloads/cmkd.html

Q. Is there a way to figure out which section (.text, .data) a virtual address belongs to?

A. When a module is loaded, its sections are mapped to corresponding usage regions. You can use this **!address** command:

```
0:000> !address 000000013fd7ef08
Usage:                Image
Allocation Base:      00000001`3fd70000
Base Address:         00000001`3fd7d000
End Address:          00000001`3fd80000
Region Size:          00000000`00003000
Type:                 01000000 MEM_IMAGE
State:                00001000 MEM_COMMIT
Protect:              00000004 PAGE_READWRITE
More info:            lmv m ApplicationN
More info:            !lmi ApplicationN
More info:            ln 0x13fd7ef08


0:000> !address esp
Usage:                Stack
Allocation Base:      00000000`00210000
Base Address:         00000000`0030c000
End Address:          00000000`00310000
Region Size:          00000000`00004000
Type:                 00020000 MEM_PRIVATE
State:                00001000 MEM_COMMIT
Protect:              00000004 PAGE_READWRITE
More info:            ~0k


0:000> !address rip
Usage:                Image
Allocation Base:      00000000`778c0000
Base Address:         00000000`778c1000
End Address:          00000000`779c4000
Region Size:          00000000`00103000
Type:                 01000000 MEM_IMAGE
State:                00001000 MEM_COMMIT
Protect:              00000020 PAGE_EXECUTE_READ
More info:            lmv m ntdll
More info:            !lmi ntdll
More info:            ln 0x7790f9fa
```

Q. How did you find the start address of **!teb** you need to use?

A. You can use the ~ command:

```
0:000> ~
.  0  Id: b6c.614 Suspend: 0 Teb: 000007ff`fffde000 Unfrozen
   1  Id: b6c.66c Suspend: 0 Teb: 000007ff`fffdc000 Unfrozen
   2  Id: b6c.a88 Suspend: 0 Teb: 000007ff`fffda000 Unfrozen
```

Q. If you can include information when and when not to look at the 64-bit stack, in your material, it would be good.

A. Here's an article that provides an example of manual parameter reconstruction on x64 Windows platforms:

https://www.dumpanalysis.org/blog/index.php/2009/09/04/manual-parameter-reconstruction-on-x64-windows-systems/

Q. How did you figure the double free from the stack trace?

A. There might be small variations in stack traces, especially if we enable different options using *gflags.exe*. Please refer to this article:

http://www.dumpanalysis.org/blog/index.php/2007/08/19/crash-dump-analysis-patterns-part-23a/

Q. When using **!cs** on complete memory dumps I have captured, I get bad symbols for NTDLL (error 3) on multiple different dumps. Even though running **.symfix** and **.reload** before didn't help, do you know why this happens?

A. I would recommend enabling verbose symbol loading:

```
0:000> !sym noisy
noisy mode - symbol prompts on

0:000> .reload
```

The first four episodes from https://www.debugging.tv discussed symbol troubleshooting in some detail.

Q. Do you have a block to teach some basics on how to read disassembly?

A. I would recommend "Practical Foundations of Windows Debugging, Disassembling, Reversing" book:

https://www.dumpanalysis.org/practical-foundations-windows-debugging-disassembling-reversing

Also, there's an excellent **Hacker Disassembling Uncovered** book by Kris Kaspersky.

Q. If a system process is hanging and preventing other processes from functioning, what is the best way to find what is the cause and what is causing it?

A. I would recommend analyzing its stack traces and compare with the normal ones. There could be blocked threads.

Q. Dump analysis provides good info about system hangs, is there any good information on how to incorporate that with perfmon logs and procmon logs?

A. Of course, you can correlate dynamic software behavior seen in logs to a static memory picture. For example, if you know PID.TID, you can check past behavior from a log, and if you see TID messages in the log abruptly stopped, you can inspect a memory dump, or if you see a CPU spiking thread in a dump you can inspect a log.

Q. How conceptually can a thread "own" a critical section?

A. Please refer to this MSDN article detailing critical section internals:

Q. Is there a prefixing convention (e.g.: ! .) for commands?

A. Commands that start with '**!**' are implemented in debugging extension DLLs. Commands that start with '**.**' are meta-commands implemented by a debugger. To get the latter list, use the **.help** command.

Q. How do you create memory dumps?

A. Please find this presentation with slides outlining different methods with corresponding article links:

https://www.patterndiagnostics.com/files/LegacyWindowsDebugging.pdf

Q. Is the **!pe** extension command only available in WinDbg (X86)? I tried the WinDbg (X64) version, and I'm getting a "no export pe found" message.

A. I think the main reason for that message is that either your process memory dump was from a 32-bit process, and you need 32-bit WinDbg to load the 32-bit SOS extension, or if your dump is from a 64-bit process and the **!analyze –v** command didn't load that extension automatically, so you need to use the **.load** command and specify a full path to *sos.dll* from .NET Framework folder.

Q. How to increase the command window buffer in WinDbg?

A. It may be possible to use a programmatic solution (external or internal via a debugger extension) to find a RichEdit edit window with the "Command" title and send EM_EXLIMITTEXT message to it. Alternatively, you can use the **.logopen** command to open a log file, and you can open that file for reading at any time in parallel to WinDbg for inspection of the earlier output.

Q. What is ChildEBP in the **k** command output?

A. These are values of the EBP register from the caller function saved on a stack by a callee. These values are commonly used to manually reconstruct a stack trace because they link function calls together.

```
0:000> k
ChildEBP RetAddr
0024f9a0 772c199a ntdll!KiFastSystemCallRet
0024f9a4 772c19cd user32!NtUserGetMessage+0xc
0024f9c0 00b9149c user32!GetMessageW+0x33
0024fa00 00b91971 notepad!WinMain+0xec
0024fa90 76193833 notepad!_initterm_e+0x1a1
0024fa9c 776fa9bd kernel32!BaseThreadInitThunk+0xe
0024fadc 00000000 ntdll!_RtlUserThreadStart+0x23

0:000> dps 0024f9c0 L3
0024f9c0  0024fa00
0024f9c4  00b9149c notepad!WinMain+0xec
0024f9c8  0024f9e4

0:000> dps 0024fa00 L3
0024fa00  0024fa90
0024fa04  00b91971 notepad!_initterm_e+0x1a1
```

340

```
0024fa08   00b90000 notepad!_imp__RegQueryValueExW <PERF> (notepad+0x0)

0:000> dps 0024fa90 L3
0024fa90   0024fa9c
0024fa94   76193833 kernel32!BaseThreadInitThunk+0xe
0024fa98   7ffd9000

0:000> dps 0024fa9c L3
0024fa9c   0024fadc
0024faa0   776fa9bd ntdll!_RtlUserThreadStart+0x23
0024faa4   7ffd9000
```

For an example of a manual stack reconstruction on x86 platforms, please see this case study:

https://www.dumpanalysis.org/blog/index.php/2007/07/25/reconstructing-stack-trace-manually/

Q. Does Task Manager send requests to check for hang condition?

A. Any application can send window messages with a timeout to check if windows are responsive or not. For example, using the *SendMessageTimeout* function with SMTO_ABORTIFHUNG flag value:

https://learn.microsoft.com/en-gb/windows/win32/api/winuser/nf-winuser-sendmessagetimeouta

Q. What if I need symbols for Citrix modules?

A. You can get Citrix symbol server path information either from www.windbg.org or this article:

https://support.citrix.com/article/CTX118622/how-to-use-the-citrix-symbol-server-to-obtain-debug-symbols

Q. When troubleshooting process termination, if you configure a default postmortem debugging tool and if you do not get a dump from a specific process, can you assume it exits gracefully?

A. Sometimes, when you get very nasty abnormal behavior such as stack overflows, a process may terminate without WER or default postmortem debugger involved. Configure LocalDumps on modern Windows systems. On legacy Windows systems prior to Windows Vista, you can also try monitoring your process with ADPlus in crash mode. Please look at this short tutorial:

https://www.dumpanalysis.org/blog/index.php/2008/09/12/adplus-in-21-seconds-and-13-steps/

Q. Why does WinDbg complain about the "Second Chance Exception"? Why not a first chance or a third chance?

A. I assume you refer to this message as "*first/second chance not available.*" This is a normal situation when a process memory dump is not saved under a debugger. If you run a process under a debugger such as WinDbg, it will have a (first) chance to see an exception before it is processed by a thread exception handling code, if there is any. Then at this point a saved process memory dump will be a first chance exception memory dump. In the debugger, you can dismiss that exception, and if it wasn't handled, control is returned to the debugger again for (second) processing, and at that point, a second chance exception memory dump can be saved. For additional information and examples, please visit this page: https://www.dumpanalysis.org/blog/index.php/first-chance-exceptions-explained/

Q. Why are all threads "Unfrozen" in a process memory dump? Does unfrozen thread ever change to frozen, and why would it do that? Why are other threads suspended?

A. A thread can be frozen if a process is under debugger control. If the debugger resumes process execution, all threads resume except the frozen thread. So if you didn't use **~<n> f** command in a debugger or saved your process memory dump by other means, all threads will be unfrozen. A thread can be suspended by OS or through API. In such cases, its suspend count will be increased. Normally a thread suspend count is 0, and there is a pattern otherwise (**Suspended Thread**):

https://www.dumpanalysis.org/blog/index.php/2008/02/06/crash-dump-analysis-patterns-part-47/

Q. What are FPO and non-FPO mean in a stack trace?

A. This is the so-called Frame Pointer Omission on 32-bit Windows platforms when EBP is reused as a general-purpose register, thus making stack reconstruction difficult without special support from symbol files. For an example, please refer to the same name pattern:

https://www.dumpanalysis.org/blog/index.php/2008/02/13/crash-dump-analysis-patterns-part-49/

On x64 Windows platforms, FPO is not used.

Q. Can a thread own more than one critical section, and if so will it be listed as the output of **!cs** command?

A. Yes, this frequently happens, and each such owned (locked) critical section will be listed with the same owner thread stack trace.

Q. Can a critical section lock count be more than one? Will that be the indication of a deadlock?

A. A deadlock assumes at least 2 threads are mutually locked, so two critical sections with a non-zero lock count are necessary. If you have just one critical section with a lock count of more than one, then it is more likely that we have multiple threads blocked waiting for that critical section to be released (a critical section wait chain):

https://www.dumpanalysis.org/blog/index.php/2007/12/19/crash-dump-analysis-patterns-part-42b/

Q. What is exactly a frame? Are there stack frame IDs or numbers?

A. A frame is a fragment of stack memory region containing values of called function parameters, the saved return address of a caller function, local variables, and information to link with other frames. It is possible to see frame numbers from the **kn** command (or any variant such as **kvn**) and switch between them using the **.frame** command:

```
0:000> kn
 # Child-SP          RetAddr           Call Site
00 00000000`0011fa98 00000000`76ffe6fa user32!ZwUserGetMessage+0xa
01 00000000`0011faa0 00000000`ffe56eca user32!GetMessageW+0x34
```

```
02 00000000`0011fad0 00000000`ffe5cf8b notepad!WinMain+0x176
03 00000000`0011fb50 00000000`770ecdcd notepad!IsTextUTF8+0x24f
04 00000000`0011fc10 00000000`7723c6e1 kernel32!BaseThreadInitThunk+0xd
05 00000000`0011fc40 00000000`00000000 ntdll!RtlUserThreadStart+0x1d

0:000> .frame 2
02 00000000`0011fad0 00000000`ffe5cf8b notepad!WinMain+0x176
```

Q. What is the stack size limit for 32 and 64?

A. It depends on the execution space. User space thread stack usually expands up to 1Mb, but that is configurable via a linking option:

```
0:001> k
Child-SP          RetAddr           Call Site
00000000`0071eb58 00000000`77985ac2 ntdll!ZwWaitForSingleObject+0xa
00000000`0071eb60 00000000`77985c65 ntdll!RtlReportSqmEscalation+0xfc2
00000000`0071ec50 00000000`77985cca ntdll!RtlReportException+0xb5
00000000`0071ecd0 00000000`77986b05 ntdll!RtlReportException+0x11a
00000000`0071ed00 00000000`778d4f48 ntdll!RtlUnhandledExceptionFilter+0x325
00000000`0071ed30 00000000`778f4f6d ntdll!_C_specific_handler+0x9c
00000000`0071eda0 00000000`778d5b2c ntdll!RtlCompareUnicodeString+0x8d
00000000`0071edd0 00000000`778d60fe ntdll!RtlTimeToSecondsSince1970+0x63c
00000000`0071f4b0 00000000`77986ab2 ntdll!RtlRaiseException+0x23e
00000000`0071faf0 00000000`77987176 ntdll!RtlUnhandledExceptionFilter+0x2d2
00000000`0071fbc0 00000000`779884a2 ntdll!EtwEnumerateProcessRegGuids+0x216
00000000`0071fbf0 00000000`77989e34 ntdll!RtlQueryProcessLockInformation+0x952
00000000`0071fc20 00000000`7792c05d ntdll!RtlLogStackBackTrace+0x444
00000000`0071fc50 00000000`77662a8a ntdll!LdrGetProcedureAddress+0x1439d
00000000`0071fcd0 00000001`3fb81258 kernel32!HeapFree+0xa
00000000`0071fd00 00000001`3fb8111c ApplicationO+0x1258
00000000`0071fd30 00000001`3fb812e7 ApplicationO+0x111c
00000000`0071fd70 00000001`3fb81391 ApplicationO+0x12e7
00000000`0071fda0 00000000`7765f33d ApplicationO+0x1391
00000000`0071fdd0 00000000`778f2cc1 kernel32!BaseThreadInitThunk+0xd
00000000`0071fe00 00000000`00000000 ntdll!RtlUserThreadStart+0x21

0:001> !address 00000000`0071edd0
Usage:                    <unclassified>
Allocation Base:          00000000`00620000
Base Address:             00000000`0071d000
End Address:              00000000`00720000
Region Size:              00000000`00003000
Type:                     00020000 MEM_PRIVATE
State:                    00001000 MEM_COMMIT
Protect:                  00000004 PAGE_READWRITE

0:001> ~3s
ntdll!ZwDelayExecution+0xa:
00000000`7790f9fa c3              ret

0:003> k 20
Child-SP          RetAddr           Call Site
00000000`00931ca8 000007fe`fdde1203 ntdll!ZwDelayExecution+0xa
00000000`00931cb0 00000001`3fb88b58 KERNELBASE!SleepEx+0xb3
00000000`00931d50 00000001`3fb889e0 ApplicationO+0x8b58
00000000`00931d80 00000001`3fb877b4 ApplicationO+0x89e0
00000000`00931db0 00000000`7790f001 ApplicationO+0x77b4
00000000`00931e80 00000001`3fb81023 ntdll!RtlRestoreContext+0x2e2
```

```
00000000`00933ff0 00000001`3fb81028 Application0+0x1023
00000000`00934030 00000001`3fb81028 Application0+0x1028
00000000`00934070 00000001`3fb81028 Application0+0x1028
00000000`009340b0 00000001`3fb81028 Application0+0x1028
00000000`009340f0 00000001`3fb81028 Application0+0x1028
00000000`00934130 00000001`3fb81028 Application0+0x1028
00000000`00934170 00000001`3fb81028 Application0+0x1028
00000000`009341b0 00000001`3fb81028 Application0+0x1028
00000000`009341f0 00000001`3fb81028 Application0+0x1028
00000000`00934230 00000001`3fb81028 Application0+0x1028
00000000`00934270 00000001`3fb81028 Application0+0x1028
00000000`009342b0 00000001`3fb81028 Application0+0x1028
00000000`009342f0 00000001`3fb81028 Application0+0x1028
00000000`00934330 00000001`3fb81028 Application0+0x1028
00000000`00934370 00000001`3fb81028 Application0+0x1028
00000000`009343b0 00000001`3fb81028 Application0+0x1028
00000000`009343f0 00000001`3fb81028 Application0+0x1028
00000000`00934430 00000001`3fb81028 Application0+0x1028
00000000`00934470 00000001`3fb81028 Application0+0x1028
00000000`009344b0 00000001`3fb81028 Application0+0x1028
00000000`009344f0 00000001`3fb81028 Application0+0x1028
00000000`00934530 00000001`3fb81028 Application0+0x1028
00000000`00934570 00000001`3fb81028 Application0+0x1028
00000000`009345b0 00000001`3fb81028 Application0+0x1028
00000000`009345f0 00000001`3fb81028 Application0+0x1028
00000000`00934630 00000001`3fb81028 Application0+0x1028
```

```
0:003> !address 00000000`00934330
Usage:                  <unclassified>
Allocation Base:        00000000`00930000
Base Address:           00000000`00931000
End Address:            00000000`00a30000
Region Size:            00000000`000ff000
Type:                   00020000 MEM_PRIVATE
State:                  00001000 MEM_COMMIT
Protect:                00000004 PAGE_READWRITE
```

Q. When running the **kv** command, what is the *Args to Child*? What is the meaning of those addresses?

A. These may be function parameters such as *func(p1, p2, p3);* They are taken from the stack because before the function is called, parameter addresses are pushed to it (in C language, for example, from right to left). So they are taken by WinDbg from the stack before the return address, even if a function doesn't have any parameters.

Q. Why does WinDbg warn about the wrong symbols?

A. This is because the module name and some function names (the so-called exported functions) are found in the dump file, but WinDbg doesn't have symbol files to map addresses to function names correctly, for example:

```
*** ERROR: Symbol file could not be found. Defaulted to export symbols for kernel32.dll
```

Q. If I do not have symbols or, even worse, if I have outdated symbols for the loaded modules, how can I know that I do not have the right symbols loaded?

344

A. WinDbg complains about symbol files because it tries to compare timestamps. Please find the first 3 Debugging TV Frames episodes 0x01, 0x02, and 0x03 dedicated to symbol file troubleshooting:

www.debugging.tv

Q. Is it possible to go up the call stack in the dump and see variables as we do during live debugging in Visual Studio?

A. Yes, we can. Please find this comparative case for WinDbg and GDB:

https://www.dumpanalysis.org/blog/index.php/2007/07/22/gdb-for-windbg-users-part-6/

and also Debugging TV Frames episode 0x18 on www.debugging.tv

Q. What is the difference between the following? As I understand, if an application is built from several DLLs, then the module name is the DLL name. But process and image names are the same, aren't they?

```
PROCESS_NAME:  ApplicationL.exe
MODULE_NAME: ApplicationL
IMAGE_NAME:  ApplicationL.exe
```

A. A module name is usually without an extension. EXE file format is the same as for DLL, so they are all modules.

Q. After opening a crash dump, is it possible to open another dump without closing WinDbg?

A. Yes, it is possible; please see a case study for the **.opendump** command:

http://www.dumpanalysis.org/blog/index.php/2010/01/06/windbg-shortcuts-opendump/

Q. The **!analyze -v** says this:

```
STACK_COMMAND:  !heap ; ~1s; .ecxr ; kb
```

What is this command trying to say? Is there any hint to trying these commands?

A. This might be what **!analyze** does to get output for parsing and guessing. Sometimes you might get some hints, learn, and try commands.

Q. In the following stack trace, 010b11f0 is the address from where the execution continues after *kernel32!HeapFree* is done. Are 00740000 00000000 007416c0 passed to the HeapFree method?

```
ChildEBP RetAddr  Args to Child
0070fab8 010b11f0 00740000 00000000 007416c0 kernel32!HeapFree+0x14
0070faf8 010b1274 007416c0 15517953 00000000 ApplicationL!free+0x6e
```

A. For most functions, you can check parameters and their number from MSDN. *HeapFree* takes three parameters:

```
BOOL WINAPI HeapFree(
  _In_  HANDLE hHeap,
  _In_  DWORD dwFlags,
```

```
    _In_   LPVOID lpMem
);
```

So they are all passed. Please be aware that on x64 Windows, the values from Args to Child array will not match to passed parameters because they were passed by registers.

Q. The **!heap** gives the following output.

```
Error address: 00740f28
Heap handle: 00740000
Error type heap_failure_multiple_entries_corruption (4)
Last known valid blocks: before - 007409e8, after - 007416b8
Stack trace:
                77b6fc76: ntdll!RtlpAnalyzeHeapFailure+0x0000025b
                77b29ef1: ntdll!RtlpCoalesceFreeBlocks+0x00000060
                77ad2d07: ntdll!RtlpFreeHeap+0x000001f4
                77ad2bf2: ntdll!RtlFreeHeap+0x00000142
                752914d1: kernel32!HeapFree+0x00000014
                010b11f0: ApplicationL!free+0x0000006e
                010b1274: ApplicationL!_callthreadstart+0x0000001b
                010b1310: ApplicationL!_threadstart+0x00000076
                75293677: kernel32!BaseThreadInitThunk+0x0000000e
                77ad9f02: ntdll!__RtlUserThreadStart+0x00000070
                77ad9ed5: ntdll!_RtlUserThreadStart+0x0000001b
```

The heap handle 00740000, and parameters passed to the method 00740000 00000000 007416c0 match! Does this mean, ApplicationL calls *free* function with a NULL pointer because BUGCHECK_STR says so?

A. No, *free* wasn't called with a NULL pointer. However, heap block headers contained NULL pointers due to previous corruption or so, and during heap compaction, it resulted in the NULL pointer access violation you see in the exception record. Please note that heap corruption is usually detected much later and from different code; for example, one module can corrupt the heap during thread execution, and it can be detected after some time by another module in another thread.

Q. If we want to see the C statement executed, how can we see that?

A. You can use **.srcpath** command to set the source code path. Please find the live Debugging TV presentation (episode 0x18) on www.debugging.tv.

Q. To capture a crash dump, do we need to use the MiniDumpWriteDump API? If we need to use *MiniDumpWriteDump* API, then does the MINIDUMP_TYPE enum decide the information that gets recorded into the crash dump?

A. To capture a dump file, we advise using an external tool to avoid process corruption interference as outlined in this article:

https://www.dumpanalysis.org/blog/index.php/2012/07/02/architecture-of-process-memory-dump-capture-done-right/.

External method links are provided in this presentation:
https://www.patterndiagnostics.com/files/LegacyWindowsDebugging.pdf

Q. WinDbg supports side-by-side installation, so is it fine if we open an x64 dump in the x86 version of WinDbg?

A. Yes, it is. We also use x86 WinDbg to open x64 dumps during some course exercises.

Q. **.chain** WinDbg command lists WinDbg extensions. How can you know the commands exposed by each WinDbg extension?

A. Usually, extensions implement a **help** command, for example:

```
0:000> !exts.help
acl <address> [flags]          - Displays the ACL
atom <address>                 - Displays the atom or table(s) for the process
avrf [-? | parameters]         - Displays or modifies App Verifier settings
cs [-? | parameters]           - Displays critical sections for the process
cxr                            - Obsolete, .cxr is new command
dlls [-h | parameters]         - Displays loaded DLLS
exr                            - Obsolete, .exr is new command
findthis [-? | options]        - Search the registers for the this pointer
gflag [-?|<value>]             - Displays the global flag
heap [-? | parameters]         - Displays heap info
help                           - Displays this list
kuser                          - Displays KUSER_SHARED_DATA
peb [address]                  - Displays the PEB structure
psr <value>|@ipsr [flags]      - Displays an IA64 Processor Status Word
sd <address> [flags]           - Displays the SECURITY_DESCRIPTOR
shipassert                     - Displays ship asserts
sid <address> [flags]          - Displays the SID
slist [-? | parameters]        - Displays singly-linked list
stl [options] <varname>        - Dumps an STL variable
stltree [options] <address>    - Dumps an STL set, map, multiset, or multimap
teb [address]                  - Displays the TEB structure
tls <slot | -1> [teb | 0]      - Dumps TLS slots. !tls /? for usage
token [-n|-?] <handle|addr>    - Displays TOKEN
tp <command>                   - Dump threadpool information

Type ".hh [command]" for more detailed help
```

Q. How to find available extension DLLs?

A. To find the available extension, please look at your Debugging Tools for Windows folders such as \winext, \winxp, etc. There is also a list of 3rd party extensions on www.windbg.org.

Q. What would you suggest reading on the internals of exception processing?

A. You can start with these articles:

https://www.dumpanalysis.org/blog/index.php/interrupts-and-exceptions-explained/

Q. Do you have any examples of malware analysis?

A. Please find a live analysis case study from this presentation on Victimware:

https://www.youtube.com/watch?v=YaE7DhSGMJc

Q. Does the machine (32-bit vs. 64-bit) have relevance for .NET Framework dumps?

A. Because you need to load an extension DLL (SOS) appropriate to the architecture of a process from where dumps were acquired, you need to use that architecture WinDbg version. For example, if your analysis machine is 64-bit, but a dump is from a 32-bit process, even if it was running on an x64 system, you need to use the 32-bit version of WinDbg. This only applies to .NET Framework analysis. You can analyze unmanaged stacks using any version of WinDbg.

Q. Does the user mode stack trace database also include memory release info?

A. No, it only includes allocations. In the case of a single extensive leak, it is usually obvious which stack trace corresponds to it, such as in our P14 exercise. For more complex scenarios, to compare logs from different times and find out differences, you can use the UMDH tool:

https://learn.microsoft.com/en-us/windows-hardware/drivers/debugger/using-umdh-to-find-a-user-mode-memory-leak

Q. Is it possible to troubleshoot access violation of a program that runs fine on all machines except one system?

A. Yes, we should compare process memory dumps. There may be a 3rd party **Hooksware** DLL in the problem scenario that is absent in all other systems, the so-called **Changed Environment** pattern:

https://www.dumpanalysis.org/blog/index.php/2007/03/19/crash-dump-analysis-patterns-part-10/

There might also be runtime DLL differences.

Q. I would love it if you point to some case studies where WinDbg scripts/plugins were developed to automate something.

A. Please look at some scripts in Software Diagnostics Library:

https://www.dumpanalysis.org/blog/index.php/category/windbg-scripts/

Also, please check this introduction to WinDbg scripts for C/C++ users:

https://www.dumpanalysis.org/WCDA/WCDA-Sample-Chapter.pdf

"Advanced Windows Memory Dump Analysis with Data Structures" training course also includes an exercise that uses the recent WinDbg JavaScript engine:

https://www.dumpanalysis.org/advanced-windows-memory-dump-analysis-book

Triple Dereference

Reprinted with corrections from Memory Dump Analysis Anthology, Volume 1, Revised Edition, pages 188 – 190.

WinDbg commands like **dpp** allow us to do double dereference in the following format:

```
pointer *pointer **pointer
```

For example:

```
0:000> dpp 004015a2
004015a2  00405068 7c80929c kernel32!GetTickCount
```

There are cases where we need triple dereference (or even quadruple dereference) done on a range of memory. Here we can utilize WinDbg scripts. The key is to use **$p** pseudo-register which shows the last value of **d*** commands (**dd**, **dps**, etc.):

```
.for (r $t0=00000000`004015a2, $t1=4; @$t1 >= 0; r $t1=$t1-1, $t0=$t0+$ptrsize) { dps
@$t0 l1; dps $p l1; dps $p l1; .printf "\n" }
```

where **$t0** and **$t1** are pseudo-registers holding the starting address of a memory block (we use 64-bit format) and the number of objects to be triple dereferenced and displayed. **$ptrsize** is a pointer size. The script is platform independent (can be used on both 32-bit and 64-bit target). For example:

```
004015a2  00405068 component!_imp__GetTickCount
00405068  7c80929c kernel32!GetTickCount
7c80929c  fe0000ba

004015a6  458df033
458df033  ????????
458df033  ????????

004015aa  15ff50f0
15ff50f0  ????????
15ff50f0  ????????

004015ae  00405064 component!_imp__QueryPerformanceCounter
00405064  7c80a427 kernel32!QueryPerformanceCounter
7c80a427  8b55ff8b

004015b2  33f4458b
33f4458b  ????????
33f4458b  ????????
```

If we want quadruple dereferenced memory, we just need to add the additional **dps @$t0 l1;** to **.for** loop body. With this script, even double dereference looks much better because it shows symbol information for the first dereference too, whereas **dpp** command shows symbol name only for the second dereference.

Another less "elegant" variation without **$p** pseudo-register uses **poi** operator, but we need a **.catch** block to prevent the script termination on invalid memory access:

```
0:000> .for (r $t0=00000000`004015a2, $t1=4; @$t1 >= 0; r $t1=$t1-1, $t0=$t0+$ptrsize)
{ .catch { dps $t0 l1; dps poi($t0) l1; dps poi(poi($t0)) l1; }; .printf "\n" }

004015a2  00405068 component!_imp__GetTickCount
00405068  7c80929c kernel32!GetTickCount
7c80929c  fe0000ba


004015a6  458df033
458df033  ????????
Memory access error at ') '


004015aa  15ff50f0
15ff50f0  ????????
Memory access error at ') '


004015ae  00405064 component!_imp__QueryPerformanceCounter
00405064  7c80a427 kernel32!QueryPerformanceCounter
7c80a427  8b55ff8b


004015b2  33f4458b
33f4458b  ????????
Memory access error at ') '
```

We can also use **!list** extension but more formatting is necessary:

```
0:000> .for (r $t0=00000000`004015a2, $t1=4; @$t1 >= 0; r $t1=$t1-1, $t0=$t0+$ptrsize)
{ .printf "%p:\n--------\n\n", $t0; !list -x "dps @$extret l1" $t0; .printf "\n" }
004015a2:
---------
004015a2  00405068 component!_imp__GetTickCount
00405068  7c80929c kernel32!GetTickCount
7c80929c  fe0000ba
fe0000ba  ????????
Cannot read next element at fe0000ba
004015a6:
---------
004015a6  458df033
458df033  ????????
Cannot read next element at 458df033
004015aa:
---------
004015aa  15ff50f0
15ff50f0  ????????
Cannot read next element at 15ff50f0
004015ae:
---------
004015ae  00405064 component!_imp__QueryPerformanceCounter
00405064  7c80a427 kernel32!QueryPerformanceCounter
7c80a427  8b55ff8b
8b55ff8b  ????????
```

```
Cannot read next element at 8b55ff8b
004015b2:
---------
004015b2  33f4458b
33f4458b  ????????
Cannot read next element at 33f4458b
```

The advantage of **!list** is in unlimited number of pointer dereferences until invalid address is reached.

Large Heap Allocations

Reprinted with corrections from Memory Dump Analysis Anthology, Volume 2, Revised Edition, pages 137 − 139.

To check heap data structures and how they change in the case of heap **Memory Leaks** we can write the minimal C program that allocates memory in a loop using *malloc* function. If we run it, VM size grows very fast, and we save process memory dumps at 200Mb and 500Mb. When checking heap segments, we see that they had not increased although the process was allocating 0x1000000 chunks of heap memory:

```
0:000> !heap 0 0
Index   Address   Name       Debugging options enabled
  1:    00260000
    Segment at 0000000000260000 to 0000000000360000 (00008000 bytes committed)
  2:    00360000
    Segment at 0000000000360000 to 0000000000370000 (00004000 bytes committed)
  3:    00440000
    Segment at 0000000000440000 to 0000000000450000 (00010000 bytes committed)
    Segment at 0000000000450000 to 0000000000550000 (00021000 bytes committed)
  4:    00560000
    Segment at 0000000000560000 to 0000000000570000 (00010000 bytes committed)
    Segment at 0000000000570000 to 0000000000670000 (0003a000 bytes committed)
```

It can be puzzling because the inspection of virtual memory shows those chunks as belonging to heap regions:

```
0:000> !address
...
    0000000009700000 : 0000000009700000 - 0000000001002000
                    Type      00020000 MEM_PRIVATE
                    Protect   00000004 PAGE_READWRITE
                    State     00001000 MEM_COMMIT
                    Usage     RegionUsageHeap
                    Handle    0000000000560000
    000000000a702000 : 000000000a702000 - 000000000000e000
                    Type      00000000
                    Protect   00000001 PAGE_NOACCESS
                    State     00010000 MEM_FREE
                    Usage     RegionUsageFree
    000000000a710000 : 000000000a710000 - 0000000001002000
                    Type      00020000 MEM_PRIVATE
                    Protect   00000004 PAGE_READWRITE
                    State     00001000 MEM_COMMIT
                    Usage     RegionUsageHeap
                    Handle    0000000000560000
    000000000b712000 : 000000000b712000 - 0000000004aee000
                    Type      00000000
                    Protect   00000001 PAGE_NOACCESS
                    State     00010000 MEM_FREE
                    Usage     RegionUsageFree
...
```

However large allocations for a process heap go to a separate linked list:

```
0:000> !peb
PEB at 000007fffffdb000

0:000> dt _PEB 000007fffffdb000
ntdll!_PEB
...
   +0x0f0 ProcessHeaps    : 0x00000000`77fa3460  -> 0x00000000`00260000
...

0:000> dq 0x00000000`77fa3460
00000000`77fa3460  00000000`00260000 00000000`00360000
00000000`77fa3470  00000000`00440000 00000000`00560000
00000000`77fa3480  00000000`00000000 00000000`00000000
00000000`77fa3490  00000000`00000000 00000000`00000000
00000000`77fa34a0  00000000`00000000 00000000`00000000
00000000`77fa34b0  00000000`00000000 00000000`00000000
00000000`77fa34c0  00000000`00000000 00000000`00000000
00000000`77fa34d0  00000000`00000000 00000000`00000000

0:000> dt _HEAP 00000000`00260000
ntdll!_HEAP
...
   +0x090 VirtualAllocdBlocks : _LIST_ENTRY [ 0x00000000`00260090 - 0x260090 ]
...

0:000> dl 00000000`00260000+90 10 2
00000000`00260090  00000000`00260090 00000000`00260090

0:000> dl 00000000`00360000+90 10 2
00000000`00360090  00000000`00360090 00000000`00360090

0:000> dl 00000000`00440000+90 10 2
00000000`00440090  00000000`00440090 00000000`00440090

0:000> dl 00000000`00560000+90 10 2
00000000`00560090  00000000`00670000 00000000`0a710000
00000000`00670000  00000000`01680000 00000000`00560090
00000000`01680000  00000000`02690000 00000000`00670000
00000000`02690000  00000000`036a0000 00000000`01680000
00000000`036a0000  00000000`046b0000 00000000`02690000
00000000`046b0000  00000000`056c0000 00000000`036a0000
00000000`056c0000  00000000`066d0000 00000000`046b0000
00000000`066d0000  00000000`076e0000 00000000`056c0000
00000000`076e0000  00000000`086f0000 00000000`066d0000
00000000`086f0000  00000000`09700000 00000000`076e0000
00000000`09700000  00000000`0a710000 00000000`086f0000
00000000`0a710000  00000000`00560090 00000000`09700000
```

We see that the last process heap has large allocations directly from virtual memory, for example:

```
0:000> !address 00000000`0a710000
    000000000a710000 : 000000000a710000 - 0000000001002000
                    Type      00020000  MEM_PRIVATE
                    Protect   00000004  PAGE_READWRITE
                    State     00001000  MEM_COMMIT
                    Usage     RegionUsageHeap
                    Handle    0000000000560000
```

Actually, if we use heap statistics option for **!heap** command we see these large allocations (shown in smaller font for visual clarity):

```
0:000> !heap -s
LFH Key                   : 0x000000a4e8aa078c
         Heap       Flags      Reserv  Commit  Virt   Free  List    UCR  Virt  Lock  Fast
                               (k)     (k)     (k)    (k)   length       blocks cont. heap
0000000000260000 00000002     1024     32      32     7     1       1    0      0     L
0000000000360000 00008000      64      16      16    12     1       1    0      0
0000000000440000 00001002     1088    196     196     4     1       1    0      0    LFH
Virtual block: 0000000000670000 - 0000000000670000
Virtual block: 0000000001680000 - 0000000001680000
Virtual block: 0000000002690000 - 0000000002690000
Virtual block: 00000000036a0000 - 00000000036a0000
Virtual block: 00000000046b0000 - 00000000046b0000
Virtual block: 00000000056c0000 - 00000000056c0000
Virtual block: 00000000066d0000 - 00000000066d0000
Virtual block: 00000000076e0000 - 00000000076e0000
Virtual block: 00000000086f0000 - 00000000086f0000
Virtual block: 0000000009700000 - 0000000009700000
Virtual block: 000000000a710000 - 000000000a710000
0000000000560000 00001002     1088    296     296    18     3       1    11     0    LFH
```

The dump file can be downloaded to play with: https://www.dumpanalysis.org/pub/LargeHeapAllocations.zip

9 781912 636921